ARMSTRONG'S HANDBOOK
OF HUMAN RESOURCE MANAGEMENT PRACTICE

ARMSTRONG'S HANDBOOK
OF HUMAN RESOURCE MANAGEMENT PRACTICE

11TH EDITION

Michael Armstrong

KOGAN PAGE
London and Philadelphia

Publisher's note

Every possible effort has been made to ensure that the information contained in this book is accurate at the time of going to press, and the publisher and authors cannot accept responsibility for any errors or omissions, however caused. No responsibility for loss or damage occasioned to any person acting, or refraining from action, as a result of the material in this publication can be accepted by the editor, the publisher or any of the authors.

First edition published in 1977 as *A Handbook of Personnel Management Practice* by Kogan Page Limited
Seventh edition published in 1999 as *A Handbook of Human Resource Management Practice*
Eleventh edition published in 2009 as *Armstrong's Handbook of Human Resource Management Practice*

120 Pentonville Road
London N1 9JN
United Kingdom
www.koganpage.com

525 South 4th Street, #241
Philadelphia PA 19147
USA

ISBN 978 0 7494 5242 1

British Library Cataloguing-in-Publication Data

A CIP record for this book is available from the British Library.

Library of Congress Cataloging-in-Publication Data

Armstrong, Michael, 1928–
Armstrong's handbook of human resource management practice / Michael Armstrong. -- Eleventh ed.
p. cm.
Rev. ed. of: A handbook of human resource management practice. 10th ed. 2006.
Includes bibliographical references and index.
ISBN 978-0-7494-5242-1
1. Personnel management --Handbooks, manuals, etc. I. Armstrong, Michael, 1928– Handbook of human resource management practice. II. Title. III. Title: Handbook of human resource management practice.
HF5549.17.A76 2009
658.3--dc22
2008053904

Typeset by Saxon Graphics Ltd, Derby
Printed and bound in India by Replika Press Pvt Ltd

Contents in Brief

Contents

Supporting Resources for Instructors and Students

As a reader of *Armstrong's Handbook of Human Resource Management Practice*, you have automatic access to a range of additional resources designed to enhance your experience and use of the book. Full details are provided below.

For lecturers and instructors

Resources include:

- Session outlines for each of the 62 chapters.
- Glossaries of key concepts and terms for 60 chapters.
- Questions for each chapter.
- A selection of multiple choice questions.
- Bibliographies for 59 chapters.
- Fifty case studies.
- Two hundred and thirty-seven PowerPoint slides.

The lecturer resources are contained within the Free Resources section of the Kogan Page website – www.koganpage.com/resources. Using the left-hand menu, go to the *Academic Resources* section, click on *Lecturer Resources* and follow the instructions online.

For students

Resources include:

- Student learning notes – with key learning points for each chapter.
- A glossary of key concepts and terms.

- Multiple choice questions.
- Case studies.
- A guide to taking CIPD exams, including an analysis of question papers from May 2005 to May 2008.

The student resources are contained within the Free Resources section of the Kogan Page website – www.koganpage.com/resources. Using the left-hand menu, go to the *Academic Resources* section, click on *Student Resources* and follow the instructions online.

List of Figures

List of Tables

Preface

This eleventh edition of *Armstrong's Handbook of Human Resource Management Practice* contains many additions and revisions. It covers major developments in the theory and practice of human resource management in the last three years. There are new chapters on the impact of HRM, corporate social responsibility, high performance work systems, employee engagement, change management, resourcing strategy and practice and employee well-being. Significant changes and improvements have been made to most of the other chapters. The plan of the book is illustrated in the 'route map' in Figure 0.1.

The design of the book has been radically updated, with the aim of providing a text that encourages and facilitates better learning. Chapters contain key concepts and terms, learning outcomes, key learning points, questions and further reading; allowing students to recap, reflect and test their learning.

The companion website provides further resources for both students and lecturers. Students can expand on their learning and are provided with help and advice on taking examinations. Lecturers are provided with a range of resources, including PowerPoint slides and support notes for teaching.

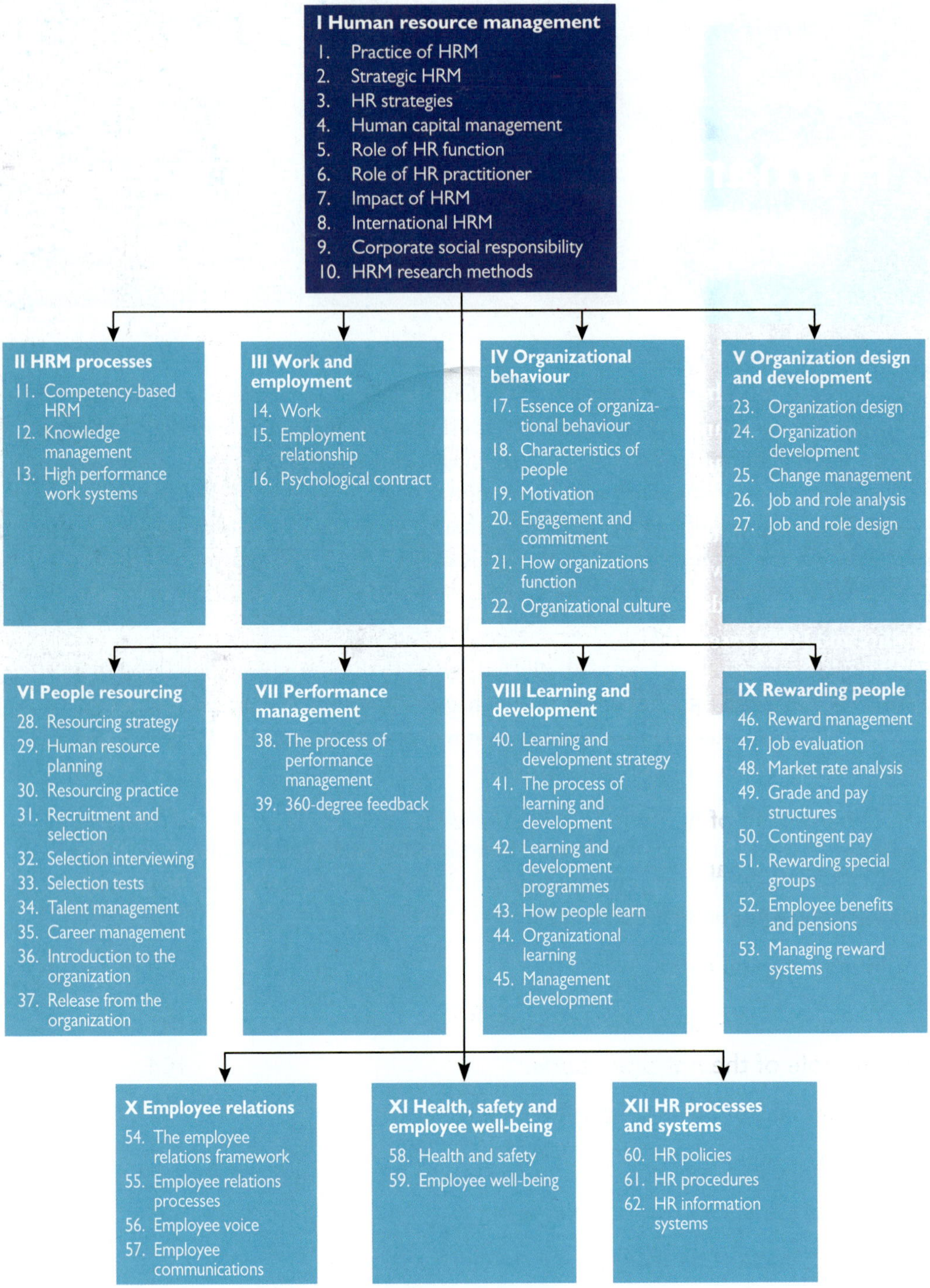
I Human resource management
1. Practice of HRM
2. Strategic HRM
3. HR strategies
4. Human capital management
5. Role of HR function
6. Role of HR practitioner
7. Impact of HRM
8. International HRM
9. Corporate social responsibility
10. HRM research methods
II HRM processes
11. Competency-based HRM
12. Knowledge management
13. High performance work systems
III Work and employment
14. Work
15. Employment relationship
16. Psychological contract
IV Organizational behaviour
17. Essence of organizational behaviour
18. Characteristics of people
19. Motivation
20. Engagement and commitment
21. How organizations function
22. Organizational culture
V Organization design and development
23. Organization design
24. Organization development
25. Change management
26. Job and role analysis
27. Job and role design
VI People resourcing
28. Resourcing strategy
29. Human resource planning
30. Resourcing practice
31. Recruitment and selection
32. Selection interviewing
33. Selection tests
34. Talent management
35. Career management
36. Introduction to the organization
37. Release from the organization
VII Performance management
38. The process of performance management
39. 360-degree feedback
VIII Learning and development
40. Learning and development strategy
41. The process of learning and development
42. Learning and development programmes
43. How people learn
44. Organizational learning
45. Management development
IX Rewarding people
46. Reward management
47. Job evaluation
48. Market rate analysis
49. Grade and pay structures
50. Contingent pay
51. Rewarding special groups
52. Employee benefits and pensions
53. Managing reward systems
X Employee relations
54. The employee relations framework
55. Employee relations processes
56. Employee voice
57. Employee communications
XI Health, safety and employee well-being
58. Health and safety
59. Employee well-being
XII HR processes and systems
60. HR policies
61. HR procedures
62. HR information systems

Figure 0.1 *Armstrong's Handbook of Human Resource Management Practice* route map

- Evaluate the range of systems on offer in terms of how they report, and how easy and quick it is to produce the types of report you need on a regular basis. Look at how reports are presented; can you download them into an Excel spreadsheet or into Access so that you can manipulate the data yourself? How easy is it to do a mail merge with the information reported?
- When buying an off-the-shelf system, don't customize it unless it's critical. Each time the system is upgraded, it's these modifications that may cause you difficulties. If you do have modifications, budget for these to be managed on an ongoing basis.

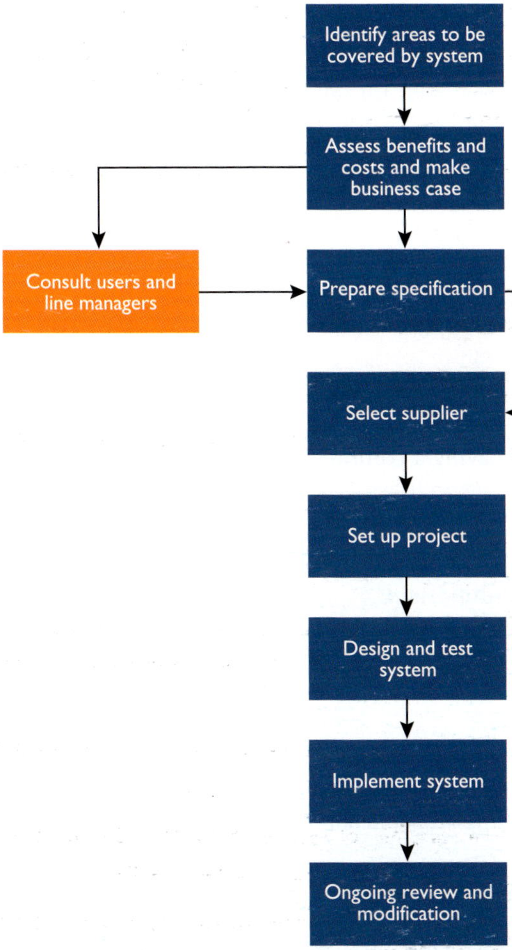

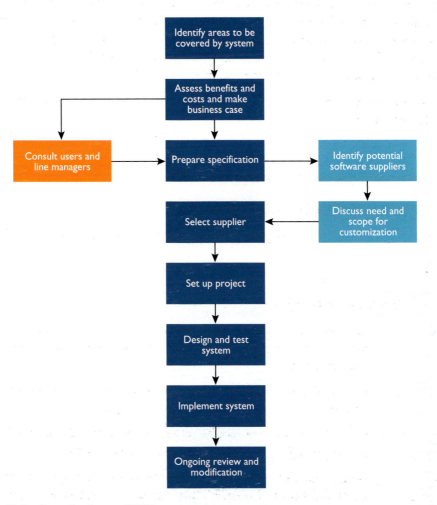

Figure 62.1 Introducing an HRIS

HR information systems – key learning points

Reasons for using an HRIS

Top five reasons are (CIPD, 2007d):

1. To improve quality of information available.
2. To reduce administrative burden on the HR department.
3. To improve speed at which information is available.
4. To improve flexibility of information to support business planning.
5. To improve services to employees.

Functions of an HRIS

Top five uses of an HRIS (CIPD, 2007d):

1. Absence management.
2. Training and development.
3. Rewards.
4. Managing diversity.
5. Recruitment and selection.

Features of an HRIS

The features of particular interest in an HRIS system are the use of software, integration with other IT systems in the organization, use of the intranet and provisions for self-service.

Introducing an HRIS

See Figure 62.1.

Questions

1. What are the main reasons for having a comprehensive human resource information system?
2. What are the five most popular applications of an HRIS?
3. What is self-service and why is it important?

References

CIPD (2005b) *People Management and Technology: Progress and potential*, CIPD, London

CIPD (2007d) *HR and Technology: Impact and advantages*, CIPD, London

Kettley, P and Reilly, P (2003) *e-HR: An introduction*, Report No 398, Institute of Employment Studies, Brighton

Tannenbaum, S (1990) HRIS: user group implications, *Journal of Systems Management*, **41** (1), pp 27–32

Appendices

Appendix A

Example of Employee Engagement and Commitment Survey

Please circle the number that most closely matches your opinion.

		Strongly agree	Agree	Disagree	Strongly disagree
Engagement					
1.	I am very satisfied with the work I do	1	2	3	4
2.	My job is interesting	1	2	3	4
3.	I know exactly what I am expected to do	1	2	3	4
4.	I am prepared to put myself out to do my work	1	2	3	4
5.	My job is not very challenging	1	2	3	4
6.	I am given plenty of freedom to decide how to do my work	1	2	3	4
7.	I get plenty of opportunities to learn in this job	1	2	3	4
8.	The facilities/equipment/tools provided are excellent	1	2	3	4
9.	I do not get adequate support from my boss	1	2	3	4
10.	My contribution is fully recognized	1	2	3	4
11.	The experience I am getting now will be a great help in advancing my future career	1	2	3	4
12.	I find it difficult to keep up with the demands of my job	1	2	3	4
13.	I have no problems in achieving a balance between my work and my private life	1	2	3	4
14.	I like working for my boss	1	2	3	4
15.	I get on well with my work colleagues	1	2	3	4
Commitment					
16.	I think this organization is a great place to work	1	2	3	4
17.	I believe I have a good future in this organization	1	2	3	4
18.	I intend to go on working for this organization	1	2	3	4
19.	I am not happy about the values of this organization – the ways in which it conducts its business	1	2	3	4
20.	I believe that the products/services provided by this organization are excellent	1	2	3	4

Appendix B
Example of Performance Management Survey

Please indicate how you felt about performance management by recording your reactions to the following statements. State:

A If you fully agree
B If you partly agree
C If you disagree

1. I am quite satisfied that the objectives I agreed were fair.
2. I felt that the meeting to agree objectives and standards of performance helped me to focus on what I should be aiming to achieve.
3. I received good feedback from my manager on how I was doing.
4. My manager was always prepared to provide guidance when I ran into problems at work.
5. The performance review meeting was conducted by my manager in a friendly and helpful way.
6. My manager fully recognized my achievements during the year.
7. If any criticisms were made during the review meeting, they were acceptable because they were based on fact, not opinion.
8. I was given plenty of opportunity by my manager to discuss the reasons for any of my work problems.
9. I felt generally that the comments made by my manager at the meeting were fair.
10. I felt motivated after the meeting.
11. The meeting ended with a clear plan of action for the future with which I agreed.
12. The action I have taken since the meeting has led to a distinct improvement in my performance.

Appendix C
Example of Reward Survey

Please circle the number that most closely matches your opinion.

		Strongly agree	Agree	Disagree	Strongly disagree
1.	My contribution is adequately rewarded	1	2	3	4
2.	Pay increases are handled fairly	1	2	3	4
3.	I feel that my pay does not reflect my performance	1	2	3	4
4.	My pay compares favourably with what I could get elsewhere	1	2	3	4
5.	I am not paid fairly in comparison with other people doing similar work in the organization	1	2	3	4
6.	I think the organization's pay policy is overdue for a review	1	2	3	4
7.	Grading decisions are made fairly	1	2	3	4
8.	I am not clear how decisions about my pay are made	1	2	3	4
9.	I understand how my job has been graded	1	2	3	4
10.	I get good feedback on my performance	1	2	3	4
11.	I am clear about what I am expected to achieve	1	2	3	4
12.	I like my job	1	2	3	4
13.	The performance pay scheme encourages better performance	1	2	3	4
14.	I am proud to work for the organization	1	2	3	4
15.	I understand how my pay can progress	1	2	3	4
16.	The job evaluation scheme works fairly	1	2	3	4
17.	The benefits package compares well with those in other organizations	1	2	3	4
18.	I would like more choice about the benefits I receive	1	2	3	4
19.	I feel motivated after my performance review meeting	1	2	3	4
20.	I do not understand the pay policies of the organization	1	2	3	4

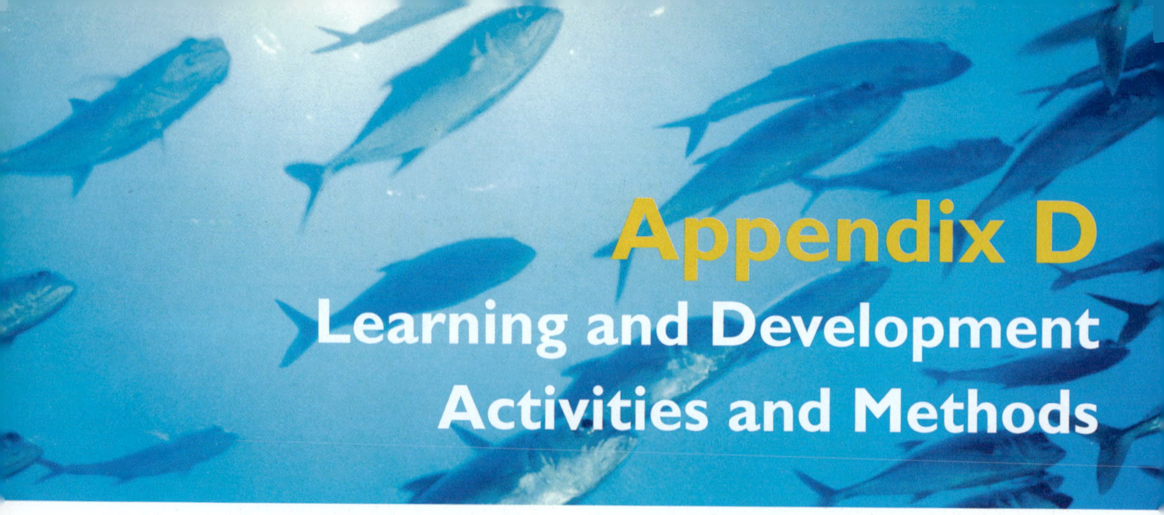

Appendix D
Learning and Development Activities and Methods

The following learning and development activities are described in this appendix:

- action learning
- coaching
- discussion
- instruction
- mentoring
- outdoor learning
- simulation
- case study
- corporate university
- group exercises
- lecture
- modern apprenticeship
- role playing

Action learning

Action learning, as developed by Revans (1989) is a method of helping managers develop their talents by exposing them to real problems. They are required to analyse them, formulate recommendations, and then take action. It accords with the belief that managers learn best by doing rather than being taught. Revans produced the following formula to describe his concept: L (learning) = P (programmed learning) + Q (questioning, insight).

A typical action learning programme brings together a group, or 'set', of four or five managers to solve the problem. They help and learn from each other, but an external consultant, or 'set adviser', sits in with them regularly. The project may last several months, and the set meets frequently, possibly one day a week. The adviser helps the members of the set to learn from one another and clarifies the process of action learning. This process involves change embedded in the web of relationships called 'the client system'. The web comprises at least three separate networks: the power network, the information network, and the motivational network (this is what Revans means by 'who can, who knows, and who cares'). The forces for change are already there within the client system and it is the adviser's role to point out the dynamics of this system as the work of diagnosis and implementation proceeds.

The group or set has to manage the project like any other project, deciding on objectives, planning resources, initiating action and monitoring progress. But all the time, with the help of their adviser, they are learning about the management processes involved as they actually happen.

Case study

A case study is a history or description of an event or set of circumstances that is analysed by trainees to diagnose the causes of a problem and work out how to solve it. Case studies are mainly used in courses for managers and team leaders, based on the belief that managerial competence and understanding can best be achieved through the study and discussion of real events.

Case studies should aim to promote enquiry, the exchange of ideas, and the analysis of experience so that the trainees can discover the underlying principles the case study is designed to illustrate. They are not light relief, nor are they a means of reducing the load on the instructor. Trainers have to work hard to define the learning points that must come out of each case, and they must work even harder to ensure that these points do emerge.

The danger of case studies is that they are often perceived by trainees to be irrelevant to their needs, even if based on fact. Consequently, the analysis is superficial and the situation is unrealistic. It is the trainer's job to avoid these dangers by ensuring that the participants are not allowed to get away with half-baked comments. Trainers have to challenge assumptions and force people to justify their reasoning. Above all, they have to seize every chance to draw out the principles they want to illustrate from the discussion and to get the group to see how these are relevant to their own working situation.

Coaching

Coaching is a personal (usually one-to-one) on-the-job approach to helping people develop their skills and levels of competence. A structured and purposeful dialogue is at the heart of coaching. The coach uses feedback and brings an objective perspective. The need for coaching may arise from formal or informal performance reviews, but opportunities for coaching will emerge during normal day-to-day activities.

Coaching as part of the normal process of management consists of:

- making people aware of how well they are performing by, for example, asking them questions to establish the extent to which they have thought through what they are doing;
- controlled delegation – ensuring that individuals not only know what is expected of them but also understand what they need to know and be able to do to complete the

task satisfactorily; this gives managers an opportunity to provide guidance at the outset – guidance at a later stage may be seen as interference;

- using whatever situations may arise as opportunities to promote learning;
- encouraging people to look at higher-level problems and how they would tackle them.

A common framework used by coaches is the GROW model:

'G' is for the goal of coaching, which needs to be expressed in specific measurable terms that represent a meaningful step towards future development.

'R' is for the reality check – the process of eliciting as full a description as possible of what the person being coached needs to learn.

'O' is for option generation – the identification of as many solutions and actions as possible.

'W' is for wrapping up – when the coach ensures that the individual being coached is committed to action.

Coaching will be most effective when the coach understands that his or her role is to help people to learn and individuals are motivated to learn. They should be aware that their present level of knowledge or skill or their behaviour needs to be improved if they are going to perform their work satisfactorily. Individuals should be given guidance on what they should be learning and feedback on how they are doing and, because learning is an active not a passive process, they should be actively involved with their coach, who should be constructive, building on strengths and experience.

Coaching may be informal but it has to be planned. It is not simply checking from time to time on what people are doing and then advising them on how to do it better. Nor is it occasionally telling people where they have gone wrong and throwing in a lecture for good measure. As far as possible, coaching should take place within the framework of a general plan of the areas and direction in which individuals will benefit from further development. Coaching plans can and should be incorporated into the personal development plans set out in a performance agreement.

Coaching should provide motivation, structure and effective feedback if managers have the required skills and commitment. As coaches, managers believe that people can succeed, that they can contribute to their success and that they can identify what people need to be able to do to improve their performance.

Corporate university

A corporate university is an institution set up and run by an organization, often with outside help, in which education and learning take place. As Carter *et al* (2002) point out:

The term 'corporate university' is interpreted in different ways. For some, it is specific and refers to the use of academic terminology to describe and raise the status of training and development and, perhaps, also implies a relationship with one or more 'real' conventional universities who co-design or accredit the company's programmes. For others, the term is interpreted more broadly as an umbrella that describes the creation and marketing of internal brands for all the learning and development opportunities an organization provides.

For example, BAe Systems operates a virtual university, which has a strategic partnership policy that allows it to co-design programmes with the help of conventional universities. In contrast, Lloyds TSB runs its training function just as though it were a university, with faculties for each development area. The aim is to align training and development with business strategy and use the concept as an internal brand, letting employees know that it is investing in them.

Discussion

The objectives of using discussion techniques are to:

- get the audience to participate actively in learning;
- give people an opportunity of learning from the experience of others;
- help people to gain understanding of other points of view;
- develop powers of self-expression.

The aim of the facilitator is to guide the group's thinking. He or she may, therefore, be more concerned with shaping attitudes than imparting new knowledge. The facilitator has unobtrusively to stimulate people to talk, guide the discussion along predetermined lines (there must be a plan and an ultimate objective), and provide interim summaries and a final summary.

The following techniques can be used to get active participation:

- Ask for contributions by direct questions.
- Use open-ended questions that will stimulate thought.
- Check understanding; make sure that everyone is following the argument.
- Encourage participation by providing support rather than criticism.
- Prevent domination by individual members of the group by bringing in other people and asking cross-reference questions.
- Avoid dominating the group yourself. The leader's job is to guide the discussion, maintain control and summarize from time to time. If necessary, 'reflect' opinions expressed by individuals back to the group to make sure they find the answer for themselves. The leader's job is to help them reach a conclusion, not to do it for them.

- Maintain control – ensure that the discussion is progressing along the right lines towards a firm conclusion.

Group exercises

In a group exercise the trainees examine problems and develop solutions to them as a group. The problem may be a case study or it could be one entirely unrelated to everyday work. The aims of an exercise of this kind are to give members practice in working together and to obtain insight into the way in which groups behave in tackling problems and arriving at decisions.

Group exercises can be used as part of a team-building programme and to develop interactive skills. They can be combined with other techniques such as the discovery method, encouraging participants to find out things for themselves and work out the techniques and skills they need to use.

Instruction

Job instruction techniques should be based on skills analysis and learning theory, as discussed in Chapters 26 and 43. The sequence of instruction should follow six stages:

1. Preparation for each instruction period means that the trainer must have a plan for presenting the subject matter and using appropriate teaching methods, visual aids and demonstration aids. It also means preparing trainees for the instruction that is to follow. They should want to learn. They must perceive that the learning will be relevant and useful to them personally. They should be encouraged to take pride in their job and to appreciate the satisfaction that comes from skilled performance.
2. Presentation should consist of a combination of telling and showing – explanation and demonstration.
3. Explanation should be as simple and direct as possible: the trainer explains briefly the ground to be covered and what to look for. He or she makes the maximum use of films, charts, diagrams and other visual aids. The aim should be to teach first things first and then proceed from the known to the unknown, the simple to the complex, the concrete to the abstract, the general to the particular, the observation to reasoning, the whole to the parts and back to the whole again.
4. Demonstration is an essential stage in instruction, especially when the skill to be learnt is mainly a 'doing skill'. Demonstration takes place in three steps:
   - The complete operation is shown at normal speed to show the trainee how the task should be carried out eventually.
   - The operation is demonstrated slowly and in correct sequence, element by element, to indicate clearly what is done and the order in which each task is carried out.

- The operation is demonstrated again slowly, at least two or three times, to stress the how, when and why of successive movements.

5. Practice consists of the learner imitating the instructor and then constantly repeating the operation under guidance. The aim is to reach the target level of performance for each element of the total task, but the instructor must constantly strive to develop coordinated and integrated performance; that is, the smooth combination of the separate elements of the task into a whole job pattern.
6. Follow up continues during the training period for all the time required by the learner to reach a level of performance equal to that of the normal experienced worker in terms of quality, speed and attention to safety. During the follow-up stage, the learner will continue to need help with particularly difficult tasks or to overcome temporary set-backs that result in a deterioration of performance. The instructor may have to repeat the presentation for the elements and supervise practice more closely until the trainee regains confidence or masters the task.

Lecture

A lecture is a talk with little or no participation except a question and answer session at the end. It is used to transfer information to an audience with controlled content and timing. When the audience is large and there is no scope to break it up into discussion groups, there may be no alternative to a 'straight lecture'.

The effectiveness of a lecture depends on the ability of the speaker to present material with the judicious use of visual aids. But there are limits on the amount an inert audience can absorb. However effective the speaker, it is unlikely that more than 20 per cent of what was said will be remembered at the end of the day. After a week, all will be forgotten unless the listeners have put some of their learning into practice. For maximum effectiveness, the lecture must never be longer than 30 or 40 minutes; it must not contain too much information (if the speaker can convey three new ideas that more than half of the audience understands and remembers, the lecture will have been successful); it must reinforce learning with appropriate visual aids (but not too many); and it must clearly indicate the action that should be taken to make use of the material.

Mentoring

Mentoring is the process of using specially selected and trained individuals to provide guidance, pragmatic advice and continuing support that will help the person or persons allocated to them to learn and develop. Mentors prepare individuals to perform better in the future and groom them for higher and greater things, ie career advancement.

Mentoring is a method of helping people to learn and develop, as distinct from coaching which is a relatively directive means of increasing people's competence. Mentoring promotes learning on the job, which is always the best way of acquiring the particular skills and knowledge the job holder needs. Mentoring also complements formal training by providing those who benefit from it with individual guidance from experienced managers who are 'wise in the ways of the organization'.

Mentors provide people with:

- advice in drawing up self-development programmes or learning contracts;
- general help with learning programmes;
- guidance on how to acquire the necessary knowledge and skills to do a new job;
- advice on dealing with any administrative, technical or people problems individuals meet, especially in the early stages of their careers;
- information on 'the way things are done around here' – the corporate culture and its manifestations in the shape of core values and organizational behaviour (management style);
- coaching in specific skills;
- help in tackling projects – not by doing it for them but by pointing them in the right direction, helping people to help themselves;
- a parental figure with whom individuals can discuss their aspirations and concerns and who will lend a sympathetic ear to their problems.

There are no standard mentoring procedures, although it is essential to select mentors who are likely to adopt the right non-directive but supportive approach to the person or persons they are dealing with. They must then be carefully briefed and trained in their role.

Modern apprenticeship

Modern apprenticeships were originally introduced by the government as a means of developing key skills. Their main features are:

- open to those aged 16–24;
- provide alternate on-the-job and off-the job experience and training;
- linked to NVQ qualifications;
- frameworks developed by Skills Sector Councils and adapted to meet local needs;
- possible to progress to further or higher education.

The problems with modern apprenticeships have included variability between sectors, concentration on traditional sectors, the number of apprentices is not increasing, concern about the NVQ framework, and poor quality trainers and assessors.

Outdoor learning

Outdoor learning involves exposing individuals to various 'Outward Bound' type activities: sailing, mountain walking, rock climbing, canoeing, caving, etc. It means placing participants, operating in teams, under pressure to carry out physical activities that are completely unfamiliar to them. The rationale is that these tests are paradigms of the sort of challenges people have to meet at work, but their unfamiliar nature means that they can learn more about how they act under pressure as team leaders or team members. Outdoor learning involves a facilitator helping participants to learn individually and collectively from their experiences.

Role playing

Role playing is used to give managers, team leaders or sales representatives practice in dealing with face-to-face situations such as interviewing, conducting a performance review meeting, counselling, coaching, dealing with a grievance, selling, leading a group or running a meeting. It develops interactive skills and gives people insight into the way in which people behave and feel. In role playing, the participants act out a situation by assuming the roles of the characters involved. The situation will be one in which there is interaction between two people or within a group. It should be specially prepared with briefs written for each participant explaining the situation and, broadly, their role in it. Alternatively, role playing could emerge naturally from a case study when the trainees are asked to test their solution by playing the parts of those concerned.

The technique of 'role reversal', in which a pair playing, say, a manager and a team leader run through the case and then exchange roles and repeat it, gives extra insight into the feelings involved and the skills required.

Role playing enables trainees to get expert advice and constructive criticism from the trainer and their colleagues in a protected training situation. It can help to increase confidence as well as developing skills in handling people. The main difficulties are either that trainees are embarrassed or that they do not take the exercise seriously and overplay their parts.

Simulation

Simulation is a training technique that combines case studies and role playing to obtain the maximum amount of realism in classroom training. The aim is to facilitate the transfer of what has been learnt off-the-job to on-the-job behaviour by reproducing, in the training room, situations that are as close as possible to real life. Trainees are thus given the opportunity to practise behaviour in conditions identical to or at least very similar to those they will meet when they complete the course.

References

Carter A, Hirsh, W and Aston, J (2002) *Resourcing the Training and Development Function*, Report No 390, Institute of Employment Studies, Brighton

Revans, R W (1989) *Action Learning*, Blond and Briggs, London

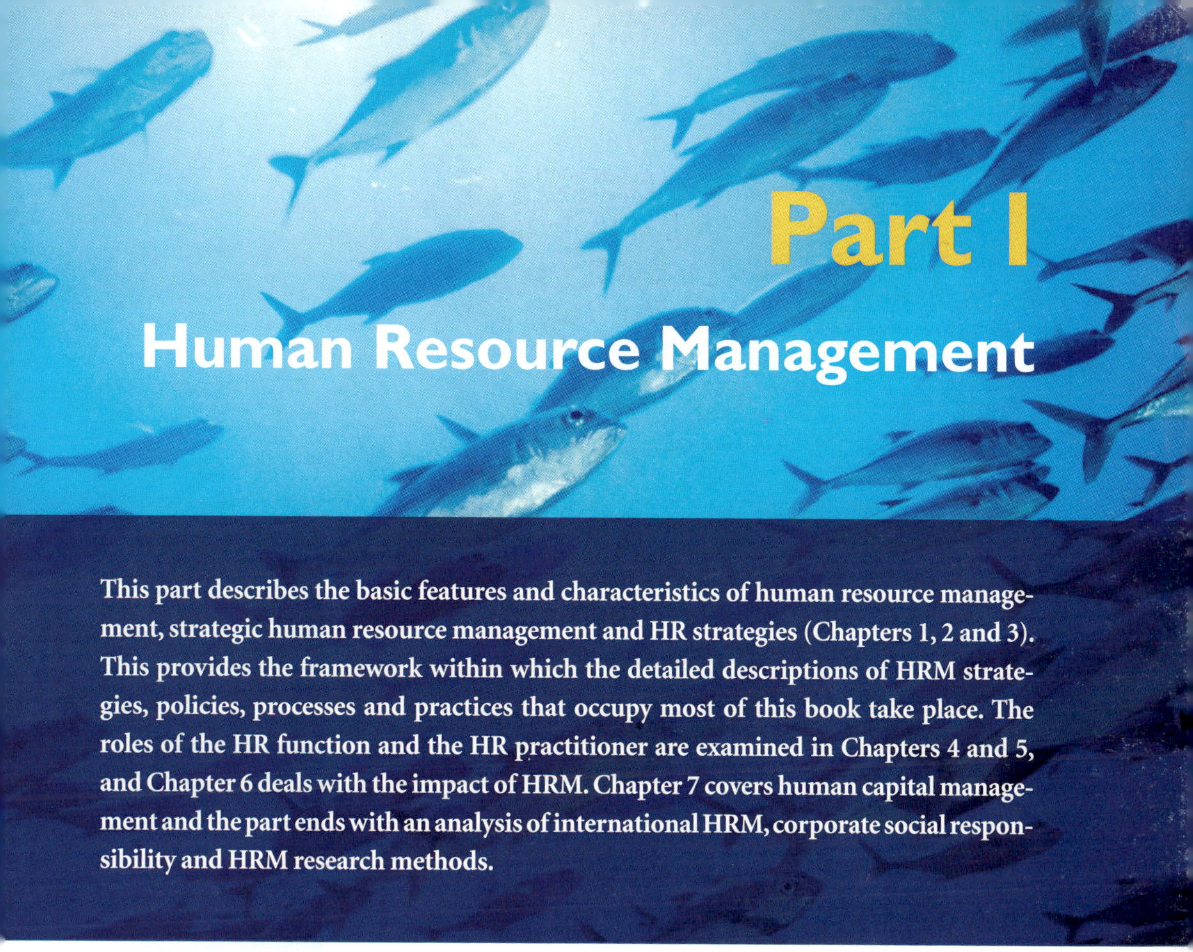

Part I

Human Resource Management

This part describes the basic features and characteristics of human resource management, strategic human resource management and HR strategies (Chapters 1, 2 and 3). This provides the framework within which the detailed descriptions of HRM strategies, policies, processes and practices that occupy most of this book take place. The roles of the HR function and the HR practitioner are examined in Chapters 4 and 5, and Chapter 6 deals with the impact of HRM. Chapter 7 covers human capital management and the part ends with an analysis of international HRM, corporate social responsibility and HRM research methods.

Part I contents

1 The Practice of Human Resource Management

Key concepts and terms

- AMO theory
- Commitment
- Contingency theory
- The hard version of HRM
- The Harvard framework
- HRM systems
- Human resource management (HRM)
- The matching model of HRM
- Mutuality
- Pluralistic employee relations
- The resource-based view
- The soft version of HRM
- Strategic integration

Learning outcomes

On completing this chapter you should be able to define these key concepts. You should also be able to:

- Define the objectives of HRM
- Describe the characteristics of HRM
- Appreciate the reservations expressed about HRM
- Appreciate the ethical dimensions of HRM
- Define the policy goals of HRM
- Understand how HRM developed as a concept
- Understand the context in which HRM operates

Introduction

The practice of human resource management (HRM) is concerned with all aspects of how people are employed and managed in organizations. It covers activities such as strategic HRM, human capital management, corporate social responsibility, knowledge management, organization development, resourcing (human resource planning, recruitment and selection, and talent management), performance management, learning and development, reward management, employee relations, employee well-being and health and safety and the provision of employee services. HRM practice has a strong conceptual basis drawn from the behavioural sciences and from strategic management, human capital and industrial relations theories. This foundation has been built with the help of a multitude of research projects.

The aim of this chapter is to provide a general introduction to the practice and underpinning concepts of HRM. It covers the definition of HRM, the objectives of HRM, HRM theory, the characteristics of HRM, the components of HRM systems, the development of HRM as an approach to managing people, the views expressed about HRM by key commentators, the context within which HRM functions, and the ethical dimensions that affect HR policy and practice.

Human resource management defined

Human resource management (HRM) is a strategic, integrated and coherent approach to the employment, development and well-being of the people working in organizations.

Other definitions of HRM

> *Human resource management involves all management decisions and action that affect the nature of the relationship between the organization and its employees – its human resources. (Beer et al, 1984)*
>
> *HRM comprises a set of policies designed to maximize organizational integration, employee commitment, flexibility and quality of work. (Guest, 1987)*

HRM consists of the following propositions:

> *That human resource policies should be integrated with strategic business planning and used to reinforce an appropriate (or change an inappropriate)*

organizational culture, that human resources are valuable and a source of competitive advantage, that they may be tapped most effectively by mutually consistent policies that promote commitment and which, as a consequence, foster a willingness in employees to act flexibly in the interests of the 'adaptive organization's' pursuit of excellence. (Legge, 1989)

Human resource management is a distinctive approach to employment management which seeks to achieve competitive advantage through the strategic deployment of a highly committed and capable workforce, using an integrated array of cultural, structural and personnel techniques. (Storey, 1995)

HRM is: 'The management of work and people towards desired ends.' (Boxall et al, 2007)

HRM is concerned with how organizations manage their workforce (Grimshaw and Rubery, 2007)

The objectives of HRM

The overall purpose of human resource management is to ensure that the organization is able to achieve success through people. HRM aims to increase organizational effectiveness and capability – the capacity of an organization to achieve its goals by making the best use of the resources available to it. Ulrich and Lake (1990) remarked that: 'HRM systems can be the source of organizational capabilities that allow firms to learn and capitalize on new opportunities.' But HRM has an ethical dimension which means that it must also be concerned with the rights and needs of people in organizations through the exercise of social responsibility.

Dyer and Holder (1998) analysed management's HR goals under the headings of contribution (what kind of employee behaviour is expected?), composition (what headcount, staffing ratio and skill mix?), competence (what general level of ability is desired?) and commitment (what level of employee attachment and identification?).

SOURCE REVIEW

HRM policy goals, David Guest (1987, 1989a, 1989b, 1991)

1. Strategic integration: the ability of the organization to integrate HRM issues into its strategic plans, ensure that the various aspects of HRM cohere, and provide for line managers to incorporate an HRM perspective into their decision making.
2. High commitment: behavioural commitment to pursue agreed goals, and attitudinal commitment reflected in a strong identification with the enterprise.
3. High quality: this refers to all aspects of managerial behaviour that bear directly on the quality of goods and services provided, including the management of employees and investment in high quality employees.
4. Flexibility: functional flexibility and the existence of an adaptable organization structure with the capacity to manage innovation.

The policy goals for HRM identified by Caldwell (2004) included managing people as assets that are fundamental to the competitive advantage of the organization, aligning HRM policies with business policies and corporate strategy, and developing a close fit of HR policies, procedures and systems with one another.

Theories of HRM

The practice of HRM is underpinned by a number of theories. The categories of HRM theory listed by Guest (1997) and Boselie *et al* (2005) are listed below.

SOURCE REVIEW

Theories of HRM, David Guest (1997)

1. Strategic theories – in the UK the implicit but untested hypothesis is that good fit (between HR practice and the internal and external context) will be associated with superior performance. In the United States the focus has been more on classifying types of HR strategy. The hypothesis is that firms that have a fit between business strategy, structure and HRM policy will have superior performance.
2. Descriptive theories – these either list areas of HR policy and outcomes (Beer *et al*, 1984) or adopt a systems approach, describing the relationships between levels (Kochan *et al*, 1986). They are largely non-prescriptive.
3. Normative theories – these are normative in the sense that they establish a norm or standard pattern in the form of prescribed best practice. These take a considerable risk in implying 'one best way'.

Theories of HRM, Boselie *et al* (2005)

1. Contingency theory – HRM is influenced by the organization's environment and circumstances (Legge, 1978).
2. The resource-based view – HRM delivers added value through the strategic development of the organization's rare, hard to imitate and hard to substitute human resources (Barney, 1991, 1995).
3. AMO theory – the formula Performance = Ability + Motivation + Opportunity to Participate provides the basis for developing HR systems that attend to employees' interests, namely their skill requirements, motivations and the quality of their job (Appelbaum *et al*, 2000; Bailey *et al*, 2001; Boxall and Purcell, 2003).

Characteristics of HRM

HRM was regarded by Storey (1989) as a 'set of interrelated policies with an ideological and philosophical underpinning'. He listed four aspects that constitute the meaningful version of HRM:

1. a particular constellation of beliefs and assumptions;
2. a strategic thrust informing decisions about people management;
3. the central involvement of line managers; and
4. reliance upon a set of 'levers' to shape the employment relationship.

As Boselie *et al* (2005) explained, HRM:

> *responds accurately and effectively to the organization's environment and complements other organizational systems (cf contingency theory) and delivers 'added value' through the strategic development of the organization's rare, inimitable and non-substitutable resources, embodied – literally – in its staff (cf the resource-based view).*

The characteristics of HRM are that it is diverse, strategic and commitment-oriented, adopts a unitary rather than pluralist viewpoint, is founded on the belief that people should be treated as assets and is a management-driven activity. HRM tends to focus on business values although there is a growing body of opinion (eg Guest, 2002) that it has also to be concerned with employee-centred outcomes. In its fully developed form, HRM functions as a system. As Schuler (1992) indicated, HRM links, integrates and coheres.

The diversity of HRM

There are no universal characteristics of HRM. Many models exist, and practices within different organizations are diverse, often only corresponding to the conceptual version of HRM in a few respects. Boxall *et al* (2007) remarked that: 'Human resource management covers a vast array of activities and shows a huge range of variations across occupations, organizational levels, business units, firms, industries and societies.'

A distinction was made by Storey (1989) between the 'hard' and 'soft' versions of HRM. The hard version emphasizes that people are important resources through which organizations achieve competitive advantage. These resources have therefore to be acquired, developed and deployed in ways that will benefit the organization. The focus is on the quantitative, calculative and business-strategic aspects of managing human resources in as 'rational' a way as for any other economic factor.

The soft version of HRM has its roots in humanism – an approach devoted to human interests that views people as responsible and progressive beings. It also traces its origins to the human relations school founded by Elton Mayo (1933), which believed that productivity was directly related to job satisfaction and that the output of people will be high if they like their co-workers and are given pleasant supervision. But this is a fairly remote connection. The soft version of HRM as described by Storey (1989) involves 'treating employees as valued assets, a source of competitive advantage through their commitment, adaptability and high quality (of skills, performance and so on)'. It therefore views employees, in the words of Guest (1999b), as means rather than objects, but it does not go as far as following Kant's (1781) advice: 'Treat people as ends unto themselves rather than as means to an end.' The soft approach to HRM stresses the need to gain the commitment (the 'hearts and minds') of employees through involvement, communication, leadership and other methods of developing a high-commitment, high-trust organization. Attention is also drawn to the key role of organizational culture.

In 1998, Karen Legge defined the 'hard' model of HRM as a process emphasizing 'the close integration of human resource policies with business strategy which regards employees as a resource to be managed in the same rational way as any other resource being exploited for maximum return'. In contrast, the soft version of HRM sees employees as 'valued assets and as a source of competitive advantage through their commitment, adaptability and high level of skills and performance'.

It has, however, been observed by Truss (1999) that 'even if the rhetoric of HRM is soft, the reality is often hard, with the interests of the organization prevailing over those of the individual'. Research carried out by Gratton *et al* (1999) found that in the eight organizations they studied, a mixture of hard and soft HRM approaches was identified. This suggested to the researchers that the distinction between hard and soft HRM was not as precise as some commentators have implied.

But as Dyer and Holder (1998) emphasized: 'HRM goals vary according to competitive choices, technologies or service tangibles, characteristics of their employees (eg could be different for managers), the state of the labour market and the societal regulations and national culture.' And Boxall *et al* (2007) noted that: 'The general motives of HRM are multiple.'

The strategic nature of HRM

Perhaps the most significant feature of HRM is the importance attached to strategic integration. Legge (1989) argued that one of the common themes of the typical definitions of HRM is that human resource policies should be integrated with strategic business planning. Keith Sisson (1990) suggested that a feature increasingly associated with HRM is the emphasis on the integration of HR policies both with one another and with business planning more generally. John Storey (1989) believes that: 'The concept locates HRM policy formulation firmly at the strategic level and insists that a characteristic of HRM is its internally coherent approach.'

The commitment-oriented nature of HRM

One of the aims of HRM is to promote commitment – the strength of an individual's identification with, and involvement in, a particular organization. It was noted by Karen Legge (1995) that human resources 'may be tapped most effectively by mutually consistent policies that promote commitment and which, as a consequence, foster a willingness in employees to act flexibly in the interests of the "adaptive organization's" pursuit of excellence'.

However, this emphasis on commitment has been criticized from the earliest days of HRM. Guest (1987) asked: 'commitment to what?' and Fowler (1987) has stated:

> *At the heart of the concept is the complete identification of employees with the aims and values of the business – employee involvement but on the company's terms. Power in the HRM system, remains very firmly in the hands of the employer. Is it really possible to claim full mutuality when at the end of the day the employer can decide unilaterally to close the company or sell it to someone else?*

Focus on mutuality

The importance of mutuality (the belief that management and employees share the same concerns and it is therefore in both their interests to work together) was emphasized by Walton (1985a) as follows:

> *The new HRM model is composed of policies that promote mutuality – mutual goals, mutual influence, mutual respect, mutual rewards, mutual responsibility. The theory is that policies of mutuality will elicit commitment which in turn will yield both better economic performance and greater human development.*

The concept of mutuality is based on the notion of unitary employee relations, described below.

Unitary and pluralist employee relations

HRM is characterized by a unitarist rather than a pluralist view of employee relations with the emphasis on individual contracts, not collective agreements. A unitarist view expresses the belief that people in organizations share the same goals and work as members of one team. The pluralist view recognizes that the interests of employees will not necessarily coincide with their employers and suggests that the unitary view is naïve, unrealistic and against the interest of employees.

Treating people as assets or human capital

The notion that people should be regarded as assets rather than variable costs, in other words, treated as human capital, was originally advanced by Beer *et al* (1984). HRM philosophy, as mentioned by Legge (1995), holds that 'human resources are valuable and a source of competitive advantage'. Armstrong and Baron (2002) stated that:

> *People and their collective skills, abilities and experience, coupled with their ability to deploy these in the interests of the employing organization, are now recognized as making a significant contribution to organizational success and as constituting a major source of competitive advantage.*

Focus on business values

The concept of hard HRM is based on a management- and business-oriented philosophy. It is concerned with the total interests of the organization – the interests of the members of the organization are recognized but subordinated to those of the enterprise. Hence the importance attached to strategic integration and strong cultures, which flow from top management's vision and leadership, and which require people who will be committed to the strategy, who will be adaptable to change and who fit the culture.

In 1995 Legge noted that HRM policies are adapted to drive business values and are modified in the light of changing business objectives and conditions. She suggested that evidence indicated more support for the hard versions of HRM than the soft version.

Organization- versus employee-centred outcomes

In line with labour process theory, Thompson and Harley (2007) asserted that; 'What is happening is a process of "capitalizing on humanity" rather than investing in human capital.' The emphasis may have been on the business orientation of HRM but there is a growing body of opinion that there is more to HRM than that. This is the employee-centred and ethical dimension of HRM, discussed at the end of the chapter.

Grant and Shields (2002) argued that the emphasis typically placed on the business case for HRM suggests a one-sided focus on organizational outcomes at the expense of employees. It was noted by Paauwe (2004) that:

> *Added value represents the harsh world of economic rationality, but HRM is also about moral values... The yardstick of human resource outcomes is not just economic rationality – a stakeholder perspective is required, ie develop and maintain sustainable relationships with all the relevant stakeholders, not just customers and shareholders.*

Kochan (2007) contended that:

> *The HR profession has always had a special professional responsibility to balance the needs of the firm with the needs, aspirations and interests of the workforce and the values and standards society expects to be upheld at work... A regime which provides human beings no deep reason to care about one another cannot long preserve its legitimacy.*

Ulrich and Brockbank (2005a) believe that 'caring and listening to employees remains a centre piece of HR work'.

HRM as a system

An open systems view of HRM has been developed by Wright and Snell (1998). An open system is dependent on the environment for inputs, which are transformed during throughput to produce outputs that are exchanged in the environment. Wright and Snell defined an open HRM system as a competence model of organizations. Skills and abilities are treated as inputs from the environment; employee behaviours are treated as throughput; and employee satisfaction and performance are treated as outputs.

In its traditional form, HRM, as pointed out by Boselie *et al* (2005), can be viewed as 'a collection of multiple discrete practices with no explicit or discernible link between them'. In contrast 'the more strategically minded systems approach views HRM as an integrated and coherent bundle of mutually reinforcing practices'. As Kepes and Delery (2007) comment, a defining characteristic of HRM is that HRM systems and not individual HRM practices are the source of competitive advantage. 'Coherent and internally aligned systems form powerful connections that create positive synergistic effects on organizational outcomes.'

As illustrated in Figure 1.1 an HRM system brings together HR philosophies that describe the overarching values and guiding principles adopted in managing people, HR strategies that define the direction in which HRM intends to go, HR policies that provide guidelines defining how these values, principles and the strategies should be applied and implemented in specific areas of HRM, HR processes that comprise the formal procedures and methods used to put HR strategic plans and policies into effect, linked HR practices that consist of the approaches used in managing people, and HR programmes that enable HR strategies, policies and practices to be implemented according to plan. Becker and Gerhart (1996) have classified these components into three levels: the system architecture (guiding principles), policy alternatives, and processes and practices.

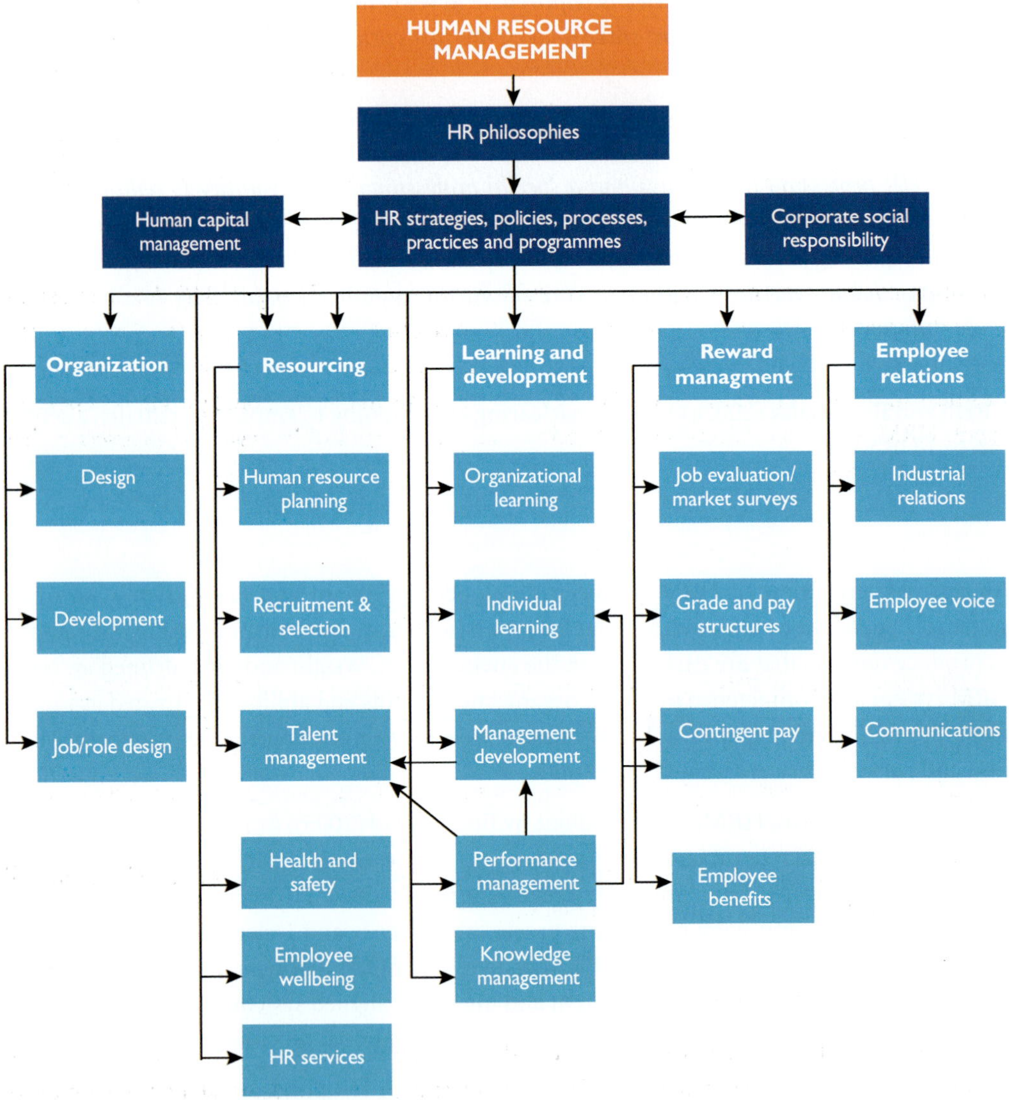

Figure 1.1 The HRM system

The development of the concept of HRM

The terms 'human resource management' (HRM) and 'human resources' (HR) have virtually replaced the term 'personnel management' as a description of the processes involved in managing people in organizations, although what is now described as HRM is in practice often synonymous with what used to be described as personnel management. In the early days of HRM it was suggested by Armstrong (1987) that:

> *HRM is regarded by some personnel managers as just a set of initials or old wine in new bottles. It could indeed be no more and no less than another name for personnel management, but as usually perceived, at least it has the virtue of emphasizing the virtue of treating people as a key resource, the management of which is the direct concern of top management as part of the strategic planning processes of the enterprise. Although there is nothing new in the idea, insufficient attention has been paid to it in many organizations.*

However, commentators such as Guest (1987) and Storey (1995) regard HRM as a substantially different model built on unitarism (employees share the same interests as employers), individualism, high commitment and strategic alignment (integrating HR strategy with the business strategy). It is claimed that HRM is more holistic than traditional personnel management. HRM has also emphasized the notion that people should be regarded as assets rather than variable costs.

Origins of the concept of HRM

The concept of HRM was first defined by Bakke (1966) who wrote that:

> *The general type of activity in any function of management... is to use resources effectively for an organizational objective... The function which is related to the understanding, maintenance, development, effective employment, and integration of the potential in the resource of 'people' I shall call simply the human resources function.*

However, HRM did not emerge in a fully fledged form until the 1980s in the 'matching model' and the Harvard framework, described below.

The matching model of HRM

One of the first detailed statements of the HRM concept was made by the Michigan school (Fombrun *et al*, 1984). They held that HR systems and the organization structure should be managed in a way that is congruent with organizational strategy (hence the name 'matching model'). They further explained that there is a human resource cycle that consists of four generic processes or functions that are performed in all organizations: selection, appraisal, rewards and development.

The Harvard framework

The other pioneers of HRM in the 1980s were the Harvard school of Beer *et al* (1984) who developed what Boxall (1992) calls the 'Harvard framework'. This framework is based on their belief that the problems of historical personnel management can only be solved:

> *when general managers develop a viewpoint of how they wish to see employees involved in and developed by the enterprise, and of what HRM policies and practices may achieve those goals. Without either a central philosophy or a strategic vision – which can be provided only by general managers – HRM is likely to remain a set of independent activities, each guided by its own practice tradition.*

Beer and his Harvard colleagues believed that 'Today, many pressures are demanding a broader, more comprehensive and more strategic perspective with regard to the organization's human resources.' These pressures have created a need for: 'A longer-term perspective in managing people and consideration of people as potential assets rather than merely a variable cost.' They were the first to underline the HRM tenet that it belongs to line managers. The Harvard school suggested that HRM had two characteristic features: 1) line managers accept more responsibility for ensuring the alignment of competitive strategy and HR policies, and 2) HR has the mission of setting policies that govern how HR activities are developed and implemented in ways that make them more mutually reinforcing.

Reservations about HRM

For some time HRM was a controversial topic, especially in academic circles. The main reservations have been that HRM promises more than it delivers and that its morality is suspect.

HRM promises more than it can deliver

Noon (1992) has commented that HRM has serious deficiencies as a theory: 'It is built with concepts and propositions, but the associated variables and hypotheses are not made explicit. It is too comprehensive… If HRM is labelled a "theory" it raises expectations about its ability to describe and predict.'

Guest (1991) believed that HRM is an 'optimistic but ambiguous concept'; it is all hype and hope. Mabey *et al* (1998) followed this up by asserting that 'the heralded outcomes (of HRM) are almost without exception unrealistically high'. To put the concept of HRM into practice involves strategic integration, developing a coherent and consistent set of employment policies, and gaining commitment. This requires high levels of determination and competence at all levels of management and a strong and effective HR function staffed by business-oriented people. It may be difficult to meet these criteria, especially when the proposed HRM culture conflicts with the established corporate culture and traditional managerial attitudes and behaviour.

Gratton *et al* (1999) were convinced on the basis of their research that there was 'a disjunction between rhetoric and reality in the area of human resource management between HRM theory and HRM practice, between what the HR function says it is doing and that practice as perceived by employers, and between what senior management believes to be the role of the HR function, and the role it actually plays'. In their conclusions they refer to the 'hyperbole and rhetoric of human resource management'.

Caldwell (2004) believed that HRM 'is an unfinished project informed by a self-fulfilling vision of what it should be'.

The above comments were based on the assumption that there is a single monolithic form of HRM. This is not the case. HRM comes in all sorts of shapes and sizes. Sometimes, as Armstrong (1987) commented, it is just new wine in old bottles – personnel management under another name. It has to be conceded that many organizations that think they are practising HRM as described earlier are not doing so, at least to the full extent. It is difficult, and it is best not to expect too much. For example, most of the managements who hurriedly adopted performance-related pay as an HRM device that would act as a lever for change have been sorely disappointed.

However, the research conducted by Guest and Conway (1997) covering a stratified random sample of 1,000 workers established that a notably high level of HRM was found to be in place. This contradicts the view that management has tended to 'talk up' the adoption of HRM practices. The HRM characteristics covered by the survey included the opportunity to express grievances and raise personal concerns on such matters as opportunities for training and development, communication about business issues, single status, effective systems for dealing with bullying and harassment at work, making jobs interesting and varied, promotion from within, involvement programmes, no compulsory redundancies, performance-related pay, profit sharing and the use of attitude surveys.

The morality of HRM

HRM is accused by many academics of being manipulative if not positively immoral. Willmott (1993) remarked that HRM operates as a form of insidious 'control by compliance' when it emphasizes the need for employees to be committed to do what the organization wants them to do. It preaches mutuality but the reality is that behind the rhetoric it exploits workers. It is, as Keenoy (1990) asserted, a wolf in sheep's clothing. Scott (1994) thought that HRM was a form of deceit, 'using subtle approaches to incorporate workers in an organizational way of thinking and in effect brainwashing them to become willing slaves'.

Legge (1998) pointed out that:

> *Sadly, in a world of intensified competition and scarce resources, it seems inevitable that, as employees are used as means to an end, there will be some who will lose out. They may even be in the majority. For these people, the soft version of HRM may be an irrelevancy, while the hard version is likely to be an uncomfortable experience.*

The accusation that HRM treats employees as means to an end is often made. However, it could be argued that if organizations exist to achieve ends, which they obviously do, and if those ends can only be achieved through people, which is clearly the case, the concern of management for commitment and performance from those people is not unnatural and is not attributable to the concept of HRM – it existed in the good old days of personnel management before HRM was invented. What matters is how management treat people as ends and what management provide in return.

Much of the hostility to HRM expressed by a number of academics is based on the belief that it is against the interests of workers, ie, that it is managerialist. However, the Guest and Conway (1997) research established that the reports of workers on outcomes showed that a higher number of HR practices were associated with higher ratings of fairness, trust and management's delivery of their promises. Those experiencing more HR activities also felt more secure in and more satisfied with their jobs. Motivation was significantly higher for those working in organizations where more HR practices were in place. In summary, as commented by Guest (1999b), it appears that workers like their experience of HRM. These findings appear to contradict the 'radical critique' view produced by academics such as Mabey *et al* (1998) and the others quoted above that HRM has been ineffectual, pernicious (ie managerialist) or both. Some of those who adopt this stance tend to dismiss favourable reports from workers about HRM on the grounds that they have been brainwashed by management. But there is no evidence to support this view.

Moreover, as Armstrong (2000) pointed out:

> *HRM cannot be blamed or given credit for changes that were taking place anyway. For example, it is often alleged to have inspired a move from pluralism to unitarism in industrial relations. But newspaper production was moved from Fleet Street to Wapping by Murdoch, not because he had read a book about HRM but as a means of breaking the print unions' control.*

Contradictions in the reservations about HRM

Guest (1999b) has suggested that there are two contradictory concerns about HRM. The first as formulated by Legge (1995, 1998) is that while management rhetoric may express concern for workers, the reality is harsher. And Keenoy (1997) complained that: 'The real puzzle about HRMism is how, in the face of such apparently overwhelming critical refutation, it has secured such influence and institutional presence.'

Other writers, however, simply observe that HRM does not work. Scott (1994), for example, stated that both management and workers were captives of their history and found it very difficult to let go of their traditional adversarial orientations.

But these contentions are contradictory. Guest (1999b) remarked that; 'It is difficult to treat HRM as a major threat (though what it is a threat to is not always made explicit) deserving of serious critical analysis while at the same time claiming that it is not practiced or is ineffective.'

The context of HRM

HRM processes take place within the context of the internal and external environment of the organization. HR practitioners will gain credibility and make a greater strategic contribution if they can analyse the impact of external events on company policies and practices. They need to be aware of the fact that what the organization does and what they need to do will depend to a large extent on its external and internal environments. They need to understand contingency theory.

Contingency theory

Contingency theory tells us that definitions of HR aims, policies and strategies, lists of activities and analyses of the role of the HR department are valid only if they are related to the situation of the organization. Legge (1978) in her influential book, *Power, Innovation and Problem Solving in Personnel Management* was the first commentator to insist that a contingent approach should be adopted to personnel management, ie, 'the design and implementation of policy that matches, or is contingent upon specified organizational requirements and circumstances'.

As Paauwe (2004) explained:

> *Contingency theory states that the relationship between the relevant independent variables (eg HRM policies and practices) and the dependent variable (performance) will vary according to the influences such as company size, age and technology, capital intensity, degree of unionization, industry/sector ownership and location.*

Contingency theory is associated with the concept of fit – the need to achieve congruence between an organization's HR strategies, policies and practices and its business strategies within the context of its external and internal environment.

Contextual factors

The contextual factors that influence HR policies and practices are the external and internal environments of the organization.

The external environment

The external environment consists of social, political, legal and economic developments and competitive pressures. Global competition in mature production and service sectors is increasing. This is assisted by easily transferable technology and reductions in international trade barriers. Customers are demanding more as new standards are reached through international competition. Organizations are reacting to this competition by becoming 'customer-focused', speeding up response times, emphasizing quality and continuous improvement, accelerating the introduction of new technology, operating more flexibly and 'losing cost'. The pressure has been for businesses to become 'lean and mean', downsizing and cutting out layers of management and supervision. They are reducing permanent staff to a core of essential workers, increasing the use of peripheral workers (sub-contractors, temporary staff) and 'outsourcing' work to external service providers.

The internal environment

The following aspects of the internal environment will affect HR policy and practice:

- the type of business or organization – private, public or voluntary sector; manufacturing or service;
- the size of the organization;
- the age or maturity of the organization;
- the technology or key activities of the business will determine how work is organized, managed and carried out;
- the type of people employed, eg professional staff, knowledge workers, technicians, administrators, production workers, sales and customer service staff;
- the organization's culture – the established pattern of values, norms, beliefs, attitudes and assumptions that shape the ways in which people behave and things get done.

The ethical dimension

As Boxall *et al* (2007) point out: 'While HRM does need to support commercial outcomes (often called "the business case"), it also exists to serve organizational needs for social legitimacy.' This means exercising social responsibility, ie being concerned for the interests (well-being) of employees and acting ethically with regard to the needs of people in the organization and the community.

Within the organization the requirement is to:

- treat people equally in terms of the opportunities for employment, learning and development provided for them;
- treat people according to the principle of procedural justice (Adams, 1965 and Leventhal, 1980), ie the ways in which people are managed are fair, consistent, transparent and properly consider the views and needs of employees;
- treat people according to the principles of distributive justice (Adams, 1965 and Leventhal, 1980), ie rewards are distributed to them according to their contribution and they receive what was promised to them;
- treat people according to the principles of natural justice, ie individuals should know the standards they are expected to achieve and the rules to which they are expected to conform, they should be given a clear indication of where they are failing or what rules have been broken and, except in cases of gross misconduct, they should be given a chance to improve before disciplinary action is taken;
- avoid treating people as mere factors of production;
- be concerned with the well-being of employees as well as the pursuit of commercial gain;
- offer as much security of employment as possible;
- provide a working environment that protects the health and safety of employees and minimizes stress;
- act in the interests of providing a reasonable balance for employees between their life and their work;
- protect employees against harmful practices at work, eg bullying, harassment and discrimination.

The practice of HRM – key learning points

The objectives of HRM

- To ensure that the organization is able to achieve success through people.
- To increase organizational effectiveness and capability.
- To be concerned with the rights and needs of people in organizations through the exercise of social responsibility.

The policy goals of HRM (Guest)

- strategic integration;
- high commitment;
- high quality;
- flexibility.

The characteristics of HRM

- diverse (hard and soft);
- strategic;
- commercial orientation;
- focus on mutuality;
- unitary view;
- people treated as assets or human capital;
- focus on business values;
- organization-centred orientation.

How HRM developed as a concept

Emerged in the 1980s in the form of the Harvard framework and the matching model.

Reservations expressed about HRM

- promises more than it can deliver;
- manipulative – 'control by compliance' (Willmott);
- managerialist.

The context in which HRM operates

HRM practice contingent on the circumstances in which the organization operates, ie its internal and external environment.

Appreciate the ethical dimensions of HRM

HRM must exercise social responsibility – it must be concerned with the interests (well-being) of employees and act ethically with regard to the needs of people in the organization and the community.

Questions

1. You are head of human resources in a medium-sized manufacturing company. Your new chief executive mentions to you that in her last firm they had a personnel manager and asks you to explain the difference, if any.
2. At a meeting of trustees the chief executive of a medium-sized charity proposed that a director of human resources should be appointed. Two trustees protested that the term 'human resources' implied that employees would just be treated as factors of production not as people. How would you respond?
3. John Storey wrote in 1995 that: 'Human resource management is a distinctive approach to employment management which seeks to achieve competitive advantage through the strategic deployment of a highly committed and capable workforce, using an integrated array of cultural, structural and personnel techniques.' Examine the approach to HRM in your own organization or any other organization known to you and analyse the extent to which Storey's description of HRM applies.
4. Your local branch of the CIPD has asked you either to propose or oppose (your choice) a motion to the effect that 'This house agrees with the statement of Keenoy and Anthony in 1992 that HRM is no more than a rhetoric masking the intensification and commodification of labour.' Prepare the case either for or against the motion.
5. Harley and Hardy (2004) wrote that 'Managers can use the language of HRM to establish the legitimacy of their practices, even if the latter bear little resemblance to the former.' What is the meaning and significance of this statement?

References

Adams, J S (1965) Injustice in social exchange, in (ed) L Berkowitz, *Advances in Experimental Psychology*, Academic Press, New York

Appelbaum, E, Bailey, T, Berg, P and Kalleberg, A L (2000) *Manufacturing Advantage: Why high performance work systems pay off*, ILR Press, Ithaca, NY

Armstrong, M (1987) Human resource management: a case of the emperor's new clothes, *Personnel Management*, August, pp 30–35

Armstrong, M (2000) The name has changed but has the game remained the same?, *Employee Relations*, **22** (6), pp 576–89

Armstrong, M and Baron, A (2002) *Strategic HRM: The route to improved business performance*, CIPD, London

Bailey, T, Berg, P and Sandy, C (2001) The effect of high performance work practices on employee earnings in the steel, apparel and medical electronics and imaging industries, *Industrial and Labor Relations Review*, **54** (2A), pp 525–43

Bakke, E W (1966) *Bonds of Organization: An appraisal of corporate human relations,* Archon, Hamden

Barney, J B (1991) Firm resources and sustained competitive advantage, *Journal of Management Studies,* **17** (1), pp 99–120

Barney, J B (1995) Looking inside for competitive advantage, *Academy of Management Executive,* **9** (4), pp 49–61

Becker, B E and Gerhart, S (1996) The impact of human resource management on organizational performance: progress and prospects, *Academy of Management Journal,* **39** (4), pp 779–801

Beer, M, Spector, B, Lawrence, P, Quinn Mills, D and Walton, R (1984) *Managing Human Assets,* The Free Press, New York

Boselie, P, Dietz, G and Boon, C (2005) Commonalities and contradictions in HRM and performance research, *Human Resource Management Journal,* **15** (3), pp 67–94

Boxall, P F (1992) Strategic HRM: a beginning, a new theoretical direction, *Human Resource Management Journal,* **2** (3) pp 61–79

Boxall, P F and Purcell, J (2003) *Strategy and Human Resource Management,* Palgrave Macmillan, Basingstoke

Boxall, P F, Purcell J and Wright P (2007) The goals of HRM, in (eds) P Boxall, J Purcell and P Wright, *Oxford Handbook of Human Resource Management,* Oxford University Press, Oxford

Caldwell, R (2004) Rhetoric, facts and self-fulfilling prophesies: exploring practitioners' perceptions of progress in implementing HRM, *Industrial Relations Journal,* **35** (3), pp 196–215

Dyer, L and Holder, G W (1998) Strategic human resource management and planning, in (ed) L Dyer, *Human Resource Management: Evolving roles and responsibilities,* Bureau of National Affairs, Washington DC

Fowler, A (1987) When chief executives discover HRM, *Personnel Management,* January, p 3

Fombrun, C J, Tichy, N M and Devanna, M A (1984) *Strategic Human Resource Management,* Wiley, New York

Grant, D and Shields, J (2002) In search of the subject: researching employee reactions to human resource management, *Journal of Industrial Relations,* **44** (3), pp 178–93

Gratton, L A, Hailey, V H, Stiles, P and Truss, C (1999) *Strategic Human Resource Management,* Oxford University Press, Oxford

Grimshaw, D and Rubery, J (2007) Economics and HRM, in (eds) P Boxall, J Purcell and P Wright, *Oxford Handbook of Human Resource Management,* Oxford University Press, Oxford

Guest, D E (1987) Human resource management and industrial relations, *Journal of Management Studies,* **14** (5), pp 503–21

Guest, D E (1989a) Human resource management: its implications for industrial relations', in (ed) J Storey, *New Perspectives in Human Resource Management,* Routledge, London

Guest, D E (1989b) Personnel and HRM: can you tell the difference? *Personnel Management,* January, pp 48–51

Guest, D E (1991) Personnel management: the end of orthodoxy, *British Journal of Industrial Relations,* **29** (2), pp 149–76

Guest, D E (1997) Human resource management and performance; a review of the research agenda, *The International Journal of Human Resource Management,* **8** (3), 263–76

Guest, D E (1999b) Human resource management: the workers' verdict, *Human Resource Management Journal,* **9** (2), pp 5–25

Guest, D E (2002) Human resource management, corporate performance and employee well-being: building the worker into HRM, *Journal of Industrial Relations,* **44** (3), pp 335–58

Guest, D E and Conway, N (1997) *Employee Motivation and the Psychological Contract,* IPD, London

Harley B and Hardy, C (2004) Firing blanks? An analysis of discursive struggle in HRM, *Journal of Management Studies,* **41** (3), pp 377–400

Kant, I (1781) *Critique of Pure Reason,* Dover Publications (2003), Mineola, NY

Keenoy, T (1990) HRM: a case of the wolf in sheep's clothing, *Personnel Review,* **19** (2), pp 3–9

Keenoy, T (1997) HRMism and the images of re-presentation, *Journal of Management Studies,* **34** (5), pp 825–41

Keenoy, T and Anthony, P (1992) HRM: metaphor, meaning and morality, in (eds) P Blyton and P Turnbull, *Reassessing Human Resource Management,* Sage Publications, London

Kepes, S and Delery, J E (2007) HRM systems and the problem of internal fit, in (eds) P Boxall, J Purcell and P Wright, *Oxford Handbook of Human Resource Management,* Oxford University Press, Oxford

Kochan, T A (2007) Social legitimacy of the HR profession, in (eds) P Boxall, J Purcell and P Wright, *Oxford Handbook of Human Resource Management,* Oxford University Press, Oxford

Kochan, T A, Katz, H and McKersie, R (1986) *The Transformation of American Industrial Relations,* Basic Books, New York

Legge, K (1978) *Power, Innovation and Problem Solving in Personnel Management,* McGraw-Hill, Maidenhead

Legge, K (1989) Human resource management: a critical analysis, in (ed) J Storey, *New Perspectives in Human Resource Management,* Routledge, London

Legge, K (1995) *Human Resource Management: Rhetorics and realities,* Macmillan, London

Legge, K (1998) The morality of HRM, in (eds) C Mabey, D Skinner and T Clark, *Experiencing Human Resource Management,* Sage, London

Leventhal, G S (1980) What should be done with equity theory? in (eds) G K Gergen, M S Greenberg and R H Willis, *Social Exchange: Advances in Theory and Research,* Plenum, New York

Mabey, C, Skinner, D and Clark, T (1998) *Experiencing Human Resource Management,* Sage, London

Mayo, E (1933) *Human Problems of an Industrial Civilisation,* Macmillan, London

Noon, M (1992) HRM: a map, model or theory?, in (eds) P Blyton and P Turnbull, *Reassessing Human Resource Management,* Sage Publications, London

Paauwe, J (2004) *HRM and performance: Achieving long term viability,* Oxford University Press, Oxford

Schuler, R S (1992) Strategic human resource management: linking people with the strategic needs of the business, *Organizational Dynamics,* **21** (1), pp 18–32

Scott, A (1994) *Willing Slaves: British workers under human resource management,* Cambridge University Press, Cambridge

Sisson, K (1990) Introducing the Human Resource Management Journal, *Human Resource Management Journal,* **1** (1), pp 1–11

Storey, J (1989) From personnel management to human resource management, in (ed) J Storey, *New Perspectives on Human Resource Management,* Routledge, London

Storey, J (ed) (1995) *Human Resource Management: A critical text,* Routledge, London

Thompson, P and Harley, B (2007) HRM and the worker: labour process perspectives, in (eds) P Boxall, J Purcell and P Wright, *Oxford Handbook of Human Resource Management,* Oxford University Press, Oxford

Truss, C (1999) Soft and hard models of HRM, in (eds) L Gratton, V H Hailey, P Stiles, and C Truss, *Strategic Human Resource Management,* Oxford University Press, Oxford

Ulrich, D and Brockbank, W (2005a) *The HR Value Proposition,* Harvard Press, Cambridge, MA

Ulrich, D and Lake, D (1990) *Organizational Capability: Competing from the inside out,* Wiley, New York

Walton, R E (1985a) From control to commitment in the workplace, *Harvard Business Review*, March–April, pp 77–84

Willmott, H (1993) Strength is ignorance, slavery is freedom: Managing culture in modern organizations, *Journal of Management Studies,* **30** (4), pp 515–52

Wright, P M and Snell, S A (1998) Towards a unifying framework for exploring fit and flexibility in strategic human resource management, *Academy of Management Review,* **23** (4), pp 756–72

2 Strategic Human Resource Management

Key concepts and terms

- Best fit
- Best practice
- Bundling
- Competitive advantage
- Configuration
- Human resource advantage
- Lifecycle model
- Resource-based view
- Strategic configuration
- Strategic fit
- Strategic HRM
- Strategic management
- Strategy

Learning outcomes

On completing this chapter you should be able to define these key concepts. You should also understand:

- The conceptual basis of strategic HRM
- How strategy is formulated
- The resource-based view and its implications
- The significance of the concepts of 'best practice' and 'best fit'
- The practical implications of strategic HRM theory
- The fundamental characteristics of strategy
- The aims of strategic HRM
- The three HRM 'perspectives' of Delery and Doty
- The significance of bundling

Introduction

As Baird and Meshoulam (1988) remarked: 'Business objectives are accomplished when human resource practices, procedures and systems are developed and implemented based on organizational needs, that is, when a strategic perspective to human resource management is adopted.' The aim of this chapter is to explore what this involves. It starts with an introduction to the basis of strategic human resource management (strategic HRM) provided by the concepts of human resource management and strategic management. It then covers a definition of strategic human resource management (strategic HRM) and its aims; an analysis of its underpinning concepts – the resource-based view and strategic fit; and a description of how strategic HRM works, namely the universalistic, contingency and configurational perspectives defined by Delery and Doty (1996) and the three approaches associated with those perspectives – best practice, best fit and bundling. The chapter ends with discussions on the reality of strategic HRM and the practical implications of the theories reviewed earlier.

The conceptual basis of strategic HRM

Boxall (1996) explained that strategic HRM 'is the interface between HRM and strategic management'. It takes the notion of HRM as a strategic, integrated and coherent approach and develops that in line with the concept of strategic management. This is an approach to management that involves taking a broad and long-term view of where the business or part of the business is going and managing activities in ways that ensure this strategic thrust is maintained.

As defined by Pearce and Robinson (1988): 'Strategic management is the set of decisions and actions resulting in the formulation and implementation of strategies designed to achieve the objectives of an organization.' According to Kanter (1984) its purpose is to: 'elicit the present actions for the future' and become 'an action vehicle – integrating and institutionalizing mechanisms for change'. The concept of strategic management is built on the concept of strategy, as considered below.

The concept of strategy

Strategy is the approach selected to achieve defined goals in the future. According to Chandler (1962) it is: 'The determination of the long-term goals and objectives of an enterprise, and the adoption of courses of action and the allocation of resources necessary for carrying out those goals.'

Strategy has three fundamental characteristics. First, it is forward looking. It is about deciding where you want to go and how you mean to get there. It is concerned with both ends and means. In this sense a strategy is a declaration of intent: 'This is what we want to do and this is how we intend to do it.' Strategies define longer-term goals but they also cover how those goals will be attained. They guide purposeful action to deliver the required result. A good strategy is one that works, one that in Abell's (1993) phrase enables organizations to adapt by 'mastering the present and pre-empting the future'. As Boxall (1996) explained: 'Strategy should be understood as a framework of critical ends and means.'

The second characteristic of strategy is that the organizational capability of a firm (its capacity to function effectively) depends on its resource capability (the quality and quantity of its resources and their potential to deliver results). This is the resource-based view, based on the ideas of Penrose (1959) who wrote that: the firm is 'an administrative organization and a collection of productive resources'. It was expanded by Wernerfelt (1984) who explained that strategy 'is a balance between the exploitation of existing resources and the development of new ones'. Resource-based strategy theorists such as Barney (1991, 1995) argued that sustained competitive advantage stemmed from the acquisition and effective use of bundles of distinctive resources that competitors cannot imitate. The resource-based view is a major element in strategic HRM, as discussed later in this chapter.

The third characteristic of strategy is strategic fit – the need when developing HR strategies to achieve congruence between them and the organization's business strategies within the context of its external and internal environment. The focus is upon the organization and the world around it. To maximize competitive advantage a firm must match its capabilities and resources to the opportunities available in its environment. The concept of fit or integration is also a major feature of strategic HRM.

The formulation of strategy

The formulation of corporate strategy is best described as a process for developing a sense of direction, making the best use of resources and ensuring strategic fit. It has often been described as a logical, step-by-step affair, the outcome of which is a formal written statement that provides a definitive guide to the organization's intentions. Many people still believe and act as if this were the case, but it is a misrepresentation of reality. In practice the formulation of strategy can never be as rational and linear a process as some writers describe it or as some managers attempt to make it.

The difficulty is that strategies are often based on the questionable assumption that the future will resemble the past. Some years ago, Heller (1972) had a go at the cult of long-range planning: 'What goes wrong' he wrote, 'is that sensible anticipation gets converted into foolish numbers: and their validity always hinges on large loose assumptions.'

Strategy formulation is not necessarily a deterministic, rational and continuous process, as was pointed out by Mintzberg (1987). He believe that, rather than being consciously and systematically developed, strategy reorientation happens in what he calls brief 'quantum loops'. A strategy, according to Mintzberg, can be deliberate – it can realize the intentions of senior management, for example to attack and conquer a new market. But this is not always the case. In theory, he says, strategy is a systematic process: first we think, then we act; we formulate, then we implement. But we also 'act in order to think'. In practice, 'a realized strategy can emerge in response to an evolving situation' and the strategic planner is often 'a pattern organizer, a learner if you like, who manages a process in which strategies and visions can emerge as well as be deliberately conceived'. This concept of 'emergent strategy' conveys the essence of how in practice organizations develop their business and HR strategies.

Mintzberg was even more scathing about the weaknesses of strategic planning in his 1994 article in the *Harvard Business Review* on 'The rise and fall of strategic planning'. He contends that 'the failure of systematic planning is the failure of systems to do better than, or nearly as well as, human beings'. He went on to say that:

> *Far from providing strategies, planning could not proceed without their prior existence... real strategists get their hands dirty digging for ideas, and real strategies are built from the nuggets they discover... sometimes strategies must be left as broad visions, not precisely articulated, to adapt to a changing environment.*

He emphasized that strategic management is a learning process as managers of firms find out what works well in practice for them.

SOURCE REVIEW

A realistic view of strategy

Tyson (1997) pointed out that, realistically, strategy:

- has always been emergent and flexible – it is always 'about to be', it never exists at the present time;
- is not only realized by formal statements but also comes about by actions and reactions;
- is a description of a future-oriented action that is always directed towards change;
- is conditioned by the management process itself.

The process of strategic HRM as defined below has to take account of these features of strategy.

Strategic HRM defined

Strategic HRM is an approach that defines how the organization's goals will be achieved through people by means of HR strategies and integrated HR policies and practices.

Strategic HRM can be regarded as a mind set underpinned by certain concepts rather than a set of techniques. It provides the foundation for strategic reviews in which analyses of the organizational context and existing HR practices lead to choices on strategic plans for the development of overall or specific HR strategies (see Chapter 3). Strategic HRM involves the exercise of strategic choice (which is always there) and the establishment of strategic priorities

But strategic HRM is not just about strategic planning. It is also concerned with the implementation of strategy and the strategic behaviour of HR specialists working with their line management colleagues on an everyday basis to ensure that the business goals of the organization are achieved and its values are put into practice. The strategic role of HR practitioners is examined in Chapter 5.

Aims of strategic HRM

The fundamental aim of strategic HRM is to generate organizational capability by ensuring that the organization has the skilled, engaged, committed and well-motivated employees it needs to achieve sustained competitive advantage. It has two main objectives: first to achieve integration – the vertical alignment of HR strategies with business strategies and the horizontal integration of HR strategies. The second objective is to provide a sense of direction in an often turbulent environment so that the business needs of the organization and the individual and collective needs of its employees can be met by the development and implementation of coherent and practical HR policies and programmes. In accordance with the resource-based view, the strategic goal will be to 'create firms which are more intelligent and flexible than their competitors' (Boxall, 1996) by hiring and developing more talented staff and by extending their skills base.

Schuler (1992) stated that:

> *Strategic human resource management is largely about integration and adaptation. Its concern is to ensure that: 1) human resources (HR) management is fully integrated with the strategy and strategic needs of the firm; 2) HR policies cohere both across policy areas and across hierarchies; and 3) HR practices are adjusted, accepted and used by line managers and employees as part of their everyday work.*

As Dyer and Holder (1988) remarked, strategic HRM provides 'unifying frameworks which are at once broad, contingency based and integrative'. The rationale for strategic HRM is the perceived advantage of having an agreed and understood basis for developing and implementing approaches to people management that take into account the changing context in which the firm operates and its longer-term requirements.

Strategic HRM is based on two key concepts, namely, the resource-based view and strategic fit.

The resource-based view of strategic HRM

To a very large extent, the philosophy and approaches to strategic HRM are underpinned by the resource-based view. This states that it is the range of resources in an organization, including its human resources, that produces its unique character and creates competitive advantage.

Barney (1991, 1995) stated that competitive advantage arises first when firms within an industry are heterogeneous with respect to the strategic resources they control and second, when these resources are not perfectly mobile across firms and thus heterogeneity can be long lasting. Creating sustained competitive advantage therefore depends on the unique resources and capabilities that a firm brings to competition in its environment. These resources include all the experience, knowledge, judgement, risk-taking propensity and wisdom of individuals associated with a firm. For a firm resource to have the potential for creating sustained competitive advantage it should have four attributes: it must be valuable, rare, imperfectly imitable and non-substitutable. To discover these resources and capabilities, managers must look inside their firm for valuable, rare and costly-to-imitate resources, and then exploit these resources through their organization.

The significant link between the resources and capabilities of a firm and its strategies was summarized by Grant (1991) as follows.

SOURCE REVIEW

The significance of the resource-base view, Grant (1991)

The resources and capabilities of a firm are the central considerations in formulating its strategy: they are the primary constants upon which a firm can establish its identity and frame its strategy, and they are the primary sources of the firm's profitability. The key to a resource-based approach to strategy formulation is understanding the relationships between resources, capabilities, competitive advantage, and profitability – in particular, an understanding of the mechanisms through which competitive advantage can be sustained over time. This requires the design of strategies which exploit to maximum effect each firm's unique characteristics.

Wright *et al* (2001) noted that there are three important components of HRM that constitute a resource for the firm and are influenced by HR practices or the HR system:

1. The human capital pool comprised of the stock of employee knowledge, skills, motivation and behaviours.
2. The flow of human capital through the firm – the movement of people and of knowledge.
3. The dynamic processes through which organizations change and/or renew themselves.

They suggested that HR practices are the primary levers through which the firm can change the pool of human capital as well as attempt to change the employee behaviours that lead to organizational success.

Resource-based strategic HRM can produce what Boxall and Purcell (2003) referred to as human resource advantage. The aim is to develop strategic capability. This means strategic fit between resources and opportunities, obtaining added value from the effective deployment of resources, and developing people who can think and plan strategically in the sense that they understand the key strategic issues and ensure that what they do supports the achievement of the business's strategic goals. In line with human capital theory, the resource-based view emphasizes that investment in people increases their value to the firm.

The strategic goal emerging from the resource-based view will be to 'create firms which are more intelligent and flexible than their competitors' (Boxall, 1996) by hiring and developing more talented staff and by extending their skills base. Resource-based strategy is therefore concerned with the enhancement of the human or intellectual capital of the firm. As Ulrich (1998) commented: 'Knowledge has become a direct competitive advantage for companies selling ideas and relationships. The challenge to organizations is to ensure that they have the capability to find, assimilate, compensate and retain the talented individuals they need.'

The significance of the resource-based view of the firm is that it highlights the importance of a human capital management approach to HRM and provides the justification for investing in people through resourcing, talent management and learning and development programmes as a means of enhancing organizational capability.

However, it should be remembered that the original resource-based view as expressed by Barney (1991, 1995) referred to all the strategic resources associated with a firm, not just human resources. This is pointed out by Mueller (1996) in a challenging comment, as follows.

SOURCE REVIEW

The resources covered by the resource-based view, Mueller (1996)

Empirical analyses conducted within a resource-based view framework have shown that in fact most companies value their company and product reputation – even though obviously sustained by employees – as their most important asset, followed in third place by employee know-how. It is difficult to see, for example, what could be more important for Glaxo than its patents, or for British Airways its landing spots at London Heathrow Airport.

Often people alone cannot sustain the success of the 'super star' of corporate performance... It is more fruitful to look at how different strategic assets sustain each other, rather than engage in a sterile debate about which are analytically prior or more important. Human resources have to be seen within the context of the firm's broad array of resources: employees are central for a firm to retain its valued product reputation, but also vice versa; a highly reputable company will find it easier to attract highly qualified employees.

Strategic fit

As explained by Wright and McMahan (1992) strategic fit refers to the two dimensions that distinguish strategic HRM:

> *First, vertically, it entails the linking of human resource management practices with the strategic management processes of the organization. Second, horizontally, it emphasizes the coordination or congruence among the various human resource management practices.*

Perspectives on strategic HRM

Taking into account the concepts of the resource-based view and strategic fit, Delery and Doty (1996) contended that 'organizations adopting a particular strategy require HR practices that are different from those required by organizations adopting different strategies' and that organizations with 'greater congruence between their HR strategies and their (business) strategies should enjoy superior performance'. They identified the three HRM perspectives set out below.

SOURCE REVIEW

Perspectives on HRM, Delery and Doty (1996)

1. The universalistic perspective – some HR practices are better than others and all organizations should adopt these best practices. There is a universal relationship between individual 'best' practices and firm performance.
2. The contingency perspective – in order to be effective, an organization's HR policies must be consistent with other aspects of the organization. The primary contingency factor is the organization's strategy. This can be described as 'vertical fit'.
3. The configurational perspective – this is an holistic approach that emphasizes the importance of the pattern of HR practices and is concerned with how this pattern of independent variables is related to the dependent variable of organizational performance. In its general sense, configuration has been defined by Huczynski and Buchanan (2007) as: 'The structures, processes, relationships and boundaries through which an organization operates.'

This typology provided the basis for what has become the most commonly used classification of approaches as advocated by Richardson and Thompson (1999), which was to adopt the terms 'best practice' and 'best fit' for the universalistic and contingency perspectives, and 'bundling' as the third approach. This followed the classification made by Guest (1997) of fit as an ideal set of practices, fit as contingency and fit as bundles.

The best practice approach

This approach is based on the assumption that there is a set of best HRM practices that are universal in the sense that they are best in any situation, and that adopting them will lead to superior organizational performance.

A number of lists of 'best practices' have been produced, the best known of which was produced by Pfeffer (1998a), namely:

1. employment security;
2. selective hiring;
3. self-managed teams;
4. high compensation contingent on performance;
5. training to provide a skilled and motivated workforce;

6. reduction of status differentials;
7. sharing information.

The following list was drawn up by Guest (1999):

1. Selection and the careful use of selection tests to identify those with potential to make a contribution.
2. Training, and in particular a recognition that training is an ongoing activity.
3. Job design to ensure flexibility, commitment and motivation, including steps to ensure that employees have the responsibility and autonomy fully to use their knowledge and skills.
4. Communication to ensure that a two-way process keeps everyone fully informed.
5. Employee share ownership programmes to increase employees' awareness of the implications of their actions on the financial performance of the firm.

Delery and Doty (1996) identified seven strategic HR practices, ie ones that are related to overall organizational performance: the use of internal career ladders, formal training systems, results-oriented appraisal, performance-based compensation, employment security, employee voice and broadly defined jobs.

High-performance work systems as described in Chapter 12 can incorporate best practice characteristics, eg the US Department of Labor (1993), Appelbaum *et al* (2000), Sung and Ashton (2005) and Thompson and Heron (2005). Another list for high commitment practices was produced by Wood and Albanese (1995).

Problems with the best practice model

The 'best practice' rubric has been attacked by a number of commentators. Cappelli and Crocker-Hefter (1996) comment that the notion of a single set of best practices has been overstated: 'There are examples in virtually every industry of firms that have very distinctive management practices… Distinctive human resource practices shape the core competencies that determine how firms compete.'

Purcell (1999) has also criticized the best practice or universalist view by pointing out the inconsistency between a belief in best practice and the resource-based view that focuses on the intangible assets, including HR, that allow the firm to do better than its competitors. He asks how can 'the universalism of best practice be squared with the view that only some resources and routines are important and valuable by being rare and imperfectly imitable?'

In accordance with contingency theory, which emphasizes the importance of interactions between organizations and their environments so that what organizations do is dependent on the context in which they operate, it is difficult to accept that there is any such thing as universal best practice. What works well in one organization will not necessarily work well in another because it may not fit its strategy, culture, management style, technology or working practices.

However, a knowledge of what is assumed to be best practice can be used to inform decisions on what practices are most likely to fit the needs of the organization, as long as it is understood why a particular practice should be regarded as a best practice and what needs to be done to ensure that it will work in the context of the organization. Becker and Gerhart (1996) argue that the idea of best practice might be more appropriate for identifying the principles underlying the choice of practices, as opposed to the practices themselves. Perhaps it is best to think of 'good practice' rather than 'best practice'.

The best fit approach

The best fit approach is in line with contingency theory. It emphasizes that HR strategies should be congruent with the context and circumstances of the organization. 'Best fit' can be perceived in terms of vertical integration or alignment between the organization's business and HR strategies. There are three models, namely: lifecycle, competitive strategy, and strategic configuration.

The lifecycle best fit model

The lifecycle model is based on the theory that the development of a firm takes place in four stages: start-up, growth, maturity and decline. This is in line with product lifecycle theory. The basic premise of this model was expressed by Baird and Meshoulam (1988) as follows:

> *Human resource management's effectiveness depends on its fit with the organization's stage of development. As the organization grows and develops, human resource management programmes, practices and procedures must change to meet its needs. Consistent with growth and development models it can be suggested that human resource management develops through a series of stages as the organization becomes more complex.*

Best fit and competitive strategies

Three strategies aimed at achieving competitive advantage have been identified by Porter (1985):

1. Innovation – being the unique producer.
2. Quality – delivering high quality goods and services to customers.
3. Cost leadership – the planned result of policies aimed at 'managing away expense'.

It was contended by Schuler and Jackson (1987) that to achieve the maximum effect it is necessary to match the role characteristics of people in an organization with the preferred strategy. Accordingly, they produced the descriptions of appropriate role behaviours set out in Table 2.1.

Table 2.1 Role behaviours appropriate for different strategies, Schuler and Jackson (1987)

Innovative	Quality	Cost-leadership strategy
• High degree of creative behaviour • A longer-term focus • A relatively high level of cooperation and interdependent behaviour • A moderate degree of concern for quantity • An equal degree of concern for process and results • A greater degree of risk taking • A high tolerance of ambiguity and unpredictability	• Relatively repetitive and predictable behaviours • A more long-term or intermediate focus • A modest amount of cooperative, interdependent behaviour • A high concern for quality • A modest concern for quantity of output • High concern for process (how the goods or services are made or delivered) • Low risk-taking activity • Commitment to the goals of the organization	• Relatively repetitive and predictable behaviours • A rather short-term focus • Primarily autonomous or individual activity • Modest concern for quality • High concern for quantity of output • Primary concern for results • Low risk-taking activity • A relatively high degree of comfort with stability

Strategic configuration

Another approach to best fit is the proposition that organizations will be more effective if they adopt a policy of strategic configuration (Delery and Doty, 1996) by matching their strategy to one of the ideal types defined by theories such as those produced by Miles and Snow (1978). This increased effectiveness is attributed to the internal consistency or fit between the patterns of relevant contextual, structural and strategic factors.

Miles and Snow (1978) identified four types of organizations, classifying the first three types as 'ideal' organizations:

1. Prospectors, which operate in an environment characterized by rapid and unpredictable changes. Prospectors have low levels of formalization and specialization and high levels of

decentralization. They have relatively few hierarchical levels.

2. Defenders, which operate in a more stable and predictable environment than prospectors and engage in more long-term planning. They have more mechanistic or bureaucratic structures than prospectors and obtain coordination through formalization, centralization, specialization and vertical differentiation.

3. Analysers, which are a combination of the prospector and defender types. They operate in stable environments like defenders and also in markets where new products are constantly required, like prospectors. They are usually not the initiators of change like prospectors but they follow the changes more rapidly than defenders.

4. Reactors, which are unstable organizations existing in what they believe to be an unpredictable environment. They lack consistent well-articulated strategies and do not undertake long-range planning.

Comments on the concept of best fit

The best fit model seems to be more realistic than the best practice model. As Dyer and Holder (1988) pointed out: 'The inescapable conclusion is that what is best depends'. It can therefore be claimed that best fit is more important than best practice. But there are limitations to the concept. Paawue (2004) emphasized that: 'It is necessary to avoid falling into the trap of "contingent determinism" (ie claiming that the context absolutely determines the strategy). There is, or should be, room for making strategic choices.'

There is a danger of mechanistically matching HR policies and practices with strategy. It is not credible to claim that there are single contextual factors that determine HR strategy, and internal fit cannot therefore be complete. As Boxall *et al* (2007) assert: 'It is clearly impossible to make all HR policies reflective of a chosen competitive or economic mission; they may have to fit with social legitimacy goals'. And Purcell (1999) commented that: 'The search for a contingency or matching model of HRM is also limited by the impossibility of modelling all the contingent variables, the difficulty of showing their interconnection, and the way in which changes in one variable have an impact on others'.

Best fit models tend to be static and don't take account of the processes of change. They neglect the fact that institutional forces shape HRM – it cannot be assumed that employers are free agents able to make independent decisions.

Bundling

As Richardson and Thompson (1999) comment: 'A strategy's success turns on combining vertical or external fit and horizontal or internal fit.' They conclude that a firm with bundles of associated HR practices should have a higher level of performance, provided it also achieves high levels of fit with its competitive strategy.

'Bundling' is the development and implementation of several HR practices together so that they are inter-related and therefore complement and reinforce each other. This is the process of horizontal integration, which is also referred to as the use of 'complementarities' (MacDuffie, 1995) who explained the concept of bundling as follows:

> *Implicit in the notion of a 'bundle' is the idea that practices within bundles are interrelated and internally consistent, and that 'more is better' with respect to the impact on performance, because of the overlapping and mutually reinforcing effect of multiple practices.*

Dyer and Reeves (1995) note that: 'The logic in favour of bundling is straightforward… Since employee performance is a function of both ability and motivation, it makes sense to have practices aimed at enhancing both.' Thus there are several ways in which employees can acquire needed skills (such as careful selection and training) and multiple incentives to enhance motivation (different forms of financial and non-financial rewards). Their study of various models listing HR practices that create a link between HRM and business performance found that the activities appearing in most of the models were involvement, careful selection, extensive training and contingent compensation.

On the basis of his research in flexible production manufacturing plants in the United States, MacDuffie (1995) noted that employees will exercise discretionary effort only if they 'believe that their individual interests are aligned with those of the company, and that the company will make a reciprocal investment in their well-being'. This means that flexible production techniques have to be supported by bundles of high-commitment human resource practices such as employment security, pay that is partly contingent on performance, a reduction of status barriers between managers and workers, and investment in building worker skills. The research indicated that plants using flexible production systems that bundle human resource practices into a system that is integrated with production/business strategy, outperform plants using more traditional mass production systems in both productivity and quality.

Following research in 43 automobile processing plants in the United States, Pil and MacDuffie (1996) established that when a high-involvement work practice is introduced in the presence of complementary HR practices, not only does the new work practice produce an incremental improvement in performance but so do the complementary practices.

The aim of bundling is to achieve high performance through coherence, which is one of the four 'meanings' of strategic HRM defined by Hendry and Pettigrew (1986). Coherence exists when a mutually reinforcing set of HR policies and practices have been developed that jointly contribute to the attainment of the organization's strategies for matching resources to organizational needs, improving performance and quality and, in commercial enterprises, achieving competitive advantage.

The process of bundling HR strategies is an important aspect of the concept of strategic HRM. In a sense, strategic HRM is holistic; it is concerned with the organization as a total system or entity and addresses what needs to be done across the organization as a whole. It is not interested in isolated programmes and techniques, or in the ad hoc development of HR practices.

Bundling can take place in a number of ways. For example, competency frameworks can be devised that are used in assessment and development centres and to specify recruitment standards, identify learning and development needs, indicate the standards of behaviour or performance required and serve as the basis for human resource planning. They could also be incorporated into performance management processes in which the aims are primarily developmental and competencies are used as criteria for reviewing behaviour and assessing learning and development needs. Job evaluation could be based on levels of competency, and competency-based pay systems could be introduced. Grade structures can define career ladders in terms of competency requirements (career family structures) and thus provide the basis for learning and development programmes. They can serve the dual purpose of defining career paths and pay progression opportunities. The development of high-performance, high-commitment or high-involvement systems (see Chapters 3 and 12) is in effect bundling because it groups a number of HR practices together to produce synergy and thus makes a greater impact.

The problem with the bundling approach is that of deciding what is the best way to relate different practices together. There is no evidence that one bundle is generally better than another.

The reality of strategic HRM

Strategic HRM, as this chapter has shown, has been a happy hunting ground for academics over many years. But what does all this conceptualizing mean in real life? What can practitioners learn from it as they go about their business?

Before answering these questions it is worth recalling the rationale for strategic HRM, which is that it is the basis for developing and implementing approaches to people management that take into account the changing context in which the firm operates and its longer-term requirements. It should also be borne in mind that strategic HRM is a mindset that only becomes real when it produces actions and reactions that can be regarded as strategic, either in the form of overall or specific HR strategies or strategic behaviour on the part of HR professionals working alongside line managers.

As modelled in Figure 2.1, strategic HRM is about both HR strategies and the strategic management role of HR professionals. There is always choice about those strategies and the strategic role of HR.

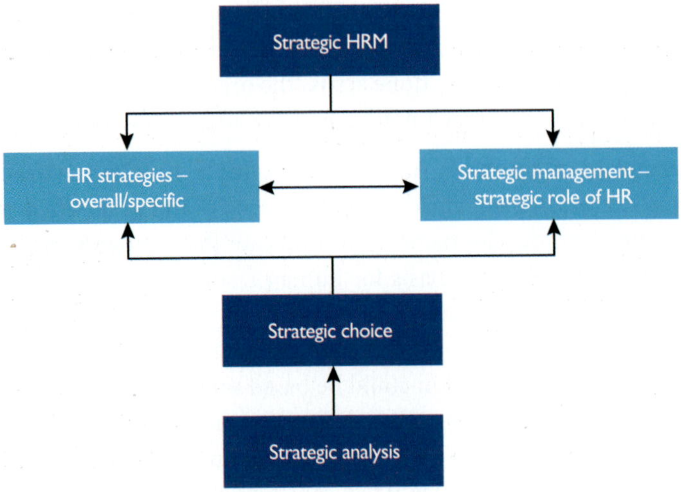

Figure 2.1 Strategic HRM model

Practical implications of strategic HRM theory

It was famously remarked by McGregor (1960) that there is nothing as practical as a good theory, ie one that has been based on rigorous field research and, probably, tested by further research. This is certainly the case with strategic HR theory, which is based on thorough research and testing and, once the jargon has been discarded, has a strong common sense appeal.

The theory 1) addresses major people issues which affect or are affected by the strategic plans of the organization, 2) provides an agreed and understood basis for developing and implementing approaches to people management that take into account the changing context in which the firm operates and its longer-term requirements, 3) ensures that business and HR strategy and functional HR strategies are aligned with one another, and 4) is the rationale for HR practitioners acting as strategic partners. The significant features of strategic HRM are set out below.

The significant features of strategic HRM

- Creating sustained competitive advantage depends on the unique resources and capabilities that a firm brings to competition in its environment (Baron, 2001).
- Competitive advantage is achieved by ensuring that the firm has higher quality people than its competitors (Purcell *et al*, 2003).

- The competitive advantage based on the effective management of people is hard to imitate (Barney, 1991, 1995).
- The challenge is to achieve organizational capability, ensuring that businesses are able to find, assimilate, reward and retain the talented individuals they need (Ulrich, 1998).
- It is unwise to pursue so-called 'best practice' (the 'universalistic' perspective of Delery and Doty, 1996) without being certain that what happens elsewhere would work in the context of the organization.
- 'Best fit' (the 'contingency' perspective of Delery and Doty, 1996) is preferable to 'best practice' as long as the organization avoids falling into the trap of 'contingent determinism' by allowing the context to determine the strategy (Paawue, 2004).
- The search for best fit is limited by the impossibility of modelling all the contingent variables, the difficulty of showing their interconnection, and the way in which changes in one variable have an impact on others (Purcell, 1999).
- Best fit can be pursued in a number of ways, namely by fitting the HR strategy to its position in its lifecycle of start-up, growth, maturity or decline (Baird and Meshoulam, 1988), or the competitive strategy of innovation, quality or cost leadership (Porter, 1985), or to the organization's 'strategic configuration' (Delery and Doty, 1996), eg the typology of organizations as prospectors, defenders and analysers defined by Miles and Snow (1978).
- Improved performance can be achieved by 'bundling', ie the development and implementation of several HR practices together so that they are inter-related and therefore complement and reinforce each other (MacDuffie, 1995).

Strategic HRM – key learning points

The conceptual basis of strategic HRM

Strategic HRM is the interface between HRM and strategic management. It takes the notion of HRM as a strategic, integrated and coherent approach and develops that in line with the concept of strategic management (Boxall, 1996).

The fundamental characteristics of strategy

- forward looking;
- the organizational capability of a firm depends on its resource capability;

Strategic HRM – key learning points (continued)

- strategic fit – the need when developing HR strategies to achieve congruence between them and the organization's business strategies within the context of its external and internal environment.

How strategy is formulated

An emergent and flexible process of developing a sense of direction, making the best use of resources and ensuring strategic fit.

The aim of strategic HRM

To generate organizational capability by ensuring that the organization has the skilled, engaged, committed and well-motivated employees it needs to achieve sustained competitive advantage.

Implications of the resource-based view

The creation of firms which are 'more intelligent and flexible than their competitors' (Boxall, 1996) by hiring and developing more talented staff and by extending the skills base.

The three HRM 'perspectives' of Delery and Doty (1996)

1. Universalistic perspective – some HR practices are better than others and all organizations should adopt these best practices.
2. Contingency – in order to be effective, an organization's HR policies must be consistent with other aspects of the organization.
3. Configurational – relating HRM to the 'configuration' of the organization in terms of its structures and processes.

The concepts of 'best practice' and 'best fit'

- The concept of best practice is based on the assumption that there is a set of best HRM practices which are universal in the sense that they are best in any situation, and that adopting them will lead to superior organizational performance. This concept of universality is criticized because it takes no account of the local context.
- The concept of best fit emphasizes that HR strategies should be congruent with the context and circumstances of the organization. 'Best fit' can be perceived in terms of vertical integration or alignment between the organization's business and HR strategies.
- It is generally accepted that best fit is more important than best practice.

The significance of bundling

The process of bundling HR strategies is an important aspect of the concept of strategic HRM which is concerned with the organization as a total system or entity and addresses what needs to be done across the organization as a whole.

Strategic HRM – key learning points (continued)

The practical implications of strategic HRM theory

The theory addresses major people issues which affect or are affected by the strategic plans of the organization. It provides the rationale for HR practitioners acting as strategic partners on an everyday basis.

Questions

1. A junior colleague in your HR department has sent you an e-mail to the effect that: 'During the course of my studies I have come across the phrase "best fit is more important than best practice". What does this mean exactly and what is its significance to us?' Produce a reply.

2. Your chief executive has sent you the following e-mail: 'I have just returned from a one-day management conference in which an academic kept on referring to "the resource based view" and its significance. What is it and how relevant is it, if at all, to what we are doing here?' Produce a reply.

3. You are the recently appointed HR director of a medium-sized distribution company based in Dartford with a staff of 350 including 130 drivers. After three months you have decided that the crucial HR issues facing the company are the high rate of turnover of drivers (35 per cent last year), an unacceptable level of road accidents, and an unsatisfactory climate of employee relations (there is a recognized union for drivers which is militant and hostile and no formal procedures for employee communications or consultation). In spite of this the company is doing reasonably well although it is felt by the board that is should do better and there are plans for opening a new distribution centre in Essex. You have received an e-mail from the finance director who is preparing the company's business plan and asks for your proposals on what needs to be done in HR to support it.

References

Abell, D F (1993) *Managing with Dual Strategies: Mastering the present, pre-empting the future*, Free Press, New York

Appelbaum, E, Bailey, T, Berg, P and Kalleberg, A L (2000) *Manufacturing Advantage: Why high performance work systems pay off*, ILR Press, Ithaca, NY

Baird, L and Meshoulam, I (1988) Managing two fits of strategic human resource management, *Academy of Management Review*, **13** (1), pp116–28

Barney, J B (1991) Firm resources and sustained competitive advantage, *Journal of Management Studies*, **17** (1), pp 99–120

Barney, J B (1995) Looking inside for competitive advantage, *Academy of Management Executive*, **9** (4), pp 49–61

Baron, D (2001) Private policies, corporate policies and integrated strategy, *Journal of Economics and Management Strategy*, **10** (7), pp 7–45

Becker, B E and Gerhart, S (1996) The impact of human resource management on organizational performance: progress and prospects, *Academy of Management Journal*, **39** (4), pp 779–801

Boxall, P F (1996) The strategic HRM debate and the resource-based view of the firm, *Human Resource Management Journal*, **6** (3), pp 59–75

Boxall, P F and Purcell, J (2003) *Strategy and Human Resource Management*, Palgrave Macmillan, Basingstoke

Boxall, P F, Purcell J and Wright P (2007) The goals of HRM, in (eds) P Boxall, J Purcell and P Wright, *Oxford Handbook of Human Resource Management*, Oxford University Press, Oxford

Cappelli, P and Crocker-Hefter, A (1996) Distinctive human resources are firms' core competencies, *Organizational Dynamics*, Winter, pp 7–22

Chandler, A D (1962) *Strategy and Structure*, MIT Press, Boston, MA

Delery, J E and Doty, H D (1996) Modes of theorizing in strategic human resource management: tests of universality, contingency and configurational performance predictions, *Academy of Management Journal*, **39** (4), pp 802–35

Dyer, L and Holder, G W (1998) Strategic human resource management and planning, in (ed) L Dyer, *Human Resource Management: Evolving roles and responsibilities*, Bureau of National Affairs, Washington DC

Dyer, L and Reeves, T (1995) Human resource strategies and firm performance: what do we know and where do we need to go? *The International Journal of Human Resource Management*, **6** (3), pp 656–70

Grant, R M (1991) The resource-based theory of competitive advantage: implications for strategy formation, *California Management Review*, **33** (3), pp 14–35

Guest, D E (1997) Human resource management and performance; a review of the research agenda, *The International Journal of Human Resource Management*, **8** (3), 263–76

Guest, D E (1999) The role of the psychological contract, in (eds) S J Perkins and St John Sandringham, *Trust, Motivation and Commitment*, Strategic Remuneration Centre, Faringdon

Heller, R (1972) *The Naked Manager*, Barrie & Jenkins, London

Hendry, C and Pettigrew, A (1986) The practice of strategic human resource management, *Personnel Review*, **15**, pp 2–8

Huczynski, A A and Buchanan, D A (2007) *Organizational Behaviour*, 6th edn, FT Prentice Hall, Harlow

Kanter, R M (1984) *The Change Masters*, Allen & Unwin, London

MacDuffie, J P (1995) Human resource bundles and manufacturing performance, *Industrial Relations Review*, **48** (2), pp 199–221

McGregor, D (1960) *The Human Side of Enterprise*, McGraw-Hill, New York

Miles, R E and Snow, C C (1978) *Organizational Strategy: Structure and process*, McGraw Hill, New York

Mintzberg, H (1987) Crafting strategy, *Harvard Business Review*, July–August, pp 66–74

Mintzberg, H (1994) The rise and fall of strategic planning, *Harvard Business Review*, January–February, pp 107–14

Mueller, F (1996) Human resources as strategic assets: an evolutionary resource-based approach, *Journal of Management Studies*, **33** (6), pp 757–85

Paauwe, J (2004) *HRM and performance: Achieving long term viability*, Oxford University Press, Oxford

Pearce, J A and Robinson, R B (1988) *Strategic Management: Strategy Formulation and Implementation*, Irwin, Georgetown, Ontario

Penrose, E (1959) *The Theory of the Growth of the Firm*, Blackwell, Oxford

Pfeffer, J (1998a) *The Human Equation*, Harvard Business School Press, Boston, MA

Pil, F K and MacDuffie, J P (1996) The adoption of high-involvement work practices, *Industrial Relations*, **35** (3), pp 423–55

Porter, M E (1985) *Competitive Advantage: Creating and sustaining superior performance*, New York, The Free Press

Purcell, J (1999) Best practice or best fit: chimera or cul-de-sac, *Human Resource Management Journal*, **9** (3), pp 26–41

Purcell, J, Kinnie, K, Hutchinson, Rayton, B and Swart, J (2003) *People and Performance: How people management impacts on organisational performance*, CIPD, London

Richardson, R and Thompson, M (1999) *The Impact of People Management Practices on Business Performance: A literature review*, Institute of Personnel and Development, London

Schuler, R S (1992) Strategic human resource management: linking people with the strategic needs of the business, *Organizational Dynamics*, **21** (1), pp 18–32

Schuler, R S and Jackson, S E (1987) Linking competitive strategies with human resource management practices, *Academy of Management Executive*, **9** (3), pp 207–19

Sung, J and Ashton, D (2005) *High Performance Work Practices: Linking strategy and skills to performance outcomes*, DTI in association with CIPD, available at http://www.cipd.co.uk/subjects/corpstrtgy/

Thompson, M and Heron, P (2005) Management capability and high performance work organization, *The International Journal of Human Resource Management*, **16** (6), pp 1029–48

Tyson, S (1997) Human resource strategy: a process for managing the contribution of HRM to organizational performance, *The International Journal of Human Resource Management*, **8** (3), pp 277–90

Ulrich, D (1998) A new mandate for human resources, *Harvard Business Review*, January–February, pp 124–34

US Department of Labor (1993) *High Performance Work Practices and Work Performance*, US Government Printing Office, Washington DC

Wernerfelt, B (1984) A resource-based view of the firm, *Strategic Management Journal*, **5** (2), pp 171–80

Wood, S and Albanese, M (1995) Can we speak of a high commitment management on the shop floor? *Journal of Management Studies*, **32** (2), pp 215–47

Wright, P M and McMahan, G C (1992) Theoretical perspectives for SHRM, *Journal of Management*, **18** (2), pp 295–320

Wright, P M, Dunford, B B and Snell, SA (2001) Human resources and the resource-based view of the firm, *Journal of Management*, **27** (6), pp 701–21

3
HR Strategies

Key concepts and terms

- High commitment management
- High performance management
- HR strategy
- High involvement management
- Horizontal fit
- Vertical fit

Learning outcomes

On completing this chapter you should be able to define these key concepts. You should also understand:

- The purpose of HR strategy
- Specific HR strategy areas
- How HR strategy is formulated
- How the vertical integration of business and HR strategies is achieved
- How HR strategies can be set out
- General HR strategy areas
- The criteria for a successful HR strategy
- The fundamental questions on the development of HR strategy
- How horizontal fit (bundling) is achieved
- How HR strategies can be implemented

Introduction

As described in Chapter 2, strategic HRM is a mindset that leads to strategic actions and reactions, either in the form of overall or specific HR strategies or strategic behaviour on the part of HR professionals. This chapter focuses on HR strategies and answers the following questions: What are HR strategies? What are the main types of overall HR strategies? What are the main areas in which specific HR strategies are developed? What are the criteria for an effective HR strategy? How should HR strategies be developed? How should HR strategies be implemented?

What are HR strategies?

HR strategies set out what the organization intends to do about its human resource management policies and practices and how they should be integrated with the business strategy and each other. They are described by Dyer and Reeves (1995) as 'internally consistent bundles of human resource practices'. Richardson and Thompson (1999) suggest that:

> *A strategy, whether it is an HR strategy or any other kind of management strategy must have two key elements: there must be strategic objectives (ie things the strategy is supposed to achieve), and there must be a plan of action (ie the means by which it is proposed that the objectives will be met).*

The purpose of HR strategies is to articulate what an organization intends to do about its human resource management policies and practices now and in the longer term, bearing in mind the dictum of Fombrun *et al* (1984) that business and managers should perform well in the present to succeed in the future. HR strategies aim to meet both business and human needs in the organization.

HR strategies may set out intentions and provide a sense of purpose and direction, but they are not just long-term plans. As Gratton (2000) commented: 'There is no great strategy, only great execution.'

Because all organizations are different, all HR strategies are different. There is no such thing as a standard strategy and research into HR strategy conducted by Armstrong and Long (1994) and Armstrong and Baron (2002) revealed many variations. Some strategies are simply very general declarations of intent. Others go into much more detail. But two basic types of HR strategies can be identified; these are: 1) general strategies such as high-performance working, and 2) specific strategies relating to the different aspects of human resource management such as learning and development and reward.

General HR strategies

General strategies describe the overall system or bundle of complementary HR practices that the organization proposes to adopt or puts into effect in order to improve organizational performance. The three main approaches are summarized below.

1. High-performance management

High-performance management or high-performance working aims to make an impact on the performance of the organization in such areas as productivity, quality, levels of customer service, growth and profits. High-performance management practices include rigorous recruitment and selection procedures, extensive and relevant training and management development activities, incentive pay systems and performance management processes.

These practices are often called 'high-performance work systems' (HPWS) which, as defined by Appelbaum *et al* (2000), comprise practices that can facilitate employee involvement, skill enhancement and motivation. Thompson and Heron (2005) refer to them as 'high-performance work organization practices' which, they say, 'consist of work practices that invest in the skills and abilities of employees, design work in ways that enable employee collaboration in problem solving and provide incentives to motivate workers to use their discretionary effort'. This term is more frequently used than either high-commitment management or high-involvement management, although there is a degree of overlap between these approaches and an HPWS and the terms 'high performance' and 'high commitment' are sometimes used interchangeably.

2. High-commitment management

One of the defining characteristics of HRM is its emphasis on the importance of enhancing mutual commitment (Walton, 1985b). High-commitment management has been described by Wood (1996) as: 'A form of management which is aimed at eliciting a commitment so that behaviour is primarily self-regulated rather than controlled by sanctions and pressures external to the individual, and relations within the organization are based on high levels of trust.'

The following definitions expand these statements.

SOURCE REVIEW

High commitment management defined, Wood (1999)

High-commitment management is generally characterized as entailing, a) a particular orientation on the part of employers to their employees, based on an underlying conception of them as assets to be developed rather than as disposable factors of production, and b) the combined use of certain personnel practices, such as job redesign, job flexibility, problem-solving groups, team working and minimal status differences.

Approaches to achieving high commitment, Beer *et al* (1984) and Walton (1985b)

- The development of career ladders and emphasis on trainability and commitment as highly valued characteristics of employees at all levels in the organization.
- A high level of functional flexibility with the abandonment of potentially rigid job descriptions.
- The reduction of hierarchies and the ending of status differentials.
- A heavy reliance on team structure for disseminating information (team briefing), structuring work (team working) and problem solving (quality circles).

Wood and Albanese (1995) added to this list:

- job design as something management consciously does in order to provide jobs that have a considerable level of intrinsic satisfaction;
- a policy of no compulsory lay-offs or redundancies and permanent employment guarantees with the possible use of temporary workers to cushion fluctuations in the demand for labour;
- new forms of assessment and payment systems and, more specifically, merit pay and profit sharing;
- a high involvement of employees in the management of quality.

As defined above, there are many similarities between high-performance and high-commitment management. In fact, there is much common ground between the practices included in all of these approaches as Sung and Ashton (2005) comment.

SOURCE REVIEW

Comparison of approaches, Sung and Ashton (2005)

In some cases high performance work practices are called 'high commitment practices' (Walton, 1985a) or 'high involvement management' (Lawler, 1986). More recently they have been termed 'high performance organizations' (Lawler *et al*, 1998) or 'high-involvement' work practices (Wood *et al*, 2001). Whilst these studies are referring to the same general phenomena the use of different 'labels' has undoubtedly added to the confusion.

However, a study of the literature shows that the most frequently used term is 'high-performance management', which is why in this book it is given more detailed consideration in Chapter 12.

3. High-involvement management

As defined by Benson *et al* (2006): 'High-involvement work practices are a specific set of human resource practices that focus on employee decision making, power, access to information, training and incentives.' The term 'high involvement' was used by Lawler (1986) to describe management systems based on commitment and involvement, as opposed to the old bureaucratic model based on control. The underlying hypothesis is that employees will increase their involvement with the company if they are given the opportunity to control and understand their work. He claimed that high-involvement practices worked well because they acted as a synergy and had a multiplicative effect. This approach involves treating employees as partners in the enterprise whose interests are respected and who have a voice on matters that concern them. It is concerned with communication and involvement. The aim is to create a climate in which a continuing dialogue between managers and the members of their teams takes place in order to define expectations and share information on the organization's mission, values and objectives. This establishes mutual understanding of what is to be achieved and a framework for managing and developing people to ensure that it will be achieved.

The practices included in a high-involvement system have sometimes expanded beyond this original concept and included high-performance practices. For example, as noted above, high-performance practices usually include relevant training and incentive pay systems. Sung and Ashton (2005) include high-involvement practices as one of the three broad areas of a high-performance work system (the other two being human resource practices and reward and commitment practices).

Examples of general HR strategies

A local authority

As expressed by the chief executive of this borough council, their HR strategy is about:

> *having a very strong focus on the overall effectiveness of the organization, its direction and how it's performing; there is commitment to, and belief in, and respect for individuals, and I think that these are very important factors.*

A public utility

> *The only HR strategy you really need is the tangible expression of values and the implementation of values... unless you get the human resource values right you can forget all the rest. (Managing Director)*

A manufacturing company

> *The HR strategy is to stimulate changes on a broad front aimed ultimately at achieving competitive advantage through the efforts of our people. In an industry of fast followers, those who learn quickest will be the winners. (HR Director)*

A retail stores group

> *The biggest challenge will be to maintain (our) competitive advantage and to do that we need to maintain and continue to attract very high calibre people. The key differentiator on anything any company does is fundamentally the people, and I think that people tend to forget that they are the most important asset. Money is easy to get hold of, good people are not. All we do in terms of training and manpower planning is directly linked to business improvement. (Managing Director)*

Specific HR strategies

Specific HR strategies set out what the organization intends to do in areas such as:

- Human capital management – obtaining, analysing and reporting on data that inform the direction of value-adding people management, strategic, investment and operational decisions.
- Corporate social responsibility – a commitment to managing the business ethically in order to make a positive impact on society and the environment.

- Organization development – the planning and implementation of programmes designed to enhance the effectiveness with which an organization functions and responds to change.
- Engagement – the development and implementation of policies designed to increase the level of employees' engagement with their work and the organization.
- Knowledge management – creating, acquiring, capturing, sharing and using knowledge to enhance learning and performance.
- Resourcing – attracting and retaining high quality people.
- Talent management – how the organization ensures that it has the talented people it needs to achieve success.
- Learning and development – providing an environment in which employees are encouraged to learn and develop.
- Reward – defining what the organization wants to do in the longer term to develop and implement reward policies, practices and processes that will further the achievement of its business goals and meet the needs of its stakeholders.
- Employee relations – defining the intentions of the organization about what needs to be done and what needs to be changed in the ways in which the organization manages its relationships with employees and their trade unions.
- Employee well-being – meeting the needs of employees for a healthy, safe and supportive work environment.

Criteria for an effective HR strategy

An effective HR strategy is one that works in the sense that it achieves what it sets out to achieve. Its particular requirements are set out below.

Criteria for an effective HR strategy

- It will satisfy business needs.
- It is founded on detailed analysis and study, not just wishful thinking.
- It can be turned into actionable programmes that anticipate implementation requirements and problems.
- It is coherent and integrated, being composed of components that fit with and support each other.

- It takes account of the needs of line managers and employees generally as well as those of the organization and its other stakeholders. As Boxall and Purcell (2003) emphasize: 'HR planning should aim to meet the needs of the key stakeholder groups involved in people management in the firm.'

How should HR strategies be formulated?

SOURCE REVIEW

Propositions about the formulation of HR strategy, Boxall (1993)

- The strategy formation process is complex, and excessively rationalistic models that advocate formalistic linkages between strategic planning and HR planning are not particularly helpful to our understanding of it.
- Business strategy may be an important influence on HR strategy but it is only one of several factors.
- Implicit (if not explicit) in the mix of factors that influence the shape of HR strategies is a set of historical compromises and trade-offs from stakeholders.

Strategic options and choices

The process of formulating HR strategies involves generating strategic HRM options and then making appropriate strategic choices. It has been noted by Cappelli (1999) that: 'The choice of practices that an employer pursues is heavily contingent on a number of factors at the organizational level, including their own business and production strategies, support of HR policies, and cooperative labour relations.' The process of developing HR strategies involves the adoption of a contingent approach in generating strategic HRM options and then making appropriate strategic choices. There is seldom if ever one right way forward.

'Inside-out' and 'outside-in' approaches to formulating HR strategies

Research conducted by Wright *et al* (2004) identified two approaches that can be adopted by HR to strategy formulation: the inside-out approach and the outside-in approach. They made the following observations about the HR-strategy linkage:

> *At the extreme, the 'inside-out' approach begins with the status quo HR function (in terms of skills, processes, technologies, etc) and then attempts (with varying degrees of success) to identify linkages to the business (usually through focusing on 'people issues'), making minor adjustments to HR activities along the way... On the other hand, a few firms have made a paradynamic shift to build their HR strategies from the starting point of the business. Within these 'outside-in' HR functions, the starting point is the business, including the customer, competitor and business issues they face. The HR strategy then derives directly from these challenges to create real solutions and add real value.*

They suggested that 'the most advanced linkage was the "integrative" linkage in which the senior HR executive was part of the top management team, and was able to sit at the table and contribute during development of the business strategy'.

In reality HR strategies are more likely to flow from business strategies, which will be dominated by product/market and financial considerations. But there is still room for HR to make a useful, even essential contribution at the stage when business strategies are conceived, for example, by focusing on resource issues. This contribution may be more significant if strategy formulation is an emergent or evolutionary process – HR strategic issues will then be dealt with as they arise during the course of formulating and implementing the corporate strategy.

Issues in developing HR strategies

Five fundamental questions that need to be asked in developing HR strategies have been posed by Becker and Huselid (1998):

1. What are the firm's strategic objectives?
2. How are these translated into unit objectives?
3. What do unit managers consider are the 'performance drivers' of those objectives?
4. How do the skills, motivation and structure of the firm's workforce influence these performance drivers?
5. How does the HR system influence the skills, motivation and structure of the workforce?

But many different routes may be followed when formulating HR strategies – there is no one right way. On the basis of their research in 30 well-known companies, Tyson and Witcher (1994) commented that: 'The different approaches to strategy formation reflect different ways to manage change and different ways to bring the people part of the business into line with business goals.'

In developing HR strategies, process may be as important as content. Tyson and Witcher (1994) also noted from their research that: 'The process of formulating HR strategy was often as important as the content of the strategy ultimately agreed. It was argued that by working through strategic issues and highlighting points of tension, new ideas emerged and a consensus over goals was found.'

There are two key issues to be addressed in developing HR strategies: achieving vertical fit or integration and achieving horizontal fit or integration (bundling).

1. Achieving vertical fit – integrating business and HR strategies

Wright and Snell (1998) suggest that seeking fit requires knowledge of the business strategy, knowledge of the skills and behaviour necessary to implement the strategy, knowledge of the HRM practices necessary to elicit those skills and behaviours, and the ability quickly to develop and implement the desired system of HRM practices.

When considering how to integrate business and HR strategies it should be remembered that business and HR issues influence each other and in turn influence corporate and business unit strategies. It is also necessary to note that in establishing these links, account must be taken of the fact that strategies for change have also to be integrated with changes in the external and internal environments. Fit may exist at a point in time but circumstances will change and fit no longer exists. An excessive pursuit of 'fit' with the status quo will inhibit the flexibility of approach that is essential in turbulent conditions.

An illustration of how HR strategies could fit vertically with one or other of the competitive strategies listed by Porter (1985) is given in Table 3.1.

Table 3.1 Achieving vertical fit between HR and business strategies

HR strategy	Competitive strategy		
	Achieve competitive advantage through innovation	Achieve competitive advantage through quality	Achieve competitive advantage through cost-leadership
Resourcing	Recruit and retain high quality people with innovative skills and a good track record in innovation	Use sophisticated selection procedures to recruit people who are likely to deliver quality and high levels of customer service	Develop core/periphery employment structures; recruit people who are likely to add value; if unavoidable, plan and manage downsizing humanely

Table 3.1 *continued*

HR strategy	Competitive strategy		
	Achieve competitive advantage through innovation	Achieve competitive advantage through quality	Achieve competitive advantage through cost-leadership
Learning and development	Develop strategic capability and provide encouragement and facilities for enhancing innovative skills and enhancing the intellectual capital of the organization	Encourage the development of a learning organization, develop and implement knowledge management processes, support total quality and customer care initiatives with focused training	Provide training designed to improve productivity; inaugurate just-in-time training which is closely linked to immediate business needs and can generate measurable improvements in cost-effectiveness
Reward	Provide financial incentives and rewards and recognition for successful innovations	Link rewards to quality performance and the achievement of high standards of customer service	Review all reward practices to ensure that they provide value for money and do not lead to unnecessary expenditure

The factors that can make the achievement of good vertical fit difficult are:

- The business strategy may not be clearly defined – it could be in an emergent or evolutionary state, which would mean that there would be little or nothing with which to fit the HR strategy.
- Even if the business strategy is clear, it may be difficult to determine precisely how HR strategies could help in specific ways to support the achievement of particular business objectives – a good business case can only be made if it can be demonstrated that there will be a measurable link between the HR strategy and business performance in the area concerned.
- Even if there is a link, HR specialists do not always have the strategic capability to make the connection – they need to be able to see the big picture, understand the business drivers and appreciate how HR policies and practices can impact on them.

- Barriers exist between top management and HR – the former may not be receptive because they don't believe this is necessary and HR is not capable of persuading them that they should listen, or HR lacks access to top management on strategic issues, or HR lacks credibility with top management as a function that knows anything about the business or should even have anything to do with the business.

It is up to HR practitioners in their strategic role to overcome these problems by getting to know what the business is aiming to do and what drives it (this should be possible even when strategies are 'emergent'), understanding just how HR practices make an impact, and achieving access to strategic business decision making by demonstrating their credibility as an integral part of the management of the business.

2. Achieving horizontal fit (bundling)

Horizontal fit or integration is achieved when the various HR strategies cohere and are mutually supporting. This can be attained by the process of 'bundling', which is carried out by first identifying appropriate HR practices; second, assessing how the items in the bundle can be linked together so that they become mutually reinforcing; and finally drawing up programmes for the development of these practices, paying particular attention to the links between them.

The use of high-performance, high-involvement or high-commitment systems as described earlier in this chapter is an integrating process. The essence of these systems is that they each consist of a set of complementary work practices that are developed and maintained as a whole. Other integrating activities or processes are talent management, performance management and the use of competencies.

The factors that inhibit the achievement of horizontal fit are difficulties in:

- deciding which bundles are likely to be best;
- actually linking practices together – it is always easier to deal with one practice at a time;
- managing the interdependencies between different parts of a bundle;
- convincing top management and line managers that bundling will benefit the organization and them.

These can be overcome by dedicated HR professionals, but it is hard work.

Setting out the strategy

There is no standard model of how an HR strategy should be set out; it all depends on the circumstances of the organization. But the typical areas that may be covered in a written strategy are set out below.

Typical areas that may be covered in a written HR strategy

- Basic considerations – business needs in terms of the key elements of the business strategy; environmental factors and analysis (SWOT/PESTLE) and cultural factors – possible helps or hindrances to implementation.
- Content – details of the proposed HR strategy.
- Rationale – the business case for the strategy against the background of business needs and environmental/cultural factors.
- Implementation plan – an action programme, definitions of responsibilities and resource requirements and arrangements for communication, consultation, involvement and training.
- Costs and benefits analysis – an assessment of the resource implications of the plan (costs, people and facilities) and the benefits that will accrue, for the organization as a whole, for line managers and for individual employees. (So far as possible these benefits should be quantified in terms of added value or return on investment.)

Implementing HR strategies

All too often, 80 per cent of the time spent on strategic management is devoted to designing strategies and only 20 per cent is spent on planning their implementation. It should be the other way round. It is necessary to plan with implementation in mind.

Because strategies tend to be expressed as abstractions, they must be translated into programmes with clearly stated objectives and deliverables. It is necessary to avoid saying, in effect: 'We need to get from here to there but we don't care how.' Getting strategies into action is not easy. Too often, strategists act like Mr Pecksmith who was compared by Dickens (1843) to 'a direction-post which is always telling the way to a place and never goes there'.

The term 'strategic HRM' has been devalued in some quarters; sometimes to mean no more than a few generalized ideas about HR policies, at other times to describe a short-term plan, for example, to increase the retention rate of graduates. It must be emphasized that HR strategies are not just programmes, policies, or plans concerning HR issues that the HR department happens to feel are important. Piecemeal initiatives do not constitute strategy.

The problem with strategic HRM as noted by Gratton *et al* (1999) is that too often there is a gap between what the strategy states will be achieved and what actually happens to it. The factors they identified as contributing to creating this say/do gap between the strategy as designed and the strategy as implemented include:

- the tendency of employees in diverse organizations only to accept initiatives they perceive to be relevant to their own areas;
- the tendency of long-serving employees to cling to the status quo;
- complex or ambiguous initiatives may not be understood by employees or will be perceived differently by them, especially in large, diverse organizations;
- it is more difficult to gain acceptance of non-routine initiatives;
- employees will be hostile to initiatives if they are believed to be in conflict with the organization's identity, eg downsizing in a culture of 'job-for-life';
- the initiative is seen as a threat;
- inconsistencies between corporate strategies and values;
- the extent to which senior management is trusted;
- the perceived fairness of the initiative;
- the extent to which existing processes could help to embed the initiative;
- a bureaucratic culture, which leads to inertia.

Barriers to the implementation of HR strategies

Each of the factors listed by Gratton *et al* (1999) can create barriers to the successful implementation of HR strategies. Other major barriers include failure to understand the strategic needs of the business, inadequate assessment of the environmental and cultural factors that affect the content of the strategies, and the development of ill-conceived and irrelevant initiatives, possibly because they are current fads or because there has been an ill-digested analysis of best practice that does not fit the organization's requirements. These problems are compounded when insufficient attention is paid to practical implementation problems, the important role of line managers in implementing strategies, and the need to have established supporting processes for the initiative (eg, performance management to support performance pay).

Approaches to implementation

An implementation programme that overcomes these barriers needs to be based on:

- a rigorous preliminary analysis of the strategic needs of the business and how the strategy will help to meet them;

- a communication programme that spells out what the strategy is, what it is expected to achieve and how it is to be introduced;
- the involvement of those who will be concerned with the strategy, eg line managers, in identifying implementation problems and how they should be dealt with;
- the preparation of action plans that indicate who does what and when;
- project managing the implementation in a way that ensures that the action plans are achieved.

HR strategies – key learning points

Purpose of HR strategy

To articulate what an organization intends to do about its human resource management policies and practices now and in the longer term.

General HR strategy areas

High-performance management, high-commitment management and high-involvement management

Specific HR strategy areas

Human capital management, corporate social responsibility, organization development, engagement, knowledge management, employee resourcing, talent management, learning and development, reward, employee relations, and employee well-being.

Criteria for an effective HR strategy

- satisfies business needs;
- founded on detailed analysis and study;
- can be turned into actionable programmes;
- is coherent and integrated;
- takes account of the needs of line managers and employees generally as well as those of the organization and its other stakeholders.

Fundamental questions on the development of HR strategy

- What are the firm's strategic objectives and how are these translated into unit objectives?
- What are the 'performance drivers' of those objectives and how do the skills, motivation and structure of the firm's workforce influence these performance drivers?
- How does the HR system influence the skills, motivation and structure of the workforce?

How the vertical integration of business and HR strategies is achieved

Understand what the business is aiming to do and what drives it, and how HR practices make an impact on these drivers.

HR strategies – key learning points (continued)

How horizontal fit (bundling) is achieved

Identify appropriate HR practices, assess how these items can be bundled together so that they become mutually reinforcing, and draw up programmes for the development of these practices, paying particular attention to the links between them.

How HR strategies can be set out

The format will vary but may typically be set out under the following headings:

- Basic considerations.
- Content.
- Rationale.
- Implementation plan.
- Costs and benefits analysis.

How HR strategies can be implemented

- Analyse business needs and how the HR strategy will help to meet them.
- Communicate full information on the strategy and what it is expected to achieve.
- Involve those concerned in identifying implementation problems and how they should be dealt with.
- Prepare action plans.
- Plan and execute a programme of project management that ensures that the action plans are achieved.

Questions

1. Critically evaluate the following statement by Lester Digman (1990): 'Since most strategic decisions are event-driven rather than programmed they are unplanned. Accordingly they should be seen in terms of preferences, choices and matches rather than exercises in applied logic.'
2. You have been asked to write an article for your CIPD branch newsletter on 'What are the main characteristics of an HR strategy?' You have also been asked to include examples from your own organization or a published article or book. Draft an outline of the article.
3. A colleague says to you: 'It's all very well talking about integrated HR strategy but what does it mean for us?' Reply.

Questions (continued)

4. Prepare a presentation for your fellow students on 'What makes a good HR strategy?' Illustrate with examples.
5. You have received an e-mail from your boss, the HR director, with the message: 'We hear a lot about integrating the HR strategy with the business strategy but what does this mean? What are the problems in doing it? How do we overcome these problems?' Reply.
6. Thompson and Harley (2007) wrote that the move has not been to abandon control in favour of commitment (cf Walton, 1985a) but towards the introduction of softer controls, ie 'towards practices intended to generate commitment through a combination of culture-led changes and delegation of authority'. Soft controls are presented as a package of high-commitment practices. To what extent is this picture of high-commitment practices as manipulative true?

References

Appelbaum, E, Bailey, T, Berg, P and Kalleberg, A L (2000) *Manufacturing Advantage: Why high performance work systems pay off*, ILR Press, Ithaca, NY

Armstrong, M and Baron, A (2002) *Strategic HRM: The route to improved business performance*, CIPD, London

Armstrong, M and Baron, A (2004) *Managing Performance: Performance management in action*, CIPD, London

Armstrong, M and Long, P (1994) *The Reality of Strategic HRM*, IPD, London

Becker, B E and Huselid, M A (1998) High performance work systems and firm performance: a synthesis of research and managerial implications, *Research on Personnel and Human Resource Management*, **16,** pp 53–101, JAI Press, Stamford, CT

Beer, M, Spector, B, Lawrence, P, Quinn Mills, D and Walton, R (1984) *Managing Human Assets*, The Free Press, New York

Benson, G S, Young, S M and Lawler, E E (2006) High involvement work practices and analysts' forecasts of corporate performance, *Human Resource Management*, **45** (4), pp 519–27

Boxall, P F (1993) The significance of human resource management: a reconsideration of the evidence, *The International Journal of Human Resource Management*, **4** (3), pp 645–65

Boxall, P F and Purcell, J (2003) *Strategy and Human Resource Management*, Palgrave Macmillan, Basingstoke

Cappelli, P (1999) *Employment Practices and Business Strategy*, Oxford University Press, New York

Dickens, C (1843) *Martin Chuzzlewit* , Chapman & Hall, London

Digman, L A (1990) *Strategic management – Concepts, decisions, cases*, Irwin, Homewood, IL

Dyer, L and Reeves, T (1995) Human resource strategies and firm performance: what do we know and where do we need to go?, *The International Journal of Human Resource Management*, **6** (3), pp 656–70

Fombrun, C J, Tichy, N M and Devanna, M A (1984) *Strategic Human Resource Management*, Wiley, New York

Gratton, L A (2000) Real step change, *People Management*, 16 March, pp 27–30

Gratton, L A, Hailey, V H, Stiles, P and Truss, C (1999) *Strategic Human Resource Management*, Oxford University Press, Oxford

Lawler, E E (1986) *High Involvement Management*, Jossey-Bass, San Francisco, CA

Lawler, E E, Mohrman, S and Ledford, G (1998) *Strategies for High Performance Organizations: Employee involvement, TQM, and re-engineering programs in Fortune 1000*, Jossey-Bass, San Francisco, CA

Porter, M E (1985) *Competitive Advantage: Creating and sustaining superior performance*, New York, The Free Press

Richardson, R and Thompson, M (1999) *The Impact of People Management Practices on Business Performance: A literature review*, IPD, London

Sung, J and Ashton, D (2005) *High Performance Work Practices: Linking strategy and skills to performance outcomes*, DTI in association with CIPD, available at http://www.cipd.co.uk/subjects/corpstrtgy/

Thompson, P and Harley, B (2007) HRM and the worker: labour process perspectives, in (eds) P Boxall, J Purcell and P Wright, *Oxford Handbook of Human Resource Management*, Oxford University Press, Oxford

Thompson, M and Heron, P (2005) Management capability and high performance work organization, *The International Journal of Human Resource Management*, **16** (6), pp 1029–48

Tyson, S and Witcher, M (1994) Human resource strategy emerging from the recession, *Personnel Management*, August, pp 20–23

Walton, R E (1985a) From control to commitment in the workplace, *Harvard Business Review*, March–April, pp 77–84

Walton, R E (1985b) Towards a strategy of eliciting employee commitment based on principles of mutuality, in (eds) R E Walton and P R Lawrence, *HRM Trends and Challenges*, Harvard Business School Press, Boston, MA

Wood, S (1996) High commitment management and organization in the UK, *The International Journal of Human Resource Management*, **7** (1), pp 41–58

Wood, S (1999) Human resource management and performance, *International Journal of Management Reviews*, **1** (4), pp 397–413

Wood, S and Albanese, M (1995) Can we speak of a high commitment management on the shop floor? *Journal of Management Studies*, **32** (2), pp 215–47

Wood, S, de Menezes, L M and Lasaosa, A (2001) High involvement management and performance, Paper delivered at the Centre for Labour Market Studies, University of Leicester, May

Wright, P M and Snell, S A (1998) Towards a unifying framework for exploring fit and flexibility in strategic human resource management, *Academy of Management Review*, **23** (4), pp 756–72

Wright, P M, Snell, S A and Jacobsen, H H (2004) Current approaches to HR strategies: inside-out versus outside-in, *Human Resource Planning*, **27** (4), pp 36–46

4 Human Capital Management

Key concepts and terms

- Human capital
- Human capital advantage
- Human process advantage
- Human capital monitor (Andrew Mayo)
- Intangible resources
- Organizational capital
- Social capital
- Human capital management
- Human capital index (Watson Wyatt)
- Human capital measurement
- Intellectual capital
- Metrics
- Organizational performance model (Mercer HR Consulting)

Learning outcomes

- The concept of human capital
- Constituents of human capital
- Importance of human capital measurement (HCM)
- Approaches to measurement
- Factors affecting choice of measurement
- Characteristics of human capital
- Significance of human capital theory
- Reasons for interest in HCM
- Measurement elements
- Criteria for HCM data for managers

Introduction

The concept 'human capital management' (HCM) is based on the concept of human capital as explained in the first part of this chapter. The next three sections describe the processes of human capital management – measurement, internal and external reporting. The chapter concludes with a note on introducing HCM.

Human capital management defined

HCM is concerned with obtaining, analysing and reporting on data that inform the direction of value-adding people management, strategic, investment and operational decisions at corporate level and at the level of front line management. It is, as emphasized by Kearns (2005), ultimately about value.

HCM is concerned with purposeful measurement, not just measurement. The defining characteristic of HCM is the use of metrics to guide an approach to managing people that regards them as assets and emphasizes that competitive advantage is achieved by strategic investments in those assets through employee engagement and retention, talent management and learning and development programmes. HCM provides a bridge between HR and business strategy.

The concept of human capital

Individuals generate, retain and use knowledge and skill (human capital) and create intellectual capital. Their knowledge is enhanced by the interactions between them (social capital) and generates the institutionalized knowledge possessed by an organization (organizational capital). These concepts of human, intellectual, social and organizational capital are explained below.

Human capital

Human capital consists of the knowledge, skills and abilities of the people employed in an organization. The term was originated by Schultz (1961) who elaborated his concept in 1981 as follows: 'Consider all human abilities to be either innate or acquired. Attributes... which are valuable and can be augmented by appropriate investment will be human capital.' A more detailed definition was put forward by Bontis *et al* (1999), as follows.

SOURCE REVIEW

Human capital defined, Bontis *et al* (1999)

Human capital represents the human factor in the organization; the combined intelligence, skills and expertise that gives the organization its distinctive character. The human elements of the organization are those that are capable of learning, changing, innovating and providing the creative thrust which if properly motivated can ensure the long-term survival of the organization.

Scarborough and Elias (2002) believe that: 'The concept of human capital is most usefully viewed as a bridging concept – that is, it defines the link between HR practices and business performance in terms of assets rather than business processes.' They point out that human capital is to a large extent 'non-standardized, tacit, dynamic, context dependent and embodied in people'. These characteristics make it difficult to evaluate human capital bearing in mind that the 'features of human capital that are so crucial to firm performance are the flexibility and creativity of individuals, their ability to develop skills over time and to respond in a motivated way to different contexts'.

It is indeed the knowledge, skills and abilities of individuals that create value, which is why the focus has to be on means of attracting, retaining, developing and maintaining the human capital they represent. Davenport (1999) comments that:

> *People possess innate abilities, behaviours and personal energy and these elements make up the human capital they bring to their work. And it is they, not their employers, who own this capital and decide when, how and where they will contribute it. In other words, they can make choices. Work is a two-way exchange of value, not a one-way exploitation of an asset by its owner.*

The choices they make include how much discretionary behaviour they are prepared to exercise in carrying out their role (discretionary behaviour refers to the discretion people at work can exercise about the way they do their job and the amount of effort, care, innovation and productive behaviour they display). They can also choose whether or not to remain with the organization.

The constituents of human capital

Human capital consists of intellectual, social and organizational capital.

Intellectual capital

The concept of human capital is associated with the overarching concept of intellectual capital, which is defined as the stocks and flows of knowledge available to an organization. These can be regarded as the intangible resources associated with people which, together with tangible resources (money and physical assets), comprise the market or total value of a business. Bontis (1998) defines intangible resources as the factors other than financial and physical assets that contribute to the value-generating processes of a firm and are under its control.

Social capital

Social capital is another element of intellectual capital. It consists of the knowledge derived from networks of relationships within and outside the organization. The concept of social capital has been defined by Putnam (1996) as 'the features of social life – networks, norms and trust – that enable participants to act together more effectively to pursue shared objectives'. It is important to take into account social capital considerations, that is the ways in which knowledge is developed through interaction between people. Bontis *et al* (1999) point out that it is flows as well as stocks that matter. Intellectual capital develops and changes over time and a significant part is played in these processes by people acting together.

Organizational capital

Organizational capital is the institutionalized knowledge possessed by an organization that is stored in databases, manuals, etc (Youndt, 2000). It is often called 'structural capital' (Edvinson and Malone, 1997), but the term 'organizational capital' is preferred by Youndt because, he argues, it conveys more clearly that this is the knowledge that the organization actually owns.

The significance of human capital theory

The added value that people can contribute to an organization is emphasized by human capital theory. It regards people as assets and stresses that investment by organizations in people will generate worthwhile returns. Human capital theory is associated with the resource-based view of the firm as developed by Barney (1991). This proposes that sustainable competitive advantage is attained when the firm has a human resource pool that cannot be imitated or substituted by its rivals. Boxall (1996) refers to this situation as one that confers 'human capital advantage'. But he also notes (1996, 1999) that a distinction should be made between 'human capital advantage' and 'human process advantage'. The former results from employing people with competitively valuable knowledge and skills, much of it tacit. The latter, however, follows from the establishment of difficult to imitate, highly evolved processes within the firm, such as cross-departmental cooperation and executive development. Accordingly, 'human resource advantage', the superiority of one firm's labour management over another's, can be thought of as the product of its human capital and human process advantages.

An approach to people management based on human capital theory involves obtaining answers to the questions set out below.

Questions on people management raised by human capital theory

- What are the key performance drivers that create value?
- What skills do we have?
- What skills do we need now and in the future to meet our strategic aims?
- How are we going to attract, develop and retain these skills?
- How can we develop a culture and environment in which organizational and individual learning takes place that meets both our needs and the needs of our employees?
- How can we provide for both the explicit and tacit knowledge created in our organization to be captured, recorded and used effectively?

Human capital theory helps to:

- determine the impact of people on the business and their contribution to shareholder value;
- demonstrate that HR practices produce value for money in terms, for example, of return on investment;
- provide guidance on future HR and business strategies;
- provide data that will inform strategies and practices designed to improve the effectiveness of people management in the organization.

Human capital measurement

Human capital measurement has been defined by IDS (2004) as being 'about finding links, correlations and, ideally, causation, between different sets of (HR) data, using statistical techniques'. As Becker *et al* (2001) emphasize:

> *The most potent action HR managers can take to ensure their strategic contribution is to develop a measurement system that convincingly showcases HR's impact on business performance. [They must] understand how the firm creates value and how to measure the value creation process.*

The primary aim of HCM is to assess the impact of human resource management practices and the contribution made by people to organizational performance. Methods of measuring impact and contribution based upon human capital data have therefore to be developed.

The need for human capital measurement

There is an overwhelming case for evolving methods of valuing human capital as an aid to people management decision making. This may mean identifying the key people management drivers and modelling the effect of varying them. The need is to develop a framework within which reliable information can be collected and analysed such as added value per employee, productivity and measures of employee behaviour (attrition and absenteeism rates, the frequency/severity rate of accidents, and cost savings resulting from suggestion schemes).

Becker *et al* (2001) refer to the need to develop a 'high-performance perspective' in which HR and other executives view HR as a system embedded within the larger system of the firm's strategy implementation. They state that: 'The firm manages and measures the relationship between these two systems and firm performance.'

Reasons for the interest in measurement

The recognized importance of achieving human capital advantage has led to an interest in the development of methods of measuring the value and impact of that capital, as indicated below.

Reasons for the interest in measuring the value and impact of human capital

- Human capital constitutes a key element of the market worth of a company. A research study conducted in 2003 (CFO Research Studies) estimated that the value of human capital represented over 36 per cent of total revenue in a typical organization.
- People in organizations add value and there is a case for assessing this value to provide a basis for HR planning and for monitoring the effectiveness and impact of HR policies and practices.

- The process of identifying measures and collecting and analysing information relating to them will focus the attention of the organization on what needs to be done to find, keep, develop and make the best use of its human capital.
- Measurements can be used to monitor progress in achieving strategic HR goals and generally to evaluate the effectiveness of HR practices.
- You cannot manage unless you measure.

However, three voices have advised caution about measurement. Leadbeater (2000) observed that measuring can 'result in cumbersome inventories which allow managers to manipulate perceptions of intangible values to the detriment of investors. The fact is that too few of these measures are focused on the way companies create value and make money'. The Institute of Employment Studies (Hartley, 2005) emphasized that reporting on human capital is not simply about measurement. Measures on their own such as those resulting from benchmarking are not enough; they must be clearly linked to business performance.

Research carried out by Professor Harry Scarborough and Juanita Elias of Warwick University (Scarborough and Elias, 2002) found that it is not what organizations decide to measure that is important but the process of measurement itself. As they noted:

> *In short, measures are less important that the activity of measuring – of continuously developing and refining our understanding of the productive role of human capital within particular settings, by embedding such activities in management practices, and linking them to the business strategy of the firm.*

This sentiment is echoed by Donkin (2005), when he says, 'It is not the measuring itself that is the key to successful human capital management but the intentions behind the measuring and the resulting practices that emerge.'

Approaches to measurement

Three approaches to measurement are described below.

1. The human capital index – Watson Wyatt

On the basis of a survey of companies that have linked together HR management practices and market value, Watson Wyatt (2002) identified four major categories of HR practice that could be linked to increases in shareholder value creation. These are:

total rewards and accountability	16.5 per cent
collegial, flexible workforce	9.0 per cent
recruiting and retention excellence	7.9 per cent
communication integrity	7.1 per cent

2. The organizational performance model – Mercer HR Consulting

As described by Nalbantian *et al* (2004) the organizational performance model developed by Mercer HR Consulting is based on the following elements: people, work processes, management structure, information and knowledge, decision making and rewards, each of which plays out differently within the context of the organization, creating a unique DNA. If these elements have been developed piecemeal, as often happens, the potential for misalignment is strong and it is likely that human capital is not being optimized, creating opportunities for substantial improvement in returns. Identifying these opportunities requires disciplined measurement of the organization's human capital assets and the management practices that affect their performance. The statistical tool, 'Internal Labour Market Analysis' used by Mercer draws on the running record of employee and labour market data to analyse the actual experience of employees rather than stated HR programmes and policies. Thus gaps can be identified between what is required in the workforce to support business goals and what is actually being delivered.

3. The human capital monitor – Andrew Mayo

Andrew Mayo (2001) has developed the 'human capital monitor' to identify the human value of the enterprise or 'human asset worth', which is equal to 'employment cost × individual asset multiplier'. The latter is a weighted average assessment of capability, potential to grow, personal performance (contribution) and alignment to the organization's values set in the context of the workforce environment (ie how leadership, culture, motivation and learning are driving success). The absolute figure is not important. What does matter is that the process of measurement leads you to consider whether human capital is sufficient, increasing, or decreasing, and highlights issues to address. Mayo advises against using too many measures and instead, to concentrate on a few organization-wide measures that are critical in creating shareholder value or achieving current and future organizational goals.

A number of other areas for measurement and methods of doing so have been identified by Mayo (1999, 2001). He believes that value added per person is a good measure of the effectiveness of human capital, especially for making inter-firm comparisons. But he considers that the most critical indicator for the value of human capital is the level of expertise possessed by an organization. He suggests that this could be analysed under the headings of identified organizational core competencies. The other criteria he mentions are measures of satisfaction derived from employee opinion surveys and levels of attrition and absenteeism.

Measurement data

Main HCM data used for measurement

- Basic workforce data – demographic data (numbers by job category, sex, race, age, disability, working arrangements, absence and sickness, turnover and pay).
- People development and performance data – learning and development programmes, performance management/potential assessments, skills and qualifications.
- Perceptual data – attitude/opinion surveys, focus groups, exit interviews.
- Performance data – financial, operational and customer.

A summary of human capital measures and their possible uses is given in Table 4.1.

Table 4.1 A summary of human capital measures and their possible uses

Measures	Possible use – analysis leading to action
Work-force composition – sex, race, age, full-time, part-time	Analyse the extent of diversity Assess the implications of a preponderance of employees in different age groups, eg extent of loses through retirement Assess the extent to which the organization is relying on part-time staff
Length of service distribution	Indicate level of success in retaining employees Indicate preponderance of long or short-serving employees Enable analyses of performance of more experienced employees to be assessed
Skills analysis/assessment – graduates, professionally/technically qualified, skilled workers	Assess skill levels against requirements Indicate where steps have to be taken to deal with shortfalls
Attrition – employee turnover rates for different categories of management and employees	Indicate areas where steps have to be taken to increase retention rates Provide a basis for assessing levels of commitment

Table 4.1 *continued*

Measures	Possible use – analysis leading to action
Attrition – cost of	Support business case for taking steps to reduce attrition
Absenteeism/sickness rates	Identify problems and need for more effective attendance management policies
Average number of vacancies as a percentage of total workforce	Identify potential shortfall problem areas
Total pay roll costs (pay and benefits)	Provide data for productivity analysis
Compa-ratio – actual rates of pay as a percentage of policy rates	Enable control to be exercised over management of pay structure
Percentage of employees in different categories of contingent pay or payment-by-result schemes	Demonstrate the extent to which the organization believes that pay should be related to contribution
Total pay review increases for different categories of employees as a percentage of pay	Compare actual with budgeted payroll increase costs Benchmark pay increases
Average bonuses or contingent pay awards as a % of base pay for different categories of managers and employees	Analyse cost of contingent pay Compare actual and budgeted increases Benchmark increases
Outcome of equal pay reviews	Reveal pay gap between male and female employees
Personal development plans completed as a percentage of employees	Indicate level of learning and development activity
Training hours per employee	Indicate actual amount of training activity (note that this does not reveal the quality of training achieved or its impact)
Percentage of managers taking part in formal management development programmes	Indicate level of learning and development activity
Internal promotion rate (% of promotions filled from within)	Indicate extent to which talent management programmes are successful
Succession planning coverage (% of managerial jobs for which successors have been identified)	Indicate extent to which talent management programmes are successful
Percentage of employees taking part in formal performance reviews	Indicate level of performance management activity

Table 4.1 *continued*

Measures	Possible use – analysis leading to action
Distribution of performance ratings by category of staff and department	Indicate inconsistencies, questionable distributions and trends in assessments
Accident severity and frequency rates	Assess health and safety programmes
Cost savings/revenue increases resulting from employee suggestion schemes	Measure the value created by employees

Human capital internal reporting

Analysing and reporting human capital data to top management and line managers will lead to better informed decision making about what kind of actions or practices will improve business results, increased ability to recognize problems and take rapid action to deal with them, and the scope to demonstrate the effectiveness of HR solutions and thus support the business case for greater investment in HR practices. The process of reporting the data internally and the inferences obtained from them is therefore a vital part of HCM. It is necessary to be clear about what data is required and how it will be communicated and used.

The factors affecting the choice of what should be reported in the form of metrics are:

- the type of organization – measures are context dependent;
- the business goals of the organization;
- the business drivers of the organization, ie the factors that contribute to the achievement of business goals, such as increases in revenue, control of costs, customer service, quality, innovation, expansion through mergers and acquisitions, product development and market development;
- the existing key performance indicators (KPIs) used in the organization;
- the use of a balanced scorecard which enables a comprehensive view of performance to be taken by reference to four perspectives: financial, customer, innovation and learning and internal processes;
- the availability of data;
- the use of data – measures should only be selected that can be put to good use in guiding strategy and reporting on performance;

- the manageability of data – there may be a wide choice of metrics and it is essential to be selective in the light of the above analysis so that the burden of collecting, analysing and evaluating the data is not too great and people do not suffer from information overload; remember that the cost of perfection is prohibitive, the cost of sensible approximation is less.

Human capital information is usually reported internally in the form of management reports providing information for managers, often through the intranet and on dashboards. However, this information will not be valued by managers unless:

- it is credible, accurate and trustworthy;
- they understand what it means for them personally and how it will help them to manage their team;
- it is accompanied by guidance as to what action can be taken;
- they have the skills and abilities to understand and act upon it.

It is not enough simply to give managers and other stakeholders information on human capital. It must be accompanied by effective analysis and explanation if they are going to understand and act upon it in the interests of maximizing organizational performance.

Human capital external reporting

The EC Accounts Modernization Directive requires companies to prepare a business review. This has to disclose information that is necessary for the understanding of the development, performance or position of the business of the company including the analysis of key financial and other performance indicators, and information relating to environmental and employee matters, social and community issues, and any policies of the company in relation to these matters and their effectiveness.

A framework (Table 4.2) for external reporting has been produced by the CIPD (2003).

Table 4.2 Framework for external reporting

Principle	Features of framework
Add value to the decision making undertaken by stakeholder groups in respect of human capital, with value added exceeding the costs of information gathered	Information should be relevant to the identification of human capital and should be available in both narrative form and as quantitative indicators The information-gathering requirement should be clearly defined and should not be too costly

Table 4.2 *continued*

Principle	Features of framework
Balance the advantages of comparability with other organizations with the need for flexibility to reflect particular contexts	There should be a distinction between primary and secondary indicators
Provide information on possible institutional barriers to the effective development and utilization of human capital within firms	Indicators to highlight possible barriers to the under-utilization of human capital based on sex, age or race
Reflect the dynamic and context-dependent nature of human capital	There should be multiple categories of indicators to reflect the acquisition, development, management and performance of human capital
Be future-oriented to highlight the contribution of human capital to future performance	The framework should incorporate information on both the near-term and the long-term, highlighting both investments in and depreciation of human capital. It should provide information not only on human capital stocks but also on the management and utilization of the flow of human capital

Introducing HCM

As Baron and Armstrong (2007) point out, it is important to emphasize the notion of HCM as a journey. It is not an all or nothing affair. It does not have to depend on a state-of-the-art HR database or the possession of advanced expertise in statistical analysis. It is not all that difficult to record and report on basic data and, although some degree of analytical ability is required, it is to be hoped, nay expected, that any self-respecting HR professional will have that skill.

At the beginning of the journey an organization may do no more than collect basic HR data on, for instance, employee turnover and absence. But anyone who goes a little bit further, and analyses that data to draw conclusions on trends and causation leading to proposals on the action required that are supported by that analysis, is into HCM. Not in a big way perhaps, but it is a beginning. At the other end of the scale there are the highly sophisticated approaches to HCM operated by such organizations as Nationwide and the Royal Bank of Scotland. This might be the ultimate destination of HCM but it can be approached on a step-by-step basis.

Human capital management – key learning points

The concept of human capital

Individuals generate, retain and use knowledge and skill (human capital) and create intellectual capital. Human capital 'defines the link between HR practices and business performance in terms of assets rather than business processes' (Scarborough and Elias, 2002).

Characteristics of human capital

Human capital is non-standardized, tacit, dynamic, context dependent and embodied in people (Scarborough and Elias, 2002).

Constituents of human capital

Human capital consists of intellectual capital, social capital and organizational capital.

Significance of human capital

Human capital theory regards people as assets and stresses that investment by organizations in people will generate worthwhile returns.

Importance of human capital measurement

Measuring and valuing human capital is an aid to people management decision making.

Reasons for interest in human capital measurement

- Human capital constitutes a key element of the market worth of a company.
- People in organizations add value.
- Focus attention on what needs to be done to make the best use of human capital.
- Monitor progress in achieving strategic HR goals and evaluate HR practices.
- You cannot manage unless you measure.

Approaches to measurement

- The human capital index, Watson Wyatt.
- The organizational performance model, Mercer HR Consulting.
- The human capital monitor, Andrew Mayo.

Measurement elements

Workforce data, people development data, perceptual data and performance data.

Factors affecting choice of measurement

- Type of organization; its business goals and drivers.
- The existing key performance indicators (KPIs).
- Use of a balanced score card.
- The availability, use and manageability of data.

Criteria for HCM data as a guide to managers

Data will only be useful for managers if:

- the data are credible, accurate and trustworthy;
- they understand what it means for them;
- they are accompanied by guidance as to what action can be taken;
- they have the skills and abilities to understand and act upon them.

Questions

1. Your finance director has asked you: 'What is the difference between human resource management and human capital management? And whether or not they are different, why should we bother with the latter?'
2. What is social capital and why is it significant?
3. You have given a presentation on human capital management at a local conference. At question time a member of the audience gets up and says: 'This is all very well, but it sounds as if we will have to do an awful lot of work in getting a full programme of HCM off the ground (eg collecting, analysing and reporting on performance statistics) and I don't think that we have the resources to do it and even if we had, that it would be a cost-effective use of our time'. Respond.

References

Barney, J B (1991) Firm resources and sustained competitive advantage, *Journal of Management Studies*, **17** (1), pp 99–120

Baron, A and Armstrong, M (2007) *Human Capital Management: Achieving added value through people*, Kogan Page, London

Becker, B E, Huselid, M A and Ulrich, D (2001) *The HR Score card: Linking people, strategy, and performance*, Harvard Business School Press, Boston, MA

Bontis, N (1998) Intellectual capital: an exploratory study that develops measures and models, *Management Decision*, **36** (2), pp 63–76

Bontis, N, Dragonetti, N C, Jacobsen, K and Roos, G (1999) The knowledge toolbox: a review of the tools available to measure and manage intangible resources, *European Management Journal*, 17 (4), pp 391–402

Boxall, P F (1996) The strategic HRM debate and the resource-based view of the firm, *Human Resource Management Journal*, **6** (3), pp 59–75

Boxall, P (1999) Human resource strategy and competitive advantage: a longitudinal study of engineering consultancies, *Journal of Management Studies*, **36** (4), pp 443–63

CFO Research Services (2003) *Human Capital Management: The CFO's perspective*, CFO Publishing, Boston, MA

CIPD (2003) *Human Capital: External reporting framework*, CIPD, London

Davenport, T O (1999) *Human Capital*, Jossey-Bass, San Francisco, CA

Donkin, R (2005) *Human Capital Management: A management report*, Croner, London

Edvinson, L and Malone, M S (1997) *Intellectual Capital: Realizing your company's true value by finding its hidden brainpower*, Harper Business, New York

Hartley, V (2005) *Open for Business: HR and human capital reporting*, IIES, Brighton

IDS (2004) Searching for the magic bullet, *HR Study 783*, IDS London

Kearns, P (2005) *Evaluating the ROI from Learning*, CIPD, London

Leadbeater, C (2000) *Living on Thin Air: The new economy*, Viking, London

Mayo, A (1999) Making human capital meaningful, *Knowledge Management Review*, January/February, pp 26–29

Mayo, A (2001) *The Human Value of the Enterprise: Valuing people as assets*, Nicholas Brealey, London

Nalbantian, R, Guzzo, R A, Kieffer, D and Doherty, J (2004), *Play to Your Strengths: Managing your internal labour markets for lasting competitive advantage*, McGraw-Hill, New York

Putnam, R (1996) Who killed civic America?, *Prospect*, March, pp 66–72

Scarborough, H and Elias, J (2002) *Evaluating Human Capital*, CIPD, London

Schultz, T W (1961) Investment in human capital, *American Economic Review*, **51**, March, pp 1–17

Schultz, T W (1981) *Investing in People: The economics of population quality*, University of California Press, CA

Watson Wyatt Worldwide (2002) *Human Capital Index: Human capital as a lead indicator of shareholder value*, Watson Wyatt Worldwide, Washington DC

Youndt, M A (2000) Human resource considerations and value creation: the mediating role of intellectual capital, Paper delivered at National Conference of US Academy of Management, Toronto, August

5 The Role and Organization of the HR Function

Key concepts and terms

- Benchmarking
- Boundary management
- Business partner
- Centre of expertise
- Offshoring
- Output criteria
- Outsourcing
- Process criteria
- Service level agreement
- Shared service centre
- Transactional activities
- Transformational activities
- The Ulrich three-legged stool model
- Utility analysis

Learning outcomes

On completing this chapter you should be able to define these key concepts. You should also understand:

- The role of the HR function
- The diversity of the HR function
- Guidelines on organizing the function
- Quantitative criteria for evaluating the HR function
- Key points for measuring HR performance
- The HR scorecard
- Using management consultants
- HR budgeting
- The activities of the HR function
- The Ulrich three-legged stool model
- The dimensions of HR effectiveness
- How HR people can demonstrate their effectiveness
- Methods of measuring HR effectiveness
- Outsourcing
- Marketing the HR function
- The HR role of line managers

Introduction

This chapter describes the role of the HR function as a key part of the process of managing organizations. It dwells on the role of the function to provide advice, guidance and HR services. Emphasis is given to the strategic role of the function, which is to provide continuing support to the achievement of the strategic objectives of the organization, to advise on business strategies as affected by HR considerations and to ensure that HR strategies are integrated with business strategies.

The chapter starts with an analysis of the role of the HR function and then deals with its organization and how its effectiveness can be evaluated. Next it covers various aspects of the work of the function, namely the use of shared service centres, outsourcing and management consultants. Consideration is also given to marketing HR and HR budgeting. Bearing in mind the comment by Boxall *et al* (2007) that 'HRM is not just what HR departments do', the chapter ends with an examination of the HR role of line managers.

The role of the HR function

The role of the HR function is to take initiatives and provide guidance, support and services on all matters relating to the organization's employees. Essentially, the HR function is in the delivery business – providing the advice and services that enable organizations to get things done through people.

The function ensures that HR strategies, policies and practices are introduced and maintained that cater for everything concerning the employment, development and well-being of people and the relationships that exist between management and the workforce. It plays a major part in the creation of an environment that enables people to make the best use of their capacities, to realize their potential to the benefit of both the organization and themselves and, by improving the quality of working life, to achieve satisfaction through their work

Increasingly the role of the HR function is seen to be business-oriented – contributing to the achievement of sustained competitive advantage. But one of the issues explored by Francis and Keegan (2006) is the tendency for a focus on business performance outcomes to obscure the importance of employee well-being in its own right. They quote the view of Ulrich and Brockbank (2005b) that 'caring, listening to, and responding to employees remains a centrepiece of HR work'. The HR function and its members have to be aware of the ethical dimensions of their work, as described at the end of Chapter 1.

The activities of the HR function

The activities carried out within an HR function can be divided into two broad categories: 1) strategic (transformational), which is largely concerned with the alignment and implementation of HR and business strategies, and 2) transactional, which covers the main HR service delivery activities of resourcing, learning and development, reward and employee relations. The HR function is involved in devising HR strategies, policies and practices that meet the needs of the organization and its members and support the attainment of sustained competitive advantage. But as Hope-Hailey *et al* (2005) emphasize, competitive advantage lies in employees themselves, not in HRM practices. They point out that: 'The HR department needs to go beyond designing effective HRM policies and practices to ensure that these practices are implemented appropriately and are accepted by employees in order to achieve the intended results.'

The 2006 survey by IRS of the work of the HR function (Crail, 2006) asked respondents to state what were the most time consuming and most important issues facing their HR departments. The replies are summarized in Table 5.1.

Table 5.1 Issues facing HR departments

HR Issue	Most time-consuming (%)	Most important (%)
Recruitment/resourcing	27.3	16.8
Administration	16.4	1.9
Absence	12.7	7.7
Pay and benefits	12.7	19.4
Employee relations	9.1	10.3
Training and development	4.2	10.3
Strategic activities	0.0	10.3

As might be expected, recruitment was the most time-consuming, although not the most important issue. Training and development was not very time-consuming but quite important. Strategic activities were believed to be important but were not mentioned at all as being time-consuming. The emphasis is on transactional activities.

Variations in the role

The role of the HR function and the practice of human resource management vary immensely in different organizations. As Sisson (1995) has commented, HR management is not a single homogeneous occupation – it involves a variety of roles and activities that differ from one organization to another and from one level to another in the same organization. And Tyson (1987) has claimed that the HR function is often 'balkanized' – not only is there a variety of roles and activities but these tend to be relatively self-centred, with little passage between them. Hope-Hailey *et al* (1998) believe that HR could be regarded as a 'chameleon function' in the sense that the diversity of practice established by their research suggests that 'contextual variables dictate different roles for the function and different practices of people management'.

The organization of the HR function

The organization and staffing of the HR function clearly depends on the size of the business, the extent to which operations are decentralized, the type of work carried out, the kind of people employed and the role assigned to the HR function. The amount of diversity was noted by Crail (2006) on the basis of an IRS survey.

The IRS 2008 survey of HR roles and responsibilities (Crail, 2008) found that the median HR specialist to employee ratio was 108 employees to each practitioner. But it varies considerably. At the upper quartile the ratio was 1:150 and at the lower quartile it was 1:63. Broadly, the larger the organization, the higher the ratio of employees to practitioners.

Guidelines on organizing HR

There are no absolute rules for organizing the function but the following are commonly assumed guidelines.

Guidelines on organizing the HR function

- The head of the function should report directly to the chief executive and be a member of the top management team involved in the formulation of business strategy.
- In a decentralized organization, operational units should be responsible for their own HR management affairs within the framework of broad strategic and policy guidelines from the centre.
- The professional members of the function should have 'strategic capability' in the sense of understanding the strategic imperatives of the organization and having the skills required to contribute to the formulation and achievement of strategic goals and 'act as catalysts for change, anticipating problems and making things happen' (Hutchinson and Wood, 1995).
- Increased responsibility for HR matters should be devolved to line managers where appropriate.

A development in the direction of establishing a model for the organization of the HR function which has excited much interest in recent years is the Ulrich 'three-legged stool' as described by Robinson (2006) and discussed below. But many HR departments are still run on traditional lines and what this involves is also discussed later.

The Ulrich three-legged stool model

The three-legged stool model for the organization of the HR function emerged from Dave Ulrich's work in the 1990s (Ulrich 1995, 1997a, 1997b, 1998). It divides the function into the following three parts.

1. Centres of expertise

These specialize in the provision of high level advice and services on key HR activities. The CIPD survey on the changing HR function (CIPD, 2007a) found that they existed in 28 per cent of respondents' organizations. The most common expertise areas were training and development (79 per cent), recruitment (67 per cent), reward (60 per cent) and employee relations (55 per cent).

2. Strategic business partners

These work with line managers to help them reach their goals through effective strategy formulation and execution (Ulrich and Brockbank, 2005b). They are often 'embedded' in business units or departments. The concept of business partnering is considered in more detail in Chapter 5.

3. Shared service centres

These handle all the routine 'transactional' services across the business. These include such activities as recruitment, absence monitoring and advice on dealing with employee issues such as discipline and absenteeism. Shared service centres are dealt with in more detail later in this chapter.

Although this Ulrich model has attracted a great deal of attention, the CIPD 2007 survey found that only 18 per cent of respondents had implemented all three legs, although 47 per cent had implemented one or two elements with business partners being the most common (29 per cent).

As Reilly (2007) commented, respondents to the survey mentioned problems in introducing the new model. These included difficulties in defining roles and accountabilities, especially those of business partners, who risk being 'hung, drawn and quartered by all sides', according to one HR director. At the same time, the segmented nature of the structure gives rise to 'boundary management' difficulties, for example when it comes to separating out transactional tasks from the work of centres of expertise. The model can also hamper communication between those engaged in different HR activities. Other impediments were technological failure, inadequate resources in HR and skills gaps.

But some benefits were reported by survey respondents. Centres of expertise provide higher quality advice. Business partners exercise better business focus, line managers are more engaged, and the profile of HR is raised, while the introduction of shared services results in improved customer service and allows other parts of HR to spend more time on value-adding activities.

Hope-Hailey *et al* (2005) raised questions about the Ulrich model on the basis of their research in a bank. Their conclusions are given below.

SOURCE REVIEW

Conclusions by Hope-Hailey *et al* (2005) on the Ulrich model

The conflict of simultaneously balancing both a process-oriented and a people-oriented role resulted in the HR department siding with management, and largely neglecting relations with employees by making this the responsibility of line management. The identification of this fundamental conflict raises serious questions about the role of the HR function. Is it possible for the function to meet both employee and business needs by operating simultaneously in all four segments within Ulrich's model? Or is Ulrich's model at best based on a unitarist perspective and at worst overly naïve about the nature of organizational life as lived by the people researched in this case?

Standard approaches to organizing the HR function

There is no such thing as a typical HR department but Crail (2006) used the responses from 179 organizations to an IRS survey of the HR function to produce a model of a 'standard' HR department. He suggested that this:

> *might consist of a team of 12 people serving a workforce of around 1,200 (on average, there was one HR practitioner or assistant for every 102 employees). The team would have a director, three managers, one supervisor, three HR officers and four assistants. Such a team would typically include a number of professionally qualified practitioners, particularly at senior level, and would enjoy good access to the company's most senior executives.*
>
> *Although having ambitions to being more proactive, both as a business partner and strategic contributor to organizational decision making, our 'standard' HR department would still consider that it spends too much time on administration. Some attempts to*

deal with this would have been made by shifting people management responsibilities to line managers – not always with entirely positive results. Despite this, our HR department's own perception is that it has won greater respect and enjoyed greater influence over the way the organization is run in recent years – partially because the environment has changed and HR is seen as the source of knowledge on legal and regulatory requirements, but largely thanks to its own efforts.

Evaluating the HR function

It is necessary to evaluate the contribution of the HR function in order to ensure that it is effective at both the strategic level and in terms of service delivery and support. The prime criteria for evaluating the work of the function are its ability to operate strategically and its capacity to deliver the levels of services required.

Research conducted by the Institute of Employment Studies (Hirsh, 2008) discovered that the factors that correlated most strongly with line managers' and employees' satisfaction with HR were:

- being well supported in times of change;
- HR giving good advice to employees;
- being well supported when dealing with difficult people or situations;
- HR getting the basics right.

However, the results showed that HR could do better in each of these areas. The conclusions reached were that HR must find out what its customers need and what their experiences of HR services are. HR has to be responsive – clear about what it is there for and what services it offers, and easy to contact.

In evaluation it is useful to remember the distinction made by Tsui and Gomez-Mejia (1988) between process criteria – how well things are done, and output criteria – the effectiveness of the end-result. A 'utility analysis' approach as described by Boudreau (1988) can be used. This focuses on the impact of HR activities measured wherever possible in financial terms (quantity), improvements in the quality of those activities, and cost/benefit (the cost of the activities in relation to the benefits they provide). The dimensions of HR effectiveness have been defined by Huselid *et al* (1997) as follows.

SOURCE REVIEW

The dimensions of HR effectiveness, Huselid *et al* (1997)

- Strategic HRM – the delivery of services in a way that supports the implementation of the firm's strategy.
- Technical HRM – the delivery of HR basics such as recruitment, compensation and benefits.

The methods that can be used to evaluate these dimensions are described below.

Quantitative criteria

These consist of:

- Organizational: added value per employee, profit per employee, sales value per employee, costs per employee and added value per £ of employment costs.
- Employee behaviour: retention and turnover rates, absenteeism, sickness, accident rates, grievances, disputes, references to employment tribunals, successful suggestion scheme outcomes.
- HR service levels and outcomes: time to fill vacancies, time to respond to applicants, ratio of acceptances to offers made, cost of replies to advertisements, training days per employee, time to respond to and settle grievances, measurable improvements in organizational performance as a result of HR practices, ratio of HR costs to total costs, ratio of HR staff to employees, the achievement of specified goals.

A summary of measures and their possible uses is given in Table 5.2.

Table 5.2 Measures of HR effectiveness and their use

Measures	Possible use – analysis leading to action
Achievement of agreed service delivery levels: time to fill vacancies response rates to requests for services or advice provision of required information provision of required training provision of advice on employment law issues handling grievances and employee concerns handling industrial relations issues	Identify strengths and weaknesses and areas for development or improvement
Outcomes of employee opinion surveys	Assess impact of HR policies and practices on motivation, engagement and commitment
Attrition levels	Assess effectiveness of HR's recruitment, induction and reward policies and processes
Absenteeism	Assess effectiveness of HR's absence management policies
Grievances	Assess effectiveness of HR's grievance handling processes
Ratio of HR costs to total costs	Assess cost-effectiveness of HR
Cost of recruitment	Exercise control over HR costs
Cost of outsourcing	
Cost of using consultants	
Ratio of HR staff to total number of employees	Exercise control over HR staffing levels Benchmark with other comparable organizations

User reactions

The internal customers of HR (the users of HR services) can provide important feedback on HR effectiveness. Users can be asked formally to assess the extent to which the members of the HR function demonstrate their abilities in the following ways.

How members of the HR function can demonstrate their effectiveness

- Understand the business strategy and act in ways that support its achievement.
- Anticipate business needs and produce realistic proposals on how HR can help to meet them.
- Show that they are capable of meeting performance standards and deadlines for the delivery of HR initiatives and projects.
- Provide relevant, clear, convincing and practical advice.
- Provide efficient and effective services with regard to response, delivery times and quality.
- Generally reveal their understanding and expertise.

Service level agreements

A service level agreement (SLA) is an agreement between the provider of HR services and the customers who use the service on the level of service that should be provided. It sets out the nature of the service provided, the volume and quality to be achieved by the service and the response times the provider must attain after receiving requests for help. The agreement provides the basis for monitoring and evaluating the level of service.

Employee satisfaction measures

The degree to which employees are satisfied with HR policies and practices can be measured by attitude surveys. These can obtain opinions on such matters as their work, their pay, how they are treated, their views about the company and their managers, how well they are kept informed, the opportunities for learning and career development and their working environment and facilities.

Benchmarking

In addition to internal data it desirable to benchmark HR services. This means comparing what the HR function is doing with what is happening in similar organizations. This may involve making direct comparisons using quantified performance data or exchanging information on 'good practice' that can be used to indicate where changes are required to existing HR practices or to provide guidance on HR innovations. Organizations such as Saratoga provide benchmarking data under standardized and therefore comparable headings for their clients.

SOURCE REVIEW

Key points for measuring HR performance, Likierman (2005)

- Agree objectives against budget assumptions; this will ensure HR's role reflects changes in strategy implementation.
- Use more sophisticated measures – get underneath the data and look not only at the figures but at the reasons behind them.
- Use comparisons imaginatively, including internal and external benchmarking.
- Improve feedback through face-to-face discussion rather than relying on questionnaires.
- Be realistic about what performance measures can deliver – many measurement problems can be mitigated, not solved.

The HR scorecard

The HR scorecard developed by Beatty *et al* (2003) follows the same principle as the balanced scorecard, ie it emphasizes the need for a balanced presentation and analysis of data. The four headings of the HR scorecard are:

1. HR competencies – administrative expertise, employee advocacy, strategy execution and change agency.
2. HR practices – communication, work design, selection, development, measurement and rewards.
3. HR systems – alignment, integration and differentiation.
4. HR deliverables – workforce mindset, technical knowledge, and workforce behaviour.

These are all influenced by the factors that determine the strategic success of the organization, ie operational excellence, product leadership and customer intimacy.

Preferred approach to evaluation

There is much to be said for the systematic HR scorecard approach although some organizations may have to develop their own headings as a basis for evaluation. There are plenty of typical measures but no standard set exists. Perhaps, as Guest and Peccei (1994) suggest:

> *The most sensible and important indicator of HRM effectiveness will be the judgements of key stakeholders... The political, stakeholder, perspective on organizations*

acknowledges that it is the interpretation placed on effectiveness in organizations and the attributions of credit and blame that are derived from them that matter most in judging effectiveness. In other words, at the end of the day, it is always the qualitative interpretation by those in positions of power that matters most.

But they recognized 'the desirability of also developing clearly specified goals and quantitative indicators, together with financial criteria'.

Finally, in evaluating the HR function it is well worth bearing in mind the following wise words of Ulrich and Brockbank (2005a).

SOURCE REVIEW

Valuing HR, Ulrich and Brockbank (2005a)

Value is defined by the receivers of HR work – the investors, customers, line managers and employees – more than by the givers. HR is successful if and when its stakeholders perceive that it produces value. Delivering what matters most to stakeholders focuses on the deliverables (outcomes of HR) rather than on the doables (activities of HR).

HR shared service centres

An HR shared service centre is an HR unit or an outsourced facility that provides HR services that are available to a number of parties in the organization. The customer or user defines the level of the service and decides which services to take up. Thus, 'the user is the chooser' (Ulrich, 1995). A basic HR shared service centre carries out various routine administrative activities such as recruitment administration, pensions and benefits administration, payroll changes and absence monitoring. This can be extended to cover advice on employment matters such as the handling of disciplinary issues and grievances. A centre may use call-centre technology and/or provide self-service facilities for line managers and employees though an intranet system.

The organizations covered by the research conducted by Reilly (2000) on behalf of the Institute of Employment Studies identified one or more of the following reasons for providing shared services:

- HR will be consumer driven, more accessible, more professional;
- the quality of HR services will be improved in terms of using better processes, delivery to specification, time and budget, incorporation of good practice, the achievement of greater consistency and accuracy;
- the process can help to achieve organizational flexibility – a common service will support customers during business change;
- it can support the repositioning of HR so that it moves from a purely operational to a more strategic role.

The advantages of shared services include lower costs, better quality, more efficient resourcing and better customer service. But there are disadvantages, which include loss of face-to-face contact, deskilling administrative jobs and, potentially, remoteness from the users.

Outsourcing HR work

Increasingly, HR services that would previously have been regarded as a business's own responsibility to manage are now routinely being purchased from external suppliers. Managements are facing Tom Peters' (1988) challenge: 'prove it can't be subcontracted'. The formal policy of a major global corporation reads: 'Manufacture only those items – and internally source only those support services – that directly contribute to, or help to maintain, our competitive advantage.'

The HR function is well positioned to outsource some of its activities to agencies or firms that act as service providers in such fields as training, recruitment, executive search, occupational health and safety services, employee welfare and counselling activities, childcare, payroll administration and legal advisory services. HR functions that have been given responsibility for other miscellaneous activities such as catering, car fleet management, facilities management and security (because there is nowhere else to put them) may gladly outsource them to specialist firms.

The criteria used in selecting outsourcing providers include having a justifiable reason for employing consultants, examining their previous work, making sure they can deliver what they say they will, ensuring assignment objectives are specified, and ensuring implementation, The benefits of outsourcing include reduced cost, access to expertise not available within HR, increased flexibility and speed of response, and freeing-up HR to focus on more value-adding activities. But there can be problems. Some firms unthinkingly outsource core activities on an ad hoc basis to gain short-term advantage while others find that they are being leveraged by their suppliers to pay higher rates. Firms may focus on a definition of the core activities and those that can be outsourced, which may be justified at the time but did not take account of the future. Additionally, a seemingly random policy of outsourcing can lead to lower employee morale and to a 'who next' atmosphere.

To minimize problems careful consideration should be given to the case for outsourcing. It is necessary to assess each potential area with great care in order to determine whether it can and should be outsourced and exactly what such outsourcing is intended to achieve. The questions to be answered include: is the activity a core one or peripheral? How efficiently is it run at present? What contribution does it make to the qualitative and financial well-being of the organization? This is an opportunity to re-engineer the HR function, subjecting each activity to critical examination to establish whether the services can be provided from within or outside the organization, if at all. Outsourcing may well be worthwhile if it is certain that it can deliver a better service at a lower cost.

The approach to using and selecting outsourcing providers should include having a justifiable reason for employing them, examining their previous work, making sure they can deliver what they say they will, ensuring assignment objectives and service delivery standards are agreed, and specifying how they should communicate and the matters that need to be discussed and agreed during the period that assignments are carried out.

Offshoring

To save costs UK organizations can employ people overseas to carry out work on their behalf. Call centres are typical examples.

Using management consultants

Management consultants provide expertise and resources to assist in development and change. They may act as service providers in such fields as recruitment, executive search and training. They also provide outside help and guidance to their clients by advising on the introduction of new systems or procedures or by going through processes of analysis and diagnosis to produce recommendations or to assist generally in the improvement of organizational performance.

Selecting and using consultants

The steps required in selecting and using consultants effectively are:

1. Define the business need – what added value consultants will provide.
2. Justify their use in terms of their expertise, objectivity and ability to bring resources to bear that might otherwise be unavailable – if the need has been established in cost–benefit terms the use of external consultants rather than internal resources has to be justified.

3. Define clearly the objectives of the exercise in terms of the end-results and deliverables.
4. Invite three or four firms or independent consultants to submit proposals.
5. Select the preferred consultants on the basis of their proposal and an interview (a 'beauty contest'). The criteria should be the degree to which the consultants understand the need, the relevance and acceptability of their proposed deliverables and programme of work, the capacity of the firm and the particular consultants to deliver, whether the consultants will be able to adapt to the culture and management style of the organization, the extent to which they are likely to be acceptable to the people with whom they will work, and the cost (but as for service providers, not the ultimate consideration).
6. Take up references before confirming the appointment.
7. Agree and sign a contract – this should always be in writing and should set out deliverables, timing and costs, methods of payment and arrangements for termination.
8. Agree a detailed project programme.
9. Monitor the progress of the assignment carefully without unduly interfering in the day-to-day work of the consultants, and evaluate the outcomes.

Legal implications

A consultancy assignment can be cancelled if either party has clearly failed to meet the terms of the contract (whether this is a formal contract or simply an exchange of letters). Clients can also sue consultants for professional negligence if they believe that their advice or actions have caused financial or some other form of measurable loss. Professional negligence is, however, not always easy to prove, especially in HR assignments. Consultants can always claim that their advice was perfectly good but that it has been used incorrectly by the client (this may also be difficult to prove). Suing consultants can be a messy business and should only be undertaken when it is felt that they (or their insurers) should pay for their mistakes and thus help to recoup the client's losses. It should also be remembered that independent consultants and even some small firms may not have taken out professional liability insurance. If that is the case, all the aggrieved client who sues would do is to bankrupt them, which may give the client some satisfaction but could be a somewhat pointless exercise. The latter problem can be overcome if the client only selects consultants who are insured.

Marketing the HR function

Top management and line managers are the internal customers whose wants and needs the HR function must identify and meet. How can this be done?

First, it is necessary to understand the needs of the business and its critical success factors – where the business is going, how it intends to get there and what are the things that are going to make the difference between success and failure. These data need to be converted into what are in effect marketing plans for the development of products and services to meet ascertained needs – of the business and its managers and employees. The plan should establish the costs of introducing and maintaining these initiatives and the benefits that will be obtained from them. Every effort must be made to quantify these benefits in financial terms.

The next step in the marketing process is to persuade management that this is a product or service the business needs. This means making out the business case – spelling out its benefits in terms of added value and the impact it will make on the performance of the business and indicating what financial and people resources will be required.

This approach is akin to 'branding' in product planning, which identifies the product or service, spells out the benefits it provides and differentiates it from other services, thus bringing it to the attention of customers and enhancing its image. Presentation is important through logos and distinctive brochures. Some HR departments brand products with an immediately identifiable name such as 'Genome' or 'Gemini'. Others 'brand' their intranet portal by means of a special design and use the same motif on other internal written communications.

HR budgeting

HR budgets are prepared like any other functional department budget in the stages set out below.

Stages in the preparation of HR budgets

1. Define functional objectives and plans.
2. Forecast the activity levels required to achieve objectives and plans in the light of company budget guidelines and assumptions on future business activity levels and any targets for reducing overheads or for maintaining them at the same level.
3. Assess the resources (people and finance) required to enable the activity levels to be achieved.
4. Cost each activity area – the sum of these costs will be the total budget.

Budgets need to be justified and protected. Justification means ensuring in advance that objectives and plans are generally agreed – there should be no surprises in a budget submitted to top management. A cast-iron business case should then be prepared to support the forecast levels of activity in each area and, on a cost/benefit basis, to justify any special expenditure. Ideally, the benefit should be defined in terms of a return on investment expressed in financial terms.

The best way to protect a budget it to provide in advance a rationale for each area of expenditure that proves that it is necessary and will justify the costs involved. The worst thing that can happen is to be forced onto the defensive. If service delivery standards (service level agreements) are agreed and achieved, these will provide a further basis for protecting the budget.

The HR role of front line managers

HR can initiate new policies and practices but it is the line that has the main responsibility for implementing them. In other words, 'HR proposes but the line disposes.' As Guest (1991) says, 'HRM is too important to be left to personnel managers.'

If line managers are not inclined favourably towards what HR wants them to do they won't do it, or if compelled to, they will be half-hearted about it. On the basis of their research, Guest and King (2004) noted that 'better HR depended not so much on better procedures but better implementation and ownership of implementation by line managers'.

As pointed out by Purcell *et al* (2003) high levels of organizational performance are not achieved simply by having a range of well-conceived HR policies and practices in place. What makes the difference is how these policies and practices are implemented. That is where the role of line managers in people management is crucial: 'The way line managers implement and enact policies, show leadership in dealing with employees and in exercising control come through as a major issue'. Purcell *et al* noted that dealing with people is perhaps the aspect of their work in which line managers can exercise the greatest amount of discretion and they can use that discretion by not putting HR's ideas into practice. As they point out, it is line managers who bring HR policies to life.

A further factor affecting the role of line managers is their ability to do the HR tasks assigned to them. People-centred activities such as defining roles, interviewing, reviewing performance, providing feedback, coaching and identifying learning and development needs all require special skills. Some managers have them: many don't. Performance-related pay schemes sometimes fail because of untrained line managers.

Hutchinson and Purcell (2003) made the following recommendations on how to improve the quality of the contribution line managers make to people management.

SOURCE REVIEW

Improving the quality of line managers as people managers, Hutchinson and Purcell (2003)

- Provide them with time to carry out their people management duties, which are often superseded by other management duties.
- Select them carefully with much more attention being paid to the behavioural competencies required.
- Support them with strong organizational values concerning leadership and people management.
- Encourage the development of a good working relationship with their own managers.
- Ensure they receive sufficient skills training to enable them to perform their people management activities such as performance management.

To which can be added that better implementation and better ownership by line managers of HR practices is more likely to be achieved if:

- the practice demonstrably benefits them;
- they are involved in the development and, importantly, the testing of the practices;
- the practice is not too complicated, bureaucratic or time-consuming;
- their responsibilities are defined and communicated clearly; and
- they are provided with the guidance, support and training required to implement the practice.

Role and organization of the HR function – key learning points

The role of the HR function

To take initiatives and provide guidance, support and services on all matters relating to the organization's employees.

The activities of the HR function

- Strategic (transformational) activities concerned with the alignment and implementation of HR and business strategies.
- Transactional – the main HR service delivery activities of resourcing, learning and development, reward and employee relations.

Role and organization of the HR function – key learning points (continued)

The diversity of the HR function

HR management involves a variety of roles and activities that differ from one organization to another and from one level to another in the same organization.

Guidelines on organizing the function

- The head of the function should report directly to the chief executive and be a member of the top management team involved in the formulation of business strategy.
- Operational units should be responsible for their own HR management affairs within the framework of broad strategic and policy guidelines from the centre.
- The professional members of the function should have 'strategic capability'.
- Increased responsibility for HR matters should be devolved to line managers.

The criteria for evaluating the effectiveness of the HR function

Its ability to operate strategically and its capacity to deliver the levels of services required.

The dimensions of HR effectiveness

- Strategic HRM – the delivery of services in a way that supports the implementation of the firm's strategy.
- Technical HRM – the delivery of HR basics such as recruitment, compensation and benefits.

Quantitative criteria for evaluating the HR function

Organizational (added value per employee, etc), employee behaviour and levels of service delivery.

How HR people can demonstrate their effectiveness

- Understand the business strategy.
- Anticipate business needs and propose realistically how HR can help to meet them.
- Show that they are capable of meeting performance standards.
- Provide relevant, clear, convincing and practical advice.
- Provide efficient and effective services.
- Generally reveal their understanding and expertise.

Methods of measuring HR effectiveness

User reaction, employee satisfaction measures, benchmarking.

The HR scorecard (Beatty *et al*, 2003)

The four headings are HR competencies, HR practices, HR systems and HR deliverables.

Outsourcing

Benefits include reduced cost, access to expertise not available within HR, increased

Role and organization of the HR function – key learning points (continued)

flexibility and speed of response, and freeing-up HR to focus on more value-adding activities. Problems include suppliers increasing charges, short-term decisions on what can be outsourced, lower employee morale.

Use of management consultants

Provide expertise and may act as service providers in recruitment, executive search and training.

Marketing the HR function

Persuade management that HR is a service to the business needs by making out the business case – spelling out its benefits in terms of added value and the impact it will make on performance.

HR budgeting

Budgets need to be justified and protected. Justification means ensuring in advance that objectives and plans are generally agreed. Protection means providing in advance a rationale for each area of expenditure (a business case) that proves it is necessary and will justify the costs involved.

The HR role of line managers

HR can initiate new policies and practices but it is the line that has the main responsibility for implementing them. Better ownership by line managers of HR practices is more likely to be achieved if:

- the practice demonstrably benefits them;
- they are involved in the development and the testing of the practices;
- the practice is not too complicated, bureaucratic or time-consuming;
- their responsibilities are defined and communicated clearly; and
- they are provided with the guidance, support and training required to implement the practice.

Questions

1. Some time ago (1987) Professor Shaun Tyson produced the following prediction: 'Personnel work can be seen to be subject to conflicting and powerful pressures which are leading to the balkanization of the personnel role. The territory which could once have been delineated as personnel country, is being invaded, sold-off, subdivided and put under lease to consultants, sub-specialists and line managers, whose crosscutting alliances do not correspond to a coherent, separate function.' To what extent has this happened since then? If not, what has happened?

Questions (continued)

2. Peter Reilly made these comments in 2006 on the three-legged Ulrich model: 'The model has many advantages, not least that it aims to centralize activities where there are scale advantages and also keep close to customers where decentralization is necessary. But it's not an easy structure to work with... Splitting the function into three distinct areas has created boundary disputes and sometimes left a hole at the very heart of HR operations... One consequence of this division of labour is that lines of accountability are not always clearly defined... The end result may be a remote service that does not attend to the areas where managers need most assistance.' Drawing on research, what can be done to avoid these problems?

3. As head of HR services you have received the following e-mail from your boss, the group head of HR: 'I note that one of the findings of the CIPD 2007 report on the changing HR function was that: "Three-quarters of survey respondents would like to go further in the transfer of people management responsibilities to the line. It seems obstacles to progress appear to be line manager priorities, their skills, the time available to them for people management tasks and poor manager self service." I believe that we have all these problems: line managers go through the motions as far as their people management responsibilities are concerned and are too busy anyhow to pay proper attention to them. Even if they are interested and have the time, they lack the skills, for example in interviewing and conducting performance reviews and we are woefully slow in extending our HR information system to provide for self-service. What should we do about these problems?' Reply to this e-mail.

References

Beatty, R W, Huselid, M A and Schneier, C E (2003) Scoring on the business scorecard, *Organizational Dynamics*, **32** (2), pp 107–21

Boudreau, J W (1988) Utility analysis, in (ed) L Dyer, *Human Resource Management: Evolving roles and responsibilities*, Bureau of National Affairs, Washington, DC

Boxall, P F, Purcell J and Wright P (2007) The goals of HRM, in (eds) P Boxall, J Purcell and P Wright, *Oxford Handbook of Human Resource Management*, Oxford University Press, Oxford

CIPD (2007a) *The Changing HR Function*, CIPD, London

Crail, M (2006) HR roles and responsibilities 2006: benchmarking the HR function, *IRS Employment Review 839*, 20 January, pp 9–15

Crail, M (2008) HR roles and responsibilities 2008: benchmarking the HR function, *IRS Employment Review 888*, 3 January, pp 1–8

Francis, H and Keegan A (2006) The changing face of HRM: in search of balance, *Human Resource Management Journal*, **16** (3), pp 231–49

Guest, D E (1991) Personnel management: the end of orthodoxy, *British Journal of Industrial Relations*, **29** (2), pp 149–76

Guest, D E and King, Z (2004) Power, innovation and problem solving: the personnel managers' three steps to heaven?, *Journal of Management Studies*, **41** (3), pp 401–23

Guest, D E and Peccei, R (1994) The nature and causes of effective human resource management, *British Journal of Industrial Relations*, June, pp 219–42

Hirsh, W (2008) What do people want from you?, *People Management*, 18 September, pp 23–26

Hope-Hailey, V, Farndale, E and Truss, C (2005) The HR department's role in organizational performance, *Human Resource Management Journal*, **15** (3), pp 49–66

Hope-Hailey, V, Gratton, L, McGovern, P, Stiles, P and Truss, C (1998) A chameleon function? HRM in the '90s, *Human Resource Management Journal*, **7** (3), pp 5–18

Huselid, M A, Jackson, S E and Schuler, R S (1997) Technical and strategic human resource management effectiveness as determinants of firm performance, *Academy of Management Journal*, **40** (1), pp 171–88

Hutchinson, S and Purcell, J (2003) *Bringing Policies to Life: The vital role of front line managers in people management*, CIPD, London

Hutchinson, S and Wood, S (1995) *Personnel and the Line: Developing the employment relationship*, IPD, London

Likierman, A (2005) How to measure the performance of HRM, *People Management*, 11 August, pp 44–45

Peters, T (1988) *Thriving on Chaos*, Macmillan, London

Purcell, J, Kinnie, K, Hutchinson, S, Rayton, B and Swart, J (2003) *People and Performance: How people management impacts on organisational performance*, CIPD, London

Reilly, P (2000) *HR Shared Services and the Re-alignment of HR*, Institute for Employment Studies, Brighton

Reilly, P (2006) Falling between two stools, *People Management*, 23 November, p 36

Reilly, P (2007) Facing up to the facts, *People Management*, 20 September, pp 43–45

Robinson, V (2006) Three legs good?, *People Management*, 26 October, pp 63–64

Sisson, K (1995) Human resource management and the personnel function, in (ed) J Storey, *Human Resource Management: A critical text*, Routledge, London

Tsui, A S and Gomez-Mejia, L R (1988) Evaluating human resource effectiveness, in (ed) L Dyer, *Human Resource Management: Evolving roles and responsibilities*, Bureau of National Affairs, Washington DC
Tyson, S (1987) The management of the personnel function, *Journal of Management Studies*, **24** (5), pp 523–32
Ulrich, D (1995) Shared services: from vogue to value, *Human Resource Planning*, **18** (3), pp 12–23
Ulrich, D (1997a) *Human Resource Champions*, Harvard Business School Press, Boston, Mass
Ulrich, D (1997b) Measuring human resources: an overview of practice and a prescription for results, *Human Resource Management*, **36** (3), pp 303–20
Ulrich, D (1998) A new mandate for human resources, *Harvard Business Review*, January–February, pp 124–34
Ulrich, D and Brockbank, W (2005a) *The HR Value Proposition*, Harvard Press, Cambridge, MA
Ulrich, D and Brockbank, W (2005b) Role call, *People Management*, 16 June, pp 24–28

6

The Role of the HR Practitioner

Key concepts and terms

- Business partner
- Continuous professional development
- Employee advocate
- Impression management
- Process consulting
- The HR thinking performer role
- Conformist innovators
- Deviant innovators
- Evidence-based management
- Organizational capability
- Strategic partner
- Value-added approach

Learning outcomes

On completing this chapter you should be able to define these key concepts. You should also know about:

- The basic role of HR practitioners
- The strategic role
- The change agent role
- The service provision role
- Models of HR roles
- Gaining support from line managers
- Professionalism
- HR effectiveness
- Continuous professional development
- The business partner role
- The strategic activities of HR practitioners
- The internal consultancy role
- The guardian of values role
- Gaining buy-in from top management
- Ethical considerations
- Ambiguities and conflict in the role
- HR competencies

Introduction

This chapter is concerned with what HR professionals do and how they do it, bearing in mind the comment of Boxall and Purcell (2003) that 'HRM does not belong to HR specialists'. HRM also belongs to the line managers who get results through people.

This chapter starts with an analysis of the basic role of HR professionals (and then deals with the business partner role, the strategic role, the change agent role, the internal consultant role and the service delivery role). It continues with descriptions of the various models of the HR role. A number of issues that affect the role of HR people are then explored; these comprise gaining support and commitment, role ambiguity, role conflict, ethics, and professionalism. The chapter concludes with a discussion of the qualities and competencies required by HR practitioners.

The basic role

The roles of HR practitioners vary widely according to the extent to which they are generalist (eg, HR director, HR manager, business partner), or specialist (eg, head of learning and development, head of talent management, head of reward), the level at which they work (strategic, executive or administrative), the needs of the organization, the context within which they work and their own capabilities.

Roles can be proactive, reactive or a mixture of both. At a strategic level, HR people take on a proactive role. Research conducted by Hoque and Noon (2001) established that: 'The growing number of specialists using the HR title are well qualified, are more likely to be involved in strategic decision-making processes and are most likely to be found in workplaces within which sophisticated methods and techniques have been adopted.' As such, they act as business partners, develop integrated HR strategies, intervene, innovate, operate as internal consultants and volunteer guidance on matters concerning upholding core values, ethical principles and the achievement of consistency. They focus on business issues and working with line managers to deliver performance targets. They contribute to improving organizational capability – the capacity of the organization to perform effectively and thus reach its goals. They act as change agents and internal consultants, as discussed later in this chapter.

In some situations they play a mainly reactive role. They spend much of their time doing what they are told or asked to do, responding to requests for services or advice. They provide the administrative systems required by management. This is what Storey (1992a) refers to as the non-interventionary role, in which HR people merely provide a service to meet the demands of management and front line managers. But many HR practitioners are involved in service delivery and the importance of this aspect of their work should not be underestimated. Service delivery includes transactional activities such as recruitment, training and advisory services.

Finally, HR practitioners are, or should be, concerned with upholding the ethical values of their firm. These aspects of their role are also examined below.

SOURCE REVIEW

The four roles of HR professionals, Ulrich (1998)

1. Managing strategic human resources.
2. Managing employee contribution.
3. Managing transformation and change.
4. Managing HR infrastructures to support line managers.

The extent to which HR specialists were carrying out these roles was researched by Guest and King (2004) who found that there was little emphasis on the first three. Instead, the focus appeared to be placed on managing infrastructures.

The business partner role

The concept of HR practitioners as business partners has become very popular. In essence, the concept is that, as business partners, HR specialists share responsibility with their line management colleagues for the success of the enterprise and get involved with them in implementing business strategy and running the business. They are often 'embedded' in business units or departments.

This concept was first mooted in 1985 by Shaun Tyson. He used the term 'business manager' rather than 'business partner' but it is much the same. He stated that personnel specialists carrying out this role integrate their activities closely with management and ensure that they serve a long-term strategic purpose. They have the capacity to identify business opportunities, to see the broad picture and to understand how their role can help to achieve the company's business objectives. They anticipate needs, act flexibly and are proactive. This is a clear case of a prophet not being honoured in their own country. In 1998, 13 years later, Dave Ulrich seized the HR community's imagination with his similar concept of the HR executive as a 'strategic partner'.

In describing his strategic partner model, Ulrich maintained that as champions of competitiveness in creating value, HR executives can deliver excellence by becoming partners with senior and line managers in strategy execution, helping to improve planning from the conference room to the marketplace and impelling and guiding serious discussion of how the company should be organized to carry out its strategy. He suggested that HR should join forces with operating managers in systematically assessing the importance of any new initiatives they propose and obtaining answers to the following questions: Which ones are really aligned with strategy implementation? Which ones should receive immediate attention and which can wait? Which ones, in short, are truly linked to business results?

As business partners HR practitioners work closely with their line management colleagues. They are aware of business strategies and the opportunities and threats facing the organization. They are capable of analysing organizational strengths and weaknesses and diagnosing the issues facing the enterprise and their human resource implications. They know about the critical success factors that will create competitive advantage and they adopt a 'value added' approach when making a convincing business case for innovations.

The term 'value added' looms large in the concept of the HR business partner. In accounting language, where the phrase originated, added value is defined as the value added to the cost of raw materials and bought-in parts by the process of production and distribution. In HR speak, a value added approach means creating value through HR initiatives that make a significant contribution to organizational success.

Strictly speaking, added value is measured by the extent to which the value of that contribution exceeds its cost or generates a return on investment. But the term is often used more generally to signify the business-oriented approach HR professionals are expected to adopt and how it contributes to the creation of value by the firm. Adding value is about improving performance and results – getting more out of an activity than was put into it. Francis and Keegan (2006) report the following comment from a recruitment consultant, which illustrates how the term has become popular: 'Most HR professionals will now have "value added" stamped on their foreheads, because they are always being asked to think in terms of the business objectives and how what they do supports the business objectives and the business plan.'

However, it can be argued that too much has been made of the business partner model. Perhaps it is preferable to emphasize that the role of HR professionals is to be part of the business rather than merely being partners. Tim Miller, Group HR Director of Standard Chartered Bank, as reported by Smethurst (2005), dislikes the term:

> *'Give me a break!' he says. 'It's so demeaning. How many people in marketing or finance have to say they are a partner in the business? Why do we have to think that we're not an intimate part of the business, just like sales, manufacturing and engineering? I detest and loathe the term and I won't use it'.*

Another leading Group HR Director, Alex Wilson of BT as reported by Pickard (2005), is equally hostile. He says:

> *The term worries me to death. HR has to be an integral and fundamental part of developing the strategy of the business. I don't even like the term 'close to the business' because, like 'business partner' it implies we are working alongside our line management colleagues but on a separate track, rather than people management being an integral part of the business.*

There is also the danger of over-emphasizing the glamorous albeit important role of business or strategic partner at the expense of the service delivery aspect of the HR specialist's role. As an HR specialist commented to Caldwell (2004): 'My credibility depends on running an extremely efficient and cost-effective administrative machine... If I don't get that right, and consistently, then you can forget about any big ideas.' Another person interviewed during Caldwell's research referred to personnel people as 'reactive pragmatists', a view which in many organizations is in accord with reality. And Syrett (2006) commented that: 'Whatever strategic aspirations senior HR practitioners have, they will amount to nothing if the function they represent cannot deliver the essential transactional services their internal line clients require.'

The problem of the over-emphasis on the business partner role has been influenced by the erroneous belief that Ulrich was simply focusing on HR executives as business partners. This has had the unfortunate effect of implying that it was their only worthwhile function. However, Ulrich cannot be blamed for this. In 1998 he gave equal emphasis to the need for HR people to be administrative experts, employee champions and change agents, and this was confirmed in a revised model (Ulrich and Brockbank, 2005a).

The strategic role of HR specialists

There may be some reservations about the focus on the business partner role but there is a universal chorus of approval for the notion that HR professionals need to be strategic, although not everyone is clear about what being strategic means. This is therefore defined below.

The strategic role of HR specialists varies according to whether they are operating at strategic levels (as HR directors or heads of the HR function, heads of centres of expertise or key HR functions, and strategic business partners) or at a transactional level (as an HR officer, adviser or assistant delivering basic HR services such as recruitment or training, or working in an HR shared service centre).

The strategic roles of HR specialists

- To formulate and implement in conjunction with their management colleagues forward-looking HR strategies that are aligned to business objectives and integrated with one another.

- To contribute to the development of business strategies. In doing so they adopt an 'outside-in' approach as described by Wright *et al* (2004) in which the starting point is the business, including the customer, competitor and business issues it faces. The HR strategy then derives directly from these challenges to create real solutions and add real value.
- They work alongside their line management colleagues to provide on an everyday basis continuous support to the implementation of the business or operational strategy of the organization, function or unit.

To carry out these roles, they need to:

- understand the strategic goals of the organization or unit and appreciate the business imperatives and performance drivers relative to these goals;
- comprehend how sustainable competitive advantage can be obtained through the human capital of the organization or unit and know how HR practices can contribute to the achievement of strategic goals;
- contribute to the development for the business of a clear vision and a set of integrated values;
- ensure that senior management understands the HR implications of its business strategy;
- be aware of the broader context (the competitive environment and the business, economic, social and legal factors that affect it) in which the organization operates;
- understand the kinds of employee behaviour required successfully to execute the business strategy;
- think in terms of the bigger and longer-term picture of where HR should go and how it should get there;
- be capable of making a powerful business case for any proposals on the development of HR strategies;
- act as a change agent in developing the organization and its culture and as an internal consultant in advising on what needs to be done and how to do it (these two aspects of the strategic role are considered at the end of this section);
- understand how the ethical dimensions of HR policy and practice fit into the present and future picture;
- believe in and practice evidence-based management (recommendations on strategy and its implementation are always backed up by hard data).

The strategic contribution of HR advisers or assistants

The role of HR advisers or assistants is primarily that of delivering effective HR services within their function or as a member of an HR service centre. While they will not be responsible for the formulation of HR strategies they may contribute to them within their own speciality. They will need to understand the business goals of the departments or managers for whom they provide services in order to ensure that these services support the achievement of those goals.

Strategic activities

Strategic activities consist of formulating HR strategies as described in Chapter 3 and providing continuous support to line managers in implementing their business or operational strategies. They involve being proactive in identifying issues that can be addressed through major or relatively minor HR initiatives. Examples of the sort of issues that may need to be dealt with are poor performance or productivity, low quality, inadequate levels of service to customers, recruitment and selection failures, skills shortages, poor retention rates (high levels of labour turnover), high levels of absenteeism, high levels of accidents, occupational health problems and too many disputes or grievances. In all these and many other problem areas a strategic approach involves:

- understanding the business or operational strategy and appreciating the performance drivers required to implement it;
- analysing how the issue is affecting those drivers;
- diagnosing the causes of any problems;
- identifying possible actions and reviewing them in conjunction with line management and employees to select the preferred option;
- preparing a proposal to deal with the issue, including a business case setting out the benefits against the costs;
- developing and implementing the new or revised policy or practice taking into account the following guidelines.

Guidelines for HR innovations

- Be clear on what has to be achieved and why.
- Ensure that what you do fits the strategy, culture and circumstances of the organization.

- Don't follow fashion – do your own thing as long as it is relevant and fits the organization's needs.
- Keep it simple – over-complexity is a common reason for failure.
- Don't rush – it will take longer than you think.
- Don't try to do too much at once – an incremental approach is generally best.
- Assess resource requirements and costs.
- Pay close attention to project planning and management.
- Remember that the success of the innovation rests as much on the effectiveness of the process of implementation (line manager buy-in and skills are crucial) as it does on the quality of the concept, if not more so.
- Pay close attention to change management approaches – communicate, involve and train.

The change agent role

The implementation of strategy means that HR specialists have to act as change agents, facilitating change by providing advice and support on its introduction and management. Caldwell (2001) categorizes HR change agents in four dimensions.

SOURCE REVIEW

HR specialists as change agents – the four dimensions, Caldwell (2001)

1. Transformational change – a major change that has a dramatic effect on HR policy and practice across the whole organization.
2. Incremental change – gradual adjustments of HR policy and practices that affect single activities or multiple functions.
3. HR vision – a set of values and beliefs that affirm the legitimacy of the HR function as a strategic business partner.
4. HR expertise – the knowledge and skills that define the unique contribution the HR professional can make to effective people management.

Change management processes and the role of HR in managing change and transformation are given more detailed consideration in Chapter 25.

The internal consultancy role

As internal consultants, HR practitioners function like external management consultants, working alongside their colleagues – their clients – in analysing problems, diagnosing issues and proposing solutions. They will be involved in the development of HR processes or systems and in 'process consulting'. The latter deals with process areas such as organization, team building and objective setting.

The service delivery role

The basic role of HR specialists is to deliver services to internal customers. These include management, line managers, team leaders and employees. The services may be general, covering all aspects of HRM or services may only be provided in one or two areas by specialists. The focus may be on the requirements of management (eg, resourcing), or it may extend to all employees (eg, health and safety).

The aims are to provide effective services that meet the needs of the business, its management and its employees and to administer them efficiently.

Guidance and advice

The services delivered by HR people comprise both the transactional services such as recruitment and training, and the provision of guidance and advice to management. At the highest level, this will include recommendations on HR strategies that have been evidence-based, ie developed by processes of analysis of the facts followed by diagnosis to address strategic issues arising from business needs and human, organizational or environmental factors. They will also provide advice on issues concerning culture change and approaches to the improvement of process capability – the ability of the organization to get things done through people. The aim will be to achieve human resource process advantage (Boxall, 1996, 1999), which is the competitive advantage achieved by organizations when they have better HR processes and practices than their rivals.

Guidance will be given to managers to ensure that consistent decisions are made on such matters as performance ratings, pay increases and disciplinary actions. At all levels, guidance may be provided on HR policies and procedures and the implications of employment legislation. In the latter area, HR practitioners are concerned with compliance – ensuring that legal requirements are met.

A balance has to be struck between the amount of freedom that can be devolved to line managers and the need to be consistent and meet social and legal obligations.

The guardian of values role

HR practitioners may act as the guardians of the organization's values and ethical standards concerning people. They point out when behaviour conflicts with those values or where proposed actions will be inconsistent with them. In a sense, their roles require them to act as the 'conscience' of management – a necessary role but not an easy one to play. Ulrich (1998) called this the 'employee champion' role.

Models of HR roles

A number of models classifying the types of roles played by HR specialists have been produced, as summarized below. These simplify the complex roles that HR professionals often have to play which, in different contexts or times, may change considerably or may mean adopting varied approaches to meet altering circumstances. They are therefore not universal but they do provide some insight into the different ways in which HR specialists operate.

Karen Legge (1978)

Two types of HR managers are described in this model. 1) Conformist innovators, who go along with their organization's ends and adjust their means to achieve them. Their expertise is used as a source of professional power to improve the position of their departments. 2) Deviant innovators, who attempt to change this means/ends relationship by gaining acceptance for a different set of criteria for the evaluation of organizational success and their contribution to it.

The Tyson and Fell (1986) model

This is the classic model that describes three types of practitioner:

1. The clerk of works – all authority for action is vested in line managers. HR policies are formed or created after the actions that created the need. Policies are not integral to the business and are short term and ad hoc. Authority is vested in line managers and HR activities are largely routine – employment and day-to-day administration.
2. The contracts manager – policies are well established, often implicit, with a heavy industrial relations emphasis, possibly derived from an employer's association. The HR department will use fairly sophisticated systems, especially in the field of employee relations. The HR manager is likely to be a professional or very experienced in industrial relations. He or she will not be on the board and, although having some authority to 'police' the implementation of policies, acts mainly in an interpretative, not a creative or innovative, role.

3. The architect – explicit HR policies exist as part of the corporate strategy. Human resource planning and development are important concepts and a long-term view is taken. Systems tend to be sophisticated. The head of the HR function is probably on the board and his or her power is derived from professionalism and perceived contribution to the business.

Although relevant at the time this model does not express the complexities of the HR role as later ones do, and the emphasis on industrial relations in the contracts manager role no longer accords with the realities of industrial relations in the 21st century.

Kathleen Monks (1992)

The four types of practitioner identified by Kathleen Monks following research in 97 organizations in Ireland extended those developed by Tyson and Fell:

1. Traditional/administrative – in this model the personnel practitioners have mainly a support role with the focus on administrative matters, record keeping and adherence to rules and regulations.
2. Traditional/industrial relations – personnel practitioners concentrate on industrial relations, giving their other functions lower priority.
3. Innovative/professional – personnel specialists are professional and expert. They aim to remove traditional practices and replace them with improved human resource planning, recruitment, human resource development and reward policies and practices.
4. Innovative/sophisticated – personnel specialists are on the board, take part in integrating HR and business strategies, and are recognized as making an important contribution to organizational success. They develop and deliver sophisticated services in each of the main HR areas.

John Storey (1992b)

Storey's model suggests a two-dimensional map: interventionary/non-interventionary and strategic/tactical, as illustrated in Figure 6.1. From this he identifies four roles:

1. Change makers (interventionary/strategic), which is close to the HRM model.
2. Advisers (non-interventionary/strategic) who act as internal consultants, leaving much of HR practice to line managers
3. Regulators (interventionary/tactical) who are 'managers of discontent' concerned with formulating and monitoring employment rules.
4. Handmaidens (non-interventionary/tactical) who merely provide a service to meet the demands of line managers.

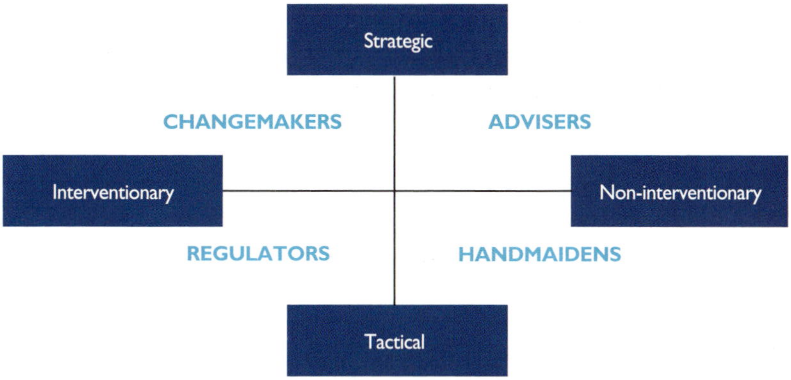

Figure 6.1 The John Storey model of personnel management
(Source: Storey, 1992b)

Peter Reilly (2000)

The different roles that practitioners can play as described by Reilly are illustrated in Figure 6.2. He suggests that it is the 'strategist/integrator' that is most likely to make the longest-term strategic contribution. The 'administrator/controller' is likely to make a largely tactical short-term contribution, while the 'adviser/consultant' falls between the two.

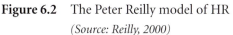

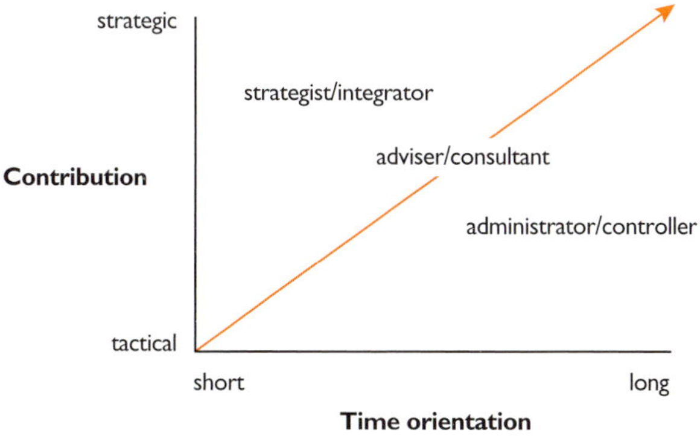

Figure 6.2 The Peter Reilly model of HR
(Source: Reilly, 2000)

Dave Ulrich and Wayne Brockbank (2005a and 2005b)

In 1998 Dave Ulrich produced his model in which he suggested that as champions of competitiveness in creating and delivering value, HR professionals carry out the roles of strategic partners, administrative experts, employee champions and change agents. The response to this formulation concentrated on the business partner role. Ulrich in conjunction with Wayne Brockbank reformulated the 1998 model in 2005, listing the following roles:

- Employee advocate – focuses on the needs of today's employees through listening, understanding and empathizing.
- Human capital developer – in the role of managing and developing human capital (individuals and teams), focuses on preparing employees to be successful in the future.
- Functional expert – concerned with the HR practices that are central to HR value, acting with insight on the basis of the body of knowledge they possess. Some are delivered through administrative efficiency (such as technology or process design), and others through policies, menus and interventions. Necessary to distinguish between the foundation HR practices – recruitment, learning and development, rewards, etc – and the emerging HR practices such as communication, work process and organization design, and executive leadership development.
- Strategic partner – consists of multiple dimensions: business expert, change agent, strategic HR planner, knowledge manager and consultant, combining them to align HR systems to help accomplish the organization's vision and mission, helping managers to get things done, and disseminating learning across the organization.
- Leader – leading the HR function, collaborating with other functions and providing leadership to them, setting and enhancing the standards for strategic thinking and ensuring corporate governance.

Ulrich and Brockbank (2005b) explained that the revised formulation was in response to the changes in HR roles they have observed recently. They commented on the importance of the employee advocate role, noting that HR professionals spend on average about 19 per cent of their time on employee relations issues. They explained that as a profession, HR possesses a body of knowledge that allows HR people to act with insight. Functional expertise enables them to create menus of choice for their business and thus identify options that are consistent with business needs rather than merely those they are able to provide. The additional heading of 'human capital developer' was introduced because of the increased emphasis on viewing people as critical assets and to recognize the significance of HR's role in developing the workforce. The concept of strategic partner remains broadly the same as before but the additional heading of 'HR leader' was introduced to highlight the importance of leadership by HR specialists of their own function – 'before they can develop other leaders, HR professionals must exhibit the leadership skills they expect in others'.

Gaining support and commitment

HR practitioners mainly get results by persuasion based on credibility and expertise. Management and employees can create blockages and barriers and their support and commitment needs to be gained, which is not always easy. As Guest and Hoque (1994) note: 'By exerting influence, HR managers help to shape the framework of HR policy and practice.' Line managers may make the day-to-day decisions, therefore influencing skills are necessary for HR specialists.

But there is a constant danger of HR professionals being so overcome by the beauty and truth of their bright ideas that they expect everyone else – management and employees alike – to fall for them immediately. Sometimes, as pointed out by Marchington (1995), HR people may go in for 'impression management' – aiming to make an impact on senior managers and colleagues through publicizing high profile innovations. HR specialists who aim to draw attention to themselves simply by promoting the latest flavour of the month, irrespective of its relevance or practicality, are falling into the trap that Peter Drucker, anticipating Marchington, described as follows.

SOURCE REVIEW

What personnel administrators worry about, Drucker (1995)

The constant worry of all personnel administrators is their inability to prove that they are making a contribution to the enterprise. Their preoccupation is with the search for a 'gimmick' which will impress their management colleagues.

Blockages and barriers within management

Managers will block or erect barriers to what the HR function believes to be progress if they are not persuaded that it will benefit both the organization and themselves at an acceptable cost (money and their time and trouble).

Blockages and barriers from employees

Employees will block or set up barriers to 'progress' or innovations if they feel they conflict with their own interests. They are likely, with reason, to be cynical about protestations that what is good for the organization will always be good for them.

Getting buy-in from top management

Buy-in from top management is achievable by processes of marketing the HR function and persuasion. Boards and senior managers, like anyone else, are more likely to be persuaded to take a course of action if their support is gained in the ways described below.

Gaining support from top management

- Demonstrate that the proposal will meet both the needs of the organization and their own personal needs.
- Base the proposal on a compelling and realistic business case that spells out the benefits and the costs and, as far as possible, is justified either in added value terms (ie the income generated by the proposal will significantly exceed the cost of implementing it), and/or on the basis of a return on investment (ie the cost of the investment, say in training, is justified by the financial returns in such terms as increased productivity).
- Prove that the innovation has already worked well within the organization (perhaps as a pilot scheme) or represents 'good practice' (it has worked well elsewhere), which is likely to be transferable to the organization.
- Show that the proposal will increase the business's competitive edge, for example enlarging the skill base or multi-skilling to ensure that it can achieve competitive advantage through innovation and/or reducing time-to-market.
- Specify how the proposal can be implemented without too much trouble, for example not taking up a lot of managers' time, or not meeting with strong opposition from line managers, employees or trade unions (it is as well to check the likely reaction before launching a proposal).
- Indicate that the innovation will add to the reputation of the company by showing that it is a 'world class' organization, ie what it does is as good as, if not better than, the world leaders in the sector in which the business operates (a promise that publicity will be achieved through articles in professional journals, press releases and conference presentations will help).

- Emphasize that the innovation will enhance the 'employer brand' of the company by making it a 'best place to work'.
- Ensure that the proposal is brief, to the point and well argued – it should take no more than five minutes to present orally and should be summarized in writing on the proverbial one side of one sheet of paper (supplementary details can be included in appendices).

Gaining the support and commitment of line management

This can sometimes be more difficult than gaining the support of top management. Line managers can be cynical or realistic about innovation – they have seen it all before and/or they believe it won't work (sometimes with good reason). Innovations pushed down from the top can easily fail.

Gaining line management support requires providing an answer to the question, 'What's in it for me?' Managers need to be convinced that the innovation will help them to achieve better results without imposing unacceptable additional burdens on them. New or revised employment practices that take up precious time and involve paperwork will be treated with particular suspicion. Many line managers, often from bitter experience, resent the bureaucracy that can surround and, indeed, engulf the over-engineered systems favoured by some HR people, such as traditional performance appraisal schemes.

Obtaining support requires market research and networking – getting around to talk to managers about their needs and testing new ideas to obtain reactions. The aim is to build up a body of information that will indicate approaches that are likely to be most acceptable, and therefore will most probably work, or at least to suggest areas where particular efforts will need to be made to persuade and educate line management. It is also useful to form 'strategic alliances' with influential managers who are enthusiastic about the innovation and will not only lend it vocal support but will also cooperate in pilot-testing it. On the principle that 'nothing succeeds like success', support for new HR practices can often be achieved by demonstrating that it has worked well elsewhere in the organization.

Gaining commitment will be easier if managers know that they have been consulted and that their opinions have been listened to and acted upon. It is even better to involve them as members of project teams or task forces in developing the new process or system. This is the way to achieve ownership and therefore commitment.

Gaining the support and commitment of employees

When it comes to new employment practices, employees often react in the same way as managers. They will tend to resist change, wanting to know 'What's in it for us?' They also want to know the hidden agenda – 'Why does the company really want to introduce a performance management process? Will it simply be used as a means of gaining evidence for disciplinary proceedings? Or is it even going to provide the information required to select people for redundancy?' As far as possible this kind of question needs to be answered in advance.

Employee commitment is also more likely if they are kept well-informed of what is proposed, why it has been proposed and how it will affect them. It will be further enhanced if they participate in the development of the new employment practice and if they know that their contributions have been welcomed and acted upon.

Ethical considerations

HR specialists are concerned with ethical standards in two ways: their conduct and values as professionals, and the ethical standards of their firms.

Professional conduct

The CIPD Code of Professional Conduct states that:

> *In the public interest and in the pursuit of its objects, the Chartered Institute of Personnel and Development is committed to the highest possible standards of professional conduct and competency. To this end members:*
>
> - *are required to exercise integrity, honesty, diligence and appropriate behaviour in all their business, professional and related personal activities;*
> - *must act within the law and must not encourage, assist or act in collusion with employees, employers or others who may be engaged in unlawful conduct.*

Professional ethical standards

As explained by Farnham (2008), professional ethics are the moral principles and values governing professional behaviour. The ethical principles of the HR profession imply that HR specialists need to take account of the dignity and rights of employees when taking employment decisions. These include having clear, fair terms and conditions of employment, healthy and safe working conditions, fair remuneration, promoting equal opportunities and employment diversity, encouraging employees to develop their skills, and not discriminating or harassing employees. The ethical frameworks for judging HR practices are basic rights, organizational justice, respecting individuals, and community of purpose. There are many instances where these principles conflict with organizational objectives. These include HR issues such as flexibility, work intensification, use of some sophisticated HR techniques such as performance-related pay and socialization programmes, and activities promoting closer managerial monitoring of employee performance.

HR professionals are part of management. But there will be occasions when in their professional capacity HR specialists should speak out against plans or actions that are not in accord with management's ethical standards or values. And they should do their best to promote ethical standards and influence changes in core values where they feel they are necessary. They must not tolerate injustice or inequality of opportunity. If redundancies are inevitable as a result of business-led 'slimming down' or 'taking costs out of the business' processes, they should ensure that the organization takes whatever steps it can to mitigate detrimental effects by, for example, relying primarily on natural wastage and voluntary redundancy or, if people have to go involuntarily, doing whatever they can to help them find other jobs (outplacement).

HR specialists may often find themselves in a hard-nosed, entrepreneurial environment. But this does not mean that they can remain unconcerned about developing and helping to uphold the core values of the organization in line with their own values on the ethical principles that govern how people should be managed. These may not always be reconcilable, and if this is strongly the case, the HR professional may have to make a choice on whether he or she can remain with the organization.

Professionalism in human resource management

If the term is used loosely, HR specialists are 'professional' when they display expertise in doing their work and act responsibly. A professional occupation such as medicine or law could, however, be defined as one that gives members of its association exclusive rights to practise their profession. A profession in this context is not so much an occupation as a means of controlling an occupation. Human resource management is obviously not in this category.

The nature of professional work was defined by the Hayes Committee (1972) as follows.

SOURCE REVIEW

The nature of professional work, Hayes Committee (1972)

Work done by the professional is usually distinguished by its reference to a framework of fundamental concepts linked with experience rather than by impromptu reaction to events or the application of laid down procedures. Such a high level of distinctive competence reflects the skilful application of specialized education, training and experience. This should be accompanied by a sense of responsibility and an acceptance of recognized standards.

By these standards an institution such as the CIPD carries out all the functions of a professional body except that of giving its members the exclusive right to practice.

A later analysis was produced by Fletcher (2004), who stated that a professional ethos is characterized by the following ingredients:

- the opportunity to display high levels of autonomy;
- the ability to apply some independence of judgement;
- self-discipline and adherence to some aspirational performance standards;
- the possession of specialized knowledge and skills;
- power and status based on expertise;
- operating, and being guided by, a code of ethics;
- allegiance to a professional body.

Ambiguities in the role of HR practitioners

The activities and roles of HR specialists and the demands made upon them as described above appear to be quite clear cut but, in Thurley's (1981) words, HR practitioners can be 'specialists in ambiguity'. There are a number of reasons for this, as discussed below, but as Watson (1977) emphasized, much management activity is typically messy and ambiguous.

Three ambiguities in the role were highlighted by Legge (1978). First, there is an ambiguity in the overlap between personnel management as a set of activities for all managers, and as a specialist function. This may arise because the role of HR practitioners is ill-defined (they are unsure of where they stand), their status is not fully recognized, or top management and line managers have equivocal views about their value to the organization. Second, ambiguity occurs because it is often difficult to define success in personnel management, to determine who or what was responsible for success or failure and to identify the unique contributions of the personnel function. Third, personnel managers sit in an uncomfortable position where they are seen as part of management but also have a special relationship to, and responsibility for, the workers. The research conducted by Guest and King (2004), which involved interviews with 48 executives from 18 organizations, established that the first two ambiguities listed by Legge still existed, but the third one has become less of an issue because of the more clear-cut alignment of HR with management.

Ambiguity in the role of HR people can result in confusion between ideals and reality. Tyson and Fell (1986) see a contrast between the ideologies and actual realities of organizational life to which HR managers, 'as organization men or women', have to conform. This ambiguity is reflected in the comments that have been made about the role of the HR function. For example, Mackay and Torrington (1986) suggested that: 'Personnel management is never identified with management interests, as it becomes ineffective when not able to understand and articulate the aspirations of the work force.'

In complete contrast, Tyson and Fell (1986) believe that:

> *Classical personnel management has not been granted a position in decision-making circles because it has frequently not earned one. It has not been concerned with the totality of the organization but often with issues which have not only been parochial but esoteric to boot.*

Ambiguity continues in the age of Ulrich. As Hope-Hailey *et al* (2005) point out: 'Ulrich highlighted that HR professionals must be both strategic and operational, yet the potential role conflict this could engender was not addressed.' Caldwell (2004) reached the following conclusions on the basis of his research.

SOURCE REVIEW

Summary of conclusions on the role of HR practitioners, Caldwell (2004)

There is the issue of 'powerlessness' or the marginality of HR practitioners in management decision-making processes, especially at a strategic level. The HR function has an inward-looking tendency to identify professional expertise mainly with administrative concerns over who controls HR activities, rather than questions of HR practices or who has responsibility for implementing HR policy.

Conflict in the HR contribution

One of the questions HR practitioners sometimes have to ask themselves is 'Who is the client – the company or the employee?' HR professionals may have to walk a fine line between serving the company that pays their salary and looking after the interests of employees. They may be involved in counselling employees over work problems. This can only be carried out successfully if the employee trusts the HR practitioner to maintain confidentiality. But something might be revealed that is of interest to management and this places the counsellor in a dilemma – to betray or not to betray the trust? There is no pat answer to this question, but the existence of a code of professional conduct, a set of values and a company ethical code can provide guidance.

HR specialists, as Thurley (1981) put it, often 'work against the grain'. Their values may be different from those of line managers and this is a potential cause of conflict. But conflict is inevitable in organizations that are pluralistic societies, the members of which have different frames of reference and interests, particularly self-interest. Management may have their own priorities: 'increase shareholder value', 'keep the City happy', 'innovate', 'get the work done'. Employees might have a completely different set: 'pay me well and equitably', 'give me security', 'provide good working conditions', 'treat me fairly'. HR specialists may find themselves somewhere in the middle.

Conflicts in the HR contribution can arise in the following ways:

- A clash of values – line managers may simply regard their workers as factors of production to be used, exploited and dispensed with in accordance with organizational imperatives.
- Different priorities – management's priority may be to add value – make more out of less – and if this involves getting rid of people that's too bad. HR people may recognize the need to add value but not at the expense of employees.
- Freedom versus control – line managers may want the freedom to get on with things their own way, interpreting company policies to meet their needs; and the thrust for devolution has encouraged such feelings. But HR specialists will be concerned about the achievement of a consistent and equitable approach to managing people and implementing HR policies. They will also be concerned with the attainment of a proper degree of compliance to employment and health and safety law. They may be given the responsibility for exercising control, and conflict is likely if they use this authority too rigidly.
- Disputes – if unions are recognized, HR specialists may be involved in conflict during the process of resolution. Even when there are no unions, there may be conflict with individuals or groups of employees about the settlement of grievances.

As Follett (1924) wrote, there is the possibility that conflict can be creative if an integrative approach is used to settle it. This means clarifying priorities, policies and roles, using agreed procedures to deal with grievances and disputes, bringing differences of interpretation out into the open and achieving consensus through a solution that recognizes the interests of both parties – a win–win process. Resolving conflict by the sheer exercise of power (win–lose) will only lead to further conflict. Resolving conflict by compromise may lead to both parties being dissatisfied (lose–lose).

The qualities required by HR professionals

Ulrich (1997a) stated that it was necessary to shift the focus of what HR people do to what they deliver. Gratton (2000) stressed the need for HR practitioners to: 'Understand the state of the company, the extent of the embedding of processes and structures throughout the organization, and the behaviour and attitudes of individual employees.' She believes that 'The challenge is to implement the ideas' and the solution is to 'build a guiding coalition by involving line managers', which means 'creating issue-based cross-functional action teams that will initially make recommendations and later move into action'. This approach 'builds the capacity to change'.

What effective HR practitioners do

Effective HR practitioners:

- Operate strategically – they have the ability to see the big picture and take, and implement, a strategic and coherent view of the whole range of HR policies, processes and practices in relation to the business as a whole; they ensure that their innovations and services are aligned to business needs and priorities while taking account of the needs of employees and other stakeholders.
- Have the capability to facilitate change, initiating it when necessary and acting as a stabilizing force in situations where change would be damaging (this is considered in more detail in Chapter 25).
- Appreciate organizational and individual needs; against a background of their knowledge of organizational behaviour, they understand how organizations function and the factors affecting individual motivation and commitment, they are capable of analysing and diagnosing the people requirements of the organization and proposing and implementing appropriate action.
- Are business-like – they have to demonstrate that they can make value-added contributions.
- Are persuasive – they present the proposals and recommendations emerging from their interventions persuasively, making out a compelling business case; innovations and

ideas are sold to management on the basis of the practical and, wherever possible, measurable benefits that will result from their implementation (it is not the idea itself that is saleable but the result it can achieve).

- Use an 'evidence-based management' approach (as defined by Rousseau, 2006: 'Evidence-based management means translating principles based on best evidence into organizational practices. Through evidence-based management, practising managers develop into experts informed by social science and organizational research').
- Deliver their services efficiently and effectively.

Competencies for HR professionals

Two broad competencies for HR professionals were identified by Huselid *et al* (1997): first, professional HR capabilities relating to the delivery of traditional HRM activities such as recruiting, selection and compensation, and second, business-related competencies reflecting an understanding of the business and the implementation of competitive strategy. A competency framework is set out in Table 6.1.

Table 6.1 Competency framework for HR professionals

Business awareness	Understands: (1) the business environment, the competitive pressures the organization faces and the impact of external events on organizational policies and practices, (2) the drivers of high performance and the business strategy, (3) the business's key activities and processes and how these affect business strategies, (4) how HR policies and practices impact on business performance, and puts this to good use
Strategic capability	(1) Seeks involvement in business strategy formulation and contributes to the development of the strategy, (2) contributes to the development for the business of a clear vision and a set of integrated values, (3) develops and implements coherent HR strategies which are aligned to the business strategy and integrated with one another, (4) works closely with line management to support the achievement of corporate, unit or functional strategies, (5) understands the importance of human capital measurement, introduces measurement systems and ensures that good use is made of them
Organizational effectiveness	(1) Contributes to the analysis and diagnosis of people issues and proposes practical solutions, (2) helps to develop resource capability by ensuring that the business has the skilled, committed and engaged workforce it needs, (3) helps to develop process capability by influencing the design of work systems to make the best use of people, (4) pursues an 'added value' approach to innovation and service delivery

Table 6.1 *continued*

Capacity as an internal consultant	(1) Carries out the analysis and diagnosis of people issues and proposes practical solutions, (2) adopts interventionist style to meet client needs, acts as catalyst, facilitator and expert as required, (3) uses process consultancy approaches to resolve people problems, (4) coaches clients to deal with their own problems, transfers skills
Effective service delivery	(1) Anticipates requirements and sets up and operates appropriate services, (2) provides efficient and cost-effective services in each HR area; (3) responds promptly and efficiently to requests for HR services, help and advice, (4) promotes the empowerment of line managers to make HR decisions but provides guidance as required
Acts in the interests of employees	Takes action to advance and protect the interests and well-being of employees
Continuous professional development	(1) Continually develops professional knowledge and skills, (2) benchmarks good HR practice, (3) keeps in touch with new HR concepts, practices and techniques, (4) keeps up-to-date with HR research and its practical implications

HR competency areas

Research conducted at the University of Michigan Business School (Brockbank *et al*, 1999) established the key competency areas (domains) and their components; these are set out in Table 6.2.

Table 6.2 Key competency areas

Competency domain	Components
1. Personal credibility	Live the firm's values, maintain relationships founded on trust, act with an 'attitude' (a point of view about how the business can win, backing up opinion with evidence)
2. Ability to manage change	Drive change: ability to diagnose problems, build relationships with clients, articulate a vision, set a leadership agenda, solve problems, and implement goals.
3. Ability to manage culture	Act as 'keepers of the culture', identify the culture required to meet the firm's business strategy, frame culture in a way that excites employees, translates desired culture into specific behaviours, encourages executives to behave consistently with the desired culture

Table 6.2 *continued*

Competency domain	Components
4. Delivery of human resource practices	Expert in speciality, able to deliver state-of-the-art innovative HR practices in such areas as recruitment, employee development, compensation and communication
5. Understanding of the business	Strategy, organization, competitors, finance, marketing, sales, operations and IT

(Source: Brockbank et al, *1999)*

Developing competence through evidence-based management

Pfeffer and Sutton (2006) provided the following advice to HR professionals on developing their competence through evidence-based management:

- Use data to identify where the greatest improvement opportunities are. This will help the organization to understand what their real, as distinct from their assumed, problems are and what is causing them.
- Know what the literature says about HR practices and use that knowledge to design more effective ways of doing things.
- Run experiments and gather information on how well things are working, building up a spirit of inquiry and learning, and a commitment to gathering data and doing the necessary analysis to make decisions based on fact. This approach can be contrasted with acting on hunches, or '… on belief, ideology, casual benchmarking, what they want or hope for, what they have done in the past, what they seem to be good or experienced in doing'.
- Have a commitment to acting upon such data in order to design more effective HR systems and processes and to ensure that those that already exist do no harm to those who use them or are affected by their use.
- Develop the right mindset – embracing learning and enquiry and tolerating failure – your own as well as that of others.

HR professionals as 'thinking performers'

The CIPD (2005a) has stated that:

> *All personnel and development specialists must be thinking performers. That is, their central task is to be knowledgeable and competent in their various fields and to be able*

> *to move beyond compliance to provide a critique of organizational policies and procedures and to advise on how organizations should develop in the future.*

This concept can be interpreted as meaning that HR professionals have to think carefully about what they are doing in the context of their organization and within the framework of a recognized body of knowledge, and they have to perform effectively in the sense of delivering advice, guidance and services that will help the organization to achieve its strategic goals.

Legge (1995) made a similar point when she referred to HRM as a process of 'thinking pragmatism'. Harrison (2007) commented that the 'thinking performer' philosophy focuses on the ways in which HR fields of activity should link to produce a whole that is greater than the sum of its parts, on strategic awareness and on evidence-based practice. The emphasis is on holistic thinking, on contextualization and on best fit rather than best practice.

Ulrich (1997a) cites the need for HR practice to be guided by HR theory as follows.

SOURCE REVIEW

The need for HR theory, Ulrich (1997a)

To make HR practices more than isolated acts managers and HR professionals must master the theory behind HR work; they need to be able to explain conceptually how and why HR practices lead to their outcomes... Regardless of the preferred theory, managers and HR professionals should extract from it a higher level of reasoning for their day-to-day work and thus better explain why their work accomplishes its goals.

Continuous professional development

As defined by the CIPD, continuous professional development (CPD) is the process that enables the integration of learning with work in ways relevant to the learner, is self-directed and contributes to the learner's development needs. The benefits to individuals include becoming better learners, profiting from learning opportunities, managing self-development, helping career advancement, and improving professional standing. The benefits to organizations include better contributions by individuals to organizational goals and objectives, improved performance for the organization, and the ability to help others learn and develop themselves to enhance their work performance and their organizational commitment.

CPD for individual HR professionals is about lifelong development. For the organization it is concerned with improving organizational capability and is linked with the concepts of knowledge management (see Chapter 12) and the learning organization (see Chapter 40).

Role of the HR practitioner – key learning points

The basic role of HR practitioners

The role varies considerably but it is basically about providing advice, guidance and services on all matters affecting people.

The business partner role

As business partners HR specialists share responsibility with their line management colleagues for the success of the enterprise and get involved with them in implementing business strategy and running the business.

The strategic role

To a) formulate and implement forward-looking HR strategies that are aligned to business objectives and integrated with one another; b) contribute to the development of business strategies; and c) work alongside their line management colleagues to provide on an everyday basis continuous support to the implementation of the strategy of the organization, function or unit.

The strategic activities of HR practitioners

Strategic activities consist of formulating HR strategies and providing continuous support to line managers in implementing their business or operational strategies. They involve being proactive in identifying issues that can be addressed through major or relatively minor HR initiatives.

The change agent role

HR specialists act as change agents, facilitating change by providing advice and support on its introduction and management.

The internal consultancy role

As internal consultants, HR practitioners work alongside their colleagues – their clients – in analysing problems, diagnosing issues and proposing solutions.

The service provision role

The basic role of HR specialists is that of providing services to internal customers. The services may be general, covering all aspects of HRM, or services may only be provided in one or two areas.

The guardian of values role

HR practitioners may act as the guardians of the organization's values and ethical standards concerning people. They point out when behaviour conflicts with those values or where proposed actions will be inconsistent with them.

Models of HR roles

A number of models of HR roles exist. One of the best known ones was devised by Tyson and Fell (1986), which listed three roles: the clerk of works (mainly administrative), the contracts manager (more sophisticated with

Role of the HR practitioner – key learning points (continued)

an employee relations focus) and the architect (strategic/innovative). The other is by Ulrich and Brockbank (2005a and b), which identified four roles: employee advocate, human capital developer, functional expert and strategic partner.

Gaining support from top management

- Demonstrate that the proposal will meet organizational needs.
- Base the proposal on a compelling and realistic business case that shows that the innovation will increase the business's competitive edge.
- Prove that the innovation has already worked well within the organization (in a pilot scheme) or elsewhere.
- Specify how the proposal can be implemented without too much trouble.
- Indicate that the innovation will add to the reputation of the company.
- Emphasize that the innovation will enhance the 'employer brand' of the company.
- Ensure that the proposal is brief, to the point and well argued.

Gaining support from line managers

Managers need to be convinced that the innovation helps them to achieve better results without imposing unacceptable additional burdens on them.

Ethical considerations

HR specialists should speak out against plans or actions that are not in accord with management's ethical standards or values.

Professionalism

HR specialists are professional when they display expertise in doing their work and act responsibly.

Ambiguities and conflict in the role

HR practitioners have to be 'specialists in ambiguity'. Conflict may arise because of a clash of values, different priorities and the need for HR to exercise a measure of control over the people management activities of managers.

HR effectiveness

Effective HR practitioners operate strategically, facilitate change, understand organizational and individual needs, are business-like and persuasive, and deliver their services efficiently and effectively.

HR competencies

The main competencies required by HR professionals are: business awareness, strategic capability, organizational effectiveness, capacity as an internal consultant, effective service delivery, acting in the interests of employees and continuous professional development.

Questions

1. Tim Miller, Group Head of HR, Standard Chartered Bank, as reported by Jane Pickard (2005) said that: 'HR is about helping managers to manage people and I want them to be engaged in building performance through people and involved in the cost of people as well. Of course, they have to understand HR processes, performance management and reward and so on. But it's how they configure and embed their products and make them part of the business that matters.' Comment on this statement against the background of the business partner concept.
2. HR professionals become strategic partners when they participate in the process of defining the business strategy, when they ask questions that move the strategy to action and when they design HR practices that align with the business (Ulrich, 1997a). What evidence is available from research that this is happening today?
3. Raymond Caldwell made the following somewhat dispiriting comment in 2004 on the basis of his research: 'Overall there is the issue of "powerlessness" or the marginality of personnel practitioners in management decision-making processes, especially at a strategic level. Closely related to this is the relative inability of the personnel function to maintain or defend the experience of their specialist expertise from encroachment or control by managerial intervention. In addition, there are issues of lack of clarity or accountability in specifying the goals, business outcomes, or the contribution of the personnel function, especially when compared to other management functions.' Drawing on other research and your own experience, comment on the validity of this assertion. If there is something in it, what can be done?
4. What do you think of the following remarks made by an HR director interviewed by Guest and King in their research published in 2004? 'One of the problems for any HR function is the separation between the tactical stuff and the strategic stuff and I guess that I am now at a level where I ought to be – I hesitate to use the word; it is so overused – but I ought to be being strategic; the reality is that 70 per cent of my job is tactical. And by the way if I didn't do it I wouldn't have any credibility.'

References

Boxall, P F (1996) The strategic HRM debate and the resource-based view of the firm, *Human Resource Management Journal*, **6** (3), pp 59–75

Boxall, P (1999) Human resource strategy and competitive advantage: a longitudinal study of engineering consultancies, *Journal of Management Studies*, **36** (4), pp 443–63

Boxall, P F and Purcell, J (2003) *Strategy and Human Resource Management*, Palgrave Macmillan, Basingstoke

Brockbank, W, Ulrich, D and Beatty, D (1999) HR professional development: creating the future creators at the University of Michigan Business School, *Human Resource Management*, **38,** Summer, pp 111–17

Caldwell, R (2001) Champions, adapters, consultants and synergists: the new change agents in HRM, *Human Resource Management Journal*, **11** (3), pp 39–52

Caldwell, R (2004) Rhetoric, facts and self-fulfilling prophesies: exploring practitioners' perceptions of progress in implementing HRM, *Industrial Relations Journal*, **35** (3), pp 196–215

CIPD (2005a) *The Thinking Performer*, CIPD.co.uk

Drucker, P (1995) The information executives truly need, *Harvard Business Review*, Jan–Feb, pp 54–62

Farnham, D (2008) *Examiner's Report* (May), CIPD.co.uk

Fletcher, C (2004) *Appraisal and Feedback: Making performance review work*, 3rd edn, CIPD, London

Follett, M P (1924) *Creative Experience*, Longmans Green, New York

Francis, H and Keegan A (2006) The changing face of HRM: in search of balance, *Human Resource Management Journal*, **16** (3), pp 231–49

Gratton, L A (2000) Real step change, *People Management*, 16 March, pp 27–30

Guest, D E and Hoque, K (1994) Yes, personnel management does make the difference, *Personnel Management*, November, pp 40–44

Guest, D E and King, Z (2004) Power, innovation and problem solving: the personnel managers' three steps to heaven?, *Journal of Management Studies*, **41** (3), pp 401–23

Harrison, R (2007) Still room for improvement in learning and development after a decade of PQS, *People Management*, 1 November, p 47

Hayes Committee on Personnel Management (1972) *Training for the Management of Human Resources*, Department of Employment, HMSO, London

Hope-Hailey, V, Farndale, E and Truss, C (2005) The HR department's role in organizational performance, *Human Resource Management Journal*, **15** (3), pp 49–66

Hoque, K and Noon, M (2001) Counting angels: a comparison of personnel and HR specialists, *Human Resource Management Journal*, **11** (3), pp 5–22

Huselid, M A, Jackson, S E and Schuler, R S (1997) Technical and strategic human resource management effectiveness as determinants of firm performance, *Academy of Management Journal*, **40** (1), pp 171–88

Legge, K (1978) *Power, Innovation and Problem Solving in Personnel Management*, McGraw-Hill, Maidenhead

Legge, K (1995) *Human Resource Management: Rhetorics and realities*, Macmillan, London

Mackay, L and Torrington, D (1986) *The Changing Nature of Personnel Management*, IPD, London

Marchington, M (1995) Fairy tales and magic wands: new employment practices in perspective, *Employee Relations*, Spring, pp 51–66

Monks, K (1992) Models of personnel management: a means of understanding the diversity of personnel practices, *Human Resource Management Journal*, **3** (2), pp 29–41

Pfeffer, J and Sutton, R I (2006) A matter of fact, *People Management*, 28 September, p 24

Pickard, J (2005) Part not partner, *People Management*, 27 October, pp 48–50

Reilly, P (2000) *HR Shared Services and the Re-alignment of HR*, Institute for Employment Studies, Brighton

Rousseau, D M (2006) Is there such a thing as evidence-based management?, *Academy of Management Review*, **31** (2), pp 256–69

Smethurst, S (2005) The long and winding road, *People Management*, 28 July, pp 25–29

Storey, J (1992a) *New Developments in the Management of Human Resources*, Blackwell, Oxford

Storey, J (1992b) HRM in action: the truth is out at last, *Personnel Management*, April, pp 28–31

Syrett, M (2006) Four reflections on developing a human capital measurement capability, in *What's the Future for Human Capital?*, CIPD, London

Thurley, K (1981) Personnel management: a case for urgent treatment, *Personnel Management*, August, pp 24–29

Tyson, S (1985) Is this the very model of a modern personnel manager? *Personnel Management*, May, pp 22–25

Tyson, S and Fell, A (1986) *Evaluating the Personnel Function*, Hutchinson, London

Ulrich, D (1997a) *Human Resource Champions*, Harvard Business School Press, Boston, MA

Ulrich, D (1998) A new mandate for human resources, *Harvard Business Review*, January–February, pp 124–34

Ulrich, D and Brockbank, W (2005a) *The HR Value Proposition*, Harvard Press, Cambridge, MA

Ulrich, D and Brockbank, W (2005b) Role call, *People Management*, 16 June, pp 24–28

Watson, A (1977) *The Personnel Managers*, Routledge and Kegan Paul, London

Wright, P M, Snell, S A and Jacobsen, H H (2004) Current approaches to HR strategies: inside-out versus outside-in, *Human Resource Planning*, **27** (4), pp 36–46

7 The Impact of HRM on Performance

Key concepts and terms

- The AMO formula
- Discretionary effort
- Organizational capability
- Performance
- Contingency theory
- Expectancy theory
- Organizational effectiveness
- Reversed causality

Learning outcomes

On completing this chapter you should be able to define these key concepts. You should also know about:

- Outcomes of research on the link between HRM and firm performance
- HRM and individual performance
- How HR practices make an impact
- Problems of establishing a link
- The link between HRM and organizational performance

Introduction

As Guest (1997) argues: 'The distinctive feature of HRM is its assumption that improved performance is achieved through the people in the organization.' If, therefore, appropriate HR policies and processes are introduced, it can also be assumed that HRM will make a substantial impact on firm performance. To back up these assumptions three questions need to be answered: What is performance? What impact does HRM make on performance? How does HRM make that impact?

The concept of performance covers both *what* has been achieved and *how* it has been achieved. Firm performance can be measured in a number of different ways. The most obvious way to measure what has been achieved, and the approach used in many studies, is by reference to key performance indicators (KPIs), which are usually to do with financial results (profitability) or productivity. Measuring the 'how' is more difficult. It has to rely extensively on qualitative assessments of organizational capability or effectiveness. Organizational capability is defined as the capacity of a firm to function effectively in order to compete and deliver results. Organizational effectiveness is defined as the capacity of an organization to achieve its goals by making effective use of the resources available to it.

What impact HRM makes may be nice to know, if only to demonstrate to dubious chief executives and line managers that HRM is a good thing. A considerable amount of research has been conducted recently on the impact of HRM, which is discussed in the first section of this chapter. But it is also necessary to understand how that impact is made in order to justify, develop and implement effective HR policies and practices. Ulrich (1997a) comments that managers and HR professionals 'need to be able to explain conceptually how and why HR practices lead to their outcomes'.

The impact made by HRM

The holy grail sought by many human resource management researchers is to establish that HRM practices demonstrably cause improvements in organizational performance. Practitioners too would like to be able to justify their existence by saying to their bosses and their colleagues that this is the case. Much research as summarized in Table 7.1 has been carried over the last decade or so, most of which at least shows that there is a link between good HRM practice and firm performance.

Table 7.1 Research on the link between HRM and firm performance

Researcher(s)	Methodology	Outcomes
Arthur (1990, 1992, 1994)	Data from 30 US strip mills used to assess impact on labour efficiency and scrap rate by reference to the existence of either a high commitment strategy or a control strategy	Firms with a high commitment strategy had significantly higher levels of both productivity and quality than those with a control strategy

Table 7.1 *continued*

Researcher(s)	Methodology	Outcomes
Huselid (1995)	Analysis of the responses of 968 US firms to a questionnaire exploring the use of high performance work practices	Productivity is influenced by employee motivation; financial performance is influenced by employee skills, motivation and organizational structures
Huselid and Becker (1996)	An index of HR systems in 740 firms was created to indicate the degree to which each firm adopted a high performance work system	Firms with high values on the index had economically and statistically higher levels of performance
Becker *et al* (1997)	Outcomes of a number of research projects were analysed to assess the strategic impact on shareholder value of high performance work systems	High performance systems make an impact as long as they are embedded in the management infrastructure.
Patterson *et al* (1997)	The research examined the link between business performance and organization culture and the use of a number of HR practices	HR practices explained significant variations in profitability and productivity (19% and 18% respectively). Two HR practices were particularly significant: (1) the acquisition and development of employee skills and (2) job design including flexibility, responsibility and variety
Appelbaum *et al* (2000)	Study of the impact of high performance work systems (HPWSs) in 44 manufacturing facilities – over 4,000 employees were surveyed.	HPWSs produced strong positive effects on performance. They are associated with workshop practices that raise the levels of trust, increase workers' intrinsic reward from work and thereby enhance organizational commitment.
Guest *et al* (2000a)	An analysis of the 1998 WERS survey which sampled some 2,000 workplaces and obtained the views of about 28,000 employees	A strong association exists between HRM and both employee attitudes and workplace performance

Table 7.1 *continued*

Researcher(s)	Methodology	Outcomes
Guest *et al* (2000b)	The Future of Work Survey covered 835 private sector organizations. Interviews were carried out with 610 HR professionals and 462 chief executives	A greater use of HR practices is associated with higher levels of employee commitment and contribution and is in turn linked to higher levels of productivity and quality of services
Thompson (2002)	A study of the impact of high performance work practices such as team working, appraisal, job rotation, broad-banded grade structures and sharing of business information in UK aerospace establishments	The number of HR practices and the proportion of the workforce covered appeared to be the key differentiating factor between more and less successful firms
West *et al* (2002)	Research conducted in 61 UK hospitals obtaining information on HR strategy, policy and procedures from chief executives and HR directors and mortality rates	An association between certain HR practices and lower mortality rates was identified. As noted by Professor West: 'If you have HR practices that focus on effort and skill; develop people's skills; encourage co-operation, collaboration, innovation and synergy in teams for most, if not all employees, the whole system functions and performs better'.
Guest *et al* (2003)	An exploration of the relationship between HRM and performance in 366 UK companies using objective and subjective performance data and cross-sectional and longitudinal data	Some evidence was shown of an association between HRM, as described by the number of HR practices in use, and performance, but there was no convincing indication that the greater application of HRM is likely to result in improved corporate performance

Table 7.1 *continued*

Researcher(s)	Methodology	Outcomes
Purcell *et al* (2003)	A University of Bath longitudinal study of 12 companies to establish how people management impacts on organizational performance	The most successful companies had 'the big idea'. They had a clear vision and a set of integrated values. They were concerned with sustaining performance and flexibility. Clear evidence existed between positive attitudes towards HR policies and practices, levels of satisfaction, motivation and commitment, and operational performance. Policy and practice implementation (not the number of HR practices adopted) is the vital ingredient in linking people management to business performance and this is primarily the task of line managers.

Comments on the research

The methodology used in many of the studies listed in Table 7.1 was to measure the association between the number of HR practices used by the firm and the financial results achieved by the firm, treating the number of practices as the input variable and profit or market value as the dependent variable. Purcell *et al* (2003) have cast doubts on the validity of this approach.

SOURCE REVIEW

Validity of HRM and performance research, Purcell *et al* (2003)

Our study has demonstrated convincingly that research which only asks about the number and extent of HR practices can never be sufficient to understand the link between HR practices and business performance... It is misleading to assume that simply because HR practices are present they will be implemented as intended.

In 1997 David Guest commented that: 'At present the studies report a promising association between HRM and outcomes, but we are not yet in a position to assert cause and effect'. Ulrich (1997a) has pointed out that: 'HR practices seem to matter; logic says it is so; survey findings confirm it. Direct relationships between performance and attention to HR practices are often fuzzy, however, and vary according to the population sampled and the measures used.' And Purcell *et al* (2003) noted that 'Measures which use profit or shareholder value are too remote from the practice of people management to be useful.' Any attempt to prove that good HR practice generates high economic returns has to confront the objection that there might be any number of reasons for high economic performance which have nothing to do with HRM.

Wood and Paauwe produced comprehensive analyses of studies of the HRM/performance link.

SOURCE REVIEW

A view on HRM/performance link studies, Stephen Wood (1999)

This empirical work (15 studies) 'has concentrated on assessing the link between practices and performance, with an increasing disregard for the mechanisms linking them. This has meant that there has been no systematic link between HR outcomes and performance. Moreover, there has been an increasing neglect of the psychological processes that mediate or moderate the link between HR practices and performance'.

Another view on HRM/performance link studies, Jaap Paauwe (2004)

Research on HR and performance has been based on a narrow-minded definition of performance which involves the use of limited analytical frameworks based on simple input/output reasoning. So there is a substantial negligence of the process itself, the actors and stakeholders involved, the administrative heritage and institutional values. A systems based approach is required which includes HRM practices and policies as input variables, HRM outcomes as intermediate variables and firm performance indicators as the dependent variables. Contingency variables such as size and technology need to be used as control variables.

Reference was made by Boselie *et al* (2005) to the causal distance between an HRM input and an output such as financial performance: 'Put simply, so many variables and events, both internal and external, affect organizations that this direct linkage strains credibility.'

Another problem is the assumption some people make that correlations indicate causality – if variable A is associated with variable B then A has caused B. It might, but again it might not. This is linked to the issue of 'reversed causality' which is the assumption, as Purcell *et al* (2003) put it, 'that more HR practices leads to higher economic return when it just as possible that it is successful firms that can afford more extensive (and expensive) HRM practices'. They also comment that when successful firms invest heavily in HRM they may do so to help sustain high performance.

How HRM strategies make an impact

As Guest *et al* (2000b) comment, much of the research has demonstrated an association between HRM and performance but leaves uncertainties about cause and effect. However, they do state that 'HRM is essentially concerned with achieving results through full and effective utilization of human resources.' They go on to suggest that: 'This is only likely to be achieved through a set of appropriate practices resulting in high quality, flexible and committed employees.'

Wood (1999) noted that the quality of the research base supporting the relationship between HRM and performance is weak. Even if it were stronger, it is not enough simply to produce evidence that HR practices lead to high performance; it is necessary to understand how they produce this effect. This was the subject of research by Rogg *et al* (2001) who suggested that HRM affects performance by first influencing climate, which then determines performance. They also argued that the direct links between HRM practices and performance are relatively weak as it is not HRM practices themselves that affect performance, but rather the extent to which they lead to a favourable climate. In 2003 the 'black box' research by Purcell *et al* explored the unknown link between inputs and outcomes. Their conclusion was that HR practice feeds in as an 'ingredient' in the workplace and, through various mechanisms, feeds out through the other side as improved performance.

The HRM factors affecting high performance for both individuals and organizations need to be considered.

HRM and individual performance

There are three factors that affect the level of individual performance: motivation, ability and opportunity to participate. The first two factors were highlighted by Vroom (1964) who made the following suggestions on the basis of his research.

SOURCE REVIEW

Factors affecting individual performance, Vroom (1964)

The effects of motivation on performance are dependent on the level of ability of the worker, and the relationship of ability to performance is dependent on the motivation of the worker. The effects of ability and motivation on performance are not additive but interactive. The data presently available on this question suggest something more closely resembling the multiplicative relationship depicted in the formula: Performance = f (Ability × Motivation).

Vroom is therefore suggesting that people need both ability and motivation to perform well and that if either ability or motivation is zero there will be no effective performance.

Vroom also pioneered expectancy theory which, as developed by Porter and Lawler (1968), proposes that high individual performance depends on high motivation plus possession of the necessary skills and abilities and an appropriate role and understanding of that role. From this, as Guest (1997) claims:

> *It is a short step to specify the HR practices that encourage high skills and abilities, for example careful selection and high investment in training; high motivation, for example employee involvement and possibly performance-related pay; and an appropriate role structure and role perception, for example job design and extensive communication and feedback… We therefore have a theory that links HRM practices to processes that facilitate high individual performance.*

Research carried out by Bailey *et al* (2001) in 45 establishments focused on the 'opportunity to participate' factor as it affects performance. They noted that 'organizing the work process so that non-managerial employees have the opportunity to contribute discretionary effort is the central feature of a high performance work system'. (This was one of the earlier uses of the term 'discretionary effort'.) They stated that the other two components of a high performance work system were incentives and skills.

The 'AMO' formula put forward by Boxall and Purcell (2003) is a combination of the Vroom and Bailey *et al* ideas. This model asserts that performance is a function of Ability + Motivation + Opportunity to Participate (note that the relationship is additive not multiplicative). HRM practices therefore impact on individual performance if they encourage discretionary effort, develop skills and provide people with the opportunity to perform.

HRM and organizational performance

It may be possible to detect an association between HRM practices and the economic performance of firms. But because of all the other factors involved, it may be difficult if not impossible to demonstrate that the HR practices caused the high performance. As contingency theory tells us, what happens in organizations will be influenced, even governed, by their internal and external environment. There is also the problem of reversed causality – HR practices may have resulted in high performance but high performance may have encouraged the use of sophisticated HR practices.

Any theory about the impact of HRM on organizational performance must be based on three propositions:

1. That HR practices can make a direct impact on employee characteristics such as engagement, commitment, motivation and skill.
2. If employees have these characteristics it is probable that organizational performance in terms of productivity, quality and the delivery of high levels of customer service will improve.
3. If such aspects of organizational performance improve, the financial results achieved by the organization will improve.

Note, however, that are two intermediate factors between HRM and financial performance (employee characteristics affected by HRM and the impact of those characteristics on non-financial performance). According to these propositions, HRM does not make a direct impact. The relationship is further complicated by the other two factors mentioned above: the contingency variables and the possibility of reversed causality. A model of the impact of HRM taking all these considerations into account is shown in Figure 7.1.

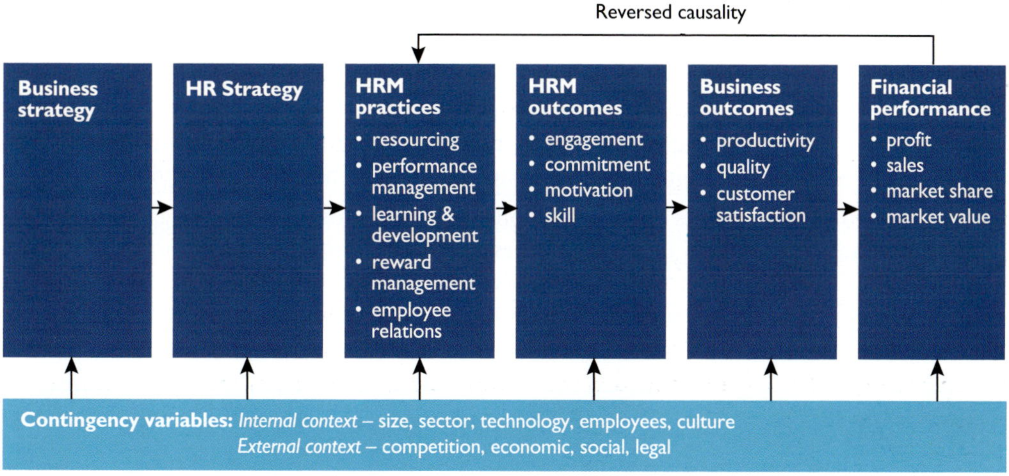

Figure 7.1 Impact of HRM on organizational performance

The case-based research by Purcell *et al* (2003) strongly indicated that the key to activating what they called the 'People–Performance' link lies not only in well-crafted 'bundles' of HR practices, but in their conjunction with a powerful and cohering organizational vision (or 'Big Idea') and corporate leadership, together with front-line leadership's action and use of its discretionary power.

How HRM practices make an impact

How HRM practices make an impact is summarized in Table 7.2.

Table 7.2 The HR practices that impact on performance

HR practice area	How it impacts
Attract, develop and retain high quality people	Match people to the strategic and operational needs of the organization. Provide for the acquisition, development and retention of talented employees, who can deliver superior performance, productivity, flexibility, innovation, and high levels of personal customer service and who 'fit' the culture and the strategic requirements of the organization
Talent management	Ensure that the talented and well motivated people required by the organization to meet present and future needs are available
Job and work design	Provides individuals with stimulating and interesting work and gives them the autonomy and flexibility to perform these jobs well. Enhance job satisfaction and flexibility which encourages greater performance and productivity
Learning and development	Enlarge the skill base and develop the levels of competence required in the workforce. Encourage discretionary learning which happens when individuals actively seek to acquire the knowledge and skills that promote the organization's objectives. Develop a climate of learning – a growth medium in which self-managed learning as well as coaching, mentoring and training flourish
Managing knowledge and intellectual capital	Focus on organizational as well as individual learning and provide learning opportunities and opportunities to share knowledge in a systematic way. Ensure that vital stocks of knowledge are retained and improve the flow of knowledge, information and learning within the organization

Table 7.2 *continued*

HR practice area	How it impacts
Increasing engagement, commitment and motivation	Encourage productive discretionary effort by ensuring that people are positive and interested in their jobs, that they are proud to work for the organization and want to go on working there and that they take action to achieve organizational and individual goals
Psychological contract	Develop a positive and balanced psychological contract which provides for a continuing, harmonious relationship between the employee and the organization
High performance management	Develop a performance culture which encourages high performance in such areas as productivity, quality, levels of customer service, growth, profits, and, ultimately, the delivery of increased shareholder value. Empower employees to exhibit the discretionary behaviours most closely associated with higher business performance such as risk taking, innovation, and knowledge sharing. of knowledge and establishing trust between managers and their team members
Reward management	Develops motivation and job engagement by valuing people in accordance with their contribution
Employee relations	Develops involvement practices and an employee relations climate which encourages commitment and cooperation.
Working environment – core values, leadership, work/life balance, managing diversity, secure employment	Develop 'the big idea' (Purcell *et al*, 2003), ie a clear vision and a set of integrated values. Make the organization 'a great place to work'

Impact of HRM – key learning points

Outcomes of research on the link between HRM and firm performance

- Firms with a high commitment strategy had significantly higher levels of both productivity and quality than those with a control strategy. (Arthur, 1992)
- Productivity is influenced by employee motivation; financial performance is influenced by employee skills, motivation and organizational structures. (Huselid, 1995)
- Firms with high values on the index had economically and statistically

Impact of HRM – key learning points (continued)

higher levels of performance. (Huselid and Becker, 1996)

- High performance systems make an impact as long as they are embedded in the management infrastructure. (Becker *et al*, 1997)
- HR practices explained significant variations in profitability and productivity. (Patterson *et al*, 1997)
- High performance work systems produced strong positive effects on performance. (Appelbaum *et al*, 2000)
- A strong association exists between HRM and both employee attitudes and workplace performance. (Guest *et al*, 2000a)
- A greater use of HR practices is associated with higher levels of employee commitment and contribution and is in turn linked to higher levels of productivity and quality of services. (Guest *et al*, 2000b)
- The number of HR practices and the proportion of the workforce covered appeared to be the key differentiating factors between more and less successful firms. (Thompson, 2002)
- If you have HR practices that focus on effort and skill; develop people's skills; encourage cooperation, collaboration, innovation and synergy in teams for most, if not all employees, the whole system functions and performs better. (West *et al*, 2002)
- Some evidence was shown of an association between HRM, as described by the number of HR practices in use, and performance, but there was no convincing indication that the greater application of HRM is likely to result in improved corporate performance. (Guest *et al*, 2003)
- Clear evidence existed between positive attitudes towards HR policies and practices, levels of satisfaction, motivation and commitment, and operational performance. (Purcell *et al*, 2003)

Problems of establishing a link

- At present the studies report a promising association between HRM and outcomes, but we are not yet in a position to assert cause and effect. (David Guest, 1997)
- HR practices seem to matter; logic says it is so; survey findings confirm it. Direct relationships between performance and attention to HR practices are often fuzzy, however, and vary according to the population sampled and the measures used. (Ulrich, 1997a)
- Measures which use profit or shareholder value are too remote from the practice of people management to be useful. (Purcell *et al*, 2003)

HRM and individual performance

The factors that affect the level of individual performance are motivation, ability and opportunity to participate.

Impact of HRM – key learning points (continued)

Link between HRM and organizational performance

Three propositions on the link: a) HR practices can make a direct impact on employee characteristics such as engagement, commitment, motivation and skill; b) if employees have these characteristics it is probable that organizational performance in terms of productivity, quality and the delivery of high levels of customer service will improve; and c) if such aspects of organizational performance improve, the financial results achieved by the organization will improve.

How HR practices make an impact

Summarized in Table 7.2.

Questions

1. The research conducted by Guest and King (2004) elicited the following response from one HR director: 'We read ad nauseum about why aren't HR directors on the main board and my answer to this would be, because not enough of them have been able to prove that HR can contribute. It is there, it is there to be done.' How can it be done?
2. Guest *et al* (2003) noted that: 'Much of the published research has shown an association between HRM and performance, either at the same point in time or over time. The demonstration of an association is an important step in advancing research but leaves uncertainties about cause and effect.' The research conducted by Guest and his colleagues did reveal a positive association between HRM and profitability but did not support the assumption that HRM led to the higher profitability. Can you identify any research projects that have established cause and effect? If not, what is the point of all this research?
3. What are the practical implications of the following comment made by Hope-Hailey *et al* (2005) made in introducing the findings of their research on HR and organizational performance? 'Sustained competitive advantage thus lies in the employees themselves, not in HRM practices, as these do not meet the criteria of value, rarity, inimitability and non-substitutability. Therefore, the HR department needs to go beyond designing effective HRM policies and practices to ensure that these practices are implemented appropriately and are accepted by employees to achieve the intended results.'

References

Appelbaum, E, Bailey, T, Berg, P and Kalleberg, A L (2000) *Manufacturing Advantage: Why high performance work systems pay off*, ILR Press, Ithaca, NY

Arthur, J (1990) Industrial Relations and Business Strategies in American Steel Minimills, unpublished PhD dissertation, Cornell University

Arthur, J (1992) The link between business strategy and industrial relations systems in American steel mills, *Industrial and Labor Relations Review*, **45** (3), pp 488–506

Arthur, J (1994) Effects of human resource systems on manufacturing performance and turnover, *Academy of Management Review*, **37** (4), pp 670–87

Bailey, T, Berg, P and Sandy, C (2001) The effect of high performance work practices on employee earnings in the steel, apparel and medical electronics and imaging industries, *Industrial and Labor Relations Review*, **54** (2A), pp 525–43

Becker, B E, Huselid, M A, Pickus, P S and Spratt, M F (1997) HR as a source of shareholder value: research and recommendations, *Human Resource Management*, Spring, **36** (1), pp 39–47

Boselie, P, Dietz, G and Boon, C (2005) Commonalities and contradictions in HRM and performance research, *Human Resource Management Journal*, **15** (3), pp 67–94

Boxall, P F and Purcell, J (2003) *Strategy and Human Resource Management*, Palgrave Macmillan, Basingstoke

Guest, D E (1997) Human resource management and performance; a review of the research agenda, *The International Journal of Human Resource Management*, **8** (3), 263–76

Guest, D E and King Z (2004) Power, innovation and problem-solving: the personnel managers' three steps to heaven? *Journal of Management Studies*, **41** (3) pp 401–23

Guest, D E, Michie, J, Sheehan, M and Conway, N (2000a) *Employee Relations, HRM and Business Performance: An analysis of the 1998 workplace employee relations survey*, CIPD, London

Guest, D E, Michie, J, Sheehan, M, Conway, N and Metochi, M (2000b) *Effective People Management: Initial findings of future of work survey*, Chartered Institute of Personnel and Development, London

Guest, D E, Michie, J, Conway, N and Sheehan, M (2003) Human resource management and corporate performance in the UK, *British Journal of Industrial Relations*, **41** (2), pp 291–314

Hope-Hailey, V, Farndale, E and Truss, C (2005) The HR department's role in organizational performance, *Human Resource Management Journal*, **15** (3), pp 49–66

Huselid, M A (1995) The impact of human resource management practices on turnover, productivity and corporate financial performance, *Academy of Management Journal*, **38** (3), pp 635–72

Huselid, M A and Becker, B E (1996) Methodological issues in cross-sectional and panel estimates of the human resource-firm performance link, *Industrial Relations*, **35** (3), pp 400–22

Paauwe, J (2004) *HRM and performance: Achieving long term viability*, Oxford University Press, Oxford

Patterson, M G, West, M A, Lawthom, R and Nickell, S (1997) *Impact of People Management Practices on Performance*, Institute of Personnel and Development, London

Porter, L W and Lawler, E E (1968) *Managerial Attitudes and Performance*, Irwin-Dorsey, Homewood, IL

Purcell, J, Kinnie, K, Hutchinson, S, Rayton, B and Swart, J (2003) *People and Performance: How people management impacts on organisational performance*, CIPD, London

Rogg, K L, Schmidt, D L, Shull C and Schmitt, N (2001) Human resource practices, organizational climate, and customer satisfaction, *Journal of Management*, **27** (4), pp 431–49

Thompson, M (2002) *High Performance Work Organization in UK Aerospace*, The Society of British Aerospace Companies, London

Ulrich, D (1997a) *Human Resource Champions*, Harvard Business School Press, Boston, MA

Vroom, V (1964) *Work and Motivation*, Wiley, New York

West, M A, Borrill, C S, Dawson, C, Scully, J, Carter, M, Anclay, S, Patterson, M and Waring, J (2002) The link between the management of employees and patient mortality in acute hospitals, *International Journal of Human Resource Management*, **13** (8), pp 1299–310

Wood, S (1999) Human resource management and performance, *International Journal of Management Reviews*, **1** (4), pp 397–413

8 International HRM

Key concepts and terms

- Convergence
- Globalization
- Host-based pay
- Divergence
- Home-based pay

Learning outcomes

On completing this chapter you should be able to define these key concepts. You should also know about:

- The meaning of international HRM
- The impact of globalization
- Factors affecting the choice between convergence and divergence
- Managing expatriates
- Issues in international HRM
- International environmental and cultural differences
- Global HR policies

Introduction

It has been stated by Brewster *et al* (2005) that: 'A critical challenge for organizations from both the public and private sectors in the twenty-first century is the need to operate across national boundaries.' In this chapter consideration is given to how organizations respond to this challenge through the practice of international HRM. The chapter includes a definition of international HRM, an examination of the issues involved in international HRM, the practice of global HRM and the management of expatriates.

International HRM defined

International human resource management is the process of managing people across international boundaries by multinational companies. It involves the worldwide management of people, not just the management of expatriates.

Companies that function globally comprise international and multinational firms. International firms are those where operations take place in subsidiaries overseas that rely on the business expertise or manufacturing capacity of the parent company; they may be highly centralized with tight controls. Multinational firms are ones in which a number of businesses in different countries are managed as a whole from the centre; the degree of autonomy they have will vary.

Dr Michael Dickman of the Cranfield School of Management, as reported by Welfare (2006), believes that the main contrast between national and global HR practice is the need to see the bigger picture: 'The difference is the higher complexity and the need for sensitivity to different cultures and different business environments.' He stated that understanding the local context is key and an international HR person needs to be asking questions such as: What is the business environment here? What is the role of the trade unions? What is the local labour law? Are these people different? Are their motivation patterns different?

Issues in international HRM

There are a number of issues that specifically affect the practice of international as distinct from domestic HRM. These are the impact of globalization, the influence of environmental and cultural differences, the extent to which HRM policy and practice should vary in different countries (convergence or divergence), and the approaches used to employ and manage expatriates.

Globalization

Globalization is the process of international economic integration in worldwide markets. It involves the development of single international markets for goods or services accompanied by an accelerated growth in world trade.

Any company that has economic interests or activities extending across a number of international boundaries is a global company. This involves a number of issues not present when the activities of the firm are confined to one country. As Ulrich (1998) put it: 'Globalization requires organizations to move people, ideas, products and information around the world to meet local needs.'

SOURCE REVIEW

The distinction between international and global HRM, Brewster *et al* (2005)

Traditionally, international HR has been about managing an international workforce – the higher level organizational people working as expatriates, frequent commuters, cross-cultural team members and specialists involved in international knowledge transfer. Global HRM is not simply about these staff. It concerns managing all HRM activities, wherever they are, through the application of global rule sets.

Bartlett and Ghoshal (1991) argue that the main issue for multinational companies is the need to manage the challenges of global efficiency and multinational flexibility – 'the ability of an organization to manage the risks and exploit the opportunities that arise from the diversity and volatility of the global environment'.

Research conducted over a number of years by Brewster and Sparrow (2007) has shown that the nature of international human resource management is changing fast. Among some of the larger international organizations, these changes have created a completely different approach to international human resource management, one we have dubbed 'globalized HRM'. Whereas international human resource management has tended to operate in the same way as local HRM but on a wider scale, globalized HRM exploits the new technologies available to manage all the company's staff around the world in the same way that it has traditionally managed staff in the home country.

Environmental differences

Environmental differences between countries have to be taken into account in managing globally. As described by Gerhart and Fang (2005), these include 'differences in the centrality of markets, institutions, regulations, collective bargaining and labour-force characteristics'. For example: in Western Europe, collective bargaining coverage is much higher than in countries like the United States, Canada and Japan. Works councils are mandated by law in Western European countries like Germany, but not in Japan or the United States. In China, Eastern Europe and Mexico, labour costs are significantly lower than in Western Europe, Japan and the United States.

Cultural differences

Cultural differences must also be taken into account. Hiltrop (1995) noted the following HR areas that may be affected by national culture:

- decisions of what makes an effective manager;
- giving face-to-face feedback;
- readiness to accept international assignments;
- pay systems and different concepts of social justice;
- approaches to organizational structuring and strategic dynamics.

The significance of cultural differences was the influential message delivered by Hofstede (1980, 1991). He defined culture as 'the collective mental programming of people in an environment', referred to cultural values as broad tendencies 'to prefer certain states of affairs over others', and described organizations as 'culture-bound'. Using worldwide data on IBM employees he identified four national cultural dimensions: uncertainty avoidance, masculinity/femininity, power distance and individualism/collectivism.

One of the conclusions Hofstede reached was that the cultural values within a nation are substantially more similar than the values of individuals from different nations. This has been taken up by subsequent commentators such as Adler (2002) who claimed that Hofstede's study explained 50 per cent of the difference between countries in employees' attitudes and behaviours. But this view has been challenged by Gerhart and Fang (2005). They subjected Hofstede's findings to further analysis and established that at the level of the individual as distinct from the country, only 2 to 4 per cent was explained by national differences and that therefore 'Hofstede's study should not be interpreted as showing that national culture explains 50 per cent of behaviours'. They also established from Hofstede's data that culture varies more between organizations than countries. In their view, cross-country cultural differences, while real, have been over-estimated and may well pale in importance when compared with other unique country characteristics when it comes to explaining the effectiveness of HR practices. But they accepted that national culture differences can be critical and that insensitivity to national culture differences can and does result in business failure (as well as failure and career consequences for individual managers.

On the basis of research conducted in 30 multinational companies by the Global HR Research Alliance (the Judge Business School, University of Cambridge and Cornell, Insead, Erasmus and Tilburg Universities) Stiles (2007) commented that 'while national cultural differences were not unimportant, organizational culture actually had more influence on HR practice'. The conclusion from the research was that: 'To think there is one best way to manage human resources is simplistic and wrong, but the variation and contextualization of HR, at least for the companies we studied, owes little to national culture.'

Convergence and divergence

According to Brewster *et al* (2002) the effectiveness of global HRM depends on 'the ability to judge the extent to which an organization should implement similar practices across the world (convergence) or adapt them to suit local conditions (divergence)'. The dilemma facing all multinational corporations is that of achieving a balance between international consistency and local autonomy. They have to decide on the extent to which their HR policies should either 'converge' worldwide to be basically the same in each location, or 'diverge' to be differentiated in response to local requirements.

SOURCE REVIEW

Convergence and divergence issues, Perkins and Shortland (2006)

Strategic choices surrounding employment relationships may be influenced primarily by 'home country' values and practices. But those managing operations in one or a range of host country environments face the challenge of transplanting 'ethnocentric' principles, justifying the consequential policies and practices in their interactions with local managers, other employees and external representatives.

There is a natural tendency for managerial traditions in the parent company to shape the nature of key decisions, but there are strong arguments for giving as much local autonomy as possible in order to ensure that local requirements are sufficiently taken into account. Hence the mantra 'Think globally but act nationally.' This leads to the fundamental assumption made by Bartlett and Ghoshal (1991) that: 'Balancing the needs of coordination, control and autonomy and maintaining the appropriate balance are critical to the success of the multinational company.' As Brewster *et al* (2005) point out:

> *Where global integration and coordination are important, subsidiaries need to be globally integrated with other parts of the organization and/or strategically coordinated by the parent. In contrast, where local responsiveness is important, subsidiaries will have far greater autonomy and there is less need for integration.*

Brewster (2004) believes that convergence may be increasing as a result of the power of the markets, the importance of cost, quality and productivity pressures, the emergence of transaction cost economies, the development of like-minded international cadres and benchmarking 'best practice'. Stiles (2007) notes that common practices across borders may be appropriate: 'Organizations seek what works and for HR in multinational companies, the range of options is limited to a few common practices that are believed to secure high performance.' Brewster *et al* (2005) think that it is quite possible for some parts of an HR system to converge while other parts may diverge. But there is choice and they have listed the following factors affecting it.

SOURCE REVIEW

Factors affecting the choice between convergence and divergence, Harris and Brewster (1999)

- The extent to which there are well-defined local norms.
- The degree to which an operating unit is embedded in the local environment.
- The strength of the flow of resources – finance, information and people – between the parent and the subsidiary.
- The orientation of the parent to control.
- The nature of the industry – the extent to which it is primarily a domestic industry at local level.
- The specific organizational competencies, including HRM, that are critical for achieving competitive advantage in a global environment.

Dickmann, as reported by Welfare (2006), instanced organizations such as IBM and Oxfam that operate a model based on universal principles or values across the organization that are then implemented differently at regional or national level. He suggested that the extent of integration or convergence depends on the business model of the organization:

If the company is basically a McDonald's, where there are only limited local variations but the product is essentially the same all over the world, then the approach is likely to be different to a company like Unilever, whose products and processes tend to be much more responsive to the local market.

Global HR policies and practices

The research conducted by Brewster *et al* (2005) identified three processes that constitute global HRM: talent management/employee branding, international assignments management, and managing an international workforce. They found that organizations such as Rolls Royce had set up centres of excellence operating on a global basis. They observed that global HR professionals are acting as the guardians of culture, operating global values and systems.

It was established by the Global HR Research Alliance study (Stiles, 2007) that global HR policies and practices were widespread in the areas of maintaining global performance standards, the use of common evaluation processes, common approaches to rewards, the development of senior managers, the application of competency frameworks and the use of common performance management criteria.

Generally the research has indicated that while global HR policies in such areas as talent management, performance management and reward may be developed, communicated and supported by centres of excellence, often through global networking, a fair degree of freedom has frequently been allowed to local management to adopt their own practices in accordance with the local context as long as in principle these are consistent with global policies.

Managing expatriates

Expatriates are people working overseas on long- or short-term contracts who can be nationals of the parent company or 'third country nationals' (TCNs) – nationals of countries other than the parent company who work abroad in subsidiaries of that company.

The management of expatriates is a major factor determining success or failure in an international business. Expatriates are expensive; they can cost three or four times as much as the employment of the same individual at home. They can be difficult to manage because of the problems associated with adapting to and working in unfamiliar environments, concerns about their development and careers, difficulties encountered when they re-enter their parent company after an overseas assignment, and how they should be remunerated. Policies to address all these issues are required, as described below.

Resourcing policies

The challenge is that of resourcing international operations with people of the right calibre. As Perkins (1997) observes, it is necessary for businesses to 'remain competitive with their employment offering in the market place, to attract and retain high quality staff with worldwide capabilities'.

Policies are required on the employment of local nationals and the use of expatriates for long periods or shorter assignments. The advantages of employing local nationals are that they:

- are familiar with local markets, the local communities, the cultural setting and the local economy;
- speak the local language and are culturally assimilated;
- can take a long-term view and contribute for a long period (as distinct from expatriates who are likely to take a short-term perspective);
- do not take the patronizing (neo-colonial) attitude that expatriates sometimes adopt.

Expatriates may be required to provide the experience and expertise that local nationals lack, at least for the time being. But there is much to be said for a long-term resourcing policy that states that the aim is to fill all or the great majority of posts with local people. Parent companies that staff their overseas subsidiaries with local nationals always have the scope to 'parachute in' specialist staff to deal with particular issues such as the start-up of a new product or service.

Recruitment and selection policies

Policies for recruitment and selection should deal with specifying requirements, providing realistic previews and preparation for overseas assignments.

Role specifications

Role specifications should take note of the behaviours required for those who work internationally. Leblanc (2001) suggested that they should be able to:

- recognize the diversity of overseas countries;
- accept differences between countries as a fact and adjust to these differences effectively;
- tolerate and adjust to local conditions;
- cope in the long term with a large variety of foreign contexts;
- manage local operations and personnel abroad effectively;

- gain acceptance as a representative of one's company abroad;
- obtain and interpret information about foreign national contexts (institutions, legislations, practices, market specifics, etc);
- inform and communicate effectively with a foreign environment about the home company's policies;
- take into account the foreign environment when negotiating contracts and partnerships;
- identify and accept adjustments to basic product specifications in order to meet the needs of the foreign market;
- develop elements of a common framework for company strategies, policies and operations;
- accept that the practices that will operate best in an overseas environment will not necessarily be the same as the company's 'home' practices.

Realistic previews

At interviews for candidates from outside the organization, and when talking to internal staff about the possibility of an overseas assignment, it is advisable to have a policy of providing a realistic preview of the job. The preview should provide information on the overseas operation, any special features of the work, what will need to be done to adjust to local conditions, career progression overseas, re-entry policy on completion of the assignment, pay, and special benefits such as home leave and children's education.

Preparation policy

The preparation policy for overseas assignments should include the provision of cultural familiarization for the country/ies in which the expatriate will work (sometimes called 'acculturization'), the preferred approach to leading and working in international teams, and the business and HR policies that will apply.

Training policy

Tarique and Caligiri (1995) propose that the following steps should be taken to design a training programme for expatriates:

1. Identify the type of global assignment, eg technical, functional, tactical, developmental or strategic/executive.
2. Conduct a cross-cultural training needs analysis covering organizational analysis and requirements, assignment analysis of key tasks and individual analysis of skills.

3. Establish training goals and measures – cognitive (eg understanding the role of cultural values and norms) and affective (modifying perception about culture and increasing confidence in dealing with individual behaviours to form adaptive behaviours such as interpersonal skills).
4. Develop the programme – the content should cover both general and specific cultural orientation; a variety of methods should be used.
5. Evaluate training given.

Career management policy

Special attention has to be paid to managing the careers of expatriates as part of their experience overseas, or on return permanently or for a period to their home country.

Assimilation and review policies

Assimilation policies will provide for the adaptation of expatriates to overseas posts and their progress in them to be monitored and reviewed. This may take the form of conventional performance management processes but additional information may be provided on potential and the ability of individuals to cope with overseas conditions. Where a number of expatriates are employed it is customary for someone at headquarters to have the responsibility of looking after them.

Re-entry policies

Re-entry policies should be designed to minimize the problems that can arise when expatriates return to their parent company after an overseas posting. They want to be assured that they will be given positions appropriate to their qualifications, and they will be concerned about their careers, suspecting that their overseas experience will not be taken into account. Policies should allow time for expatriates to adjust. The provision of mentors or counsellors is desirable.

Pay and allowances policies

The factors that are likely to impact on the design of reward systems, as suggested by Bradley *et al* (1999) are the corporate culture of the multinational enterprise, expatriate and local labour markets, local cultural sensitivities and legal and institutional factors. They refer to the choice that has to be made between seeking internal consistency by developing common reward policies to facilitate the movement of employees across borders and preserve internal equity, and responding to pressures to conform to local practices. But they point out that: 'Studies of cultural differences suggest that reward system design and management need to be tailored to local values to enhance the performance of overseas operations.' Although, as Sparrow (1999) asserts: 'Differences in international reward are not just a consequence of cultural differences, but also of differences in international influences, national business systems and the role and competence of managers in the sphere of HRM.'

The policy of most organizations is to ensure that expatriates are no worse off because they have been posted abroad. In practice, various additional allowances or payments, such as hardship allowances, mean that they are usually better off financially than if they had stayed at home. The basic choice for expatriates is whether to adopt a home-based or host-based policy.

Home-based pay

The home-based pay approach aims to ensure that the value of the remuneration (pay, benefits and allowances) of expatriates is the same as in their home country. The home-base salary may be a notional one for long-term assignments (ie the salary that it is assumed would be paid to expatriates were they employed in a job of equivalent level at the parent company). For shorter-term assignments it may be the actual salary of the individual. The notional or actual home-base salary is used as the foundation upon which the total remuneration package is built. This is sometimes called the 'build-up' or 'balance sheet' approach.

The salary 'build-up' starts with the actual or notional home-base salary. To it is added a cost of living adjustment that is applied to 'spendable income' – the portion of salary that would be used at home for everyday living. It usually excludes income tax, social security, pensions and insurance and can exclude discretionary expenditure on major purchases or holidays on the grounds that these do not constitute day-to-day living expenses.

The expatriate's salary would then consist of the actual or notional home-base salary plus the cost of living adjustment. In addition, it may be necessary to adjust salaries to take account of the host country's tax regime to achieve tax equalization. Moves of less than a year that might give rise to double taxation require particular attention.

Some or all of the following allowances may be added to this salary:

- 'incentive to work abroad' premium;
- hardship and location;
- housing and utilities;
- school fees;
- 'rest and recuperation' leave.

Host-based pay

The host-based pay approach provides expatriates with salaries and benefits such as company cars and holidays that are in line with those given to nationals of the host country in similar jobs. This method ensures equity between expatriates and host country nationals. It is adopted by companies using the so-called 'market rate' system, which ensures that the salaries of expatriates match the market levels of pay in the host country.

Companies using the host-based approach commonly pay additional allowances such as school fees, accommodation and medical insurance. They may also fund long-term benefits like social security, life assurance and pensions from home.

The host-based method is certainly equitable from the viewpoint of local nationals, and it can be less expensive than home-based pay. But it may be much less attractive as an inducement for employees to work abroad, especially in unpleasant locations, and it can be difficult to collect market rate data locally to provide a basis for setting pay levels.

International HRM – key learning points

The meaning of international HRM

International human resource management is the process of managing people across international boundaries by multinational companies. It involves the worldwide management of people, not just the management of expatriates.

Issues in international HRM

International HRM issues comprise the impact of globalization, the influence of environmental and cultural differences, the extent to which HRM policy and practice should vary in different countries (convergence or divergence), and the approaches used to employ and manage expatriates.

The impact of globalization

Globalization requires organizations to move people, ideas, products and information around the world to meet local needs (Ulrich, 1998).

International environmental differences

Environmental differences between countries have to be taken into account in managing globally. These include markets, institutions, regulations, collective bargaining and labour-force characteristics.

International cultural differences

National cultural differences can be critical and insensitivity to them can result in business failure (as well as failure and career consequences for individual managers).

Factors affecting the choice between convergence and divergence (Harris and Brewster, 1999)

- The extent to which there are well-defined local norms.

International HRM – key learning points (continued)

- The degree to which an operating unit is embedded in the local environment.
- The strength of the flow of resources between the parent and the subsidiary.
- The orientation of the parent to control.
- The nature of the industry.
- The specific organizational competencies, including HRM, that are critical for achieving competitive advantage in a global environment.

Global HR policies

Three processes that constitute global HRM are: talent management/employee branding, international assignments management, and managing an international workforce (Brewster *et al*, 2005).

Managing expatriates

Expatriates can be difficult to manage because of the problems associated with adapting to and working in unfamiliar environments, concerns about their development and careers, difficulties encountered when they re-enter their parent company after an overseas assignment, and how they should be remunerated. Special policies for them are required, covering:

- recruitment and selection;
- assimilation and review;
- training;
- career management;
- re-entry;
- pay and allowances (home-based or host-based pay).

Questions

1. The conclusions reached by Brewster *et al* (2005) after their extensive research were that: 'Our study has revealed an increasing emphasis on globalizing HR processes, with intense discussion around what needs to be global, regional or national. This new definition of global HR positions the global HR professional as the guardian of culture, operating global values and systems.' What do you think this means in practice for anyone involved in international HRM?
2. You are director of HRM (international) for an international firm operating mainly in Africa. The business strategy is to expand operations into the Far East, starting in Malaysia. A number of medium-sized firms based in Kuala Lumpur have been

Questions (continued)

identified as possibilities for acquisition. It will, however, be necessary to place a number of expatriates in those firms to facilitate the acquisition and ensure that their operations fit into the strategic pattern envisaged for the company. Due diligence has established that these firms have a number of capable executives who are paid above the going rate locally. However, their pay is well below the level of remuneration that would be required to attract and retain expatriates to work there. You have been asked by the managing director, international operations, to propose a remuneration policy for expatriates. What do you recommend and why?

3. The chief executive officer of one of your company's overseas subsidiaries has e-mailed you as follows: 'I have come across the terms "convergence" and "divergence" in an *Economist* article about managing international businesses. Apparently they refer to the choice of how far either employment conditions should be standardized worldwide or local companies should adopt their policies. In these terms we are pretty convergent. Are there any arguments I could use to achieve a more divergent policy for us?' Draft your reply.

References

Adler, N J (2002) *International Dimensions of Organizational Behaviour*, South-Western, Cincinnati, OH

Bartlett, C A and Ghoshal, S (1991) *Managing across Borders: The transnational solution*, London Business School, London

Bradley, P, Hendry, C and Perkins, P (1999) Global or multi-local? The significance of international values in reward strategy, in (eds) C Brewster and H Harris, *International HRM: Contemporary issues in Europe*, Routledge, London

Brewster, C (2004) European perspectives of human resource management, *Human Resource Management Review*, **14** (4), pp 365–82

Brewster, C and Sparrow, P (2007) Advances in technology inspire a fresh approach to international HRM, *People Management*, 8 February, p 48

Brewster, C, Harris, H and Sparrow, P (2002) *Globalizing HR*, CIPD, London

Brewster, C, Sparrow, P and Harris, H (2005) Towards a new model of globalizing HRM, *The International Journal of Human Resource Management*, **16** (6), pp 949–70

Gerhart, B and Fang, M (2005) National culture and human resource management: assumptions and evidence, *The International Journal of Human Resource Management*, **16** (6), pp 971–86

Harris, H and Brewster, C (1999) International human resource management: the European contribution, in (eds) C Brewster and H Harris, *International HRM: Contemporary issues in Europe*, Routledge, London

Hiltrop, J M (1995) The changing psychological contract: the human resource challenge of the 1990s, *European Management Journal*, **13** (3), pp 286–94

Hofstede, G (1980) *Cultural Consequences: International differences in work-related values*, Sage, Beverley Hills, CA

Hofstede, G (1991) *Culture and Organization: Software of the mind*, Sage, London

Leblanc B (2001) European competitiveness – some guidelines for companies, in (ed) M H Albrecht, *International HRM*, Blackwell, Oxford

Perkins, S J (1997) *Internationalization: The people dimension*, Kogan Page, London

Perkins, S J and Shortland, S M (2006) *Strategic International Human Resource Management*, Kogan Page, London

Sparrow, P R (1999) *The IPD Guide on International Recruitment, Selection and Assessment*, IPD, London

Stiles, P (2007) A world of difference?, *People Management*, 15 November, pp 36–41

Tarique, I and Caligiri, P (1995) Training and development of international staff, in (eds) A-W Herzorg and J V Ruyssevelde, *International Human Resource Management*, Sage Publications, London

Ulrich, D (1998) A new mandate for human resources, *Harvard Business Review*, January–February, pp 124–34

Welfare, S (2006) A whole world out there: managing global HR, *IRS Employment Review*, **862,** 29 December, pp 8–12

9 Corporate Social Responsibility

Key concepts and terms

- Corporate social responsibility (CSR)
- Strategic CSR
- Stakeholder theory

Learning outcomes

On completing this chapter you should be able to define these key concepts. You should also know about:

- The meaning of corporate social responsibility
- CSR activities
- Developing a CSR strategy
- CSR strategy
- The rationale for CSR

Introduction

Corporate social responsibility (CSR) is exercised by organizations when they conduct their business in an ethical way, taking account of the social, environmental and economic impact of how they operate, and going beyond compliance. As defined by McWilliams *et al* (2006) CSR refers to the actions taken by businesses 'that further some social good beyond the interests of the firm and that which is required by law'.

CSR has also been described by Husted and Salazar (2006) as being concerned with 'the impact of business behaviour on society' and by Porter and Kramer (2006) as a process of integrating business and society. The latter argued that to advance CSR, 'We must root it in a broad understanding of the interrelationship between a corporation and society while at the same time anchoring it in the strategies and activities of specific companies.'

The CIPD, in *Making CSR Happen: the contribution of people management* (Redington, 2005) placed more emphasis on CSR in the workplace when it defined it as: 'The continuing commitment by business to behave ethically and contribute to economic development while improving the quality of life of the workforce and their families as well as of the local community and society at large.'

CSR was justified by the CIPD (2007b) as a relevant and important HR activity because:

> *HR is responsible for the key systems and processes underpinning effective delivery. Through HR, CSR can be given credibility and aligned with how businesses run. CSR could be integrated into processes such as the employer brand, recruitment, appraisal, retention, motivation, reward, internal communication, diversity, coaching and training.*

Strategic CSR defined

Strategic CSR is about deciding initially the extent to which the firm should be involved in social issues and then creating a corporate social agenda – considering what social issues to focus on and to what extent. As Porter and Kramer (2006) emphasize, strategy is always about choice. They suggest that organizations that 'make the right choices and build focused, proactive and integrated social initiatives in concert with their core strategies will increasingly distance themselves from the pack'. They also believe that: 'It is through strategic CSR that the company will make the greatest social impact and reap the greatest business benefits.' Baron (2001) points out that CSR is what a firm does when it provides 'a public good in conjunction with its business and marketing strategy'.

CSR strategy needs to be integrated with the business strategy but it is also closely associated with HR strategy. This is because it is concerned with socially responsible behaviour both outside and within the firm – with society generally and with the internal community. In the latter case this means creating a working environment where personal and employment rights are upheld and HR policies and practices provide for the fair and ethical treatment of employees.

CSR activities

CSR activities as listed by McWilliams *et al* (2006) include incorporating social characteristics or features into products and manufacturing processes, adopting progressive human resource management practices, achieving higher levels of environmental performance through recycling and pollution abatement and advancing the goals of community organizations.

SOURCE REVIEW

The CSR activities of 120 leading British companies, Business in the Community (2007)

1. Community – skills and education, employability and social exclusion were frequently identified as key risks and opportunities. Other major activities were support for local community initiatives and being a responsible and safe neighbour.
2. Environment – most companies reported climate change and resource-use as key issues for their business; 85 per cent of them managed their impacts through an environmental management system.
3. Marketplace – the issues most frequently mentioned by companies were research and development, procurement and supply chain, responsible selling, responsible marketing and product safety. There was a rising focus on fair treatment of customers, providing appropriate product information and labelling, and on the impacts of products on customer health.
4. Workplace – this was the strongest management performing area as most companies have established employment management frameworks that can cater for workplace issues as they emerge. Companies recognized the crucial role of employees to achieve responsible business practices. Increasing emphasis was placed on internal communications and training to raise awareness and understanding of why CSR is relevant to them and valuable for the business. More attention was being paid to health and well-being issues as well as the traditional safety agenda. More work was being done on diversity, both to ensure the business attracts a diverse workforce and to communicate the business case for diversity internally.

Business in the Community also reported a growing emphasis on responsible business as a source of competitive advantage as firms move beyond minimizing risk to creating opportunities. A survey conducted by Industrial Relations Services (Egan, 2006) found that:

- most employers believe that employment practices designed to ensure the fair and ethical treatment of staff can boost recruitment and retention;
- relatively few employers are strongly convinced of a positive link to business performance or productivity;
- the issue of ethics in employment is often viewed as part of a broader social responsibility package;
- policies on ethical employment most commonly cover HR practice in the areas of recruitment, diversity, redundancy/dismissal proceedings and employee involvement.

The rationale for CSR

Stakeholder theory as first propounded by Freeman (1984) suggests that managers must satisfy a variety of constituents (eg workers, customers, suppliers, local community organizations) who can influence firm outcomes. According to this view, it is not sufficient for managers to focus exclusively on the needs of stockholders or the owners of the corporation. Stakeholder theory implies that it can be beneficial for the firm to engage in certain CSR activities that non-financial stakeholders perceive to be important.

A different view was expressed by Theodore Levitt, marketing expert. In his 1958 *Harvard Business Review* article, 'The dangers of social responsibility', he warned that 'government's job is not business, and business's job is not government'. Milton Friedman (1970), the Chicago monetarist, expressed the same sentiment. His maxim was that the social responsibility of business is to maximize profits within the bounds of the law. He argued that the mere existence of CSR was an agency problem within the firm in that it was a misuse of the resources entrusted to managers by owners, which could be better used on value-added internal projects or returned to the shareholders.

Generally, however, academics at least have been in favour of CSR and there is plenty of evidence both in the UK and the United States that many firms are pursuing CSR policies.

SOURCE REVIEW

Arguments supporting CSR, Porter and Kramer (2006)

1. The moral appeal – the argument that companies have a duty to be good citizens. The US business association Business for Social Responsibility (2007) asks its members 'to achieve commercial success in ways that honour ethical values and respect people, communities and the natural environment'.
2. Sustainability – an emphasis on environmental and community stewardship. As expressed by the World Business Council for Sustainable Social Development (2006) this involves 'meeting the needs of the present without compromising the ability of future generations to meet their own needs'.
3. Licence to operate – every company needs tacit or explicit permission from government, communities and other stakeholders to do business.
4. Reputation – CSR initiatives can be justified because they improve a company's image, strengthen its brand, enliven morale and even raise the value of its stock.

The rationale for CSR as defined by Hillman and Keim (2001) is based on two propositions. First, there is a moral imperative for businesses to 'do the right thing' without regard to how such decisions affect firm performance (the social issues argument) and second, firms can achieve competitive advantage by tying CSR activities to primary stakeholders (the stakeholders argument). Their research in 500 firms implied that investing in stakeholder management may be complementary to shareholder value creation and could indeed provide a basis for competitive advantage as important resources and capabilities are created that differentiate a firm from its competitors. However, participating in social issues beyond the direct stakeholders may adversely affect a firm's ability to create shareholder wealth.

It can be argued, as do Moran and Ghoshal (1996), 'that what is good for society does not necessarily have to be bad for the firm, and what is good for the firm does not necessarily have to come at a cost to society'. It could be argued, more cynically, that there is room for enlightened self-interest that involves doing well by doing good.

Much research has been conducted into the relationship between CSR and firm performance, with mixed results. For example, Russo and Fouts (1997) found that there was a positive relationship between environmental performance and financial performance. Hillman and Keim (2001) found that if the socially responsible activity were directly related to primary stakeholders, then investments may benefit not only stakeholders but also result in increased shareholder wealth. However, participation in social issues beyond the direct stakeholders may adversely affect a firm's ability to create shareholder wealth.

Developing a CSR strategy

The basis for developing a CSR strategy is provided by the following competency framework of the CSR Academy (2006), which is made up of six characteristics.

CSR competency framework

1. Understanding society – understanding how business operates in the broader context and knowing the social and environmental impact that the business has on society.
2. Building capacity – building the capacity of others to help manage the business effectively. For example, suppliers understand the business's approach to the environment and employees can apply social and environmental concerns in their day-to-day roles.
3. Questioning business as usual – individuals continually questioning the business in relation to a more sustainable future and being open to improving the quality of life and the environment.
4. Stakeholder relations – understanding who the key stakeholders are and the risks and opportunities they present. Working with them through consultation and taking their views into account.
5. Strategic view – ensuring that social and environmental views are included in the business strategy so that they are integral to the way the business operates.
6. Harnessing diversity – respecting that people are different, which is reflected in fair and transparent business practices.

To develop and implement a CSR strategy based on these principles it is necessary to:

- understand the business and social environment in which the firm operates;
- understand the business and HR strategies and how the CSR strategy should be aligned to them;
- know who the stakeholders are (including top management) and find out their views and expectations on CSR;
- identify the areas in which CSR activities might take place by reference to their relevance in the business context of the organization and an evaluation of their significance to stakeholders;

- prioritize as necessary on the basis of an assessment of the relevance and significance of CSR to the organization and its stakeholders and the practicalities of introducing the activity or practice;
- draw up the strategy and make the case for it to top management and the stakeholders;
- obtain approval for the CSR strategy from top management and key stakeholders;
- communicate information on the whys and wherefores of the strategy comprehensively and regularly;
- provide training to employees on the skills they need in implementing the CSR strategy;
- measure and evaluate the effectiveness of CSR.

Corporate social responsibility – key learning points

The meaning of corporate social responsibility (CSR)

CSR refers to the actions taken by businesses that further some social good beyond the interests of the firm and that which is required by law. It is concerned with the impact of business behaviour on society and can be regarded as a process of integrating business and society.

CSR strategy

CSR strategy determines how socially responsible behaviour is exercised both outside and within the firm.

CSR activities

CSR activities include incorporating social characteristics or features into products and manufacturing processes, adopting progressive human resource management practices, achieving higher levels of environmental performance through recycling and pollution abatement, and advancing the goals of community organizations.

The rationale for CSR

There are two arguments for CSR (Hillman and Keim, 2001). First, there is a moral imperative for businesses to 'do the right thing' without regard to how such decisions affect firm performance (the social issues argument) and second, firms can achieve competitive advantage by tying CSR activities to primary stakeholders (the stakeholders argument).

Developing a CSR strategy

- Identify the areas in which CSR activities might take place by reference to their relevance in the business context of the organization and an evaluation of their significance to stakeholders.

Corporate social responsibility – key learning points (continued)

- Prioritize as necessary on the basis of an assessment of the relevance and significance of CSR to the organization and its stakeholders and the practicalities of introducing the activity or practice.
- Draw up the strategy and make the case for it to top management and the stakeholders in order to obtain their approval.
- Communicate information on the strategy comprehensively and regularly.
- Provide training to employees on the skills they need in implementing the CSR strategy.

Questions

1. What does the concept of corporate social responsibility (CSR) mean and what are the main activities involved? Review the situation in your own organization and identify what CSR activities are taking place and what more could be done.
2. Comment on the following remarks: 'The most important thing a corporation can do for society, and for any community, is contribute to a prosperous economy' (Porter and Kramer, 2006). 'Profits should be a reflection not of corporate greed but a vote of confidence from society that what is offered by a firm is valued' (Matsushita, 2000).
3. You have been asked by your HR director to produce a memorandum setting out the business case on why the company should develop a more active corporate responsibility strategy. You looked at the research conducted by IRS (Egan, 2006) and came across the following information: 'The main motivation for employers in engaging in community and charitable work seem to be varied and sometimes interlinked. The following factors were cited by 12 organizations each: to enhance corporate image/reputation, to promote the business and to improve employee satisfaction and motivation. The desire to help others was mentioned by 10, with seven wishing to help employee development and four hoping to boost recruitment and retention. Two organizations each mentioned the aims of enhancing profitability, helping acquire public sector contracts and helping to acquire other contracts. Just one employer was motivated by a sense of moral obligation.' Taking into account these varied arguments, produce the business case.

References

Baron, D (2001) Private policies, corporate policies and integrated strategy, *Journal of Economics and Management Strategy*, **10** (7), pp 7–45

Business for Social Responsibility (2007) *Annual report*, web@BSR.org

Business in the Community (2007) *Benchmarking Responsible Business Practice*, bitc.org.uk

CIPD (2007b) *Corporate Social Responsibility*, CIPD Fact Sheet, www.cipd.co.uk

CSR Academy (2006) *The CSR Competency Framework*, Stationery Office, Norwich

Egan, J (2006) Doing the decent thing: CSR and ethics in employment, *IRS Employment Review*, **858,** 3 November, pp 9–16

Freeman, R E (1984) *Strategic Management: A stakeholder perspective*, Prentice Hall, Englewood Cliffs, NJ

Friedman, M (1970) The social responsibility of business is to increase its profits, *New York Times Magazine*, September, p 13

Hillman, A and Keim, G (2001) Shareholder value, stakeholder management and social issues: what's the bottom line?, *Strategic Management Journal*, **22** (2), pp 125–39

Husted, B W and Salazar, J (2006) Taking Friedman seriously: maximizing profits and social performance, *Journal of Management Studies*, **43** (1), pp 75–91

Levitt, T (1958) The dangers of social responsibility, *Harvard Business Review*, September–October, pp 41–50

McWilliams, A, Siegal, D S and Wright, P M (2006) Corporate social responsibility: strategic implications, *Journal of Management Studies*, **43** (1), pp 1–12

Matsushita, A (2000) Common sense talk, *Asian Productivity Organization News*, **30** (8), p 4

Moran, P and Ghoshal, S (1996) Value creation by firms, *Best Paper Proceedings*, Academy of Management Annual Meeting, Cincinnati, OH

Porter, M E and Kramer, M R (2006) Strategy and society: the link between competitive advantage and corporate social responsibility, *Harvard Business Review*, December, pp 78–92

Redington, I (2005) *Making CSR Happen: The contribution of people management*, CIPD, London

Russo, M V and Fouts, P A (1997) A resource-based perspective on corporate environmental performance and profitability, *Academy of Management Review*, **40** (3), pp 534–59

World Business Council for Sustainable Social Development (2006) *From Challenge to Opportunity: The role of business in tomorrow's society*, WBCSSD, Geneva

10 Human Resource Management Research Methods

Key concepts and terms

- Central tendency
- Chi-squared test
- Correlation
- Critical evaluation
- Deduction
- Dispersion
- Evidence-based
- Experimental design
- Falsification
- Frequency
- Grounded theory
- Hypothesis
- Induction
- Likert scale
- Linear regression
- Multivariate analysis
- Null hypothesis
- Paradigm
- Phenomenology
- Primary source
- Positivism
- Proposition
- Qualitative research
- Quantitative research
- Reductionism
- Regression
- The research question
- Secondary source
- Significance
- Theory

Learning outcomes

On completing this chapter you should be able to define these key concepts. You should also know about:

- The nature of research
- Planning and conducting research programmes
- Approaches to research
- The basics of statistical analysis
- Research philosophy
- Literature reviews
- Methods of collecting data

Introduction

HRM specialists and those studying for HR professional qualifications may be involved in conducting or taking part in research projects. Postgraduate students will almost certainly do so. Qualified HR specialists should keep up to date as part of their continuous professional development by studying publications such as those produced by the CIPD, which present research findings, or by reading articles in HR journals such as *People Management* or academic journals based on research. Students must extend their understanding of HRM through reading about research findings.

The purpose of this chapter is to explain what is involved in planning and conducting research projects. This will be done against the background of a review of the nature and philosophy of research. Descriptions will be given of the main approaches used by researchers, including literature reviews, quantitative and qualitative methods and collecting and analysing data.

The nature of research

Research is concerned with establishing what is and from this predicting what will be. It does not decide what ought to be; that is for human beings interpreting the lessons from research in their own context. Research is about the conception and testing of ideas. This is an inductive, creative and imaginative process, although new information is normally obtained within the framework of existing theory and knowledge. Logic and rational argument are methods of testing ideas after they have been created.

What emerges from research is a theory – a well-established explanatory principle that has been tested and can be used to make predictions of future developments. A theory is produced by clear, logical and linear development of argument with a close relationship between information, hypothesis and conclusion. Quality of information is a criterion for good research as is the use of critical evaluation techniques, which are described later in this chapter.

The production of narratives that depict events (case studies) or the collection of data through surveys, are elements in research programmes but they can stand alone as useful pieces of information that illustrate practice.

Research methodology is based on research philosophy and uses a number of approaches, as described later. There is usually a choice about which philosophy or approach or which combination of them should be used.

The characteristics of good research

The characteristics of good research, as identified by Phillips and Pugh (1987) are first, it is based on an open system of thought that requires continually testing, review and criticism of other ideas and a willingness to hazard new ideas. Second, the researcher must always be prepared to examine data critically, and to request the evidence behind conclusions drawn by others. Third, the researcher should always try to generalize the research but within stated limits. This means attempting to extract understanding from one situation and to apply it to as many other situations as possible.

Research philosophy

Research can be based on a philosophy of positivism or phenomenology.

Positivism

Positivism is the belief that researchers should focus on facts (observable reality), look for causality and fundamental laws, reduce phenomena to their simplest elements (reductionism), formulate hypotheses and then test them. Researchers are objective analysts. The emphasis in positivism is on quantifiable observations that lend themselves to statistical analysis. It tends to be deductive (see page 187).

Phenomenology

Phenomenology focuses more on the meaning of phenomena than on the facts associated with them. Researchers adopting this philosophy try to understand what is happening. Their approach is holistic, covering the complete picture, rather than reductionist. Researchers collect and analyse evidence, but their purpose is to use this data to develop ideas that explain the meaning of things. They believe that reality is socially constructed rather than objectively determined. Using a phenomenological approach means that the research unfolds as it proceeds – early evidence is used to indicate how to move on to the next stage of evidence collection and analysis, and so on. It tends to be inductive (see page 187).

Table 10.1 Alternative research philosophies

Advantages and disadvantages of alternative research philosophies (Easterby-Smith *et al*, 1991)			
Positivism		**Phenomenology**	
Advantages	**Disadvantages**	**Advantages**	**Disadvantages**
• Wide coverage of the range of situations • Can be fast and economical • May be relevant to policy decisions when statistics are aggregated in large samples	• Methods tend to be flexible and artificial • Not very effective in understanding processes or the significance people attach to actions • Not very helpful in generating theories • Because they focus on what is or what has been recently, they make it hard for policy makers to infer what actions should take place in the future	• Can look at change processes over time • Help to understand people's meanings • Help to adjust to new issues and ideas as they emerge • Contribute to the development of new theories • Gather data that is seen as natural rather than artificial	• Data gathering can take up a great deal of time and resources • The analysis and interpretation of data may be difficult • May be harder than a positivist approach to control pace, progress and endpoints • Policy makers may give low credibility to a phenomenological study

As Valentin (2006) has commented:

> *A positivist perspective has dominated mainstream management research and theory. This assumes a broad consensus concerning the goals and practices of management. Management is seen as a purely instrumental process, objective, neutral, simply concerned with methods to ensure control and efficiency in organizations.*

Planning and conducting research programmes

Against this background, the steps required to plan and conduct a research programme are as follows:

1. Define research area. This should be one that interests the researcher and has a clear link to an accepted theory or an important issue that is worth exploring. The research should generate fresh insights into the topic. It is necessary to undertake background reading at this stage by means of a preliminary review of the literature (particularly academic journals but also books, especially those based on research) to identify what has already been achieved in this area and any gaps (academic articles often include proposals for further research). The context within which the research is to be carried out needs to be explained and justified.
2. Formulate initial research question. This provides a rationale for the research. It is in effect a statement that answers the questions: 'What is this research project intended to address and what is its potential contribution to increasing knowledge?' At this stage it is based on the outcome of the initial work carried out in Step 1 but it will be refined and reformulated at a later stage when more information about the research has been made available.
3. Review literature. A literature review will focus mainly on academic journals. The aim is to establish what is already known about the topic, identify existing theoretical frameworks and find out what other relevant research has been carried out. The conduct of literature reviews is considered in more detail on page 180 of this chapter.
4. Develop theoretical framework. It is necessary to conduct the research within a clear theoretical framework. This will set out the models, concepts and theories that can be drawn on and developed to provide an answer to the research question. If an appropriate framework does not exist, a grounded theory approach (see page 188) may be required in which the researcher uses empirical evidence directly to establish the concepts and relationships that will be contained in the theory adopted as the research framework. It is important to be clear about the assumptions, conditions and limitations within which the investigation is taking place.
5. Finalize the research question. The initial research question needs to be finalized in the light of the outcome of the earlier steps. The final research question will identify the issues to be explored and the problems to be investigated. It will include a statement of intent that will set out what the research is to achieve. This statement leads to the formulation of the hypotheses or propositions that will be tested by survey or experiment during the research programme.
6. Formulate hypotheses or propositions. An hypothesis provisionally states a relationship between two concepts in such a way that the consequences of the statement being true can be tested. Hypotheses (there may be more than one) indicate the form the research project

will take in the shape of obtaining and analysing the evidence required to test them. Hypotheses may be attached to the statement of the research question. A proposition is a proposal put forward as an explanation of an event, a possible situation or a form of behaviour that will be tested by the research.

7. Design the research. This means considering initially what research philosophy will be adopted. Is it to be positivist, phenomenological, or both? It is then necessary to establish the methodology. A decision will need to be made on the extent to which the research will be quantitative, qualitative or, again, a combination of the two (see page 181). Methods of collecting and analysing evidence and testing hypotheses or propositions will be described. The sources of evidence and how they will be accessed will be identified. This will include the analysis of primary and secondary source documents, further literature reviews, surveys and field work. The design must clearly indicate how it will address the research question and be consistent with the theoretical framework. If at a later stage this is shown not to be the case, then the design will have to be amended.
8. Draw up research programme. This will cover how the research will be conducted, the timetable and the resources (funding, people, software, etc) required. Careful project planning is essential.
9. Prepare and submit proposal. This will justify the research by setting out the research question and the proposed methodology. It will also describe the programme and the resources required.
10. Conduct the research project. This includes obtaining and analysing the evidence from the various sources needed to answer the research question and prove or disprove hypotheses. The significance of the findings in relation to the research question and the hypotheses will be discussed and reference will be made to relevant information provided in the literature. This involves an extended literature review (see page 180), data collection (see pages 182–87) the use of critical evaluation processes (see pages 189–91) and the use of statistical analysis where relevant (see pages 191–95).
11. Develop conclusions. These draw together all the evidence. They provide the answer to the research question and explain why hypotheses have been accepted or rejected. The significance of the findings will also be assessed in terms of how they contribute to the development of existing knowledge and understanding. Any limitations to the study should also be mentioned.
12. Make recommendations. These set out management guidelines emerging from the research. They may also indicate any follow-up actions required if the research has been conducted within an organization.

Further guidance on conducting HRM research programmes is provided by Anderson (2004).

The ethics of research

There are a number of ethical issues that affect research. They include the need for researchers generally to act with integrity, for example in their dealings with the organization in which they are researching and the people they deal with. They must also respect the rights of participants by not publishing any information that might harm their interests and to be honest about their role when participating in research, especially when they are participating observers.

Literature reviews

Literature reviews or searches are essential preliminary steps in any research project. They often focus on articles in academic journals although textbooks may also be consulted, especially if they are based on research. It is necessary to know what has already been covered and the theories that have been developed to provide leads and reference points or as the basis for a grounded theory approach.

Literature searches in academic journals are much easier now by means of the Business Source Corporate database made available through EBSCO. CIPD members can access this through the CIPD website, on which about 350 journals are available. In most cases articles can be downloaded free of charge although some journals restrict this service for the first 12 months after publication. Searches can be made by subject matter, but unless the research is refined a huge number of references may be turned up – searching 'performance management' produces more than 6,000 results! The search can be extended through the references included in articles. A checklist to use when evaluating an article or text is given below.

Literature evaluation checklist

- To what extent is the article/text relevant to my research?
- What was the aim of the article/text?
- To what extent was this aim achieved?
- Are the findings supported by rigorous and convincing research?
- Does the article/text present new and interesting ideas or perspectives?
- Is the article/text clear and persuasive?
- To what extent do I agree with the views expressed?

Quantitative and qualitative methods of research

One of the key decisions to be made in planning and conducting a research programme is the extent to which quantitative methods (which broadly follow the positivist philosophy) or qualitative methods (which broadly follow the phenomenological philosophy) are used.

Quantitative research

Quantitative research is empirical – based on the collection of factual data that is measured and quantified. It answers research questions from the viewpoint of the researcher. It may involve a considerable amount of statistical analysis using methods for collecting the data through questionnaires, surveys, observation and experiment. The collection of data is distinct from its analysis.

Qualitative research

Qualitative research aims to generate insights into situations and behaviour so that the meaning of what is happening can be understood. It emphasizes the interpretation of behaviour from the viewpoint of the participants. It is based on evidence that may not be easily reduced to numbers. It makes use of interviews, case studies and observation but it may also draw on the information obtained from surveys. It may produce narratives or 'stories' describing situations, events or processes.

Comparison and use of quantitative or qualitative research

Quantitative research measures and predicts, whereas qualitative research describes and understands; see Table 10.2.

Table 10.2 Contrasts between quantitative and qualitative research (Bryman and Bell, 2007)

Quantitative research	Qualitative research
numbers	words
researcher distant	researcher close
macro	micro
hard data	soft data
theory testing	theory building
static	process
structured	unstructured

As Valentin (2006) notes, mainstream management journals, especially US ones, focus on empirical research using quantitative methodologies. There is a growing trend in the UK to follow suit, but in Europe there is greater preference for qualitative over quantitative methods, with case studies being a popular approach, at least for HRD (human resource development) research.

However, the distinction between qualitative and quantitative research is sometimes blurred. Easterby-Smith *et al* (1991) mention that increasingly researchers argue that an attempt should be made to mix methods to some extent because this will provide more perspectives on the phenomena to be investigated.

Methods of collecting data

The main methods of collecting data are interviews, questionnaires, surveys, case studies, observation, diaries and experimental designs.

Interviews

Interviews are an important research method. They obtain factual data and insights into attitudes and feelings and can take three forms:

1. Structured, which means that they are entirely concerned with obtaining answers to a pre-prepared set of questions. This ensures that every topic is covered and minimizes variations between respondents. But they may be too rigid and inhibit spontaneous and revealing reactions.
2. Unstructured, which means that no questions have been prepared in advance and the person being interviewed is left free to talk about the subject without interruption or intervention. Such 'non-directive' interviews are supposed to provide greater insight into the interviewee's perspective, avoid fitting respondents into predetermined categories and enable interviewers to explore issues as they arise. But they can be inconsequential and lead to poor data that are difficult to analyse.
3. Semi-structured, which means that the areas of interest have been predetermined and the key questions to be asked or information to be obtained have been identified. The interview may have a checklist but does not follow this rigidly. This approach enables the interviewer to phrase questions and vary their order to suit the special characteristics of each interviewee. It may avoid the problems of the completely structured or unstructured interview but it does require a considerable degree of skill on the part of the interviewer.

Interviews are basically qualitative but they can become more quantitative by the use of content analysis. This records the number of times reference is made in an interview to the key issues or areas of interest it was intended to cover.

The advantages of interviews are that they obtain information directly from people involved in the area that is being researched and can provide insights into attitudes and perspectives that questionnaires and surveys will not reveal, thus promoting in-depth understanding. They enable the interviewer to probe answers and check that questions had been understood. But the disadvantages are that:

- the construction of the interview questions may result in leading questions or bland answers;
- interviewers may influence the interviewees' reactions by imposing their own reference frame;
- respondents may tell interviewers what they want to hear;
- they are time-consuming – to set up, to conduct and to analyse;
- they require considerable interviewing skills including the abilities to recognize what is important and relevant, to probe when necessary, and to listen and to control the interview so that it covers the ground it was intended to cover.

Questionnaires

Questionnaires collect data systematically by obtaining answers on the key issues and opinions that need to be explored in a research project. They are frequently used as a means of gathering information on matters of fact or opinion. They use a variety of methods, namely closed questions that require a yes or no answer, ranking in order of importance or value, or Likert scales. The latter, named after Rensis Likert the US sociologist who invented them, ask respondents to indicate the extent to which they agree or disagree with a statement. For example, in response to a statements such as 'I like my job' the choice may be 1 strongly agree, 2 agree, 3 disagree, 4 strongly disagree. Alternatively, an extended scale may be used and respondents asked to circle the number that reflects their view about the statement (the higher the number the greater the agreement), for example:

My contribution is fully recognized   1 2 3 4 5 6 7 8 9

Extended scales facilitate the quantitative analysis of responses to questionnaires.

To construct and use a questionnaire effectively it is necessary to:

- Identify the key issues and potential questions.
- Ensure questions are clear.
- Avoid asking two questions in one item.
- Avoid leading questions that supply their own answers.

- Decide on the structure of the questionnaire including its length (not too many items) and the choice of scale.
- Code questions for ease of analysis.
- Start with simple factual questions, moving on later to items of opinion or values.
- Add variety and the opportunity to check consistency by interspersing positive statements such as 'I like working for my boss' with occasional associated negative ones such as 'I do not get adequate support from my boss'.
- Pilot test the questionnaire.
- Code results and analyse. Where rating scales have been used the analysis can be quantified for comparison purposes. Content analysis can be used to analyse narrative answers to open-ended questions.

Questionnaires are effective in gathering factual evidence but are not so useful for researchers who are investigating how or why things are happening. It is also impossible to assess the degree of subjectivity that has crept in when expressing opinions. For example, HR managers may give an opinion on the extent to which a performance-related pay scheme has in fact improved performance but the evidence to support that opinion will be lacking. This is where interviews can be much more informative.

Surveys

Surveys obtain information from a defined population of people. Typically, they are based on questionnaires but they can provide more powerful data than other methods by using a combination of questionnaires and interviews and, possibly, focus groups (groups of people gathered together to answer and discuss specific questions). When developing and administering surveys the issues are:

- The definition of the purpose of the survey and the outcomes hoped for – these must be as precise as possible.
- The population to be covered – this may involve a census of the whole population. If the population is large, sampling will be necessary (see below).
- The choice of methods – relying entirely on questionnaires may limit the validity of the findings. It is better, if time and the availability of finance permit, to complement them with interviews and, possibly, focus groups. Consideration has to be given to the extent to which triangulation (comparing the information obtained from different sources) is desirable (it usually is) and possible.
- The questions to which answers are required, whichever method is used.
- The design of questionnaires and the ways in which interview or focus groups, if used, should be structured.

- How the outcome of the survey will be analysed and presented, including the use of case studies.

In using surveys, and possibly other methods, it may not be feasible to cover the whole population (the sampling frame) and sampling will therefore be necessary. Sampling means that a proportion of the total population is selected for study and the aim is to see that this proportion represents the characteristics of the whole population. The sample must not be biased and that is why in large-scale surveys use is made of random sampling, ie the individuals covered by a survey are not selected in accordance with any criteria except that they exist in the population and can be reached by the survey. It is the equivalent of drawing numbers out of a hat. However, if the sample frame is considered to be already arranged randomly, as in the electoral roll, then structured sampling, that is, sampling at regular intervals, can be employed.

Sampling can produce varying degrees of error depending on the size of the sample. Statistical techniques can be used to establish sample errors and confidence limits. For example, they might establish that a sampling error is 3 per cent and the confidence limit is 95 per cent. This could be reasonably satisfactory, depending on the nature of the research (medical research aims to achieve 100 per cent confidence).

Case study

A case study is a description or history of an event or sequence of events in a real life setting. In learning and development, case studies are analysed by trainees to learn something by diagnosing the causes of a problem and working out how to solve it.

Case studies are used extensively in HRM research as a means of collecting empirical evidence in a real life context. Information is collected about an event or a set of events that establishes what has happened, how it happened and why it happened. Case studies provide information that contributes to the creation of a theory as part of a grounded theory approach, or the validation of an established theory. In addition, they can take the form of stories or narratives that illuminate a decision or a set of decisions, why they were taken, how they were implemented and with what result. They can illustrate a total situation and describe the processes involved and how individuals and groups behave in a social setting.

Case study protocol sets out the objectives of the research, how the case study will support the achievement of those objectives, including the evidence required, and how the work of producing the case study will be conducted. The methodology covers:

- sources of evidence – interviews, observation, documents and records;
- the need to use multiple sources of evidence (triangulation) so far as possible;
- the questions to which answers need to be obtained;

- how the case study should be set up including informing those involved of what is taking place and enlisting their support;
- the schedule of interviews and other evidence collection activities;
- how the case study database recording the evidence will be set up and maintained;
- how the case study will be presented – including the chain of evidence so that the reader can follow the argument and trace the development of events, the headings and report guidelines (these may be finalized during the course of the exercise) and whether or not the name of the organization will be revealed on publication (named cases studies are more convincing than anonymous ones);
- how approval will be sought for the publication of the case study, especially if it reveals the name of the organization.

Case studies are useful ways of collecting information on the reality of organizational life and processes. But there is a danger of the studies being no more than a story or an anecdote that does not contribute to greater knowledge or understanding. Quite a lot of skill and persistence is required from the researcher in gaining support, ensuring that relevant and revealing information is obtained and presenting the case study as a convincing narrative from which valid and interesting conclusions can be derived. All this must be done without taking a biased view, which can be difficult.

Observation

Observation of individuals or groups at work is a method of getting a direct and realistic impression of what is happening. It can be done by a detached or an involved observer, or by participant observation.

Detached observers who simply study what is going on without getting involved with the people concerned may only get a superficial impression of what is happening and may be resented by the people under observation as 'eaves-dropping'. Involved observers work closely with employees and can move around, observe and participate as appropriate. This means that they can get closer to events and are more likely to be accepted, especially if the objectives and methods have been agreed in advance. Participant observation in the fullest sense means that the researcher becomes an employee and experiences the work and the social processes that take place at first hand. This can provide powerful insights but is time-consuming and requires considerable skill and persistence.

The issues with any form of observation are getting close enough to events to understand their significance and then analysing the mass of information that might be produced in order to produce findings that contribute to answering the research question.

Diaries

Getting people to complete diaries of what they do is a method of building a realistic picture of how people, especially managers, spend their time.

Experimental designs

Experimental designs involve setting up an experimental group and a control group and then placing subjects at random in one or other group. The conditions under which the experimental group functions are then manipulated and the outcomes compared with the control group, whose conditions remain unchanged. The classic case of an experimental design was the Hawthorne experiment, the results of which had a major impact on thinking about how groups function and on the human relations movement. But this was exceptional. It is much easier to use experiments in a laboratory setting, as has been done many times with students. But there is always the feeling that such experiments do not really reflect real life conditions.

Processes involved in research

This section describes the logical, analytical and critical thinking processes that are used in research, namely deduction, induction, hypothesis testing, grounded theory, paradigms and critical evaluation.

Deduction

Research involves deduction, which is the process of using logical reasoning to reach a conclusion that necessarily follows from general or universal premises. If the premises are correct, so is the deduction. The conclusion is therefore contained within the evidence. It is not a creative or imaginative argument which produces new ideas.

Induction

Research can also be based on induction, which is the process of reaching generalized conclusions from the observation of particular instances. In contrast to deduction, inductive conclusions may be tentative but they contain new ideas. A creative leap may be required to reach them. Karl Popper (1972) referred to the problem of induction, which is that while science is seen as rational, deductive, logical, certain and objective, scientific progress seems to depend on processes that are imaginative, not entirely logical and tentative. But in research both deductive and inductive reasoning can be used in hypothesis testing.

Hypothesis testing

Formulating a hypothesis is an important element in a research project in that it provides a basis for the development of theory and the collection and analysis of data. A hypothesis is a supposition – a tentative explanation of something. It is a provisional statement that is taken to be true for the purpose of argument or a study and usually relates to an existing wider body of knowledge or theory. A hypothesis has to be tested and should be distinguished from a theory which, by definition, has been tested. A good hypothesis contains two concepts and proposes a relationship between the two. A working hypothesis is a general hypothesis that has been operationalized so that it can be tested.

Hypothesis formulation and testing use the strengths of both deductive and inductive argument; the former entirely conclusive but unimaginative, the latter tentative but creative. Induction produces ideas, deduction tests them.

To test a hypothesis, data have to be obtained that will demonstrate that the predicted consequences are true or false. Simply leaping to the conclusion that a hypothesis is true because a single cause of the consequence has been observed falls into the trap of what logicians call the 'fallacy of affirming the consequent'. There may be alternative and more valid causes. The preferred method of testing is that of denying the consequent. This is 'falsification' as advocated by Karl Popper (1959). His view was that however much data may be assembled to support a hypothesis, it is not possible to reach a conclusive proof of the truth of that hypothesis. Popper therefore proposed that it was insufficient simply to assemble confirmatory evidence. What must also be obtained is evidence that refutes the hypothesis. Only one instance of refutation is needed to falsify a theory, whereas however many confirmations of the theory exist it will still not be proved conclusively. I had the good fortune to be taught by Popper at the LSE and he illustrated his concept of falsification with swans. The hypothesis is that all swans are white and someone who stayed in Great Britain and didn't visit a zoo might think that this was the case. But a visit to Australia would lead to the discovery that swans can also be black. It is best, according to Popper, to take a falsification view and search for swans that are not white. This would mean that the original hypothesis would have to be modified to state that swans can be either white or black.

Grounded theory

Grounded theory is an inductive method of developing the general features of a theory by grounding the account in empirical observations or evidence. The researcher uses empirical evidence directly to establish the concepts and relationships that will be contained in the theory. Evidence is collected from both primary sources (ie obtained directly by the researcher from the originator of the evidence) and secondary sources (ie information that is already available in the literature or the internet). Use is made of triangulation – the corroboration of evidence by comparing what has emerged from different sources.

Paradigm

The term 'paradigm' has become popularized as meaning a way of looking at things. It is often used loosely, but properly it means the philosophical and theoretical framework of a scientific school or discipline within which theories, laws and generalizations and the experiments performed in support of them, are formulated. In other words, it is a common perspective that underpins the work of theorists so that they use the same approach to conducting research.

Critical evaluation

Critical evaluation involves making informed judgements about the value of ideas and arguments. It uses critical thinking, which is the process of analysing and evaluating the quality of ideas, theories and concepts in order to establish the degree to which they are valid and supported by the evidence (evidence-based) and the extent to which they are biased. It means reflecting on and interpreting data, drawing warranted conclusions and identifying faulty reasoning, assumptions and biases. It is necessary to test propositions using the following checklist.

Testing propositions checklist

- Was the scope of the investigation sufficiently comprehensive?
- Are the instances representative or are they selected simply to support a point of view?
- Are there contradictory instances that have not been looked for?
- Does the proposition conflict with other propositions for which there are equally good grounds?
- If there are any conflicting beliefs or contradictory items of evidence, have they been put to the test against the original proposition?
- Could the evidence lead to other equally valid conclusions?
- Are there any other factors that have not been taken into account which may have influenced the evidence and, therefore, the conclusion?

Critical evaluation requires clear thinking and the application of logical reasoning to establish the validity of a proposition, concept or idea. It is necessary to spot fallacious and misleading arguments. A fallacy is an unsound form of argument leading to an error in reasoning or a misleading impression. The most common form of fallacies that need to be discerned in other people's arguments or avoided in one's own are summarized below.

Common logical fallacies

- Sweeping statements – over-simplifying the facts or selecting instances favourable to a contention while ignoring those that conflict with it.
- Potted thinking – using slogans and catch phrases to extend an assertion in an unwarrantable fashion.
- Special pleading – focusing too much on one's own case and failing to see that there may be other points of view.
- Reaching false conclusions – forming the view that because some are then all are. An assertion about several cases is twisted into an assertion about all cases. The conclusion does not follow the premise. This is what logicians call the 'undistributed middle', which occurs when a syllogism is expressed as: All A is B. All C is B. Therefore all A is C. The conclusion all A is C is false because although everything that applies to A and C also applies to B, there is nothing in their relationship to B which connects A and C together.
- Affirming the consequent – leaping to the conclusion that a hypothesis is true because a single cause of the consequence has been observed.
- Begging the question – taking for granted what has yet to be proved.
- Chop logic – 'Contrariwise', continued Tweedledee, 'if it was so, it might be, and if it were so, it would be; but as it isn't it ain't. That's logic.' Chop logic may not always be as bad as that, but it is about drawing false conclusions and using dubious methods of argument. Examples are selecting instances favourable to a contention while ignoring those that contend with it; twisting an argument used by an opponent to mean something quite different from what was intended; diverting opponents by throwing on them the burden of proof for something they have not maintained; ignoring the point in dispute, and reiterating what has been denied and ignoring what has been asserted. Politicians know all about chop logic.

The following checklist can be used when carrying out critical evaluation.

Critical evaluation checklist

- Is the research methodology sufficiently rigorous and appropriate?
- Are the results and conclusions consistent with the methodology used and its outcomes?

- Have hypotheses been stated clearly and tested thoroughly?
- Do there appear to be any misleading errors of omission or bias?
- Are any of the arguments tendentious?
- Are inferences, findings and conclusions derived from reliable and convincing evidence?
- Has a balanced approach been adopted?
- Is the perspective adopted by the researchers stated clearly?
- Have any underlying assumptions been identified and justified?
- Have the component parts been covered in terms of their interrelationships and their relationship with the whole?
- Have these component parts been disaggregated for close examination?
- Have they been reconstructed into a coherent whole based on underlying principles?

Statistical analysis

Whichever approach or combination of approaches is used, the results have to be analysed and presented in reports, journal articles, papers or books. Quantitative research clearly involves statistical analysis. Reports on qualitative research may be largely descriptive but qualitative research is often supported by quantitative research, and statistical analysis to illuminate and support findings may still be required.

In general, the statistical analysis of quantified information is used to:

- identify and convey salient facts about the population under consideration;
- test hypotheses;
- make predictions on what is likely to happen;
- build a model that describes how a situation probably works;
- answer questions about the strength of evidence and how much certainty can be attached to predictions and models.

Statistics are used to describe and summarize data relating to a 'population', ie a homogeneous set of items with variable individual values. This involves measuring frequencies, central tendencies and dispersion. They are also used to analyse the data and the sample from which the data were obtained to measure the relationships between variables (correlation, regression and the chi-squared test), to establish the relation between cause and effect (causality) and to assess the degree of confidence that can be attached to conclusions (tests of significance). A wide variety of software is available to conduct the more sophisticated analyses.

Frequency

The number of times individual items in a population or set occur is represented in frequency distributions expressed in tabular form or graphically. Commonly used charts are illustrated in Figure 10.1.

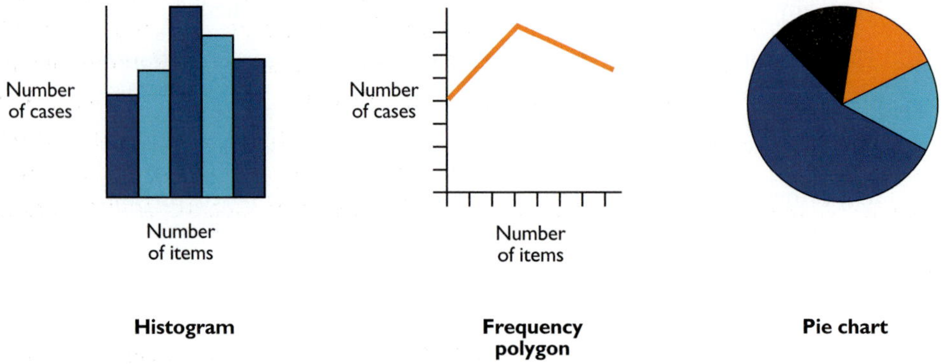

Figure 10.1 Examples of charts

Measures of central tendency

Measures of central tendency identify the middle or centre of a set of data. There are three types:

1. Arithmetic average or mean – the total of items or scores in a set divided by the number of individual items in the set. It may give a distorted picture because of large items at either end of the scale.
2. Median – the middle item in a range of items (often used in pay surveys when the arithmetic mean is likely to be distorted).
3. Mode – the most commonly occurring item.

Measures of dispersion

These are often useful to measure the extent to which the items in a set are dispersed or spread over a range of data. This can be done in four ways:

1. By identifying the upper quartile or lower quartile of a range of data. The strict definition of an upper quartile is that it is the value which 25 per cent of the values in the distribution

exceed, and the lower quartile is the value below which 25 per cent of the values in a distribution occur. More loosely, especially when looking at pay distributions, the upper and lower quartiles are treated as ranges rather than points in a scale and represent the top and the bottom 25 per cent of the distribution respectively.

2. By presenting the total range of values from top to bottom, which may be misleading if there are exceptional items at either end.
3. By calculating the inter-quartile range, which is the range between the value of the upper quartile and that of the lower quartile. This can present more revealing information of the distribution than the total range.
4. By calculating the standard deviation, which is used to indicate the extent to which the items or values in a distribution are grouped together or dispersed in a normal distribution, ie one which is reasonably symmetrical around its average. As a rule of thumb, two-thirds of the distribution will be less than one standard deviation from the mean, 95 per cent of the distribution will be less than two standard deviations from the mean, and less than 1 per cent of the distribution is more than three standard deviations from the mean. Another measure of dispersion is variance, which is the square of a standard deviation.

Correlation

Correlation represents the relationship between two variables. If they are highly correlated they are strongly connected to one another, and vice versa. In statistics, correlation is measured by the coefficient of correlation, which varies between -1 to +1 to indicate totally negative and totally positive correlations respectively. A correlation of zero means that there is no relationship between the variables. Establishing the extent to which variables are correlated is an important feature of HRM research, for example assessing the degree to which a performance management system improves organizational performance. But correlations do not indicate causal relationships. They can only show that X is associated with Y but this does not mean necessarily that X causes Y. Multiple correlation looks at the relationship between more than two variables.

Regression

Regression is another way of looking at the relationship between variables. Regression analysis examines how changes in levels of X relate to changes in levels of Y. A regression line (a trend line or line of best fit) can be traced on a scattergram expressing values of one variable on one axis and values of the other variable on another axis, as shown in Figure 10.2.

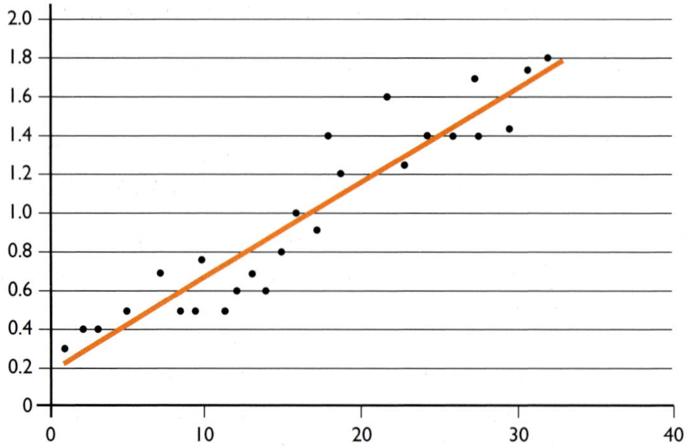

Figure 10.2 A scattergram with regression (trend) line

A trend line like this can be drawn by hand as a line of best fit but it can be calculated mathematically with greater accuracy. The distances of points from the trend line (the residuals) can be calculated as a check on the reliability of the line.

Multiple regression analysis can be conducted with the aid of a computer, which enables the values of additional variables to be predicted under various combinations of conditions.

The chi-squared test

The chi-squared test uses a statistical formula to assess the degree of agreement between the data actually obtained and that expected under a particular hypothesis.

The null hypothesis approach

A null hypothesis is a method of testing a hypothesis frequently used by researchers in which it is assumed that there is no relationship between two or more variables. It asks the question: 'Could the hypothetical relationship have been caused by chance?' If the answer is no, then the hypothesis is worth pursuing. However, it does not prove that the hypothesis is correct; it only indicates that something is worth pursuing. It can be associated with the chi-squared test.

Causality

Causality – determining the link between independent and dependent variables (cause and effect) – is a major issue in research, especially in the HRM field. As mentioned earlier, it may be relatively easy to establish correlations in the shape of a demonstration that X is associated with Y; it is much more difficult and sometimes impossible to prove that X causes Y. There are a number of reasons for this, of which the three set out below are the most important.

First, the issue is complicated because of the need to distinguish between necessary and sufficient causes:

- Necessary cause: if X is a necessary cause of Y, then the presence of Y necessarily implies the presence of X. However, the presence of X does not imply that Y will occur.
- Sufficient cause: if X is a sufficient cause of Y, then the presence of Y necessarily implies the presence of X. However, another cause Z may alternatively cause Y. If so, the presence of Y does not imply the presence of X.

Second, complications arise because of the phenomenon of multiple causation. There may be a number of factors contributing to a result. Researchers pursuing the holy grail of trying to establish what HRM contributes to organization performance are usually confronted with a number of reasons why a firm has done well in addition to adopting 'best practice' HRM, whatever that is. Statistical methods can be used to 'control' some variables, ie eliminate them from the analysis, but it is difficult if not impossible to ensure that HRM practices have been completely isolated and that their direct impact on performance has been measured. Multivariate analysis is used where there is more than one dependent variable and where the dependent variables cannot be combined.

Third, there is the phenomenon of reverse causation when a cause is pre-dated by an effect – A might have caused B but alternatively, B may have come first and be responsible for A. For example, it is possible to demonstrate that firms with effective performance management schemes do better than those without. But it might equally be the case that it is high performing firms that introduce effective performance management. It can be hard to be certain.

Tests of significance

Significance as a statistical concept refers to the degree to which an event could have occurred by chance. At the heart of statistical science lies a simple idea which is that the chance or probability of various patterns of events can be predicted. When a particular pattern is observed it is possible to work out what the chances of its occurrence may be, given our existing state of knowledge or by making certain assumptions. If something has been observed that is unlikely to have occurred by chance, this occurrence can be accepted as significant. The problem is that any attempt to reach general conclusions may have to rely on fragmentary data. It is usually necessary to rely on samples of the population being studied and all sampling is subject to experimental error – the result can only be expressed in terms of probability and confidence limits will have to be placed on it. These can be calculated in terms of the standard error that might be expected from a sample. A standard error is the estimated standard deviation of a sample mean from a true mean. This implies that on approximately 95 per cent of occasions the estimate of the mean provided by the sample will be within two standard errors of the true mean.

HRM research methods – key learning points

The nature of research

Research is concerned with establishing what is and from this predicting what will be. It is about the conception and testing of ideas.

Research philosophy

Research design can be based on a philosophy of positivism or phenomenology. *Positivism* is the belief that researchers should focus on facts (observable reality), look for causality and fundamental laws. *Phenomenology* is concerned more with the meaning of phenomena than the facts associated with them.

Planning and conducting research programmes

1. Define research area.
2. Formulate initial research question.
3. Review literature.
4. Assess existing theoretical frameworks.
5. Formalize the research question.
6. Formulate hypotheses.
7. Establish the methodology.
8. Draw up research programme.
9. Prepare and submit proposal.
10. Collect and analyse evidence.
11. Develop conclusions.

Literature review

Literature reviews or searches are essential preliminary steps in any research project. They often focus on articles in academic journals although textbooks may also be consulted, especially if they are based on research.

Approaches to research

Research can be quantitative or qualitative. It can use inductive or deductive methods. It involves the testing of hypotheses and may adopt a grounded theory approach, ie an inductive method of developing the general features of a theory by grounding the account in empirical observations or evidence. Use may be made of paradigms – common perspectives that underpin the work of theorists so that they use the same approach to conducting research. Informed judgements about the value of ideas and arguments are made through critical evaluation. It makes use of critical thinking, which is the process of analysing and evaluating the quality of ideas, theories and concepts in order to establish the degree to which they are valid and supported by the evidence.

Methods of collecting data

- Interviews obtain factual data and insights into attitudes and feelings and can be structured, unstructured or semi-structured.
- Questionnaires collect data systematically by obtaining answers on the key issues and opinions that need to be explored in a research project.
- Surveys obtain information from a defined population of people.

HRM research methods – key learning points (continued)

- Case studies collect empirical evidence in a real life context.

The basics of statistical analysis

The statistical analysis of quantified information is used to:

- identify and convey salient facts about the population under consideration;
- test hypotheses;
- make predictions on what is likely to happen;
- build a model that describes how a situation probably works;
- answer questions about the strength of evidence and how much certainty can be attached to predictions and models.

Questions

1. You have been invited to contribute to a workshop in your local university on research management skills. This will involve making a short presentation on 'Using surveys in HR research.' Outline what you will say and why.
2. A friend who is studying for an MA in HRM has sent you the following e-mail: 'I understand that when you did your MA you carried out research making extensive use of case studies. Could you please explain to me how case studies are used and when it is appropriate to do so?' Provide a convincing reply.
3. What are the main advantages and disadvantages of interviews as a means of collecting data in HRM research?
4. A colleague is planning a research project and asks you in an e-mail to explain the differences between quantitative and qualitative research and the circumstances when they are best used. Produce a justified response.

References

Anderson, V (2004) *Research Methods in HRM*, CIPD, London

Bryman, A and Bell, E (2007) *Business Research Methods*, 2nd edn, Oxford University Press, Oxford

Easterby-Smith, M, Thorpe, R and Lowe, A (1991) *Management Research: An introduction*, Sage, London

Phillips, E M and Pugh, D S (1987) *How to Get a PhD*, Open University Press, Milton Keynes

Popper, K (1959) *The Logic of Scientific Discovery*, Hutchinson, London
Popper, K (1972) *Conjectures and Refutations*, Routledge and Kegan Paul, London
Valentin, C (2006) Researching human resource development: emergence of a critical approach to HRD enquiry, *International Journal of Training and Development*, **10** (1), pp 17–29

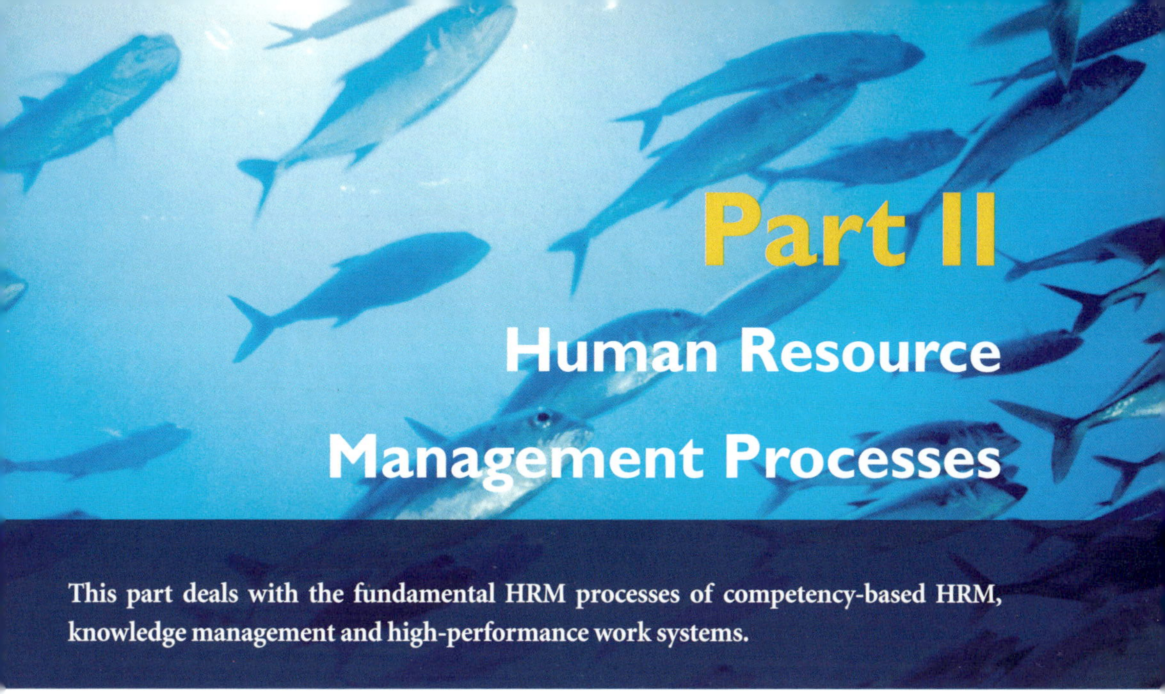

Part II
Human Resource Management Processes

This part deals with the fundamental HRM processes of competency-based HRM, knowledge management and high-performance work systems.

Part II contents

11 Competency-based HRM

Key concepts and terms

- Behavioural competencies
- Competency-based HRM
- Competency framework
- Emotional intelligence
- Technical competencies
- Behavioural indicators
- Competency
- Criterion referencing
- Role-specific competencies

Learning outcomes

On completing this chapter you should be able to define these key concepts. You should also know about:

- The different types of competencies
- Reasons for using competencies
- Applications of competency-based HRM
- Keys to success in using competencies
- The contents of competency frameworks
- Coverage of competencies
- How to develop a competency framework
- Competencies and emotional intelligence

Introduction

Competency-based HRM is about using the notion of competency and the results of competency analysis to inform and improve the processes of performance management, recruitment and selection, employee development and employee reward. It therefore has an important part to play in all the major HR activities.

The concept of competency is essentially about performance. Mansfield (1999) defines competency is 'an underlying characteristic of a person that results in effective or superior performance'. Rankin (2002) describes competencies as 'definitions of skills and behaviours that organizations expect their staff to practice in their work' and explains their meaning as follows.

SOURCE REVIEW

The meaning of competencies, Rankin (2004)

Competencies represent the language of performance. They can articulate both the expected outcomes from an individual's efforts and the manner in which these activities are carried out. Because everyone in the organization can learn to speak this language, competencies provide a common, universally understood means of describing expected performance in many different contexts.

Competency-based HR is primarily based on the concepts of behavioural and technical competencies as defined in the first section of this chapter. But it is also associated with the use of National and Scottish National Vocational qualifications (NVQs/SNVQs), examined in the first section. The next five sections of the chapter concentrate on the application and use of behavioural and technical competencies under the following headings: competency frameworks; reasons for using competencies; use of competencies; guidelines on the development of competency frameworks; and keys to success in using competencies. The final section describes the associated concept of emotional intelligence.

Types of competencies

The three types of competencies are behavioural competencies, technical competencies and NVQs and SNVQs.

1. Behavioural competencies

Behavioural competencies define behavioural expectations, ie the type of behaviour required to deliver results under such headings as team working, communication, leadership and decision making. They are sometimes known as 'soft skills'. Behavioural competencies are usually set out in a competency framework.

The behavioural competency approach was first advocated by McClelland (1973). He recommended the use of criterion-referenced assessment. Criterion referencing or validation is the process of analysing the key aspects of behaviour that differentiate between effective and less effective performance.

But the leading figure in defining and popularizing the concept of competency was Boyatzis (1982). He conducted research that established that there was no single factor but a range of factors that differentiated successful from less successful performance. These factors included personal qualities, motives, experience and behavioural characteristics.

SOURCE REVIEW

Competency defined, Boyatzis (1982)

A capacity that exists in a person that leads to behaviour that meets the job demands within the parameters of the organizational environment and that, in turn, brings about desired results.

The 'clusters' of competencies he identified were goal and action management, directing subordinates, human resource management and leadership. He made a distinction between threshold competencies, which are the basic competencies required to do a job, and performance competences, which differentiate between high and low performance.

2. Technical competencies

Technical competencies define what people have to know and be able to do (knowledge and skills) to carry out their roles effectively. They are related to either generic roles (groups of similar roles), or to individual roles ('role-specific competencies'). They are not usually part of a behavioural-based competency framework although of course the two are closely linked when considering and assessing role demands and requirements. Guidelines on defining technical competencies are provided in Chapter 26.

The term 'technical competency' has been adopted fairly recently to avoid the confusion that existed between the terms 'competency' and 'competence'. Competency, as mentioned above, is about behaviours, while competence as defined by Woodruffe (1990) is: 'A work-related concept which refers to areas of work at which the person is competent. Competent people at work are those who meet their performance expectations.' Competences are sometimes known as 'hard skills'. The terms 'technical competencies' and 'competences' are closely related, although the latter has a particular and more limited meaning when applied to NVQs/SNVQs, as discussed below.

3. NVQ/SNVQ competences

The concept of competence was conceived in the UK as a fundamental part of the process of developing standards for NVQs/SNVQs. These specify minimum standards for the achievement of set tasks and activities expressed in ways that can be observed and assessed with a view to certification. An element of competence in NVQ language is a description of something that people in given work areas should be able to do. They are assessed on being competent or not yet competent. No attempt is made to assess the degree of competence.

Competency frameworks

A competency framework contains definitions of the behavioural competencies used in the whole or part of an organization. It provides the basis for the use of competencies in such areas as recruitment, performance management, learning and development and reward. A survey by Competency and Emotional Intelligence (2006/7) established that the 49 frameworks reviewed had a total of 553 competency headings. Presumably, many of these overlapped. The typical number of competencies was seven, rising to eight where the frameworks apply solely to managers.

Competency headings

The most common competencies in frameworks are people skills, although outcome-based skills, such as focusing on results and solving problems, are also popular. The competency headings included in the frameworks of 20 per cent or more of the organizations responding to the survey are shown in Table 11.1. The first seven of these are used in over 50 per cent of the respondents.

Table 11.1 Incidence of different competency headings

Competency heading	Summary definition	% used
Team orientation	The ability to work cooperatively and flexibly with other members of the team with a full understanding of the role to be played as a team member	86
Communication	The ability to communicate clearly and persuasively, orally or in writing	73
People management	The ability to manage and develop people and gain their trust and cooperation to achieve results	67
Customer focus	The exercise of unceasing care in looking after the interests of external and internal customers to ensure that their wants, needs and expectations are met or exceeded	65
Results orientation	The desire to get things done well and the ability to set and meet challenging goals, create own measures of excellence and constantly seek ways of improving performance	59
Problem solving	The capacity to analyse situations, diagnose problems, identify the key issues, establish and evaluate alternative courses of action and produce a logical, practical and acceptable solution	57
Planning and organizing	The ability to decide on courses of action, ensuring that the resources required to implement the action will be available and scheduling the programme of work required to achieve a defined end-result	51
Technical skills	Possession of the knowledge, understanding and expertise required to carry out the work effectively	49
Leadership	The capacity to inspire individuals to give of their best to achieve a desired result and to maintain effective relationships with individuals and the team as a whole	43
Business awareness	The capacity continually to identify and explore business opportunities, understand the business needs and priorities of the organization and constantly to seek methods of ensuring that the organization becomes more business-like	37
Decision making	The capacity to make sound and practical decisions that deal effectively with the issues and are based on thorough analysis and diagnosis	37
Change-orientation	The ability to manage and accept change	33

Table 11.1 *continued*

Competency heading	Summary definition	% used
Developing others	The desire and capacity to foster the development of members of his or her team, providing feedback, support, encouragement and coaching	33
Influence and persuasion	The ability to convince others to agree on or to take a course of action	33
Initiative	The capacity to take action independently and to assume responsibility for one's actions	29
Interpersonal skills	The ability to create and maintain open and constructive relationships with others, to respond helpfully to their requests and to be sensitive to their needs	29
Strategic orientation	The capacity to take a long-term and visionary view of the direction to be followed in the future	29
Creativity	The ability to originate new practices, concepts and ideas	26
Information management	The capacity to originate and use information effectively	26
Quality focus	The focus on delivering quality and continuous improvement	24
Self-confidence and assertiveness	Belief in oneself and standing up for one's own rights	24
Self-development	Managing one's own learning and development	22
Managing	Managing resources, people, programmes and projects.	20

Examples

The following are two examples of competency frameworks. The first is a fairly simple set of competency headings used in a charity mainly for recruitment purposes; the second is an example of part of a competency framework in a housing association illustrating the use of positive and negative examples for one competency heading. The purpose of these is to extend the broad definition of a competency by providing examples of positive and negative behaviours. The simple definitions in the first examples may not prove sufficient guidance in using the competency framework, especially for performance management.

Example of a competency framework used in a charity

- Achievement/results orientation The desire to get things done well and the ability to set and meet challenging goals, create own measures of excellence and constantly seek ways of improving performance.
- Business awareness. The capacity continually to identify and explore business opportunities, understand the business opportunities and priorities of the organization and constantly to seek methods of ensuring that the organization becomes more business-like.
- Communication. The ability to communicate clearly and persuasively, orally or in writing.
- Customer focus. The exercise of unceasing care in looking after the interests of external and internal customers to ensure that their wants, needs and expectations are met or exceeded.
- Developing others. The desire and capacity to foster the development of members of his or her team, providing feedback, support, encouragement and coaching.
- Flexibility. The ability to adapt to and work effectively in different situations and to carry out a variety of tasks.
- Leadership. The capacity to inspire individuals to give of their best to achieve a desired result and to maintain effective relationships with individuals and the team as a whole.
- Planning. The ability to decide on courses of action, ensuring that the resources required to implement the action will be available and scheduling the programme of work required to achieve a defined end-result.
- Problem solving. The capacity to analyse situations, diagnose problems, identify the key issues, establish and evaluate alternative courses of action and produce a logical, practical and acceptable solution.
- Teamwork. The ability to work cooperatively and flexibly with other members of the team with a full understanding of the role to be played as a team member.

Table 11.2 Reasons for using competencies

Example of competency definition illustrated with indicators in a housing association	
Competency definition	Constantly seeking ways of improving the quality of services, the relevance and appeal of those services to the needs of customers and clients and their effectiveness
Competency requirement	• Set targets for improvement • Develop and implement programmes for implementing change • Contribute to the development of quality assurance and control processes and ensure that they are implemented
Positive indicators	• Encourages the development of new ideas and methods especially those concerned with the provision of quality • Conscious of the factors that enable change to take place smoothly • Discusses ideas with colleagues and customers and formulates views on how to improve services and processes
Negative indicators	• Doesn't try anything that hasn't been done before • Complacent, believes that there is no room for improvement • Follows previous practices without considering whether there is any need to change

The two prime reasons for organizations to use competencies as established by Miller *et al* (2001) were first, that the application of competencies to appraisal, training and other personnel processes will help to increase the performance of employees; and second, that competencies provide a means of articulating corporate values so that their requirements can be embodied in HR practices and be readily understood by individuals and teams within the organization. Other reasons include the use of competencies as a means of achieving cultural change and of raising skill levels.

Coverage of competencies

SOURCE REVIEW

Coverage of competencies, Miller *et al* (2001)

- 22 per cent covered the whole work force with a single set or framework of core competencies (modified in a further 10 per cent of employers by the incorporation of additional behavioural competencies for managers and other staff);
- 48 per cent confined competencies to specific work groups, functions or departments;
- 20 per cent have a core competency framework that covers all staff in respect of behavioural competencies, alongside sets of technical competencies in functions or departments.

Subsequent research (Rankin, 2002) found that 25 per cent of employers using behavioural competencies had a core framework, and 19 per cent supplemented the core framework with additional competencies for single groups such as managers.

The 'menu' approach

Rankin notes that 21 per cent of respondents adopted a 'menu' approach. This enables competencies to be selected that are relevant to generic or individual roles. Approaches vary. Some organizations provide guidelines on the number of competencies to be selected (eg four to eight) and others combine their core framework with a menu so that users are required to select the organization-wide core competencies and add a number of optional ones.

Role-specific competencies

Role-specific competencies are also used by some organizations for generic or individual roles. These may be incorporated in a role profile in addition to information about the key output or result areas of the role. This approach is likely to be adopted by employers who use competencies in their performance management processes, but role-specific competencies also provide the basis for person specifications used in recruitment and for the preparation of individual learning programmes.

Graded competencies

A further, although less common, application of competencies is in graded career or job family structures (career or job families consist of jobs in a function or occupation such as marketing, operations, finance, IT, HR, administration or support services that are related through the activities carried out and the basic knowledge and skills required, but in which the levels of responsibility, knowledge, skill or competence needed differ). In such families, the successive levels in each family are defined in terms of competencies as well as the key activities carried out (career and job family structures are described in Chapter 49).

Applications of competency-based HRM

The Competency and Emotional Intelligence 2006/7 survey found that 95 per cent of respondents used behavioural competencies and 66 per cent used technical competencies. It was noted that because the latter deal with specific activities and tasks they inevitably result in different sets of competencies for groups of related roles, functions or activities. The top four areas where competencies were applied are:

1. Learning and development – 82 per cent.
2. Performance management – 76 per cent.
3. Selection – 85 per cent.
4. Recruitment – 55 per cent.

Only 30 per cent of organizations link competencies to reward. The ways in which these competencies are used are described below.

Learning and development

Role profiles, which are either generic (covering a range of similar jobs) or individual (role-specific), can include statements of the technical competencies required. These can be used as the basis for assessing the levels of competency achieved by individuals and so identifying their learning and development needs.

Career family grade structures (see Chapter 49) can define the competencies required at each level in a career family These definitions provide a career map showing the competencies people need to develop in order to progress their career.

Competencies are also used in development centres, which help participants build up their understanding of the competencies they require now and in the future so that they can plan their own self-directed learning programmes.

Performance management

Competencies in performance management are used to ensure that performance reviews do not simply focus on outcomes but also consider the behavioural aspects of how the work is carried out, which determine those outcomes. Performance reviews conducted on this basis are used to inform personal improvement and development plans and other learning and development initiatives.

As noted by Rankin (2004): 'Increasingly, employers are extending their performance management systems to assess not only objectives but also qualitative aspects of the job.' The alternative approaches are, 1) the assessment has to be made by reference to the whole set of core competencies in the framework, or 2) the manager and the individual carry out a joint assessment of the latter's performance and agree on the competencies to be assessed, selecting those most relevant to the role. In some cases the assessment is linked to defined levels of competency.

Use of behavioural indicators

Guidance on assessing levels of competency can be provided by the use of behavioural indicators that define how the effective use of a behavioural competency can be demonstrated in a person's day-to-day work (an example is given in Chapter 26).

Recruitment and selection

The language of competencies is used in many organizations as a basis for the person specification that is set out under competency headings as developed through role analysis. The competencies defined for a role are used as the framework for recruitment and selection.

A competencies approach can help to identify which selection techniques such as psychological testing are most likely to produce useful evidence. It provides the information required to conduct a structured interview in which questions can focus on particular competency areas to establish the extent to which candidates meet the specification as set out in competency terms.

In assessment centres, competency frameworks are used to define the competency dimensions that distinguish high performance. This indicates what exercises or simulations are required and the assessment processes that should be used.

Reward management

In the 1990s, when the competency movement came to the fore, the notion of linking pay to competencies – competency-related pay – emerged. But it has never taken off; only 8 per cent of the respondents to the e-reward 2004 survey of contingent pay used it. However, more recently the concept of contribution-related pay has emerged, which provides for people to be rewarded according to both the results they achieve and their level of competence, and the e-reward 2004 survey established that 33 per cent of respondents had introduced it.

Another application of competencies in reward management is that of career family grade and pay structures.

Developing a competency framework

The competency framework should be as simple to understand and use as possible. The language should be clear and jargon-free. Without clear language and examples it can be difficult to assess the level of competency achieved. When defining competencies, especially when they are used for performance management or competency-related pay, it is essential to ensure that they can be assessed. They must not be vague or overlap with other competencies and they must specify clearly the sort of behaviour that is expected and the level of technical or functional skills (competencies) required to meet acceptable standards. As Rankin (2002) suggests, it is helpful to address the user directly ('you will...') and give clear and brief examples of how the competency needs to be performed.

Developing a behavioural competency framework that fits the culture and purpose of the organization and provides a sound basis for a number of key HR processes is not an undertaking to be taken lightly. It requires a lot of hard work, much of it concerned with involving staff and communicating with them to achieve understanding and buy-in. The steps required are described below.

Step 1. Programme launch

Decide on the purpose of the framework and the HR processes for which it will be used. Make out a business case for its development, setting out the benefits to the organization in such areas as improved performance, better selection outcomes, more focused performance management, employee development and reward processes. Prepare a project plan that includes an assessment of the resources required and the costs.

Step 2. Involvement and communication

Involve line managers and employees in the design of the framework (Stages 3 and 4) by setting up a task force. Communicate the objectives of the exercise to staff.

Step 3. Framework design – competency list

First, get the task force to draw up a list of the core competencies and values of the business – what it should be good at doing and the values it believes should influence behaviour. This provides a foundation for an analysis of the competencies required by people in the organization. The aim is to identify and define the behaviours that contribute to the achievement of organizational success and there should be a powerful link between these people competencies and the organization's core competencies (more guidance on defining competencies is provided in Chapter 26).

The list can be drawn up by brainstorming. The list should be compared with examples of other competency frameworks. The purpose of this comparison is not to replicate other lists. It is essential to produce a competency framework that fits and reflects the organization's own culture, values, core competencies and operations. But referring to other lists will help to clarify the conclusions reached in the initial analysis and serve to check that all relevant areas of competency have been included. When identifying competencies, care must be taken to avoid bias because of sex or race.

Step 4. Framework design – definition of competencies

Care needs to be exercised to ensure that definitions are clear and unambiguous and that they will serve their intended purpose. If, for example, one of the purposes is to provide criteria for conducting performance reviews, then it is necessary to be certain that the way the competency is defined together with supporting examples will enable fair assessments to be made. The following four questions have been produced by Mirabile (1998) to test the extent to which a competency is valid and can be used:

- Can you describe the competency in terms that others understand and agree with?
- Can you observe it being demonstrated or failing to be demonstrated?
- Can you measure it?
- Can you influence it in some way, eg by training, coaching or some other method of development?

It is also important at this stage to ensure that definitions are not biased.

Step 5. Define uses of the competency framework

Define exactly how it is intended the competency framework should be used, covering such applications as performance management, recruitment, learning and development, and reward.

Step 6. Test the framework

Test the framework by gauging the reactions of a balanced selection of line managers and other employees to ensure that they understand it and believe that it is relevant to their roles. Also pilot-test the framework in live situations for each of its proposed applications.

Step 7. Finalize the framework

Amend the framework as necessary following the tests and prepare notes for guidance on how it should be used.

Step 8. Communicate

Let everyone know the outcome of the project – what the framework is, how it will be used and how people will benefit. Group briefings and any other suitable means should be used.

Step 9. Train

Give line managers and HR staff training in how to use the framework.

Step 10. Monitor and evaluate

Monitor and evaluate the use of the framework and amend it as required.

The process of analysing competencies is discussed in more detail in Chapter 26.

Keys to success in using competencies

- Frameworks should not be over-complex.
- There should not be too many headings in a framework – seven or eight will often suffice.
- The language used should be clear and jargon-free.
- Competencies must be selected and defined in ways that ensure that they can be assessed by managers – the use of 'behavioural indicators' is helpful.
- Frameworks should be regularly updated.

Competencies and emotional intelligence

In 1998 Goleman defined emotional intelligence as covering self-management, self-awareness, social awareness and social skills (see Chapter 18 for a full description). These components encompass many of the areas covered by typical competency frameworks. Miller *et al* (2001) found that one-third of employers covered by their survey had consciously included emotional intelligence-type factors such as interpersonal skills in their frameworks.

Dulewicz and Higgs (1999) have produced a detailed analysis of how the emotional intelligence elements of self-awareness, emotional management, empathy, relationships, communication and personal style correspond to competencies such as sensitivity, flexibility, adaptability, resilience, impact, listening, leadership, persuasiveness, motivating others, energy, decisiveness and achievement motivation. They conclude that there are distinct associations between competency modes and elements of emotional intelligence.

However, as noted by Miller *et al* (2001) a quarter of the employers they surveyed have provided or funded training that is based on emotional intelligence. The most common areas are leadership skills, people management skills and team working.

Competency-based HRM – key learning points

The different types of competencies

The three types of competencies are behavioural competencies, technical competencies and NVQs/SNVQs.

The contents of competency frameworks (the most popular headings)

- Team orientation.
- Communication.
- People management.
- Customer focus.
- Results orientation.
- Problem solving.
- Planning and organizing.
- Technical skills.
- Leadership.

Coverage of competencies (Rankin, 2002)

- 22 per cent covered the whole work force.
- 48 per cent confined competencies to specific work groups, functions or departments.
- 20 per cent have a core competency framework that covers all staff in respect of behavioural competencies, alongside sets of technical competencies in functions/departments.

Uses of competencies (Competency and Emotional Intelligence, 2006/7)

- Learning and development – 82 per cent.
- Performance management – 76 per cent.
- Selection – 85 per cent.
- Recruitment – 55 per cent.
- Reward – 30 per cent.

How to develop a competency framework

- Decide on the purpose of the framework and the HR processes for which it will be used.
- Make out a business case for its development, setting out the benefits.
- Prepare a project plan that includes an assessment of the resources required and the costs. Involve line

Competency-based HRM – key learning points (continued)

managers and employees in the design of the framework.

- Communicate the objectives of the exercise to staff.
- Draw up a list of the core competencies of the business.
- Define the competencies for inclusion in a competency framework.
- Test and finalize and communicate framework.

Keys to success in using competencies

- Frameworks should not be over-complex.
- There should not be too many headings in a framework – seven or eight will often suffice.
- The language used should be clear and jargon-free.
- Competencies must be selected and defined in ways that ensure that they can be assessed by managers – the use of 'behavioural indicators' is helpful.
- Frameworks should be regularly updated.

Competencies and emotional intelligence

The emotional intelligence elements of self-awareness, emotional management, empathy, relationships, communication and personal style correspond to competencies such as sensitivity, flexibility, adaptability, resilience, impact, listening, leadership, persuasiveness, motivating others, energy, decisiveness and achievement motivation.

Questions

1. Your managing director says to you that she is getting confused by the terms 'competency' and 'emotional intelligence'. She asks you to clarify the differences between them, if any, and what their significance is to the organization. Draft your response.
2. You have been asked to deliver a talk at a local conference on the use of competency frameworks and their advantages and disadvantages. Prepare you lecture outline.
3. It is felt by your boss that the existing competence framework in your organization is out of date. He has asked you to propose a programme for updating it that will not take too much time or trouble. Draft a programme.

References

Boyatzis, R (1982) *The Competent Manager*, Wiley, New York

Competency and Emotional Intelligence (2004) Benchmarking survey, *Competency and Emotional Intelligence*, **12** (1), pp 4–6

Competency and Emotional Intelligence (2006/7) *Raising Performance Through Competencies: The annual benchmarking survey*, Competency and Emotional Intelligence, London

Dulewicz, V and Higgs, M (1999) The seven dimensions of emotional intelligence, *People Management*, 28 October, p 53

e-reward (2004) *Survey of Contingent Pay*, e-reward.co.uk, Stockport

Goleman, D (1998) *Working With Emotional Intelligence*, Bloomsbury, London

McClelland, D C (1973) Testing for competence rather than intelligence, *American Psychologist*, **28** (1), pp 1–14

Mansfield, B (1999) What is 'competence' all about?, *Competency*, **6** (3), pp 24–28

Miller, L, Rankin, N and Neathey, F (2001) *Competency Frameworks in UK Organizations*, CIPD, London

Mirabile, R J (1998) Leadership competency development, competitive advantage for the future, *Management Development Forum*, **1** (2), pp 1–15

Rankin, N (2002) Raising performance through people: the ninth competency survey, *Competency and Emotional Intelligence*, January, pp 2–21

Rankin, N (2004) Benchmarking survey, *Competency and Emotional Intelligence*, **12** (1), pp 4–6

Woodruffe, C (1990) *Assessment Centres*, IPM, London

12 Knowledge Management

Key concepts and terms

- Communities of practice
- Explicit knowledge
- Knowledge
- Tacit knowledge
- Data
- Information
- Knowledge management

Learning outcomes

On completing this chapter you should be able to define these key concepts. You should also know about:

- The purpose and significance of knowledge management
- Knowledge management systems
- The contribution HR can make to knowledge management
- Knowledge management strategies
- Knowledge management issues

Introduction

Knowledge management is concerned with storing and sharing the wisdom, understanding and expertise accumulated in an organization about its processes, techniques and operations. It treats knowledge as a key resource. As Ulrich (1998) points out: 'Knowledge has become a direct competitive advantage for companies selling ideas and relationships.'

There is nothing new about knowledge management. Hansen *et al* (1999) remark that: 'For hundreds of years, owners of family businesses have passed on their commercial wisdom to children, master craftsmen have painstakingly taught their trades to apprentices, and workers have exchanged ideas and know-how on the job.' But they also remark that: 'As the foundation of industrialized economies has shifted from natural resources to intellectual assets, executives have been compelled to examine the knowledge underlying their business and how that knowledge is used.'

Knowledge management is as much if not more concerned with people and how they acquire, exchange and disseminate knowledge as it is about information technology. That is why it has become an important area for HR practitioners who are in a strong position to exert influence in this aspect of people management. Scarborough *et al* (1999) believe that they should have 'the ability to analyse the different types of knowledge deployed by the organization (and) to relate such knowledge to issues of organizational design, career patterns and employment security'.

The concept of knowledge management is closely associated with intellectual capital theory, as described in Chapter 4, in that it refers to the notions of human, social and organizational or structural capital. It is also linked to the concepts of organizational learning as discussed in Chapter 44. This chapter covers the concepts of knowledge and knowledge management and the actions that can be taken to deal with it.

Knowledge management defined

Knowledge management is 'any process or practice of creating, acquiring, capturing, sharing and using knowledge, wherever it resides, to enhance learning and performance in organizations' (Scarborough *et al*, 1999). They suggest that it focuses on the development of firm-specific knowledge and skills that are the result of organizational learning processes. Knowledge management is concerned with both stocks and flows of knowledge. Stocks included expertise and encoded knowledge in computer systems. Flows represent the ways in which knowledge is transferred from people to people or from people to a knowledge database. Knowledge management has also been defined by Tan (2000) as: 'The process of systematically and actively managing and leveraging the stores of knowledge in an organization.'

Scarborough and Carter (2000) describe knowledge management as 'the attempt by management to actively create, communicate and exploit knowledge as a resource for the organization'. They suggest that this attempt has the following components.

SOURCE REVIEW

Components of knowledge management, Scarborough and Carter (2000)

- In technical terms knowledge management involves centralizing knowledge that is currently scattered across the organization and codifying tacit forms of knowledge.
- In social and political terms, knowledge management involves collectivizing knowledge so that it is no longer the exclusive property of individuals or groups.
- In economic terms, knowledge management is a response by organizations to the need to intensify their creation and exploitation of knowledge.

Knowledge management involves transforming knowledge resources by identifying relevant information and then disseminating it so that learning can take place. Knowledge management strategies promote the sharing of knowledge by linking people with people and by linking them to information so that they learn from documented experiences.

Knowledge is possessed by organizations and the people in organizations. Organizational operational, technical and procedural knowledge can be stored in databanks and found in presentations, reports, libraries, policy documents and manuals. It can also be moved around the organization through information systems and by traditional methods such as meetings, workshops, courses, 'master classes' and written publications. The intranet provides an additional and very effective medium for communicating knowledge. A more recent development is that of 'communities of practice' defined by Wenger and Snyder (2000) as 'groups of people informally bound together by shared expertise and a passion for joint enterprise'.

People in organizations have knowledge that will not necessarily be shared formally or even informally with their colleagues. It may have been acquired through their own experiences at work. This individual knowledge may be crucial to the interests of the business and could be lost if it remains locked up in the minds of employees or taken elsewhere by them if they leave the organization. If this knowledge is important, one of the key issues in knowledge management is how it can be identified and disseminated.

The concept of knowledge

Knowledge is defined as what people understand about things, concepts, ideas, theories, procedures, practices and 'the way we do things around here'. It can be described as 'know-how' or, when it is specific, expertise. A distinction was made by Ryle (1949) between 'knowing how' and 'knowing that'. Knowing how is the ability of a person to perform tasks, and knowing that is holding pieces of knowledge in one's mind. Blackler (1995) noted that: 'Knowledge is multifaceted and complex, being both situated and abstract, implicit and explicit, distributed and individual, physical and mental, developing and static, verbal and encoded.'

Nonaka (1991) suggested that knowledge is held either by individuals or collectively. In Blackler's (1995) terms, embodied or embraced knowledge is individual and embedded, and cultural knowledge is collective. It can be argued (Scarborough and Carter, 2000) that knowledge emerges from the collective experience of work and is shared between members of a particular group or community.

Explicit and tacit knowledge

Nonaka (1991) and Nonaka and Takeuchi (1995) stated that knowledge is either explicit or tacit. Explicit knowledge can be codified – it is recorded and available and is held in databases, in corporate intranets and intellectual property portfolios. Tacit knowledge exists in people's minds. It is difficult to articulate in writing and is acquired through personal experience. As suggested by Hansen *et al* (1999), it includes scientific or technological expertise, operational know-how, insights about an industry and business judgement. The main challenge in knowledge management is how to turn tacit knowledge into explicit knowledge.

Data, information and knowledge

A distinction can be made between data, information and knowledge:

- data consists of the basic facts – the building blocks – for information and knowledge;
- information is data that have been processed in a way that is meaningful to individuals; it is available to anyone entitled to gain access to it. As Drucker (1988) wrote, 'information is data endowed with meaning and purpose';
- knowledge is information put to productive use; it is personal and often intangible and it can be elusive – the task of tying it down, encoding it and distributing it is tricky.

The purpose and significance of knowledge management

As explained by Blake (1998), the purpose of knowledge management is to capture a company's collective expertise and distribute it to 'wherever it can achieve the biggest payoff'. This is in accordance with the resource-based view of the firm, which suggests that the source of competitive advantage lies within the firm (ie in its people and their knowledge), not in how it positions itself in the market. Trussler (1998) commented that 'the capability to gather, lever and use knowledge effectively will become a major source of competitive advantage in many businesses over the next few years'. A successful company is a knowledge-creating company.

Knowledge management is about getting knowledge from those who have it to those who need it in order to improve organizational effectiveness. In the information age, knowledge rather than physical assets or financial resources is the key to competitiveness. In essence, as pointed out by Mecklenburg *et al* (1999): 'Knowledge management allows companies to capture, apply and generate value from their employees' creativity and expertise.'

Knowledge management strategies

Two approaches to knowledge management strategy have been identified by Hansen *et al* (1999).

1. The codification strategy

Knowledge is carefully codified and stored in databases where it can be accessed and used easily by anyone in the organization. Knowledge is explicit and is codified using a 'people-to-document' approach. This strategy is therefore document-driven. Knowledge is extracted from the person who developed it, made independent of that person and re-used for various purposes. It will be stored in some form of electronic repository for people to use and allows many people to search for and retrieve codified knowledge without having to contact the person who originally developed it. This strategy relies largely on information technology to manage databases and also on the use of the intranet.

2. The personalization strategy

Knowledge is closely tied to the person who has developed it and is shared mainly through direct person-to-person contacts. This is a 'person-to-person' approach that involves ensuring that tacit knowledge is passed on. The exchange is achieved by creating networks and encouraging face-to-face communication between individuals and teams by means of informal conferences, workshops, communities of practice, brainstorming and one-to-one sessions.

Hansen *et al* (1999) state that the choice of strategy should be contingent on the organization; what it does, how it does it, and its culture. Thus consultancies such as Ernst & Young using knowledge to deal with recurring problems may rely mainly on codification so that recorded solutions to similar problems are easily retrievable. Strategy consultancy firms such as McKinsey or Bains, however, will rely mainly on a personalization strategy to help them to tackle the high-level strategic problems they are presented with that demand the provision of creative, analytically rigorous advice. They need to channel individual expertise and they find and develop people who are able to use a person-to-person knowledge-sharing approach effectively. In this sort of firm, directors or experts can be established who can be approached by consultants by telephone, e-mail or personal contact.

The research conducted by Hansen *et al* (1999) established that companies that use knowledge effectively pursue one of these strategies predominantly and use the second strategy to support the first. Those who try to excel at both strategies risk failing at both.

Knowledge management systems

A survey of 431 US and European firms by Rugles (1998) found that the following systems were used.

SOURCE REVIEW

Use of knowledge management systems, Rugles (1998)

- Creating an intranet (47 per cent).
- Creating 'data warehouses', ie large physical databases that hold information from a wide variety of sources (33 per cent).
- Using decision support systems that combine data analysis and sophisticated models to support non-routine decision-making (33 per cent).
- Using 'groupware', ie information communication technologies such as e-mail or Lotus Notes discussion bases to encourage collaboration between people to share knowledge (33 per cent).
- Creating networks or communities of practice or interest of knowledge workers to share knowledge (24 per cent).
- Mapping sources of internal expertise by, for example, producing 'expert yellow pages' and directories of communities (18 per cent).

Knowledge management issues

The various approaches referred to above do not provide easy answers. The issues that need to be addressed in developing knowledge management processes are discussed below.

The pace of change

One of the main issues in knowledge management is how to keep up with the pace of change and identify what knowledge needs to be captured and shared.

Relating knowledge management strategy to business strategy

As Hansen *et al* (1999) show, it is not knowledge per se but the way it is applied to strategic objectives that is the critical ingredient in competitiveness. They point out that 'competitive strategy must drive knowledge management strategy' and that management have to answer the question: 'How does knowledge that resides in the company add value for customers?' Mecklenburg *et al* (1999) argue that organizations should 'start with the business value of what they gather. If it doesn't generate value, drop it'.

Technology and people

Technology may be central to companies adopting a codification strategy but for those following a personalization strategy, IT is best used in a supportive role. As Hansen *et al* (1999) comment:

> *In the codification model, managers need to implement a system that is much like a traditional library – it must contain a large cache of documents and include search engines that allow people to find and use the documents they need. In the personalization model, it's more important to have a system that allows people to find other people.*

Scarborough *et al* (1999) suggest that 'technology should be viewed more as a means of communication and less as a means of storing knowledge'. Knowledge management is more about people than technology. As research by Davenport (1996) established, managers get two-thirds of their information from face-to-face or telephone conversations.

There is a limit to how much tacit knowledge can be codified. In organizations relying more on tacit than explicit knowledge, a person-to-person approach works best, and IT can only support this process; it cannot replace it.

The significance of process and social capital and culture

Blackler (1995) emphasized that a preoccupation with technology may mean that too little attention is paid to the processes (social, technological and organizational) through which knowledge combines and interacts in different ways. The key processes are the interactions between people. This is the social capital of an organization, ie the 'network of relationships (that) constitute a valuable resource for the conduct of social affairs' (Nahpiet and Ghoshal, 1998). Social networks can be particularly important in ensuring that knowledge is shared. Trust is also required – people are not willing to share knowledge with those whom they do not trust.

The culture of the company may inhibit knowledge sharing. The norm may be for people to keep knowledge to themselves as much as they can because 'knowledge is power'. An open culture will encourage people to share their ideas and knowledge.

Knowledge workers

Knowledge workers as defined by Drucker (1993) are individuals who have high levels of education and specialist skills combined with the ability to apply these skills to identify and solve problems. As Argyris (1991) comments: 'The nuts and bolts of management... increasingly consists of guiding and integrating the autonomous but interconnected work of highly skilled people.' Knowledge management is about the management and motivation of knowledge workers who create knowledge and will be the key players in sharing it.

The contribution of HR to knowledge management

HR can make an important contribution to knowledge management simply because knowledge is shared between people; it is not just a matter of capturing explicit knowledge through the use of information technology. The role of HR is to ensure that the organization has the intellectual capital it needs. The resource-based view of the firm emphasizes, in the words of Cappelli and Crocker-Hefter (1996), that 'distinctive human resource practices help to create unique competences that differentiate products and services and, in turn, drive competitiveness'.

Ten ways in which HR can contribute to knowledge management

1. Help to develop an open culture in which the values and norms emphasize the importance of sharing knowledge.
2. Promote a climate of commitment and trust.
3. Advise on the design and development of organizations that facilitate knowledge sharing through networks, teamwork and communities of practice (groups of people who share common interests in certain aspects of their work).
4. Advise on resourcing policies and provide resourcing services that ensure that valued employees who can contribute to knowledge creation and sharing are attracted and retained.

5. Advise on methods of motivating people to share knowledge and rewarding those who do so.
6. Help in the development of performance management processes that focus on the development and sharing of knowledge.
7. Develop processes of organizational and individual learning that will generate and assist in disseminating knowledge.
8. Set up and organize workshops, conferences, seminars, communities of practice and symposia that enable knowledge to be shared on a person-to-person basis.
9. In conjunction with IT, develop systems for capturing and, as far as possible, codifying explicit and tacit knowledge.
10. Generally, promote the cause of knowledge management with senior managers to encourage them to exert leadership and support knowledge management initiatives.

Knowledge management – key learning points

The purpose and significance of knowledge management

Knowledge management is about getting knowledge from those who have it to those who need it in order to improve organizational effectiveness.

Knowledge management strategies

The codification strategy – knowledge is carefully codified and stored in databases where it can be accessed and used easily by anyone in the organization. Knowledge is explicit and is codified using a 'people-to-document' approach.

The personalization strategy – knowledge is closely tied to the person who has developed it and is shared mainly through direct person-to-person contacts. This is a 'person-to-person' approach that involves ensuring that tacit knowledge is passed on.

Knowledge management systems

- Creating an intranet.
- Creating 'data warehouses'.
- Using decision support systems.
- Using 'groupware', ie information communication technologies such as e-mail or Lotus Notes discussion bases.
- Creating networks or communities of practice or interest of knowledge workers.

Knowledge management issues

- The pace of change.

Knowledge management – key learning points (continued)

- Relating knowledge management strategy to business strategy.
- IT is best used in a supportive role.
- Attention must be paid to the processes (social, technological and organizational) through which knowledge combines and interacts in different ways.
- The significance of knowledge workers must be appreciated.

The contribution HR can make to knowledge management

- Help to develop an open culture that emphasizes the importance of sharing knowledge.
- Promote a climate of commitment and trust.
- Advise on the design and development of organizations that facilitate knowledge sharing.
- Ensure that valued employees who can contribute to knowledge creation and sharing are attracted and retained.
- Advise on methods of motivating people to share.
- Help in the development of performance management processes that focus on the development and sharing of knowledge.
- Develop processes of organizational and individual learning that will generate and assist in disseminating knowledge.
- Set up and organize workshops, conferences and communities of practice and symposia that enable knowledge to be shared on a person-to-person basis.
- In conjunction with IT, develop systems for capturing and, as far as possible, codifying explicit and tacit knowledge.
- Generally, promote the cause of knowledge management with senior managers.

Questions

1. In the new knowledge economy, HR practitioners should be helping their organizations to ensure the creation and application of business-relevant knowledge in the workplace. Outline and justify the kind of help that HR staff in your organization should provide.
2. Many organizations are now introducing knowledge-sharing initiatives and processes. Outline one approach that you would like to see introduced in your organization, justifying how it would be of benefit to the business.

Questions (continued)

3. Your managing director has sent you the following e-mail: 'I have been hearing about the concept of communities of interest. What are they, would they be useful in our company and, if so, how should we introduce them?' Draft your reply.
4. The following questions were posed by Swart *et al* (2003) for the CIPD on knowledge-intensive firms:
   - What are the key characteristics of knowledge-intensive organizations?
   - What are the particular knowledge-intensive situations that are important for the success of organizations?
   - Which people management practices are particularly valuable in helping to manage these situations successfully?

Drawing on the Swart *et al* and other research, provide answers to these questions.

References

Argyris, C (1991) Teaching smart people how to learn, *Harvard Business Review*, May–June, pp 54–62

Blackler, F (1995) Knowledge, knowledge work and experience, *Organization Studies*, **16** (6), pp 16–36

Blake, P (1988) The knowledge management explosion, *Information Today*, **15** (1), pp 12–13

Cappelli, P and Crocker-Hefter, A (1996) Distinctive human resources are firms' core competencies, *Organizational Dynamics*, Winter, pp 7–22

Davenport, T H (1996) Why re-engineering failed: the fad that forgot people, *Fast Company*, Premier Issue, pp 70–74

Drucker, P (1988) The coming of the new organization, *Harvard Business Review*, January–February, pp 45–53

Drucker, P (1993) *Post-Capitalist Society*, Butterworth-Heinemann, Oxford

Hansen, M T, Nohria, N and Tierney, T (1999) What's your strategy for managing knowledge?, *Harvard Business Review*, March–April, pp 106–16

Mecklenberg, S, Deering, A and Sharp, D (1999) Knowledge management: a secret engine of corporate growth, *Executive Agenda*, **2**, pp 5–15

Nahpiet, J and Ghoshal, S (1998) Social capital, intellectual capital and the organizational advantage, *Academy of Management Review*, **23** (2), pp 242–66

Nonaka, I (1991) The knowledge creating company, *Harvard Business Review*, Nov–Dec, pp 96–104

Nonaka, I and Takeuchi, H (1995) *The Knowledge Creating Company*, Oxford University Press, New York

Rugles, R (1998) The state of the notion, *Californian Management Review*, **40** (3), pp 80–89

Ryle, G (1949) *The Concept of Mind*, Oxford University Press, Oxford

Scarborough, H and Carter, C (2000) *Investigating Knowledge Management*, CIPD, London

Scarborough, H, Swan, J and Preston, J (1999) *Knowledge Management: A literature review*, Institute of Personnel and Development, London

Swart, J, Kinnie, N and Purcell, J (2003) *People and Performance in Knowledge-intensive Firms: A comparison of six research and technology organisations*, CIPD, London

Tan, J (2000) Knowledge management – just more buzzwords?, *British Journal of Administrative Management*, March/April, pp 10–11

Trussler, S (1998) The rules of the game, *Journal of Business Strategy*, **19** (1), pp 16–19

Ulrich, D (1998) A new mandate for human resources, *Harvard Business Review*, January–February, pp 124–34

Wenger, E and Snyder, W M (2000) Communities of practice: the organizational frontier, *Harvard Business Review*, January–February, pp 33–41

13 High-performance Work Systems

Key concepts and terms

- High-commitment management
- High-involvement management
- High-performance management
- Performance management model
- High-commitment model
- High-performance culture
- High-performance work system (HPWS)

Learning outcomes

On completing this chapter you should be able to define these key concepts. You should also know about:

- The characteristics of a high-performance culture
- The components of a HPWS
- Developing high-performance work systems
- The characteristics of a high-performance work system (HPWS)
- Impact of high-performance work systems

Introduction

Organizations are in the business of achieving sustained high performance. They do this through the systems of work they adopt but these systems are managed and operated by people. Ultimately, therefore, high-performance working is about improving performance through people. The aim is to achieve a high-performance culture as defined in the first section of this chapter. This can be done through the development and implementation of high-performance work systems (defined in the second section of his chapter), which incorporate to varying degrees processes of high performance, high commitment and high involvement management, as described in Chapter 3.

High-performance working can involve the two 'ideal type' approaches to HRM identified by Guest (2007): 1) the 'high-commitment' model – 'a move from external control through management systems, technology and supervision to self-control by workers or teams of workers, who, because of their commitment to the organization, would exercise responsible autonomy and control in the interests of the organization'. The emphasis is on intrinsic control and intrinsic rewards. 2) The 'performance management model' in which management retains much of the control – 'the focus is on the adoption of practices designed to maximize high performance by ensuring high levels of competence and motivation.' The emphasis is on external control and extrinsic rewards.

According to Guest, reconciling these has been attempted through high-performance work systems. These achieve high performance by ensuring that HR practices are adopted 'that lead to workers having high ability/competence, high motivation, and an opportunity to contribute through jobs that provide the discretion, autonomy and control required to use their knowledge and skills and to exercise motivation'. The focus is on performance and not the well-being of employees.

High-performance culture

The aim of a HPWS is to achieve a high-performance culture, one in which the values, norms and HR practices of an organization combine to create a climate in which the achievement of high levels of performance is a way of life.

Characteristics of a high-performance culture

- Management defines what it requires in the shape of performance improvements, sets goals for success and monitors performance to ensure that the goals are achieved.
- Alternative work practices are adopted such as job redesign, autonomous work teams, improvement groups, team briefing and flexible working.

- People know what's expected of them – they understand their goals and accountabilities.
- People feel that their job is worth doing, and there is a strong fit between the job and their capabilities.
- People are empowered to maximize their contribution.
- There is strong leadership from the top that engenders a shared belief in the importance of continuing improvement.
- There is a focus on promoting positive attitudes that result in an engaged, committed and motivated workforce.
- Performance management processes are aligned to business goals to ensure that people are engaged in achieving agreed objectives and standards.
- Capacities of people are developed through learning at all levels to support performance improvement and people are provided with opportunities to make full use of their skills and abilities.
- A pool of talent ensures a continuous supply of high performers in key roles.
- People are valued and rewarded according to their contribution.
- People are involved in developing high-performance practices.
- There is a climate of trust and teamwork, aimed at delivering a distinctive service to the customer.
- A clear line of sight exists between the strategic aims of the organization and those of its departments and its staff at all levels.

High-performance work system defined

There are many definitions of a high-performance work system (HPWS) and high-performance working. In their seminal work, *Manufacturing Advantage: Why high performance work systems pay off*, Appelbaum *et al* (2000) stated that high-performance work systems facilitate employee involvement, skill enhancement and motivation. An HPWS is 'generally associated with workshop practices that raise the levels of trust within workplaces and increase workers' intrinsic reward from work, and thereby enhance organizational commitment'. They define high performance as a way of organizing work so that front-line workers participate in decisions that have a real impact on their jobs and the wider organization.

It is sometimes believed that high-performance work systems are just about HR policies and initiatives. But as Godard (2004) suggested, they are based on both alternative work practices and high-commitment employment practices. He called this the 'high-performance paradigm' and described it as follows.

SOURCE REVIEW

The high-performance work paradigm, Godard (2004)

Alternative work practices that have been identified include: 1) alternative job design practices, including work teams (autonomous or non-autonomous), job enrichment, job rotation and related reforms; and 2) formal participatory practices, including quality circles or problem-solving groups, town hall meetings, team briefings and joint steering committees. Of these practices, work teams and quality circles can be considered as most central to the high-performance paradigm. High-commitment employment practices that have been identified include: 1) sophisticated selection and training, emphasizing values and human relations skills as well as knowledge skills; 2) behaviour-based appraisal and advancement criteria; 3) single status policies; 4) contingent pay systems, especially pay-for-knowledge, group bonuses, and profit sharing; 5) job security; 6) above-market pay and benefits; 7) grievance systems; and others.

However, research conducted by Armitage and Keble-Allen (2007) indicated that people management basics formed the foundation of high-performance working. They identified the following three themes underpinning the HPWS concept.

Themes underpinning the HPWS concept

- An open and creative culture that is people-centred and inclusive, where decision taking is communicated and shared through the organization.
- Investment in people through education and training, loyalty, inclusiveness and flexible working.
- Measurable performance outcomes such as benchmarking and setting targets, as well as innovation through processes and best practice.

Sung and Ashton (2005) defined what they call 'high-performance work practices' as a set or 'bundle' of 35 complementary work practices covering three broad areas:

1. High employee involvement work practices – eg self-directed teams, quality circles and sharing/access to company information.
2. Human resource practices – eg sophisticated recruitment processes, performance appraisals, mentoring and work redesign.
3. Reward and commitment practices – eg various financial rewards, family-friendly policies, job rotation and flexi hours.

Characteristics of a high-performance work system

A high-performance work system is described by Becker and Huselid (1998) as: 'An internally consistent and coherent HRM system that is focused on solving operational problems and implementing the firm's competitive strategy.' They suggest that such a system 'is the key to the acquisition, motivation and development of the underlying intellectual assets that can be a source of sustained competitive advantage'. This is because it has the following characteristics.

Characteristics of an HPWS

- It links the firm's selection and promotion decisions to validated competency models.
- It is the basis for developing strategies that provide timely and effective support for the skills demanded to implant the firm's strategies.
- It enacts compensation and performance management policies that attract, retain and motivate high-performance employees.

Nadler and Gerstein (1992) have characterized an HPWS as a way of thinking about organizations. It can play an important role in strategic human resource management by helping to achieve a 'fit' between information, technology, people and work.

High-performance work systems provide the means for creating a performance culture. They embody ways of thinking about performance in organizations and how it can be improved. They are concerned with developing and implementing bundles of complementary practices which, as an integrated whole, will make a much more powerful impact on performance than if they were dealt with as separate entities.

Becker *et al* (2001) have stated that the aim of such systems is to develop a 'high-performance perspective in which HR and other executives view HR as a system embedded within the larger system of the firm's strategy implementation'. As Nadler (1989) commented, they are deliberately introduced in order to improve organizational, financial and operational performance.

'High-performance work systems' are also known as 'high-performance work practices' (Sung and Ashton, 2005). Thompson and Heron (2005) referred to them as 'high-performance work organizations' that 'invest in the skills and abilities of employees, design work in ways that enable employee collaboration in problem solving, and provide incentives to motivate workers to use their discretionary effort'. The terms 'high-performance system' and 'high-commitment system' often seem to be used interchangeably. There is indeed much common ground between the practices included in high-performance, high-commitment and high-involvement work systems, as described in Chapter 3 although, following Godard (2004) there may be more emphasis in a high-performance work system on alternative work practices. Sung and Ashton (2005) noted that:

> *In some cases high-performance work practices are called 'high commitment practices' (Walton, 1985b) or 'high-involvement management' (Lawler, 1986). More recently they have been termed 'high-performance organizations' (Lawler et al, 1998, Ashton and Sung, 2002) or 'high-involvement' work practices (Wood et al, 2001). Whilst these studies are referring to the same general phenomena the use of different 'labels' has undoubtedly added to the confusion.*

The term 'high-performance work system' (HPWS) is the one most commonly used in both academic and practitioner circles and it is therefore adopted in this chapter. But it is recognized that high commitment and high involvement are both important factors in the pursuit of high performance. The notions incorporated in these practices therefore need to be incorporated in any programme for improving organizational effectiveness wherever they add to the basic concepts of a high-performance work system.

Components of an HPWS

There is no generally accepted definition of an HPWS and there is no standard list of the features or components of such a system. Appelbaum and Batt (1994) identified six models: US lean production, US team production, German diversified quality production, Italian flexible specialization, Japanese lean production and Swedish socio-technical systems. These systems vary in the degree of autonomy they give the workforce, the nature of the supporting human resource practices, and the extent to which the gains from the systems are shared.

In spite of this problem of definition, an attempt to define the basic components of an HPWS was made by Shih *et al* (2005) as follows:

- Job infrastructure – workplace arrangements that equip workers with the proper abilities to do their jobs, provide them with the means to do their jobs, and give them the motivation to do their jobs. These practices must be combined to produce their proper effects.

- Training programmes to enhance employee skills – investment in increasing employee skills, knowledge and ability.
- Information sharing and worker involvement mechanisms – to understand the available alternatives and make correct decisions.
- Compensation and promotion opportunities that provide motivation – to encourage skilled employees to engage in effective discretionary decision making in a variety of environmental contingencies.

Many other descriptions of high-performance systems include lists of desirable practices and therefore embody the notion of 'best practice' or the 'universalistic' approach described in Chapter 2. Lists vary considerably, as is shown in the selection set out in Table 13.1. Gephart (1995) noted that research has not clearly identified any single set of high-performance practices. Becker *et al* (1997) remarked that: 'Organizational high-performance work systems are highly idiosyncratic and must be tailored carefully to each firm's individual situation to achieve optimum results.' And Sung and Ashton (2005) commented: 'It would be wrong to seek one magic list.' It all depends on the context.

Table 13.1 Lists of HR practices in high-performance work systems

US Department of Labor (1993)	Appelbaum *et al* (2000)	Sung and Ashton (2005)	Thompson and Heron (2005)
• Careful and extensive systems for recruitment, selection and training • Formal systems for sharing information with employees • Clear job design • High-level participation processes • Monitoring of attitudes	• Work is organized to permit front-line workers to participate in decisions that alter organizational routines • Workers require more skills to do their jobs successfully, and many of these skills are firm-specific • Workers experience greater	• High-involvement work practices – eg self-directed teams, quality circles, and sharing/access to company information • Human resource practices – eg sophisticated recruitment processes, performance appraisals, work redesign	• Information sharing. • Sophisticated recruitment • Formal induction programme • Five or more days of off-the-job training in the last year • Semi or totally autonomous work teams; continuous improvement teams; problem-

Table 13.1 *continued*

US Department of Labor (1993)	Appelbaum *et al* (2000)	Sung and Ashton (2005)	Thompson and Heron (2005)
• Performance appraisals • Properly functioning grievance procedures • Promotion and compensation schemes that provide for the recognition and reward of high-performing employees	autonomy over their job tasks and methods of work • Incentive pay motivates workers to extend extra effort on developing skills • Employment security provides front-line workers with a long-term stake in the company and a reason to invest in its future	and mentoring • Reward and commitment practices – eg various financial rewards, family friendly policies, job rotation and flexi hours	solving groups • Interpersonal skill development • Performance feedback • Involvement – works council, suggestion scheme, opinion survey • Team-based rewards, employee share ownership scheme, profit-sharing scheme.

However, Ashton and Sung (2002) noted that the practices may be more effective when they are grouped together in 'bundles'. For example, the isolated use of quality circles is not as effective as when the practice is supported by wider employee involvement/empowerment practices.

Godard (2004) suggested that that there is a general assumption that the benefit of an HPWS increases with the number of practices adopted. However, it is often argued that high-performance practices are complementary to, and hence interact with, each other, so that their true potential is not fully realized unless they are adopted in combination or as part of a full-blown high-performance system (the complementarities thesis). It is also sometimes argued that these effects are not fully realized unless integrated with or matched to a particular employer strategy (the 'matching' thesis).

It is possible to interpret these descriptions of HPWS activities as in effect incorporating the high-commitment principle that jobs should be designed to provide intrinsic satisfaction and the high-involvement principle of treating employees as partners in the enterprise whose interests are respected and who have a voice on matters that concern them.

Impact of high-performance work systems

A considerable number of studies as summarized below have been conducted that demonstrate that the impact of high-performance work systems is positive.

US Department of Labor (1993)

In a survey of 700 organizations the US Department of Labor found that firms that used innovative human resource practices show a significantly higher level of shareholder and gross return on capital.

King (1995)

King cites a survey of Fortune 1000 companies in the United States revealing that 60 per cent of those using at least one practice, increasing the responsibility of employees in the business process, reported that the result was an increase in productivity while 70 per cent reported an improvement in quality.

He examined the impact of the use of one practice. A study of 155 manufacturing firms showed that those which had introduced a formal training programme experienced a 19 per cent larger rise in productivity over three years than firms that did not introduce a training programme. Research into the use of gainsharing in 112 manufacturing firms revealed that defect and downtime rates fell 23 per cent in the first year after the approach was introduced. His review of 29 studies on the effects of workplace participation on productivity indicated that 14 had a positive effect on productivity, only two had negative effects and the rest were inconclusive.

However, he noted that such work practices may have only a limited effect unless they are elements of a coherent work system. Further research examined changes over time in 222 firms and found that these and other practices are associated with even greater productivity when implemented together in systems.

He concluded that the evidence suggest that it is the use of comprehensive systems of work practices in firms that is most closely associated with stronger firm performance. Yet he noted that 'the nature of the relationship between high-performance work practices and productivity is not clear'.

Varma *et al* (1999)

A survey of 39 organizations was conducted by Varma *et al* to examine the antecedents, design and effectiveness of high-performance initiatives. Results indicated that HPWSs are primarily initiated by strong firms that are seeking to become stronger. First and foremost, firms reported that in general their HPWS:

- had a significant impact on financial performance;
- created a positive culture change in the organization (eg, cooperation and innovation);
- created higher degrees of job satisfaction among employees;
- positively influenced the way in which work was designed;
- led to marked improvement in communication processes within the organization.

In particular, the use of team-based and non-financial rewards was closely related to improved performance, as was rewarding people for improving their competencies.

Appelbaum *et al* (2000)

A multifaceted research design was used by the authors in their study of the impact of HPWSs. This included management interviews, the collection of plant performance and data surveys of workers on their experiences with workshop practices. Nearly 4,400 employees were surveyed and 44 manufacturing facilities were visited. The findings of the research were that:

- in the steel industry HPWSs produced strong positive effects on performance, for example, substantial increases in uptime;
- in the apparel industry the introduction of a 'module system' (ie group piecework rates linked to quality as well as quantity rather than individual piecework, plus multi-skilling) dramatically speeded up throughput times, meeting consumer demands for fast delivery;
- in the medical electronics and imaging industry those using an HPWS ranked highly on eight diverse indicators of financial performance and production efficiency and quality.

The impact of HPWS on individual workers was to enhance:

- trust by sharing control and encouraging participation;
- intrinsic rewards because workers are challenged to be creative and use their skills and knowledge – discretion and autonomy are the task-level decisions most likely to enhance intrinsic rewards;
- organizational commitment through opportunity to participate, and incentives that make people feel that organizational relationships are beneficial for them;
- job satisfaction because of participation, perception of fairness in pay and adequate resources to do jobs (inadequate resources is a cause of dissatisfaction, as is working in an unsafe or unclean environment).

They concluded that taken as a whole, the results suggested that the core characteristics of HPWSs – having autonomy over task-level decision making, membership of self-directing production and off-line teams and communication with people outside the work group – generally enhance workers' levels of organizational commitment and satisfaction:

> *HPWSs are generally associated with workshop practices that raise the levels of trust within workplaces and increase workers' intrinsic reward from work, and thereby enhance organizational commitment. Wages are higher as well... The adoption of HPWSs sets positive productivity dynamics in motion.*

Sung and Ashton (2005)

This survey of high-performance work practices (HPWP) was conducted in 294 UK companies. It provided evidence that the level of HPWP adoption as measured by the number of practices in use is linked to organizational performance. Those adopting more of the practices as 'bundles' had greater employee involvement and were more effective in delivering adequate training provision, managing staff and providing career opportunities.

Combs *et al* (2006)

A meta-analysis of 92 studies showed a link between high performance HR practices and organization performance. The three sets of influential HR practices identified were those that: 1) increased skills; 2) empower employees; and 3) improve motivation. HPWSs also improve the internal social structure within organizations, which facilitates communication and cooperation among employees.

Ericksen (2007)

Research was conducted in 196 small businesses to test the hypothesis that HPWSs create a human resource advantage by aligning key employee attributes and the strategic goals of the firm and by adapting their workforce attributes in response to new strategic circumstances. Dynamic workforce alignment exists when firms have 'the right types of people, in the right places, doing the right things right', and when adjustments are readily made to their workforces as the situation changes.

The research showed that there was a strong positive relationship between workforce alignment and sales growth when adaptation was high.

Reservations about the impact of an HPWS

Research conducted by Ramsay *et al* (2000) aimed to explore linkages from HPWS practices to employee outcomes and via these to organizational performance. They referred to the existence of the 'black box', meaning that while the introduction of an HPWS may be associated with improved performance, no researchers have yet established how this happens. Their research was based on data from the UK 1998 Workplace Employee Relations Survey. They commented that 'the widely held view that positive performance outcomes from HPWS flow via positive employee outcomes has been shown to be highly questionable', a finding that ran counter to most of the other studies. They admit that their analysis was 'perhaps too simplistic to capture the complex reality of the implementation and operation of HPWS', but they note, realistically, that 'there are major limitations to the strategic management of labour which severely constrain the potential for innovative approaches to be implemented successfully'.

Godard (2001) concluded, following his research in Canada, that the actual effects of HPWSs can vary considerably and many have a limited lifespan. Following further research, Godard (2004) commented that:

> *The full adoption of this (high-performance) paradigm may not yield outcomes that are appreciably more positive than those yielded by practices that have long been associated with good management, including professional personnel practices (eg job ladders, employment security, grievance systems, formal training, above-market pay), group work organization, information sharing and accommodative union relations policies... There may be positive effects in some workplaces. However, these effects may be inherently more limited than assumed and, in a great many workplaces, may not be sufficient to justify full adoption.*

Farnham (2008) summed up the reservations about the high-performance or high-commitment model by referring to issues about the direction of the causality in the black box, lack of consistency in the practices included in the bundle, variations in the proxies used to measure high-commitment HRM, variations in the proxies used to measure performance, relying on the self-report scores of HR managers, doubts about how much autonomy organizations have introduced in decision making in practice, and doubts about the universal application of high-commitment HRM as an approach to HR strategy.

These reservations usefully modify the often starry-eyed enthusiasm for the notion of high-performance working and emphasize that it is not an easy option. But it is difficult to argue against the basic concept and there is enough evidence that it is effective to encourage its development as described below, albeit being realistic about what is possible and how well it will work.

Developing a high-performance work system

A high-performance work system has to be based on a high-performance strategy that sets out intentions and plans on how a high-performance culture can be created and maintained. The strategy has to be aligned to the context of the organization and to its business strategy. Every organization will therefore develop a different strategy, as is illustrated by the case study examples set out in Table 13.2.

Table 13.2 Examples of high-performance working ingredients

Organization	High-performance working ingredients
Halo Foods	• A strategy that maintains competitiveness by increasing added value through the efforts and enhanced capability of all staff • The integration of technical advance with people development • Continuing reliance on team-working and effective leadership, with innovation and self and team management skills
Land Registry	• Organizational changes to streamline processes, raise skill levels and release talents • Managers who could see that the problems were as much cultural as organizational • Recruitment of people whose attitudes and aptitudes match the needs of high performance work practices
Meritor Heavy Vehicle Braking Systems	• Skill enhancement, particularly of management and self management skills using competence frameworks • Team-working skills and experience used on improvement projects • Linking learning, involvement and performance management
Orangebox	• A strategy that relies on constant reinvention of operational capability • Engagement and development of existing talent and initiative in productivity improvement • Increasing use of cross-departmental projects to tackle wider opportunities
Perkinelmer	• A vision and values worked through by managers and supervisors • Engagement of everyone in the organization and establishment of a continuous improvement culture • Learning as a basis for change
United Welsh Housing Association	• Linking of better employment relations with better performance • Using staff experience to improve customer service • Focusing management development on the cascading of a partnership culture

(Source: Stevens, 2005)

Approach to developing an HPWS

The approach to developing an HPWS is based on an understanding of what the goals of the business are, what work arrangements are appropriate to the attainment of those goals and how people can contribute to their achievement. This leads to an assessment of what type of performance culture is required.

The development programme requires strong leadership from the top. Stakeholders – line managers, team leaders, employees and their representatives – should be involved as much as possible through surveys, focus groups and workshops.

The development programme

The steps required to develop an HPWS are described below.

1. Analyse the business strategy

- Where is the business going?
- What are the strengths and weaknesses of the business?
- What threats and opportunities face the business?
- What are the implications of the above on the type of work practices and people required by the business, now and in the future?

2. Define the desired performance culture of the business and the objectives of the exercise

Use the list of characteristics of a high-performance culture as set out at the beginning of this chapter as a starting point and produce a list that is aligned to the culture and context of the business and a statement of the objectives of developing an HPWS. Answer the questions:

- What differences do we want to make to working arrangements?
- How do we want to treat people differently?
- What do we want people to do differently?

3. Analyse the existing arrangements

Start from the headings defined at Stage 2 and analyse against each heading:

- What is happening now in the form of practices, attitudes and behaviours?
- What should be happening?

- What do people feel about it? (The more involvement in this analysis from all stakeholders the better.)

4. Identify the gaps between what is and what should be

Clarify specific practices where there is considerable room for improvement.

5. Draw up a list of practices that need to be introduced or improved

At this stage only a broad definition should be produced of what ideally needs to be done.

6. Establish complementarities

Identify the practices that can be linked together in 'bundles' to complement and support one another.

7. Assess practicality

The ideal list of practices, or preferably, bundles of practices, should be subjected to a reality check:

- Is it worth doing? What's the business case in terms of added value? What contribution will it make to supporting the achievement of the organization's strategic goals?
- Can it be done?
- Who does it?
- Do we have the resources to do it?
- How do we manage the change?

8. Prioritize

In the light of the assessment of practicalities, decide on the priorities that should be given to introducing new or improved practices. A realistic approach is essential. There will be limits on how much can be done at once or any future time. Priorities should be established by assessing:

- the added value the practice will create;
- the availability of the resources required;
- anticipated problems in introducing the practice, including resistance to change by stakeholders (too much should not be made of this: change can be managed, but there is much to be said for achieving some quick wins);
- the extent to which they can form bundles of mutually supporting practices.

9. Define project objectives

Develop the broad statement of objectives produced at Stage 2 and define what is to be achieved, why and how.

10. Get buy-in

This should start at the top with the chief executive and members of the senior management team, but so far as possible it should extend to all the other stakeholders (easier if they have been involved at earlier stages and if the intentions have been fully communicated).

11. Plan the implementation

This is where things become difficult. Deciding what needs to be done is fairly easy; getting it done is the hard part. The implementation plan needs to cover:

- who takes the lead – this must come from the top of the organization: nothing will work without it;
- who manages the project and who else is involved;
- the timetable for development and introduction;
- the resources (people and money required);
- how the change programme will be managed, including communication and further consultation;
- the success criteria for the project.

12. Implement

Too often, 80 per cent of the time spent on introducing an HPWS is devoted to planning and only 20 per cent on implementation. It should be the other way round. Whoever is responsible for implementation must have considerable project and change management skills.

High-performance work systems – key learning points

The key characteristics of a high-performance culture

- People know what's expected of them – they understand their goals and accountabilities.
- People feel that their job is worth doing, and there is a strong fit between the job and their capabilities.
- Management defines what it requires in the shape of performance

High-performance work systems – key learning points (continued)

improvements, sets goals for success and monitors performance to ensure that the goals are achieved.

- There is a focus on promoting positive attitudes that result in an engaged, committed and motivated workforce.
- Performance management processes are aligned to business goals to ensure that people are engaged in achieving agreed objectives and standards.
- Capacities of people are developed through learning at all levels to support performance improvement.

The characteristics of a high-performance work system (HPWS)

- Links the firm's selection and promotion decisions to validated competency models.
- A basis for developing strategies that provide timely and effective support for the skills demanded to implement the firm's strategies.
- Enacts compensation and performance management policies that attract, retain and motivate high performance employees.

The components of an HPWS

There is no 'magic list' of best practices for an HPWS although they work best if bundled together. The lists that have been produced include sophisticated HR practices in such areas as recruitment, learning and development, performance management and reward processes.

Impact of high-performance work systems

A considerable number of studies have been conducted that demonstrate that the impact of high-performance work systems is positive.

Developing high-performance work systems

The approach to developing an HPWS is based on an understanding of what the goals of the business are and how people can contribute to their achievement. This leads to an assessment of what type of performance culture is required.

Questions

1. You have received an e-mail from your operations director to the effect that he is confused by the terms 'high performance', 'high commitment' and 'high involvement' management. He wants to know what the differences are between them, if any. He would also like your views on how any of them might benefit the company, particularly distribution and customer service. Draft a reply.
2. What has recent research told us about the extent to which high-performance working leads to improved levels of organizational performance?
3. Your managing director has asked you to draft a paper for the board on why the organization should introduce a high-performance work system. Prepare the paper explaining what such as system would look like and how it might be developed.

References

Appelbaum, E, and Batt, R (1994) *The New American Workplace*, Cornell University Press, Ithaca, NY

Appelbaum, E, Bailey, T, Berg, P and Kalleberg, A L (2000) *Manufacturing Advantage: Why high performance work systems pay off*, ILR Press, Ithaca, NY

Armitage, A and Keble-Allen, D (2007) Why people management basics form the foundation of high-performance working, *People Management*, 18 October, p 48

Ashton, D and Sung, (2002) *Supporting Workplace Learning for High performance*, ILO, Geneva

Becker, B E and Huselid, M A (1998) High performance work systems and firm performance: a synthesis of research and managerial implications, *Research on Personnel and Human Resource Management*, **16,** pp 53–101, JAI Press, Stamford, CT

Becker, B E, Huselid, M A and Ulrich, D (2001) *The HR Score card: Linking people, strategy, and performance*, Harvard Business School Press, Boston, MA

Becker, B E, Huselid, M A, Pickus, P S and Spratt, M F (1997) HR as a source of shareholder value: research and recommendations, *Human Resource Management*, Spring, **36** (1), pp 39–47

Combs, J, Liu, Y, Hall, A and Ketchan, D (2006) How much do high performance work practices matter? A meta-analysis of their effects on organizational performance, *Personnel Psychology* **59** (3), pp 501–28

Ericksen, J (2007) High performance work systems: dynamic workforce alignment and firm performance, *Academy of Management Proceedings*, pp 1–6

Farnham, D (2008) *Examiner's Report* (May), CIPD.co.uk

Gephart, M A (1995) The road to high performance: steps to create a high-performance workplace, *Training and Development*, June, p 29

Godard, J (2001) Beyond the high-performance paradigm? An analysis of variation in Canadian managerial perceptions of reform programme effectiveness, *British Journal of Industrial Relations* **39** (1), pp 25–52

Godard, J (2004) A critical assessment of the high-performance paradigm, *British Journal of Industrial Relations*, **42** (2), pp 349–78

Guest, D (2007) HRM: Towards a new psychological contract, in (eds) P Boxall, J Purcell and P Wright, *Oxford Handbook of Human Resource Management*, Oxford University Press, Oxford

King, J (1995) High performance work systems and firm performance, *Monthly Labour Review*, May, pp 29–36

Lawler, E E (1986) *High Involvement Management*, Jossey-Bass, San Francisco, CA

Lawler, E E, Mohrman, S and Ledford, G (1998) *Strategies for High Performance Organizations: Employee involvement, TQM, and re-engineering programs in Fortune 1000*, Jossey-Bass, San Francisco, CA

Nadler, D A (1989) Organizational architecture for the corporation of the future, *Benchmark*, Fall, 12–13

Nadler, D A and Gerstein, M S (1992) Designing high-performance work systems: organizing people, technology, work and information, *Organizational Architecture*, Summer, pp 195–208

Ramsay, H, Scholarios, D and Harley, B (2000) Employees and high-performance work systems: testing inside the black box, *British Journal of Industrial Relations*, **38** (4), pp 501–31

Shih, H-A, Chiang, Y-H and Hsu, C-C (2005) Can high performance work systems really lead to better performance?, *Academy of Management Conference Paper*, pp 1–6

Stevens, J (2005) *High Performance Wales: Real experiences, real success*, Wales Management Council, Cardiff

Sung, J and Ashton, D (2005) *High Performance Work Practices: Linking strategy and skills to performance outcomes*, DTI in association with CIPD, available at http://www.cipd.co.uk/subjects/corpstrtgy/

Thompson, M and Heron, P (2005) Management capability and high performance work organization, *The International Journal of Human Resource Management*, **16** (6), pp 1029–48

US Department of Labor (1993) *High Performance Work Practices and Work Performance*, US Government Printing Office, Washington DC

Varma, A, Beatty, R W, Schneier, C E and Ulrich, D O (1999) High performance work systems: exciting discovery or passing fad?, *Human Resource Planning*, **22** (1), pp 26–37

Walton, R E (1985b) Towards a strategy of eliciting employee commitment based on principles of mutuality, in (eds) R E Walton and P R Lawrence, *HRM Trends and Challenges*, Harvard Business School Press, Boston, MA

Wood, S, de Menezes, L M and Lasaosa, A (2001) High involvement management and performance, Paper delivered at the Centre for Labour Market Studies, University of Leicester, May

Workplace Employee Relations Survey (2004) HMSO, Norwich

Part III

Work and Employment

This part of the handbook is concerned with the factors affecting employment in organizations. It explores the nature of work, the employment relationship and the important concept of the psychological contract.

Part III contents

14 Work

Key concepts and terms

- Financial flexibility
- Functional flexibility
- Numerical flexibility
- Work
- The flexible firm
- The lean organization
- Portfolio career

Learning outcomes

On completing this chapter you should be able to define these key concepts. You should also know about:

- The nature of work
- Feelings about work
- The future of work
- The essential components of work
- Organizational factors affecting work: the flexible firm and the lean firm

Introduction

The nature and meaning of work need to be taken into account when developing employment policies and practices. The aim of this chapter is to provide the basic information required to do this. This comprises the nature and significance of work for people, the factors that affect how work takes place within organizations, changes in the pattern of employment and the future of work.

The nature of work

Work is the exertion of effort and the application of knowledge and skills to achieve a purpose. Most people work to earn a living – to make money. But they also work because of the other satisfactions it brings, such as doing something worthwhile, a sense of achievement, prestige, recognition, the opportunity to use and develop abilities, the scope to exercise power, and companionship. Gallie *et al* (1994), quoting research conducted by the Social Change and Economic Life Initiative, found that 67 per cent of the people questioned worked for money but a surprisingly high proportion (27 per cent) said they worked for the intrinsic rewards money provides ('expressive reasons').

Within organizations, the nature of the work carried out by individuals and what they feel about it is governed by the employment relationship and the psychological contract, as considered in Chapters 15 and 16 respectively.

SOURCE REVIEW

Essential components of work, Thomas (1999)

- Work produces or achieves something (it is not an end in itself).
- Work involves a degree of obligation or necessity (it is a task set either by others or ourselves).
- Work involves effort and persistence (it is not wholly pleasurable, although there may be pleasurable elements in it).

The meaning of work

Research conducted by the Roffey Park Institute found that 70 per cent of employees were looking for 'more meaning in the workplace'. As the authors of the report, Holbeche and Springett (2004) commented:

> *The search for meaning appears to be part of a fundamental human need to feel of value and to make a difference... People need and want to belong to communities in which they can make meaningful contributions. Work, for many people, provides a source of identity and a feeling of togetherness. It gives us a sense of our status in society.*

As Noon and Blyton (2007) pointed out, work is regarded by many people as a central life activity – research has established that in terms of importance, respondents judged work to be second only to their family. They suggested that the significance of work arises through the work ethic, ie a feeling that it is morally necessary to work and seek paid employment rather than being idle.

Feelings about work

Research into employee motivation and the psychological contract by Guest *et al* (1996) and Guest and Conway (1997) obtained the following responses from the people they surveyed:

- work remains a central interest in the lives of most people;
- if they won the Lottery, 39 per cent would quit work and most of the others would continue working;
- asked to select the three most important things they look for in a job, 70 per cent of respondents cited pay, 62 per cent wanted interesting and varied work and only 22 per cent were looking for job security;
- 35 per cent claimed that they were putting in so much effort that they could not work any harder and a further 34 per cent claimed they were working very hard.

The 2004 Workplace Employee Relations Survey (WERS) covering 700,000 workplaces and 22.5 million employees established on how they felt at work. The results are summarized in Table 14.1.

Table 14.1 Feelings at work (WERS, 2004)

The job makes you feel:	All of the time %	Most of the time %	Some of the time %	Occasionally %	Never %
Tense	4	15	42	27	12
Calm	3	30	29	27	11
Relaxed	2	10	35	32	21
Worried	2	10	35	32	21
Uneasy	2	8	28	33	29
Content	5	33	30	22	11

This does not present an unduly gloomy picture. The percentage of people feeling either tense or calm some, more or all of the time was much the same. An equal number of people were never relaxed or worried and rather more were never uneasy; 69 per cent were content all, most or some of the time. The WERS survey also revealed that job-related well-being was higher in small organizations and workplaces than in large ones, higher among union members, falls with increased education and is U-shaped with regard to age (ie higher amongst younger and older employees than amongst the middle-aged).

An analysis by Brown *et al* (2008) of changes in job satisfaction between the 1998 and 2004 WERS surveys found significant increases in satisfaction with the sense of achievement from work together with improvements in perceptions of job security, the climate of employment relations and managerial responsiveness.

SOURCE REVIEW

Commitment to work, Gallie and White (1993)

Stronger:

- the more qualifications a person has;
- the more successful they feel they have been in their career;
- the higher they value 'hard work';
- the more they feel they have personal control over their destiny;
- the higher their preference for their current job;
- the lower their preference for 'an easy life';
- the higher their attachment to their current organization.

Organizational factors affecting work

The nature of work alters as organizations change in response to new demands and environmental pressures. The notions of the flexible firm and the 'lean' organization are particularly significant.

The flexible firm

The flexible firm is one in which there is structural and operational flexibility. The concept originated in the work of Doeringer and Priore (1971) and Loveridge and Mok (1979) but was popularized by Atkinson (1984).

Structural flexibility is present when the core of permanent employees is supplemented by a peripheral group of part-time employees, employees on short- or fixed-term contracts or subcontracted workers. The forms of operational flexibility are set out below.

Forms of operational flexibility

1. Functional flexibility, which is sought so that employees can be redeployed quickly and smoothly between activities and tasks. Functional flexibility may require multiskilling – workers who possess and can apply a number of skills, for example, both mechanical and electrical engineering, or multitasking – workers who carry out a number of different tasks, for example in a work team.
2. Numerical flexibility, which is sought so that the number of employees can be quickly and easily increased or decreased in line with even short-term changes in the level of demand for labour.
3. Financial flexibility, which provides for pay levels to reflect the state of supply and demand in the external labour market and also means the use of flexible pay systems that facilitate either functional or numerical flexibility.

Atkinson (1984) suggested that the growth of the flexible firm has involved the break-up of the labour force into increasingly peripheral, and therefore numerically flexible, groups of workers clustered around a numerically stable core group that will conduct the organization's key, firm-specific activities. This is usually called the 'core-periphery' view of the firm.

At the core, the focus is on functional flexibility. Shifting to the periphery, numerical flexibility becomes more important. As the market grows, the periphery expands to take up slack; as growth slows, the periphery contracts. In the core, only tasks and responsibilities change; the workers here are insulated from medium-term fluctuations in the market and can therefore enjoy a measure of job security, whereas those in the periphery are exposed to them.

Several concerns about the concept of the flexible firm have been raised by Marchington and Wilkinson (1996). First, it tends to fuse together description, prediction and prescription into a self-fulfilling prophesy. Second, the evidence of a significant increase in 'flexible firms' and flexibility within firms is lacking. Third, it is not a recent phenomenon – the proportion of people working part-time has grown for decades. Fourth, there are doubts about the costs and benefits of flexibility – sub-contracted workers can be expensive and part-time workers may have higher levels of absenteeism and lack commitment.

The lean organization

The term 'lean production' was popularized by Womack and Jones (1970) in *The Machine that Changed the World.* But the drive for leaner methods of working was confined initially to the car industry, as in Toyota, one of the pioneers of lean production, or more loosely, 'world class manufacturing'.

Lean production aims to add value by minimizing waste in terms of materials, time, space and people. Production systems associated with leanness include just-in-time, supply chain management, material resources planning and zero defects/right first time.

The concept of 'leanness' has since been extended to non-manufacturing organizations. This can often be number-driven and is implemented by means of a reduction in headcounts (downsizing) and a reduction in the number of levels of management and supervision (delayering). But there is no standard model of what a lean organization looks like. According to research conducted by Kinnie *et al* (1996) firms select from a menu the methods that meet their business needs. These include, other than delayering or the negative approach of downsizing, positive steps such as team-based work organizations, cross-functional management and development teams, emphasis on horizontal business processes rather than vertical structures, and HRM policies aimed at high performance and commitment and including communication programmes and participation in decision making.

Changes in the pattern of employment

Changes in the pattern of employment include the shift to a service-sector economy, the increasing number of female and part-time employees, greater employment flexibility, the changing size and distribution of the public sector, growth in the numbers of knowledge workers, growth in self-employment and the changing age structure.

The following analysis of the pattern of employment was made by ESRC (2008):

- In the third quarter of 2006 there were 29 million people employed in the UK and 1.7 million unemployed.

- Financial and business services account for about one in five jobs in the UK compared with about one in eight in 1986.
- In 1986 more than one in four jobs held by men were in manufacturing. By 2006 this had fallen to less than one in seven.
- The number of people in the UK normally working over 45 hours per week generally rose from 1992/93 until it peaked in the autumn of 1997. Since then it has been steadily in decline: now only one in five workers puts in a 45-plus hour week.

Career expectations

It is often said that the days of the lifelong career are over, especially for white-collar workers, and that the job security they previously enjoyed no longer exists. The evidence from the ESRC (2000) survey showed that this was not the case. Job tenure has not fallen but has in fact increased on average from six years and two months to seven years and four months. For men there has been a small decrease but for women there has been a significant increase.

The future of work

Futurologists, as noted by Nolan and Wood (2003), have been busy forecasting what is going to happen to work. Charles Handy (1984) was one of the first. He offered the notions of 'portfolio workers' who frequently changed their careers, a new 'knowledge economy' and the collapse of work in traditional industries. The full employment society, he claimed, was becoming the part-employment society. 'Labour and manual skills were yielding to knowledge as the basis for new business and new work... Hierarchies and bureaucracies were being supported by emerging networks and partnership and the one-organization career was becoming rarer.'

Pessimists such as Bridges (1995) and Rifkin (1995) have argued that growing insecurity, widening social divisions and higher levels of unemployment are the inevitable consequences of structural change, new information and communication technologies. Alternatively, optimists such as Leadbeater (2000) have held out the prospect of a world with limitless possibilities for creative, cooperative and socially useful work. But as Nolan and Wood (2003) comment, the evidence on work and employment patterns in Britain (see above) confounds many of these claims: 'Complexity, unevenness and the enduring features in the structure and relations of employment are crowded out by visions of universal paradigm shifts.'

Work – key learning points

The nature of work

Most people work to earn a living. But they also work because of the other satisfactions it brings, such as doing something worthwhile, a sense of achievement, prestige, recognition, the opportunity to use and develop abilities, the scope to exercise power, and companionship.

The essential components of work

- Work produces or achieves something (it is not an end in itself).
- Work involves a degree of obligation or necessity (it is a task set either by others or ourselves).
- Work involves effort and persistence (it is not wholly pleasurable, although there may be pleasurable elements in it).

Feelings about work

Work remains a central interest in the lives of most people.

Organizational factors affecting work

The nature of work alters as organizations change in response to new demands and environmental pressures. The notions of the flexible firm and the 'lean' organization are particularly significant.

The future of work

Futorologists have predicted various fundamental changes, 'paradigm shifts', in the nature of work but as Nolan and Wood (2003) comment, 'complexity, unevenness and the enduring features in the structure and relations of employment are crowded out by visions of universal paradigm shifts'.

Questions

1. What are the main changes that have taken place in the pattern of employment in recent years? Explain how these changes have affected your organization.
2. Your operations director, who is in charge of a large distribution centre and an associated customer service department, has asked you to explain how flexible working may benefit his operations, taking into account that there are marked seasonal fluctuations in customer demand. Prepare a memorandum that sets out the different types of flexibility available and suggests which of these might be appropriate.
3. Your managing director has sent you the following e-mail: 'I have heard about lean production but are the concepts involved applicable in any way to a firm like ours, which is not involved in manufacturing?' Draft your reply.

References

Atkinson, J (1984) Manpower strategies for flexible organizations, *Personnel Management*, August, pp 28–31

Bridges, M (1995) *Job Shift: How to prosper in a world without jobs*, Nicolas Brealey, London

Brown, A, Forde, C, Spencer, D and Charlwood, A (2008) Changes in HRM and job satisfaction, 1998–2004: evidence from the Workplace Employment Relations Survey, *Human Resource Management Journal*, **18** (3), pp 237–56

Doeringer, P and Priore, M (1971) *Internal Labour Markets and Labour Market Analysis*, Heath, Lexington, DC

ESRC (2000) *Working in Britain Survey*, ESRC Data Archives, University of Essex

ESRC (2008) *UK Fact Sheet – Workers in the UK*, www.esrc.ac.uk

Gallie, D and White, M (1993) *Employee Commitment and the Skills Revolution*, Policy Studies Institute, London

Gallie, D, Marsh, C and Vogler, C (1994) *Social Changes and the Experience of Unemployment*, Oxford University Press, Oxford

Guest, D E and Conway, N (1997) *Employee Motivation and the Psychological Contract*, IPD, London

Guest, D E, Conway, N and Briner, T (1996) *The State of the Psychological Contract in Employment*, IPD, London

Handy, C (1984) *The Future of Work*, Blackwell, Oxford

Holbeche, L and Springett, N (2004) *In Search of Meaning at Work*, Roffey Park Institute, Horsham

Kinnie, N, Hutchinson, S, Purcell, J, Rees, C, Scarborough, H and Terry, M (1996) *The People Management Implications of Leaner Methods of Working*, IPD, London

Leadbeater, C (2000) *Living on Thin Air: The new economy*, Viking, London

Loveridge, R and Mok, A (1979) *Theories of Labour Market Segmentation: A critique*, Martinus Nijhoff, The Hague

Marchington, M and Wilkinson, A (1996) *Core Personnel and Development*, Institute of Personnel and Development, London

Nolan, P and Wood, S (2003) Mapping the future of work, *British Journal of Industrial Relations*, **41** (2), pp 165–74

Noon, M and Blyton, P (2007) *The Realities of Work*, Palgrave Macmillan, Basingstoke

Rifkin, J (1995) *The End of Work: The decline of the global labour force and the dawn of the new economy*, Putnam, New York

Thomas, K (1999) Introduction, in (ed) K Thomas, *The Oxford Book of Work*, Oxford University Press, Oxford

Womack, J and Jones, D (1970) *The Machine that Changed the World*, Rawson, New York

Workplace Employee Relations Survey (2004) HMSO, Norwich

15 The Employment Relationship

Key concepts and terms

- Agency theory
- Exchange theory
- Labour process theory
- The pay–work bargain
- Procedural justice
- Relationship contract
- Trust
- The employment relationship
- High trust organization
- Mutuality
- Pluralist framework of reference
- Psychological contract
- Transactional contract
- Unitary framework of reference

Learning outcomes

On completing this chapter you should be able to define these key concepts. You should also know about:

- Basis of the employment relationship
- What is happening to the employment relationship
- Developing a high trust organization
- Employment relationship contracts
- Managing the employment relationship
- Theories explaining the employment relationship

Introduction

The employment relationship is one that is established whenever employers and employees work together. A positive employment relationship is required, one in which there is trust and mutuality – the state that exists when management and employees are interdependent and both benefit from this interdependency. Such a relationship provides a foundation for employment and employee relations policies, including the development of a climate of mutual trust. It governs much of what organizations need to be aware of in developing and applying human resource management and employee relations processes, policies and procedures. These need to be considered in terms of what they will or will not contribute to furthering a productive and rewarding relationship between all the parties concerned. This chapter describes the employment relationship, how it is managed and how a climate of trust can be created. Theories about the relationship are summarized at the end of the chapter.

The employment relationship defined

Organizations consist of employers and employees who relate to one another This is the employment relationship, which may be expressed formally by what Rubery *et al* (2002) regarded as its cornerstone, namely the contract of employment. In law an employee is someone working for an employer who has the ultimate right to tell the worker what to do. In the UK, the Employment Rights Act (1996) defines an 'employee' as a person who works under a contract of employment, the tacit assumption being that 'the employer' is the other party to the contract. This is sometimes called 'the pay–work bargain'. The employment relationship can additionally be defined formally by such means as procedure agreements and work rules.

But the employment relationship is also an informal and constant process that happens whenever an employer has dealings with an employee, and vice versa. Underpinning the employment relationship is the psychological contract, which expresses certain assumptions and expectations about what managers and employees have to offer and are willing to deliver. This is discussed in more detail in Chapter 16. The dimensions of the employment relationship as described by Kessler and Undy (1996) are shown in Figure 15.1.

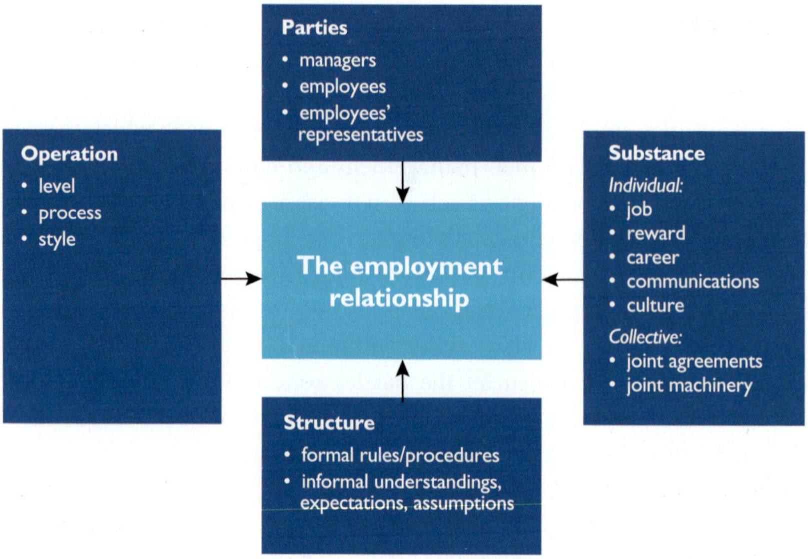

Figure 15.1 Dimensions of the employment relationship

The basis of the employment relationship

The starting point of the employment relationship is an undertaking by an employee to provide skill and effort to the employer in return for which the employer provides the employee with a salary or a wage (the pay–work bargain). Initially the relationship is founded on a legal contract. This may be a written contract, but the absence of such a contract does not mean that no contractual relationship exists. Employers and employees still have certain implied legal rights and obligations. The employer's obligations include the duty to pay salary or wages, provide a safe workplace, to act in good faith towards the employee and not to act in such a way as to undermine the trust and confidence of the employment relationship. The employee has corresponding obligations, which include obedience, competence, honesty and loyalty.

The employment relationship exists at different levels in the organization (management to employees generally, and managers to individual employees and their representatives or groups of people). The operation of the relationship will also be affected by processes such as communication and consultation, and by the management style prevailing throughout the organization or adopted by individual managers.

An important point to remember about the employment relationship is that, generally, it is the employer that has the power to dictate the contractual terms unless they have been fixed by collective bargaining. Individuals, except when they are much in demand, have little scope to vary the terms of the contract imposed upon them by employers. Inevitably there are conflicts of interest between employers that want to control compliant and high-performing employees and the employees who want to maintain their rights to 'a fair day's pay for a fair day's work'.

Employment relationship contracts

Two types of contracts defining the employment relationship have been distinguished by MacNeil (1985) and Rousseau and Wade-Benzoni (1994), namely relationship contracts and transactional contracts.

Types of employment relationship contracts

- Transactional contracts are formal contracts that have well-described terms of exchange between employer and employees, which are often expressed financially. They contain specified performance requirements.
- Relational contracts are largely informal contracts with more abstract terms and refer to an open-ended membership of the organization. Performance requirements attached to this continuing membership are incomplete or ambiguous.

There is also the psychological contract, which is implied rather than stated.

More specifically, the employment relationship is governed by express agreements between employers and employees including contracts of employment, the terms implied by common law and statutory requirements.

Express agreements

Express agreements consist of written contracts of employment but they may be conveyed orally at an interview or even set out in an advertisement. In addition, express terms may be included in collective agreements or works rules.

Contracts of employment

A formal contract is an agreement between two or more parties which the law will enforce. The essential elements that have to be present to make a contract enforceable are as follows:

- there must have been an offer by one party that has been accepted by the other party;
- there must be an intention to create legal relations;

- the terms agreed by the parties must be sufficiently certain to be enforceable;
- the agreement must be supported by consideration (ie some form of payment).

Contracts contain:

- express terms – those defined in writing or orally (eg pay, hours, holidays, pensions);
- implied terms – those that can be implied into the contract of employment by nature of the relationship, by the conduct of the parties or by custom and practice (note that an implied term cannot override or exclude an expressly agreed term or a term expressly included by statute);
- terms implied by statute – the duty of the parties to conform to statutory law.

Contracts may also include a statement of the duties involved in the job, ideally with a flexibility clause such as: 'the employee will perform such duties and will be responsible to such person, as the company may from time to time require'. In certain cases it may be stated that: 'The employee will work at different locations as required by the company.'

Contracts may consist of one or a number of documents:

- the letter of appointment;
- a written statement of express terms;
- other documents, such as staff handbooks, works rules, or collective agreements that are incorporated into the contract by being expressly referred to in the letter of appointment or written statement.

Common law

The common law obligations of employers include the duty to pay wages, provide work, cooperate with the employee, and take reasonable care of the health and safety of the employee. Employees, in turn, are expected to cooperate with the employer, be faithful to the employer, and take reasonable care in performing their duties.

Statutory requirements – written particulars

Written particulars (a statutory statement) of the main terms and conditions of employment must be given to all employees who work eight or more hours a week, within two months of starting work. Changes to terms have to be notified individually. The written statement must contain or refer to particulars of the following:

- the name of the employer and the employee;
- starting date;

- commencement of continuous service;
- the scale or rate of remuneration, or the method of calculating remuneration;
- the intervals at which remuneration is paid (eg weekly, monthly);
- hours of work and normal working hours;
- entitlement to holidays, including public holidays;
- entitlement to holiday pay, including entitlement to accrued holiday pay on terminating employment;
- provision of sick pay, if any;
- pensions and pension schemes;
- the length of notice the employee is obliged to give and is entitled to receive to terminate his or her contract of employment;
- the title of the job the employee is employed to do;
- the disciplinary rules that apply to the employee (or reference can be made to a document specifying these rules, which is reasonably accessible to the employee);
- in firms with 20 or more workers, employees will be entitled to additional information on how the company's training policy affects them.

What is happening to the employment relationship

Gallie *et al* (1998), in their analysis of the outcome of their Employment in Britain research programme, noted that while there have been shifts in the ways in people are employed, 'the evidence for a major change in the nature of the employment relationship was much less convincing'. But they did note a number of developments, as listed below.

SOURCE REVIEW

Developments in the employment relationship, Gallie *et al* (1998)

- New forms of management, often based explicitly or implicitly on HRM principles and emphasizing individual contracts rather than collective bargaining.
- There was some increase in task discretion but there was no evidence of a significant decline in managerial control; indeed, in some important respects control was intensified.
- Supervisory activity was still important.
- Integrative forms of management policy were centred on non-manual employees.

- The great majority of employees continued to attach a high level of importance to the intrinsically motivating aspects of work.
- The higher the level of skill, the more people were involved with their work.
- The raising of skill levels and the granting of increased discretion to employers are key factors in improving the quality of work experience.
- High levels of commitment to the organization can reduce absenteeism and labour turnover but there was no evidence that organizational commitment 'added anything over and above other organizational and task characteristics with regard to the quality of work performance'.

Managing the employment relationship

The dynamic and often nebulous nature of the employment relationship increases the difficulty of managing it. The problem is compounded because of the multiplicity of the factors that influence the contract – the culture of the organization, the prevailing management style, the values, espoused and practised, of top management, the existence or non-existence of a climate of trust, day-to-day interactions between employees and line managers, and the HR policies and practices of the business.

The latter are particularly important. The nature of the employment relationship is strongly influenced by HR actions. These cover all aspects of HRM. How people are treated in such areas as recruitment, performance reviews, promotion, career development, reward, involvement and participation, grievance handling, disciplinary procedures and redundancy will be particularly important. The ways in which people are required to carry out their work (including flexibility and multi-skilling), how performance expectations are expressed and communicated, how work is organized and how people are managed will also make a significant impact on the employment relationship. HR specialists can contribute to the development of a positive and productive employment relationship in the following ways:

- during recruitment interviews – presenting the unfavourable as well as the favourable aspects of a job in a 'realistic job preview';
- in induction programmes – communicating to new starters the organization's HR policies and procedures and its core values, indicating to them the standards of performance expected in such areas as quality and customer service, and spelling out requirements for flexibility;
- by issuing and updating employee handbooks that reinforce the messages delivered in induction programmes;

- by encouraging the development of performance management processes that ensure that performance expectations are agreed and reviewed regularly;
- by encouraging the use of personal development plans that spell out how continuous improvement of performance can be achieved, mainly by self-managed learning;
- by using learning and development programmes to underpin core values and define performance expectations;
- by ensuring through manager and team leader training that managers and team leaders understand their role in managing the employment relationship through such processes as performance management and team leadership;
- by encouraging the maximum amount of contact between managers and team leaders and their team members to achieve mutual understanding of expectations and to provide a means of two-way communications;
- by adopting a general policy of transparency – ensuring that on all matters that affect them, employees know what is happening, why it is happening and the impact it will make on their employment, development and prospects;
- by developing HR procedures covering grievance handling, discipline, equal opportunities, promotion and redundancy and ensuring that they are implemented fairly and consistently;
- by developing and communicating HR policies covering the major areas of employment, development, reward and employee relations;
- by ensuring that the reward system is developed and managed to achieve equity, fairness, consistency and transparency in all aspects of pay and benefits;
- generally, by advising on employee relations procedures, processes and issues that further good collective relationships.

These approaches to managing the employment relationship cover all aspects of people management. It is important to remember, however, that this is a continuous process. The effective management of the relationship means ensuring that values are upheld and that a transparent, consistent and fair approach is adopted in dealing with all aspects of employment. It is also important to remember that perhaps the best way of improving the employment relationship is to develop a high trust organization.

Developing a high trust organization

A high trust organization is one in which high levels of trust exist between employees and management. A climate of trust is an essential ingredient in a positive employment relationship. Trust, as defined by the *Oxford English Dictionary,* is a firm belief that a person may be relied on. An alternative definition has been provided by Shaw (1997) to the effect that trust is the 'belief that those on whom we depend will meet our expectations of them'. These expectations are dependent on 'our assessment of another's responsibility to meet our needs'.

It has been suggested by Herriot *et al* (1998) that trust should be regarded as social capital – the fund of goodwill in any social group that enables people within it to collaborate with one another. Thompson (1998) sees trust as a 'unique human resource capability that helps the organization fulfil its competitive advantage' – a core competency that leads to high business performance. Thus there is a business need to develop a high trust organization, as described below.

SOURCE REVIEW

A high trust organization, Fox (1973)

In a high trust organization, participants share certain ends or values; bear towards each other a diffuse sense of long-term obligations; offer each other spontaneous support without narrowly calculating the cost or anticipating any short-term reciprocation; communicate honestly and freely; are ready to repose their fortunes in each other's hands; and give each other the benefit of any doubt that may arise with respect to goodwill or motivation.

This ideal state may seldom, if ever, be attained, but it does represent a picture of an effective organization in which, as Thompson (1998) noted, trust 'is an outcome of good management'. He also commented that a number of writers have generally concluded that trust is 'not something that can, or should, be directly managed'. He cites Sako (1994) who wrote that: 'Trust is a cultural norm which can rarely be created intentionally because attempts to create trust in a calculative manner would destroy the effective basis of trust.'

In the end trust is not to do with managing people or processes, but is more about relationships and mutual support. Trust is created and maintained by managerial behaviour and by the development of better mutual understanding of expectations – employers of employees, and employees of employers.

Clearly, the sort of behaviour that is most likely to engender trust is when management is honest with people, keeps its word (delivers the deal) and practices what it preaches. Organizations that espouse core values ('people are our greatest asset') and then proceed to ignore them will be low-trust organizations.

More specifically, trust will be developed if management acts fairly, equitably and consistently, if a policy of transparency is implemented, if intentions and the reasons for proposals or decisions are communicated both to employees generally and to individuals, if there is full involvement in developing reward processes, and if mutual expectations are agreed through performance management.

Failure to meet these criteria, wholly or in part, is perhaps the main reason why so many performance-related pay schemes have not lived up to expectations. The starting point is to understand and apply the principles of distributive and procedural justice.

When do employees trust management?

Management is more likely to be trusted by employees when the latter:

- believe that the management means what it says;
- observe that management does what it says it is going to do – suiting the action to the word;
- know from experience that management, in the words of Guest and Conway (1998), 'delivers the deal – it keep its word and fulfils its side of the bargain';
- feel they are treated justly.

Distributive, procedural and natural justice

To treat people justly is to deal with them fairly and equitably. Leventhal (1980), following Adams (1965), distinguished between distributive and procedural justice, and the principle of natural justice has been enshrined in employment law, especially the law dealing with dismissal.

Distributive justice refers to how rewards are distributed. People will feel that they have been treated justly in this respect if they believe that rewards have been distributed in accordance with their contributions, that they receive what was promised to them and that they get what they need.

Procedural justice refers to the ways in which managerial decisions are made and personnel procedures are managed. The five factors that affect perceptions of procedural justice as identified by Tyler and Bies (1990) are:

1. Adequate consideration of an employee's viewpoint.
2. Suppression of personal bias towards an employee.
3. Applying criteria consistently across employees.
4. Providing early feedback to employees about the outcome of decisions.
5. Providing employees with an adequate explanation of decisions made.

Natural justice refers to how people are treated in disciplinary and dismissal cases. The three principles are:

1. Individuals should know the standards of performance they are expected to meet and the rules to which they are expected to conform.
2. They should be given a clear indication of where they are failing or what rules they have broken.
3. Except in cases of gross misconduct, they should be given an opportunity to improve before disciplinary action is taken.

Renewing trust

As suggested by Herriot *et al* (1988), if trust is lost, a four-step programme is required for its renewal:

1. Admission by top management that it has paid insufficient attention in the past to employees' diverse needs.
2. A limited process of contracting whereby a particular transition to a different way of working for a group of employees is done in a form that takes individual needs into account.
3. Establishing 'knowledge-based' trust, which is based not on a specific transactional deal but on a developing perception of trustworthiness.
4. Achieving trust based on identification in which each party empathizes with each other's needs and therefore takes them on board themselves (although this final state is seldom reached in practice).

Theories explaining the employment relationship

The meaning of the employment relationship has been explained in a number of theories, summarized below.

Labour process theory

Labour process theory was originally formulated by Karl Marx (translated in 1976). His thesis was that surplus is appropriated from labour by paying it less than the value it adds to the labour process. Capitalists therefore design the labour process to secure the extraction of surplus value. The human capacity to produce is subordinated to the exploitative demands of the capitalist, which is an alien power confronting the worker who becomes a 'crippled monstrosity by furthering his skill as if in a forcing house through the suppression of a whole world of productive drives and inclinations'.

Considerably later, a version of labour process theory was set out by Braverman (1974). His view was that the application of modern management techniques, in combination with mechanization and automation, secures the real subordination of labour and de-skilling of work in the office as well as the shop floor. He stated that the removal of all forms of control from the worker is 'the ideal towards which management tends, and in pursuit of which it uses every productive innovation shaped by science'. He saw this as essentially the application of 'Taylorism' (ie F W Taylor's concept of scientific management, meaning the use of systematic observation and measurement, task specialism and, in effect, the reduction of workers to the level of efficiently functioning machines).

Braverman's notion of labour process theory has been criticized as being simplistic by subsequent commentators such as Littler and Salaman (1982) who argue that there are numerous determinants in the control of the labour process. And Friedman (1977) believes that Braverman's version neglects the diverse and sophisticated character of management control as it responds not only to technological advances but also to changes in the degree and intensity of worker resistance and new product and labour market conditions. Storey (1985) has commented that 'the labour process bandwagon… is now holed and patched beyond repair'.

But labour process theory continues to thrive in different forms. It was claimed by Edwards (1990) that relationships between capital and labour are ones of 'structured antagonism'. Newton and Findlay (1996) believed that labour process theory explains how management has at its disposal a range of mechanisms through which control is exercised: 'Job performance and its assessment are at the heart of the labour process.' Management, according to Newton and Findlay is constantly seeking ways to improve the effectiveness of control mechanisms to achieve compliance. Managers 'try to squeeze the last drop of surplus value' out of their labour.

Thompson and Harley (2007) noted that: 'The notion of the workplace as contested terrain is a central motif of labour process theory.' They pointed out that what is happening is a process of 'capitalizing on humanity' rather than investing in human capital. However, they did comment that; 'In the employment relationship there will always be (actual and potential) conflict, but simultaneously there will be shared interests.' And they suggested that: 'In an environment where employee skills and commitment are central to organizational success, it is precisely by giving more that organizations will gain more.'

Agency theory

Agency or principal agent theory indicates that principals (owners and managers) have to develop ways of monitoring and controlling the activities of their agents (staff). Agency theory suggests that principals may have problems in ensuring that agents do what they are told. It is necessary to clear up ambiguities by setting objectives and monitoring performance to ensure that objectives are achieved.

Agency theory has been criticized by Gomez-Mejia and Balkin (1992) as 'managerialist'. As Armstrong (1996) wrote: 'It looks at the employment relationships purely from management's point of view and regards employees as objects to be motivated by the carrot and stick. It is a dismal theory, which suggests that people cannot be trusted.'

Exchange theory

Exchange theory sets out to explain organizational behaviour in terms of the rewards and costs incurred in the interaction between employers and employees. There are four concepts:

1. Rewards – payoffs that satisfy needs emerging from the interactions between individuals and their organizations.
2. Costs – fatigue, stress, anxiety, punishments and the value of rewards that people have lost because of lack of opportunity.
3. Outcomes – rewards minus costs: if positive the interaction yields a 'profit' and this is satisfactory as long as it exceeds the minimum level of expectation.
4. Level of comparisons – people evaluate the outcome of an interaction against the profit they are foregoing elsewhere.

Unitary and pluralist frames of reference

One of the often expressed aims of human resource management is to increase the commitment of people to the organization by getting them to share its views and values and integrate their own work objectives with those of the organization. This concept adopts a unitary frame of reference; in other words, as expressed by Gennard and Judge (2005), organizations are assumed to be 'harmonious and integrated, all employees sharing the organizational goals and working as members of one team'. Alternatively, the pluralist perspective as expressed by Cyert and March (1963) sees organizations as coalitions of interest groups and recognizes the legitimacy of different interests and values. Organizational development programmes which, amongst other things, aim to increase commitment and teamwork, adopt a unitary framework. But it can be argued that this is a managerialist assumption and that the legitimate interests of the other members of a pluralist society – the stakeholders – will have their own interests that should be respected.

The employment relationship – key learning points

Basis of the employment relationship

An undertaking by an employee to provide skill and effort to the employer in return for which the employer provides the employee with a salary or a wage. The employer's obligations also include the duty to provide a safe workplace, to act in good faith towards the employee and not to act in such a way as to undermine the trust and confidence of the employment relationship. The employee has corresponding obligations, which include obedience, competence, honesty and loyalty.

Employment relationship contracts

The three types of employment relationship contracts are transactional, relational and psychological.

Three of the more important developments in the employment relationship (Gallie *et al*, 1998) are:

1. New forms of management, often based explicitly or implicitly on HRM principles and emphasizing individual contracts rather than collective bargaining.
2. There was some increase in task discretion but there was no evidence of a significant decline in managerial control; indeed, in some important respects control was intensified.
3. The higher the level of skill, the more people were involved with their work.

Managing the employment relationship

The dynamic and often nebulous nature of the employment relationship and the multiplicity of the factors that influence the contract increase the difficulty of managing it.

Developing a high trust organization

A high trust organization exists when management is honest with people, keeps its word (delivers the deal) and practices what it preaches. Trust is created and maintained by managerial behaviour and by the development of better mutual understanding of expectations – employers of employees, and employees of employers.

Theories explaining the employment relationship

The theories explaining the employment relationship are labour process theory, agency theory and exchange theory.

Questions

1. What is the basis and the main features of the employment relationship?
2. It was claimed by Edwards (1990) that relationships between capital and labour are ones of 'structured antagonism'. What does this mean and to what extent is it true?

Questions (continued)

3. What is labour process theory and how relevant is it in explaining the employment relationship?
4. After a meeting of the works council the chief executive turned to you and said, 'I'm worried, they don't seem to trust us. What can we do about it?' Write an e-mail to her to explain what needs to be done.

References

Adams, J S (1965) Injustice in social exchange, in (ed) L Berkowitz, *Advances in Experimental Psychology*, Academic Press, New York

Armstrong M (1996) *A Handbook of Personnel Management Practice*, 6th edn, Kogan Page, London

Braverman, H (1974) *Labour and Monopoly Capital*, Monthly Review Press, New York

Cyert, R M and March, J G (1963) *A Behavioural Theory of the Firm*, Prentice-Hall, Englewood Cliffs, NJ

Edwards, P K (1990) Understanding conflict in the labor process: the logic and anatomy of struggle, in *Labor Process Theory*, Macmillan, London

Fox, A (1973) *Beyond Contract*, Faber and Faber, London

Friedman, A (1977) *Industry and Labour: Class structure and monopoly capitalism*, Macmillan, London

Gallie, D, White, M, Cheng, Y and Tomlinson, M (1998) *Restructuring the Employment Relationship*, The Clarendon Press, Oxford

Gennard, J and Judge, G (2005) *Employee Relations*, 3rd edn, CIPD, London

Gomez-Mejia, L R and Balkin, D B (1992) *Compensation: Organizational strategy and firm performance*, South-Western Publishing, CA

Guest, D E and Conway, N (1998) *Fairness at Work and the Psychological Contract*, IPD, London

Herriot, P, Hirsh, W and Riley, P (1988) *Trust and Transition: Managing the employment relationship*, Wiley, Chichester

Kessler, S and Undy, R (1996) *The New Employment Relationship: Examining the psychological contract*, IPM, London

Leventhal, G S (1980) What should be done with equity theory?, in (eds) G K Gergen, M S Greenberg and R H Willis, *Social Exchange: Advances in theory and research*, Plenum, New York

Littler, C and Salaman, (1982) Bravermania and beyond: recent theories of the labour process, *Sociology*, **16** (2), pp 215–69

Macneil, R (1985) Relational contract: what we do and do not know, *Wisconsin Law Review*, pp 483–525

Marx, K (1867, translated in 1976) *Capital*, Harmondsworth, Penguin

Newton, T and Findlay, P (1996) Playing god? The performance of appraisal, *Human Resource Management Journal*, **6** (3), pp 42–56

Rousseau, D M and Wade-Benzoni, K A (1994) Linking strategy and human resource practices: how employee and customer contracts are created, *Human Resource Management*, **33** (3), pp 463–89

Rubery, J, Earnshaw, J, Marchington, M, Cooke, F L and Vincent, S (2002) Changing organizational forms and the employment relationship, *Journal of Management Studies*, **39** (5), pp 645–72

Sako, M (1994) The informational requirement of trust in supplier relations: evidence from Japan, the UK and the USA, unpublished

Shaw, R B (1997) *Trust in the Balance*, Jossey-Bass, San Francisco, CA

Storey, J (1985) The means of management control, *Sociology*, **19** (2), pp 193–212

Thompson, M (1998) Trust and reward, in (eds) S Perkins and St John Sandringham, *Trust, Motivation and Commitment: A reader*, Strategic Remuneration Research Centre, Faringdon

Thompson, P and Harley, B (2007) HRM and the worker: labour process perspectives, in (eds) P Boxall, J Purcell and P Wright, *Oxford Handbook of Human Resource Management*, Oxford University Press, Oxford

Tyler, T R and Bies, R J (1990) Beyond formal procedures: the interpersonal context of procedural justice, in (ed) J S Carrol, *Applied Social Psychology and Organizational Settings*, Lawrence Erlbaum, Hillsdale, NJ

16

The Psychological Contract

Key concepts and terms

- Employability
- Social exchange theory
- The psychological contract

Learning outcomes

On completing this chapter you should be able to define these key concepts. You should also know about:

- The psychological contract defined
- The significance of the psychological contract
- Changes to the psychological contract
- How psychological contracts develop
- The psychological contract and the employment relationship
- The core of the psychological contract
- The state of the psychological contract
- Developing a positive psychological contract

Introduction

The psychological contract underpins the employment relationship. This chapter defines the psychological contract, explains its significance and describes how it is changing.

The psychological contract defined

A psychological contract is a set of unwritten expectations that exist between individual employees and their employers. As Guest (2007) noted, it is concerned with: 'The perceptions of both parties to the employment relationship, organization and individual, of the reciprocal promises and obligations implied in that relationship.' A psychological contract is a system of beliefs that encompasses the actions employees believe are expected of them and what response they expect in return from their employer and, reciprocally, the actions employers believe are expected of them and what response they expect in return from their employees.

The concept of the psychological contract is commonly traced back to the early work of Argyris (1957) and to social exchange theory (Blau, 1964). The latter explains social change and stability as a process of negotiated exchanges between parties. However, the key developments leading to its current use as an analytical framework were provided mainly by Schein (1965), who explained that: 'The notion of a psychological contract implies that there is an unwritten set of expectations operating at all times between every member of an organization and the various managers and others in that organization.' This definition was amplified by Rousseau and Wade-Benzoni (1994) as follows.

SOURCE REVIEW

Psychological contracts, Rousseau and Wade-Benzoni (1994)

Psychological contracts refer to beliefs that individuals hold regarding promises made, accepted and relied upon between themselves and another. (In the case of organizations, these parties include an employee, client, manager, and/or organization as a whole.) Because psychological contracts represent how people interpret promises and commitments, both parties in the same employment relationship (employer and employee) can have different views regarding specific terms.

Within organizations, as Katz and Kahn (1966) pointed out, every role is basically a set of behavioural expectations. These expectations are often implicit – they are not defined in the employment contract. Basic models of motivation such as expectancy theory (Vroom, 1964) and operant conditioning (Skinner, 1974) maintain that employees behave in ways they expect will produce positive outcomes. But they do not necessarily know what to expect.

SOURCE REVIEW

Expectations in the psychological contract, Rousseau and Greller (1994)

The ideal contract in employment would detail expectations of both employee and employer. Typical contracts, however, are incomplete due to bounded rationality which limits individual information seeking, and to a changing organizational environment that makes it impossible to specify all conditions up front. Both employee and employer are left to fill up the blanks.

Employees may expect to be treated fairly as human beings, to be provided with work that uses their abilities, to be rewarded equitably in accordance with their contribution, to be able to display competence, to have opportunities for further growth, to know what is expected of them and to be given feedback (preferably positive) on how they are doing. Employers may expect employees to do their best on behalf of the organization – 'to put themselves out for the company' – to be fully committed to its values, to be compliant and loyal, and to enhance the image of the organization with its customers and suppliers. Sometimes these assumptions are justified – often they are not. Mutual misunderstandings can cause friction and stress and lead to recriminations and poor performance, or to a termination of the employment relationship.

To summarize in the words of Guest and Conway (1998), the psychological contract lacks many of the characteristics of the formal contract: 'It is not generally written down, it is somewhat blurred at the edges, and it cannot be enforced in a court or tribunal.'

SOURCE REVIEW

The psychological contract as defined by Guest *et al* (1996)

The psychological contract is concerned with assumptions, expectations, promises and mutual obligations. It creates attitudes and emotions which form and govern behaviour. A psychological contract is implicit. It is also dynamic – it develops over time as experience accumulates, employment conditions change and employees re-evaluate their expectations.

The psychological contract and the employment relationship

The psychological contract is best seen as a metaphor; a word or phrase borrowed from another context that helps us make sense of our experience. The psychological contract is a way of interpreting the state of the employment relationship.

As described by Guest *et al* (1996), the psychological contract may provide some indication of the answers to the two fundamental employment relationship questions that individuals pose: 'What can I reasonably expect from the organization?' and 'What should I reasonably be expected to contribute in return?' But it is unlikely that the psychological contract and therefore the employment relationship will ever be fully understood by either party.

The aspects of the employment relationship covered by the psychological contact will include from the employee's point of view:

- how they are treated in terms of fairness, equity and consistency;
- security of employment;
- scope to demonstrate competence;
- career expectations and the opportunity to develop skills;
- involvement and influence;
- trust in the management of the organization to keep their promises.

From the employer's point of view, the psychological contract covers such aspects of the employment relationship as competence, effort, compliance, commitment and loyalty.

SOURCE REVIEW

What employees and employers want, Guest *et al* (1996)

While employees may want what they have always wanted – security, a career, fair rewards, interesting work and so on – employers no longer feel able or obliged to provide these. Instead, they have been demanding more of their employees in terms of greater input and tolerance of uncertainty and change, while providing less in return, in particular less security and more limited career prospects.

The core of the psychological contract

A model of the psychological contract as formulated by Guest *et al* (1996) suggests that the core of the contract can be measured in terms of fairness of treatment, trust, and the extent to which the explicit deal or contract is perceived to be delivered. The full model is illustrated in Figure 16.1.

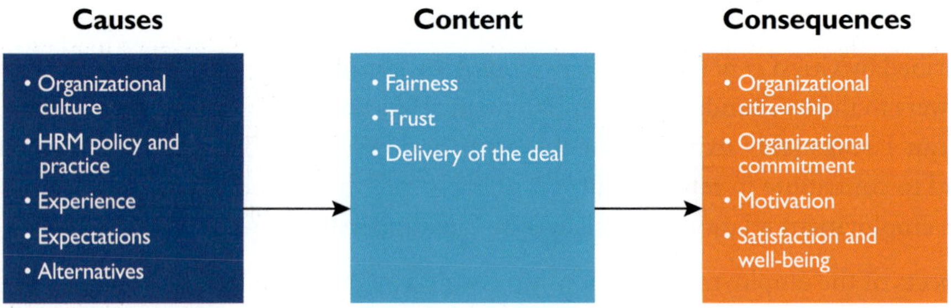

Figure 16.1 A model of the psychological contract

The significance of the psychological contract

As suggested by Spindler (1994): 'A psychological contract creates emotions and attitudes which form and control behaviour'. Its significance was summarized by Sims (1994) as follows.

SOURCE REVIEW

The significance of the psychological contract, Sims (1994)

A balanced psychological contract is necessary for a continuing, harmonious relationship between the employee and the organization. However, the violation of the psychological contract can signal to the participants that the parties no longer shared (or never shared) a common set of values or goals.

The concept highlights the fact that employee/employer expectations take the form of unarticulated assumptions. Disappointments on the part of management as well as employees may therefore be inevitable. These disappointments can, however, be alleviated if management appreciate that one of their key roles is to manage expectations, which means clarifying what they believe employees should achieve, the competences they should possess and the values they should uphold. And this is a matter not just of articulating and stipulating these requirements but of discussing and agreeing them with individuals and teams.

The psychological contract governs the continuing development of the employment relationship, which is constantly evolving over time. But how the contract is developing and the impact it makes may not be fully understood by any of the parties involved. Spindler (1994) comments that: 'In a psychological contract the rights and obligations of the parties have not been articulated much less agreed to. The parties do not express their expectations and, in fact, may be quite incapable of doing so.'

People who have no clear idea about what they expect may, if such unexpressed expectations have not been fulfilled, have no clear idea why they have been disappointed. But they will be aware that something does not feel right. And a company staffed by 'cheated' individuals who expect more than they get is heading for trouble.

Schein (1965) made the following points about the importance of the psychological contract.

SOURCE REVIEW

Effectiveness and organizational commitment depend on the following, Schein (1965)

1. The degree to which people's expectations of what the organization will provide to them and what they owe the organization in return matches what the organization's expectations are of what it will give and get in return.
2. The nature of what is actually to be exchanged (assuming there is some agreement) – money in exchange for time at work; social need satisfaction and security in exchange for hard work and loyalty; opportunities for self-actualization and challenging work in exchange for high productivity, high quality work, and creative effort in the service of organizational goals; or various combinations of these and other things.

The research conducted by Guest and Conway (2002) led to the conclusion that:

> *The management of the psychological contract is a core task of management and acknowledged as such by many senior HR and employment relations managers, and shows that it has a positive association with a range of outcomes within the employment relationship and is a useful way of conceptualizing that relationship.*

Changes to the psychological contract

The nature of the psychological contract is changing in many organizations in response to changes in their external and internal environments. The ways in which psychological contracts are changing as suggested by Hiltrop (1995) are shown in Table 16.1.

Table 16.1 Changes in the psychological contract

From	To
• Imposed relationship (compliance, command and control • Permanent employment relationship	• Mutual relationship (commitment, participation and involvement) • Variable employment relationship – people and skills only obtained and retained when required

Table 16.1 *continued*

From	To
• Focus on promotion • Finite duties • Meeting job requirements • Emphasis on job security and loyalty to the company • Training provided by the organization	• Focus on lateral career development • Multiple roles • Add value • Emphasis on employability and loyalty to own career skills • Opportunities for self-managed learning

Hiltrop suggests that a new psychological contract is emerging – one that is more situational and short-term and which assumes that each party is much less dependent on the other for survival and growth. He believes that in its most naked form, the new contract could be defined as follows:

> *There is no job security. The employee will be employed as long as he or she adds value to the organization, and is personally responsible for finding new ways to add value. In return, the employee has the right to demand interesting and important work, has the freedom and resources to perform it well, receives pay that reflects his or her contribution, and gets the experience and training needed to be employable here or elsewhere.*

State of the psychological contract 2004

The 2004 Workplace Employee Relations Survey (published in 2005) surveyed 21,624 employees in workplaces employing more than 10 people about their level of job satisfaction. The results are shown in Table 16.2.

Table 16.2 Job satisfaction (WERS, 2004)

	Very satisfied %	Satisfied %	Neither %	Dissatisfied %	Very dissatisfied %
Sense of achievement	18	52	19	8	3
Scope for using initiative	20	52	19	8	3

Table 16.2 *continued*

	Very satisfied %	Satisfied %	Neither %	Dissatisfied %	Very dissatisfied %
Influence over job	12	15	28	11	3
Training	11	40	26	16	7
Pay	4	31	26	28	13
Job security	13	50	22	11	5
Work itself	17	55	19	7	3
Involvement in decision making	8	30	39	17	6

The only area in which there was more dissatisfaction than satisfaction was pay. A higher proportion than might have been expected (72 per cent) was satisfied or very satisfied with the work itself and equally high percentages were satisfied with regard to having a sense of achievement and scope for using initiative.

How psychological contracts develop

Psychological contracts are not developed by means of a single transaction; they evolve over time and can be multi-faceted. There are many contract makers who exert influence over the whole duration of an employee's involvement with an organization. Spindler (1994) comments that:

> *Every day we create relationships by means other than formal contracts... As individuals form relationships they necessarily bring their accumulated experience and developed personalities with them. In ways unknown to them what they expect from the relationship reflects the sum total of their conscious and unconscious learning to date.*

The problem with psychological contracts is that employees are often unclear about what they want from the organization or what they can contribute to it. Some employees are equally unclear about what they expect from their employees.

Because of these factors, and because a psychological contract is essentially implicit, it is likely to develop in an unplanned way with unforeseen consequences. Anything that management does or is perceived as doing that affects the interests of employees will modify the psychological contract. Similarly the actual or perceived behaviour of employees, individually or collectively, will affect an employer's concept of the contract.

Developing and maintaining a positive psychological contract

As Guest *et al* (1996) point out:

> *A positive psychological contract is worth taking seriously because it is strongly linked to higher commitment to the organization, higher employee satisfaction and better employment relations. Again this reinforces the benefits of pursuing a set of progressive HRM practices.*

They also emphasize the importance of a high-involvement climate and suggest in particular that HRM practices such as the provision of opportunities for learning, training and development, focus on job security, promotion and careers, minimizing status differentials, fair reward systems and comprehensive communication and involvement processes will all contribute to a positive psychological contract. The steps required to develop a positive psychological contract are shown below.

Steps required to develop a positive psychological contract

- Define expectations during recruitment and induction programmes.
- Communicate and agree expectations as part of the continuing dialogue that is implicit in good performance management practices.
- Adopt a policy of transparency on company policies and procedures and on management's proposals and decisions as they affect people.
- Generally treat people as stakeholders, relying on consensus and cooperation rather than control and coercion.

On the basis of their research, Guest and Conway (2002) emphasize the importance of communication in shaping the psychological contract, especially at the recruitment and induction stage when promises and commitments can be made by employers on such matters as interesting work, learning and development opportunities, not to make unreasonable demands on employees, feedback on performance, fair treatment, work/life balance, a reasonable degree of security and a safe working environment. They concluded that following the recruitment and induction stage, communication is most effective if it is personal and job-related. Top-down communication is less important. They also stressed that a positive psychological contract can only be achieved if management keeps its word – if it does not breach the contract.

The psychological contract – key learning points

The psychological contract defined

A psychological contract is a set of unwritten expectations that exist between individual employees and their employers. It is a system of beliefs that encompasses the actions employees believe are expected of them and what response they expect in return from their employer, and, reciprocally, the actions employers believe are expected of them and what response they expect in return from their employees.

The psychological contract and the employment relationship

The aspects of the employment relationship covered by the psychological contact will include from the employee's point of view:

- how they are treated in terms of fairness, equity and consistency;
- security of employment;
- scope to demonstrate competence;
- career expectations and the opportunity to develop skills;
- involvement and influence;
- trust in the management of the organization to keep their promises.

From the employer's point of view, the psychological contract covers such aspects of the employment relationship as competence, effort, compliance, commitment and loyalty.

The core of the psychological contract

The core of the psychological contract can be measured in terms of fairness of treatment, trust, and the extent to which the explicit deal or contract is perceived to be delivered.

The significance of the psychological contract

A psychological contract creates emotions and attitudes that form and control behaviour (Spindler, 1994).

Changes to the psychological contract

The nature of the psychological contract is changing in many organizations in response to changes in their external and internal environments. For example, there is more focus on mutuality, a variable employment relationship and employability.

The state of the psychological contract

A national survey (WERS) in 2004 found that the only area in which there was more dissatisfaction than satisfaction was pay. A higher proportion than might have been expected (72 per cent) was satisfied or very satisfied with the work itself and equally

The psychological contract – key learning points

high percentages were satisfied with regard to having a sense of achievement and scope for using initiative.

How psychological contracts develop

Psychological contracts are not developed by means of a single transaction; they evolve over time and can be multi-faceted.

Steps required to develop a positive psychological contract

- Define expectations during recruitment and induction programmes.
- Communicate and agree expectations as part of the continuing dialogue that is implicit in good performance management practices.
- Adopt a policy of transparency on company policies and procedures and on management's proposals and decisions as they affect people.
- Generally treat people as stakeholders, relying on consensus and cooperation rather than control and coercion.

Questions

1. You have been asked to write a short piece for your CIPD branch magazine on the psychological contract and its significance. Prepare an outline of the article.
2. You have been asked by your managing director to let her have a brief report on what your company can do to develop a more positive psychological contract. Prepare the report.
3. How do psychological contracts develop?

References

Argyris, C (1957) *Personality and Organization*, Harper & Row, New York

Blau, P (1964) *Exchange and power in social life*, Wiley, New York

Guest, D (2007) HRM: Towards a new psychological contract, in (eds) P Boxall, J Purcell and P Wright, *Oxford Handbook of Human Resource Management*, Oxford University Press, Oxford

Guest, D E and Conway, N (1998) *Fairness at Work and the Psychological Contract*, IPD, London

Guest, D E and Conway, N (2002) Communicating the psychological contract: an employee perspective, *Human Resource Management Journal*, **12** (2), pp 22–39

Guest, D E, Conway, N and Briner, T (1996) *The State of the Psychological Contract in Employment*, IPD, London

Hiltrop, J M (1995) The changing psychological contract: the human resource challenge of the 1990s, *European Management Journal*, **13** (3), pp 286–94
Katz, D and Kahn, R (1966) *The Social Psychology of Organizations*, John Wiley, New York
Rousseau, D M and Greller, M M (1994) Human resource practices: administrative contract makers, *Human Resource Management*, **33** (3), pp 385–401
Rousseau, D M and Wade-Benzoni, K A (1994) Linking strategy and human resource practices: how employee and customer contracts are created, *Human Resource Management*, **33** (3), pp 463–89
Schein, E H (1965) *Organizational Psychology*, Prentice-Hall, Englewood Cliffs, NJ
Sims, R R (1994) Human resource management's role in clarifying the new psychological contract, *Human Resource Management*, **33** (3), pp, 373–82
Skinner, B F (1974) *About Behaviourism*, Cape, London
Spindler, G S (1994) Psychological contracts in the workplace: a lawyer's view, *Human Resource Management*, **33** (3) pp 325–33
Vroom, V (1964) *Work and Motivation*, Wiley, New York
Workshop Employee Relations Survey (2004) DTI, London

Part IV

Organizational Behaviour

As defined by Huczyinski and Buchanan, 2007 organizational behaviour is concerned with 'the study of the structure, functioning and performance of organizations, and the behaviour of groups and individuals within them'.

The purpose of this part of the book is to outline a basic set of concepts and to provide analytical tools that will enable HR specialists to diagnose organizational behaviour and to take appropriate actions. Following an introduction to the concept of organizational behaviour (Chapter 17), a general analysis of the characteristics of individuals at work is provided (Chapter 18).

The notions of individual motivation, employee engagement and commitment are then explored in Chapters 19, 20 and 21. These terms are sometimes confused but are distinguished in this part as follows:

- Motivation is the strength and direction of behaviour and the factors that influence people to behave in certain ways in carrying out their work.
- Employee engagement takes place when people at work are interested in and positive, even excited, about their jobs and are prepared to go the extra mile to get them done to the best of their ability.
- Organizational commitment is the strength of an individual's identification with, and involvement in, a particular organization.

Thus, motivation could be regarded as task-oriented, engagement could be seen as job-oriented and commitment seen as organization-oriented.

The part ends with a description of how organizations function (Chapter 22) and an examination of the concept of organizational culture (Chapter 23).

Part IV contents

Reference

Huczynski, A A and Buchanan, D A (2007) *Organizational Behaviour,* 6th edn, FT Prentice Hall, Harlow

17 The Essence of Organizational Behaviour

Key concepts and terms

- Behavioural science
- Process theory
- Variance theory
- Organizational behaviour
- Social sciences

Learning outcomes

On completing this chapter you should be able to define these key concepts. You should also know about:

- The characteristics of organizational behaviour
- The sources and applications of organization behaviour theory
- The factors affecting organizational behaviour
- The significance of organizational behaviour theory

Introduction

People perform their roles within complex systems called organizations. The study of organizational behaviour focuses on people within the context of their organizations – analysing and understanding what they do, how they do it and the factors that affect their behaviour. The aim is to provide the basis for developing HR policies and practices which will lead to improved organizational capability.

Organizational behaviour defined

'Organizational behaviour' is the term used to describe how people within their organizations act, individually or in groups, and how organizations function, in terms of their structure, processes and culture. As noted by Wood (1995) it was first used in the late 1950s. The following are three other definitions:

- The study of the structure, functioning and performance of organizations, and the behaviour of groups and individuals within them. (Pugh, 1971)
- The interdisciplinary body of knowledge and field of research, concerned with how formal organizations, behaviour of people in organizations, and salient features of their context and environment, evolve and take shape, why all these things happen the way they do, and what purposes they serve. (Sorge and Warner, 1997)
- The study of human behaviour, attitudes, and performance within an organizational setting; drawing on theory, methods and principles from such disciplines as psychology, sociology, political science and cultural anthropology to learn about individuals, groups, structure and processes. (Ivancevich *et al*, 2008)

Characteristics of organizational behaviour

The following characteristics of organizational behaviour have been identified by Ivancevich *et al* (2008):

SOURCE REVIEW

Characteristics of organizational behaviour, Ivancevich *et al* (2008)

1. It is a way of thinking about individuals, groups and organizations.
2. It is multidisciplinary – it uses principles, models, theories and methods from other disciplines.
3. There is a distinctly humanistic orientation – people and their attitudes, perceptions, learning capacities, feelings and goals are of major importance.
4. It is performance-orientated – it deals with the factors affecting performance and how it can be improved.
5. The use of scientific method is important in studying variables and relationships.
6. It is applications-orientated in the sense of being concerned with providing useful answers to questions which arise when managing organizations.

Note that organization behaviour is described in this analysis as multidisciplinary, not interdisciplinary as mentioned by Sorge and Warner (1997). Huczynski and Buchanan (2007) pointed out that:

> *This is an area where the contributions of the different social and behavioural sciences can be integrated. The extent of that integration, however, is comparatively weak. Multidisciplinary means drawing from a number of different subjects. Interdisciplinary suggests that different subjects collaborate with each other. Full interdisciplinary collaboration is rare.*

Organizational behaviour and the social and behavioural sciences

Organizational behaviour studies make considerable use of social and behavioural science methodologies which involve the use of scientific procedures. The social sciences include the disciplines of psychology, social psychology, sociology, anthropology, economics and political science.

Behavioural science is mainly concerned with psychology and sociology. It was defined by Kelly (1969) as: 'The field of enquiry dedicated to the study of human behaviour through sophisticated but rigorous methods'. The term 'behavioural science' was first used to describe a Ford Foundation research programme at Harvard in 1950. It became prominent in the 1960s and 1970s and formed the basis for the behavioural science school of organization as discussed in Chapter 21. It played an important part in the earlier manifestations of organizational development as covered in Chapter 24 and influenced the quality of working life movement in the 1970s and the principles of job design as described in Chapter 27.

Explaining organizational behaviour

Two ways of explaining organizational behaviour have been described by Mohr (1982): variance theory and process theory.

Variance theory

Variance theory explains the causes of organizational behaviour by reference to the independent or causal variables which cause a change and result in dependent variables – the outcomes of the change. Variance theory involves the definition and precise measurement of the variables.

Process theory

Process theory explains organizational behaviour by producing narratives which provide probable explanations of the outcomes of a series of events.

Factors affecting organizational behaviour

The actions, reactions and interactions of people that constitute organizational behaviour are influenced by the following factors.

Factors affecting organizational behaviour

- The characteristics of people at work – individual differences, attitudes, personality, attributions, orientation and the roles they play.
- How people are motivated.
- The process of employee engagement.
- The process of organizational commitment.

- How organizations function.
- Organizational culture.

The sources and applications of organizational behaviour theory

Figure 17.1 summarizes how each of the main organization behaviour disciplines contributes first to different aspects of organization behaviour theory, which in turn influence HR practices.

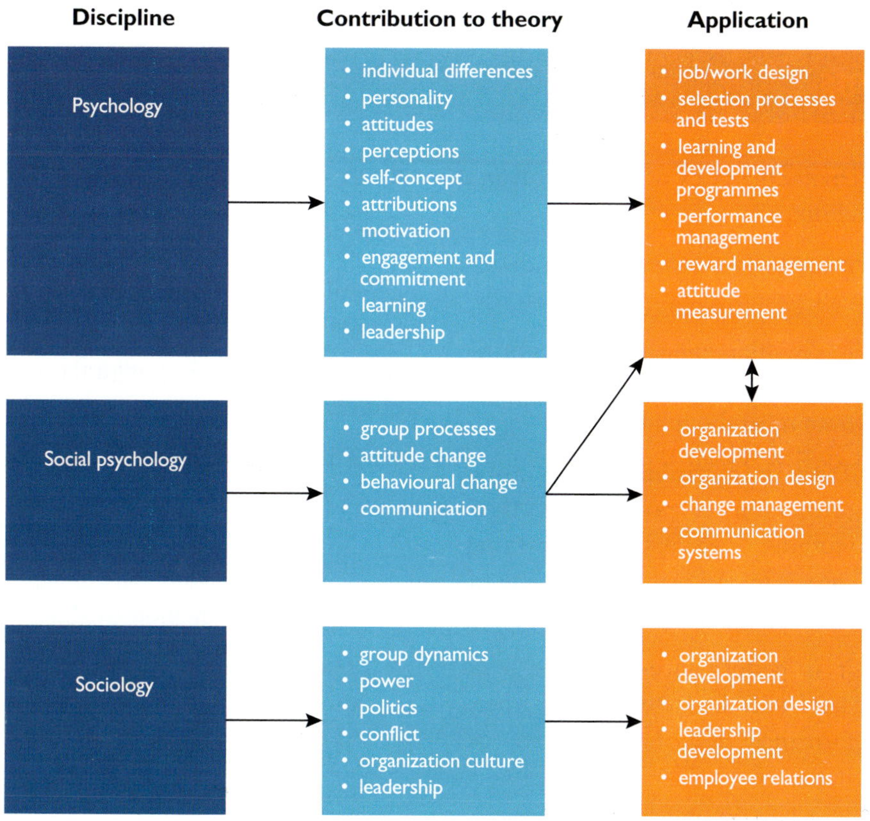

Figure 17.1 The sources and applications of organization behaviour theory

The significance of organizational behaviour theory

All managers and HR specialists are in the business of influencing behaviour in directions that will meet business needs. An understanding of organizational processes and skills in the analysis and diagnosis of organizational behaviour is therefore important. As Nadler and Tushman (1980) wrote:

> *The manager needs to understand the patterns of behaviour that are observed to predict in what direction behaviour will move (particularly in the light of managerial action), and to use this knowledge to control behaviour over the course of time. Effective management action requires that the manager be able to diagnose the system he or she is working in.*

The essence of organizational behaviour – key learning points

The characteristics of organizational behaviour

- It is a way of thinking about individuals, groups and organizations.
- It is multidisciplinary – it uses principles, models, theories and methods from other disciplines.
- There is a distinctly humanistic orientation – people and their attitudes, perceptions, learning capacities, feelings and goals are of major importance.
- It is performance-orientated – it deals with the factors affecting performance and how it can be improved.
- The use of scientific method is important in studying variables and relationships.
- It is applications-orientated in the sense of being concerned with providing useful answers to questions which arise when managing organizations.

The factors affecting organizational behaviour

- The characteristics of people at work – individual differences, attitudes, personality, attributions, orientation and the roles they play.
- How people are motivated.
- The process of employee engagement.
- The process of organizational commitment.
- How organizations function.
- Organizational culture.

The essence of organizational behaviour – key learning points (continued)

The sources and applications of organization behaviour theory

The sources comprise the disciplines of psychology, social psychology and sociology. Contributions are based on an understanding of individual differences, leadership, group processes and concepts such as motivation, engagement and commitment. Applications cover all aspects of people management and development.

The significance of organizational behaviour theory

All managers and HR specialists are in the business of influencing behaviour in directions that will meet business needs. An understanding of organizational processes and skills in the analysis and diagnosis of organizational behaviour is therefore important.

Questions

1. A colleague e-mails you to the effect that she missed a session on organizational behaviour in her course at the local college of further education. She asks you to recall what you learned about the subject when you took the course and for your opinion on its importance. Reply.
2. What are the characteristics of organizational behaviour?
3. What are the factors that affect organizational behaviour?

References

Huczynski, A A and Buchanan, D A (2007) *Organizational Behaviour*, 6th edn, FT Prentice Hall, Harlow

Ivancevich, J M, Konopaske, R and Matteson, M T (2008) *Organizational Behaviour and Management*, 8th edn, McGraw-Hill/Irwin, New York

Kelly, J (1969) *Organizational Behaviour*, Irwin, Homewood, Ill

Mohr, L B (1982) *Explaining Organizational Behaviour: The limits and possibility of theory and research*, Jossey-Bass, San Francisco, CA

Nadler, D A and Tushman, M L (1980) A congruence model for diagnosing organizational behaviour, in (ed) R H Miles, *Resource Book in Macro-organizational Behaviour*, Goodyear Publishing, Santa Monica, CA

Pugh, D S (ed) (1971) *Organization Theory: Selected readings*, Penguin Books, Harmondsworth

Sorge, A and Warner, M (eds) (1997) *The Handbook of Organizational Behaviour*, Thomson Business Press, London

Wood, J (1995) Mastering management: organizational behaviour, *Financial Times*, Mastering Management supplement

18 Characteristics of People

Key concepts and terms

- Ability
- Attitudes
- Attribution theory
- Bounded rationality
- Emotional intelligence
- Emotions
- Self-efficacy
- Intelligence
- Orientation to work
- Perception
- Personality
- Psychological climate
- Roles

Learning outcomes

On completing this chapter you should be able to define these key concepts. You should also know about:

- Individual differences
- Personality theories
- Types of behaviour
- Variations in personal characteristics
- Emotional intelligence characteristics

Introduction

To manage people effectively, it is necessary to take into account the factors that affect how they behave at work. This means understanding the significance of individual differences, the characteristics of people that explain how they act and the types of behaviour that feature in organizational life.

Individual differences

The development of HR processes and the design of organizations are often predicated on the belief that everyone is the same and will behave rationally when faced with change or other demands. But the behaviour of people differs because of their characteristics and individual differences and it is not always rational.

The management of people would be much easier if everyone were the same, but they aren't. As discussed below, they are, of course, different because of variations in personal characteristics and the influence of their background (the culture in which they were brought up); sex, race or disability are also considered factors by some people although holding these views readily leads to discrimination. In addition, there will be differences in ability, intelligence, personality, background and the environment in which they were brought up.

Variations in personal characteristics

The headings under which personal characteristics can vary have been classified by Mischel (1968) as follows.

SOURCE REVIEW

Variations in personal characteristics, Mischel (1968)

- Competencies – abilities and skills.
- Constructs – the conceptual framework that governs how people perceive their environment.
- Expectations – what people have learnt to expect about their own and others' behaviour.
- Values – what people believe to be important.
- Self-regulatory plans – the goals people set themselves and the plans they make to achieve them.

These are affected by environmental or situational variables, including the type of work individuals carry out; the culture, climate and management style in the organization; the social group within which they work; and the 'reference groups' that individuals use for comparative purposes (eg comparing conditions of work or pay between one category of employee and another).

The influence of background and culture

Individual differences may be a function of people's background, which will include the environment and culture in which they have been brought up and now exist. Levinson (1978) suggested that 'individual life structure' is shaped by three types of external event: the socio-cultural environment, the roles people play and the relationships they have, and the opportunities and constraints that enable or inhibit them to express and develop their personality.

Differences arising from sex, race or disability

It is futile, dangerous and invidious to make assumptions about inherent differences between people because of their sex, race or disability. If there are differences in behaviour at work these are more likely to arise from environmental and cultural factors than from differences in fundamental personal characteristics. The work environment undoubtedly influences feelings and behaviour for all these categories. Arnold *et al* (1991) referred to research that established that working women as a whole 'experienced more daily stress, marital dissatisfaction, and ageing worries, and were less likely to show overt anger than either housewives or men'. Ethnic minorities may find that the selection process is biased against them, promotion prospects are low and that they are subject to other overt or subtle forms of discrimination. The behaviour of disabled people can also be affected by the fact that they are not given equal opportunities. There is, of course, legislation against discrimination in each of those areas but this cannot prevent the more covert forms of prejudice.

Influences on behaviour at work

Behaviour at work is dependent on both the personal characteristics of individuals, as considered below, and the situation in which they are working. These factors interact, and this theory of behaviour is sometimes called 'interactionism'. It is because of the process of interaction and because there are so many variables in personal characteristics and situations that behaviour is difficult to analyse and predict. It is generally assumed that attitudes determine behaviour but there is not such a direct link as most people suppose. As Arnold *et al* (1991) comment, research evidence has shown that: 'People's avowed feelings and beliefs about someone or something seemed only loosely related to how they behaved towards it.'

SOURCE REVIEW

Environmental influences on behaviour, James and Sells (1981)

- Role characteristics such as role ambiguity and conflict (see the last section of this chapter).
- Job characteristics such as autonomy and challenge.
- Leader behaviours including goal emphasis and work facilitation.
- Work group characteristics including cooperation and friendliness.
- Organizational policies that directly affect individuals such as the reward system.

Personal characteristics

The personal characteristics that affect people's behaviour at work are their ability, intelligence, personality, attitudes, emotions and emotional intelligence.

Abilities

Ability is the quality possessed by people that makes an action possible. Abilities have been analysed by Burt (1954) and Vernon (1961). They classified them into two major groups:

V:ed – standing for verbal, numerical, memory and reasoning abilities.

K:m – standing for spatial and mechanical abilities, as well as perceptual (memory) and motor skills relating to physical operations such as eye/hand coordination and mental dexterity.

They also suggested that overriding these abilities there is GMA, or general mental ability, which accounts for most variations in performance. It is interesting to note that, as established by Schmidt and Hunter (1998) following a meta-analysis of 85 years of research findings, for selecting people without previous experience the most valid predictor of future performance and learning was GMA.

Alternative classifications have been produced by:

- Thurstone (1940) – spatial ability, perceptual speed, numerical ability, verbal meaning, memory, verbal fluency and inductive reasoning.
- Gagne (1977) – intellectual skills, cognitive (understanding and learning) skills, verbal and motor skills.

- Argyle (1989) – judgement, creativity and social skills.

Intelligence

Intelligence has been defined as:

- 'The capacity to solve problems, apply principles, make inferences and perceive relationships.' (Argyle, 1989)
- 'The capacity for abstract thinking and reasoning with a range of different contents and media.' (Toplis *et al*, 1991)
- 'The capacity to process information.' (Makin *et al*, 1996)
- 'What is measured by intelligence tests.' (Wright and Taylor, 1970)

The last, tautological definition is not facetious. As an operational definition, it can be related to the specific aspects of reasoning, inference, cognition (ie knowing, conceiving) and perception (ie understanding, recognition) that intelligence tests attempt to measure.

General intelligence, as noted above, consists of a number of mental abilities that enable a person to succeed at a wide variety of intellectual tasks that use the faculties of knowing and reasoning. The mathematical technique of factor analysis has been used to identify the constituents of intelligence, such as Thurstone's (1940) multiple factors listed above.

An alternative approach to the analysis of intelligence was put forward by Guilford (1967), who distinguished five types of mental operation: thinking, remembering, divergent production (problem solving that leads to unexpected and original solutions), convergent production (problem solving that leads to the one, correct solution) and evaluating.

Personality

Personality has been defined by Huczynski and Buchanan (2007) as: 'The psychological qualities that influence an individual's characteristic behaviour patterns in a stable and distinctive manner.' As noted by Ivancevich *et al* (2008), personality appears to be organized into patterns that are, to some degree, observable and measurable and involves both common and unique characteristics – every person is different from every other person in some respects but similar to other persons in other respects. Personality is a product of both nature (hereditary) and nurture (the pattern of life experience). Personality can be described in terms of traits or types.

The trait concept of personality

Traits are predispositions to behave in certain ways in a variety of different situations. They have been classified as the 'big five' as follows.

SOURCE REVIEW

Personality traits – the big five, Costa and McRae (1992)

1. Openness.
2. Conscientiousness.
3. Extraversion.
4. Agreeableness.
5. Neuroticism.

The assumption that people are consistent in the ways they express these traits is the basis for making predictions about their future behaviour. We all attribute traits to people in an attempt to understand why they behave in the way they do. As Chell (1987) explained: 'This cognitive process gives a sense of order to what might otherwise appear to be senseless uncoordinated behaviours. Traits may therefore be thought of as classification systems, used by individuals to understand other people's and their own behaviour.' But the trait theory of personality has been attacked by people such as Mischel (1981). The main criticisms have been as follows:

- People do not necessarily express the same trait across different situations or even the same trait in the same situation. Different people may exhibit consistency in some traits and considerable variability in others.
- Classical trait theory, as formulated by Cattell (1963), assumes that the manifestation of trait behaviour is independent of the situations and the persons with whom the individual is interacting. This assumption is questionable, given that trait behaviour usually manifests itself in response to specific situations.
- Trait attributions are a product of language – they are devices for speaking about people and are not generally described in terms of behaviour.

Type theories of personality

Type theory identifies a number of types of personality that can be used to categorize people and may form the basis of a personality test. The types may be linked to descriptions of various traits.

One of the most widely used type theories is that of Jung (1923). He identified four major preferences of people:

1. relating to other people – extraversion or introversion;
2. gathering information – sensing (dealing with facts that can be objectively verified), or intuitive (generating information through insight);
3. using information – thinking (emphasizing logical analysis as the basis for decision making), or feeling (making decisions based on internal values and beliefs);
4. making decisions – perceiving (collecting all the relevant information before making a decision), or judging (resolving the issue without waiting for a large quantity of data).

This theory of personality forms the basis of personality tests such as the Myers-Briggs Types Indicator.

Eysenck (1953) produced a well known typology. He identified three personality traits: extroversion/introversion, neuroticism and psychoticism, and classified people as stable or unstable extroverts or introverts. For example, a stable introvert is passive, careful, controlled and thoughtful, while a stable extrovert is lively, outgoing, responsive and sociable.

As Makin *et al* (1996) comment, studies using types to predict work-related behaviours are less common and may be difficult to interpret: 'In general it would be fair to say that their level of predictability is similar to that for trait measures.'

Attitudes

An attitude can broadly be defined as a settled mode of thinking. Attitudes are evaluative. As Makin *et al* 1996 say, 'Any attitude contains an assessment of whether the object to which it refers is liked or disliked.' Attitudes are developed through experience but they are less stable than traits and can change as new experiences are gained or influences absorbed. Within organizations they are affected by cultural factors (values and norms), the behaviour of management (management style), policies such as those concerned with pay, recognition, promotion and the quality of working life, and the influence of the 'reference group' (the group with whom people identify). Sometimes there may be a discrepancy between attitudes and behaviour, ie someone may believe in one thing such as being fair to people but act differently. This is called 'cognitive dissonance'.

Emotions

Emotions are feelings such as anger, fear, sadness, joy, anticipation and acceptance; they arouse people and therefore influence their behaviour. The mildest forms of emotions are called 'moods', which are low intensity, long-lasting emotional states.

Emotional intelligence

Emotional intelligence is a combination of skills and abilities such as self-awareness, self-control, empathy and sensitivity to the feelings of others. The notion of emotional intelligence was first defined by Salovey and Mayer (1990), who proposed that it involves the capacity to perceive emotion, integrate emotion in thought, understand emotion and manage emotions effectively.

Goleman (1995) popularized the concept. He defined emotional intelligence as 'The capacity for recognizing our own feelings and that of others, for motivating ourselves, for managing emotions well in ourselves as well as others.' He defined its four components as follows.

SOURCE REVIEW

Components of emotional intelligence, Goleman (1995)

1. Self-management – the ability to control or redirect disruptive impulses and moods and regulate your own behaviour coupled with a propensity to pursue goals with energy and persistence. The six competencies associated with this component are self-control, trustworthiness and integrity, initiative, adaptability – comfort with ambiguity, openness to change and strong desire to achieve.
2. Self-awareness – the ability to recognize and understand your moods, emotions and drives as well as their effect on others. This is linked to three competencies: self-confidence, realistic self-assessment and emotional self-awareness.
3. Social awareness – the ability to understand the emotional makeup of other people and skill in treating people according to their emotional reactions. This is linked to six competencies: empathy, expertise in building and retaining talent, organizational awareness, cross-cultural sensitivity, valuing diversity and service to clients and customers.
4. Social skills – proficiency in managing relationships and building networks to get the desired result from others and reach personal goals and the ability to find common ground and build rapport. The five competencies associated with this component are: leadership, effectiveness in leading change, conflict management, influence/communication, and expertise in building and leading teams.

According to Goleman it is not enough to have a high IQ (intelligence quotient); emotional intelligence is also required. Since Goleman's contribution, the following three major models of emotional intelligence, as summarized by Clarke (2007), that have dominated the writing in this area are as follows:

1. Personality models have become the most popular theory of emotional intelligence following Goleman. Here, emotional intelligence is viewed as comprising a range of emotional dispositions as well as competences, from individual traits to a number of learnt capabilities. These are all contained within five separate elements of emotional intelligence: self-awareness, motivation, self-regulation, empathy, and adeptness in relationships.
2. Mixed models – comprising aspects of personality as well as abilities to perceive emotional intelligence and manage emotions – have abounded, with arguably the most developed being that by Bar-On (1997). This model includes 15 subscales underpinning five dimensions of an individual's emotional quotient (EQ). These are identified as: intrapersonal EQ (including emotional self-awareness), interpersonal EQ, adaptability, stress management, and general mood. The most notable distinction of this model is the far wider array of elements that make up emotional intelligence, in addition to those that might be more strictly considered as emotional abilities.
3. The ability model, however, views emotional intelligence far more narrowly, comprising a set of four cognitive abilities that involve the capacity to identify, reason with, and utilize emotions effectively. The construct is made up of four branches: the ability to perceive emotion, the ability to integrate emotion to facilitate thought, the ability to understand emotions, and the ability to manage and regulate emotions.

As Clarke comments, of all these models, the first two have come under criticism in terms of the ambiguity associated with the areas included and the measurement approaches employed. The ability model has received more positive commentary as possessing greater validity. Research is now showing some exciting implications, particularly as regards a clear link between this set of emotional abilities, transformational leadership and the quality of individuals' social relationships.

Types of behaviour

The types of behaviour associated with individual differences are perception, attribution, orientation, roles and bounded rationality.

Perception

Perception is the intuitive understanding, recognition and interpretation of things and events. Behaviour will be influenced by the perceptions of individuals about the situation they are in.

The term 'psychological climate' has been coined by James and Sells (1981) to describe how perceptions give the situation psychological significance and meaning.

Perception has been defined by Ivancevitch *et al* (2008) as: 'The process by which an individual gives meaning to the environment. It involves organizing and interpreting various stimuli into a psychological experience.' Perception is empirical in that it is based on the individual's past experience. Different people will therefore perceive the same thing in different ways. As Ivancevitch *et al* comment: 'While we think we are describing some objective reality, we are in fact describing our subjective reactions to that reality.' And it is this perception of reality that shapes behaviour. To a large extent people interpret the events and the actions of others from their own viewpoint. They see what they want to see.

Attribution theory

Attribution theory is concerned with how people assign causes to events. It involves perceptions about why things happen or why people behave in the way they do. Behaviour is often influenced by the perceived causes of events rather than the events themselves. Attribution theory explains how we make judgements about people at work. We make an attribution when we perceive and describe other people's actions and try to discover why they behaved in the way they did. We can also make attributions about our own behaviour. Heider (1958) has pointed out that: 'In everyday life we form ideas about other people and about social situations. We interpret other people's actions and we predict what they will do under certain circumstances.'

In attributing causes to people's actions we distinguish between what is in the person's power to achieve and the effect of environmental influence. A personal cause, whether someone does well or badly, may, for example, be the amount of effort displayed, while a situational cause may be the extreme difficulty of the task.

SOURCE REVIEW

Criteria for deciding whether behaviour is attributable to personal rather than external (situational) causes, Kelley (1967)

1. Distinctiveness – the behaviour can be distinguished from the behaviour of other people in similar situations.
2. Consensus – if other people agree that the behaviour is governed by some personal characteristic.
3. Consistency over time – whether the behaviour is repeated.
4. Consistency over modality (ie the manner in which things are done) – whether or not the behaviour is repeated in different situations.

Attribution theory is also concerned with the way in which people attribute success or failure to themselves. Research by Weiner (1974) and others has indicated that when people with high achievement needs have been successful they ascribe this to internal factors such as ability and effort. High achievers tend to attribute failure to lack of effort and not lack of ability. Low achievers tend not to link success with effort but to ascribe their failures to lack of ability.

Self-efficacy

The concept of self-efficacy was developed by Bandura (1982) who defined it as 'how well one can execute courses of action required to deal with prospective situations'. It is concerned with an individual's self-belief that he or she will be able to accomplish certain tasks, achieve certain goals or learn certain things. Research by Grandey (2000) established that individuals high on self-efficacy tended to perform at a higher level.

Orientation to work

Orientation theory examines the factors that are instrumental, ie serve as a means of accomplishing something, in directing people's choices about work. An orientation is a central organizing principle that underlies people's attempts to make sense of their lives. In relation to work, as defined by Guest (1984): 'An orientation is a persisting tendency to seek certain goals and rewards from work which exists independently of the nature of the work and the work content.' The concept of orientation stresses the role of the social environment factor as a key factor affecting motivation.

Orientation theory is primarily developed from fieldwork carried out by sociologists rather than from laboratory work conducted by psychologists. Goldthorpe *et al* (1968) studied skilled and semi-skilled workers in Luton and, in their findings, they stressed the importance of instrumental orientation, that is, a view of work as a means to an end, a context in which to earn money to purchase goods and leisure. The research team found that the 'affluent` workers they interviewed valued work largely for extrinsic reasons.

In their research carried out with blue-collar workers in Peterborough, Blackburn and Mann (1979) found a wider range of orientations. They suggested that different ones could come into play with varying degrees of force in different situations. The fact that workers, in practice, had little choice about what they did contributed to this diversity – their orientations were affected by the choice or lack of choice presented to them and this meant that they might be forced to accept alternative orientations. They commented that: 'An obsession with wages clearly emerged... A concern to minimize unpleasant work was also widespread.' Surprisingly, perhaps, they also revealed that the most persistent preference of all was for outside work, 'a fairly clear desire for a combination of fresh air and freedom'.

Roles

When faced with any situation, eg carrying out a job, people have to enact a role in order to manage that situation. This is sometimes called the 'situation-act model'. As described by Chell (1985), the model indicates that: 'The person must act within situations: situations are rule-governed and how a person behaves is often prescribed by these socially acquired rules. The person thus adopts a suitable role in order to perform effectively within the situation.'

At work, the term 'role' describes the part played by individuals in fulfilling their work requirements. Roles therefore indicate the specific forms of behaviour required to carry out a particular task or the group of tasks contained in a position or job. The concept of a role emphasizes the fact that people at work are, in a sense, always acting a part: they are not simply reciting the lines but are interpreting them in terms of their own perceptions of how they should behave in relation to the context in which they work, especially with regard to their interactions with other people.

Role theory, as formulated by Katz and Kahn (1966) states that the role individuals occupy at work, and elsewhere, exists in relation to other people – their role set, which consists of the individuals with whom a role-holder interacts and therefore influences and is also influenced by them. Members of a role set have expectations about the individuals' roles, and if they live up to these expectations they will have successfully performed the role.

Performance in a role is a product of the situation individuals are in (the organizational context and the direction or influence exercised from above or elsewhere in the organization) and their own skills, competencies, attitudes and personality. Situational factors are important, but the role individuals perform can both shape and reflect their personalities. Stress and inadequate performance result when roles are ambiguous, incompatible, or in conflict with one another.

Role problems

- Role ambiguity – when individuals are unclear about what their role is, what is expected of them, or how they are getting on, they may become insecure or lose confidence in themselves.
- Role incompatibility – stress and poor performance may be caused by roles having incompatible elements, as when there is a clash between what other people expect from the role and what individuals believe is expected of them.
- Role conflict – this happens when, even if roles are clearly defined and there are no incompatible elements, individuals have to carry out two antagonistic roles. For example, conflict can exist between the roles of individuals at work and their roles at home.

Bounded rationality

The extent to which people behave rationally is limited by their capacity to understand the complexities of the situation they are in and their emotional reactions to it. This is the concept of bounded rationality – while people by their own lights are reasoned in their own behaviour, the reasoning behind their behaviour is influenced by 'human frailties and demands from both within and outside the organization' (Miller *et al*, 1999). As Harrison (2005) put it:

> *Some of the factors that pull players away from a purely rational approach include confused, excessive, incomplete or unreliable data, incompetent processing or communicating of information, pressures of time, human emotions and differences in individuals' cognitive processes, mental maps and reasoning capacity.*

Implications for HR specialists

The main implications for HR specialists of the factors that affect individuals at work are summarized below.

Individual differences

When designing jobs, preparing learning and development programmes, assessing and counselling staff, developing reward systems and dealing with grievances and disciplinary problems, it is necessary to remember that all people are different. What fulfils one person may not fulfil another. Abilities, aptitudes and intelligence differ widely and it is necessary to take particular care in fitting the right people to the right jobs and giving them the right training. Personalities, attitudes and emotions also differ. It is important to focus on how to manage diversity. This should take account of individual differences, which will include any issues arising from the employment of women, people from different ethnic groups, those with disabilities and older people. The predictive effectiveness of general mental ability (GMA) tests as selection aids should be noted.

Judgements on personality

Personality should not be judged or measured simplistically in terms of stereotyped traits. People are complex and they change, and account has to be taken of this. The problem for HR specialists and managers in general is that, while they have to accept and understand these differences and take full account of them, they have ultimately to proceed on the basis of fitting them to the requirements of the situation, which are essentially what the organization needs to achieve. There is always a limit to the extent to which an organization that relies on collective effort to achieve its goals can adjust itself to the specific needs of individuals. But the organization has to appreciate that the pressures it places on people can result in stress and therefore can become counter-productive.

Perceptions and attributions

We tend to see things from our own frame of reference when we ascribe motives to other people and attempt to establish the causes of their behaviour. We must be careful not to make simplistic judgements about causality (ie what has motivated someone's behaviour) – for ourselves as well as in respect of others – especially when we are assessing performance.

Self-efficacy

In operating performance management and reward systems and providing training we must try to develop self-belief – the confidence people have in their own abilities and capacity to perform well.

Orientation theory

The significance of orientation theory is that it stresses the importance of the effect of environmental factors on the motivation to work.

Role theory

Role theory helps us to understand the need to clarify with individuals what is expected of them in behavioural terms and to ensure when designing jobs that they do not contain any incompatible elements. We must also be aware of the potential for role conflict so that steps can be taken to minimize stress.

Bounded rationality

Don't expect everyone to behave rationally, especially when confronted with change. Use techniques of communication and involvement to overcome irrational reactions.

Characteristics of people – key learning points

Individual differences

The development of HR processes and the design of organizations are often based on the belief that everyone is the same and will behave rationally when faced with change or other demands. But the behaviour of people differs because of their characteristics and individual differences and it is not always rational.

Variations in personal characteristics

These result from differences in:

- competencies – abilities and skills;
- constructs – the conceptual framework that governs how people perceive their environment;
- expectations – what people have learnt to expect about their own and others' behaviour;
- values – what people believe to be important;
- self-regulatory plans – the goals people set themselves and the plans they make to achieve them.

Personality theories

Personality is a product of both nature (hereditary) and nurture (the pattern of life experience). Personality can be described in terms of traits or types.

Emotional intelligence characteristics

- Self-management.
- Self-awareness.
- Social awareness.
- Social skills.

Types of behaviour

The types of behaviour associated with individual differences are perception, attribution, orientation, roles and bounded rationality.

Role theory

The role individuals occupy at work, and elsewhere, exists in relation to other people – their role set, which consists of the individuals with whom a role-holder interacts and therefore influences and is also influenced by them.

Questions

1. What is personality?
2. You have been asked to explain trait theory to your fellow students. You are expected to submit the theory to critical examination.
3. What problems can occur in carrying out roles?

References

Argyle, M (1989) *The Social Psychology of Work*, Penguin, Harmondsworth

Arnold, J, Robertson, I T and Cooper, C L (1991) *Work Psychology*, Pitman, London

Bandura, A (1982) Self-efficacy mechanism in human agency, *American Psychologist*, **37**, pp 122–47

Bar-On, R (1997) *Bar-On Emotional Quotient Inventory: A measure of emotional intelligence*, Technical Manual, Multi-Health Systems, Toronto

Blackburn, R M and Mann, R (1979) *The Working Class in the Labour Market*, Macmillan, London

Burt, C (1954) The differentiation of intellectual ability, *British Journal of Educational Psychology*, **24**, pp 45–67

Cattell, R B (1963) *The Sixteen Personality Factor Questionnaire*, Institute for Personality and Ability Training, Ill

Chell, E (1985) *Participation and Organisation*, Macmillan, London

Chell, E (1987) *The Psychology of Behaviour in Organisations*, Macmillan, London

Clarke, N (2007) Be selective when choosing emotional intelligence training, *People Management*, 3 May, p 47

Costa, P and McRae, R R (1992) *NEO PI-R: Professional manual*, Psychological Assessment Resources, Odessa, FL

Eysenck, H J (1953) *The Structure of Human Personality*, Methuen, London

Gagne, R M (1977) *The Conditions of Learning*, 3rd edn, Rinehart and Winston, New York

Goldthorpe, J H, Lockwood, D C, Bechofer, F and Platt, J (1968) *The Affluent Worker: Industrial attitudes and behaviour*, Cambridge University Press, Cambridge

Goleman, D (1995) *Emotional Intelligence*, Bantam, New York

Grandey, A (2000) Emotion regulation in the work place: a new way to conceptualize emotional labour, *Journal of Occupational Psychology*, **5**, pp 95–110

Guest, D E (1984) What's new in motivation, *Personnel Management*, May, pp 30–33

Guilford, J P (1967) *The Nature of Human Intelligence*, McGraw-Hill, New York

Harrison, R (2005) *Learning and Development*, 4th edn, CIPD, London

Heider, F (1958) *The Psychology of Interpersonal Relationships*, Wiley, New York

Huczynski, A A and Buchanan, D A (2007) *Organizational Behaviour*, 6th edn, FT Prentice Hall, Harlow

Ivancevich, J M, Konopaske, R and Matteson, M T (2008) *Organizational Behaviour and Management*, 8th edn, McGraw-Hill/Irwin, New York

James, R and Sells, S B (1981) Psychological climate: theoretical perspectives and empirical research, in (ed) D Magnusson, *Towards a Psychology of Situations: An interactional perspective*, Erlbaum, Hillsdale, NJ

Jung, C (1923) *Psychological Types*, Routledge Kegan Paul, London

Katz, D and Kahn, R (1966) *The Social Psychology of Organizations*, John Wiley, New York

Kelley, H H (1967) Attribution theory in social psychology, in (ed) D Levine, *Nebraska Symposium on Motivation*, University of Nebraska Press, Lincoln, NB

Levinson, D (1978) *The Seasons of Man's Life*, Knopf, New York

Makin, P, Cooper, C and Cox, C (1996) *Organizations and the Psychological Contract*, BPS Books, Leicester

Miller, S, Hickson, D J and Wilson, D C (1999) Decision-making in organizations, in (eds) S R Clegg, C Hardy and W R Nord, *Managing Organizations: Current issues*, Sage, London

Mischel, W (1968) *Personality and Assessment*, Wiley, New York
Mischel, W (1981) *Introduction to Personality*, Holt, Rinehart and Winston, New York
Salovey, P and Mayer, J D (1990) Emotional intelligence, *Imagination, Cognition and Personality*, **9**, pp 185–211
Schmidt, F L and Hunter, J E (1998) The validity and utility of selection methods in personnel psychology: practical and theoretical implications of 85 years of research findings, *Psychological Bulletin*, **124** (2), pp 262–74
Thurstone, L L (1940) Current issues in factor analysis, *Psychological Bulletin*, **30**, pp 26–38
Toplis, J, Dulewicz, V, and Fletcher, C (1991) *Psychological Testing*, Institute of Personnel Management, London
Vernon, P E (1961) *The Structure of Human Abilities*, Methuen, London
Weiner, B (1974) *Achievement Motivation and Attribution Theory*, General Learning Press, New Jersey
Wright, D S and Taylor, A (1970) *Introducing Psychology*, Penguin, Harmondsworth

19 Motivation

Key concepts and terms

- Content or needs theory
- Discretionary behaviour
- Equity theory
- ERG theory
- Expectancy theory
- Extrinsic motivation
- Goal theory
- Herzberg's two-factor theory
- Instrumentality
- Instrumentality theory
- Intrinsic motivation
- Maslow's hierarchy of needs
- McGregor's theory X and theory Y
- McClelland's need theory
- Motivation
- Process or cognitive theory
- Quality of working life
- Reinforcement theory
- Social learning theory
- Valency–instrumentality–expectancy theory

Learning outcomes

On completing this chapter you should be able to define these key concepts. You should also know about:

- The process of motivation
- Motivation theories
- Motivation strategies
- Types of motivation
- Motivation and money

Introduction

High performance is achieved by well-motivated people who are prepared to exercise discretionary effort. Even in fairly basic roles, Hunter *et al* (1990) found that the difference in value-added discretionary performance between 'superior' and 'standard' performers was 19 per cent. For highly complex jobs it was 48 per cent.

To motivate people it is necessary to appreciate how motivation works. This means understanding motivation theory and how the theory can be put into practice, as discussed in this chapter.

Motivation defined

A motive is a reason for doing something. Motivation is concerned with the strength and direction of behaviour and the factors that influence people to behave in certain ways. The term 'motivation' can refer variously to the goals individuals have, the ways in which individuals chose their goals and the ways in which others try to change their behaviour.

SOURCE REVIEW

The three components of motivation, Arnold *et al* (1991)

1. Direction – what a person is trying to do.
2. Effort – how hard a person is trying.
3. Persistence – how long a person keeps on trying.

Motivating other people is about getting them to move in the direction you want them to go in order to achieve a result. Motivating yourself is about setting the direction independently and then taking a course of action that will ensure that you get there. Motivation can be described as goal-directed behaviour. People are motivated when they expect that a course of action is likely to lead to the attainment of a goal and a valued reward – one that satisfies their needs and wants.

Well-motivated people engage in discretionary behaviour – in the majority of roles there is scope for individuals to decide how much effort to exert. Such people may be self-motivated, and as long as this means they are going in the right direction to attain what they are there to achieve, then this is the best form of motivation. Most of us, however, need to be motivated to a greater or lesser degree. There are two types of motivation, and a number of theories explaining how it works as discussed below.

Types of motivation

The two types of motivation are intrinsic motivation and extrinsic motivation.

Intrinsic motivation

Intrinsic motivation can arise from the self-generated factors that influence people's behaviour. It is not created by external incentives. It can take the form of motivation by the work itself when individuals feel that their work is important, interesting and challenging and provides them with a reasonable degree of autonomy (freedom to act), opportunities to achieve and advance, and scope to use and develop their skills and abilities. Deci and Ryan (1985) suggested that intrinsic motivation is based on the needs to be competent and self-determining (that is, to have a choice).

Intrinsic motivation can be enhanced by job or role design. According to an early writer on the significance of the motivational impact of job design (Katz, 1964): 'The job itself must provide sufficient variety, sufficient complexity, sufficient challenge and sufficient skill to engage the abilities of the worker.' In their job characteristics model, Hackman and Oldham (1974) emphasized the importance of the core job dimensions as motivators, namely skill variety, task identity, task significance, autonomy and feedback.

Extrinsic motivation

Extrinsic motivation occurs when things are done to or for people to motivate them. These include rewards, such as incentives, increased pay, praise, or promotion; and punishments, such as disciplinary action, withholding pay, or criticism.

Extrinsic motivators can have an immediate and powerful effect, but will not necessarily last long. The intrinsic motivators, which are concerned with the 'quality of working life' (a phrase and movement that emerged from this concept), are likely to have a deeper and longer-term effect because they are inherent in individuals and their work and not imposed from outside in such forms as incentive pay.

Motivation theories

There are a number of motivation theories which, in the main, are complementary to one another. The leading theories are listed and described below and summarized in Table 19.1. The most significant ones are those concerned with expectancy, goal setting and equity, which are classified as process or cognitive theories.

Table 19.1 Summary of motivation theories

Category	Type	Theorist(s)	Summary of theory	Implications
Instrumentality	Taylorism	Taylor (1911)	If we do one thing it leads to another. People will be motivated to work if rewards and punishments are directly related to their performance	Basis of crude attempts to motivate people by incentives. Often used as the implied rationale for performance-related pay although this is seldom an effective motivator
Reinforcement	The motivation process	Hull (1951)	As experience is gained in satisfying needs people perceive that certain actions help to achieve goals while others are unsuccessful. The successful actions are repeated when a similar need arises	Provides feedback which positively reinforces effective behaviour
Needs (content) theory	Hierarchy of needs	Maslow (1954)	A hierarchy of five needs exist: physiological, safety, social, esteem, self-fulfilment. Needs at a higher level only emerge when a lower need is satisfied	Focuses attention on the various needs that motivate people and the notion that a satisfied need is no longer a motivator. The concept of a hierarchy has no practical significance
	ERG theory	Alderfer (1972)	Three fundamental needs: existence, relatedness and growth	A simpler and more convincing approach to Maslow's on the motivation provided by needs

Table 19.1 *continued*

Category	Type	Theorist(s)	Summary of theory	Implications
Needs (content) theory *continued*	Managerial needs theory	McClelland (1973)	Managers have three fundamental needs: achievement, affiliation and power	Draws attention to the needs of managers and the important concept of 'achievement motivation'
Process/ cognitive theory	Expectancy theory	Vroom (1964), Porter and Lawler (1968)	Effort (motivation) depends on the likelihood that rewards will follow effort and that the reward is worthwhile	The key theory informing approaches to rewards, ie that they must be a link between effort and reward (line of sight), the reward should be achievable and should be worthwhile
	Goal theory	Latham and Locke (1979)	Motivation will improve if people have demanding but agreed goals and receive feedback	Provides the rationale for performance management, goal setting and feedback
	Equity theory	Adams (1965)	People are better motivated if treated equitably	Need to have equitable reward and employment practices.
	Social learning theory	Bandura (1977)	Emphasizes the importance of internal psychological factors, especially expectancies about the value of goals and the individual's ability to reach them	Influences performance management and learning and development practices

Table 19.1 *continued*

Category	Type	Theorist(s)	Summary of theory	Implications
Two-factor model	Related to needs theory	Herzberg *et al* (1957)	Two groups of factors affect job satisfaction: (1) those intrinsic to the work itself; (2) those extrinsic to the job (extrinsic motivators or hygiene factors) such as pay and working conditions	Identifies a number of fundamental needs ie achievement, recognition, advancement, autonomy and the work itself. Influences approaches to job design (job enrichment). Underpins the proposition that reward systems should provide for both financial and non-financial rewards
Theory X and theory Y	General approaches to motivation	McGregor (1960)	Theory X is the traditional view that people must be coerced into performing; theory Y is the view that people will exercise self-direction and self-direction in the service of objectives to which they are committed	Emphasizes the importance of commitment, rewards and integrating individual and organizational needs

Leading motivation theories

- Reinforcement theory.
- Instrumentality theory.
- Content or needs theory.
- Process or cognitive theory.

- Herzberg's two-factor (motivation-hygiene) theory.
- McGregor's theory X and theory Y.

Instrumentality theory

'Instrumentality' is the belief that if we do one thing it will lead to another. In its crudest form, instrumentality theory states that people only work for money.

The theory emerged in the second half of the 19th century with its emphasis on the need to rationalize work and on economic outcomes. It assumes that people will be motivated to work if rewards and penalties are tied directly to their performance; thus the awards are contingent upon effective performance. Instrumentality theory has its roots in the scientific management methods of Taylor (1911), who wrote: 'It is impossible, through any long period of time, to get workmen to work much harder than the average men around them unless they are assured a large and permanent increase in their pay.'

This theory provides a rationale for incentive pay, albeit a dubious one. It is based on the principle of reinforcement. Motivation using this approach has been and still is widely adopted and can be successful in some circumstances. But it is based exclusively on a system of external controls and fails to recognize a number of other human needs. It also fails to appreciate the fact that the formal control system can be seriously affected by the informal relationship existing between workers.

Reinforcement theory

As experience is gained in taking action to satisfy needs; people perceive that certain actions help to achieve their goals while others are less successful. Some actions bring rewards; others result in failure or even punishment. Reinforcement theory as developed by Hull (1951) suggests that successes in achieving goals and rewards act as positive incentives and reinforce the successful behaviour, which is repeated the next time a similar need emerges. The more powerful, obvious and frequent the reinforcement, the more likely it is that the behaviour will be repeated until, eventually, it can become a more or less unconscious reaction to an event. Conversely, failures or punishments provide negative reinforcement, suggesting that it is necessary to seek alternative means of achieving goals. This process has been called 'the law of effect'.

The associated concept of operant conditioning (Skinner, 1974) explains that new behaviours or responses become established through particular stimuli, hence conditioning – getting people to repeat behaviour by positive reinforcement in the form of feedback and knowledge of results. The concept suggests that people behave in ways they expect will produce positive outcomes. It is linked to expectancy theory, as described later in this chapter and also contributes to learning theory (see Chapter 41).

The degree to which experience shapes future behaviour does, of course, depend, first, on the extent to which individuals correctly perceive the connection between the behaviour and its outcome and, second, on the extent to which they are able to recognize the resemblance between the previous situation and the one that now confronts them. Perceptive ability varies between people as does the ability to identify correlations between events. For these reasons, some people are better at learning from experience than others, just as some people are more easily motivated than others.

It has been suggested that behavioural theories based on the principle of reinforcement or the law of effect are limited because they imply, in Allport's (1954) phrase, a 'hedonism of the past'. They assume that the explanation of the present choices of individuals is to be found in an examination of the consequences of their past choices. Insufficient attention is paid in the theories to the influence of expectations, and no indication is given of any means of distinguishing in advance the class of outcomes that would strengthen responses and those that would weaken them.

Content (needs) theory

The theory focuses on the content of motivation in the shape of needs. Its basis is the belief that an unsatisfied need creates tension and a state of disequilibrium. To restore the balance a goal is identified that will satisfy the need, and a behaviour pathway is selected that will lead to the achievement of the goal and the satisfaction of the need. All behaviour is therefore motivated by unsatisfied needs. This process is modelled in Figure 19.1 below:

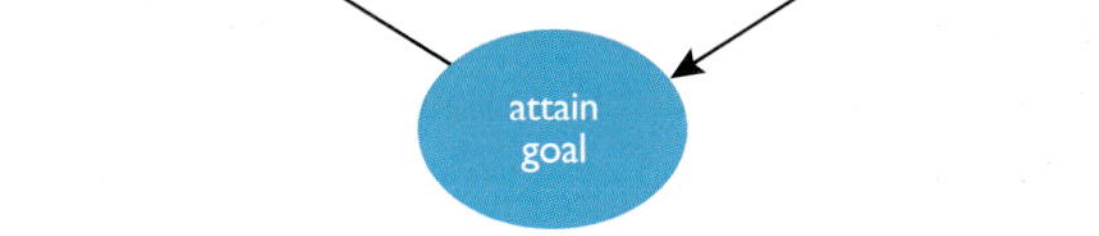

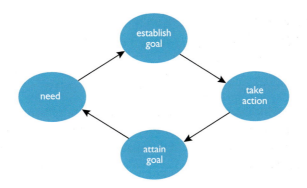

Figure 19.1 The process of motivation

There are three points that emerge from this model. First, people have a multiplicity of needs depending on themselves and the situation they are in. Second, they can select all sorts of goals and actions to satisfy those needs. Third, while we can observe their behaviour we cannot be certain of the needs and goals that motivated it. It is unwise to assume that any one approach to motivation will appeal to all affected by it. Motivation policies and practices must recognize that people are different.

Needs theory has been developed by Maslow, Alderfer and McClelland, as described below.

Maslow's hierarchy of needs

The most famous classification of needs is the one formulated by Maslow (1954). He suggested that there are five major need categories that apply to people in general, starting from the fundamental physiological needs and leading through a hierarchy of safety, social and esteem needs to the need for self-fulfilment, the highest need of all. When a lower need is satisfied the next highest becomes dominant and the individual's attention is turned to satisfying this higher need. The need for self-fulfilment, however, can never be satisfied. 'Man is a wanting animal'; only an unsatisfied need can motivate behaviour and the dominant need is the prime motivator of behaviour. Psychological development takes place as people move up the hierarchy of needs, but this is not necessarily a straightforward progression. The lower needs still exist, even if temporarily dormant as motivators, and individuals constantly return to previously satisfied needs.

Maslow's needs hierarchy has an intuitive appeal and has been very popular. But it has not been verified by empirical research such as that conducted by Wahba and Bridwell (1979), and it has been criticized for its apparent rigidity (different people may have different priorities and it is difficult to accept that needs progress steadily up the hierarchy) and for the misleading simplicity of Maslow's conceptual language. In fact, Maslow himself expressed doubts about the validity of a strictly ordered hierarchy.

ERG theory (Alderfer)

Alderfer (1972) devised a theory of human needs that postulated three primary categories:

1. Existence needs such as hunger and thirst – pay, fringe benefits and working conditions are other types of existence needs.
2. Relatedness needs, which acknowledge that people are not self-contained units but must engage in transactions with their human environment – acceptance, understanding, confirmation and influence are elements of the relatedness process.
3. Growth needs, which involve people in finding the opportunities 'to be what they are most fully and to become what they can'.

McClelland's achievement–affiliation–power needs

An alternative way of classifying needs was developed by McClelland (1961), who based it mainly on studies of managers. He identified three needs as being most important:

1. The need for achievement, defined as the need for competitive success measured against a personal standard of excellence.
2. The need for affiliation, defined as the need for warm, friendly, compassionate relationships with others.
3. The need for power, defined as the need to control or influence others.

Different individuals have different levels of these needs. Some have a greater need for achievement, others a stronger need for affiliation, and still others a stronger need for power. While one need may be dominant, however, this does not mean that the others are non-existent.

The three needs may be given different priorities at different levels of management. Achievement needs are particularly important for success in many junior and middle management jobs where it is possible to feel direct responsibility for task accomplishment. But in senior management positions a concern for institutionalized as opposed to personal power becomes more important. A strong need for affiliation is not so significant at any level.

Process theory

In process theory, the emphasis is on the psychological processes or forces that affect motivation, as well as on basic needs. It is also known as 'cognitive theory' because it is concerned with people's perceptions of their working environment and the ways in which they interpret and understand it. According to Guest (1992), process theory provides a much more relevant approach to motivation that replaces the theories of Maslow and Herzberg which, he claims, have been shown by extensive research to be wrong.

Process or cognitive theory can certainly be more useful to managers than needs theory because it provides more realistic guidance on motivation techniques. The main processes are expectations, goal achievement and feelings about equity.

Expectancy theory

Expectancy theory states that motivation will be high when people know what they have to do to get a reward, expect that they will be able to get the reward and expect that the reward will be worthwhile.

The concept of expectancy was originally contained in the valency–instrumentality–expectancy (VIE) theory formulated by Vroom (1964). Valency stands for value, instrumentality is the belief that if we do one thing it will lead to another, and expectancy is the probability that action or effort will lead to an outcome.

The strength of expectations may be based on past experiences (reinforcement), but individuals are frequently presented with new situations – a change in job, payment system, or working conditions imposed by management – where past experience is an inadequate guide to the implications of the change. In these circumstances, motivation may be reduced.

Motivation is only likely when a clearly perceived and usable relationship exists between performance and outcome, and the outcome is seen as a means of satisfying needs. This explains why extrinsic financial motivation – for example, an incentive or bonus scheme – works only if the link (line of sight) between effort and reward is clear and the value of the reward is worth the effort. It also explains why intrinsic motivation arising from the work itself can be more powerful than extrinsic motivation; intrinsic motivation outcomes are more under the control of individuals, who can place greater reliance on their past experiences to indicate the extent to which positive and advantageous results are likely to be obtained by their behaviour.

This theory was developed by Porter and Lawler (1968) into a model that follows Vroom's ideas by suggesting that there are two factors determining the effort people put into their jobs: first the value of the rewards to individuals in so far as they satisfy their needs for security, social esteem, autonomy, and self-actualization, and second the probability that rewards depend on effort, as perceived by individuals – in other words, their expectations about the relationships between effort and reward. Thus, the greater the value of a set of awards and the higher the probability that receiving each of these rewards depends upon effort, the greater the effort that will be expended in a given situation.

But, as Porter and Lawler emphasize, mere effort is not enough. It has to be effective effort if it is to produce the desired performance. The two variables additional to effort that affect task achievement are 1) ability – individual characteristics such as intelligence, knowledge, skills, and 2) role perceptions – what individuals want to do or think they are required to do. These are good from the viewpoint of the organization if they correspond with what it thinks the individual ought to be doing. They are poor if the views of the individual and the organization do not coincide. A model of their theory is shown in Figure 19.2.

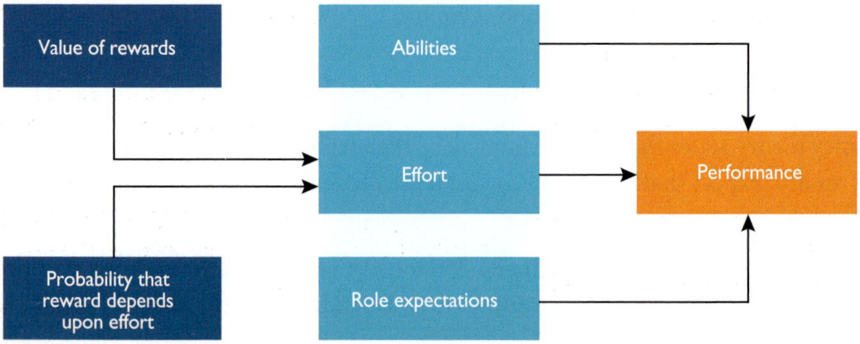

Figure 19.2 Motivation model (Porter and Lawler)

Goal theory

Goal theory as developed by Latham and Locke (1979) states that motivation and performance are higher when individuals are set specific goals, when goals are difficult but accepted, and when there is feedback on performance. Participation in goal setting is important as a means of getting agreement to the setting of higher goals. Difficult goals must be agreed and their achievement reinforced by guidance and advice. Finally, feedback is vital in maintaining motivation, particularly towards the achievement of even higher goals.

Goal theory is in line with the 1960s concept of management by objectives (a process of managing, motivating and appraising people by setting objectives or goals and measuring performance against those objectives). But management by objectives or MBO fell into disrepute because it was tackled bureaucratically without gaining the real support of those involved and, importantly, without ensuring that managers were aware of the significance of the processes of agreement, reinforcement and feedback, and were skilled in practising them. Goal theory, however, plays a key part in performance management, as described in Chapter 38.

Social learning theory

Social learning theory as developed by Bandura (1977) combines aspects of both behavioural and expectancy theory. It recognizes the significance of the basic behavioural concept of reinforcement as a determinant of future behaviour but also emphasizes the importance of internal psychological factors, especially expectancies about the value of goals and the individual's ability to reach them. The term 'reciprocal determinism' is used to denote the concept that while the situation will affect individual behaviour, individuals will simultaneously influence the situation.

Robertson and Cooper (1983) have pointed out that 'there are many similarities between social learning theory and expectancy theory in their joint emphasis on expectancies, individual goals and values and the influence of both person and situational factors'.

Equity theory

Equity theory (Adams, 1965) is concerned with the perceptions people have about how they are being treated as compared with others. To be dealt with equitably is to be treated fairly in comparison with another group of people (a reference group) or a relevant other person. Equity involves feelings and perceptions and it is always a comparative process. It is not synonymous with equality, which means treating everyone the same, since this would be inequitable if they deserve to be treated differently.

Equity theory states, in effect, that people will be better motivated if they are treated equitably and demotivated if they are treated inequitably. It explains only one aspect of the processes of motivation and job satisfaction, although it may be significant in terms of morale.

There are two forms of equity: distributive equity, which is concerned with the fairness with which people feel they are rewarded in accordance with their contribution and in comparison with others; and procedural equity, which is concerned with the perceptions employees have about the fairness with which company procedures in such areas as performance appraisal, promotion and discipline are being operated.

Herzberg's two-factor model

The two-factor model of satisfiers and dissatisfiers was developed by Herzberg *et al* (1957) following an investigation into the sources of job satisfaction and dissatisfaction of accountants and engineers. It was assumed that people have the capacity to report accurately the conditions that made them satisfied and dissatisfied with their jobs. Accordingly, the subjects were asked to tell their interviewers about the times during which they felt exceptionally good and exceptionally bad about their jobs and how long their feelings persisted. It was found that the accounts of 'good' periods most frequently concerned the content of the job, particularly achievement, recognition, advancement, responsibility, and the work itself. On the other hand, accounts of 'bad' periods most frequently concerned the context of the job. Company policy and administration, supervision, salary and working conditions more frequently appeared in these accounts than in those told about 'good' periods. The main implications of this research, according to Herzberg *et al*, were explained as follows.

SOURCE REVIEW

Implications of their research as explained by Herzberg *et al* (1957)

The wants of employees divide into two groups. One group revolves around the need to develop in one's occupation as a source of personal growth. The second group operates as an essential base to the first and is associated with fair treatment in compensation, supervision, working conditions and administrative practices. The fulfilment of the needs of the second group does not motivate the individual to high levels of job satisfaction and to extra performance on the job. All we can expect from satisfying this second group of needs is the prevention of dissatisfaction and poor job performance.

The second group forms the hygiene factors in the medical use of the term, meaning preventive and environmental. Herzberg pointed out that while financial incentives may motivate in the short term, the effect quickly wears off.

Herzberg's two-factor theory has been strongly attacked by, for example, Opsahl and Dunnette (1966). The research method has been criticized because no attempt was made to measure the relationship between satisfaction and performance. It has been suggested that the two-factor nature of the theory is an inevitable result of the questioning method used by the interviewers. It has also been suggested that wide and unwarranted inferences have been drawn from small and specialized samples and that there is no evidence to suggest that the satisfiers do improve productivity.

In spite of these criticisms the Herzberg two-factor theory continues to thrive; partly because it is easy to understand and seems to be based on 'real life' rather than academic abstractions, and partly because it convincingly emphasizes the positive value of the intrinsic motivating factors. It is also in accord with a fundamental belief in the dignity of labour and the Protestant ethic – that work is good in itself. As a result, Herzberg had immense influence on the job enrichment movement, which sought to design jobs in a way that would maximize the opportunities to obtain intrinsic satisfaction from work and thus improve the quality of working life.

McGregor's Theory X and Y

Douglas McGregor (1960) produced his analysis of the different views about people and how they should be motivated. Theory X is the traditional view that the average human dislikes work and wishes to avoid responsibility and that, therefore, 'most people must be coerced, controlled, directed, threatened with punishment to get them to put forward adequate effort towards organizational objectives'. In contrast, theory Y emphasizes that people will exercise self-direction in the service of objectives to which they are committed and that commitment to objectives is a function of the rewards associated with their achievement.

Motivation and money

Money, in the form of pay or some other sort of remuneration, is the most obvious extrinsic reward. Money seems to provide the carrot most people want.

Doubts were cast on the effectiveness of money by Herzberg *et al* (1957) because, they claimed, while the lack of it can cause dissatisfaction, its provision does not result in lasting satisfaction. There is something in this, especially for people on fixed salaries or rates of pay who do not benefit directly from an incentive scheme. They may feel good when they get an increase; apart from the extra money, it is a highly tangible form of recognition and an effective means of helping people to feel that they are valued. But this feeling of euphoria can rapidly die away. Other dissatisfactions from Herzberg's list of hygiene factors, such as working conditions or the quality of management, can loom larger in some people's minds when they fail to get the satisfaction they need from the work itself. However, it must be re-emphasized that different people have different needs and wants. Some will be much more motivated by money than others. What cannot be assumed is that money motivates everyone in the same way and to the same extent. Thus it is naïve to think that the introduction of a performance-related pay scheme will miraculously transform everyone overnight into well-motivated, high-performing individuals.

Nevertheless, money is a powerful force because it is linked directly or indirectly to the satisfaction of many needs. Money may in itself have no intrinsic meaning, but it acquires significant motivating power because it comes to symbolize so many intangible goals. It acts as a symbol in different ways for different people, and for the same person at different times.

But do financial incentives motivate people? The answer is yes, for those people who are strongly motivated by money and whose expectations that they will receive a financial reward are high. But less confident employees may not respond to incentives that they do not expect to achieve. It can also be argued that extrinsic rewards may erode intrinsic interest – people who work just for money could find their tasks less pleasurable and may not, therefore, do them so well. What we do know is that a multiplicity of factors is involved in performance improvements and many of those factors are interdependent.

Money can therefore provide positive motivation in the right circumstances not only because people need and want money but also because it serves as a highly tangible means of recognition. But badly designed and managed pay systems can demotivate. Another researcher in this area was Jaques (1961), who emphasized the need for such systems to be perceived as being fair and equitable. In other words, the reward should be clearly related to effort or level of responsibility and people should not receive less money than they deserve compared with their fellow workers. Jaques called this the 'felt-fair' principle.

Motivation strategies

Motivation strategies aim to create a working environment and to develop policies and practices that will provide for higher levels of performance from employees. The factors affecting them and the HR contribution are summarized in Table 19.2.

Table 19.2 Factors affecting motivation strategies and the HR contribution

Factors affecting motivation strategies	The HR contribution
• The complexity of the process of motivation means that simplistic approaches based on instrumentality theory are unlikely to be successful.	• Avoid the trap of developing or supporting strategies that offer prescriptions for motivation based on a simplistic view of the process or fail to recognize individual differences

Table 19.2 *continued*

Factors affecting motivation strategies	The HR contribution
• People are more likely to be motivated if they work in an environment in which they are valued for what they are and what they do. This means paying attention to the basic need for recognition	• Encourage the development of performance management processes which provide opportunities to agree expectations and give positive feedback on accomplishments • Develop reward systems which provide opportunities for both financial and non-financial rewards to recognize achievements. Bear in mind, however, that financial rewards systems are not necessarily appropriate and the lessons of expectancy, goal and equity theory need to be taken into account in designing and operating them
• The need for work which provides people with the means to achieve their goals, a reasonable degree of autonomy, and scope for the use of skills and competences should be recognized	• Advise on processes for the design of jobs which take account of the factors affecting the motivation to work, providing for job enrichment in the shape of variety, decision-making responsibility and as much control as possible in carrying out the work
• The need for the opportunity to grow by developing abilities and careers	• Provide facilities and opportunities for learning through such means as personal development planning processes as well as more formal training • Develop career planning processes
• The cultural environment of the organization in the shape of its values and norms will influence the impact of any attempts to motivate people by direct or indirect means	• Advise on the development of a culture which supports processes of valuing and rewarding employees
• Motivation will be enhanced by leadership which sets the direction, encourages and stimulates achievement and provides support to employees in their efforts to reach goals and improve their performance generally	• Devise competence frameworks which focus on leadership qualities and the behaviours expected of managers and team leaders • Ensure that leadership potential is identified through performance management and assessment centers • Provide guidance and training to develop leadership qualities

Motivation – key learning points

The process of motivation

Motivation is goal-directed behaviour. People are motivated when they expect that a course of action is likely to lead to the attainment of a goal and a valued reward – one that satisfies their needs and wants.

Types of motivation

The two basic types are intrinsic and extrinsic motivation.

Motivation theories

There are a number of motivation theories which, in the main, are complementary to one another. The most significant theories are those concerned with expectancy, goal setting and equity, which are classified as process or cognitive theories.

Motivation and money

Money is a powerful motivating force because it is linked directly or indirectly to the satisfaction of many needs. Money may in itself have no intrinsic meaning, but it acquires significant motivating power because it comes to symbolize so many intangible goals.

Motivation strategies

Motivation strategies aim to create a working environment and to develop policies and practices that will provide for higher levels of performance from employees. They include the development of total reward systems and performance management processes, the design of intrinsically motivating jobs and leadership development programmes.

Questions

1. What is the difference between content and process theory?
2. In his seminal 1968 *Harvard Business Review* article 'One more time, how do you motivate employees', Frederick Herzberg wrote that: 'The opposite of job satisfaction is not job dissatisfaction but, rather, no job satisfaction; and similarly, the opposite of job dissatisfaction is not job satisfaction, but no job dissatisfaction.' What do you think Herzberg meant by that statement and what is its significance?
3. In his 1993 *Harvard Business Review* article, Alfie Kohn wrote: 'Do rewards work? The answer depends on what we mean by "work". Research suggests that, by and large, rewards succeed at securing one thing only: temporary compliance. When it comes to producing lasting change in attitudes and behaviour, however, rewards, like punishment, are strikingly ineffective.' What does this tell us about the power of money to motivate? Does it mean that money never motivates effectively, or what?

Questions (continued)

4. Jeffrey Pfeffer (1998b) wrote in his article on 'Six dangerous myths about pay' in the *Harvard Business Review:* 'People do work for money – but they work even more for meaning in their lives. In fact, they work to have fun. Companies that ignore this fact are essentially bribing their employees and will pay the price in a lack of loyalty and commitment.' What are the implications of this contention on policies affecting motivation in an organization?

References

Adams, J S (1965) Injustice in social exchange, in (ed) L Berkowitz, *Advances in Experimental Psychology*, Academic Press, New York

Alderfer, C (1972) *Existence, Relatedness and Growth*, New York, The Free Press

Allport, G (1954) The historical background of modern social psychology, in (ed) G Lindzey, *Theoretical Models and Personality*, Addison-Wesley, Cambridge, MA

Arnold, J, Robertson, I T and Cooper, C L (1991) *Work Psychology*, Pitman, London

Bandura, A (1977) *Social Learning Theory*, Prentice-Hall, Englewood Cliffs, NJ

Deci, E L and Ryan, R M (1985) *Intrinsic Motivation and Self-determination in Human Behaviour*, Plenum, New York

Guest, D E (1992) Motivation after Herzberg, Unpublished paper delivered at the Compensation Forum, London

Hackman, J R and Oldham, G R (1974) Motivation through the design of work: test of a theory, *Organizational Behaviour and Human Performance*, **16** (2), pp 250–79

Herzberg, F W, Mausner, B and Snyderman, B (1957) *The Motivation to Work*, Wiley, New York

Herzberg, F (1968) One more time: how do you motivate employees?, *Harvard Business Review*, January-February, pp 109–20

Hull, C (1951) *Essentials of Behaviour*, Yale University Press, New Haven CT

Hunter, J E, Schmidt, F L and Judiesch, M K (1990) Individual differences in output variability as a function of job complexity, *Journal of Applied Psychology*, **75** (1), pp 28–42

Jaques, E (1961) *Equitable Payment*, Heinemann, Oxford

Katz, D (1964) The motivational basis of organizational behaviour, *Behavioural Science*, **9**, pp 131–36

Kohn, A (1993) Why incentive plans cannot work, *Harvard Business Review*, September–October, pp 54–63

Latham, G and Locke, R (1979) Goal setting – a motivational technique that works, *Organizational Dynamics*, Autumn, pp 68–80

McClelland, D C (1973) Testing for competence rather than intelligence, *American Psychologist*, **28** (1), pp 1–14

McGregor, D (1960) *The Human Side of Enterprise*, McGraw-Hill, New York

Maslow, A (1954) *Motivation and Personality*, Harper & Row, New York

Opsahl, R C and Dunnette, M D (1966) The role of financial compensation in individual motivation, *Psychological Bulletin*, **56**, pp 94–118

Pfeffer, J (1998b) Six dangerous myths about pay, *Harvard Business Review*, May–June, pp 109–19

Porter, L W and Lawler, E E (1968) *Managerial Attitudes and Performance*, Irwin-Dorsey, Homewood, IL

Robertson, I T and Cooper, C L (1983) *Human Behaviour in Organizations*, Macdonald & Evans, Plymouth

Skinner, B F (1974) *About Behaviourism*, Cape, London

Taylor, F W (1911) *Principles of Scientific Management*, Harper, New York

Vroom, V (1964) *Work and Motivation*, Wiley, New York

Wahba, M A and Bridwell, L G (1979) Maslow reconsidered: a review of research on the need hierarchy theory, in (eds) R M Sters and L W Porter, *Motivation and Work Behaviour*, McGraw Hill, New York

20

Engagement and Commitment

Key concepts and terms

- Commitment
- Discretionary learning
- Job satisfaction
- Organization climate
- Organizational citizenship
- Discretionary behaviour
- Engagement
- Learning culture
- Unitary frame of reference

Learning outcomes

On completing this chapter you should be able to define these key concepts. You should also know about:

- Comparison of the concepts of engagement and commitment
- The factors that influence engagement
- Measuring engagement
- The meaning of organizational commitment
- Problems with the concept of commitment
- Developing a commitment strategy
- The significance of employee engagement
- Engagement strategy
- Engagement and job satisfaction
- The significance of commitment
- Factors affecting commitment
- The contribution of HR to developing commitment

Introduction

The term 'commitment' in the shape of loyalty to and identification with the firm has been around for a long time as has the notion of organizational citizenship, which is behaviour that benefits the organization but is not required as part of the job description and is therefore discretionary.

However, more recently the term 'engagement' has come to the fore. It is sometimes used very loosely as a powerful notion that embraces pretty well everything the organization is seeking with regard to the contribution and behaviour of its employees in terms of levels of job performance, willingness to do that much more and identification with the organization. It is a useful mantra for management in organizations to chant – 'We want more engagement' – without always being clear about what they mean by engagement or how it can be achieved.

Confusion is further confounded when definitions of engagement are produced that make it synonymous with commitment. For example, Porter *et al* (1974) defined commitment as: 'The relative strength of the individual's identification with and involvement in a particular organization'. But the well-respected Conference Board in the United States defined employee engagement in 2006 as 'a heightened connection that an employee feels for his or her organization'. And the equally well-respected Institute for Employment Studies in the United Kingdom stated in 2004 (Robinson *et al*) that an engaged employee is someone who believes in, and identifies with, the organization.

Of course, there is some overlap between the ideas of engagement, commitment and motivation. It could be argued that this confusion may not create much real harm – as mentioned above, 'engagement, more engagement' is a worthy slogan. But unless some attempt is made to disentangle these concepts there is a real risk that progress in putting them to good use will be slow. It is necessary, for example, to appreciate that engaged employees are not necessarily committed to their organization; that a committed employee is not necessarily motivated to work harder; and that people may be committed to the organization in terms of wanting to stay with it, possibly because they may have nowhere else to go, but are still disenchanted with their jobs.

This chapter focuses on the area where most confusion lies: engagement and commitment. The aim is to clarify what these concepts really mean – the extent to which they are different; the extent to which they overlap. This is dealt with in the first section of the chapter. The next two sections concentrate on job engagement and organizational commitment in more detail; defining what each of them means and discussing what organizations can do about them.

The concepts of engagement and commitment compared

Employee engagement and organizational commitment are two important concepts affecting work performance and the attraction and retention of employees. Essentially, as explained in more detail later in this chapter, engagement is job-oriented and commitment is organization-oriented.

This is a clear distinction, although as mentioned above, the terms can be confused. They can indeed be closely linked – high organizational commitment can be associated with increased engagement and high engagement can be associated with increased commitment. But people can be engaged with their work even when they are not committed to the organization except in so far as it gives them the opportunity to use and develop their skills. This may be the case with some knowledge workers. For example, researchers may be mainly interested in the facilities for research they are given and the opportunity to make a name for themselves. They therefore join and stay with an organization only if it gives them the opportunities they seek.

It is useful to distinguish between the two because different policies may be required to enhance job engagement than those need to increase organizational commitment. Combinations of engagement and organizational commitment are illustrated in Figure 20.1.

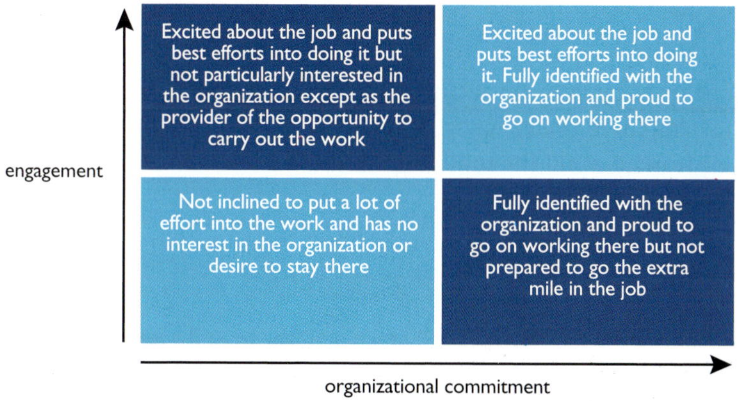

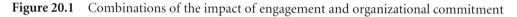

Figure 20.1 Combinations of the impact of engagement and organizational commitment

Employee engagement

Employee engagement takes place when people at work are interested in and positive, even excited about their jobs and are prepared to go the extra mile to get them done to the best of their ability. An engaged employee as defined by Bevan *et al* (1997) is someone 'who is aware of business context, and works closely with colleagues to improve performance within the job for the benefit of the organization'.

Interest in the notion of engagement was originally generated by The Hay Group which referred to it as 'engaged performance'. This was defined by Murlis and Watson (2001) as follows.

SOURCE REVIEW

The Hay Group definition of engaged performance

A result that is achieved by stimulating employees' enthusiasm for their work and directing it towards organizational success. This result can only be achieved when employers offer an implied contract to their employees that elicits specific positive behaviours aligned with the organization's goals.

This definition quite clearly focuses on performance in the job and not commitment to the organization.

Another firm of management consultants, Towers Perrin (2007), adopts a similar approach when it defined employee engagement as 'the extent to which employees put discretionary effort into their work, beyond the minimum to get the job done, in the form of extra time, brainpower or energy'.

The significance of employee engagement

The significance of employee engagement is that it is at the heart of the employment relationship. It is about what people do and how they behave in their roles and what makes them act in ways that further the achievement of the objectives of both the organization and themselves. Research reported by Watkin (2002) found that there were considerable differences in value-added discretionary performance between 'superior' and 'standard' performers. The difference in low complexity jobs was 19 per cent, in moderate-complexity jobs 32 per cent and in high-complexity jobs 48 per cent.

Engagement and discretionary behaviour

There is a close link between high levels of engagement and positive discretionary behaviour. As described by Purcell *et al* (2003) discretionary behaviour refers to the choices that people at work often have in the way they do the job and the amount of effort, care, innovation and productive behaviour they display. It can be positive when people 'go the extra mile' to achieve high levels of performance. It can be negative when they exercise their discretion to slack at their work. Discretionary behaviour is hard for the employer to define and monitor and to control the amount required. But positive discretionary behaviour is more likely to happen when people are engaged with their work.

SOURCE REVIEW

Propositions on discretionary behaviour, Purcell *et al* (2003)

- Performance-related practices only work if they positively induce discretionary behaviour, once basic staffing requirements have been met.
- Discretionary behaviour is more likely to occur when enough individuals have commitment to their organization and/or when they feel motivated to do so and/or when they gain high levels of job satisfaction.
- Commitment, motivation and job satisfaction, either together or separately, will be higher when people positively experience the application of HR policies concerned with creating an able workforce, motivating valued behaviours and providing opportunities to participate.
- This positive experience will be higher if the wide range of HR policies necessary to develop ability, motivation, and opportunity are both in place and are mutually reinforcing.
- The way HR and reward policies and practices are implemented by front line managers and the way top-level espoused values and organizational cultures are enacted by them will enhance or weaken the effect of HR policies in triggering discretionary behaviour by influencing attitudes.
- The experience of success seen in performance outcomes helps reinforce positive attitudes.

The factors that influence engagement

Research cited by IDS (2007a) has identified two key elements that have to be present if genuine engagement is to exist. The first is the rational aspect, which relates to employees' understanding of their role, where it fits in the wider organization, and how it aligns with business objectives. The second is the emotional aspect, which has to do with how people feel about the organization, whether their work gives them a sense of personal accomplishment and how they relate to their manager.

These two overall aspects can be analysed into a number of factors that influence levels of engagement, as set out below.

The work itself

The work itself can create job satisfaction leading to intrinsic motivation and increased engagement. The factors involved are interesting and challenging work, responsibility (feeling that the work is important and having control over one's own resources), autonomy (freedom to act), scope to use and develop skills and abilities, the availability of the resources required to carry out the work, and opportunities for advancement.

The work environment

An enabling, supportive and inspirational work environment creates experiences that impact on engagement by influencing how people regard their roles and carry them out. An enabling environment will create the conditions that encourage high performance and effective discretionary behaviour. These include work processes, equipment and facilities, and the physical conditions in which people work. A supportive environment will be one in which proper attention is paid to achieving a satisfactory work–life balance, emotional demands are not excessive, attention is paid to providing healthy and safe working conditions, job security is a major consideration and personal growth needs are taken into consideration. An inspirational environment will be where what John Purcell and his colleagues refer to as 'the big idea' is present – the organization has a clear vision and a set of integrated values that are 'embedded, collective, measured and managed'.

The environment is affected by the organization's climate which, as defined by French *et al* (1985), is 'the relatively persistent set of perceptions held by organization members concerning the characteristics and quality of organizational culture'. It is also directly influenced by its work and HR practices. As Purcell (2001) stated, the way HR practices are experienced by employees is affected by organizational values and operational strategies, such as staffing policies or hours of work, as well as the way they are implemented. He also emphasized that work climate – how people get on in the organization – and the experience of actually doing the job – pace, demand and stress – all influence the way employees experience the work environment. This has an important effect on how they react to HR and reward practices and how these influence organizational outcomes. Employees react in a number of different ways to practices in their organization and this affects the extent to which they want to learn more, are committed and satisfied with their jobs. This, in turn, influences engagement – how well they do their jobs and whether they are prepared to contribute discretionary effort.

Leadership

The degree to which jobs encourage engagement and positive discretionary behaviour very much depends upon the ways in which job holders are led and managed. Managers and team leaders often have considerable discretion over how jobs are designed, how they allocate work and how much they delegate and provide autonomy. They can spell out the significance of the work people do. They can give them the opportunity to achieve and develop, and provide feedback that recognizes their contribution.

Opportunities for personal growth

Most people want to get on. As Lawler put it in 2003: 'People enjoy learning – there's no doubt about it – and it touches on an important "treat people right" principle for both organizations and people: the value of continuous, ongoing training and development.' Learning is a satisfying and rewarding experience and makes a significant contribution to intrinsic motivation. Alderfer (1972) emphasized the importance of the chance to grow as a means of rewarding people. He wrote: 'Satisfaction of growth needs depends on a person finding the opportunity to be what he or she is most fully and become what he or she can.' The opportunity to grow and develop is a motivating factor that directly impacts on engagement when it is an intrinsic element of the work.

Opportunities to contribute

Engagement is enhanced if employees have a voice that is listened to. This enables them to feed their ideas and views upwards and feel that they are making a contribution.

Strategies for enhancing engagement

Engagement strategies can be developed under the headings of the factors affecting engagement set out above.

The work itself

Intrinsic motivation through the work itself and therefore engagement depends basically on the way in which work or jobs are designed which, as Lawler (1969) stressed, must provide for feedback, use of abilities and autonomy.

Approaches based on these principles, as described in Chapter 27, should be used when setting up new work systems or jobs and the strategy should include provision for guidance and advice along these lines to those responsible for such developments. But the greatest impact on the levels of engagement arising from the design of work systems or jobs is made by line managers on a day-to-day basis. The strategy should therefore include arrangements for educating them as part of a leadership development programme in the importance of good work and job design, the part they can play and the benefits to them arising from thereby enhancing engagement. Performance management, with its emphasis on agreeing role expectations, is a useful means of doing this.

The work environment

A strategy for increasing engagement through the work environment will be generally concerned with developing a culture that encourages positive attitudes to work, promoting interest and excitement in the jobs people do and reducing stress. Lands' End believes that staff who are enjoying themselves, who are being supported and developed and who feel fulfilled and respected at work, will provide the best service to customers. The thinking behind why the company wants to inspire staff is straightforward – employees' willingness to do that little bit extra arises from their sense of pride in what the organization stands for, ie quality, service and value. It makes the difference between a good experience for customers and a poor one.

The strategy also needs to consider particular aspects of the work environment, especially communication, involvement, work–life balance and working conditions. It can include the formulation and application of 'talent relationship management' policies, which are concerned with building effective relationships with people in their roles, treating individual employees fairly, recognizing their value, giving them a voice and providing opportunities for growth.

Leadership

The leadership strategy should concentrate on what line managers have to do as leaders in order to play their vital and immediate part in increasing levels of engagement. This will include the implementation of learning programmes that help them to understand how they are expected to act and the skills they need to use. The programmes can include formal training (especially for potential managers or those in their first leadership role) but more impact will be made by 'blending' various learning methods such as e-learning, coaching and mentoring.

It should also be recognized that a performance management process can provide line managers with a useful framework in which they can deploy their skills in improving performance though increased engagement. This applies particularly to the performance management activities of role definition, performance improvement planning, joint involvement in monitoring performance, and feedback. The strategy should therefore include the steps required to make performance management more effective by increasing the commitment of managers to it and developing the skills they require.

Opportunities for personal growth

A strategy for providing development and growth opportunities should be based on the creation of a learning culture. This is one that promotes learning because it is recognized by top management, line managers and employees generally as an essential organizational process to which they are committed and in which they engage continuously. Reynolds (2004) describes a learning culture as a 'growth medium' that will 'encourage employees to commit to a range of positive discretionary behaviours, including learning' and which has the following characteristics: empowerment not supervision, self-managed learning not instruction, long-term capacity building not short-term fixes. It will encourage discretionary learning, which Sloman (2003) believes takes place when individuals actively seek to acquire the knowledge and skills that promote the organization's objectives.

Specifically, the strategy should define the steps required to ensure that people have the opportunity and are given the encouragement to learn and grow in their roles. This includes the use of policies that focus on role flexibility – giving people the chance to develop their roles by making better and extended use of their talents. This means going beyond talent management for the favoured few and developing the abilities of the core people on whom the organization depends. The philosophy should be that everyone has the ability to succeed and the aim should be to 'achieve extraordinary results with ordinary people'. It includes using performance management primarily as a developmental process with an emphasis on personal development planning.

The strategy should also cover career development opportunities and how individuals can be given the guidance, support and encouragement they need if they are to fulfil their potential and achieve a successful career with the organization in tune with their talents and aspirations. The actions required to provide men and women of promise with a sequence of learning activities and experiences that will equip them for whatever level of responsibility they have the ability to reach should be included in the strategy.

Opportunities to contribute

Providing people with the opportunity to contribute is not just a matter of setting up formal consultative processes, although they can be important. It is also about creating a work environment that gives people a voice by encouraging them to have their say, and emphasizes as a core value of the organization that management at all levels must be prepared to listen and respond to any contributions their people make.

Measuring engagement

When developing engagement strategies the first step is to establish what is happening now and, in the light of that, determine what should happen in each of the areas described above. This means measuring levels of engagement regularly to identify successes and failures and analyse any gaps between what is wanted and what is actually going on. This can be done through published surveys such as those operated by Gallop, which enable benchmarking to take place with the levels of engagement achieved in other organizations. Alternatively, organizations can develop their own surveys to suit their circumstances. An example of such a survey is provided in Appendix A.

Engagement and job satisfaction

The concept of job satisfaction is closely linked to that of engagement. Job satisfaction refers to the attitudes and feelings people have about their work. Positive and favourable attitudes towards the job lead to engagement and therefore job satisfaction. Negative and unfavourable attitudes towards the job indicate job dissatisfaction.

Morale is often defined as being equivalent to job satisfaction. Thus Guion (1958) defines morale as 'the extent to which an individual's needs are satisfied and the extent to which the individual perceives that satisfaction as stemming from his [sic] total work situation'. Other definitions stress the group aspects of morale. Gilmer (1961) suggests that morale 'is a feeling of being accepted by and belonging to a group of employees through adherence to common goals'. He distinguishes between morale as a group variable, related to the degree to which group members feel attracted to their group and desire to remain a member of it, and job attitude as an individual variable related to the feelings employees have about their job.

Factors affecting job satisfaction

The level of job satisfaction is affected by intrinsic and extrinsic motivating factors, the quality of supervision, social relationships with the work group and the degree to which individuals succeed or fail in their work. Purcell *et al* (2003) believe that discretionary behaviour that helps the firm to be successful is most likely to happen when employees are well motivated and feel committed to the organization and when the job gives them high levels of satisfaction. Their research found that the key factors affecting job satisfaction were career opportunities, job influence, teamwork and job challenge.

Job satisfaction and performance

It is a commonly held and a seemingly not unreasonable belief that an increase in job satisfaction will result in improved performance. But research has not established any strongly positive connection between satisfaction and performance. A review of the extensive literature on this subject by Brayfield and Crockett (1955) concluded that there was little evidence of any simple or appreciable relationship between employee satisfaction and performance. An updated review of their analysis by Vroom (1964) covered 20 studies, in each of which one or more measures of job satisfaction or employee attitudes were correlated with one or more criteria of performance. The median correlation of all these studies was 0.14, which is not high enough to suggest a marked relationship between satisfaction and performance.

It can be argued that it is not job satisfaction that produces high performance but high performance that produces job satisfaction, and that a satisfied worker is not necessarily a productive worker and a high producer is not necessarily a satisfied worker. People are motivated to achieve certain goals and will be satisfied if they achieve these goals through improved performance. They may be even more satisfied if they are then rewarded by extrinsic recognition or an intrinsic sense of achievement. This suggests that performance improvements can be achieved by giving people the opportunity to perform, ensuring that they have the knowledge and skill required to perform, and rewarding them by financial or non-financial means when they do perform. It can also be argued that some people may be complacently satisfied with their job and will not be inspired to work harder or better. They may find other ways to satisfy their needs.

Organizational commitment

The concept of commitment plays an important part in HRM philosophy. As Guest (1987) has suggested, HRM policies are designed to 'maximize organizational integration, employee commitment, flexibility and quality of work'.

The meaning of organizational commitment

Commitment refers to attachment and loyalty. It is associated with the feelings of individuals about their organization. As defined by Porter *et al* (1974), commitment is the relative strength of the individual's identification with, and involvement in, a particular organization. The three characteristics of commitment identified by Mowday *et al* (1982) are:

1. A strong desire to remain a member of the organization.
2. A strong belief in, and acceptance of, the values and goals of the organization.
3. A readiness to exert considerable effort on behalf of the organization.

An alternative, although closely related, definition of commitment emphasizes the importance of behaviour in creating commitment. As Salancik (1977) put it: 'Commitment is a state of being in which an individual becomes bound by his [sic] actions to beliefs that sustain his activities and his own involvement.' Three features of behaviour are important in binding individuals to their acts: the visibility of the acts, the extent to which the outcomes are irrevocable, and the degree to which the person undertakes the action voluntarily. Commitment, according to Salancik, can be increased and harnessed 'to obtain support for organizational ends and interests' through such ploys as participation in decisions about actions.

The importance of commitment

There have been two schools of thought about what makes commitment important. One, the 'from control to commitment' school, was led by Walton (1985a, 1985b), the other, 'Japanese/excellence' school, is represented by writers such as Ouchi (1981), Pascale and Athos (1981) and Peters and Waterman (1982).

From control to commitment

The importance of commitment was highlighted by Walton (1985a, 1985b). His theme was that improved performance would result if the organization moved away from the traditional control-oriented approach to workforce management, which relies upon establishing order, exercising control and 'achieving efficiency in the application of the workforce'. He proposed that this approach should be replaced by a commitment strategy. Workers respond best – and most creatively – not when they are tightly controlled by management, placed in narrowly defined jobs, and treated like an unwelcome necessity, but, instead, when they are given broader responsibilities, encouraged to contribute and helped to achieve satisfaction in their work.

SOURCE REVIEW

The commitment-based approach, Walton (1985a, 1985b)

Jobs are designed to be broader than before, to combine planning and implementation, and to include efforts to upgrade operations, not just to maintain them. Individual responsibilities are expected to change as conditions change, and teams, not individuals, often are the organizational units accountable for performance. With management hierarchies relatively flat and differences in status minimized, control and lateral coordination depend on shared goals. And expertise rather than formal position determines influence.

Put like this, a commitment strategy may sound idealistic but does not appear to be a crude attempt to manipulate people to accept management's values and goals as some have suggested. In fact, Walton does not describe it as being instrumental in this manner. His prescription is for a broad HRM approach to the ways in which people are treated, jobs are designed and organizations are managed. He believes that the aim should be to develop 'mutuality', a state that exists when management and employees are interdependent and both benefit from this interdependency.

The Japanese/excellence school

Attempts made to explain the secret of Japanese business success in the 1970s by such writers as Ouchi (1981) and Pascale and Athos (1981) led to the theory that the best way to motivate people is to get their full commitment to the values of the organization by leadership and involvement. This might be called the 'hearts and minds' approach to motivation and, among other things, it popularized such devices as quality circles.

The baton was taken up by their imitators later in the 1980s. This approach to excellence was summed up by Peters and Waterman (1982) when they wrote, again, somewhat idealistically, as follows.

SOURCE REVIEW

Approach to excellence, Peters and Waterman (1982)

Trust people and treat them like adults, enthuse them by lively and imaginative leadership, develop and demonstrate an obsession for quality, make them feel they own the business, and your workforce will respond with total commitment.

Problems with the concept of commitment

A number of commentators have raised questions about the concept of commitment. These relate to three main problem areas: 1) its unitary frame of reference, 2) commitment as an inhibitor of flexibility, and 3) whether high commitment does in practice result in improved organizational performance.

Unitary frame of reference

A comment frequently made about the concept of commitment is that it is too simplistic in adopting a unitary frame of reference; in other words, it assumes unrealistically that an organization consists of people with shared interests. It has been suggested by people like Cyert and March (1963), Mangham (1979) and Mintzberg (1983a) that an organization is really a coalition of interest groups where political processes are an inevitable part of everyday life. The pluralistic perspective recognizes the legitimacy of different interests and values and therefore asks the question, 'Commitment to what?' Thus, as Coopey and Hartley (1991) put it, 'commitment is not an all-or-nothing affair (though many managers might like it to be) but a question of multiple or competing commitments for the individual'. Legge (1989) also raises this question in her discussion of strong culture as a key requirement of HRM through 'a shared set of managerially sanctioned values'.

However, values concerned with performance, quality, service, equal opportunity and innovation are not necessarily wrong because they are managerial values. But it is not unreasonable to believe that pursuing a value such as innovation could work against the interests of employees by, for example, resulting in redundancies. And it would be quite reasonable for any employee encouraged to behave in accordance with a value supported by management to ask, 'What's in it for me?' It can also be argued that the imposition of management's values on employees without their having any part to play in discussing and agreeing them is a form of coercion.

Commitment and flexibility

It was pointed out by Coopey and Hartley (1991) that: 'The problem for a unitarist notion of organizational commitment is that it fosters a conformist approach which not only fails to reflect organizational reality, but can be narrowing and limiting for the organization.' They argue that if employees are expected and encouraged to commit themselves tightly to a single set of values and goals they will not be able to cope with the ambiguities and uncertainties that are endemic in organizational life in times of change. Conformity to 'imposed' values will inhibit creative problem solving, and high commitment to present courses of action will increase both resistance to change and the stress that invariably occurs when change takes place.

If commitment is related to tightly defined plans then this will become a real problem. To avoid it, the emphasis should be on overall strategic directions. These would be communicated to employees with the proviso that changing circumstances will require their amendment. In the meantime, however, everyone can at least be informed in general terms where the organization is heading and, more specifically, the part they are expected to play in helping the organization to get there. And if they can be involved in the decision-making processes on matters that affect them (including management's values for performance, quality and customer service), so much the better.

Values need not necessarily be restrictive. They can be defined in ways that allow for freedom of choice within broad guidelines. In fact, the values themselves can refer to such processes as flexibility, innovation and responsiveness to change. Thus, far from inhibiting creative problem solving, they can encourage it.

SOURCE REVIEW

The positive value of commitment, Walton (1985a)

Underlying all these (human resource) policies is a management philosophy, often embedded in a published statement, that acknowledges the legitimate claims of a company's multiple stakeholders – owners, employees, customers and the public. At the centre of this philosophy is a belief that eliciting employee commitment will lead to enhanced performance. The evidence shows this belief to be well founded.

However, a review by Guest (1991) of the mainly North American literature, reinforced by the limited UK research available, led him to the conclusion that: 'High organizational commitment is associated with lower labour turnover and absence, but there is no clear link to performance.'

It is probably wise not to expect too much from commitment as a means of making a direct and immediate impact on performance. It is not the same as motivation or engagement. Commitment is a wider concept and tends to be more stable over a period of time and less responsive to transitory aspects of an employee's job. It is possible to be dissatisfied with a particular feature of a job while retaining a reasonably high level of commitment to the organization as a whole.

SOURCE REVIEW

Three perspectives on relating commitment to motivation, Buchanan and Huczynski (1985)

1. The goals towards which people aim. From this perspective, goals such as the good of the company, or effective performance at work, may provide a degree of motivation for some employees, who could be regarded as committed in so far as they feel they own the goals.
2. The process by which goals and objectives at work are selected, which is quite distinct from the way in which commitment arises within individuals.
3. The social process of motivating others to perform effectively. From this viewpoint, strategies aimed at increasing motivation also affect commitment. It may be true to say that where commitment is present, motivation is likely to be strong, particularly if a long-term view is taken of effective performance.

It is reasonable to believe that strong commitment to work is likely to result in conscientious and self-directed application to do the job, regular attendance, nominal supervision and a high level of effort. Commitment to the organization will certainly be related to the intention to stay – in other words, loyalty to the company.

Factors affecting commitment

Kochan and Dyer (1993) have indicated that the factors affecting the level of commitment in what they call 'mutual commitment firms' are as follows:

- Strategic level: supportive business strategies, top management value commitment and effective voice for HR in strategy making and governance.

- Functional (human resource policy) level: staffing based on employment stabilization, investment in training and development and contingent compensation that reinforces cooperation, participation and contribution.
- Workplace level: selection based on high standards, broad task design and teamwork, employee involvement in problem solving and a climate of cooperation and trust.

SOURCE REVIEW

Key policy and practice factors influencing levels of commitment, Purcell *et al* (2003)

- Received training last year.
- Satisfied with career opportunities.
- Satisfied with the performance appraisal system.
- Think managers are good in people management (leadership).
- Find their work challenging.
- Think their firm helps them achieve a work–life balance.
- Satisfied with communication or company performance.

Developing a commitment strategy

A commitment strategy will be based on the high-commitment model described in Chapter 3. It will aim to develop commitment using, as appropriate, approaches such as those described below. When formulating the strategy, account should be taken of the reservations expressed earlier in this chapter and too much should not be expected from it. The aim will be to increase identification with the organization, develop feelings of loyalty amongst its employees, provide a context within which motivation and therefore performance will increase, reduce employee turnover, and increase job satisfaction. But too much should not be expected from campaigns to increase commitment the level of which is influenced by many factors that cannot always be manipulated as the organization would wish. It is naïve to believe that 'hearts and minds' campaigns to win commitment will transform organizational behaviour overnight.

Steps to create commitment will be concerned with both strategic goals and values. They may include initiatives to increase involvement and 'ownership', communication, leadership development, developing a sense of excitement in the job, and developing various HR policy and practice initiatives.

Developing ownership

Commitment – a sense of belonging – is enhanced if there is a feeling of 'ownership' among employees: not just in the literal sense of owning shares (although this can help) but in the sense of believing they are genuinely accepted by management as key stakeholders in the organization. This concept of 'ownership' extends to participating in decisions on new developments and changes in working practices that affect the individuals concerned. They should take part in making those decisions and feel that their ideas have been listened to and that they have contributed to the outcome.

Communication programmes

It may seem to be strikingly obvious that commitment will only be gained if people understand what they are expected to commit to. But management too often fail to pay sufficient attention to delivering the message in terms that recognize that the frame of reference for those who receive it is likely to be quite different from their own. Management's expectations will not necessarily coincide with those of employees. Pluralism prevails. And in delivering the message, the use of different and complementary channels of communication such as newsletters, briefing groups, videos, notice boards, etc is often neglected.

Leadership development

Commitment is enhanced if managers can gain the confidence and respect of their teams, and development programmes to improve the quality of leadership should form an important part of any strategy for increasing commitment. Management training can also be focused on increasing the competence of managers in specific areas of their responsibility for gaining commitment, eg performance management.

Developing HR practices that enhance commitment

The policies and practices that may contribute to the increase of commitment are learning and development, career planning, performance management, reward management, work–life balance policies and job design. Engagement strategies, as described in Chapter 19, will create feelings of excitement in the job and therefore commitment.

The contribution of HR to developing commitment

The HR function can play a major part in developing a high-commitment organization. The 10 steps it can take are:

1. Advise on methods of communicating the values and aims of management and the achievements of the organization so that employees are more likely to identify with it as one they are proud to work for.

2. Emphasize to management that commitment is a two-way process; employees cannot be expected to be committed to the organization unless management demonstrates that it is committed to them and recognizes their contribution as stakeholders.
3. Impress on management the need to develop a climate of trust by being honest with people, treating them fairly, justly and consistently, keeping its word, and showing willingness to listen to the comments and suggestions made by employees during processes of consultation and participation.
4. Develop a positive psychological contract (see Chapter 16) by treating people as stakeholders, relying on consensus and cooperation rather than control and coercion, and focusing on the provision of opportunities for learning, development and career progression.
5. Advise and assist on the establishment of partnership agreements with trade unions that emphasize unity of purpose, common approaches to working together and the importance of giving employees a voice in matters that concern them.
6. Recommend and take part in the achievement of single status for all employees (often included in a partnership agreement) so that there is no longer an 'us and them' culture.
7. Encourage management to declare a policy of employment security and ensure that steps are taken to avoid involuntary redundancies.
8. Develop performance management processes that provide for the alignment of organizational and individual objectives.
9. Advise on means of increasing employee identification with the company through rewards related to organizational performance (profit sharing or gainsharing) or employee share ownership schemes.
10. Enhance employee engagement, ie identification of employees with the job they are doing, through job design processes that aim to create higher levels of job satisfaction (job enrichment).

Engagement and commitment – key learning points

Comparison of the concepts of engagement and commitment

Engagement is job-oriented and commitment is organization-oriented. This is a clear distinction but the terms are often confused.

The significance of employee engagement

There is a close link between high levels of engagement and positive discretionary behaviour.

Engagement and commitment – key learning points (continued)

The factors that influence engagement

The first factor is the rational aspect, which relates to employees' understanding of their role, where it fits in the wider organization, and how it aligns with business objectives. The second is the emotional aspect, which has to do with how people feel about the organization, whether their work gives them a sense of personal accomplishment and how they relate to their manager.

Engagement strategy

Enhance motivation through the work itself, the work environment, leadership and opportunities for growth.

Measuring engagement

This can be done through published surveys that enable benchmarking to take place with the levels of engagement achieved in other organizations. Alternatively organizations can develop their own surveys to suit their circumstances.

Engagement and job satisfaction

The concept of job satisfaction is closely linked to that of engagement. Job satisfaction refers to the attitudes and feelings people have about their work. Positive and favourable attitudes towards the job lead to engagement and therefore job satisfaction. The level of job satisfaction is affected by intrinsic and extrinsic motivating factors, the quality of supervision, social relationships with the work group and the degree to which individuals succeed or fail in their work.

The meaning of organizational commitment

Commitment refers to attachment and loyalty. It is associated with the feelings of individuals about their organization. As defined by Porter *et al* (1974), commitment is the relative strength of the individual's identification with, and involvement in, a particular organization.

The importance of commitment

There have been two schools of thought about what makes commitment important. One, the 'from control to commitment' school, was led by Walton (1985a, 1985b); the other, 'Japanese/excellence' school, is represented by writers such as Ouchi (1981), Pascale and Athos (1981) and Peters and Waterman (1982).

Problems with the concept of commitment

There are three main problem areas: 1) its unitary frame of reference, 2) it might inhibit flexibility, and 3) it does not necessarily result in improved organizational performance.

Factors affecting commitment

Kochan and Dyer (1993) have indicated that the factors affecting the level of commitment are:

- Strategic level: supportive business strategies, top management value commitment and an effective voice for HR in strategy making and governance.

Engagement and commitment – key learning points (continued)

- Functional (human resource policy) level: staffing based on employment stabilization, investment in training and development and contingent compensation that reinforces cooperation, participation and contribution.
- Workplace level: selection based on high standards, broad task design and teamwork, employee involvement in problem solving and a climate of cooperation and trust.

Developing a commitment strategy

Steps to create commitment may include initiatives to increase involvement and 'ownership', communication, leadership development, developing a sense of excitement in the job, and developing various HR policy and practice initiatives.

The contribution of HR to developing commitment

HR can provide advice and guidance on communicating corporate values, building trust, making commitment a two-way process, developing a positive psychological contract, the development of partnership agreements, single status and increased employment security, and the use of performance management to align individual and organizational goals.

Questions

1. What is the difference between engagement and commitment?
2. Your boss e-mails you as follows: 'I keep on hearing about employee engagement but what does it really mean? Is it just another piece of HR jargon as an alternative to motivation? Is there anything we should or can do about it?' Reply.
3. You have been asked to give a talk to your colleagues in the HR department on 'What can we do to increase commitment?' Draft your presentation.

References

Alderfer, C (1972) *Existence, Relatedness and Growth*, The Free Press, New York

Bevan S, Barber, L and Robinson, D (1997) *Keeping the Best: A practical guide to retaining key employees*, Institute for Employment Studies, Brighton

Brayfield, A H and Crockett, W H (1955) Employee attitudes and employee performance, *Psychological Bulletin*, **52**, pp 346–424

Buchanan, D and Huczynski, A (1985) *Organizational Behaviour*, Prentice Hall, Englewood Cliffs, NJ

Conference Board (2006) *Employee Engagement: A review of current research and its implications*, Conference Board, New York

Coopey, J and Hartley, J (1991) Reconsidering the case for organizational commitment, *Human Resource Management Journal*, **3**, Spring, pp 18–31

Cyert, R M and March, J G (1963) *A Behavioural Theory of the Firm*, Prentice Hall, Englewood Cliffs, NJ

French, W L, Kast, F E and Rosenzweig, J E (1985) *Understanding Human Behaviour in Organizations*, Harper & Row, New York

Gilmer, B (1961) *Industrial Psychology*, McGraw-Hill, New York

Guest, D E (1984) What's new in motivation, *Personnel Management*, May, pp 30–33

Guest, D E (1987) Human resource management and industrial relations, *Journal of Management Studies*, **14** (5), pp 503–21

Guest, D E (1991) Personnel management: the end of orthodoxy, *British Journal of Industrial Relations*, **29** (2), pp 149–76

Guion, R M (1958) Industrial morale (a symposium) – the problems of terminology, *Personnel Psychology*, **11**, pp 59–64

IDS (2007a) Building an engaged workforce, *HR Studies Update*, IDS London

Kochan, T A and Dyer, L (1993) Managing transformational change: the role of human resource professionals, *International Journal of Human Resource Management*, **4** (3), pp 569–90

Lawler, E E (1969) Job design and employee motivation, *Personnel Psychology*, **22**, pp 426–35

Lawler E E (2003) *Treat People Right! How organisations and individuals can propel each other into a virtuous spiral of success*, Jossey-Bass, San Francisco, CA

Legge, K (1989) Human resource management: a critical analysis, in (ed) J Storey, *New Perspectives in Human Resource Management*, Routledge, London

Mangham, L L (1979) *The Politics of Organizational Change*, Associated Business Press, London

Mintzberg, H (1983a) *Power in and Around Organizations*, Prentice Hall, Englewood Cliffs, NJ

Mowday, R, Porter, L and Steers, R (1982) *Employee–organization Linkages: The psychology of commitment, absenteeism and turnover*, Academic Press, London

Murlis, H and Watson, S (2001) Creating employee engagement – transforming the employment deal, *Benefits and Compensation International*, **30** (8), pp 6–17

Ouchi, W G (1981) *Theory Z*, Addison-Wesley, Reading, MA

Pascale, R and Athos, A (1981) *The Art of Japanese Management*, Simon & Schuster, New York

Peters, T and Austin, N (1985) *A Passion for Excellence*, Collins, Glasgow

Peters, T and Waterman, R (1982) *In Search of Excellence*, Harper & Row, New York

Porter, L W, Steers, R, Mowday, R and Boulian, P (1974) Organizational commitment: job satisfaction and turnover amongst psychiatric technicians, *Journal of Applied Psychology*, **59**, pp 603–9

Purcell, J (2001) The meaning of strategy in human resource management, in (ed) J Storey, *Human Resource Management: A critical text*, Thompson Learning, London

Purcell, J, Kinnie, K, Hutchinson, S, Rayton, B and Swart, J (2003) *People and Performance: How people management impacts on organisational performance*, CIPD, London

Reynolds, J (2004) *Helping People Learn*, CIPD, London

Robinson, D, Perryman, S and Hayday, S (2004) *The Drivers of Employee Engagement*, Institute of Employment Studies, Brighton

Salancik, G R (1977) Commitment and the control of organizational behaviour and belief, in (eds) B M Staw and G R Salancik, *New Directions in Organizational Behaviour*, St Clair Press, Chicago, IL

Sloman, M (2003) E-learning: stepping up the learning curve, *Impact*, CIPD, January, pp 16–17

Towers Perrin (2007) *Global Workforce Study* at http://www.towersperrin.com

Vroom, V (1964) *Work and Motivation*, Wiley, New York

Walton, R E (1985a) From control to commitment in the workplace, *Harvard Business Review*, March–April, pp 77–84

Walton, R E (1985b) Towards a strategy of eliciting employee commitment based on principles of mutuality, in (eds) R E Walton and P R Lawrence, *HRM Trends and Challenges*, Harvard Business School Press, Boston, MA

Watkin, C (2002) Engage employees to boost performance, *Selection & Development Review*, **18** (2), pp 3–6

21 How Organizations Function

Key concepts and terms

- Bureaucracy
- Contingency school
- Decentralized organization
- Divisionalized organization
- Equifinality
- Flexible organization
- Formal group
- Formal organization
- Group cohesion
- Group dynamics
- Group ideology
- Group norms
- Group think
- Humanism
- Informal group
- Informal organization
- Leadership
- Leadership style
- Line and staff organization
- Matrix organization
- Networking
- Open system
- Organization
- Organization structure
- Organizing
- Organizational capability
- Post-modernism
- Process-based organization
- Reference group
- Scientific management
- Socio-technical model
- Systems theory
- Team
- Theory Y

Learning outcomes

On completing this chapter you should be able to define these key concepts and terms. You should also know about:

- The process of organizing
- Organization structures
- Organizational processes
- Teamwork
- Power
- Conflict
- Organization theory
- Types of organization
- Group behaviour
- Leadership roles
- Politics

Introduction

An organization is a group of people who exist to achieve a common purpose. Organizing is the process of making arrangements in the form of defined or understood responsibilities and relationships to enable those people to work cooperatively together. Organizations can be described as systems which, as affected by their environment, have a structure that has both formal and informal elements.

Formal structures are based on laid down hierarchies (lines of command), which are represented in organization charts. Typically, use is made of closely defined job descriptions. But to varying extents they can operate informally as well as formally by means of a network of roles and relationships that cut across formal organizational boundaries and lines of command. The processes that take place in organizations of group behaviour, interaction and networking, leadership, the exercise of power and the use of politics may well have much more effect on how organizations function than a well-defined organization chart supported by elaborate job descriptions and an organization manual. Moreover, the way in which an organization functions will be largely contingent on its purpose, technology, methods of working and external environment.

One of the most important ways in which HR specialists contribute to enhancing organizational capability (the capacity of an organization to function effectively in order to compete and deliver results) is by providing advice on how best to organize the human resources involved. That is why HR specialists need to understand how organizations work. They need to be familiar with the guidance provided by organizational theory and an analysis of the various types of organizations and the practical issues of structure and process, as covered in this chapter.

Organization theory

Organization theory aims to describe how organizations function. There are a number of schools and models, described below.

The classical school

The classical or scientific management school, as represented by Fayol (1916), Taylor (1911) and Urwick (1947) believed in control, measurement, order and formality. Organizations need to minimize the opportunity for unfortunate and uncontrollable informal relations, leaving room only for the formal ones.

The human relations school

The classical model was first challenged by Barnard (1938). He emphasized the importance of the informal organization – the network of informal roles and relationships which, for better or worse, strongly influences the way the formal structure operates. He wrote: 'Formal organizations come out of and are necessary to informal organization: but when formal organizations come into operation, they create and require informal organizations.'

The importance of informal groups and decent, humane leadership was emphasized by Roethlisberger and Dickson (1939) in their report on the Hawthorne studies, which examined at length how groups of workers behaved in different circumstances

The behavioural science school

In the late 1950s and 1960s the focus shifted to the behaviour of people in organizations. Behavioural scientists such as Argyris (1957), Herzberg *et al* (1957), McGregor (1960) and Likert (1961) adopted a humanistic point of view that is concerned with what people can contribute and how they can best be motivated:

- Argyris believed that individuals should be given the opportunity to feel that they have a high degree of control over setting their own goals and over defining the paths to these goals.
- Herzberg suggested that improvements in organization design must centre on the individual job as the positive source of motivation. If individuals feel that the job is stretching them, they will be moved to perform it well.
- McGregor developed his theory of integration (theory Y), which emphasizes the importance of recognizing the needs of both the organization and the individual and creating conditions that will reconcile these needs so that members of the organization can work together for its success and share in its rewards.

- Likert stated that effective organizations function by means of supportive relationships which, if fostered, will build and maintain people's sense of personal worth and importance.

The concepts of these and other behavioural scientists such as Schein (1965) provided the impetus for the organization development (OD) movement, discussed in Chapter 24.

No one can quarrel with the values expressed by the members of the behavioural science school – we are all in favour of virtue. But there are a number of grounds on which the more extreme beliefs of the school can be criticized:

- It claims that its concepts are universally applicable, yet organizations come in all shapes and sizes with different activities and operating in different contexts.
- It ignores the real commercial and technological constraints of industrial life. Instead, it reflects more of an ideological concern for personal development and the rights of the individual rather than a scientific curiosity about the factors affecting organizational efficiency. It over-reacts against the excessive formality of the classical or scientific management school by largely ignoring the formal organization.
- Its emphasis on the need to minimize conflict overlooks the point that conflict is not necessarily undesirable, and may rather be an essential concomitant of change and development.

To be fair, not all behavioural scientists were so naïve. Although McGregor's theory Y was somewhat idealistic, he at least recognized that 'industrial health does not flow automatically from the elimination of dissatisfaction, disagreement, or even open conflict. Peace is not synonymous with organizational health; socially responsible management is not co-extensive with permissive management'.

The bureaucratic model

SOURCE REVIEW

The arrival of the bureaucratic model, Perrow (1980)

In another part of the management forest, the mechanistic school was gathering its forces and preparing to outflank the forces of light. First came the numbers people – the linear programmers, the budget experts, the financial analysts. Armed with emerging systems concepts, they carried the 'mechanistic' analogy to its fullest extent – and it was very productive. Their work still goes on, largely untroubled by organizational theory; the theory, it seems clear, will have to adjust to them, rather than the other way around. Then the works of Max Weber, not translated until the 1940s, began to find their way into social science thought.

Max Weber (translated in 1946) coined the term 'bureaucracy' as a label for a type of formal organization in which impersonality and rationality are developed to the highest degree. Bureaucracy, as he conceived it, was the most efficient form of organization because it is coldly logical and because personalized relationships and non-rational, emotional considerations do not get in its way. The ideal bureaucracy, according to Weber, has the following features:

- maximum specialization;
- close job definition as to duties, privileges and boundaries;
- vertical authority patterns;
- decisions based on expert judgement, resting on technical knowledge and on disciplined compliance with the directives of superiors;
- policy and administration are separate;
- maximum use of rules;
- impersonal administration of staff.

At first, with his celebration of the efficiency of bureaucracy, Weber was received with only reluctant respect, even hostility. Many commentators were against bureaucracy. But it turned out that managers are not. They tend to prefer clear lines of communication, clear specifications of authority and responsibility, and clear knowledge of whom they are responsible to. Admittedly, in some situations, as Burns and Stalker (1961) point out, managers might want absolute clarity but they can't get it. On the other hand there are circumstances when the type of work carried out in an organization requires a bureaucratic approach in the Weberian, not the pejorative 'red tape', sense. The problem with both the human relations and bureaucratic schools of thought were that they were insufficiently related to context. It is necessary to look at how organizations worked as systems within their environment – this was the approach adopted by the systems and socio-technical schools. It is also necessary to look at how organizations have to adapt to that environment. This was done by the contingency school.

The systems school

An important insight into how organizations function was provided by Miller and Rice (1967) who stated that organizations should be treated as open systems that are continually dependent upon and influenced by their environments. The basic characteristic of the enterprise as an open system is that it transforms inputs into outputs within its environment.

As Katz and Kahn (1966) wrote: 'Systems theory is basically concerned with problems of relationship, of structure and of interdependence.' As a result there is a considerable emphasis on the concept of transactions across boundaries – between the system and its environment and between the different parts of the system. This open and dynamic approach avoided the error of the classical, bureaucratic and human relations theorists, who thought of organizations as closed systems and analysed their problems with reference to their internal structures and processes of interaction, without taking account either of external influences and the changes they impose or of the technology in the organization.

The socio-technical model

The concept of the organization as a system was extended by Emery (1959) and his Tavistock Institute colleagues (Trist *et al*, 1963) into the socio-technical model of organizations. The basic principle of this model is that in any system of organization, technical or task aspects are interrelated with the human or social aspects. The emphasis is on interrelationships between, on the one hand, the technical processes of transformation carried out within the organization and, on the other hand, the organization of work groups and the management structures of the enterprise. This approach avoided the humanistic generalizations of the behavioural scientists without falling into the trap of treating the organization as a machine.

The contingency school

The contingency school consists of writers such as Burns and Stalker (1961), Woodward (1965) and Lawrence and Lorsch (1969) who have analysed a variety of organizations and concluded that their structures and methods of operation are a function of the circumstances in which they exist. They do not subscribe to the view that there is one best way of designing an organization or that simplistic classifications of organizations as formal or informal, bureaucratic or non-bureaucratic are helpful. They are against those who see organizations as mutually opposed social systems (what Burns and Stalker refer to as the 'Manichean world of the Hawthorne studies') that set up formal against informal organizations. They also disagree with those who impose rigid principles of organization irrespective of the technology or environmental conditions.

Burns and Stalker

Burns and Stalker (1961), in their study of electronic companies in Scotland, identified two types of organizations in which the structure and processes involved were contingent on their environment. In stable conditions a highly structured or 'mechanistic' organization will emerge with specialized functions, clearly defined roles, strictly administrative routines and a hierarchical system of exercising control. However, when the environment is volatile, a rigid system of ranks and routine will inhibit the organization's speed and sensitivity of response. In these circumstances the structure is, or should be, 'organic' in the sense that it is a function of the situation in which the enterprise finds itself rather than conforming to any predetermined and rigid view of how it should operate. Perhaps the most important contribution made by Burns and Stalker was their emphasis on the need for any system to fit its own specific set of conditions. Thus they expressed the notion of strategic fit well before its time. Their conclusions are set out below.

SOURCE REVIEW

Contingency theory applied to organizations, Burns and Stalker (1961)

We desire to avoid the suggestion that either system is superior under all circumstances to the other. In particular, nothing in our experience justifies the assumption that mechanistic systems should be superseded by organic in conditions of stability. The beginning of administrative wisdom is there is no one optimum type of management system.

Woodward

Woodward (1965) formulated her ideas about organization following a research project carried out in Essex to discover whether the principles of organization laid down by the classical theorists correlate with business success when put into practice. She found that there was no significant correlation. Her conclusions after further analysis were as follows.

SOURCE REVIEW

Contingency theory applied to organizations, Woodward (1965)

When, however, the firms were grouped according to similarity of objectives and techniques of production, and classified in order of the technical complexity of their production systems, each production system was found to be associated with a characteristic pattern of organization. It appeared that technical methods were the most important factor in determining organization structure and in setting the tone of human relationships inside the firms. The widely held assumption that there are principles of management valid for all types of production systems seemed very doubtful.

Lawrence and Lorsch

Lawrence and Lorsch (1969) developed their contingency model in a study of six firms in the plastics industry. They noted that the process of reacting to complexity and change by differentiation creates a demand for effective integration if the organization as a whole is to adapt efficiently to its environment. Their conclusions are given below.

SOURCE REVIEW

Contingency and the need for differentiation and integration, Lawrence and Lorsch (1969)

As organizations deal with their external environments, they become segmented into units, each of which has as its major task the problem of dealing with a part of the conditions outside the firm… These parts of the system need to be linked together towards the accomplishment of the organization's overall purpose.

The postmodern school

The postmodern school emerged in the early 1990s when commentators observed what was happening to organizations in their efforts to cope in a turbulent and highly competitive global environment. They noted that the emphasis was first on getting the process right and not bothering about rigid structures, and second on ensuring organizational agility – the ability to respond flexibly to new challenges. Postmodernism is about challenging assumptions, taking nothing for granted. It 'deconstructs' conventional wisdom about organizations so that previously unconsidered alternative approaches are revealed. As Huczynski and Buchanan (2007) comment, postmodernism represents a fundamental challenge to the ways in which we think about organizations and organizational behaviour.

Pascale (1990) described a 'new organizational paradigm', the features of which are:

- From the image of organizations as machines, with the emphasis on concrete strategy, structure and systems, to the idea of organizations as organisms, with the emphasis on the 'soft' dimensions – style, staff and shared values.
- From a hierarchical model, with step-by-step problem solving, to a network model, with parallel nodes of intelligence that surround problems until they are eliminated.

- From the status-driven view that managers think and workers do as they are told, to a view of managers as 'facilitators', with workers empowered to initiate improvements and change.
- From an emphasis on 'vertical tasks' within functional units to an emphasis on 'horizontal tasks' and collaboration across units.
- From a focus on 'content' and the prescribed use of specific tools and techniques to a focus on 'process' and a holistic synthesis of techniques.
- From the military model to a commitment model.

Ghoshal and Bartlett (1995) focused on process when they wrote:

> *Managers are beginning to deal with their organizations in different ways. Rather than seeing them as a hierarchy of static roles, they think of them as a portfolio of dynamic processes. They see core organizational processes that overlay and often dominate the vertical, authority-based processes of the hierarchical structure.*

Organization structure

The members of the various schools were in effect commenting on the factors affecting organization structure, as considered below.

Organization structure defined

All organizations have some form of more or less formalized structure that is the framework for getting things done. As defined by Child (1977) it consists of 'all the tangible and regularly occurring features which help to shape their members' behaviour'. Structures incorporate a network of roles and relationships and are there to help in the process of ensuring that collective effort is explicitly organized to achieve specified ends.

Organizations vary in their complexity, but it is necessary to divide the overall management task into a variety of activities, to allocate these activities to the different parts of the organization and to establish means of controlling, coordinating and integrating them. The structure of an organization consists of units, functions, divisions, departments and formally constituted work teams into which activities related to particular processes, projects, products, markets, customers, geographical areas or professional disciplines are grouped together. The structure indicates who is accountable for directing, coordinating and carrying out these activities and defines management hierarchies – the 'chain of command' – thus spelling out, broadly, who is responsible to whom for what at each level in the organization.

In accordance with the principle of equifinality (Doty *et al*, 1993) there are a number of equally effective forms of structure. The type of structure adopted is often contingent on the circumstances of the organization.

Organization charts

Structures are usually described in the form of an organization chart (deplorably, sometimes called an 'organogram', especially in UK government circles). This places individuals in boxes that denote their job and their position in the hierarchy and traces the direct lines of authority (command and control) through the management hierarchies.

Organization charts are vertical in their nature and therefore misrepresent reality. They do not give any indication of the horizontal and diagonal relationships that exist within the framework between people in different units or departments, and do not recognize the fact that within any one hierarchy, commands and control information do not travel all the way down and up the structure as the chart implies. In practice information jumps (especially computer-generated information) and managers or team leaders will interact with people at levels below those immediately beneath them.

Organization charts have their uses as means of defining – simplistically – who does what and hierarchical lines of authority. But even if backed up by organization manuals (which no one reads and which are, in any case, out of date as soon as they are produced) they cannot convey how the organization really works. They may, for example, lead to definitions of jobs – what people are expected to do – but they cannot convey the roles these people carry out in the organization, the parts they play in interacting with others and the ways in which, like actors, they interpret the parts they are given in their roles.

Types of organization

The basic types of organization are described below.

Line and staff

The line and staff organization was the type favoured by the classical theorists based on a military model. Although the term is not so much used today, except when referring to line managers, it still describes many structures. The line hierarchy in the structure consists of functions and managers who are directly concerned in achieving the primary purposes of the organization, for example, manufacturing and selling or directing the organization as a whole. 'Staff' in functions such as finance, HR and engineering provide services to the line to enable them to get on with their job.

Divisionalized organizations

The process of divisionalization, as first described by Sloan (1967) on the basis of his experience in running General Motors, involves structuring the organization into separate divisions each concerned with discrete manufacturing, sales, distribution or service functions, or with serving a particular market. At group headquarters, functional departments may exist in such areas as finance, planning, personnel, legal and engineering to provide services to the divisions and, importantly, to exercise a degree of functional control over their activities. The amount of control exercised will depend on the extent to which the organization has decided to decentralize authority to strategic business units that are positioned close to the markets they serve.

Decentralized organizations

Some organizations decentralize most of their activities and retain only a skeleton headquarters staff to deal with financial control matters, strategic planning, legal issues and sometimes, but not always, HR issues, especially those concerned with senior management on an across the group or international basis (recruitment, development and remuneration).

Matrix organizations

A matrix organization consists of a functional structure consisting of a number of different disciplines and a project structure consisting of project teams drawn from the disciplines. Thus an employee can be a member of a discipline and of a project team and so have two reporting relationships. Matrix organizations are project-based. Development, design or construction projects will be controlled by project directors or managers or, in the case of a consultancy, assignments will be conducted by project leaders. Project managers will have no permanent staff except, possibly, some administrative support. They will draw the members of their project teams from discipline groups, each of which will be headed up by a director or manager who is responsible on a continuing basis for resourcing the group, developing and managing its members and ensuring that they are assigned as fully as possible to project teams. These individuals are assigned to a project team and they will be responsible to the team leader for delivering the required results, but they will continue to be accountable generally to the head of their discipline for their overall performance and contribution. The most typical form of matrix organization is a large multidiscipline consultancy.

Flexible organizations

Flexible organizations may conform broadly to the Mintzberg (1983b) category of an adhocracy in the sense that they are capable of quickly adapting to new demands and operate fluidly. They may be organized as core-periphery organization or along the lines of Handy's (1981) 'shamrock' organization, which consists of three elements: 1) the core workers (the central leaf of the shamrock) – professionals, technicians and managers; 2) the contractual fringe – contract workers; and 3) the flexible labour force consisting of temporary staff.

An organization may adopt a policy of numerical flexibility, which means that the number of employees can be quickly increased or decreased in line with changes in activity levels. The different types of flexibility are described in Chapter 13.

The process-based organization

A process-based organization is one in which the focus is on horizontal processes that cut across organizational boundaries. Traditional organization structures consist of a range of functions operating semi-independently and each with its own, usually extended, management hierarchy. Functions acted as vertical 'chimneys' with boundaries between what they did and what happened next door. Continuity of work between functions and the coordination of activities was prejudiced. Attention was focused on vertical relationships and authority-based management – the 'command and control' structure. Horizontal processes received relatively little attention. It was, for example, not recognized that meeting the needs of customers by systems of order processing could only be carried out satisfactorily if the flow of work from sales through manufacturing to distribution were treated as a continuous process and not as three distinct parcels of activity. Another horizontal process that drew attention to the need to reconsider how organizations should be structured was total quality. This is not a top-down system. It cuts across the boundaries separating organizational units to ensure that quality is built into the organization's products and services.

In a process-based organization there will still be designated functions for, say, manufacturing, sales and distribution. But the emphasis will be on how these areas work together on multi-functional projects to deal with new demands such as product/market development. Teams will jointly consider ways of responding to customer requirements. Quality and continuous improvement will be regarded as a common responsibility shared between managers and staff from each function. The overriding objective will be to maintain a smooth flow of work between functions and to achieve synergy by pooling resources from different functions in task forces or project teams.

The Mintzberg analysis

An alternative analysis of organizations was made by Mintzberg (1983b) who identified five broad types or configurations:

1. Simple structures, which are dominated by the top of the organization with centralized decision making.
2. Machine bureaucracy, which is characterized by the standardization of work processes and the extensive reliance on systems.

3. Professional bureaucracy, where the standardization of skills provides the prime coordinating mechanism.
4. Divisionalized structures, in which authority is drawn down from the top and activities are grouped together into units that are then managed according to their standardized outputs.
5. Adhocracies, where power is decentralized selectively to constellations of work that are free to coordinate within and between themselves by mutual adjustments.

Organizational processes

The structure of an organization as described in an organization chart does not give any real indication of how it functions. To understand this, it is necessary to consider the various processes that take place within the structural framework; those of interaction and networking, communication, group behaviour, leadership, power, politics and conflict.

Interaction and networking

Interactions between people criss-cross the organization creating networks for getting things done and exchanging information that are not catered for in the formal structure. 'Networking' is an increasingly important process in flexible and delayered organizations where more fluid interactions across the structure are required between individuals and teams. Individuals can often get much more done by networking than by going through formal channels. At least this means that they can canvass opinion and enlist support to promote their projects or ideas.

People also get things done in organizations by creating alliances – getting agreement on a course of action with other people and joining forces to get things done.

Communication

The communication processes used in organizations have a marked effect on how it functions, especially if they take place through the network, which can then turn into the 'grapevine'. E-mails encourage the instant flow of information (and sometimes produce information overload) but may inhibit the face-to-face interactions that are often the best ways of getting things done.

Group behaviour

Organizations consist of groups of people working together. Groups or teams exist when a number of people work together or regularly interact with one another. They may be set up formally as part of the structure or they may be informal gatherings. They can be a permanent feature of the organization or are set up or form themselves temporarily. Interactions take place within and between groups and the degree to which these processes are formalized varies according to the organizational context.

To understand and influence organizational behaviour, it is necessary to appreciate how groups behave – group process. This means considering the nature of:

- formal groups;
- informal groups;
- the processes that take place within groups;
- group ideology;
- group cohesion;
- group dynamics;
- the concept of a reference group and its impact on group members;
- the factors that make for group effectiveness.

Formal groups

Formal groups are set up by organizations to achieve a defined purpose. People are brought together with the necessary skills to carry out the tasks and a system exists for directing, coordinating and controlling the group's activities. The structure, composition and size of the group will depend largely on the nature of the task; although tradition, organizational culture and management style may exert considerable influence. The more routine or clearly defined the task is the more structured the group will be. In a highly structured group the leader will have a positive role and may well adopt an authoritarian style. The role of each member of the group will be precise and a hierarchy of authority is likely to exist. The more ambiguous the task the more difficult it will be to structure the group. The leader's role is then more likely to be supportive – she or he will tend to concentrate on encouragement and coordination rather than on issuing orders. The group will operate in a more democratic way and individual roles will be fluid and less clearly defined.

Informal groups

Informal groups are set up by people in organizations who have some affinity for one another. It could be said that formal groups satisfy the needs of the organization while informal groups satisfy the needs of their members. One of the main aims of organization design and development should be to ensure, so far as possible, that the basis upon which activities are grouped together and the way in which groups are allowed or encouraged to behave satisfy both these needs. The values and norms established by informal groups can work against the organization. This was first clearly established in the Hawthorne studies (Roethlisberger and Dickson, 1939), which revealed that groups could regulate their own behaviour and output levels irrespective of what management wanted. An understanding of the processes that take place within groups can, however, help to make them work for, rather than against, what the organization needs.

Group processes

The way in which groups function is affected by the task and by the norms in the organization. An additional factor is size. There is a greater diversity of talent, skills and knowledge in a large group, but individuals find it more difficult to make their presence felt. According to Handy (1981), for best participation and for highest all-round involvement, the optimum size is between five and seven. But to achieve the requisite breadth of knowledge the group may have to be considerably larger, and this makes greater demands on the skills of the leader in getting participation. The main processes that take place in groups as described below are interaction, task and maintenance functions, group ideology, group cohesion, group development and identification.

Interaction

Three basic channels of communication within groups were identified by Leavitt (1951) and are illustrated in Figure 21.1.

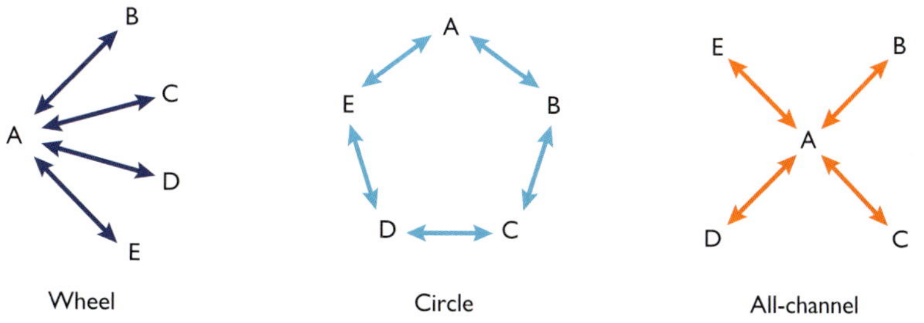

Figure 21.1 Channels of communication within groups

The characteristics of these different groups are as follows:

- Wheel groups, where the task is straightforward, work faster, need fewer messages to solve problems and make fewer errors than circle groups, but they are inflexible if the task changes.
- Circle groups are faster in solving complex problems than wheel groups.
- All-channel groups are the most flexible and function well in complex, open-ended situations.

The level of satisfaction for individuals is lowest in the circle group, fairly high in the all-channel group and mixed in the wheel group, where the leader is more satisfied than the outlying members.

Task and maintenance functions

The following functions need to be carried out in groups:

- task – initiating, information seeking, diagnosing, opinion seeking, evaluating, decision managing;
- maintenance – encouraging, compromising, peace keeping, clarifying, summarizing, standard setting.

It is the job of the group leader to ensure that these functions operate effectively. Leaderless groups can work, but only in special circumstances. A leader is almost essential, whether official or self-appointed. The style adopted by a leader affects the way the group operates. If the leader is respected, this will increase group cohesiveness and its ability to get things done. An inappropriately authoritarian style creates tension and resentment. An over-permissive style means that respect for the leader diminishes and the group does not function so effectively.

Self-managed groups are given a task do to and left to get on with it. They may or may not have a formally appointed leader.

Group dynamics

The term 'group dynamics' can be used to describe the ways in which groups are formed and group members interact. But originally, as defined by Kurt Lewin (1947), it refers to the improvement of group processes through various forms of training, eg team building, interactive skills training and T-groups ('training groups', which aim to increase sensitivity, diagnostic ability and action skills).

Group ideology

In the course of interacting and carrying out its task and maintenance functions, the group develops an ideology that affects the attitudes and actions of its members and the degree of satisfaction they feel.

Group cohesion

If the group ideology is strong and individual members identify closely with the group, it will become increasingly cohesive. Group norms or implicit rules will be evolved that define what is and is not acceptable behaviour. The impact of group cohesion can, however, result in negative as well as positive results. Janis's (1972) study of the decision-making processes of groups established that a cohesive group of individuals, sharing a common fate, exerts a strong pressure towards conformity. He coined the term 'group think' to describe the pressure for conformity in a highly cohesive group that might involve the exaggeration of irrational tendencies. He argued that a group setting can magnify weakness of judgement.

To be 'one of us' is not always a good thing in management circles. A sturdy spirit of independence, even a maverick tendency, may be more conducive to correct decision making. Team working is a good thing but so is flexibility and independent judgement. These need not be incompatible with team membership, but could be if there is too much emphasis on cohesion and conformity within the group.

Reference group

A reference group consists of the group of people with whom an individual identifies. This means that the group's norms are accepted and if in doubt about what to do or say, reference is made to these norms or to other group members before action is taken. Most people in organizations belong to a reference group and this can significantly affect the ways in which they behave.

Impact on group members

The reference group will affect individual behaviour by encouraging acceptance of group norms. This commonly goes through two stages – compliance and internalization. Initially, a group member complies in order not to be rejected by the group, although he or she may behave differently when away from the group. Progressively, however, the individual accepts the norm whether with the group or not – the group norm has been internalized. As noted by Chell (1987), pressure on members to conform can cause problems when:

- there is incompatibility between a member's personal goals and those of the group;
- there is no sense of pride in being a member of the group;
- the member is not fully integrated with the group;
- the price of conformity is too high.

Group development

Tuckman (1965) has identified four stages of group development:

1. Forming, when there is anxiety, dependence on the leader and testing to find out the nature of the situation and the task, and what behaviour is acceptable.
2. Storming, where there is conflict, emotional resistance to the demands of the task, resistance to control and even rebellion against the leader.
3. Norming, when group cohesion is developed, norms emerge, views are exchanged openly, mutual support and cooperation increase and the group acquires a sense of its identity.

4. Performing, when interpersonal problems are resolved, roles are flexible and functional, there are constructive attempts to complete tasks and energy is available for effective work.

Identification

Individuals will identify with their groups if they like the other members, approve of the purpose and work of the group and wish to be associated with the standing of the group in the organization. Identification will be more complex if the standing of the group is not good.

Teamwork

As defined by Katzenbach and Smith (1993), 'A team is a small number of people with complementary skills who are committed to a common purpose, performance goals and approach for which they hold themselves mutually accountable.' They list the characteristics of effective teams as follows:

- Teams are the basic units of performance for most organizations. They meld together the skills, experiences and insights of several people.
- Teamwork applies to the whole organization as well as specific teams. It represents 'a set of values that encourage behaviours such as listening and responding cooperatively to points of view expressed by others, giving others the benefit of the doubt, providing support to those who need it and recognizing the interests and achievements of others'.
- Teams are created and energized by significant performance challenges.
- Teams outperform individuals acting alone or in large organizational groupings, especially when performance requires multiple skills, judgements and experiences.
- Teams are flexible and responsive to changing events and demands. They can adjust their approach to new information and challenges with greater speed, accuracy and effectiveness than can individuals caught in the web of larger organizational conventions.
- High-performance teams invest much time and effort exploring, shaping and agreeing on a purpose that belongs to them, both collectively and individually. They are characterized by a deep sense of commitment to their growth and success.

Dysfunctional teams

The specification set out above is somewhat idealistic. Teams do not always work like that. They can fail to function effectively in the following ways:

- the atmosphere can be strained and over-formalized;
- either there is too much discussion, which gets nowhere, or discussion is inhibited by dominant members of the team;
- team members do not really understand what they are there to do and the objectives or standards they are expected to achieve;
- people don't listen to one another;
- disagreements are frequent and often relate to personalities and differences of opinion rather than a reasoned discussion of alternative points of view;
- decisions are not made jointly by team members;
- there is evidence of open personal attacks or hidden personal animosities;
- people do not feel free to express their opinions;
- individual team members opt out or are allowed to opt out, leaving the others to do the work;
- there is little flexibility in the way in which team members operate – people tend to use a limited range of skills on specific tasks; there is little evidence of multi-skilling;
- the team leader dominates the team; more attention is given to who takes control rather than to getting the work done;
- the team determines its own standards and norms, which may not be in accord with the standards and norms of the organization.

Team roles

The different types of roles played by team members have been defined by Belbin (1981) as follows:

- chairpersons who control the way the team operates;
- shapers who specify the ways the team should work;
- company workers who turn proposals into practical work procedures;
- plants who produce ideas and strategies;
- resource investigators who explore the availability of resources, ideas and developments outside the team;
- monitor-evaluators who analyse problems and evaluate ideas;
- team workers who provide support to team members, improve team communication and foster team spirit;
- completer-finishers who maintain a sense of urgency in the team.

An alternative classification of roles has been developed by Margerison and McCann (1986). The eight roles are:

1. Reporter-adviser: gathers information and expresses it in an easily understandable form.
2. Creator-innovator: enjoys thinking up new ideas and ways of doing things.
3. Explorer-promoter: takes up ideas and promotes them to others.
4. Assessor-developer: takes ideas and makes them work in practice.
5. Thruster-organizer: gets things done, emphasizing targets, deadlines and budgets.
6. Concluder-producer: sets up plans and standard systems to ensure outputs are achieved.
7. Controller-inspector: concerned with the details and adhering to rules and regulations.
8. Upholder-maintainer: provides guidance and help in meeting standards.

According to Margerison and McCann, a balanced team needs members with preferences for each of these eight roles.

Leadership

Leadership is the process of inspiring people to do their best to achieve a desired result. It can also be defined as the ability to persuade others willingly to behave differently. The function of team leaders is to achieve the task set for them with the help of the group. Leaders and their groups are therefore interdependent.

Leadership roles

Leaders have two main roles. First, they must achieve the task. Second, they have to maintain effective relationships between themselves and the group and the individuals in it – effective in the sense that they are conducive to achieving the task. As Adair (1973) pointed out, in fulfilling their roles, leaders have to satisfy the following needs:

1. Task needs. The group exists to achieve a common purpose or task. The leader's role is to ensure that this purpose is fulfilled. If it is not, they will lose the confidence of the group and the result will be frustration, disenchantment, criticism and, possibly, the ultimate disintegration of the group.
2. Group maintenance needs. To achieve its objectives, the group needs to be held together. The leader's job is to build up and maintain team spirit and morale.
3. Individual needs. Individuals have their own needs which they expect to be satisfied at work. The leader's task is to be aware of these needs so that where necessary they can take steps to harmonize them with the needs of the task and the group.

These three needs are interdependent. The leader's actions in one area affect both the others; thus successful achievement of the task is essential if the group is to be held together and its members motivated to give their best effort to the job. Action directed at meeting group or individual needs must be related to the needs of the task. It is impossible to consider individuals in isolation from the group or to consider the group without referring to the individuals within it. If any need is neglected, one of the others will suffer and the leader will be less successful.

The kind of leadership exercised will be related to the nature of the task and the people being led. It will also depend on the environment and, of course, on the actual leader. Analysing the qualities of leadership in terms of traits such as intelligence, initiative, self-assurance and so on has only limited value. The qualities required may be different in different situations. It is more useful to adopt a contingency approach and take account of the variables leaders have to deal with; especially the task, the group and their own position relative to the group.

Leadership style

Leadership style, often called 'management style', describes the approach managers use to deal with people in their teams. There are many styles of leadership. Leaders can be classified in extremes as follows:

- Charismatic/non-charismatic. Charismatic leaders rely on their personality, their inspirational qualities and their 'aura'. They are visionary leaders who are achievement-oriented, calculated risk takers and good communicators. Non-charismatic leaders rely mainly on their know-how (authority goes to the person who knows), their quiet confidence and their cool, analytical approach to dealing with problems.
- Autocratic/democratic. Autocratic leaders impose their decisions, using their position to force people to do as they are told. Democratic leaders encourage people to participate and involve themselves in decision taking.
- Enabler/controller. Enablers inspire people with their vision of the future and empower them to accomplish team goals. Controllers manipulate people to obtain their compliance.
- Transactional/transformational. Transactional leaders trade money, jobs and security for compliance. Transformational leaders motivate people to strive for higher-level goals.

Goleman (2000) produced an alternative list of six leadership styles: coercive, authoritative, affiliative, democratic, pacesetting and coaching.

Power

Organizations exist to get things done and in the process of doing this people or groups exercise power. Directly or indirectly, the use of power in influencing behaviour is a pervading feature of organizations, whether it is exerted by managers, specialists, informal groups or trade union officials. It is a way of getting things done, but it can be misused.

Power is the capacity to secure the dominance of one's goals or values over others. Four different types of power have been identified by French and Raven (1959):

1. Reward power – derived from the belief of individuals that compliance brings rewards; the ability to distribute rewards contributes considerably to an executive's power.
2. Coercive power – making it plain that non-compliance will bring punishment.
3. Expert power – exercised by people who are popular or admired with whom the less powerful can identify.
4. Legitimized power – power conferred by the position in an organization held by an executive.

Politics

Power and politics are inextricably mixed, and in any organization there will inevitably be people who want to achieve their satisfaction by acquiring power, legitimately or illegitimately. Kakabadse (1983) defines politics as 'a process, that of influencing individuals and groups of people to your point of view, where you cannot rely on authority'. Organizational politicians are determined to get their own way by fair or foul means.

Organizations consist of individuals who, while they are ostensibly there to achieve a common purpose, are, at the same time, driven by their own needs to achieve their own goals. Effective management is the process of harmonizing individual endeavour and ambition to the common good. Some individuals genuinely believe that using political means to achieve their goals will benefit the organization as well as themselves. Others rationalize this belief; yet others unashamedly pursue their own ends. Politics, like power, is an inevitable feature of organization. Political behaviour can be harmful when it is underhand and devious, but it can sometimes help to enlist support and overcome obstacles to getting results.

Conflict

Conflict is inevitable in organizations because they function by means of adjustments and compromises among competitive elements in their structure and membership. Conflict also arises when there is change, because it may be seen as a threat to be challenged or resisted, or when there is frustration – this may produce an aggressive reaction: fight rather than flight.

Conflict is not to be deplored. It is an inevitable result of progress and change and it can and should be used constructively.

Conflict between individuals raises fewer problems than conflict between groups. Individuals can act independently and resolve their differences. Members of groups may have to accept the norms, goals and values of their group. The individual's loyalty will usually be to his or her own group if it is in conflict with others.

How organizations function – key learning points

The process of organizing

Organizing is the process of making arrangements in the form of defined or understood responsibilities and relationships to enable people to work cooperatively together. Formal organizations have formal structures with defined hierarchies (lines of command), but to varying extents they can operate informally as well as formally by means of a network of roles and relationships that cut across formal organizational boundaries and lines of command.

Organization theory

Organization theory aims to describe how organizations function. There are a number of schools and models.

Organization structures

Organizations vary in their complexity, but it is necessary to divide the overall management task into a variety of activities, to allocate these activities to the different parts of the organization and to establish means of controlling, coordinating and integrating them.

Types of organization

The basic types of organization are line and staff, divisionalized, decentralized, matrix, and process-based.

Organizational processes

The structure of an organization as described in an organization chart does not give any real indication of how it functions. To understand this, it is necessary to consider the various processes that take place within the structural framework; those of interaction and networking, communication, group behaviour, leadership, power, politics and conflict.

Group behaviour

Organizations consist of groups of people working together. Groups or teams exist when a number of people work together or regularly interact with one another. Interactions take place within and between groups and the degree to which these processes are formalized varies according to the organizational context.

Teamwork

As defined by Katzenbach and Smith (1993), 'A team is a small number of people with complementary skills who are committed to a common purpose, performance goals and approach for which they hold themselves mutually accountable.'

Leadership roles

Leaders have two main roles. First, they must achieve the task; second, they have to

How organizations function – key learning points (continued)

maintain effective relationships between themselves and the group and the individuals in it – effective in the sense that the relationships are conducive to achieving the task.

Power

Directly or indirectly, the use of power in influencing behaviour is a pervading feature of organizations, whether it is exerted by managers, specialists, informal groups or trade union officials.

Politics

Power and politics are inextricably mixed, and in any organization there will inevitably be people who want to achieve their satisfaction by acquiring power, legitimately or illegitimately. Kakabadse (1983) defines politics as 'a process, that of influencing individuals and groups of people to your point of view, where you cannot rely on authority'. Organizational politicians are determined to get their own way by fair means or foul.

Conflict

Conflict is inevitable in organizations because they function by means of adjustments and compromises among competitive elements in their structure and membership. Conflict also arises when there is change, because it may be seen as a threat to be challenged or resisted, or when there is frustration.

Questions

1. Is individualism a good thing that should be encouraged or a bad thing that should be discouraged?
2. What does contingency theory tell us about organizations?
3. Critically evaluate the trait theory of leadership.
4. What can HR do about increasing organizational capability?

References

Adair, J (1973) *The Action-centred Leader*, McGraw-Hill, Maidenhead

Argyris, C (1957) *Personality and Organization*, Harper & Row, New York

Barnard, C (1938) *The Functions of an Executive*, Harvard University Press, Boston, MA

Belbin, M (1981) *Management Teams: Why they succeed or fail*, Heinemann, Oxford

Burns, T and Stalker, G (1961) *The Management of Innovation*, Tavistock, London

Chell, E (1987) *The Psychology of Behaviour in Organisations*, Macmillan, London

Child, J (1977) *Organization: A Guide to Problems and Practice*, Harper & Row, London

Doty, D H, Glick, W H and Huber, G P (1993) Fit, equifinality, and organizational effectiveness: a test of two configurational theories, *Academy of Management Journal*, **36** (6), pp 1196–250

Emery, F E (1959) *Characteristics of Socio-technical Systems*, Tavistock Publications, London

Fayol, H (1916) *Administration Industrielle et General*, translated by C Storrs (1949) as *General and Industrial Management*, Pitman, London

French, J R and Raven, B (1959) The basis of social power, in (ed) D Cartwright, *Studies in Social Power*, Institute for Social Research, Ann Arbor, MI

Ghoshal, S and Bartlett, C A (1995) Changing the role of top management: beyond structure to process, *Harvard Business Review*, January–February, pp 86–96

Goleman, D (2000) Leadership that gets results, *Harvard Business Review*, March/April, pp 78–90

Handy, C (1981) *Understanding Organizations*, Penguin Books, Harmondsworth

Herzberg, F W, Mausner, B and Snyderman, B (1957) *The Motivation to Work*, Wiley, New York

Huczynski, A A and Buchanan, D A (2007) *Organizational Behaviour*, 6th edn, FT Prentice Hall, Harlow

Janis, I (1972) *Victims of Groupthink*, Houghton Mifflin, Boston, MA

Kakabadse, A (1983) *The Politics of Management*, Gower, Aldershot

Katz, D and Kahn, R (1966) *The Social Psychology of Organizations*, John Wiley, New York

Katzenbach, J and Smith, D (1993) *The Magic of Teams*, Harvard Business School Press, Boston, MA

Lawrence, P R and Lorsch, J W (1969) *Developing Organizations*, Addison-Wiley, Reading, MA

Leavitt, H J (1951) Some effects of certain communication patterns on group performance, *Journal of Abnormal Psychology*, **14** (3), pp 457–81

Lewin, K (1947) Frontiers in group dynamics, *Human Relations*, **1** (1), pp 5–42

Likert, R (1961) *New Patterns of Management*, Harper & Row, New York

McGregor, D (1960) *The Human Side of Enterprise*, McGraw-Hill, New York

Margerison, C and McCann, R (1986) The Margerison/McCann team management resource: theory and application, *International Journal of Manpower*, **7** (2), pp 1–32

Miller, E and Rice, A (1967) *Systems of Organization*, Tavistock, London

Mintzberg, H (1983b) *Structure in Fives*, Prentice Hall, Englewood Cliffs, NJ

Pascale, R (1990) *Managing on the Edge*, Viking, London

Perrow, C (1980) The short and glorious history of organizational theory, in (ed) R H Miles, *Resource Book in Macro-organizational Behaviour*, Goodyear Publishing, Santa Monica, CA

Roethlisberger, F and Dickson, W (1939) *Management and the Worker*, Harvard University Press, Cambridge, MA

Schein, E H (1965) *Organizational Psychology*, Prentice Hall, Englewood Cliffs, NJ

Sloan, A P (1967) *My Years with General Motors*, Pan Books, London

Taylor, F W (1911) *Principles of Scientific Management*, Harper, New York
Trist, E L, Higgin, G W, Murray, H and Pollock, A B (1963) *Organizational Choice*, Tavistock Publications, London
Tuckman, B (1965) Development sequences in small groups, *Psychological Bulletin*, **63**, pp 123–56
Urwick, L F (1947) *Dynamic Administration*, Pitman, London
Weber, M (1946) *From Max Weber* (ed) H H Gerth and C W Mills, Oxford University Press, Oxford
Woodward, J (1965) *Industrial Organization*, Oxford University Press, Oxford

22 Organizational Culture

Key concepts and terms

- Artefacts
- Management style
- Organizational climate
- Values
- Value set
- Espoused values
- Norms
- Organizational culture
- Values in use

Learning outcomes

On completing this chapter you should be able to define these key concepts. You should also know about:

- The characteristics of organizational culture
- How organizational culture develops
- The components of organizational culture
- Measuring organizational climate
- Supporting and changing cultures
- The significance of organizational culture
- The diversity of organizational culture
- Classifications of organizational culture
- Appropriate cultures

Introduction

The culture of an organization affects the way in which people behave and has to be taken into account as a contingency factor in any programme for developing organizations and HR policies and practices. This is why it is important for HR specialists to understand the concept of organizational culture, how it affects organizations and how it can be managed, as discussed in this chapter.

Organizational culture defined

Organizational or corporate culture is the pattern of values, norms, beliefs, attitudes and assumptions that may not have been articulated but shape the ways in which people in organizations behave and things get done. 'Values' refer to what is believed to be important about how people and organizations behave. 'Norms' are the unwritten rules of behaviour.

The definition emphasizes that organizational culture is concerned with the subjective aspect of what goes on in organizations. It refers to abstractions such as values and norms that pervade the whole or part of a business, which may not be defined, discussed or even noticed. Nevertheless, culture can have a significant influence on people's behaviour. The following are some other definitions of organizational culture:

- The culture of an organization refers to the unique configuration of norms, values, beliefs and ways of behaving that characterize the manner in which groups and individuals combine to get things done. Eldridge and Crombie (1974)
- Culture is a system of informal rules that spells out how people are to behave most of the time. Deal and Kennedy (1982)
- A pattern of basic assumptions – invented, discovered or developed by a given group as it learns to cope with the problems of external adaptation and internal integration – that has worked well enough to be considered valid and, therefore, to be taught to new members as the correct way to perceive, think and feel in relation to these problems. Schein (1985)
- Culture is the commonly held beliefs, attitudes and values that exist in an organization. Put more simply, culture is 'the way we do things around here'. Furnham and Gunter (1993)

SOURCE REVIEW

Characteristics of culture, Furnham and Gunter (1993)

- It is difficult to define (often a pointless exercise).
- It is multi-dimensional, with many different components at different levels.
- It is not particularly dynamic and ever-changing (being relatively stable over short periods of time).
- It takes time to establish and therefore time to change a corporate culture.

Significance of culture, Furnham and Gunter (1993)

Culture represents the 'social glue' and generates a 'we-feeling', thus counter-acting processes of differentiations that are an unavoidable part of organizational life. Organizational culture offers a shared system of meanings which is the basis for communications and mutual understanding. If these functions are not fulfilled in a satisfactory way, culture may significantly reduce the efficiency of an organization.

Problems with the concept

But Furnham and Gunter refer to a number of problems with the concept, which include:

- how to categorize culture (what terminology to use);
- when and why corporate culture should be changed and how this takes place;
- what is the healthiest, most optimal or desirable culture.

They also point out that it is dangerous to treat culture as an objective entity 'as if everyone in the world would be able to observe the same phenomenon, whereas this is patently not the case'.

Organizational climate defined

As defined by Ivancevitch *et al* (2008), organizational climate is: 'A set of properties of the work environment, perceived directly or indirectly by the employees, that is assumed to be a major force in influencing employee behaviour.' The term 'organizational climate' is sometimes confused with organizational culture and there has been much debate on what distinguishes them from one another. In his analysis of this issue, Denison (1996) suggested that 'culture' refers to the deep structure of organizations, which is rooted in the values, beliefs and assumptions held by organizational members. In contrast, 'climate' refers to those aspects of the environment that are consciously perceived by organizational members. Rousseau (1988) stated that climate is a perception and is descriptive. Perceptions are sensations or realizations experienced by an individual. Descriptions are what a person reports of these sensations.

The debate about the meanings of these terms can become academic. It is easiest to regard organizational climate as how people perceive (see and feel about) the culture existing in their organization. As defined by French *et al* (1985) it is 'the relatively persistent set of perceptions held by organization members concerning the characteristics and quality of organizational culture'. They distinguish between the actual situations (ie culture) and the perception of it (climate).

How organizational culture develops

The values and norms that are the basis of culture are formed in four ways; first, by the leaders in the organization, especially those who have shaped it in the past. Schein (1990) indicates that people identify with visionary leaders – how they behave and what they expect. They note what such leaders pay attention to and treat them as role models. Second, as Schein also points out, culture is formed around critical incidents – important events from which lessons are learnt about desirable or undesirable behaviour. Third, as suggested by Furnham and Gunter (1993), culture develops from the need to maintain effective working relationships among organization members, and this establishes values and expectations. Finally, culture is influenced by the organization's environment. The external environment may be relatively dynamic or unchanging.

Culture is learnt over a period of time. Schein (1984) suggests that there are two ways in which this learning takes place. First, the trauma model, in which members of the organization learn to cope with some threat by the erection of defence mechanisms. Second, the positive reinforcement model, where things that seem to work become embedded and entrenched. Learning takes place as people adapt to and cope with external pressures, and as they develop successful approaches and mechanisms to handle the internal challenges, processes and technologies in their organization.

Where culture has developed over long periods of time and has become firmly embedded it may be difficult to change quickly, if at all, unless a traumatic event occurs.

The diversity of culture

The development process described above may result in a culture that characterizes the whole organization. But there may be different cultures within organizations. For example, the culture of an outward-looking marketing department may be substantially different from that of an internally-focused manufacturing function. There may be some common organizational values or norms, but in some respects these will vary between different work environments.

The components of culture

Organizational culture can be described in terms of values, norms, artefacts and management style.

Values

Values are beliefs in what is best or good for the organization and what should or ought to happen. The 'value set' of an organization may only be recognized at top level, or it may be shared throughout the business, in which case it could be described as 'value-driven'.

The stronger the values the more they will influence behaviour. This does not depend upon their having been articulated. Implicit values that are deeply embedded in the culture of an organization and are reinforced by the behaviour of management can be highly influential, while espoused values that are idealistic and are not reflected in managerial behaviour may have little or no effect. When values are acted on they are called 'values in use'.

Areas in which values may be expressed – explicitly or implicitly

- Care and consideration for people.
- Competence.
- Competitiveness.
- Customer service.
- Innovation.
- Performance.
- Quality.
- Teamwork.

Values are translated into reality through norms and artefacts, as described below. They may also be expressed through the media of language (organizational jargon), rituals, stories and myths.

Norms

Norms are the unwritten rules of behaviour, the 'rules of the game' that provide informal guidelines on how to behave. Norms tell people what they are supposed to be doing, saying, believing, even wearing. They are never expressed in writing – if they were, they would be policies or procedures. They are passed on by word of mouth or behaviour and can be enforced by the reactions of people if they are violated. They can exert very powerful pressure on behaviour because of these reactions – we control others by the way we react to them.

Typical norms

- How managers treat the members of their teams (management style) and how the latter relate to their managers.
- The prevailing work ethic, eg 'work hard, play hard', 'come in early, stay late', 'if you cannot finish your work during business hours you are obviously inefficient', 'look busy at all times', 'look relaxed at all times'.
- Status – how much importance is attached to it; the existence or lack of obvious status symbols.
- Ambition – naked ambition is expected and approved of, or a more subtle approach is the norm.
- Performance – exacting performance standards are general; the highest praise that can be given in the organization is to be referred to as 'very professional'.
- Power – recognized as a way of life; executed by political means, dependent on expertise and ability rather than position; concentrated at the top; shared at different levels in different parts of the organization.
- Politics – rife throughout the organization and treated as normal behaviour; not accepted as overt behaviour.
- Loyalty – expected, a cradle to grave approach to careers; discounted, the emphasis is on results and contribution in the short term.
- Anger – openly expressed; hidden, but expressed through other, possibly political, means.

- Approachability – managers are expected to be approachable and visible; everything happens behind closed doors.
- Formality – a cool, formal approach is the norm; forenames are/are not used at all levels; there are unwritten but clearly understood rules about dress.

Artefacts

Artefacts are the visible and tangible aspects of an organization that people hear, see or feel and which contribute to their understanding of the organization's culture. Artefacts can include such things as the working environment, the tone and language used in e-mails, letters or memoranda, the manner in which people address each other at meetings, in e-mails or over the telephone, the welcome (or lack of welcome) given to visitors and the way in which telephonists deal with outside calls. Artefacts can be very revealing.

Management style

Management style is the approach managers use to deal with people. It is also called 'leadership style', as described in Chapter 21. As defined there, it consists of the following extremes:

- Charismatic/non-charismatic.
- Autocratic/democratic.
- Enabler/controller.
- Transactional/transformational.

Most managers adopt an approach somewhere between the extremes. Some will vary it according to the situation or their feelings at the time; others will stick to the same style whatever happens. A good case can be made for using an appropriate style according to the situation but it is undesirable to be inconsistent in the style used in similar situations. Every manager has his or her own style but this will be influenced by the organizational culture, which may produce a prevailing management style that represents the behavioural norm for managers that is generally expected and adopted.

The term 'management style' can also refer to the overall approach an organization adopts to the conduct of employee relations. Purcell and Sisson (1983) identified five typical styles: authoritarian, paternalistic, consultative, constitutional and opportunist.

Classifying organizational culture

There have been many attempts to classify or categorize organizational culture as a basis for the analysis of cultures in organizations and for taking action to support or change them. Most of these classifications are expressed in four dimensions and some of the best-known ones are summarized below. Note that following the lead of Harrison (1972), there is much common ground between them.

SOURCE REVIEW

Organization ideologies, Harrison (1972)

- Power-oriented – competitive, responsive to personality rather than expertise.
- People-oriented – consensual, management control rejected.
- Task-oriented – focus on competency, dynamic.
- Role-oriented – focus on legality, legitimacy and bureaucracy.

Culture typology, based on Harrison, Handy (1981)

1. The power culture is one with a central power source that exercises control. There are few rules or procedures and the atmosphere is competitive, power-oriented and political.
2. The role culture in which work is controlled by procedures and rules and the role, or job description, is more important than the person who fills it. Power is associated with positions not people.
3. The task culture in which the aim is to bring together the right people and let them get on with it. Influence is based more on expert power than in position or personal power. The culture is adaptable and teamwork is important.
4. The person culture in which the individual is the central point. The organization exists only to serve and assist the individuals in it.

Schein (1985)

1. Power culture in which leadership resides in a few and rests on their ability and which tends to be entrepreneurial.
2. Role culture in which power is balanced between the leader and bureaucratic structure. The environment is likely to be stable and roles and rules are clearly defined.

3. Achievement culture in which personal motivation and commitment are stressed and action, excitement and impact are valued.
4. Support culture in which people contribute out of a sense of commitment and solidarity. Relationships are characterized by mutuality and trust.

Williams *et al* (1989)

1. Power orientation in which organizations try to dominate their environment and those exercising power strive to maintain absolute control over subordinates.
2. Role orientation, which emphasizes legality, legitimacy and responsibility. Hierarchy and status are important.
3. Task orientation, which focuses on task accomplishment. Authority is based on appropriate knowledge and competence.
4. People orientation in which the organization exists primarily to serve the needs of its members. Individuals are expected to influence each other through example and helpfulness.

Assessing organizational culture

A number of instruments exist for assessing organizational culture. This is not easy because culture is concerned with both subjective beliefs and unconscious assumptions (which might be difficult to measure), and with observed phenomena such as behavioural norms and artefacts. Two of the better-known instruments are summarized below.

Organizational ideology questionnaire (Harrison, 1972)

This questionnaire deals with the four orientations referred to earlier (power, role, task and self). The questionnaire is completed by ranking statements according to views on what is closest to the organization's actual position. Statements include:

- a good boss is strong, decisive and firm but fair;
- a good subordinate is compliant, hard-working and loyal;
- people who do well in the organization are shrewd and competitive, with a strong need for power;
- the basis of task assignment is the personal needs and judgements of those in authority;

- decisions are made by people with the most knowledge and expertise about the problem.

Organizational culture inventory (Cooke and Lafferty, 1989)

This instrument assesses organizational culture under 12 headings:

1. Humanistic/helpful – organizations managed in a participative and person-centred way.
2. Affiliative – organizations that place a high priority on constructive relationships.
3. Approval – organizations in which conflicts are avoided and interpersonal relationships are pleasant – at least superficially.
4. Conventional – conservative, traditional and bureaucratically controlled organizations.
5. Dependent – hierarchically controlled and non-participative organizations.
6. Avoidance – organizations that fail to reward success but punish mistakes.
7. Oppositional – organizations in which confrontation prevails and negativism is rewarded.
8. Power – organizations structured on the basis of the authority inherent in members' positions.
9. Competitive – a culture in which winning is valued and members are rewarded for out-performing one another.
10. Competence/perfectionist – organizations in which perfectionism, persistence and hard work are valued.
11. Achievement – organizations that do things well and value members who set and accomplish challenging but realistic goals.
12. Self-actualization – organizations that value creativity, quality over quantity, and both task accomplishment and individual growth.

Measuring organizational climate

Organizational climate measures attempts to assess organizations in terms of dimensions that are thought to capture or describe perceptions about the climate, such as the example given below.

SOURCE REVIEW

Questionnaire on organizational climate, Litwin and Stringer (1968)

1. Structure – feelings about constraints and freedom to act and the degree of formality or informality in the working atmosphere.
2. Responsibility – the feeling of being trusted to carry out important work.
3. Risk – the sense of riskiness and challenge in the job and in the organization; the relative emphasis on taking calculated risks or playing it safe.
4. Warmth – the existence of friendly and informal social groups.
5. Support – the perceived helpfulness of managers and co-workers; the emphasis (or lack of emphasis) on mutual support.
6. Standards – the perceived importance of implicit and explicit goals and performance standards; the emphasis on doing a good job; the challenge represented in personal and team goals.
7. Conflict – the feeling that managers and other workers want to hear different opinions; the emphasis on getting problems out into the open rather than smoothing them over or ignoring them.
8. Identity – the feeling that you belong to a company; that you are a valuable member of a working team.

Perceptions about climate can be measured by questionnaires such as that developed by Koys and DeCotiis (1991), which cover eight categories:

SOURCE REVIEW

Typical dimensions of organizational climate questionnaires (Koys and DeCotiis, 1991)

1. Autonomy – the perception of self-determination with respect to work procedures, goals and priorities.
2. Cohesion – the perception of togetherness or sharing within the organization setting, including the willingness of members to provide material risk.
3. Trust – the perception of freedom to communicate openly with members at higher organizational levels about sensitive or personal issues with the expectation that the integrity of such communication will not be violated.

4. Resource – the perception of time demands with respect to task competition and performance standards.
5. Support – the perception of the degree to which superiors tolerate members' behaviour, including willingness to let members learn from their mistakes without fear of reprisal.
6. Recognition – the perception that members' contributions to the organization are acknowledged.
7. Fairness – the perception that organizational policies are non-arbitrary or capricious.
8. Innovation – the perception that change and creativity are encouraged, including risk taking in new areas where the member has little or no prior experience.

Appropriate cultures

It is not possible to say that one culture is better than another, only that a culture is to a greater or lesser extent appropriate in the sense of being relevant to the needs and circumstances of the organization and helping rather than hindering its performance. However, embedded cultures exert considerable influence on organizational behaviour and therefore performance. If there is an appropriate and effective culture it would therefore be desirable to take steps to support or reinforce it. If the culture is inappropriate, attempts should be made to determine what needs to be changed and to develop and implement plans for change.

Furnham and Gunter (1993) considered that a culture will be more effective if 'it is consistent in its components and shared amongst organizational members, and it makes the organization unique, thus differentiating it from other organizations'.

Supporting and changing cultures

While it may not be possible to define an ideal structure or to prescribe how it can be developed, it can at least be stated with confidence that embedded cultures exert considerable influence on organizational behaviour and therefore performance. If there is an appropriate and effective culture it would be desirable to take steps to support or reinforce it. If the culture is inappropriate attempts should be made to determine what needs to be changed and to develop and implement plans for change.

Culture analysis

In either case, the first step is to analyse the existing culture. This can be done through questionnaires, surveys and discussions in focus groups or workshops. It is often helpful to involve people in analysing the outcome of surveys, getting them to produce a diagnosis of the cultural issues facing the organization and to participate in the development and implementation of plans and programmes to deal with any issues. This could form part of an organizational development programme, as described in Chapter 24. Groups can analyse the culture through the use of measurement instruments. Extra dimensions can be established by the use of group exercises such as 'rules of the club' (participants brainstorm the 'rules' or norms that govern behaviour) or 'shield' (participants design a shield, often quartered, which illustrates major cultural features of the organization). Joint exercises like this can lead to discussions on appropriate values that are much more likely to be 'owned' by people if they have helped to create them rather than having them imposed from above.

While involvement is highly desirable, there will be situations when management has to carry out the analysis and determine the actions required without the initial participation of employees. But the latter should be kept informed and brought into discussion on developments as soon as possible.

Culture support and reinforcement

Culture support and reinforcement programmes aim to preserve and underpin what is good and functional about the present culture. Schein (1985) has suggested that the most powerful primary mechanisms for culture embedding and reinforcement are:

- what leaders pay attention to, measure and control;
- leaders' reactions to critical incidents and crises;
- deliberate role modelling, teaching and coaching by leaders;
- criteria for allocation of rewards and status;
- criteria for recruitment, selection, promotion and commitment.

Culture can also be underpinned by reaffirming and operationalizing existing values through actions designed, for example, to implement total quality and customer care programmes, to provide financial and non-financial rewards for expected behaviour, to improve productivity, to promote and reward good teamwork or to develop a learning organization (see Chapter 40). Additionally, the value set of the organization can be used as headings for reviewing individual and team performance – emphasizing that people are expected to uphold the values, and induction programmes and further training can cover core values and how people are expected to achieve them.

Culture change

In theory, culture change programmes start with an analysis of the existing culture. The desired culture is then defined, which leads to the identification of a 'culture gap' that needs to be filled. This analysis can identify behavioural expectations so that development and reward processes can be used to define and reinforce them. In real life, it is not quite as simple as that. Culture is by definition deeply embedded and changing it can be a long and difficult haul.

A comprehensive change programme may be a fundamental part of an organizational transformation programme, as described in Chapter 25. But culture change programmes can focus on particular aspects of the culture, for example, performance, commitment, quality, customer service, teamwork and organizational learning. In each case the underpinning values would need to be defined. It would probably be necessary to prioritize by deciding which areas need the most urgent attention. There is a limit to how much can be done at once, except in crisis conditions.

Levers for change

Having identified what needs to be done and the priorities, the next step is to consider what levers for change exist and how they can be used. The levers could include, as appropriate:

- Performance – performance-related or contribution-related pay schemes; performance management processes; gainsharing; leadership training, skills development.
- Commitment – communication, participation and involvement programmes; developing a climate of cooperation and trust; clarifying the psychological contract.
- Quality – total quality programmes.
- Customer service – customer care programmes.
- Teamwork – teambuilding; team performance management; team rewards.
- Organizational learning – taking steps to enhance intellectual capital and the organization's resource-based capability by developing a learning organization.
- Values – gaining understanding, acceptance and commitment through involvement in defining values, performance management processes and employee development interventions.

Change management

The effectiveness of culture change programmes largely depends on the quality of change management processes. These are described in Chapter 25.

Organizational culture – key learning points

The characteristics of organizational culture (Furnham and Gunter, 1993)

- It is difficult to define (often a pointless exercise).
- It is multi-dimensional, with many different components at different levels.
- It is not particularly dynamic and ever-changing (being relatively stable over short periods of time).
- It takes time to establish and therefore time to change a corporate culture.

The significance of organizational culture (Furnham and Gunter, 1993)

Culture represents the 'social glue' and generates a 'we-feeling', thus counteracting processes of differentiations that are an unavoidable part of organizational life. Organizational culture offers a shared system of meanings that is the basis for communication and mutual understanding. If these functions are not fulfilled in a satisfactory way, culture may significantly reduce the efficiency of an organization.

How organizational culture develops

- Over a period of time.
- Through visionary leaders.
- Around critical incidents.
- From the need to maintain effective working relationships among organization members.
- By the influence of the organization's environment.

The diversity of organizational culture

There may be different cultures within organizations, although there could be some common organizational values or norms, but in some respects even these will vary between different work environments.

The components of organizational culture

Organizational culture can be described in terms of values, norms, artefacts and management/leadership style.

Classifications of organizational culture

There have been many attempts to classify or categorize organizational culture as a basis for the analysis of cultures in organizations and for taking action to support or change them. Most of these classifications are expressed in four dimensions and, following the lead of Harrison (1972), there is much common ground between them. His classification was:

- Power-oriented – competitive, responsive to personality rather than expertise.
- People-oriented – consensual, management control rejected.
- Task-oriented – focus on competency, dynamic.
- Role-oriented – focus on legality, legitimacy and bureaucracy.

Measuring organizational climate

Organizational climate measures attempts to assess organizations in terms of

Organizational culture – key learning points (continued)

dimensions that are thought to capture or describe perceptions about the climate.

Appropriate cultures

It cannot be said that one culture is better than another, only that a culture is to a greater or lesser extent appropriate in the sense of being relevant to the needs and circumstances of the organization and helping rather than hindering its performance.

Supporting and changing cultures

- It may not be possible to define an ideal culture or to prescribe how it can be developed.
- But it is certain that embedded cultures exert considerable influence on organizational behaviour and therefore performance.
- If there is an appropriate and effective culture, it would be desirable to take steps to support or reinforce it.
- If the culture is inappropriate, attempts should be made to determine what needs to be changed and to develop and implement plans for change.

Questions

1. Charles Handy (1981) made the following remarks on culture: 'In organizations there are deep-set beliefs about the way work should be organized, people rewarded, people controlled. What are the degrees of formalization required? How much planning and how far ahead? What combination of obedience and initiative is looked for in subordinates? Do work hours matter, or dress, or personal eccentricities? What about expense accounts, and secretaries, stock options and incentives? Do committees control or individuals? Are there rules and procedures or only results?' Can you explain the culture of your own organization in these terms, or any other?
2. What are core values, espoused values and values in use?
3. Can culture be managed? If so, how?
4. You have been asked to facilitate a group of employee representatives in a discussion on what should be the core values of your company. How would you set about doing it?

References

Cooke, R and Lafferty, J (1989) *Organizational Culture Inventory*, Human Synergistic, Plymouth, MI

Deal, T and Kennedy, A (1982) *Corporate Cultures*, Addison-Wesley, Reading, MA

Denison, D R (1996) What *is* the difference between organizational culture and organizational climate? A native's point of view on a decade of paradigm wars, *Academy of Management Review*, July, pp 619–54

Eldridge, J and Crombie, A (1974) *The Sociology of Organizations*, Allen & Unwin, London

French, W L, Kast, F E and Rosenzweig, J E (1985) *Understanding Human Behaviour in Organizations*, Harper & Row, New York

Furnham, A and Gunter, B (1993) *Corporate Assessment*, Routledge, London

Handy, C (1981) *Understanding Organizations*, Penguin Books, Harmondsworth

Harrison, R (1972) Understanding your organization's character, *Harvard Business Review*, **5**, pp 119–28

Ivancevich, J M, Konopaske, R and Matteson, M T (2008) *Organizational Behaviour and Management*, 8th edn, McGraw-Hill/Irwin, New York

Koys, D and De Cotiis, T (1991) Inductive measures of organizational climate, *Human Relations*, **44**, pp 265–85

Litwin, G H and Stringer, R A (1968) *Motivation and Organizational Climate*, Harvard University Press, Boston, MA

Purcell, J and Sisson, K (1983) Strategies and practice in the management of industrial relations, in (ed) G Bain, *Industrial Relations in Britain*, Blackwell, Oxford

Rousseau, D M (1988) The construction of climate in organizational research, in (ed) L C Cooper and I Robertson, *International Review of Industrial and Organizational Psychology*, Wiley, Chichester

Schein, E H (1984) Coming to a new awareness of culture, *Sloan Management Review*, Winter, pp 1–15

Schein, E H (1985) *Organizational Culture and Leadership*, Jossey-Bass, San Francisco, CA

Schein, E H (1990) Organizational culture, *American Psychologist*, **45**, pp 109–19

Williams, A, Dobson, P and Walters, M (1989) *Changing Culture: New organizational approaches*, IPA, London

Part V

Organization Design and Development

This part is concerned with the practical applications of organizational behaviour theory. It starts by looking at the processes of organizational design and development and then deals with change management, job and role analysis, and job and role development.

Part V contents

23 Organization Design

Key concepts and terms

- The dominant coalition
- Organizing
- Organizational choice
- Organization planning
- Strategic choice
- Law of the situation
- Organizations as systems
- Organizational dilemma
- Smart working

Learning outcomes

On completing this chapter you should be able to define these key concepts. You should also know about:

- The process of organizing
- Conducting an organizational review – analysis
- Conducting an organizational review – planning
- Aims of organization design
- Conducting an organizational review – diagnosis

Introduction

Organization design is the process of deciding how organizations should be structured and function.

The management of people in organizations constantly raises questions such as, who does what? How should activities be grouped together? What lines and means of communication need to be established? How should people be helped to understand their roles in relation to the objectives of the organization and the roles of their colleagues? Are we doing everything that we ought to be doing and nothing that we ought not to be doing? How can we achieve a reasonable degree of flexibility? Have we got too many unnecessary layers of management in the organization? How can we overcome what has been called by Huczynski and Buchanan (2007) 'the organizational dilemma', meaning the question of how to reconcile the potential inconsistency between individual needs and aspirations on the one hand, and the collective purpose of the organization on the other?

These are questions involving people that must concern HR specialists in their capacity of helping the business to make the best use of its human resources. HR professionals should be able to contribute to the processes of organization design or redesign, as described below, because of their understanding of the factors affecting organizational behaviour and because they are in a position to take an overall view of how the business is organized.

The process of organizing

Organizations exist to achieve a purpose. They do this through the collective efforts of the people who work in or with them. The process of organizing can be described as 'the design, development and maintenance of a system of coordinated activities in which individuals and groups of people work cooperatively under leadership towards commonly understood and accepted goals'. The key word in that definition is 'system'. Organizations are systems which, as affected by their environment, contain a set of practices or activities that fit together and interact to achieve a purpose.

The process of organizing may involve the grand design or redesign of the total structure, but most frequently it is concerned with the organization of particular functions and activities and the basis upon which the relationships between them are managed.

Organizations are not static things. Changes are constantly taking place in the business itself, in the environment in which the business operates, and in the people who work in the business. There is no such thing as an 'ideal' organization. The most that can be done is to optimize the processes involved, remembering that whatever structure evolves it will be contingent on the circumstances of the organization.

An important point to bear in mind is that organizations consist of people working more or less cooperatively together. Inevitably, and especially at managerial levels, the organization may have to be adjusted to fit the particular strengths and attributes of the people available. The result may not conform to the ideal, but it is more likely to work than a structure that ignores the human element. It is always desirable to have an ideal structure in mind, but it is equally desirable to modify it to meet particular circumstances, as long as there is awareness of the potential problems that may arise. This may seem an obvious point, but it is frequently ignored by management consultants and others who adopt a doctrinaire approach to organization, often with disastrous results.

Aims of organization design

Bearing in mind the need to take an empirical and contingent approach to organizing, as suggested above, the primary overall aim of organization design is to optimize the arrangements for conducting the affairs of the business. But another overall aim of organization design is to achieve the 'best fit' between the structure and the circumstances in which the organization operates.

The detailed aims of organization design are set out below.

Aims of organization design

- Clarify the overall purposes of the organization – the strategic goals that govern what it does and how it functions.
- Define how work should be organized to achieve that purpose, including the use of technology and other work processes.
- Define as precisely as possible the key activities involved in carrying out the work.
- Group these activities logically together to avoid unnecessary overlap or duplication.
- Provide for the integration of activities and the achievement of cooperative effort and teamwork.
- Build flexibility into the system so that organizational arrangements can adapt quickly to new situations and challenges.
- Provide for the rapid communication of information throughout the organization.

- Define the role and function of each organizational unit so that all concerned know how it plays its part in achieving the overall purpose.
- Clarify individual roles, accountabilities and authorities.
- Take account of individual needs and aspirations.
- Design jobs to make the best use of the skills and capacities of the job holders and to provide them with high levels of intrinsic motivation.
- Plan and implement organization development activities to ensure that the various processes within the organization operate in a manner that contributes to organizational effectiveness.
- Set up teams and project groups as required to be responsible for specific processing, development, professional or administrative activities or for the conduct of projects.

Conducting organization reviews

Organization reviews are conducted in the following stages.

Stages of an organization review

1. An analysis of the existing arrangements and the factors that may affect the organization now and in the future.
2. A diagnosis of the problems and issues facing the organization and what therefore needs to be done to improve the way in which the organization is structured and functions.
3. A plan to implement any revisions to the structure emerging from the diagnosis, possibly in phases. The plan may include longer-term considerations about the structure and the type of managers and employees who will be required to operate within it.
4. Implementation of the plan.

Organization analysis

The starting point for an organization review is an analysis of the existing circumstances, structure and processes of the organization and an assessment of the strategic issues that might affect it in the future. This covers the following areas.

The external environment

The economic, market, competitive, social and legal matters that may affect the organization. Plans for product-market development will be significant.

The internal environment

The mission, values, organization climate, management style, technology and processes of the organization as they affect the way it functions and should be structured to carry out its function. Technological developments may be particularly important, as well as the introduction of new processes such as just-in-time or the development of an entirely new computer system.

Strategic issues and objectives

As a background to the study it is necessary to identify the strategic issues facing the organization and its objectives. These may be considered under such headings as growth, competition and market position and standing. Issues concerning the availability of the required human, financial and physical resources would also have to be considered.

Activities

Activity analysis establishes what work is done and what needs to be done in the organization to achieve its objectives within its environment. The analysis should cover what is and is not being done, who is doing it and where, and how much is being done. An answer is necessary to the key questions: are all the activities required properly catered for? Are there any unnecessary activities being carried out, ie those that do not need to be done at all or those that could be conducted more economically and efficiently by external contractors or providers?

Structure

The analysis of structure covers how activities are grouped together, the number of levels in the hierarchy, the extent to which authority is decentralized to divisions and strategic business units (SBUs), where functions such as finance, HR and research and development are placed in the structure (eg as central functions or integrated into divisions or SBUs), and the relationships that exist between different units and functions (with particular attention being given to the way in which they communicate and cooperate with one another). Attention would be paid to such issues as the logic of the way in which activities are grouped and decentralized, the span of control of managers (the number of separate functions or people they are directly responsible for), any overlap between functions or gaps leading to the neglect of certain activities, and the existence of unnecessary departments, units, functions or layers of management.

There are no absolute standards against which an organization structure can be judged. Every organization is and should be different. There is never one right way of organizing anything and there are no absolute principles that govern organizational choice. Never follow fashion. Always do what is right in the context in which the organization exists. The fashion for de-layering organizations had much to commend it but it could go too far, leaving units and individuals adrift without any clear guidance on where they fit into the structure and how they should work with one another, and denuding the organization of key middle managers.

SOURCE REVIEW

A framework for organizational analysis, Kotter (1978)

- Key organizational processes – the major information gathering, communication, decision making, matter/energy transporting and matter/energy converting actions of the organization's employees and machines.
- External environment – an organization's 'task' environment includes suppliers, markets and competitors; the wider environment includes factors such as public attitudes, economic and political systems, laws, etc.
- Employees and other tangible assets – people, plant and equipment.
- Formal organizational requirements – systems designed to regulate the actions of employees (and machines).
- The social system – culture (values and norms) and relationships between employees in terms of power, affiliation and trust.
- Technology – the major techniques people use while engaged in organizational processes and that are programmed into machines.
- The dominant coalition The strategies and actions of the dominant coalition – those who control fundamental policy making and decision taking in the organization.

Organization diagnosis

The aim of the diagnosis is to establish the reasons for any structural problems facing the organization. The diagnosis should be made on the basis of the analysis of the external and internal environment. The organizational guidelines set out below can be used to identify causes and therefore indicate possible solutions.

Organization guidelines

There are a number of organizational guidelines that are worth bearing in mind. But they are not absolutes. Their relevance is contingent on the circumstances. The days have long gone when the classical principles of organization (line of command, span of control, etc) as formulated by Urwick (1947) and others were seen as the only basis for organization design. These principles do, however, persist in the minds of many managers. Some time ago Lupton (1975) pointed out that: 'The attraction of the classical design from the point of view of top management is that it seems to offer control.' Managers like to think they are rational and this has all the appearance of a rational approach. But without falling into the trap of believing that classical design works as it is supposed to do, the following guidelines are worth bearing in mind at all stages in an organization study and can help in the diagnosis of problems:

Allocation of work

The work that has to be done should be defined and allocated to functions, units, departments, work teams, project groups and individual positions. Related activities should be grouped together. There will be a choice between dividing work by product, process, market or geographical area.

Differentiation and integration

As Lawrence and Lorsch (1969) emphasized, it is necessary to differentiate between the different activities that have to be carried out, but it is equally necessary to ensure that these activities are integrated so that everyone in the organization is working towards the same goals.

Teamwork

Jobs should be defined and roles described in ways that facilitate and underline the importance of teamwork. Areas where cooperation is required should be highlighted. The organization should be designed and operated in such a way as to facilitate cooperation across departmental or functional boundaries. Wherever possible, self-managing teams and autonomous work groups should be set up and given the maximum amount of responsibility to run their own affairs, including planning, budgeting and exercising quality control. Networking should be encouraged in the sense of people communicating openly and informally with one another as the need arises. It is recognized that these informal processes can be more productive than rigidly 'working through channels', as set out in the organization chart. As the highly original and influential thinker about management Mary Parker Follett (1924) stressed, the primary task of management is to arrange the situation so that people cooperate of their own accord.

Flexibility

The organization structure should be flexible enough to respond quickly to change, challenge and uncertainty. Flexibility should be enhanced by the creation of core groups and using part-time, temporary and contract workers to handle extra demands. At top management level and elsewhere, a 'collegiate' approach to team operation should be considered in which people share responsibility and are expected to work with their colleagues in areas outside their primary function or skill.

Role clarification

People should be clear about their roles as individuals and as members of a team. They should know what they will be held accountable for and be given every opportunity to use their abilities in achieving objectives that they have agreed and are committed to. Role profiles should be used to define key result areas but should not act as straitjackets, restricting initiative and unduly limiting responsibility.

Decentralization

Authority to make decisions should be delegated as close to the scene of action as possible. Profit centres should be set up as strategic business units that operate close to their markets and with a considerable degree of autonomy. A multiproduct or market business should develop a federal organization with each federated entity running its own affairs, although they will be linked together by the overall business strategy.

De-layering

Organizations should be 'flattened' by stripping out superfluous layers of management and supervision in order to promote flexibility, facilitate swifter communication, increase responsiveness, enable people to be given more responsibility as individuals or teams and reduce costs.

Organization planning

Organization design leads into organization planning – assessing the implications of structural changes on future people requirements and taking steps to meet those requirements. Organization planning determines structure, relationships, roles, human resource requirements and the lines along which changes should be implemented. There is no one best design. There is always a choice. This concept of organizational choice was developed by Trist *et al* (1963), the Tavistock researchers who explained that work organization (the social system) was not absolutely determined by the technology, although it would be influenced by it.

Logical analysis will help in the evaluation of the alternatives, but the law of the situation as described originally by Follett (1924) must prevail. This states that the work that people are required to do depends on the objective requirements of the situation – not on the personal whim of a particular manager. The final choice will depend upon the context and circumstances of the organization – as Lupton (1975) pointed out, it is important to achieve best fit.

The concept of strategic choice, as developed by Child (1972, 1997), emphasized the significant contribution of leading groups (the dominant coalition) to influencing the structures of their organizations through an essentially political process. It was advanced by Child as a corrective to the view set out above that the way in which organizations are designed and structured is determined by their operational contingencies. Miles and Snow (1978) recognized how strategic choice identified the ongoing relationship between organizational agents and the environment, giving rise to what they termed the 'adaptive cycle'. They noted that: 'The strategic-choice approach essentially argues that the effectiveness of organizational adaptation hinges on the dominant coalition's perceptions of environmental conditions and the decisions it makes concerning how the organization will cope with these conditions.' In 1997 Child pointed out that strategic choice analysis regards debate and negotiation in the social networks existing in organizations as integral to decision making on organizational priorities, policies, structures and actions.

Organization structures are generally strongly influenced by personal and human considerations – the inclinations of top management, the strengths and weaknesses of management generally, the availability of people to work in the new organization and the need to take account of the feelings of those who will be exposed to change. Cold logic may sometimes have to override these considerations. If it does, then it must be deliberate and the consequences must be appreciated and allowed for when planning the implementation of the new organization.

It may have to be accepted that a logical regrouping of activities cannot be introduced in the short term because no one with the experience is available to manage the new activities, or because capable individuals are so firmly entrenched in one area that to uproot them would cause serious damage to their morale and would reduce the overall effectiveness of the new organization.

The worst sin that organization designers can commit is that of imposing their own ideology on the organization. Their job is to be eclectic in their knowledge, sensitive in their analysis of the situation and deliberate in their approach to the evaluation of alternatives.

Having planned the organization and defined structures, relationships and rules, it is necessary to consider how the new organization should be implemented. It may be advisable to stage an implementation over a number of phases, especially if new people have to be found and trained.

Smart working

Organization planning is not just about designing structures. It is also concerned with how people work, which includes how jobs are designed. This is the notion of 'smart working' in which the work environment is managed to release employees' energy and drive business performance. As defined by the Chartered Institute of Personnel and Development (CIPD, 2008d) smart working is: 'An approach to organizing work that aims to drive greater efficiency and effectiveness in achieving job outcomes through a combination of flexibility, autonomy and collaboration, in parallel with optimizing tools and working environments for employees.' The characteristics of smart working as established by the CIPD research include designing roles in which there is a higher degree of freedom to act, a philosophy of empowerment, flexible working arrangements, the development of high-performance working and the creation of high-trust working relationships.

Successful organizing

Research conducted by Whittington and Molloy (2005) identified the following steps to successful organizing:

- sustaining top management support, especially personal commitment and political support;
- avoiding piecemeal, uncoordinated change initiatives by making a strategic business case that anticipates implications across the entire organization;
- achieving substantive, rather than tokenistic, employee involvement in the change process, moving beyond communication to active engagement;
- investing in communication with external stakeholders, including customers, suppliers and financial stakeholders;
- involving HR professionals closely, right from the start – involving HR has been proved to positively impact on a range of performance outcomes;
- maintaining effective project management disciplines that are embedded in the organization;
- building skilled change management teams, with the right mix of experiences and abilities, that can work together.

Who does the work?

Organization design may be carried out by line management with or without the help of members of the HR function or internal consultants, or it may be done by outside consultants.

HR should always be involved because organization design is essentially about people and the work they do. The advantage of using outside consultants is that an entirely independent and dispassionate view is obtained. They can cut through internal organizational pressures, politics and constraints and bring experience of other organizational problems they have dealt with. Sometimes, regrettably, major changes can be obtained only by outside intervention. But there is a danger of consultants suggesting theoretically ideal organizations that do not take sufficient account of the problems of making them work with existing people. They do not have to live with their solutions as do line and HR managers. If outside consultants are used, it is essential to involve people from within the organization so they can ensure that they are able to implement the proposals smoothly.

Organization design – key learning points

The process of organizing

The process of organizing may involve the grand design or redesign of the total structure, but most frequently it is concerned with the organization of particular functions and activities and the basis upon which the relationships between them are managed.

Aims of organization design

The overall aim of organization design is to optimize the arrangements for conducting the affairs of the business. But another overall aim of organization design is to achieve the 'best fit' between the structure and these circumstances.

Conducting an organization review – analysis

The starting point for an organization review is an analysis of the existing circumstances, structure and processes of the organization and an assessment of the strategic issues that might affect it in the future. This covers the internal and external environment, strategic issues and objectives, activities and structures.

Conducting an organization review – diagnosis

The aim of the diagnosis is to establish the reasons for any structural problems facing the organization. The guidelines for the diagnosis cover: allocation of work, differentiation and integration, teamwork, flexibility, role clarification, decentralization and de-layering.

Conducting an organization review – planning

Organization planning involves assessing the implications of structural changes on future people requirements and taking steps to meet those requirements. It determines structure, relationships, roles, human resource requirements, methods of working and the lines along which changes should be implemented.

Questions

1. Are there any such things as principles of organization design?
2. Jack Welch, when CEO of General Electric, was quoted by Krames (2004) as saying: 'The way to harness the power of these people is not to protect them... but to turn them loose, and get the management layers off their backs, the bureaucratic shackles off their feet and the functional barriers out of their way.' Critically evaluate this statement from the viewpoint of its practicality in your own or any organization.
3. How do you judge the effectiveness of an organization?
4. How do you ensure that a matrix organization works well?

References

Child, J (1972) Organizational structure, environment and performance: the role of strategic choice, *Sociology*, **6** (1), pp 1–22

Child, D (1997) Strategic choice in the analysis of action, structure, organizations and environment: retrospective and prospective, *Organizational Studies*, **18** (1), pp 43–76

CIPD (2008d) *Smart Working: The impact of work organisation and job design*, CIPD, London

Follett, M P (1924) *Creative Experience*, Longmans Green, New York

Huczynski, A A and Buchanan, D A (2007) *Organizational Behaviour*, 6th edn, FT Prentice Hall, Harlow

Kotter, J (1978) *Organizational Dynamics: Diagnosis and intervention*, Addison-Wesley, Reading MA

Krames, J A (2004) *The Welch Way*, McGraw-Hill, New York

Lawrence, P R and Lorsch, J W (1969) *Developing Organizations*, Addison-Wiley, Reading, MA

Lupton, T (1975) Best fit in the design of organizations, *Personnel Review*, **4** (1), pp 15–22

Miles, R E and Snow, C C (1978) *Organizational Strategy: Structure and process*, McGraw-Hill, New York

Trist, E L, Higgin, G W, Murray, H and Pollock, A B (1963) *Organizational Choice*, Tavistock Publications, London

Urwick, L F (1947) *Dynamic Administration*, Pitman, London

Whittington, R and Molloy, E (2005) *HR's Role in Organizing: Shaping change*, CIPD, London

24 Organization Development

Key concepts and terms

- Action research
- Group dynamics
- Intervention
- Organization development (OD)
- Process consulting
- Survey feedback
- Behaviour modification
- Integrated strategic change
- Neuro-linguistic programming (NLP)
- Organizational transformation
- Sensitivity training laboratories (T-groups)
- Transactional analysis

Learning outcomes

On completing this chapter you should be able to define these key concepts. You should also know about:

- Features of organization development programmes
- Organization development activities
- The assumptions and values of organization development

Introduction

Organization development (OD) is about taking systematic steps to improve organizational capability. It is concerned with process – how things get done. In this chapter, organization development is defined, organization development strategies are examined, consideration is given to the assumptions and values of OD, and OD activities are described. Processes associated with OD for managing change and organizational transformation are dealt with in Chapter 25.

Organization development defined

Organization development is defined by Cummins and Worley (2005) as: 'The system-wide application and transfer of behavioural science knowledge to the planned development, improvement and refinement of the strategies, structures and processes that lead to organizational effectiveness'.

SOURCE REVIEW

Organization development defined, French and Bell (1990)

A planned systematic process in which applied behavioural science principles and practices are introduced into an ongoing organization towards the goals of effecting organizational improvement, greater organizational competence, and greater organizational effectiveness. The focus is on organizations and their improvement or, to put it another way, total systems change. The orientation is on action – achieving desired results as a result of planned activities.

Organization development aims to help people work more effectively together, improve organizational processes such as the formulation and implementation of strategy, and facilitate the transformation of the organization and the management of change. As expressed by Beer (1980), OD operates as: 'A system-wide process of data collection, diagnosis, action planning, intervention and evaluation.'

OD is based on behavioural science concepts, but during the 1980s and 1990s the focus shifted to a number of other approaches. Some of these, such as organizational transformation, are not entirely dissimilar to OD. Others such as change management are built on some of the basic ideas developed by writers on organization development and OD practitioners. Yet other approaches such as high-performance work systems, total quality management and performance management can be described as holistic processes that attempt to improve overall organizational effectiveness from a particular perspective. More recently, as noted by Cummins and Worley (2005), the practice of OD has gone 'far beyond its humanistic origins by incorporating concepts from organization strategy that complement the early emphasis on social processes'.

Organization development programmes

OD programmes are concerned with system-wide change and have the features described below.

Features of organization development programmes

1. They are managed, or at least strongly supported, from the top but may make use of third parties or 'change agents' to diagnose problems and to manage change by various kinds of planned activity or 'intervention'.
2. The plans for organization development are based upon a systematic analysis and diagnosis of the strategies and circumstances of the organization and the changes and problems affecting it.
3. They use behavioural science knowledge and aim to improve the way the organization copes in times of change through such processes as interaction, communication, participation, planning and conflict management.
4. They focus on ways of ensuring that business and HR strategies are implemented and change is managed effectively.

Assumptions and values of organization development

OD is based upon the assumptions and values listed below.

Assumptions and values of organization development

- Most individuals are driven by the need for personal growth and development as long as their environment is both supportive and challenging.
- The work team, especially at the informal level, has great significance for feelings of satisfaction and the dynamics of such teams have a powerful effect on the behaviour of their members.

- OD programmes aim to improve the quality of working life of all members of the organization.
- Organizations can be more effective if they learn to diagnose their own strengths and weaknesses.
- Managers often do not know what is wrong and need special help in diagnosing problems, although the outside 'process consultant' ensures that decision making remains in the hands of the client.
- The implementation of strategy involves paying close attention to the people processes involved and the management of change.

Organization development activities

Action research

This is an approach developed by Lewin (1951) that takes the form of systematically collecting data from people about process issues and feeding it back in order to identify problems and their likely causes. This provides the basis for an action plan to deal with the problem that can be implemented cooperatively by the people involved. The essential elements of action research are data collection, diagnosis, feedback, action planning, action and evaluation.

Survey feedback

This is a variety of action research in which data are systematically collected about the system and then fed back to groups to analyse and interpret as the basis for preparing action plans. The techniques of survey feedback include the use of attitude surveys and workshops to feed back results and discuss implications.

Interventions

The term 'intervention' in OD refers to core structured activities involving clients and consultants. The activities can take the form of action research, survey feedback or any of those mentioned below.

SOURCE REVIEW

The three primary tasks of the OD practitioner or interventionist, Argyris (1970)

1. Generate and help clients to generate valid information that they can understand about their problems.
2. Create opportunities for clients to search effectively for solutions to their problems, to make free choices.
3. Create conditions for internal commitment to their choices and opportunities for the continual monitoring of the action taken.

Process consultation

As described by Schein (1969), this involves helping clients to generate and analyse information they can understand and, following a diagnosis, act upon. The information will relate to organizational processes such as inter-group relations, interpersonal relations and communication. The job of the process consultant was defined by Schein as being to 'help the organization to solve its own problems by making it aware of organizational processes, of the consequences of these processes, and of the mechanisms by which they can be changed'.

Group dynamics

Group dynamics (a term coined by Lewin, 1947) are the processes that take place in groups that determine how they act and react in different circumstances. Team-building interventions can deal with permanent work teams or those set up to deal with projects or to solve particular problems. Interventions are directed towards the analysis of the effectiveness of team processes such as problem solving, decision making and interpersonal relationships, a diagnosis and discussion of the issues, and joint consideration of the actions required to improve effectiveness.

Inter-group conflict interventions

As developed by Blake *et al* (1964), these aim to improve inter-group relations by getting groups to share their perceptions of one another and to analyse what they have learnt about themselves and the other group. The groups involved meet each other to share what they have learnt, to agree on the issues to be resolved and the actions required.

Personal interventions

These include:

- neuro-linguistic programming (NLP) in which people learn to programme their reactions to others and develop unconscious strategies for interacting with them;
- sensitivity training laboratories (T-groups), which aim to increase sensitivity, diagnostic ability and action skills;
- transactional analysis – an approach to understanding how people behave and express themselves through transactions with others using the parent–adult–child model to do so;
- behaviour modification – the use of positive reinforcement and corrective feedback to change behaviour which, as developed by Luthans and Krietner (1985), involves identifying the behaviours to be modified, measuring the extent to which these behaviours occur, establishing what causes the behaviours and their consequences, developing an intervention strategy to strengthen desirable behaviours and weaken dysfunctional behaviours, and evaluating the outcome.

Integrated strategic change

Integrated strategic change methodology is a highly participative process conceived by Worley *et al* (1996). The aim is to facilitate the implementation of strategic plans. The steps required are:

1. Strategic analysis, a review of the organization's strategic orientation (its strategic intentions within its competitive environment) and a diagnosis of the organization's readiness for change.
2. Develop strategic capability – the ability to implement the strategic plan quickly and effectively.
3. Integrate individuals and groups throughout the organization into the processes of analysis, planning and implementation to maintain the firm's strategic focus, direct attention and resources to the organization's key competencies, improve coordination and integration within the organization, and create higher levels of shared ownership and commitment.
4. Create the strategy, gain commitment and support for it and plan its implementation.
5. Implement the strategic change plan, drawing on knowledge of motivation, group dynamics and change processes, dealing with issues such as alignment, adaptability, teamwork and organizational and individual learning.
6. Allocate resources, provide feedback and solve problems as they arise.

Organization development – key learning points

Features of organization development programmes

- They are managed from the top but may make use of third parties or 'change agents' to diagnose problems and to manage change by various kinds of planned activity or 'intervention'.
- The plans for organization development are based upon a systematic analysis and diagnosis of the strategies and circumstances of the organization and the changes and problems affecting it.
- They use behavioural science knowledge and aim to improve the way the organization copes in times of change through such processes as interaction, communication, participation, planning and conflict management.
- They focus on ways of ensuring that business and HR strategies are implemented and change is managed effectively.

The assumptions and values of organization development

- Most individuals are driven by the need for personal growth and development as long as their environment is both supportive and challenging.
- The work team, especially at the informal level, has great significance for feelings of satisfaction and the dynamics of such teams have a powerful effect on the behaviour of their members.
- OD programmes aim to improve the quality of working life of all members of the organization.
- Organizations can be more effective if they learn to diagnose their own strengths and weaknesses.
- Managers often do not know what is wrong and need special help in diagnosing problems, although the outside 'process consultant' ensures that decision making remains in the hands of the client.
- The implementation of strategy involves paying close attention to the people processes involved and the management of change.

Organization development activities

Action research, survey feedback, interventions, process consultation, group dynamics, inter-group conflict resolution, neuro-linguistic programming, sensitivity training, transactional analysis, behaviour modification, and integrated strategic change.

Questions

1. Organization development (OD) emerged in the 1960s as part of the behavioural science movement. Is this still valid today?
2. Can you give examples of any successful OD programmes? Draw on recent research for your answer.
3. You have been asked to give a talk to a postgraduate management conference on 'The qualities required of an effective OD practitioner'. Outline what you will say and explain its relevance for developing the capability of your own organization.
4. Why has organization development been described as a quasi-religious movement?

References

Argyris, C (1970) *Intervention Theory and Method*, Addison-Wesley, Reading, MA

Beer, M (1980) *Organization Change and Development: A systems view*, Goodyear, Santa Monica, CA

Blake, R, Shepart, H and Mouton, J (1964) Breakthrough in organizational development, *Harvard Business Review*, **42**, pp 237–58

Cummins, T G and Worley, C G (2005) *Organization Development and Change*, South Western, Mason, OH

French, W L and Bell, C H (1990) *Organization Development*, Prentice-Hall, Englewood Cliffs, NJ

Lewin, K (1947) Frontiers in group dynamics, *Human Relations*, **1** (1), pp 5–42

Lewin, K (1951) *Field Theory in Social Science*, Harper & Row, New York

Luthans, F and Kreitner, R (1985) *Organizational Behaviour Modification and Beyond*, Scott Foresman, Glenview, IL

Schein, E H (1969) *Process Consultation: Its role in organizational development*, Addison-Wesley, Reading, MA

Worley, C, Hitchin, D and Ross, W (1996) *Integrated Strategic Change: How organization development builds competitive advantage*, Addison-Wesley, Reading MA

25 Change Management

Key concepts and terms

- Change agent
- Field force analysis
- Incremental change
- Organizational transformation
- Strategic change
- Transformational change
- Change management
- Gamma change
- Operational change
- Second order change
- Transactional change

Learning outcomes

On completing this chapter you should be able to define these key concepts. You should also know about:

- Types of change
- Change models
- Overcoming resistance to change
- Strategies for organizational transformation
- The change process
- Reasons for resistance to change
- Implementing change
- The role of HR in managing change

Introduction

Change management is defined as the process of achieving the smooth implementation of change by planning and introducing it systematically, taking into account the likelihood of it being resisted.

Change, it is often said, is the only thing that remains constant in organizations. As A P Sloan wrote in *My Years with General Motors* (1967) 'The circumstances of an ever-changing market and an ever-changing product are capable of breaking any business organization if that organization is unprepared for change.' Change cannot just be allowed to happen. It needs to be managed.

As described in this chapter, to manage change it is first necessary to understand the types of change and how the process works. It is important to bear in mind that while those wanting change need to be constant about ends, they have to be flexible about means. This requires them to come to an understanding of the various models of change that have been developed and of the factors that create resistance to change and how to minimize such resistance. In the light of an understanding of these models and the phenomenon of resistance to change they will be better equipped to make use of the guidelines for change set out in this chapter.

Change often takes place incrementally but it can take the form of a transformation of the organization, and the considerations affecting the management of transformational change are discussed in the penultimate section of the chapter. The role of HR in managing change is examined in the last section of the chapter.

Types of change

There are three types of change: strategic, operational and transformational.

1. Strategic change

Strategic change is concerned with broad, long-term and organization-wide issues involving change. It is about moving to a future state that has been defined generally in terms of strategic vision and scope. It will cover the purpose and mission of the organization, its corporate philosophy on such matters as growth, quality, innovation and values concerning employees and customers, competitive positioning and strategic goals for achieving and maintaining competitive advantage and for product-market development. These goals are supported by policies concerning marketing, sales, manufacturing, product and process development, finance and human resource management.

Strategic change takes place within the context of the external competitive, economic and social environment, and the organization's internal resources, capabilities, culture, structure and systems. Its successful implementation requires thorough analysis and understanding of these factors in the formulation and planning stages. The ultimate achievement of sustainable competitive advantage relies on the qualities defined by Pettigrew and Whipp (1991), namely 'The capacity of the firm to identify and understand the competitive forces in play and how they change over time, linked to the competence of a business to mobilize and manage the resources necessary for the chosen competitive response through time.'

Strategic change, however, should not be treated simplistically as a linear process of getting from A to B that can be planned and executed as a logical sequence of events. Pettigrew and Whipp (1991) issued the following warning based on their research into competitiveness and managing change in the motor, financial services, insurance and publishing industries.

SOURCE REVIEW

Pettigrew and Whipp (1991) on strategic change

The process by which strategic changes are made seldom moves directly through neat, successive stages of analysis, choice and implementation. Changes in the firm's environment persistently threaten the course and logic of strategic changes: dilemma abounds... We conclude that one of the defining features of the process, in so far as management action is concerned, is ambiguity; seldom is there an easily isolated logic to strategic change. Instead, that process may derive its motive force from an amalgam of economic, personal and political imperatives. Their introduction through time requires that those responsible for managing that process make continual assessments, repeated choices and multiple adjustments.

2. Operational change

Operational change relates to new systems, procedures, structures or technology that will have an immediate effect on working arrangements within a part of the organization. But its impact on people can be more significant than broader strategic change and it has to be handled just as carefully.

3. Transformational change

Transformational change takes place when there are fundamental and comprehensive changes in structures, processes and behaviours that have a dramatic effect on the ways in which the organization functions.

The change process

Conceptually, the change process starts with an awareness of the need for change. An analysis of this situation and the factors that have created it leads to a diagnosis of their distinctive characteristics and an indication of the direction in which action needs to be taken. Possible courses of action can then be identified and evaluated and a choice made of the preferred action.

It is then necessary to decide how to get from here to there. Managing change during this transition state is a critical phase in the change process. It is here that the problems of introducing change emerge and have to be managed. These problems can include resistance to change, low stability, high levels of stress, misdirected energy, conflict and loss of momentum. Hence the need to do everything possible to anticipate reactions and likely impediments to the introduction of change.

The installation stage can also be painful. When planning change there is a tendency for people to think that it will be an entirely logical and linear process of going from A to B. It is not like that at all. As described by Pettigrew and Whipp (1991), the implementation of change is an 'iterative, cumulative and reformulation-in-use process'.

Change models

The best known change models are those developed by Lewin (1951) and Beckhard (1969). But other important contributions to an understanding of the mechanisms for change have been made by Thurley (1979), Bandura (1986) and Beer *et al* (1990).

Lewin

The basic mechanisms for managing change as set out by Lewin (1951) are:

- Unfreezing – altering the present stable equilibrium that supports existing behaviours and attitudes. This process must take account of the inherent threats change presents to people and the need to motivate those affected to attain the natural state of equilibrium by accepting change.
- Changing – developing new responses based on new information.
- Refreezing – stabilizing the change by introducing the new responses into the personalities of those concerned.

Lewin also suggested a methodology for analysing change that he called 'field force analysis'.

SOURCE REVIEW

Field force analysis, Lewin (1951)

- Analyse the restraining or driving forces which will affect the transition to the future state – these restraining forces will include the reactions of those who see change as unnecessary or as constituting a threat.
- Assess which of the driving or restraining forces are critical.
- Take steps both to increase the critical driving forces and to decrease the critical restraining forces.

Beckhard

According to Beckhard (1969), a change programme should incorporate the following processes.

SOURCE REVIEW

Change programme processes, Beckhard (1969)

- Set goals and define the future state or organizational conditions desired after the change.
- Diagnose the present condition in relation to these goals.
- Define the transition state activities and commitments required to meet the future state.
- Develop strategies and action plans for managing this transition in the light of an analysis of the factors likely to affect the introduction of change.

Thurley

Thurley (1979) described the following five approaches to managing change.

SOURCE REVIEW

Approaches to managing change, Thurley (1979)

1. Directive – the imposition of change in crisis situations or when other methods have failed. This is done by the exercise of managerial power without consultation.

2. Bargained – this approach recognizes that power is shared between the employer and the employed and change requires negotiation, compromise and agreement before being implemented.

3. 'Hearts and minds' – an all-embracing thrust to change the attitudes, values and beliefs of the whole workforce. This 'normative' approach (ie one that starts from a definition of what management thinks is right or 'normal') seeks 'commitment' and 'shared vision' but does not necessarily include involvement or participation.

4. Analytical – a theoretical approach to the change process using models of change such as those described above. It proceeds sequentially from the analysis and diagnosis of the situation, through the setting of objectives, the design of the change process, the evaluation of the results and, finally, the determination of the objectives for the next stage in the change process. This is the rational and logical approach much favoured by consultants – external and internal. But change seldom proceeds as smoothly as this model would suggest. Emotions, power politics and external pressures mean that the rational approach, although it might be the right way to start, is difficult to sustain.

5. Action-based – this recognizes that the way managers behave in practice bears little resemblance to the analytical, theoretical model. The distinction between managerial thought and managerial action blurs in practice to the point of invisibility. What managers think is what they do. Real life therefore often results in a 'ready, aim, fire' approach to change management. This typical approach to change starts with a broad belief that some sort of problem exists, although it may not be well defined. The identification of possible solutions, often on a trial or error basis, leads to a clarification of the nature of the problem and a shared understanding of a possible optimal solution, or at least a framework within which solutions can be discovered.

Bandura

The ways in which people change was described by Bandura (1986). He suggested that people make conscious choices about their behaviours. The information people use to make their choices comes from their environment, and their choices are based upon the things that are important to them, the views they have about their own abilities to behave in certain ways and the consequences they think will accrue to whatever behaviour they decide to engage in.

For those concerned with change management, the implications of Bandura's concept of change (which is linked to expectancy theory) are that:

- the tighter the link between a particular behaviour and a particular outcome, the more likely it is that we will engage in that behaviour;
- the more desirable the outcome, the more likely it is that we will engage in behaviour that we believe will lead to it;
- the more confident we are that we can actually assume a new behaviour, the more likely we are to try it.

To change people's behaviour, therefore, we have first to change the environment within which they work; second, convince them that the new behaviour is something they can accomplish (training is important); and third, persuade them that it will lead to an outcome that they will value. None of these steps is easy.

Beer *et al*

Michael Beer (1990) and his colleagues suggested in a seminal *Harvard Business Review* article, 'Why change programs don't produce change', that most such programmes are guided by a theory of change that is fundamentally flawed. This theory states that changes in attitudes lead to changes in behaviour. 'According to this model, change is like a conversion experience. Once people get religion, changes in their behaviour will surely follow.' They believe that this theory gets the change process exactly backwards and made the following comment on it.

SOURCE REVIEW

Beer *et al* (1990) on change

In fact, individual behaviour is powerfully shaped by the organizational roles people play. The most effective way to change behaviour, therefore, is to put people into a new organizational context, which imposes new roles, responsibilities and relationships on them. This creates a situation that in a sense 'forces' new attitudes and behaviour on people.

They prescribe six steps to effective change that concentrate on what they call 'task alignment' – reorganizing employees' roles, responsibilities and relationships to solve specific business problems in small units where goals and tasks can be clearly defined. The aim of following the overlapping steps is to build a self-reinforcing cycle of commitment, coordination and competence.

SOURCE REVIEW

Steps to achieving change, Beer *et al* (1990)

1. Mobilize commitment to change through the joint analysis of problems.
2. Develop a shared vision of how to organize and manage to achieve goals such as competitiveness.
3. Foster consensus for the new vision, competence to enact it, and cohesion to move it along.
4. Spread revitalization to all departments without pushing it from the top – don't force the issue, let each department find its own way to the new organization.
5. Institutionalize revitalization through formal policies, systems and structures.
6. Monitor and adjust strategies in response to problems in the revitalization process.

Resistance to change

People resist change because it is seen as a threat to familiar patterns of behaviour as well as to status and financial rewards. Woodward (1968) made this point clearly.

SOURCE REVIEW

Joan Woodward (1968) on resistance to change

When we talk about resistance to change we tend to imply that management is always rational in changing its direction, and that employees are stupid, emotional or irrational in not responding in the way they should. But if an individual is going to be worse off, explicitly or implicitly, when the proposed changes have been made, any resistance is entirely rational in terms of his [*sic*] own best interest. The interests of the organization and the individual do not always coincide.

However, some people will welcome change as an opportunity. These need to be identified and where feasible they can be used to help in the introduction of change as change agents. Specifically, the main reasons for resisting charge are as follows:

- The shock of the new – people are suspicious of anything that they perceive will upset their established routines, methods of working or conditions of employment. They do not want to lose the security of what is familiar to them. They may not believe statements by management that the change is for their benefit as well as that of the organization; sometimes with good reason. They may feel that management has ulterior motives and sometimes, the louder the protestations of management, the less they will be believed.
- Economic fears – loss of money, threats to job security.
- Inconvenience – the change will make life more difficult.
- Uncertainty – change can be worrying because of uncertainty about its likely impact.
- Symbolic fears – a small change that may affect some treasured symbol, such as a separate office or a reserved parking space, may symbolize big ones, especially when employees are uncertain about how extensive the programme of change will be.
- Threat to interpersonal relationships – anything that disrupts the customary social relationships and standards of the group will be resisted.
- Threat to status or skill – the change is perceived as reducing the status of individuals or as de-skilling them.
- Competence fears – concern about the ability to cope with new demands or to acquire new skills.

Overcoming resistance to change

Resistance to change can be difficult to overcome even when it is not detrimental to those concerned. But the attempt must be made. The first step is to analyse the potential impact of change by considering how it will affect people in their jobs. The reasons for resisting change set out above can be used as a checklist of where there may be problems, generally, with groups or with individuals.

The analysis should indicate what aspects of the proposed change may be supported generally or by specified individuals and which aspects may be resisted. So far as possible, the potentially hostile or negative reactions of people and the reasons for them should be identified. It is necessary to try to understand the likely feelings and fears of those affected so that unnecessary worries can be relieved and, as far as possible, ambiguities can be resolved. In making this analysis, the individual introducing the change – the change agent – should recognize that new ideas are likely to be suspect and should make ample provision for the discussion of reactions to proposals to ensure complete understanding of them.

Involvement in the change process gives people the chance to raise and resolve their concerns and make suggestions about the form of the change and how it should be introduced. The aim is to get 'ownership' – a feeling amongst people that the change is something that they are happy to live with because they have been involved in its planning and introduction – it has become *their* change.

A communication strategy to explain the proposed change should be prepared and implemented so that unnecessary fears are allayed. All the available channels, as described in Chapter 57, should be used but face-to-face communication direct from managers to individuals or through a team briefing system are best.

Implementing change

The following guidelines on implementing change were produced by Nadler and Tushman (1980).

SOURCE REVIEW

Guidelines on implementing change, Nadler and Tushman (1980)

- Motivate in order to achieve changes in behaviour by individuals.
- Manage the transition by making organizational arrangements designed to assure that control is maintained during and after the transition and by developing and communicating a clear image of the future.
- Shape the political dynamics of change so that power centres develop that support the change rather than block it.
- Build in stability of structures and processes to serve as anchors for people to hold on to – organizations and individuals can only stand so much uncertainty and turbulence, hence the emphasis by Quinn (1980) on the need for an incremental approach.

The change process will take place more smoothly with the help of credible change agents – internal or external. These are people who facilitate change by providing advice and support on its introduction and management. It is often assumed that only people from outside the organization can take on the change agent role because they are independent and do not 'carry any baggage'. They can be useful, but people from within the firm who are respected and credible can do the job well. This is often the role of HR specialists, but the use of line managers adds extra value.

Guidelines for change management

- The achievement of sustainable change requires strong commitment and visionary leadership from the top.
- Understanding is necessary of the culture of the organization and the levers for change that are most likely to be effective in that culture.
- Those concerned with managing change at all levels should have the temperament and leadership skills appropriate to the circumstances of the organization and its change strategies.
- Change is more likely to be successful if there is a 'burning platform' to justify it, ie a powerful and convincing reason for change.
- People support what they help to create. Commitment to change is improved if those affected by change are allowed to participate as fully as possible in planning and implementing it. The aim should be to get them to 'own' the change as something they want and will be glad to live with.
- The reward system should encourage innovation and recognize success in achieving change.
- Change will always involve failure as well as success. The failures must be expected and learnt from.
- Hard evidence and data on the need for change are the most powerful tools for its achievement, but establishing the need for change is easier than deciding how to satisfy it.
- It is easier to change behaviour by changing processes, structure and systems than to change attitudes or the organizational culture.
- There are always people in organizations who can act as champions of change. They will welcome the challenges and opportunities that change can provide. They are the ones to be chosen as change agents.
- Resistance to change is inevitable if the individuals concerned feel that they are going to be worse off – implicitly or explicitly. The inept management of change will produce that reaction.
- In an age of global competition, technological innovation, turbulence, discontinuity, even chaos, change is inevitable and necessary. The organization must do all it can to explain why change is essential and how it will affect everyone. Moreover, every effort must be made to protect the interests of those affected by change.

Organizational transformation

Organizational transformation is defined by Cummins and Worley (2005) as 'A process of radically altering the organization's strategic direction, including fundamental changes in structures, processes and behaviours.' Transformation involves what is called 'second order' or 'gamma' change involving discontinuous shifts in strategy, structure, processes or culture. Transformation is required when:

- significant changes occur in the competitive, technological, social or legal environment;
- major changes take place to the product lifecycle requiring different product development and marketing strategies;
- major changes take place in top management;
- a financial crisis or large downturn occurs;
- an acquisition or merger takes place.

Transformation strategies

Transformation strategies are usually driven by senior management and line managers with the support of HR rather than OD specialists. The key roles of management as defined by Tushman *et al* (1988) are envisioning, energizing and enabling.

Organizational transformation strategic plans may involve radical changes to the structure, culture and processes of the organization – the way it looks at the world. They may involve planning and implementing significant and far-reaching developments in corporate structures and organization-wide processes. The change is neither incremental (bit by bit) nor transactional (concerned solely with systems and procedures). Transactional change, according to Pascale (1990), is merely concerned with the alteration of ways in which the organization does business and people interact with one another on a day-to-day basis, and 'is effective when what you want is more of what you've already got'. He advocates a 'discontinuous improvement in capability' and this he describes as transformation.

SOURCE REVIEW

Strategies for transformational change, Beckard (1989)

1. A change in what drives the organization – for example, a change from being production-driven to being market-driven would be transformational.
2. A fundamental change in the relationships between or among organizational parts – for example, decentralization.
3. A major change in the ways of doing work – for example, the introduction of new technology such as computer-integrated manufacturing.
4. A basic, cultural change in norms, values or research systems – for example, developing a customer-focused culture.

Transformation through leadership

Transformation programmes are led from the top within the organization. They do not rely on an external 'change agent' as did traditional OD interventions, although specialist external advice might be obtained on aspects of the transformation such as strategic planning, reorganization or developing new reward processes.

The prerequisite for a successful programme is the presence of a transformational leader who, as defined by Burns (1978), motivates others to strive for higher-order goals rather than merely short-term interest. Transformational leaders go beyond dealing with day-to-day management problems: they commit people to action and focus on the development of new levels of awareness of where the future lies, and commitment to achieving that future. Burns contrasts transformational leaders with transactional leaders who operate by building up a network of interpersonal transactions in a stable situation and who enlist compliance rather than commitment through the reward system and the exercise of authority and power. Transactional leaders may be good at dealing with here-and-now problems but they will not provide the vision required to transform the future.

Managing the transition

Strategies need to be developed for managing the transition from where the organization is to where the organization wants to be. This is the critical part of a transformation programme. It is during the transition period of getting from here to there that change takes place. Transition management starts from a definition of the future state and a diagnosis of the present state. It is then necessary to define what has to be done to achieve the transformation. This means deciding on the new processes, systems, procedures, structures, products and markets to be developed. Having defined these, the work can be programmed and the resources required (people, money, equipment and time) can be defined. The strategic plan for managing the transition should include provisions for involving people in the process and for communicating to them about what is happening, why it is happening and how it will affect them. Clearly the aim is to get as many people as possible committed to the change. The eight steps required to transform an organization have been summed up by Kotter (1995) as follows.

SOURCE REVIEW

Steps to achieving organizational transformation, Kotter (1995)

1. Establish a sense of urgency – examining market and competitive realities; identifying and discussing crises, potential crises, or major opportunities.
2. Form a powerful guiding coalition – assembling a group with enough influence and power to lead change.
3. Create a vision – creating a vision to help direct the change effort and developing strategies for achieving that vision.
4. Communicate the vision – using every vehicle possible to communicate the new vision and strategies and teaching new behaviours by the example of the guiding coalition.
5. Empower others to act on the vision – getting rid of obstacles to change; changing systems or structures that seriously undermine the vision and encouraging risk taking and non-traditional ideas, activities and actions.
6. Plan for and create short-term wins – planning for visible performance improvement; creating those improvements and recognizing and rewarding employees involved in the improvements.
7. Consolidate improvements and produce still more change – using increased credibility to change systems, structures and policies that don't fit the vision; hiring, promoting and developing employees who can implement the vision and reinvigorating the process with new projects, themes and change agents.
8. Institutionalize new approaches – articulating the connections between the new behaviours and corporate success and developing the means to ensure leadership development and succession.

Transformation capability

The development and implementation of transformation strategies require special capabilities. As Gratton (1999) points out:

> *Transformation capability depends in part on the ability to create and embed processes which link business strategy to the behaviours and performance of individuals and teams. These clusters of processes link vertically (to create alignment with short-term business needs), horizontally (to create cohesion), and temporally (to transform to meet future business needs).*

The role of HR in managing change

If HR is concerned – as it should be – in playing a major role in the achievement of continuous improvement in organizational capability and individual performance, and in the HR processes that support that improvement, then it will need to be involved in facilitating change. Ulrich (1997a) believes that one of the key roles of HR professionals is to act as change agents, delivering organizational transformation and culture change.

Strategic HRM is as much if not more about managing change during the process of implementation as it is about producing long-term plans; a point emphasized by Purcell (1999) who believes that: 'We should be much more sensitive to processes of organizational change and avoid being trapped in the logic of rational choice.' In 2001 Purcell suggested that change is especially important in HRM strategies 'since their concern is with the future, the unknown, thinking of and learning how to do things differently, undoing the ways things have been done in the past, and managing its implementation'. He believes that the focus of strategy is on implementation, where HR can play a major part.

The importance of the human resource element in achieving change has been emphasized by Johnson and Scholes (1997):

> *Organizations which successfully manage change are those which have integrated their human resource management policies with their strategies and the strategic change process... training, employee relations, compensation packages and so on are not merely operational issues for the personnel department; they are crucially concerned with the way in which employees relate to the nature and direction of the firm and as such they can both block strategic change and be significant facilitators of strategic change.*

HR professionals as change agents

Caldwell (2001) categorizes HR change agents in four dimensions:

1. Transformational change – a major change that has a dramatic effect on HR policy and practice across the whole organization.
2. Incremental change – gradual adjustments of HR policy and practices that affect single activities or multiple functions.

3. HR vision – a set of values and beliefs that affirm the legitimacy of the HR function as strategic business partner.
4. HR expertise – the knowledge and skills that define the unique contribution the HR professional can make to effective people management.

Across these dimensions, the change agent roles that Caldwell suggests can be carried out by HR professionals are those of change champions, change adapters, change consultants and change synergists.

The contribution of HR to change management

HR practitioners may be involved in initiating change but they can also act as a stabilizing force in situations where change would be damaging. Mohrman and Lawler (1998) believe that:

> *The human resources function can help the organization develop the capability to weather the changes that will continue to be part of the organizational landscape. It can help with the ongoing learning processes required to assess the impact of change and enable the organization to make corrections and enhancements to the changes. It can help the organization develop a new psychological contract and ways to give employees a stake in the changes that are occurring and in the performance of the organization.*

Ulrich (1998) argues that HR professionals are 'not fully comfortable or compatible in the role of change agent', and that their task is therefore not to carry out change but to get change done. But HR practitioners are in a good position to understand possible points of resistance to change and they can help to facilitate the information flow and understanding that will help to overcome that resistance.

Gratton (2000) stresses the need for HR practitioners to: 'Understand the state of the company, the extent of the embedding of processes and structures throughout the organization, and the behaviour and attitudes of individual employees.' She believes that 'The challenge is to implement the ideas' and the solution is to 'build a guiding coalition by involving line managers', which means 'creating issue-based cross-functional action teams that will initially make recommendations and later move into action'. This approach 'builds the capacity to change'.

The contribution of HR to change management will often take the form of implementing the right tasks, structures, processes and systems to support change in line with the views of Beer *et al* (1990) as expressed earlier in this chapter. HR will also be continuously involved in developing processes for involving people in planning and managing change and communicating information on proposed changes – what they are, why they are taking place and how they will affect employees. Change often requires adopting new behaviours and acquiring different skills, and HR can organize the learning and development programmes required to do this.

Change management – key learning points

Types of change

The main types are: strategic change, operational change and transformational change.

The change process

The change process starts with an awareness of the need for change. An analysis of this situation and the factors that have created it leads to a diagnosis of their distinctive characteristics and an indication of the direction in which action needs to be taken. Possible courses of action can then be identified and evaluated and a choice made of the preferred action.

Change models

The main change models are those produced by Lewin, Beckhard, Thurley, Bandura and Beer *et al.*

Reasons for resistance to change

The shock of the new, economic fears, inconvenience, uncertainty, symbolic fears, threat to interpersonal relationships, threat to status or skills and competence fears.

Overcoming resistance to change

- Analyse the potential impact of change by considering how it will affect people in their jobs.
- Identify the potentially hostile or negative reactions of people.
- Make ample provision for the discussion of reactions to proposals to ensure complete understanding of them.
- Get 'ownership' – a feeling amongst people that the change is something that they are happy to live with because they have been involved in its planning and introduction.
- Prepare and implement a communication strategy to explain the proposed change.

Implementing change (Nadler and Tushman, 1980)

- Motivate.
- Manage the transition.
- Shape the political dynamics of change.
- Build in stability of structures and processes.

Strategies for organizational transformation (Kotter, 1995)

- Establish a sense of urgency.
- Form a powerful guiding coalition.
- Create a vision.
- Communicate.
- Empower others to act.

Change management – key learning points (continued)

- Plan for and create short-term wins.
- Consolidate improvements and producing still more change.
- Institutionalize new approaches.

The role of HR in managing change

HR specialists in their role of change agents will be continuously involved in developing processes for involving people in planning and managing change and communicating information on proposed changes – what they are, why they are taking place and how they will affect employees. Change often requires adopting new behaviours and acquiring different skills, and HR can organize the learning and development programmes required to do this.

Questions

1. Describe one well-known model of change management. Give examples of how it might work in a change programme in your organization.
2. Alfred Sloan (1967) said that his experience as CEO of General Electric demonstrated that change is the only constant thing in organizations. Do you agree with that statement and if so, what are its implications?
3. Jack Welch, a much later CEO of General Electric, said, as reported by Krames (2004): 'How do you get people into the change process? Start with reality... when everyone gets the same facts, they'll generally come to the same conclusion.' Is this true and if so, what does it tell us about change management?
4. Michael Beer wrote the following in 2001: 'There are two schools of thought about how to manage organizational change. The dominant one today espouses a top-down, drive-for-results change strategy that employs interventions like restructuring, layoffs and re-engineering. The second, much less frequently employed, espouses the development of organizational capabilities through a slower bottoms-up, unit-by-unit, high involvement approach to change. It rejects the results-driven approach as at best inadequate and at worst injurious to the development of organizational capabilities needed for sustained high performance.' Which of these two approaches do you prefer, or do you think they can both be used? If so, how?

References

Bandura, A (1986) *Social Boundaries of Thought and Action*, Prentice Hall, Englewood Cliffs, NJ

Beckhard, R (1969) *Organization Development: Strategy and Models*, Addison-Wesley, Reading, MA

Beckhard, R (1989) A model for the executive management of transformational change, in (ed) G Salaman, *Human Resource Strategies*, Sage, London

Beer, M, Eisenstat, R and Spector, B (1990) Why change programs don't produce change, *Harvard Business Review*, November–December, pp 158–66

Beer, M (2001) How to develop an organization capable of sustained high performance: embrace the drive for results-capability development paradox, *Organizational Dynamics*, **29** (4), pp 233–47

Burns, J M (1978) *Leadership*, Harper & Row, New York

Caldwell, R (2001) Champions, adapters, consultants and synergists: the new change agents in HRM, *Human Resource Management Journal*, **11** (3), pp 39–52

Cummins, T G and Worley, C G (2005) *Organization Development and Change*, South Western, Mason, OH

Gratton, L A (1999) People processes as a source of competitive advantage, in (eds) L Gratton, V H Hailey, P Stiles and C Truss, *Strategic Human Resource Management*, Oxford University Press, Oxford

Gratton, L A (2000) Real step change, *People Management*, 16 March, pp 27–30

Johnson, G and Scholes, K (1997) *Exploring Corporate Strategy*, Prentice Hall, Hemel Hempstead

Kotter, J J (1995) *A 20% solution: Using rapid re-design to build tomorrow's organization today*, Wiley, New York

Krames, J A (2004) *The Welch Way*, McGraw-Hill, New York

Lewin, K (1951) *Field Theory in Social Science*, Harper & Row, New York

Mohrman, S A and Lawler, E E (1998) The new human resources management: creating the strategic business partnership, in (eds) S A Mohrman, J R Galbraith and E E Lawler, *Tomorrow's Organization: Crafting winning capabilities in a dynamic world*, Jossey-Bass, San Francisco, CA

Nadler, D A and Tushman, M L (1980) A congruence model for diagnosing organizational behaviour, in (ed) R H Miles, *Resource Book in Macro-organizational Behaviour*, Goodyear Publishing, Santa Monica, CA

Pascale, R (1990) *Managing on the Edge*, Viking, London

Pettigrew, A and Whipp, R (1991) *Managing Change for Competitive Success*, Blackwell, Oxford

Purcell, J (1999) Best practice or best fit: chimera or cul-de-sac, *Human Resource Management Journal*, **9** (3), pp 26–41

Purcell, J (2001) The meaning of strategy in human resource management, in (ed) J Storey, *Human Resource Management: A critical text*, Thompson Learning, London

Quinn, J B (1980) Managing strategic change, *Sloane Management Review*, **11** (4/5), pp 3–30

Sloan, A P (1967) *My Years with General Motors*, Pan Books, London

Thurley, K (1979) *Supervision: A reappraisal*, Heinemann, Oxford

Tushman, M, Newman, W and Nadler, D (1988) Executive leadership and organizational evolution: managing incremental and discontinuous change, in (eds) R Kilmann and T Covin, *Corporate Transformation: Revitalizing organizations for a competitive world*, Jossey-Bass, San Francisco, CA

Ulrich, D (1997a) *Human Resource Champions*, Harvard Business School Press, Boston, MA
Ulrich, D (1998) A new mandate for human resources, *Harvard Business Review*, January–February, pp 124–34
Woodward, J (1968) Resistance to change, *Management International Review*, **8**, pp 78–93

26 Job, Role, Competency and Skills Analysis

Key concepts and terms

- Accountablity profile
- Competency analysis
- Competency modelling
- Critical-incident technique
- Descriptor
- Faults analysis
- Functional analysis
- Generic role
- Job
- Job analysis
- Job breakdown
- Job description
- Job learning analysis
- KSA (knowledge, skills and abilities statement)
- Learning specification
- Manual skills analysis
- Person specification
- Personal construct
- Repertory grid analysis
- Role
- Role analysis
- Role profile
- Skills analysis
- Task analysis

Learning outcomes

On completing this chapter you should be able to define these key concepts. You should also know about:

- Job analysis methodology and techniques
- Role analysis methodology
- Analysing technical competencies
- Job descriptions
- Behavioural competency modelling
- Skills analysis

Introduction

The analysis of jobs, roles, skills and competencies is one of the most important techniques in human resource management. It provides the information required to produce job descriptions, role profiles and person and learning specifications. It is of fundamental importance in organization and job design, recruitment and selection, performance management, learning and development, management development, career management, job evaluation and the design of grade and pay structures. These constitute most of the key HRM activities.

This chapter starts with definitions of the terms used in job and role analysis and then deals with job analysis, role analysis, competency analysis, skills analysis, job descriptions and role profiles.

Definitions

The terms 'job' and 'role' are often used interchangeably. But they are different as defined below.

Job

A job is an organizational unit which consists of a group of defined tasks or activities to be carried out or duties to be performed.

Job description

A job description defines what job holders are required to do in terms of activities, duties or tasks. They are prescriptive and inflexible, giving people the opportunity to say: 'It's not in my job description', meaning that they only need to do the tasks listed there. They are more concerned with tasks than outcomes and with the duties to be performed rather than the competencies required to perform them (technical competencies covering knowledge and skills and behavioural competencies).

Job analysis

Job analysis is the process of collecting, analysing and setting out information about the content of jobs in order to provide the basis for a job description and data for recruitment, training, job evaluation and performance management. Job analysis concentrates on what job holders are expected to do.

Role

A role has been defined by Ivancevich *et al* as 'an organized set of behaviours'. It is the part people play in their work – the emphasis is on the patterns of behaviour expected of them in order to achieve agreed outcomes. The term 'role' is sometimes used interchangeably with 'job'. But they are different. Roles are about people. Jobs are about tasks and duties. It is recognized more generally that organizations consist of people using their knowledge and skills to achieve results and working cooperatively together rather than impersonal jobs contained in the boxes of an organization chart. References are therefore nowadays made more frequently to roles, although use is still made of the terms job analysis, job design and job evaluation.

Role profile

A role profile defines outcomes, accountabilities, and competencies for an individual role. It concentrates on outcomes rather than duties and therefore provides better guidance than a job description on expectations and does not constrain people to carrying out a prescribed set of tasks. Outcomes may be expressed as key result areas – elements of the role for which clear outputs and standards can be defined, each of which makes a significant contribution to achieving its overall purpose. Alternatively, they may be termed accountabilities – areas of the role for which role holders are responsible in the form of being held to account for what they do and what they achieve.

A role profile does not prescribe in detail what has to be done to achieve the required outcomes. It therefore allows for greater flexibility than a job description and is more easily updated to reflect changing demands.

Role profiles are person-orientated. A role can be described in behavioural terms – given certain expectations, this is how the person needs to behave to meet them. Because it identifies knowledge, skill and competency requirements it also provides a better basis for recruitment and selection, performance management and learning and development purposes.

Accountability profile

An accountability profile is a type of role profile that focuses on what role holders will be held to account for in terms of what they do and what they achieve. It may be set out as a list of main accountabilities.

Generic role

A generic role is a role in which essentially similar activities are carried out by a number of people, for example a team leader or a call centre agent. In effect, it covers an occupation rather than a single role. It is described in a generic role profile.

Role analysis

Role analysis finds out what people are expected to achieve when carrying out their work and the competencies and skills required to meet those expectations. Role analysis uses similar techniques to job analysis although the objective of the analysis will be somewhat different.

Competency analysis

Competency analysis is concerned with functional analysis to determine work-based competences and behavioural analysis to establish the behavioural dimensions that affect job performance. Work-based or occupational competences refer to expectations of workplace performance and the standards and outputs that people carrying out specified roles are expected to attain. Behavioural or personal competences are the personal characteristics of individuals which they bring to their work roles.

Skills analysis

Skills analysis determines the skills required to achieve an acceptable level of performance.

Person specification

A person specification, also known as a job or role specification, sets out the education, qualifications, training, experience, personal attributes and competences a job holder requires to perform her or his job satisfactorily. Person specifications are used in recruitment and selection, as described in Chapter 31.

Learning specification

A learning specification defines the knowledge and skills needed to achieve an acceptable level of performance. It is used as the basis for devising learning and development programmes (see Chapter 42). Learning specifications may be drawn up on the basis of competency and skills analysis.

Job analysis

Job analysis produces the following information about a job:

- Overall purpose – why the job exists and, in essence, what the job holder is expected to contribute.
- Organization – to whom the job holder reports and who reports to the job holder.

- Content – the nature and scope of the job in terms of the tasks and operations to be performed and duties to be carried out.

If the outcome of the job analysis is to be used for job evaluation purposes (see Chapter 47) the job will also be analysed in terms of the factors or criteria used in the job evaluation scheme.

Job analysis methodology and techniques

The essence of job analysis is the application of systematic methods to the collection of information about job content. It is essentially about data collection and the basic steps are:

- obtain documents such as existing organization, procedure or training manuals which give information about the job;
- obtain from managers fundamental information concerning the job;
- obtain from job holders similar information about their jobs.

There are a number of job analysis techniques used for data collection as described below.

Interviews

The full flavour of a job is best obtained by interviewing job holders and checking findings with their managers or team leaders. The aim of the interview should be to obtain the relevant facts about the job, namely the job title, organizational details (reporting relationships as described in an organization chart) and a list of the tasks or duties performed by the job holder.

For recruitment, training or job evaluation purposes these basic details can be supplemented by questions designed to elicit from the job holders more information about the level of their responsibilities and the demands made upon them by the job. These can cover the amount of supervision received, the degree of discretion allowed in making decisions, the typical problems to be solved, the amount of guidance available when solving the problems, the relative difficulty of the tasks to be performed and the qualifications and skills required to carry out the work.

Conducting a job analysis interview

- Work to a logical sequence of questions which help interviewees to order their thoughts about the job.
- Probe as necessary to establish what people really do – answers to questions are often vague and information may be given by means of untypical instances.

- Ensure that job holders are not allowed to get away with vague or inflated descriptions of their work – if, for example, the interview is part of a job evaluation exercise, they would not be human if they did not present the job in the best possible light.
- Sort out the wheat from the chaff; answers to questions may produce a lot of irrelevant data which must be sifted before preparing the job description.
- Obtain a clear statement from job holders about their authority to make decisions and the amount of guidance they receive from their manager or team leader – this is not easy; if asked what decisions they are authorized to make, most people look blank because they think about their job in terms of duties and tasks rather than abstract decisions.
- Avoid asking leading questions which make the expected answer obvious.
- Allow the job holder ample opportunity to talk by creating an atmosphere of trust.

It is helpful to use a checklist when conducting the interview. Elaborate checklists are not necessary. They only confuse people. The basic questions to be answered are as follows.

Job analysis interview checklist

1. What is the title of your job?
2. To whom are you responsible?
3. Who is responsible to you? (An organization chart is helpful.)
4. What is the main purpose of your job, ie in overall terms, what are you expected to do?
5. What are the key activities you have to carry out in your role? Try to group them under no more than ten headings.
6. What are the results you are expected to achieve in each of those key activities?
7. What are you expected to know to be able to carry out your job?
8. What skills should you have to carry out your job?

The answers to these questions may need to be sorted out – they can often result in a mass of jumbled information which has to be analysed so that the various activities can be distinguished and refined to seven or eight key areas.

The advantages of the interviewing method are that it is flexible, can provide in-depth information and is easy to organize and prepare. It is therefore the most common approach. But interviewing can be time-consuming which is why in large job analysis exercises, questionnaires may be used to provide advance information about the job. This speeds up the interviewing process or even replaces the interview altogether, although this means that much of the 'flavour' of the job – ie what it is really like – may be lost.

Questionnaires

Questionnaires about their roles can be completed by role holders and approved by the role holder's manager or team leader. They are helpful when a large number of roles have to be covered. They can also save interviewing time by recording purely factual information and by enabling the analyst to structure questions in advance to cover areas which need to be explored in greater depth. The simpler the questionnaire the better: it need only cover the eight questions listed above.

The advantage of questionnaires is that they can produce information quickly and cheaply for a large number of jobs. But a substantial sample is needed and the construction of a questionnaire is a skilled job which should only be carried out on the basis of some preliminary fieldwork. It is highly advisable to pilot-test questionnaires before launching into a full-scale exercise. The accuracy of the results also depends on the willingness and ability of job holders to complete questionnaires. Many people find it difficult to express themselves in writing about their work.

Observation

Observation means studying role holders at work, noting what they do, how they do it, and how much time it takes. This method is most appropriate for routine administrative or manual roles but it seldom used because of the time it takes.

Job descriptions

Job descriptions should be based on the job analysis and should be as brief and factual as possible. The headings under which the job description should be written and notes for guidance on completing each section are set out below.

Job title

The existing or proposed job title should indicate as clearly as possible the function in which the job is carried out and the level of the job within that function. The use of terms such as 'manager', 'assistant manager' or 'senior' to describe job levels should be reasonably consistent between functions with regard to grading of the jobs.

Reporting to

The job title of the manager or team leader to whom the job holder is directly responsible should be given under this heading. No attempt should be made to indicate here any functional relationships the job holder might have to other people.

Reporting to job holder

The job titles of all the posts directly reporting to the job holder should be given under this heading. Again, no attempt should be made here to indicate any functional relationships that might exist between the job holder and other employees.

Overall purpose

This section should describe as concisely as possible the overall purpose of the job. The aim should be to convey in one sentence a broad picture of the job which will clearly distinguish it from other jobs and establish the role of the job holders and the contribution they should make towards achieving the objectives of the company and their own function or unit. No attempt should be made to describe the activities carried out under this heading, but the overall summary should lead naturally to the analysis of activities in the next section. When preparing the job description, it is often best to defer writing down the definition of overall responsibilities until the activities have been analysed and described.

Main activities, tasks or duties

The following method of describing activities, tasks or duties should be adopted:

1. Group the various activities identified by the job analysis together so that no more than seven or eight areas remain. If the number is extended much beyond that, the job description will become over-complex and it will be difficult to be specific about tasks or duties.

2. Define each activity in one sentence which starts with a verb in the active voice in order to provide a positive indication of what has to be done and eliminate unnecessary wording; for example: plan, prepare, produce, implement, process, provide, schedule, complete, dispatch, maintain, liaise with, collaborate with.

3. Describe the object of the verb (what is done) as succinctly as possible; for example: test new systems, post cash to the nominal and sales ledgers, dispatch to the warehouse packed output, schedule production, ensure that management accounts are produced, prepare marketing plans.
4. State briefly the purpose of the activity in terms of outputs or standards to be achieved for example: test new systems to ensure they meet agreed systems specifications, post cash to the nominal and sales ledgers in order to provide up-to-date and accurate financial information, dispatch the warehouse planned output so that all items are removed by carriers on the same day they are packed, schedule production in order to meet laid-down output and delivery targets, ensure that management accounts are produced which provide the required level of information to management and individual managers on financial performance against budget and on any variances, prepare marketing plans which support the achievement of the marketing strategies of the enterprise, are realistic, and provide clear guidance on the actions to be taken by the development, production, marketing and sales departments.

An example of a job description is given in Figure 26.1.

Job title: HR adviser; recruitment
Reports to: HR Service Centre Manager
Reports to job holder: none
Job purpose: To provide recruitment services to line managers for jobs below management level
Main duties:

1. Respond promptly to requests from line managers to assist in recruiting staff.
2. Produce person specifications.
3. Agree on the use of recruitment agencies and/or media advertisements or internet notifications of vacancies.
4. Brief and liaise with agencies and/or draft advertisements for jobs for approval by line managers and place advertisements or information on vacancies using the media and/or the internet.
5. Process replies and draws up short lists.
6. Conduct preliminary interviews independently or conduct short-list interviews with line managers.
7. Agree offer terms with line manager, take up references and confirm the offer.
8. Review and evaluate sources of candidates and analyse recruitment costs.

Figure 26.1 Example of job description

Role analysis and role profiles

Role analysis uses the same techniques as job analysis but the focus is on identifying inputs (knowledge and skill and competency requirements) and required outcomes (key result areas or accountabilities) rather than simply listing the tasks to be carried out.

A role profile is initially set out under the same headings as a job description ie: role title, responsible to, responsible to role holder and the purpose of the role. But it then focuses on the following aspects of the role.

Key result areas

A key result area is an element of a role for which clear outputs and outcomes can be defined, each of which makes a significant contribution to achieving the overall purpose of the role. It may be described as an accountability – an aspect of the role for which the role holder is responsible (held to account for).

The number of key result areas is unlikely to be more than seven or eight, certainly not more than 10. The basic structure of a key result area definition should resemble that of a job description task definition, ie it should be expressed in one sentence starting with an active verb. However, the content of the key result area definition should focus more on the specific purpose of the activity in terms of outputs or standards to be achieved rather than describing in detail the duties involved.

Knowledge and skills required

These should be expressed in terms of 'need to know' – the knowledge required of techniques, processes, procedures, systems and the business generally (its products or services and its competitors and customers), and 'need to be able to do' – the skills required in each area of activity.

Behavioural competencies

These are how the role holder is expected to behave when carrying out the role. These behavioural competencies may be linked to the organization's competency framework and cover such areas as team working, communication, people management and development and customer relations. An example of a role profile is given in Figure 26.2.

Role title: Database administrator
Department: Information systems
Responsible to: Database manager
Purpose of role: Responsible for the development and support of databases and their underlying environment
Key result areas:

1. Identify database requirements for all projects that require data management in order to meet the needs of internal customers.
2. Develop project plans collaboratively with colleagues to deliver against their database needs.
3. Support underlying database infrastructure.
4. Liaise with system and software providers to obtain product information and support.
5. Manage project resources (people and equipment) within predefined budget and criteria, as agreed with line manager and originating department.
6. Allocate work to and supervise contractors on day-to-day basis.
7. Ensure security of the underlying database infrastructure through adherence to established protocols and develop additional security protocols where needed.

Need to know:

- Oracle database administration.
- Operation of oracle forms SQL/PLSQL, Unix administration, shell programming.

Able to:

- Analyse and choose between options where the solution is not always obvious.
- Develop project plans and organize own workload on a timescale of 1–2 months.
- Adapt to rapidly changing needs and priorities without losing sight of overall plans and priorities.
- Interpret budgets in order to manage resources effectively within them.
- Negotiate with suppliers.
- Keep abreast of technical developments and trends, bring these into day-to-day work when feasible and build them into new project developments.

Behavioural competencies:

- Aim to get things done well and set and meet challenging goals, create own measures of excellence and constantly seek ways of improving performance.
- Analyse information from range of sources and develop effective solutions/recommendations.
- Communicate clearly and persuasively, orally or in writing, dealing with technical issues in a non-technical manner.
- Work participatively on projects with technical and non-technical colleagues.
- Develop positive relationships with colleagues as the supplier of an internal service.

Figure 26.2 Example of a role profile

Generic role profiles

As, by definition, generic role profiles cover occupations rather than individual roles, they tend to generalize more and may be somewhat simpler than individual role profiles, for example by restricting the profile to lists of key result areas and competency dimensions. An example of a generic role profile is given in Figure 26.3.

Generic role title: Team leader
Overall purpose of role: To lead teams in order to attain team goals and further the achievement of the organization's objectives.
Key result areas:

1. Agree targets and standards with team members that support the attainment of the organization's objectives.
2. Plan with team members work schedules and resource requirements that will ensure that team targets will be reached, indeed exceeded.
3. Agree performance measures and quality assurance processes with team members that will clarify output and quality expectations.
4. Agree with team members the allocation of tasks, rotating responsibilities as appropriate to achieve flexibility and the best use of the skills and capabilities of team members.
5. Coordinate the work of the team to ensure that team goals are achieved.
6. Ensure that the team members collectively monitor the team's performance in terms of achieving output, speed of response and quality targets and standards, and agree with team members any corrective action required to ensure that team goals are achieved.
7. Conduct team reviews of performance to agree areas for improvement and actions required.

Competencies:

- Build effective team relationships, ensuring that team members are committed to the common purpose.
- Encourage self-direction amongst team members but provide guidance and clear direction as required.
- Share information with team members.
- Trust team members to get on with things – not continually checking.
- Treat team members fairly and consistently.
- Support and guide team members to make the best use of their capabilities.
- Encourage self-development by example.
- Actively offer constructive feedback to team members and positively seek and be open to constructive feedback from them.
- Contribute to the development of team members, encouraging the acquisition of additional skills and providing opportunities for them to be used effectively.

Figure 26.3 Example of a generic role profile

Behavioural competency modelling

Behavioural competency modelling is the process used for identifying, analysing and describing behavioural competencies which define the behaviours that organizations expect their staff to practice in their work in order to reach an acceptable level of performance. As explained in Chapter 11, they have an important part to play in providing information which contributes to a number of HRM activities, for example, recruitment, learning and development, and performance management. Examples of competencies and competency frameworks were given in Chapter 11 and suggestions were also made about how a competency framework should be constructed. The guidance on the criteria for a fully rigorous competency definition, shown in Table 26.1, was produced by a task force set up by the Society for Industrial and Organizational Psychology (SIOP) in the United States (Shippmann *et al*, 2000) to investigate and review the practice of competency modelling.

Table 26.1 Criteria for a rigorous competency definition

Variable	Conditions required to meet high rigour criteria
Method of investigation	A logically selected mix of multiple methods are used to obtain information, eg interviews, focus groups, questionnaires
Type of descriptor content collected	Variable combinations of multiple types of information are collected, eg work activities, KSAs (knowledge, skills and abilities statements) and performance standards
Procedures for developing descriptors	Information collected from content experts using a structured protocol and a representative sample
Detail of descriptor content	Use of a number of labels representing discrete categories of content that operationally define each category and leave no room for misinterpretation
Link to business goals and strategies	Steps taken to ensure that results are aligned with the broader goals and longer-term strategies of the organization
Content review	Formal review takes place to ensure that • item level descriptions are clear • content categories do not overlap, content categories are internally consistent • items represent measurable content appropriate for the intended application
Ranking descriptor content	The set of descriptors are prioritized and ranked
Assessment of reliability	Content category labels are matched with item-level descriptors and rated according to their relative importance for successful job performance
Item retention criteria	Multiple, clear, logical criteria are consistently applied to items to determine whether content is retained or deleted.
Documentation	Clear definitions are made of the procedures to be employed in applying the competency framework

(Source: Shippmann et al, *2000)*

These are exacting criteria. The emphasis is on the systematic collection and analysis of data. There are five approaches to behavioural competency analysis. In ascending order of complexity these are:

1. expert opinion;
2. structured interview;

3. workshops;
4. critical-incident technique;
5. repertory grid analysis.

1. Expert opinion

The basic, crudest and least satisfactory method is for an 'expert' member of the HR department, possibly in discussion with other 'experts' from the same department, to draw up a list from their own understanding of 'what counts' coupled with an analysis of other published lists.

This is unsatisfactory because the likelihood of the competencies being appropriate, realistic and measurable in the absence of detailed analysis, is fairly remote. The list tends to be bland and, because line managers and job holders have not been involved, unacceptable.

2. Structured interview

This method begins with a list of competencies drawn up by 'experts' and proceeds by subjecting a number of role holders to a structured interview. The interviewer starts by identifying the key result areas of the role and goes on to analyse the behavioural characteristics which distinguish performers at different levels of competence.

The basic question is: 'What are the positive or negative indicators of behaviour which are conducive or non-conducive to achieving high levels of performance?' These may be analysed under the following headings.

Behavioural headings

- Personal drive (achievement motivation).
- Impact on results.
- Analytical power.
- Strategic thinking.
- Creative thinking (ability to innovate).
- Decisiveness.
- Commercial judgement.
- Team management and leadership.

- Interpersonal relationships.
- Ability to communicate.
- Ability to adapt and cope with change and pressure.
- Ability to plan and control projects.

Under each heading instances will be sought which illustrate effective or less effective behaviour.

One of the problems with this approach is that it relies too much on the ability of the expert to draw out information from interviewees. It is also undesirable to use a deductive approach which pre-empts the analysis with a prepared list of competency headings. It is far better to do this by means of an inductive approach which starts from specific types of behaviour and then groups them under competence headings. This can be done in a workshop by analysing positive and negative indicators to gain an understanding of the competence dimensions of an occupation or job as described below.

3. Workshops

Workshops bring a group of people together who have 'expert' knowledge or experience of the role – managers and role holders as appropriate – with a facilitator, usually but necessarily a member of the HR department or an outside consultant.

The members of the workshop begin by getting agreement to the overall purpose of the role and its key result areas. They then develop examples of effective and less effective behaviour for each area which are recorded on flipcharts. For example, one of the key result areas for a divisional HR director might be human resource planning, defined as:

> *Prepares forecasts of human resource requirements and plans for the acquisition, retention and effective utilization of employees which ensure that the company's needs for people are met.*

The positive indicators for this competency area could include:

- seeks involvement in business strategy formulation;
- contributes to business planning by taking a strategic view of longer-term human resource issues which are likely to affect business strategy;
- networks with senior management colleagues to understand and respond to the human resource planning issues they raise;

- suggests practical ways to improve the use of human resources, for example, the introduction of annual hours.

Negative indicators could include:

- takes a narrow view of HR planning – does not seem to be interested in or understand the wider business context;
- lacks the determination to overcome problems and deliver forecasts;
- fails to anticipate skills shortages; for example, unable to meet the multi-skilling requirements implicit in the new computer integrated manufacturing system;
- does not seem to talk the same language as line management colleagues – fails to understand their requirements;
- slow in responding to requests for help.

When the positive and negative indicators have been agreed the next step is to distil the competency dimensions that can be inferred from the lists. In this example they could be:

- strategic capability;
- business understanding;
- achievement motivation;
- interpersonal skills;
- communication skills;
- consultancy skills.

These dimensions might also be reflected in the analysis of other areas of competency so that, progressively, a picture of the competencies is built up which is linked to actual behaviour in the workplace.

The facilitator's job is to prompt, help the group to analyse its findings and assist generally in the production of a set of competence dimensions which can be illustrated by behaviour-based examples. The facilitator may have some ideas about the sort of headings that may emerge from this process but should not try to influence the group to come to a conclusion which it has not worked out for itself, albeit with some assistance from the facilitator.

Workshops can use the critical incident or repertory grid techniques as described below.

4. Critical-incident technique

The critical-incident technique is a means of eliciting data about effective or less effective behaviour which is related to examples of actual events – critical incidents. The technique is used with groups of job holders and/or their managers or other 'experts' (sometimes, less effectively, with individuals) as follows:

1. Explain what the technique is and what it is used for, ie 'To assess what constitutes good or poor performance by analysing events which have been observed to have a noticeably successful or unsuccessful outcome, thus providing more factual and "real" information than by simply listing tasks and guessing performance requirements.'
2. Agree and list the key result in the role to be analysed. To save time, the analyst can establish these prior to the meeting but it is necessary to ensure that they are agreed provisionally by the group, which can be told that the list may well be amended in the light of the forthcoming analysis.
3. Take each area of the role in turn and ask the group for examples of critical incidents. If, for instance, one of the job responsibilities is dealing with customers, the following request could be made: 'I want you to tell me about a particular occasion at work which involved you – or that you observed – in dealing with a customer. Think about what the circumstances were, eg who took part, what the customer asked for, what you or the other member of the staff did and what the outcome was.'
4. Collect information about the critical incident under the following headings:
   - what the circumstances were;
   - what the individual did;
   - the outcome of what the individual did.
5. Record this information on a flip chart.
6. Continue this process for each key result area.
7. Refer to the flipchart and analyse each incident by obtaining ratings of the recorded behaviour on a scale such as 1 for least effective to 5 for most effective.
8. Discuss these ratings to get initial definitions of effective and ineffective performance for each of the key result areas.
9. Refine these definitions as necessary after the meeting – it can be difficult to get a group to produce finished definitions.
10. Produce the final analysis which can list the competencies required and include performance indicators or standards of performance for each key result area.

5. Repertory grid

Like the critical incident technique, the repertory grid can be used to identify the dimensions which distinguish good from poor standards of performance. The technique is based on Kelly's

(1955) personal construct theory. Personal constructs are the ways in which we view the world. They are personal because they are highly individual and they influence the way we behave or view other people's behaviour. The aspects of the role to which these 'constructs' or judgements apply are called 'elements'.

To elicit judgements, a group of people are asked to concentrate on certain elements, which are the tasks carried out by role holders, and develop constructs about these elements. This enables them to define the qualities which indicate the essential requirements for successful performance.

The procedure followed by the analyst is known as the 'triadic method of elicitation' (a sort of three card trick) and involves the following steps:

1. Identify the tasks or elements of the role to be subjected to repertory grid analysis. This is done by one of the other forms of job analysis, eg interviewing.
2. List the tasks on cards.
3. Draw three cards at random from the pack and ask the members of the group to nominate which of the these tasks is the odd one out from the point of view of the qualities and characteristics needed to perform it.
4. Probe to obtain more specific definitions of these qualities or characteristics in the form of expected behaviour. If, for example, a characteristic has been described as the 'ability to plan and organize', ask questions such as: what sort of behaviour or actions indicate that someone is planning effectively? How can we tell if someone is not organizing his or her work particularly well?
5. Draw three more cards from the pack and repeat steps 3 and 4.
6. Repeat this process until all the cards have been analysed and there do not appear to be any more constructs to be identified.
7. List the constructs and ask the group members to rate each task on every quality, using a six or seven point scale.
8. Collect and analyse the scores in order to assess their relative importance.

Like the critical-incident technique, repertory grid analysis helps people to articulate their views by reference to specific examples. An additional advantage is that the repertory grid makes it easier for them to identify the behavioural characteristics or competencies required in a job by limiting the area of comparison through the triadic technique.

Although a full statistical analysis of the outcome of a repertory grid exercise is helpful, the most important results which can be obtained are the descriptions of what constitute good or poor performance in each element of the job.

Both the repertory grid and the critical incident techniques require a skilled analyst who can probe and draw out the descriptions of job characteristics. They are quite detailed and time-consuming but even if the full process is not followed, much of the methodology is of use in a less elaborate approach to competency analysis.

Choice of approach

Workshops are probably the best approach. They get people involved and do not rely on 'expert' opinion. Critical incident or repertory grid techniques are more sophisticated but they take more time and expertise to run.

Analysing technical competencies

The approach to the definition of technical competencies (descriptions of what people have to know and be able to do to carry out their roles effectively) differs from that used for behavioural competencies. As technical competencies are in effect competences, a functional analysis process can be used. This methodology was originally developed by Mansfield and Mitchell (1986) and Fine (1988). In essence, functional analysis focuses on the outcomes of work performance. Note that the analysis is not simply concerned with outputs in the form of quantifiable results but deals with the broader results that have to be achieved by role holders. An outcome could be a satisfied customer, a more highly motivated subordinate or a better-functioning team.

Functional analysis deals with processes such as developing staff, providing feedback and monitoring performance as well as tasks. As described by Miller et al (2001) it starts with an analysis of the roles fulfilled by an individual in order to arrive at a description of the separate components or 'units' of performance that make up that role. The resulting units consist of performance criteria, described in terms of outcomes, and a description of the knowledge and skill requirements that underpin successful performance.

Functional analysis is the method used to define competence-based standards for N/SNVQs.

Skills analysis

Skills analysis determines the skills required to achieve an acceptable standard of performance. It is mainly used for technical, craft, manual and office jobs to provide the basis for devising learning and training programmes. Skills analysis starts from a broad job analysis but goes into details of not only what job holders have to do but also the particular abilities and skills they need to do it. Skills analysis techniques are described below.

Job breakdown

The job breakdown technique analyses a job into separate operations, processes, or tasks which can be used as the elements of an instruction sequence. A job breakdown analysis is recorded in a standard format of three columns:

1. The stage column in which the different steps in the job are described – most semiskilled jobs can easily be broken down into their constituent parts.
2. The instruction column in which a note is made against each step of how the task should be done. This, in effect, describes what has to be learned by the trainee.
3. The key points column in which any special points such as quality standards or safety instructions are noted against each step so that they can be emphasized to a trainee learning the job.

Manual skills analysis

Manual skills analysis is a technique developed from work study. It isolates for instructional purposes the skills and knowledge employed by experienced workers in performing tasks which require manual dexterity. It is used to analyse short-cycle, repetitive operations such as assembly tasks and other similar factory work.

The hand, finger and other body movements of experienced operatives are observed and recorded in detail as they carry out their work. The analysis concentrates on the tricky parts of the job which, while presenting no difficulty to the experienced operative, have to be analysed in depth before they can be taught to trainees. Not only are the hand movements recorded, but particulars are also noted of the cues (visual and other senses) which the operative absorbs when performing the tasks. Explanatory comments are added when necessary.

Task analysis

Task analysis is a systematic analysis of the behaviour required to carry out a task with a view to identifying areas of difficulty and the appropriate training techniques and learning aids necessary for successful instruction. It can be used for all types of jobs but is specifically relevant to administrative tasks.

The analytical approach used in task analysis is similar to those adopted in the job breakdown and manual skills analysis techniques. The results of the analysis are usually recorded in a standard format of four columns as follows:

1. Task – a brief description of each element.
2. Level of importance – the relative significance of each task to the successful performance of the role.

3. Degree of difficulty – the level of skill or knowledge required to perform each task.
4. Training method – the instructional techniques, practice and experience required.

Faults analysis

Faults analysis is the process of analysing the typical faults which occur when performing a task, especially the more costly faults. It is carried out when the incidence of faults is high. A study is made of the job and, by questioning workers and team leaders, the most commonly occurring faults are identified. A faults specification is then produced which provides trainees with information on what faults can be made, how they can be recognized, what causes them, what effect they have, who is responsible for them, what action the trainees should take when a particular fault occurs, and how a fault can be prevented from recurring.

Job learning analysis

Job learning analysis, as described by Pearn and Kandola (1993), concentrates on the inputs and process rather than the content of the job. It analyses nine learning skills which contribute to satisfactory performance. A learning skill is one used to increase other skills or knowledge and represents broad categories of job behaviour which need to be learnt. The learning skills are the following:

- physical skills requiring practice and repetition to get right;
- complex procedures or sequences of activity which are memorized or followed with the aid of written material such as manuals;
- non-verbal information such as sight, sound, smell, taste and touch which is used to check, assess or discriminate, and which usually takes practice to get right;
- memorizing facts or information;
- ordering, prioritizing and planning, which refer to the degree to which a role holder has any responsibility for and flexibility in determining the way a particular activity is performed;
- looking ahead and anticipating;
- diagnosing, analysing and problem solving, with or without help;
- interpreting or using written manuals and other sources of information such as diagrams or charts;
- adapting to new ideas and systems.

In conducting a job learning analysis interview, the interviewer obtains information on the main aims and principal activities of the job, and then, using question cards for each of the nine learning skills, analyses each activity in more depth, recording responses and obtaining as many examples as possible under each heading.

Job, role, competency and skills analysis – key learning points

Job analysis methodology and techniques

The essence of job analysis is the application of systematic methods to the collection of information about job content. It is essentially about data collection and the basic steps are:

- obtain documents such as existing organization, procedure or training manuals which give information about the job;
- obtain from managers fundamental information concerning the job;
- obtain from job holders similar information about their jobs.

Job descriptions

Job descriptions should be based on the job analysis and should be as brief and factual as possible. The headings should be: job title, reporting to, reporting to job holder, main purpose of job, main activities, tasks or duties.

Role analysis methodology

Role analysis uses the same techniques as job analysis but the focus is on identifying inputs (knowledge and skill and competency requirements) and required outcomes (key result areas) rather than simply listing the tasks to be carried out.

Behavioural competency modelling

Behavioural competency modelling is the process used for identifying, analysing and describing behavioural competencies which define the behaviours that organizations expect their staff to practice in their work in order to reach an acceptable level of performance. The emphasis is on the systematic collection and analysis of data. There are five approaches to behavioural competency analysis. In ascending order of complexity these are: expert opinion, structured interview, workshops, critical-incident technique, and repertory grid analysis.

Analysing technical competencies

The technique of functional analysis is used which starts with an analysis of the roles fulfilled by an individual in order to arrive at a description of the separate components or 'units' of performance that make up that role. The resulting units consist of performance criteria, described in terms of outcomes, and a description of the knowledge and skill requirements that underpin successful performance.

Skills analysis

Skills analysis determines the skills required to achieve an acceptable standard of performance. It is mainly used for technical, craft, manual and office jobs to provide the basis for devising learning and training

Job, role, competency and skills analysis – key learning points (continued)

programmes. Skills analysis starts from a broad job analysis but goes into details of not only what job holders have to do but also the particular abilities and skills they need to do it. Skills analysis techniques include: job breakdown, manual skills analysis, faults analysis and job learning analysis.

Questions

1. What is the difference between a job and a role?
2. How should a job analysis interview be conducted?
3. What are the advantages and disadvantages of questionnaires as a method of analysing jobs?
4. What is job learning analysis?

References

Fine, S A (1988), Functional job analysis, in S Gael (ed) *The Job Analysis Handbook for Business, Industry and Government*, Wiley, New York

Ivancevich, J M, Konopaske, R and Matteson, M T (2008) *Organizational Behaviour and Management*, 8th edition, McGraw-Hill/Irwin, New York

Kelly, G (1955) *The Psychology of Personal Constructs*, Norton, New York

Mansfield, B and Mitchell, L (1986), *Towards a Competent Workforce*, Gower, Aldershot

Miller, L, Rankin, N and Neathey, F (2001) *Competency Frameworks in UK Organizations*, CIPD, London

Pearn, K and Kandola, R (1993) *Job Analysis*, IPM, London

Shippmann, J S, Ash R A and Battista, M (2000) The practice of competency modelling, *Personnel Psychology*, **53** (3), pp 703–40

27 Job and Role Design and Development

Key concepts and terms

- Intrinsic motivation
- Job design
- Job enrichment
- Job characteristics model
- Job enlargement
- Job rotation

Learning outcomes

On completing this chapter you should be able to define these key concepts. You should also know about:

- The factors affecting job design
- Task structure
- Role development
- The characteristics of jobs
- Approaches to job design

Introduction

This chapter deals with designing jobs and developing roles. Obtaining the information for this purpose may use the analytical techniques described in Chapter 26, but as organizations grow and introduce new activities or technology, different methods of working such as smart working (see Chapter 23) may have to be devised and this will affect the content of jobs and the purposes of roles. To obtain the maximum benefit from such developments, it is necessary to ensure that the structure of jobs or roles and the demands they make on job or role holders will enhance motivation, engagement and commitment. The contents, methods and relationships of jobs or roles must satisfy technological and organizational requirements, but they should also meet the personal needs of the individuals concerned. These two aims may not always be easy to reconcile, but the attempt must be made if the maximum benefits from technological and organizational change are to be obtained.

A distinction was made between jobs and roles at the beginning of Chapter 26. Essentially jobs consist of an impersonal list of tasks or duties. They are fixed entities, part of a machine that can be 'designed' like any other part of a machine. Routine or machine-controlled jobs exist in most organizations but, increasingly, the work carried out by people is not mechanistic. What is done, how it is done and the results achieved depend more and more on the capabilities and motivation of people and their interactions with one another and their customers, clients and suppliers. A role is the part people play in their work – the emphasis is on the patterns of behaviour expected of them in order to achieve agreed outcomes rather than a set of duties they have to carry out. Jobs are about tasks; roles are about people. This distinction means that while jobs may be designed to fit work requirements, roles are developed as people work flexibly, demonstrate that they can do more and take on different responsibilities.

This chapter starts with job design: what it is and the factors to be taken into account in carrying it out. The second part of the chapter covers role development, a much more flexible process, but the criteria for ensuring that roles help to motivate people and foster engagement and commitment are fundamentally the same as those related to job design.

Job design

Job design specifies the contents, methods and relationships of jobs in order to satisfy work requirements for productivity, efficiency and quality, meet the personal needs of the job holder and thus increase levels of employee engagement.

The process of job design is based on an analysis of the way in which work needs to be organized and what work therefore needs to be done – the tasks that have to be carried out if the purpose of the organization or an organizational unit is to be achieved. This is where the techniques of process planning and systems analysis are used to achieve improvement in organizational performance. They concentrate on the work to be done, not the worker. They may lead to a high degree of task specialization and assembly line processing; of paper work as well as physical products. More desirably, it can also lead to the maximization of individual responsibility and the opportunity to use personal skills.

It is necessary, however, to distinguish between efficiency and effectiveness. The most efficient method may maximize outputs in relation to inputs in the short run, but it may not be effective in the longer term in that it fails to achieve the overall objectives of the activity. The pursuit of short-term efficiency by imposing the maximum degree of task specialization may reduce longer-term effectiveness by demotivating job holders and increasing employee turnover and absenteeism.

Job design has to start from work requirements because that is why the job exists. When the tasks to be done have been determined it should then be the function of the job designer to consider how the jobs can be set up to provide the maximum degree of intrinsic motivation for those who have to carry them out, with a view to improving performance and productivity. Consideration has also to be given to another important aim of job design: to fulfil the social responsibilities of the organization to the people who work in it by improving the quality of working life, an aim which, as stated in Wilson's (1973) report on this subject, 'depends upon both efficiency of performance and satisfaction of the worker'.

Factors affecting job design

Job design is fundamentally affected by the technology of the organization, the changes that are taking place in that technology and the environment in which the organization operates. Job design has therefore to be considered within the context of organization design, as described in Chapter 23, but it must also take into account the following factors.

Factors affecting job design

- The characteristics of jobs.
- The characteristics of task structure.
- The process of intrinsic motivation.
- The job characteristics model.
- The implications of group activities.

The characteristics of jobs

There are three fundamental characteristics shared by all jobs:

1. Job range – the number of operations a job holder performs to complete a task.
2. Job depth – the amount of discretion a job holder has to decide job activities and job outcomes.
3. Job relationships – the interpersonal relationships between job holders and their managers and co-workers.

Task structure

Job design requires the assembly of a number of tasks into a job or a group of jobs. An individual may carry out one main task that consists of a number of interrelated elements or functions. Alternatively, task functions may be allocated to a team working closely together in a manufacturing 'cell' or customer service unit, or strung along an assembly line. In more complex jobs, individuals may carry out a variety of connected tasks (multi-tasking), each with a number of functions, or these tasks may be allocated to a team of workers or divided between them. In the latter case, the tasks may require a variety of skills that have to be possessed by all members of the team (multi-skilling) in order to work flexibly. Complexity in a job may be a reflection of the number and variety of tasks to be carried out, the different skills or competencies to be used, the range and scope of the decisions that have to be made, or the difficulty of predicting the outcome of decisions.

The internal structure of each task consists of three elements: planning (deciding on the course of action, its timing and the resources required), executing (carrying out the plan), and controlling (monitoring performance and progress and taking corrective action when required). A completely integrated job includes all these elements for each of the tasks involved. The worker, or group of workers, having been given objectives in terms of output, quality and cost targets, decides on how the work is to be done, assembles the resources, performs the work, and monitors output, quality and cost standards. Responsibility in a job is measured by the amount of authority someone has to do all these things.

The ideal arrangement from the point of view of motivation and engagement is to provide for fully integrated jobs containing all three task elements. In practice, management and team leaders are often entirely responsible for planning and control, leaving the worker responsible for execution. To a degree this is inevitable, but one of the aims of job design is often to extend the responsibility of workers into the functions of planning and control. This can involve empowerment – giving individuals and teams more responsibility for decision making and ensuring that they have the training, support and guidance to exercise that responsibility properly.

Intrinsic motivation

The case for using job design techniques is based on the premise that effective performance and genuine satisfaction in work follow mainly from the intrinsic content of the job. This is related to the fundamental concept that people are motivated when they are provided with the means to achieve their goals. Work provides the means to earn money, which as an extrinsic reward satisfies basic needs and is instrumental in providing ways of satisfying higher-level needs. But work also provides intrinsic rewards related to achievement, responsibility and the opportunity to use and develop skills that are more under the control of the worker.

Three characteristics have been distinguished by Lawler (1969) as being required in jobs if they are to be intrinsically motivating.

SOURCE REVIEW

Intrinsic motivating characteristics of jobs, Lawler (1969)

1. Feedback – individuals must receive meaningful feedback about their performance, preferably by evaluating their own performance and defining the feedback. This implies that they should ideally work on a complete product, or a significant part of it that can be seen as a whole.
2. Use of abilities – the job must be perceived by individuals as requiring them to use abilities they value in order to perform the job effectively.
3. Self-control – individuals must feel that they have a high degree of self-control over setting their own goals and over defining the paths to these goals.

The job characteristics model

A useful perspective on the factors affecting job design and motivation is provided by Hackman and Oldham's (1974) job characteristics model. They suggest that the 'critical psychological states' of 'experienced meaningfulness of work, experienced responsibility for outcomes of work and knowledge of the actual outcomes of work' strongly influence motivation, job satisfaction and performance. They identified the following characteristics of jobs that need to be taken into account in job design.

SOURCE REVIEW

Job characteristics, Hackman and Oldman (1974)

1. Variety.
2. Autonomy.
3. Required interaction.
4. Optional interaction.
5. Knowledge and skill required.
6. Responsibility.

Approaches to job design

Job design starts with an analysis of task requirements, using the job analysis techniques described in Chapter 26. These requirements will be a function of the purpose of the organization, its technology and its structure. The analysis has also to take into account the decision-making process – where and how decisions are made and the extent to which responsibility is devolved to individuals and work teams.

SOURCE REVIEW

Approaches to job design, Robertson and Smith (1985)

1. Influence skill variety by providing opportunities for people to do several tasks and by combining tasks.
2. Influence task identity by combining tasks and forming natural work units.
3. Influence task significance by forming natural work units and informing people of the importance of their work.
4. Influence autonomy by giving people responsibility for determining their own working systems.
5. Influence feedback by establishing good relationships and opening feedback channels.

These approaches are used as the basis for the methods of job design described below.

1. Job rotation

This is the movement of employees from one task to another to reduce monotony by increasing variety.

2. Job enlargement

This means combining previously fragmented tasks into one job, again to increase the variety and meaning of repetitive work.

3. Job enrichment

This goes beyond job enlargement to add greater autonomy and responsibility to a job and is based on the job characteristics approach. Job enrichment aims to maximize the interest and challenge of work by providing the employee with a job that has these characteristics:

- it is a complete piece of work in the sense that the worker can identify a series of tasks or activities that end in a recognizable and definable product;
- it affords the employee as much variety, decision-making responsibility and control as possible in carrying out the work;
- it provides direct feedback through the work itself on how well the employee is doing his or her job.

As described by Herzberg (1968), job enrichment is not just increasing the number or variety of tasks; nor is it the provision of opportunities for job rotation. These approaches may relieve boredom, but they do not result in positive increases in motivation.

4. Self-managing teams (autonomous work groups)

These are self-regulating teams who work largely without direct supervision. The philosophy on which this technique is based is a logical extension of job enrichment but is strongly influenced by socio-technical systems theory (see Chapter 21). A self-managing team enlarges individual jobs to include a wider range of operative skills (multi-skilling), decides on methods of work and the planning, scheduling and control of work, distributes tasks itself among its members and monitors its own performance, taking corrective action when required.

The advocates of self-managing teams or autonomous work groups claim that this approach offers a more comprehensive view of organizations than the rather simplistic individual motivation theories that underpin job rotation, enlargement and enrichment. Be that as it may, the strength of this system is that it does take account of the social or group factors and the technology as well as the individual motivators.

5. High-performance work design

This concentrates on setting up working groups in environments where high levels of performance can be achieved. As described by Buchanan (1987), this requires management to define what it needs in the form of methods of production and the results expected from its introduction. It involves multi-skilling – job demarcation lines are eliminated as far as possible and encouragement and training are provided for employees to acquire new skills. Self-managed teams are set up with full responsibility for planning, controlling and monitoring the work.

Choice of approach

Of the five approaches described above, it is generally recognized that although job rotation and job enlargement have their uses in developing skills and relieving monotony, they do not go to the root of the requirements for intrinsic motivation and for meeting the various motivating characteristics of jobs. These are best satisfied by using, as appropriate, job enrichment, autonomous work groups, or high-performance work design.

Role development

Role development is the continuous process through which roles are defined or modified as work proceeds and evolves. Job design as described above takes place when a new job is created or an existing job is substantially changed, often following a reorganization. But the part people play in carrying out their roles can evolve over time as people grow into them and grow with them, and as incremental changes take place in the scope of the work and the degree to which individuals have freedom to act (their autonomy). Roles will be developed as people develop in them – responding to opportunities and changing demands, acquiring new skills and developing competencies. Role development is a continuous process that takes place in the context of day-to-day work and is therefore a matter between managers and the members of their teams. It involves agreeing definitions of accountabilities, objectives and competency requirements as they evolve. When these change – as they probably will in all except the most routine jobs – it is desirable to achieve mutual understanding of new expectations.

The process of understanding how roles are developing and agreeing the implications can take place within the framework of performance management, as described in Part VII, where the performance agreement, which is updated regularly, spells out the outcomes (key result areas) and the competency requirements. It is necessary to ensure that managers, team leaders and employees generally acquire the skills necessary to define roles within the performance management framework, taking into account the principles of job design set out earlier in this chapter.

Job and role design and development – key learning points

The factors affecting job design

- The characteristics of jobs.
- The characteristics of task structure.
- The process of intrinsic motivation.
- The job characteristics model.
- The implications of group activities.

The characteristics of jobs

- Job range – the number of operations a job holder performs to complete a task.
- Job depth – the amount of discretion a job holder has to decide job activities and job outcomes.
- Job relationships – the interpersonal relationships between job holders and their managers and co-workers.

Task structure

Job design requires the assembly of a number of tasks into a job or a group of jobs. Individuals may carry out a variety of connected tasks (multi-tasking), each with a number of functions, or these tasks may be allocated to a team of workers or divided between them. The internal structure of each task consists of three elements: planning (deciding on the course of action, its timing and the resources required), executing (carrying out the plan), and controlling (monitoring performance and progress and taking corrective action when required). A completely integrated job includes all these elements for each of the tasks involved.

Approaches to job design (Robertson and Smith, 1985)

- Influence skill variety by providing opportunities for people to do several tasks and by combining tasks.
- Influence task identity by combining tasks and forming natural work units.
- Influence task significance by forming natural work units and informing people of the importance of their work.
- Influence autonomy by giving people responsibility for determining their own working systems.
- Influence feedback by establishing good relationships and opening feedback channels.

Role development

Role development is the continuous process through which roles are defined or modified as work proceeds and evolves.

Questions

1. What is the process of job design?
2. What are the factors affecting job design?
3. What are the intrinsically motivating characteristics of jobs?
4. What is the job characteristics model?
5. How is role development carried out?

References

Buchanan, D (1987) Job enrichment is dead: long live high performance work design!, *Personnel Management*, May, pp 40–43

Hackman, J R and Oldham, G R (1974) Motivation through the design of work: test of a theory, *Organizational Behaviour and Human Performance*, **16** (2), pp 250–79

Herzberg, F (1968) One more time: how do you motivate employees? *Harvard Business Review*, January–February, pp 109–120

Lawler, E E (1969) Job design and employee motivation, *Personnel Psychology*, **22**, pp 426–35

Robertson, I T and Smith, M (1985) *Motivation and Job Design*, IPM, London

Wilson, N A B (1973) *On the Quality of Working Life*, HMSO, London

Part VI

People Resourcing

People resourcing is concerned with ensuring that the organization obtains and retains the people it needs and employs them productively. It is closely associated with performance management and employee development policy and practice. It is also about those aspects of employment practice that are concerned with welcoming people to the organization and, if there is no alternative, releasing them.

Part VI contents

28 People Resourcing Strategy

Key concepts and terms

- Bundling
- Organizational capability
- Resource capability
- Human resource planning
- The resource-based view
- Talent management

Learning outcomes

On completing this chapter you should be able to define these key concepts. You should also know about:

- The objective of resourcing strategy
- Integrating business and resourcing strategies
- The strategic HRM approach to resourcing
- The components of employee resourcing strategy

Introduction

This chapter deals with people resourcing strategy, which is concerned with taking steps to ensure that the organization obtains and keeps the people it needs and employs them efficiently. It is closely associated with learning and development strategy, which sets out how the organization ensures that it has the skilled and knowledgeable workforce it needs and that a pool of talented people is created who will provide for management succession.

The objective of people resourcing strategy

The concept that the strategic capability of a firm depends on its resource capability in the shape of people (the resource-based view) provides the rationale for resourcing strategy. As explained by Grant (1991):

> *The firm's most important resources and capabilities are those which are durable, difficult to identify and understand, imperfectly transferable, not easily replicated, and in which the firm possesses clear ownership and control. These are the firm's 'crown jewels' and need to be protected; and they play a pivotal role in the competitive strategy which the firm pursues. The essence of strategy formulation, then, is to design a strategy that makes the most effective use of these core resources and capabilities.*

The aim of this strategy is to ensure that a firm achieves competitive advantage by attracting and retaining more capable people than its rivals and employing them more effectively. These people will have a wider and deeper range of skills and will behave in ways that will maximize their contribution. The organization attracts such people by being 'the employer of choice'. It retains them by providing better opportunities and rewards than others and by developing a positive psychological contract that increases commitment and creates mutual trust. Furthermore, the organization deploys its people in ways that maximize the added value they create.

The strategic HRM approach to resourcing

Strategic HRM emphasizes the importance of human resources in achieving organizational capability and therefore the need to find people whose attitudes and behaviour are likely to be congruent with what management believes to be appropriate and conducive to success. In the words of Townley (1989), organizations are concentrating more on 'the attitudinal and behavioural characteristics of employees'. This tendency has its dangers. Innovative and adaptive organizations need non-conformists, even mavericks, who can 'buck the system'. If managers recruit people 'in their own image' there is the risk of staffing the organization with conformist clones and of perpetuating a dysfunctional culture – one that may have been successful in the past but is no longer appropriate in the face of new challenges (as Pascale, 1990, exclaims, 'nothing fails like success').

The HRM approach to resourcing therefore emphasizes that matching resources to organizational requirements does not simply mean maintaining the status quo and perpetuating a moribund culture. It can and often does mean radical changes in thinking about the skills and behaviours required in the future to achieve sustainable growth and cultural change. It also means using a systematic approach, starting with human resource planning and proceeding through recruitment, selection and induction, followed by performance management, learning and development, recognition and reward.

Integrating business and resourcing strategies

The philosophy behind the strategic HRM approach to resourcing is that it is people who implement the strategic plan. As Quinn Mills (1983) has put it, the process is one of 'planning with people in mind'.

The integration of business and resourcing strategies is based on an understanding of the direction in which the organization is going and the following considerations.

Considerations affecting the integration of business and resourcing strategies

- The numbers of people required to meet business needs.
- The skills and behaviour required to support the achievement of business strategies.
- The impact of organizational restructuring as a result of rationalization, decentralization, delayering, acquisitions, mergers, product or market development, or the introduction of new technology, for example, cellular manufacturing.
- Plans for changing the culture of the organization in such areas as ability to deliver, performance standards, quality, customer service, team working and flexibility that indicate the need for people with different attitudes, beliefs and personal characteristics.

These considerations will be strongly influenced by the type of business strategies adopted by the organization and the sort of business it is in. These may be expressed in such terms as Porter's

(1985) classification of business strategic aims (innovation, quality and cost leadership) or Miles and Snow's (1978) typology of defender, prospector and analyser organizations.

Resourcing strategies exist to provide the people and skills required to support the business strategy, but they should also contribute to the formulation of that strategy. HR directors have an obligation to point out to their colleagues the human resource opportunities and constraints that will affect the achievement of strategic plans. In mergers or acquisitions, for example, the ability of management within the company to handle the new situation and the quality of management in the new business will be important considerations.

The components of people resourcing strategy

The components of employee resourcing strategy are:

- Human resource planning (often referred to, especially in the public sector, as workforce planning) – assessing future business needs, deciding on the numbers and types of people required and preparing plans for obtaining them from within or outside the organization (Chapter 29).
- Creating an employer brand – developing the organization's employee value proposition (Chapter 30).
- Retention strategy – preparing plans for retaining the people the organization needs (Chapter 30).
- Absence management strategy – planning for the control of absence (Chapter 30).
- Flexibility strategy – planning for increased flexibility in the use of human resources to enable the organization to make the best use of people and adapt swiftly to changing circumstances (Chapter 30).
- Talent management strategy – ensuring that the organization has the talented people it requires to provide for management succession and meet present and future business needs (Chapter 31).
- Recruitment and selection strategy – planning the approaches used to obtain people as described in Chapters 31 (recruitment and selection), 32 (selection interviewing) and 33 (selection tests).

Bundling resourcing strategies and activities

People resourcing is not just about recruitment and selection. It is concerned with any means available to meet the needs of the firm for certain skills and behaviours. A strategy to enlarge the skill base may start with recruitment and selection but would extend into learning and development to enhance skills and modify behaviours, and methods of rewarding people for the acquisition of extra skills. Performance management processes can be used to identify development needs (skill and behavioural) and motivate people to make the most effective use of their skills. Competency frameworks and profiles can be prepared to define the skills and behaviours required and used in selection, employee development and employee reward processes. The aim should be to develop a reinforcing bundle of strategies along these lines. Talent management is a 'bundling' process that is an aspect of resourcing.

People resourcing strategy – key learning points

Objective of resourcing strategy

To ensure that a firm achieves competitive advantage by attracting and retaining more capable people than its rivals and employing them more effectively.

The strategic HRM approach to resourcing

Strategic HRM emphasizes the importance of human resources in achieving organizational capability and therefore the need to find people whose attitudes and behaviour are likely to be congruent with what management believes to be appropriate and conducive to success.

Integrating business and resourcing strategies

- The numbers of people required to meet business needs.
- The skills and behaviour required to support the achievement of business strategies.
- The impact of organizational restructuring.
- Plans for changing the culture of the organization.

The components of employee resourcing strategy

Human resource planning includes creating an employer brand, retention strategy, absence management strategy, flexibility strategy, talent management strategy, recruitment and selection strategy.

Bundling and resourcing strategy

Resourcing strategy should include the bundling of different aspects of resourcing together so that they can be mutually supportive.

Questions

1. From a fellow student: 'The preamble to the CIPD People Resourcing syllabus says that "Many of those engaged in employee resourcing concentrate on minor incremental efficiency or system changes and on the legalistic, ethical and procedural dimensions of resourcing – instead of the added-value dimensions."' To what extent do you think this is true, both generally and with specific reference to your own organization? What evidence do you have to support your views?
2. From your chief executive: 'We are doing well but we need to do better. This will be the theme of our away day for the board in May. I want each director to make a short presentation as a basis for discussion on a key aspect of strategy in their area and how it will impact on our performance. As director of human resources I would like you to talk about our need for a people resourcing strategy, what it involves and how it will contribute to improved performance. Any information you can provide based on benchmarking or evidence from research you can provide will be welcome.'
3. From your HR director: 'We tend to use the phrase "added value" or "value-added management" rather loosely in our organization. I would be interested in your views on what it means in the context of people resourcing.'
4. From the Features Editor, *People Management*: 'We're planning a full-length piece about "adding value", and in seeking a cross-section of reader views we'd welcome your input.' What does it mean in your organization for a people resourcing professional to 'add value' and how do you know when you've done it?

References

Grant, R M (1991) The resource-based theory of competitive advantage: implications for strategy formation, *California Management Review*, **33** (3), pp 14–35

Miles, R E and Snow, C C (1978) *Organizational Strategy: Structure and process*, McGraw-Hill, New York

Pascale, R (1990) *Managing on the Edge*, Viking, London

Porter, M E (1985) *Competitive Advantage: Creating and sustaining superior performance*, New York, The Free Press

Quinn Mills, D (1983) Planning with people in mind, *Harvard Business Review*, November–December, pp 97–105

Townley, B (1989) Selection and appraisal: reconstructing social relations?, in (ed) J Storey, *New Perspectives in Human resource Management*, Routledge, London

29 Human Resource Planning

Key concepts and terms

- Demand forecasting
- Human resources planning
- Scenario planning
- Supply forecasting
- Hard human resources planning
- Ratio-trend analysis
- Soft human resources planning

Learning outcomes

On completing this chapter you should be able to define these key concepts. You should also know about:

- Aims of human resource planning
- Action planning
- Human resource planning activities

Introduction

Organizations need to know how many people and what sort of people they should have to meet present and future business requirements. This is the function of human resource planning, or workforce planning as it is sometimes called, especially in the public sector.

The purpose of this chapter is to describe how human resource planning works, bearing in mind that it is not as straightforward as it was presented when the notion of 'manpower planning' became popular in the 1960s and 70s. Human resource planning may be well established in the HRM vocabulary but it does not seem to be embedded as a key HR activity.

This chapter starts with a definition of human resource planning and continues with a discussion of its aims and the issues involved, including its link with business planning. The final section of the chapter describes the processes used, namely scenario planning, demand and supply forecasting and action planning.

Human resource planning defined

As defined by Bulla and Scott (1994), human resource planning is 'the process for ensuring that the human resource requirements of an organization are identified and plans are made for satisfying those requirements'. Reilly (2003) defined workforce planning as: 'A process in which an organization attempts to estimate the demand for labour and evaluate the size, nature and sources of supply which will be required to meet the demand.'

Hard and soft human resource planning

A distinction can be made between 'hard' and 'soft' human resource planning. The former is based on quantitative analysis to ensure that the right number of the right sort of people is available when needed. The latter, as described by Marchington and Wilkinson (1996), 'is more explicitly focused on creating and shaping the culture of the organization so that there is a clear integration between corporate goals and employee values, beliefs and behaviours'. But as they point out, the soft version becomes virtually synonymous with the whole area of human resource management.

Link to business planning

Human resource planning is an integral part of business planning. The strategic planning process defines projected changes in the types of activities carried out by the organization and the scale of those activities. It identifies the core competences the organization needs to achieve its goals and therefore its skill and behavioural requirements.

Human resource planning interprets these plans in terms of people requirements. But it may influence the business strategy by drawing attention to ways in which people could be developed and deployed more effectively to further the achievement of business goals as well as focusing on any problems that might have to be resolved to ensure that the people required will be available and will be capable of making the necessary contribution. As Quinn Mills (1983) indicates, human resource planning is:

> *a decision-making process that combines three important activities: 1) identifying and acquiring the right number of people with the proper skills, 2) motivating them to achieve high performance, and 3) creating interactive links between business objectives and people-planning activities.*

Aims of human resource planning

Human resource planning aims to ensure that the organization has the number of people with the right skills needed to meet forecast requirements. Research conducted by the Institute for Employment Studies (Reilly, 1999) established that there are a number of reasons why organizations choose to engage in some form of human resource planning. These fall into the following three groups.

Reasons for engaging in human resource planning

1. Planning for substantive reasons, that is, to have a practical effect by optimizing the use of resources and/or making them more flexible, acquiring and nurturing skills that take time to develop, identifying potential problems and minimizing the chances of making a bad decision.
2. Planning because of the process benefits, which involves understanding the present in order to confront the future, challenging assumptions and liberating thinking, making explicit decisions that can later be challenged, standing back and providing an overview and ensuring that long-term thinking is not driven out by short-term focus.
3. Planning for organizational reasons, which involves communicating plans so as to obtain support/adherence to them, linking HR plans to business plans so as to influence them, (re)gaining corporate control over operating units, and coordinating and integrating organizational decision making and actions.

Farnham (2006) explained that human resource planning is important because it encourages employers to develop clear and explicit links between their business and HR plans and to integrate the two more effectively. It allows for better control over staffing costs and numbers employed, and it enables employers to make more informed judgements about the skills and attitude mix in organizations. Human resource planning also provides a profile of current staff in terms of age, sex, disability, etc so as to move towards being an equal opportunity organization. But he commented that organizations give little time to it because of lack of resources and skills, the time and effort required and the absence of relevant data to do so.

Use of human resource planning

As Rothwell (1995) suggested: 'Apart from isolated examples, there has been little research evidence of increased use or of its success'. She explains the gap between theory and practice as arising from:

- the impact of change and the difficulty of predicting the future – 'the need for planning may be in inverse proportion to its feasibility';
- the 'shifting kaleidoscope' of policy priorities and strategies within organizations;
- the distrust displayed by of many managers of theory or planning – they often prefer pragmatic adaptation to conceptualization;
- the lack of evidence that human resource planning works.

Summarizing the problem, Taylor (2008) noted that:

> *It would seem that employers, quite simply, prefer to wait until their view of the future environment clears sufficiently for them to see the whole picture before committing resources in preparation for its arrival. The perception is that the more complex and turbulent the environment, the more important it is to wait and see before acting.*

Human resource planning is likely to be more appropriate in a stable market place, with largely passive (and static) customers, and with scope for long-term forecasting because of the predictability of demographic change. This applies to many public sector enterprises and it is happening under the name of workforce planning in, for example, local authorities and the NHS. Examples are given by the Employers' Organization for Local Government (2003).

Approaches to human resource planning

Human resource planning involves the activities listed below.

Human resource planning activities

- Scenario planning – making broad assessments of future environmental factors and their likely impact on people requirements.
- Demand forecasting – estimate future needs for people and competences by reference to corporate and functional plans and forecasts of future activity levels.
- Supply forecasting – estimate the supply of people by reference to analyses of current resources and future availability, after allowing for wastage. The forecast will also take account of labour market trends relating to the availability of skills and to demographics.
- Forecasting requirements – analyse the demand and supply forecasts to identify future deficits or surpluses with the help of models, where appropriate.
- Action planning – prepare plans to deal with forecast deficits through internal promotion, training or external recruitment. If necessary, plan for unavoidable downsizing so as to avoid any compulsory redundancies, if that is possible. Develop retention and flexibility strategies.

Although these are described as separate areas, they are closely interrelated and often overlap. For example, demand forecasts are estimates of future requirements, and these may be prepared on the basis of assumptions about the productivity of employees. But the supply forecast will also have to consider productivity trends and how they might affect the supply of people.

A flow chart of the process of human resource planning is shown in Figure 29.1 and each of the main activities is described below.

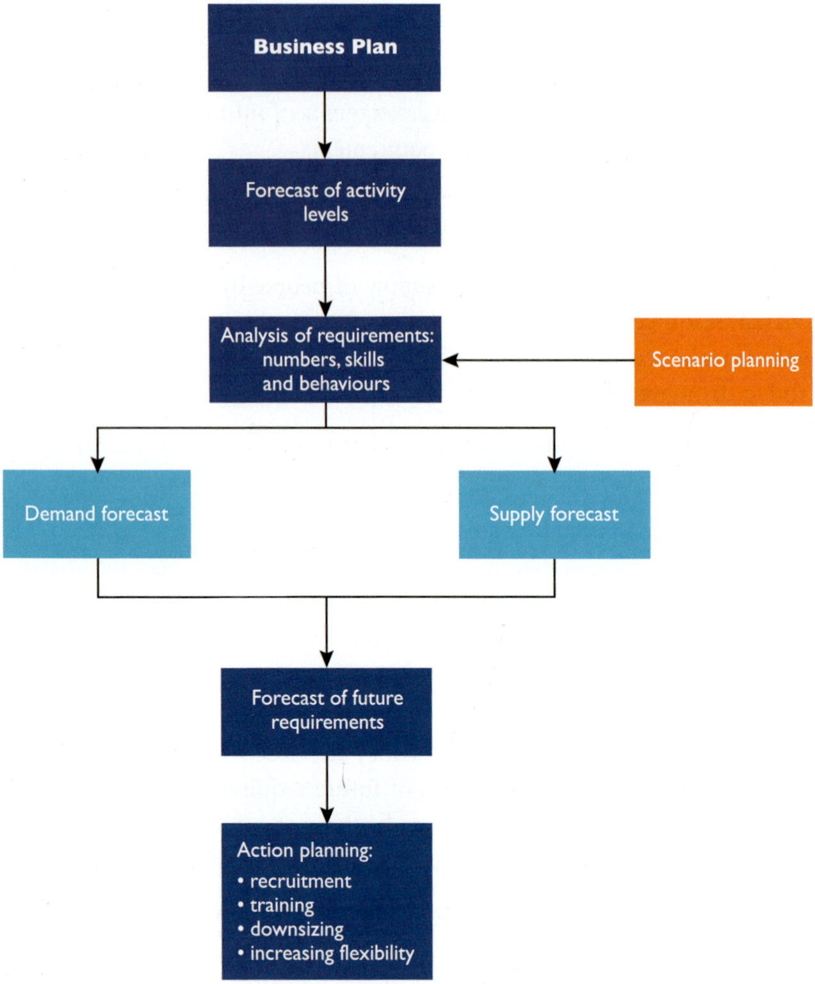

Figure 29.1 Human resource planning flow chart

Scenario planning

Scenario planning is simply an assessment of the environmental changes that are likely to affect the organization so that a prediction can be made of the possible situations that may have to be dealt with in the future. The scenario may list a range of predictions so that different responses can be considered. The scenario is best based on systematic environmental scanning, possibly using the PEST approach (an assessment of the political, economic, social and technological factors that might affect the organization). The implications of these factors on the organization's labour markets and what can be done about any human resource issues can then be considered.

Demand forecasting

Demand forecasting is the process of estimating the future numbers of people required and the likely skills and competences they will need. The basis of the forecast is the annual budget and longer-term business plan, translated into activity levels for each function and department or decisions on 'downsizing'. In a manufacturing company the sales budget would be translated into a manufacturing plan giving the numbers and types of products to be made in each period. From this information the number of hours to be worked by each skill category to make the quota for each period would be computed.

Details are required of any organization plans that would result in increased or decreased demands for employees, for example setting up a new regional organization, creating a new sales department, decentralizing a head office function to the regions. Plans and budgets for reducing employment costs and their implications on the future numbers of people to be employed would also have to be considered.

The demand forecasting methods for estimating the numbers of people required are described below.

Managerial judgement

The most typical method of forecasting used is managerial judgement. This simply requires managers to sit down, think about their future workloads, and decide how many people they need. It might be done on a 'bottom-up' basis with line managers submitting proposals for agreement by senior management.

Alternatively, a 'top-down' approach can be used, in which company and departmental forecasts are prepared by top management, possibly acting on advice from the personnel departments. These forecasts are reviewed and agreed with departmental managers. A less directive approach is for top management to prepare planning guidelines for departmental managers, setting out the planning assumptions and the targets they should try to meet.

Perhaps the best way of using managerial judgement is to adopt both the 'bottom-up' and 'top-down' approaches. Guidelines for departmental managers should be prepared that indicate broad company assumptions about future activity levels that will affect their departments. Targets are also set where necessary. Armed with these guidelines, departmental managers prepare their forecasts to a laid-down format. They are encouraged to seek help at this stage from the personnel or work study departments. Meanwhile, the personnel department, in conjunction as necessary with planning and work study departments, prepares a company human resource forecast. The two sets of forecasts can then be reviewed by a human resource planning committee consisting of functional heads. This committee reconciles with departmental managers any discrepancies between the two forecasts and submits the final amended forecast to top management for approval. This is sometimes called the 'right-angle method'.

Ratio-trend analysis

Ratio-trend analysis is carried out by studying past ratios between, say, the number of direct (production) workers and indirect (support) workers in a manufacturing plant, and forecasting future ratios, having made some allowance for changes in organization or methods. Activity level forecasts are then used to determine, in this example, direct labour requirements, and the forecast ratio of indirects to directs would be used to calculate the number of indirect workers needed.

Work study techniques

Work study techniques can be used when it is possible to apply work measurement to calculate how long operations should take and the number of people required. Work study techniques for direct workers can be combined with ratio-trend analysis to calculate the number of indirect workers needed.

Forecasting skill and competence requirements

Forecasting skill and competence requirements is largely a matter of managerial judgement. This judgement should however be exercised on the basis of a careful analysis of the impact of projected product-market developments and the introduction of new technology, either information technology or computerized manufacturing.

Supply forecasting

Supply forecasting measures the number of people likely to be available from within and outside the organization, having allowed for absenteeism, internal movements and promotions, wastage and changes in hours and other conditions of work. The supply analysis covers the following areas.

Supply analysis areas

- Existing number of people employed by occupation, skill and potential.
- Potential losses to existing resources through attrition (employee turnover).
- Potential changes to existing resources through internal promotions.
- Effect of changing conditions of work and absenteeism.
- Sources of supply from within the organization.
- Sources of supply from outside the organization in the national and local labour markets.

Forecast of future requirements

To forecast future requirements it is necessary to analyse the demand and supply forecasts to identify any deficits or surpluses. The analysis can be made with the help of spreadsheets. It can be set out as follows:

1.	Current number employed	70
2.	Annual level of turnover	10%
3.	Expected losses during year	7
4.	Balance at end year	63
5.	Number required at end year	75
6.	Number to be obtained during year (5 − 4)	12

Action planning

Action plans are derived from the broad resourcing strategies and the more detailed analysis of demand and supply factors. However, the plans often have to be short term and flexible because of the difficulty of making firm predictions about human resource requirements in times of rapid change. The planning activities start with the identification of internal resources available now or which could be made available through learning and development programmes. They continue with plans for increasing the attractiveness of working for the organization by developing an employer brand and an employee value proposition, taking steps to reduce employee turnover and absenteeism, and increasing employment flexibility. Recruitment plans, as described in Chapter 31, also need to be prepared.

Human resource planning – key learning points

Aims of human resource planning

Human resource planning aims to ensure that the organization has the number of people with the right skills needed to meet forecast requirements.

Human resource planning activities

Scenario planning, demand and supply forecasts, action planning.

Action planning

Action plans are derived from the broad resourcing strategies and the more detailed analysis of demand and supply factors.

Questions

1. You have been asked to oppose the motion, 'Human resource planning is impossible or at least a waste of time in a situation where the future is so unpredictable.' Prepare your case, which should include evidence from your own experience or research.
2. From a PhD student conducting research on human resource planning: 'Can you tell me whether your organization or any organization you know has constructed any human resource plans? If so, why and what do they look like, and if not, why not?'
3. From your manufacturing director: 'What methods are available for me to forecast the future demand for skilled staff in my production departments? We have a pretty good idea of what the order book will look like over the next three years and can deploy some reasonably sophisticated operational planning procedures. All our operations have been work studied.'

References

Bulla, D N and Scott, P M (1994) Manpower requirements forecasting: a case example, in (eds) D Ward, T P Bechet and R Tripp, *Human Resource Forecasting and Modelling*, The Human Resource Planning Society, New York

Employers' Organization for Local Government (2003) *Guide to Workforce Planning in Local Authorities*, Employers' Organization for Local Government, London

Farnham, D (2006) *Examiner's Report* (May), CIPD.co.uk

Marchington, M and Wilkinson, A (1996) *Core Personnel and Development*, Institute of Personnel and Development, London

Quinn Mills, D (1983) Planning with people in mind, *Harvard Business Review*, November–December, pp 97–105

Reilly, P (1999) *The Human Resource Planning Audit*, Cambridge Strategy Publications, Cambridge

Reilly, P (2003) *Guide to Workforce Planning in Local Authorities*, Employers' Organization for Local Government, London

Rothwell, S (1995) Human resource planning, in (ed) J Storey, *Human Resource Management: A critical text*, Routledge, London

Taylor, S (2008) *People Resourcing*, CIPD, London

30 People Resourcing Practice

Key concepts and terms

- Absence management
- Employee turnover
- Employer brand
- Employee turnover index
- Length of service analysis
- Survival rate
- The Bradford Factor
- Employee value proposition
- Employer of choice
- Half-life index
- Stability index

Learning outcomes

On completing this chapter you should be able to define these key concepts. You should also know about:

- Measuring employee turnover
- Retention planning
- Absence management
- Estimating the cost of employee turnover
- Risk of leaving analysis
- Flexibility planning

Introduction

People resourcing is largely about recruitment and selection, talent and career management, introducing people to the organization, and releasing them from it, as covered in Chapters 31 to 37. But there are six other resourcing activities, which are dealt with in this chapter, namely: developing an employee value proposition, creating an employer brand, analysing employee turnover, tackling retention problems, absence or attendance management, and achieving flexibility in the use of people.

Employee value proposition

An organization's employee value proposition consists of what an organization has to offer that prospective or existing employees would value and which would help to persuade them to join or remain with the business. It will include remuneration – which is important but can be over-emphasized compared with other elements. These non-financial factors may be crucial in attracting and retaining people and include the attractiveness of the organization, the degree to which it acts responsibly, respect – diversity and inclusion, work–life balance and opportunities for personal and professional growth.

The aim is to become 'an employer of choice', a firm people want to work for and stay with. The conclusions of Purcell *et al* (2003) on the basis of their research were as follows.

SOURCE REVIEW

On being an employer of choice, Purcell *et al* (2003)

What seems to be happening is that successful firms are able to meet people's needs both for a good job and to work 'in a great place'. They create good work and a conducive working environment. In this way they become an 'employer of choice'. People will want to work there because their individual needs are met – for a good job with prospects linked to training, appraisal and working with a good boss who listens and gives some autonomy but helps with coaching and guidance.

Employer brand

The employee value proposition can be expressed as an employer brand, defined by Walker (2007) as 'a set of attributes and qualities – often intangible – that make an organization distinctive, promise a particular kind of employment experience and appeal to people who will thrive and perform their best in its culture'. Employer branding is the creation of a brand image of the organization for prospective employees. It will be influenced by the reputation of the organization as a business or provider of services as well as its reputation as an employer.

Creating an employer brand

- Analyse what ideal candidates need and want and take this into account in deciding what should be offered and how it should be offered.
- Establish how far the core values of the organization support the creation of an attractive brand and ensure that these are incorporated in the presentation of the brand as long as they are 'values in use' (lived by members of the organization) rather than simply espoused.
- Define the features of the brand on the basis of an examination and review of each of the areas that affect the perceptions of people about the organization as 'a great place to work' – the way people are treated, the provision of a fair deal, opportunities for growth, work–life balance, leadership, the quality of management, involvement with colleagues and how and why the organization is successful.
- Benchmark the approaches of other organizations (the *Sunday Times* list of the 100 best companies to work for is useful) to obtain ideas about what can be done to enhance the brand.
- Be honest and realistic.

Employee turnover

Employee turnover (sometimes known as 'labour turnover, 'wastage' or 'attrition') is the rate at which people leave an organization. It can be disruptive and costly. The CIPD (2008a) survey of recruitment, retention and turnover found that the average rate of turnover (the number leaving as a percentage of the number employed) in the UK was 17.3 per cent. It is necessary to measure employee turnover and calculate its costs in order to forecast future losses for planning purposes and to identify the reasons that people leave the organization. Plans can then be made to attack the problems causing unnecessary turnover and to reduce costs. There are a number of different methods of measuring turnover, as described below.

Employee turnover index

The employee turnover index as set out below (sometimes referred to as the employee or labour wastage index) is the traditional formula for measuring turnover:

$$\frac{\text{Number of leavers in a specified period (usually 1 year)}}{\text{Average number of employees during the same period}} \times 100$$

This method is in common use because it is easy to calculate and to understand. It is a simple matter to work out that if last year 30 out of an average force of 150 employees left (20 per cent turnover), and this trend continues, then the company will have to recruit 108 employees during the following year to increase and to hold the workforce at 200 in that year (50 extra employees, plus 40 to replace the 20 per cent wastage of the average 200 employees employed, plus 18 to replace wastage of the 90 recruits).

This formula may be simple to use, but it can be misleading. The main objection is that the percentage may be inflated by the high turnover of a relatively small proportion of the workforce, especially in times of heavy recruitment. Thus, a company employing 1,000 people might have had an annual wastage rate of 20 per cent, meaning that 200 jobs had become vacant during the year. But this could have been spread throughout the company, covering all occupations and long- as well as short-service employees. Alternatively, it could have been restricted to a small sector of the workforce – only 20 jobs might have been affected although each of these had to be filled 10 times during the year. These are totally different situations, and unless they are understood, inaccurate forecasts would be made of future requirements and inappropriate actions would be taken to deal with the problem. The turnover index is also suspect if the average number of employees upon which the percentage is based is unrepresentative of recent trends because of considerable increases or decreases during the period in the numbers employed.

Stability index

The stability index is considered by many to be an improvement on the turnover index. The formula is:

$$\frac{\text{Number of 1 year's service or more}}{\text{Number employed 1 year ago}} \times 100$$

This index provides an indication of the tendency for longer-service employees to remain with the company, and therefore shows the degree to which there is a continuity of employment. But this too can be misleading because the index will not reveal the vastly different situations that exist in a company or department with a high proportion of long-serving employees in comparison with one where the majority of employees are short service.

Survival rate

The survival rate is the proportion of employees who are engaged within a certain period who remain with the organization after so many months or years of service. Thus, an analysis of a cohort of trainees who have completed their training might show that after two years, 10 of the original trainees were still with the company, a survival rate of 50 per cent.

The distribution of losses for each entry group, or cohort, can be plotted in the form of a survival curve, as shown in Figure 30.1.

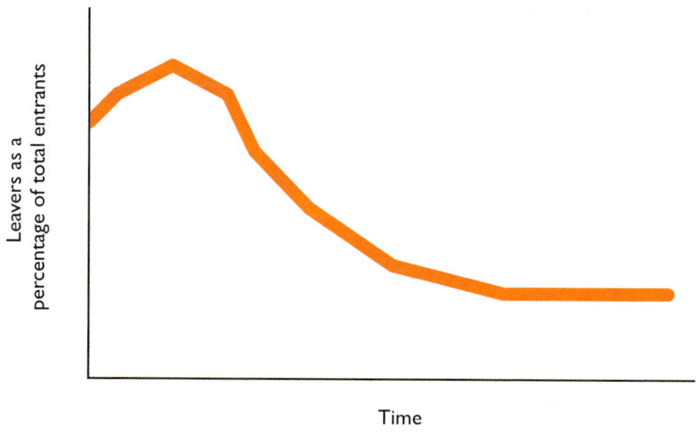

Figure 30.1 A survival curve

The basic shape of this curve has been found to be similar in many situations, although the peak of the curve may occur further along the time scale and/or may be lower when it relates to more highly skilled or trained entry cohorts. An example of a survival rate analysis is shown in Table 30.1. This indicates that half the number of recruits in any one year may be lost over the next five years, unless something can be done about the factors causing wastage.

Table 30.1 A survival rate analysis

Entry cohort	Original number	Number surviving to end of year after engagement				
		Year 1	Year 2	Year 3	Year 4	Year 5
A	40	35	28	26	22	20
B	32	25	24	19	18	17
C	48	39	33	30	25	23
D	38	32	27	24	22	19
E	42	36	30	26	23	21
Total	200	167	142	125	110	100
Average survival rate	100%	83%	71%	62%	55%	50%

Half-life index

A simpler concept derived from survival rate analysis is that of the half-life index, which is defined as the time taken for a group or cohort of starters to reduce to half its original size through the wastage process (five years in the above example). Comparisons can then be made for successive entry years or between different groups of employees to show where action may have to be taken to counter undesirable wastage trends.

Leavers' length of service analysis

This disadvantage of the stability index may be partly overcome if an analysis is also made of the average length of service of people who leave, as in Table 30.2.

This analysis is still fairly crude, because it deals only with those who leave. A more refined analysis would compare for each service category the numbers leaving with the numbers employed. If, in the example shown, the total numbers employed with less than three months' service were 80 and the total with more than five years' were 80, the proportion of leavers in each category would be, respectively, 35 per cent and 14 per cent – more revealing figures.

Table 30.2 Leavers' length of service analysis

Occupation	Leavers by length of service						Total number leaving	Average number employed	Index of employee turnover %
	Less than 3 months	3–6 months	6 months–1 year	1–2 years	3–5 years	5 or more years			
A	5	4	3	3	2	3	20	220	9
B	15	12	10	6	3	4	50	250	20
C	8	6	5	4	3	4	30	100	30
Totals	28	22	18	13	8	11	100	570	18

Choice of measurement

It is difficult to avoid using the conventional employee (labour) turnover index as the easiest and most familiar of all methods of measurement. But it needs to be supplemented with some measure of stability: an analysis of turnover or wastage as part of a human resource planning exercise requires detailed information on the length of service of leavers to identify problem areas and to provide a foundation for supply forecasts.

The cost of employee turnover

The cost of employee turnover can be considerable. The CIPD 2008(a) survey established on a small sample that the average cost per employee was £5,800, rising to £20,000 for senior managers or directors.

Cost estimates are useful as means of backing up a business case for taking action to reduce turnover. The following factors should be considered when calculating costs.

Factors affecting the cost of employee turnover

- Direct cost of recruiting replacements (advertising, interviewing, testing, etc).
- Direct cost of introducing replacements (induction cost).
- Direct cost of training replacements in necessary skills.
- Leaving costs – payroll and HR administration.
- Opportunity cost of time spent by HR and line managers in recruitment, induction and training.
- Loss of output from those leaving before they are replaced.
- Loss of output because of delays in obtaining replacements.
- Loss of output while new starters are on their learning curves acquiring the necessary knowledge and skills.

Research by Phillips (1990) found that the 'visible', ie direct, costs of recruitment accounted for only 10 to 15 per cent of total costs. By far the highest costs were associated with the inefficiencies arising while the post was vacant (33 per cent) and the inefficiency of new workers (32 per cent). On average, 12.5 months were required for executives to be comfortable in a new position and 13.5 months were required for a new employee to achieve maximum efficiency.

Retention planning

The turnover of key employees can have a disproportionate impact on the business. The people organizations wish to retain are often the ones most likely to leave. It was claimed by Reed (2001) that: 'Every worker is five minutes away from handing in his or her notice, and 150 working hours away from walking out of the door to a better offer. There is no such thing as a job for life and today's workers have few qualms about leaving employers for greener pastures.' Concerted action is required to retain talented people but there are limits to what any organization can do. It is also necessary to encourage the greatest contribution from existing talent and to value them accordingly.

Factors affecting retention

Retention strategies should be based on an understanding of the factors that affect whether or not employees leave or stay. For early-career employees (30 years and under) career advancement is significant. For mid-career employees (age 31–50) the ability to manage their careers and satisfaction from their work are important. Late-career employees (over 50) will be interested in security. It is also the case that a younger workforce will change jobs and employers more often than an older workforce, and workforces with a lot of part-timers are less stable than those with predominately full-time staff. The other factors that affect retention are:

- company image;
- recruitment, selection and deployment;
- leadership – 'employees join companies and leave managers';
- learning opportunities;
- performance recognition and rewards.

A study by Holbeche (1998) of high flyers found that the factors that aided the retention and motivation of high performers included providing challenge and achievement opportunities (eg assignments), mentors, realistic self-assessment and feedback processes.

Basis of the retention strategy

A retention strategy takes into account the retention issues the organization is facing and sets out ways in which these issues can be dealt with. This may mean accepting the reality, as mentioned by Cappelli (2000), that the market, not the company will ultimately determine the movement of employees. Cappelli believes that it may be difficult to counter the pull of the market – 'you can't shield your people from attractive opportunities and aggressive recruiters'. He suggests that: 'The old goal of HR management – to minimize overall employee turnover

– needs to be replaced by a new goal: to influence who leaves and when.' This, as proposed by Bevan *et al* (1997), could be based on risk analysis to quantify the seriousness of losing key people or of key posts becoming vacant.

Risk of leaving analysis

Risk analysis can be carried out by initially identifying potential risk areas – the key people who may leave and for each of them, as individuals or groups:

1. Estimate the likelihood of this occurring.
2. Estimate how serious the effects of a loss would be on the business.
3. Estimate the ease with which a replacement could be made and the replacement costs.

Each of the estimates could be expressed on a scale, say: very high, high, medium, low, very low. An overview of the ratings under each heading could then indicate where action may need to be taken to retain key people or groups of people.

Analysis of reasons for leaving

Risk analysis provides specific information on areas for concern. Reasons for leaving can be amongst the following.

Possible reasons for leaving

- More pay.
- Better prospects (career move).
- More security.
- More opportunity to develop skills.
- Unable to cope with job.
- Better working conditions.
- Poor relationships with manager/team leader.
- Poor relationships with colleagues.
- Bullying or harassment.
- Personal – pregnancy, illness, moving away from area, etc.

Some indication of the reasons for leaving, and therefore where action needs to be taken, can be provided by exit interviews, but they are fallible. More reliance can be placed on the results of attitude or opinion surveys to identify any areas of dissatisfaction. The retention plan should propose actions that would focus on each of the areas in which lack of commitment and dissatisfaction can arise.

Areas for action

Depending on the outcome of the risk analysis and the overall assessment of reasons for leaving, the possible actions that can be taken are as follows.

Possible actions to deal with employee turnover problems

- Deal with uncompetitive, inequitable or unfair pay systems. But as Cappelli (2000) points out, there is a limit to the extent to which people can be bribed to stay.
- Design jobs to maximize skill variety, task significance, autonomy, control over work and feedback, and ensure that they provide opportunities for learning and growth. Some roles can be 'customized' to meet the needs of particular individuals.
- Develop commitment to the work (job engagement) not only through job design but also by organizing work around projects with which people can identify more readily than the company as a whole.
- Encourage the development of social ties within the company. In the words of Cappelli (2000), 'loyalty to companies may be disappearing but loyalty to colleagues is not'.
- Ensure that selection and promotion procedures match the capacities of individuals to the demands of the work they have to do. Rapid turnover can result simply from poor selection or promotion decisions.
- Reduce the losses of people who cannot adjust to their new job – the 'induction crisis' – by giving them proper training and support when they join the organization.
- Take steps to improve work–life balance by developing policies including flexible working that recognize the needs of employees outside work.
- Eliminate as far as possible unpleasant working conditions or the imposition of too much stress on employees.
- Select, brief and train managers and team leaders so that they appreciate the positive contribution they can make to improving retention by the ways in which they lead their teams. Bear in mind that people often leave their managers rather than their organization.
- Ensure that policies for controlling bullying and harassment exist and are applied.

Absence management

Absence management is the development and application of policies and procedures designed to reduce levels of absenteeism. The CIPD (2008c) report on absence management revealed that on average employers lose eight working days for each member of staff per year and average sickness absence costs employers £666 per employee per year. Something has to be done about it. This means understanding the causes of absence, and adopting comprehensive absence management (or more positively, attendance management) policies, measuring absence and implementing procedures for the management of short- and long-term absence.

Causes of absence

The causes of absence have been analysed by Huczynski and Fitzpatrick (1989) under three headings: job situation factors, personal factors and attendance factors.

Job situation factors

Job situation factors include:

- Job scope – a high degree of task repetitiveness is associated with absenteeism, although job satisfaction itself is a contributory rather than a primary cause of absence.
- Stress – it is estimated that 40 million working days are lost each year in the UK through stress. This can be attributed to work load, poor working conditions, shift work, role ambiguity or conflict, relationships and organizational climate.
- Frequent job transfers increase absenteeism.
- Management style – the quality of management, especially that of immediate supervisors, affects the level of absenteeism.
- Physical working conditions.
- Work group size – the larger the organization the higher the absence rate.

Personal factors

- Employee values – for some workers, doing less work for the same reward improves the deal made with the employer (the effort–reward bargain). The following positive outcomes of absence have been shown by research to be particularly important to employees: break from routine, leisure time, dealing with personal business and a break from co-workers.
- Age – younger employees are more frequently absent than older ones.
- Sex – women are more prone to sickness absence than men.

- Personality – some people are absence-prone (studies have noted that between 5 and 10 per cent of workers account for about half of the total absence, while a few are never absent at all).

Attendance factors

Attendance factors include:

- Reward systems – as pay increases attendance improves.
- Sick pay schemes may increase absenteeism.
- Work group norms can exert pressure for or against attendance.

Absence policies

Absence policies should cover:

- methods of measuring absence;
- setting targets for the level of absence;
- deciding on the level of short-term absence that would trigger action, possibly using the Bradford Factor, as explained below;
- the circumstances in which disciplinary action might be taken;
- what employees must do if they are unable to attend work;
- sick pay arrangements;
- provisions for the reduction and control of absence such as return-to-work interviews;
- other steps that can be taken to reduce absence such as flexible working patterns.

Recording and measuring absence

As a basis for action, absence levels need to be recorded so that they can be measured and monitored against targets for maintaining absence at a certain level or reducing absenteeism.

An HR information system (HRIS) can provide the best means of recording absenteeism. If a self-service approach is in place, managers and team leaders can have direct access to absence records showing the incidence of absenteeism (number and lengths of absence). These data can be consolidated for use by HR in compiling absence statistics and monitoring against targets.

The most common measurement is the percentage of time available that has been lost due to absence.

The Bradford Factor

Another increasingly popular measure is the so-called 'Bradford Factor'. This index identifies persistent short-term absence by measuring the number and duration of spells of absence. Its exact origin is a mystery, although IDS (2007b) believes that it has some connection with Bradford University's School of Management. It is calculated using the formula S × S × D = Bradford points score, where S is the number of occasions of absence in the last 52 weeks and D is the total number of days' absence in the last 52 weeks. Thus, for employees with a total of 14 days' absence in a 52 week period, the Bradford score can vary enormously depending on the number of occasions involved. For example:

> one absence of 14 days is 14 points, ie 1 × 1 × 14
>
> seven absences of two days each is 686 points, ie 7 ×7 × 14
>
> 14 absences of one day each is 2,744 points, ie 14 × 14 × 14

The Bradford index can be used as a trigger to initiate action. It is typically set at 250 points so that action would be triggered if, for example, there had been 10 days absence over five spells, or seven days over six spells.

Controlling short-term absence

Short-term absence can be controlled by the following actions.

Controlling short-term absence

- Return-to-work interviews conducted by line managers, which can identify problems at an early stage and provide an opportunity for a discussion on ways of reducing absence.
- Use of trigger mechanisms such as the Bradford Factor to review attendance.
- Invoking disciplinary procedures for unacceptable absence levels.
- Training line managers in methods of controlling absence, including return-to-work interviews.
- Extending the scope for flexible working.

Managing long-term absence

CIPD (2007c) research has shown that absence of eight days or more accounts for almost 40 per cent of the time lost through absence, and absence of four weeks or more accounts for about one-fifth. The best way to manage long-term absence is to keep in contact with employees by letter, telephone or visits to discuss the situation and, where possible, plan the return to work. This plan may include modified working hours or a modified role for a period.

Flexibility planning

Flexibility planning involves taking a radical look at traditional employment patterns. This means considering the scope for more flexible working based on multi-skilling, developing a 'flexible firm' by identifying and employing core and peripheral employees, including the use of sub-contracting and outsourcing, and introducing more flexible working arrangements including job sharing, homeworking and teleworking, flexible hours, and overtime and shift working. The aim of flexibility planning is to provide for greater operational flexibility, improve the utilization of employees' skills and capacities, increase productivity and reduce employment costs.

Multi-skilling

Multi-skilling takes place when workers acquire through experience and training a range of different skills they can apply when carrying out different tasks (multi-tasking). This means that they can be used flexibly, transferring from one task to another as the occasion demands. A multi-skilling strategy will involve providing people with a variety of experience, through, for example, job rotation and secondments, and making arrangements for them to acquire new skills through training. It typically includes setting up flexible work teams, the members of which can be deployed on all or many of the tasks the team is there to carry out. This can lead to the establishment of a flexible employee resourcing policy that enables the organization to redeploy people rapidly to meet new demands. This implies abandoning the traditional job description that rigidly prescribes the tasks to be carried out and replacing it with a role profile that indicates the range of knowledge and skills the role holder needs to possess to fulfil role expectations, which include flexible working.

Core and peripheral employees

The first step is to identify the 'core' of permanent employees who are essential to the conduct of the organization's business. The core may include managers, team leaders, professional staff, knowledge workers and technicians and other workers with relevant key skills. Employees in this core group need to be flexible and adaptable. The group may mainly consist of full-time workers but core workers could be part-time.

Having identified the core group, the next step is to make the peripheral arrangements. These can include the use of temporary workers and sub-contracting work to other firms. The numbers of temporary staff can be increased or reduced to match fluctuations in the level of business activity or to cover peaks. Outsourcing of activities such as recruitment, training and payroll administration can increase operational flexibility by allowing organizations easily to adjust the amount of work outsourced as situations change.

Job sharing

This is an arrangement whereby two employees share the work of one full-time position, dividing pay and benefits between them according to the time each works. Job sharing can involve splitting days or weeks or, less frequently, working alternate weeks. The advantages of job sharing include reduced employee turnover and absenteeism because it suits the needs of individuals. Greater continuity results because if one half of the job sharing team is ill or leaves, the sharer will continue working for at least half the time. Job sharing also means that a wider employment pool can be tapped for those who cannot work full time but want permanent employment. The disadvantages are the administrative costs involved and the risk of responsibility being divided.

Homeworking

Home-based employees can carry out such roles as consultants, analysts, designers or programmers, or undertake various kinds of administrative work. The advantages are flexibility to respond rapidly to fluctuations in demand, reduced overheads and lower employment costs if the homeworkers are self-employed (care, however, has to be taken to ensure that they are regarded as self-employed for income tax and national insurance purposes).

Teleworking

This involves people working at home with a terminal linked to the main company or networked with other outworkers. Its aim is to achieve greater flexibility, rapid access to skills and the retention of skilled employees who would otherwise be lost to the company. Teleworkers can be used in a number of functions such as marketing, finance and management services. The arrangement does, however, depend for its success on the involvement and education of all employees (full-time and teleworkers), the careful selection and training of teleworkers, allocating adequate resources to them and monitoring the operation of the system.

Flexible hours arrangements

Flexible hours arrangements can be included in the flexibility plan in one or more of the following ways:

- flexible daily hours – these may follow an agreed pattern day by day according to typical or expected workloads (eg flexitime systems);

- flexible weekly hours – providing for longer weekly hours to be worked at certain peak periods during the year;
- flexible daily and weekly hours – varying daily or weekly hours or a combination of both to match the input of hours to achieve the required output. Such working times, unlike daily or weekly arrangements, may fluctuate between a minimum and a maximum;
- compressed working weeks in which employees work fewer than the five standard days;
- annual hours – scheduling employee hours on the basis of the number of hours to be worked, with provisions for the increase or reduction of hours in any given period, according to the demand for goods or services.

Overtime and shift arrangements

A flexibility plan can contain proposals to reduce overtime costs by the use of flexible hours, new shift arrangements (eg twilight shifts), time off in lieu and overtime limitation agreements. The reduction of overtime is often catered for in formal productivity deals, which include a quid pro quo in the form of increased pay for the elimination of overtime payments and the introduction of flexible work patterns.

People resourcing practice – key learning points

Measuring employee turnover

It is necessary to measure employee turnover and calculate its costs in order to forecast future losses for planning purposes and to identify the reasons that people leave the organization. Plans can then be made to tackle the problems causing unnecessary turnover and to reduce costs. The methods available are: employee turnover index, half-life index, length of service analysis, stability index, and survival rate.

Estimating the cost of employee turnover

- Direct cost of recruiting replacements.
- Direct cost of introducing replacements.
- Direct cost of training replacements.
- Leaving costs.
- Opportunity cost of time spent by HR and line managers in recruitment, etc.
- Loss of output.

Retention planning

Retention strategies should be based on an understanding of the factors that affect whether or not employees leave or stay.

People resourcing practice – key learning points

Risk of leaving analysis

- More pay.
- Better prospects (career move).
- More security.
- More opportunity to develop skills.
- Unable to cope with job.
- Better working conditions.
- Poor relationships with manager/team leader.
- Poor relationships with colleagues.
- Bullying or harassment.
- Personal – pregnancy, illness, moving away from area, etc.

Absence policy areas

- Methods of measuring absence.
- Setting targets for the level of absence.
- Deciding on the level of short-term absence that would trigger action, possibly using the Bradford Factor.
- The circumstances in which disciplinary action might be taken.
- What employees must do if they are unable to attend work.
- Sick pay arrangements.
- Provisions for the reduction and control of absence such as return-to-work interviews.
- Other steps that can be taken to reduce absence such as flexible working patterns.

Flexibility planning

Flexibility planning involves taking a radical look at traditional employment patterns. This means:

- considering the scope for more flexible working based on multi-skilling.
- Developing a 'flexible firm' by identifying and employing core and peripheral employees, including the use of sub-contracting and outsourcing.
- Introducing more flexible working arrangements, including job sharing, homeworking and teleworking, flexible hours, and overtime and shift working.

Questions

1. From the chief executive to the HR director: 'What can we do to ensure that we are an employer of choice?'

Questions (continued)

2. From the personnel and development course tutor at your local further education college: 'I should be most grateful if you would give a brief talk (20 minutes or so) to our People Resourcing students on the issues relating to developing an employer value proposition and an employee brand.' Prepare an outline of the talk.
3. From your HR director: 'We have always measured employee turnover using the traditional labour turnover index. What are its advantages and disadvantages? Are there any better alternatives?'
4. From your managing director: 'I note from your last report that employee turnover is increasing. This must be costly. How can we estimate just what that cost is to provide a business case for corrective action?'
5. From the operations director: 'Our levels of absence are going through the roof. What can we do to ensure that our line managers keep it more under control?'

References

Bevan S, Barber, I and Robinson, D (1997) *Keeping the Best: A practical guide to retaining key employees*, Institute for Employment Studies, Brighton

Cappelli, P (2000) A market-driven approach to retaining talent, *Harvard Business Review*, January–February, pp 103–11

CIPD (2008a) *Survey of Recruitment, Retention and Turnover*, CIPD, London

CIPD (2008c) *Survey of Absence Management*, CIPD, London

Holbeche, L (1998) *Motivating People in Lean Organizations*, Butterworth-Heinemann, Oxford

Huczynski, A and Fitzpatrick, M J (1989) M*anaging Employee Absence for a Competitive Edge*, Pitman, London

IDS (2007b) Absence management, *HR Study 810*, IDS London

Phillips, J D (1990) The price tag of turnover, *Personnel Journal*, December, pp 58–61

Purcell, J, Kinnie, K, Hutchinson, S, Rayton, B and Swart, J (2003) *People and Performance: How people management impacts on organisational performance*, CIPD, London

Reed, A (2001) *Innovation in Human Resource Management*, CIPD, London

Walker, P (2007) Develop an effective employer brand, *People Management*, 18 October, pp 44–5

31

Recruitment and Selection

Key concepts and terms

- Biodata
- Person specification
- Recruitment process outsourcing (RPO)
- Selection
- Knowledge, skills and abilities (KSAs)
- Recruitment
- Role profile

Learning outcomes

On completing this chapter you should be able to define these key concepts. You should also know about:

- Defining requirements
- Analysing recruitment strengths and weaknesses
- Identifying sources of candidates
- Online recruitment
- Using recruitment consultants
- References and offers
- Recruitment planning
- Analysing the requirement
- Advertising
- Using agencies and job centres
- Selection methods

Introduction

Recruitment is the process of finding and engaging the people the organization needs. Selection is that part of the recruitment process concerned with deciding which applicants or candidates should be appointed to jobs.

The recruitment and selection process

The four stages of recruitment and selection are as follows.

Recruitment and selection stages

1. Defining requirements – preparing role profiles and person specifications; deciding terms and conditions of employment.
2. Planning recruitment campaigns.
3. Attracting candidates – reviewing and evaluating alternative sources of applicants, inside and outside the company: advertising, e-recruiting, agencies and consultants.
4. Selecting candidates – sifting applications, interviewing, testing, assessing candidates, assessment centres, offering employment, obtaining references; preparing contracts of employment.

Defining requirements

The number and categories of people required may be set out in formal human resource or workforce plans from which are derived detailed recruitment plans More typically, requirements are expressed in the form of ad hoc demands for people because of the creation of new posts, expansion into new activities or areas, or the need for a replacement. These short-term demands may put HR under pressure to deliver candidates quickly.

Requirements are set out in the form of job descriptions or role profiles and person specifications. These provide the information required to draft advertisements, post vacancies on the internet, brief agencies or recruitment consultants, and assess candidates by means of interviews and selection tests.

Role profiles for recruitment purposes

Role profiles, as described in Chapter 26, define the overall purpose of the role, its reporting relationships and the key result areas. They may also include a list of the competencies required. These will be technical competencies (knowledge and skills) and any specific behavioural competencies attached to the role. The latter would be selected from the organization's competency framework and modified as required to fit the demands made on role holders. For recruiting purposes, the profile is extended to include information on terms and conditions (pay, benefits and hours of work), special requirements such as mobility, travelling or unsocial hours, and learning, development and career opportunities. The recruitment role profile provides the basis for a person specification.

Person specification

A person specification, also known as a recruitment or job specification, defines the knowledge, skills and abilities (KSAs) required to carry out the role and the education, training, qualifications and experience needed to acquire the necessary KSAs. A person specification can be set out under the following headings:

Person specification headings

- Knowledge – what the individual needs to know to carry out the role.
- Skills and abilities – what the individual has to be able to do to carry out the role.
- Behavioural competencies – the types of behaviour required for successful performance of the role. These should be role-specific, ideally based on an analysis of employees who are carrying out their roles effectively. The behaviours should also be linked to the core values and competency framework of the organization to help in ensuring that candidates will fit and support the organization's culture. As reported by Purcell *et al* (2003), companies such as Selfridges take great care to develop specifications that define the behaviours required and to use selection techniques that provide for cultural fit between the individual and the organization.
- Qualifications and training – the professional, technical or academic qualifications required or the training that the candidate should have undertaken.
- Experience – the types of achievements and activities that would be likely to predict success.
- Specific demands – anything that the role holder will be expected to achieve in specified areas, eg develop new markets or products, improve sales, productivity or levels of customer service, introduce new systems or processes.
- Special requirements – travelling, unsocial hours, mobility, etc.

Alternatively, one or other of the traditional but well-tested classification schemes developed as the framework for interviews could be used.

Table 31.1 Person specification classification schemes

Seven-point plan (Rodger, 1952)	Five-fold grading scheme (Munro-Fraser, 1954)
1. *physical make-up* – health, physique, appearance, bearing and speech	1. *impact on others* – physical make-up, appearance, speech and manner
2. *attainments* – education, qualifications, experience	2. *acquired qualifications* – education, vocational training, work experience
3. *general intelligence* – fundamental intellectual capacity	3. *innate abilities* – natural quickness of comprehension and aptitude for learning
4. *special aptitudes* – mechanical, manual dexterity, facility in the use of words or figures	4. *motivation* – the kinds of goals set by the individual, his or her consistency and determination in following them up, and success in achieving them
5. *interests* – intellectual, practical, constructional, physically active, social, artistic	5. *adjustment* – emotional stability, ability to stand up to stress and ability to get on with people
6. *disposition* – acceptability, influence over others, steadiness, dependability, self-reliance	
7. *circumstances* – availability, mobility, etc	

The biggest danger to be avoided at this stage is that of overstating the requirements. Perhaps it is natural to go for the best, but setting an unrealistically high level for candidates increases the problems of attracting applicants and results in dissatisfaction among recruits when they find their talents are not being used. Understating requirements can, of course, be equally dangerous, but it happens less frequently.

The competencies defined in the role profile form a fundamental feature of the selection process which, rightly, becomes more of a person-based than a job-based approach. They are used as the basis for structured interviews (see Chapter 32) and provide guidance on which selection techniques such as psychological testing or assessment centres are most likely to be useful.

The advantages of a competency-based approach have been summarized by Wood and Payne (1998) as follows:

- it increases the accuracy of predictions about suitability;
- it facilitates a closer match between the person's attributes and the demands of the job;
- it helps to prevent interviewers making 'snap' judgements;
- it can underpin the whole range of recruitment techniques – application forms, interviews, tests and assessment centres.

An example of the key competencies parts of a person specification for an HR recruitment specialist is given in Figure 31.1.

1 *Knowledge of:*

- all aspects of recruitment
- sources of recruits
- different media for use in recruiting
- relevant test instruments (OPQ qualified)

2 *Skills in:*

- interviewing techniques
- test administration
- role analysis

3 *Behavioural competencies:*

- able to relate well to others and use interpersonal skills to achieve desired objectives
- able to influence the behaviour and decisions of people on matters concerning recruitment and other HR or individual issues
- able to cope with change, to be flexible and to handle uncertainty
- able to make sense of issues, identify and solve problems and 'think on one's feet'
- focus on achieving results
- able to maintain appropriately directed energy and stamina, to exercise self-control and to learn new behaviours
- able to communicate well, orally and on paper

Figure 31.1 Competency-based person specification for a recruitment specialist

Recruitment planning

A recruitment plan will cover:

- the number and types of employees required to cater for expansion or new developments and make up for any deficits;
- the likely sources of candidates;
- plans for tapping alternative sources;
- how the recruitment programme will be conducted.

Attracting candidates

The first step in attracting candidates is to analyse recruitment strengths and weaknesses. The outcome of this analysis can be used to develop an employee value proposition and employer brand.

Analyse recruitment strengths and weaknesses

Attracting candidates is primarily a matter of identifying, evaluating and using the most appropriate sources of applicants. However, in cases where difficulties in attracting or retaining candidates are being met or anticipated, it may be necessary to carry out a preliminary study of the factors that are likely to attract or repel candidates – the strengths and weakness of the organization as an employer. The study could make use of an attitude survey to obtain the views of existing employees.

The analysis of strengths and weaknesses should cover such matters as the national or local reputation of the organization, pay, employee benefits and working conditions, the intrinsic interest of the job, security of employment, opportunities for education and training, career prospects, and the location of the office or plant. These need to be compared with the competition so that a list of what are, in effect, selling points, can be drawn up as in a marketing exercise, in which the preferences of potential customers are compared with the features of the product so that those aspects that are likely to provide the most appeal to the customers can be emphasized. The analysis can show where the organization needs to improve as an employer if it is to attract more or better candidates and to retain those selected.

Candidates are, in a sense, selling themselves, but they are also buying what the organization has to offer. If, in the latter sense, the labour market is a buyer's market, then the company that is selling itself to candidates must study their wants and needs in relation to what it can provide. The study can be used to develop an employee value proposition and an employee brand incorporating the features set out above and described in Chapter 30. They can help in the preparation of a better image of the organization for use on corporate websites and in advertisements, brochures or interviews.

Analyse the requirement

First it is necessary to establish how many jobs have to be filled and by when. Then turn to an existing role profile and person specification or, if not available or out of date, draw up new ones that set out information on responsibilities and competency requirements. This information can be analysed to determine the required education, qualifications and experience.

The next step is to consider where suitable candidates are likely to come from; the companies, jobs or education establishments they are in; and the parts of the country where they can be found. Next, define the terms and conditions of the job (pay and benefits).

Finally, refer to the analysis of strengths and weaknesses to assess what is likely to attract good candidates to the job or the organization so the most can be made of these factors when advertising the vacancy or reaching potential applicants in other ways. Consider also what might put them off, for example the location of the job, so that objections can be anticipated. Analyse previous successes or failures to establish what does or does not work.

Identify sources of candidates

First, consideration should be given to internal candidates. It may also be worth trying to persuade former employees to return to the organization or obtain suggestions from existing employees (referrals). If these approaches do not work the main sources of candidates are advertising, online recruiting, agencies and job centres, consultants, recruitment process outsourcing providers and direct approaches to educational establishments.

The 2008 CIPD survey of recruitment, retention and turnover found that 78 per cent used recruitment agencies, 75 per cent used their own corporate website, 75 per cent used local newspaper advertisements and 62 per cent used specialist journals (CIPD, 2008a).

There is usually a choice between different methods or combinations of them. The criteria to use when making the choice are, 1) the likelihood that it will produce good candidates, 2) the speed with which the choice enables recruitment to be completed, and 3) the costs involved, bearing in mind that there may be direct advertising costs or consultants' fees.

Advertising

Advertising has traditionally been the most obvious method of attracting candidates and it is still important, although many organizations are outsourcing recruitment to agencies or consultants or using online recruitment, as was revealed in the CIPD (2008a) survey. A conventional advertisement will have the following aims.

Aims of an advertisement

- Generate candidates – attract a sufficient number of good candidates at minimum cost.
- Attract attention – it must compete for the attention of potential candidates against other employees.
- Create and maintain interest – it has to communicate in an attractive and interesting way information about the job, the company and the terms and conditions of employment.
- Stimulate action – the message needs to be conveyed in a way that will prompt a sufficient number of replies from candidates with the right qualifications for the job.

To achieve these aims, it is necessary to carry out the actions set out below.

Decide on whether or not to use an advertising agency

When planning a campaign or recruiting key people, there is much to be said for using an advertising agency. An agency can provide expertise in producing eye-catching headlines and writing good copy. It can devise an attractive house style that promotes the employer brand and prepare layouts that make the most of the text, the logo and any 'white space' round the advertisement. Moreover, it can advise on ways of achieving visual impact by the use of illustrations and special typographical features. Finally, an agency can advise on media, help in response analysis and take up the burden of preparing and placing advertisements.

The following steps should be taken when choosing an advertising agency:

- check its experience in handling recruitment advertising;
- see examples of its work;
- check with clients on the level of service provided;
- meet the staff who will work on the advertisements;
- check the fee structure;
- discuss methods of working.

Write the copy

A recruitment advertisement should start with a compelling headline and then contain information on the following.

Information in a recruitment advertisement

- The organization.
- The job.
- The person required – qualifications, experience, etc.
- The pay and benefits offered.
- The location.
- The action to be taken.

The headline is all important. The simplest and most obvious approach is to set out the job title in bold type. To gain attention, it is advisable to quote the rate of pay and key benefits such as a company car. Applicants are suspicious of clauses such as 'salary will be commensurate with age and experience' or 'salary negotiable'. This often means either that the salary is so low that the company is afraid to reveal it, or that pay policies are so incoherent that the company has no idea what to offer until someone tells them what he or she wants.

The name of the company should be given. Do not use box numbers – if you want to be anonymous, use a consultant. Add any selling points, such as growth or diversification, and any other areas of interest to potential candidates, such as career prospects. The essential features of the job should be conveyed by giving a brief description of what the job holder will do and, as far as space permits, the scope and scale of activities. Create interest in the job but do not oversell it.

The qualifications and experience required should be stated as factually as possible. There is no point in overstating requirements and seldom any point in specifying exactly how much experience is wanted. This will vary from candidate to candidate and the other details about the job and the rate of pay should provide them with enough information about the sort of experience required. Be careful about including a string of personal qualities such as drive, determination, and initiative. These have no real meaning to candidates. Phrases such as 'proven track record' and 'successful experience' are equally meaningless. No one will admit to not having either of them.

The advertisement should end with information on how the candidate should apply. 'Brief but comprehensive details' is a good phrase. Candidates can be asked to write or e-mail their response, but useful alternatives are to ask them to telephone or to come along for an informal chat at a suitable venue.

Remember the anti-discrimination legislation. The Sex Discrimination Act 1975 makes it unlawful to discriminate in an advertisement by favouring either sex, the only exceptions being a few jobs that can be done only by one sex. Advertisements must therefore avoid sexist job titles such as 'salesman' or 'stewardess'. They must use a neutral title such as 'sales representative', or amplify the description to cover both sexes by stating 'steward or stewardess'. It is accepted, however, that certain job titles are unisex and therefore non-discriminatory. These include director, manager, executive and officer. It is best to avoid any reference to the sex of the candidate by using neutral or unisex titles and referring only to the 'candidate' or the 'applicant'. Otherwise you must specify 'man or woman' or 'he or she'.

The Race Relations Act 1976 has similar provisions, making unlawful an advertisement that discriminates against any particular race. As long as race is never mentioned or even implied in an advertisement, you should have no problem in keeping within the law.

The Age Discrimination Regulations 2006 make it unlawful to discriminate against employees on account of their age. Age limits should therefore not be included in advertisements and the wording should not indicate that people below or above a certain age are not wanted.

Design the advertisement

The main types of advertisement are:

- Classified/run-on, in which copy is run on, with no white space in or around the advertisement and no paragraph spacing or indentation. They are cheap but suitable only for junior or routine jobs.
- Classified/semi-display, in which the headings can be set in capitals, paragraphs can be indented and white space is allowed round the advertisement. They are fairly cheap and semi-display can be much more effective than run-on advertisements.
- Full display, which are bordered and in which any typeface and illustrations can be used. They can be expensive but obviously make the most impact for managerial, technical and professional jobs.

Plan the media

An advertising agency can advise on the choice of media (press, radio, television) and its cost. *British Rates and Data (BRAD)* can be consulted to give the costs of advertising in particular media.

The so-called 'quality papers' are best for managerial and professional jobs. Local papers are best for recruiting sales and office staff and manual workers. Professional and trade journals can reach specialists directly, but results can be erratic and it may be advisable to use them to supplement a national campaign.

Avoid Saturdays and be cautious about repeating advertisements in the same medium. Diminishing returns can set in rapidly.

Evaluate the response

Measure response to provide guidance on the relative cost-effectiveness of different media. Cost per reply is the best ratio.

Online recruitment

Online or e-recruitment uses the internet to advertise or 'post' vacancies, provide information about jobs and the organization and enable e-mail communication to take place between employers and candidates. The latter can apply for jobs online and can e-mail application forms and their CVs to employers or agencies. Tests can be completed online.

Some organizations are using Web 2.0 technologies to search for recruits online through social networking sites such as Facebook and MySpace. Websites such as Linkedin, which provide personal profiles, can be consulted. Other organizations are providing 'blogs' from existing employees covering their experiences in working for the organization. The main types of online recruitment sites are corporate websites, commercial job boards and agency sites.

Corporate websites

These may simply list vacancies and contact details. A more elaborate approach would consist of a dedicated website area that gives details of vacancies, person specifications, benefits and how to apply for jobs by for example completing online application forms and tests. Such areas may be linked directly to an organization's home page so that general browsers can access them. An intranet link may be available to enable internal staff to access the website. Some organizations outsource the management of their website to recruitment consultants and specialized web agencies.

Commercial job boards

These are operated by specialized firms such as Monster.co.uk and Fish4jobs.com and consist of large databanks of vacancies. Companies pay to have their jobs listed on the sites. Information about vacancies may reproduce an advertisement so that the site is simply an additional form of communication. Alternatively, some vacancies are only found online. Links may be provided to the organization's website.

Agency sites

These are run by established recruitment agencies. Candidates register online but may be expected to discuss their details in person before they are forwarded to a prospective employer.

Advantages and disadvantages of online recruiting

The advantages of online recruiting are that it can reach a wider range of possible applicants, and it is quicker and cheaper than traditional methods of advertising. More details of jobs and firms can be supplied on the site and CVs can be matched and applications can be submitted electronically. The disadvantages are that it may produce too many irrelevant or poor applications and it is still not the first choice of many job seekers.

Making the best use of online recruiting

- Consider using it in conjunction with other recruitment methods to maximize response.
- Keep the content of the site up-to-date.

- Ensure the site is accessible directly or through search engines.
- Provide contact numbers for those with technical problems.
- Take care over the wording of online copy – the criteria for good copy in conventional advertisements apply.

Using agencies and job centres

Most private agencies deal with secretarial and office staff. They are usually quick and effective but quite expensive. Agencies can charge a fee of 15 per cent or more of the first year's salary for finding someone. It can be cheaper to advertise or use the internet, especially when the company is in a buyer's market. Shop around to find the agency that suits the organization's needs at a reasonable cost.

Agencies should be briefed carefully on what is wanted. They produce unsuitable candidates from time to time but the risk is reduced if they are clear about your requirements.

The job centres operated by the government are mainly useful for manual and clerical workers and sales or call centre assistants.

Using recruitment consultants

Recruitment consultants generally advertise, interview and produce a short-list. They provide expertise and reduce workload. The organization can be anonymous if it wishes. Most recruitment consultants charge a fee based on a percentage of the basic salary for the job, usually ranging from 15 to 20 per cent.

The following steps should be taken when choosing a recruitment consultant:

- check reputation with other users;
- look at the advertisements of the various firms to obtain an idea of the quality of a consultancy and the type and level of jobs with which it deals;
- check on special expertise;
- meet the consultant who will work on the assignment to assess his or her quality;
- compare fees, although the differences are likely to be small and the other considerations are usually more important.

When using recruitment consultants it is necessary to:

- agree terms of reference;
- brief them on the organization, where the job fits in, why the appointment is to be made, terms and conditions and any special requirements;
- give them every assistance in defining the job and the person specification, including any special demands that will be made of the successful candidate in the shape of what he or she will be expected to achieve – they will do much better if they have comprehensive knowledge of what is required and what type of person is most likely to fit well into the organization;
- check carefully the proposed programme and the draft text of the advertisement;
- clarify the arrangements for interviewing and short-listing;
- clarify the basis on which fees and expenses will be charged;
- ensure that arrangements are made to deal directly with the consultant who will handle the assignment.

Using executive search consultants

Use an executive search consultant, or 'head hunter' for senior jobs where there are only a limited number of suitable people and a direct lead to them is wanted. They are not cheap. Head hunters charge a fee of 30 to 50 per cent or so of the first year's salary, but they can be quite cost-effective.

Executive search consultants first approach their own contacts in the industry or profession concerned. The good ones have an extensive range of contacts and their own data bank. They will also have researchers who will identify suitable people who may fit the specification or can provide a lead to someone else who may be suitable. The more numerous the contacts, the better the executive search consultant.

When a number of potentially suitable and interested people have been assembled, a fairly relaxed and informal meeting takes place and the consultant forwards a short-list with full reports on candidates to the client.

There are some good and some not so good executive search consultants. Do not use one unless a reliable recommendation is obtained.

Recruitment process outsourcing

'Recruitment process outsourcing' (RPO) is the term used when an organization commissions a provider to take responsibility for the end-to-end delivery of the recruitment process covering all vacancies or a selection of them. This involves liaising with hiring managers to define requirements and specifications, deciding on the best ways to attract candidates, processing applications, and setting up and facilitating interviews. Some companies do not hand over all recruitment, using RPO only for high-volume vacancies and retaining responsibility for senior and specialist jobs.

The advantages of RPO are that it can save time, bring outside expertise to bear on recruitment problems and free up HR for more value-adding activities. The disadvantage is the perception by some HR people and line managers that the provider is too remote to deal with the real issues and that there is a danger of losing control.

Educational and training establishments

Many jobs can, of course, be filled by school leavers. For some organizations the major source of recruits for training schemes will be universities and training establishments, as well as schools. Graduate recruitment is a major annual exercise for some companies, which go to great efforts to produce glossy brochures, visit campuses on the 'milk run' and use elaborate sifting and selection procedures to vet candidates, including 'biodata' and assessment centres, as described later in this chapter.

Processing applications

When the vacancy or vacancies have been advertised and a fair number of replies received, the typical sequence of steps required to process applications is as follows:

1. List the applications on a control sheet setting out name, date application received and actions taken (reject, hold, interview, short-list, offer).
2. Send a standard acknowledgement letter to each applicant unless an instant decision can be made to interview or reject.
3. The applicant may be asked to complete and return an application form by post or by e-mail to supplement a letter or CV. This ensures that all applicants are considered on the same basis – it can be very difficult to plough through a pile of letters, often ill-written and badly organized. Even CVs may be difficult to sift although their quality is likely to be higher if the applicant has been receiving advice from an 'outplacement' consultant, ie one who specializes in finding people jobs. However, to save time, trouble, expense and irritation, many recruiters prefer to make a decision on the initial letter plus CV where it is quite clear that an applicant meets or does not meet the specification, rather than ask for a form. For more senior jobs it is generally advisable to ask for a CV.
4. Compare the applications with the key criteria in the person specification and sort them initially into three categories: possible, marginal and unsuitable.
5. Scrutinize the possibles again to draw up a short-list for interview. This scrutiny could be carried out by the HR or recruitment specialist, and the manager. The numbers on the

short-list should ideally be between four and eight. Fewer than four leaves relatively little choice (although such a limitation may be forced on you if an insufficient number of good applications have been received). More than eight will mean that too much time is spent on interviewing and there is a danger of diminishing returns setting in.

6. Draw up an interviewing programme. The time you should allow for the interview will vary according to the complexity of the job. For a fairly routine job, 30 minutes or so should suffice. For a more senior job, 60 minutes or more is required. It is best not to schedule too many interviews in a day – if you try to carry out more than five or six exacting interviews you will quickly run out of steam and do neither the interviewee nor your company any justice. It is advisable to leave about 15 minutes between interviews to write up notes and prepare for the next one.
7. Invite the candidates to interview, using a standard letter where large numbers are involved. At this stage, candidates should be asked to complete an application form, if they have not already done so. There is much to be said at this stage for sending candidates more details of the organization and the job so that you do not have to spend too much time going through this information at the interview.
8. Review the remaining possibles and marginals and decide if any are to be held in reserve. Send reserves a standard 'holding' letter and send the others a standard rejection letter. The latter should thank candidates for the interest shown and inform them briefly, but not too brusquely, that they have not been successful. A typical reject letter might read as follows:

   Since writing to you on... we have given careful consideration to your application for the above position. I regret to inform you, however, that we have decided not to ask you to attend for an interview. We should like to thank you for the interest you have shown.

Biodata

A highly structured method of sifting applications is provided by the use of biodata. These are items of biographical data that are criterion-based (ie they relate to established criteria in such terms as qualifications and experience that indicate that individuals are likely to be suitable). These are objectively scored and, by measurements of past achievements, predict future behaviour.

The items of biodata consist of demographic details (sex, age and family circumstances), education and professional qualifications, previous employment history and work experience, positions of responsibility outside work, leisure interests and career/job motivation. These items are weighted according to their relative importance as predictors, and a range of scores is allocated to each one. The biodata questionnaire (essentially a detailed application form) obtains information on each item, which is then scored.

Biodata are most useful when a large number of applicants are received for a limited number of posts. Cut-off scores can then be determined, based on previous experience. These scores would indicate who should be accepted for the next stage of the selection process and who should be rejected, but they would allow for some possible candidates to be held until the final cut-off score can be fixed after the first batch of applicants have been screened.

Biodata criteria and predictors are selected by job and functional analysis, which produces a list of competences. The validity of these items as predictors and the weighting to be given to them are established by analysing the biodata of existing employees who are grouped into high or low performers. Weights are allocated to items according to the discriminating power of the response.

Biodata questionnaires and scoring keys are usually developed for specific jobs in an organization. Their validity compares reasonably well with other selection instruments but they need to be developed and validated with great care and they are only applicable when large groups of applicants have to be screened.

Application forms

Application forms set out the information on a candidate in a standardized format. They provide a structured basis for drawing up short-lists, the interview itself and for the subsequent actions in offering an appointment and in setting up personnel records. An example of a form is given in Figure 31.2.

The following suggestions have been made by Pioro and Baum (2005) on how to use application forms more effectively:

- Decide what the criteria for selection are and how these will be assessed by use of the application form.
- Keep questions clear, relevant and non-discriminatory.
- Ask for only the bare minimum of personal details.
- Widen your pool of applicants by offering different options and guidance for completing and viewing application forms.

Selection methods

The aim of selection is to assess the suitability of candidates by predicting the extent to which they will be able to carry out a role successfully. It involves deciding on the degree to which the characteristics of applicants in terms of their competencies, experience, qualifications, education and training match the person specification. It also involves using this assessment to make a choice between candidates.

APPLICATION FORM

Surname:		First name:
Address:		
Tel: (home)	Tel: (work)	E-Mail: (personal)
Position applied for:		

Education

Dates		Name of secondary school, college or university	Main subjects taken	Qualifications
From	To			

Specialized training recieved

Other qualifications and skills (including languages, keyboard skills, current driving licence, etc)

Employment history
(give details of all positions held since completing full-time education; start with your present or most recent position and work back)

Dates		Name of employer, address and nature of business including any service in the armed forces	Position and summary of main duties	Starting and leaving rate of pay	Reasons for leaving or wanting to leave
From	To				

Add any coments you wish to make to support your application

I confirm that the information given on this application form is correct

Signature of applicant .... Date ....

Figure 31.2 Example of application form (compressed)

The so-called 'classic trio' of selection methods consists of application forms, interviews and references. But to these should be added selection tests and assessment centres. Application forms were described earlier and the various types of interviews and assessment centres are described below, as is the dubious technique of graphology. The use of references is considered in the next section of this chapter. Interviewing techniques and psychological tests are dealt with separately in Chapters 32 and 33.

Individual interviews

The individual interview is the most familiar method of selection. It involves face-to-face discussion and provides the best opportunity for the establishment of close contact – rapport – between the interviewer and the candidate. A structured interview, as described in Chapter 32, is one that is built around a set of predetermined questions that may be related to the competencies required as set out in the person specification or typical situations faced by holders of the role for which the candidate is being considered. If only one interviewer is used, there is more scope for a biased or superficial decision, and this is one reason for using a second interviewer or an interviewing panel.

Interviewing panels

Two or more people gathered together to interview one candidate may be described as an 'interviewing panel'. The most typical situation is that in which an HR specialist and line managers see the candidate at the same time. This has the advantage of enabling information to be shared and reducing overlaps. The interviewers can discuss their joint impressions of the candidate's behaviour at the interview and modify or enlarge any superficial judgements.

Selection boards or panels

Selection boards are more formal and, usually, larger interviewing panels convened because there are a number of parties interested in the selection decision. Their only advantage is that they enable a number of different people to have a look at the applicants and compare notes on the spot. The disadvantages are that the questions tend to be unplanned and delivered at random, the prejudices of a dominating member of the board can overwhelm the judgements of the other members, and the candidates are unable to do justice to themselves because they are seldom allowed to expand. Selection boards tend to favour the confident and articulate candidate, but in doing so they may miss the underlying weaknesses of a superficially impressive individual. They can also underestimate the qualities of those who happen to be less effective in front of a formidable board, although they would be fully competent in the less formal or less artificial situations that would face them in the job.

Assessment centres

Assessment centres assemble a group of candidates and use a range of assessment techniques over a concentrated period (one or two days) with the aim of providing a more comprehensive and balanced view of the suitability of individual members of the group.

Because an assessment centre gives the opportunity to observe actual behaviour in work-related situations, some 'reality' scenarios from the company may be used. Assessment centres are based on an understanding of the competencies they are trying to investigate and use systematic methods for measuring the degree to which each applicant fulfils them. The main characteristics of assessment centres are that:

- exercises are used to capture and simulate the key dimensions of the job. These may include one-to-one role-plays and group exercises; it is assumed that performance in these simulations predicts behaviour on the job;
- candidates are interviewed and tested;
- performance is measured in several dimensions in terms of the competencies required to achieve the target level of performance in a particular job or at a particular level in the organization;
- several candidates or participants are assessed together to allow interaction and to make the experience more open and participative;
- several trained assessors or observers are used to increase the objectivity of assessments.

Assessment centres provide opportunities for indicating the extent to which candidates match the culture of the organization. This will be established by observation of their behaviour in different but typical situations, and the range of the tests and structured interviews that are part of the proceedings. Assessment centres also give candidates a better feel for the organization and its values so that they can decide for themselves whether or not they are likely to fit.

The case for assessment centres is that they obtain much more information about candidates than conventional interviews, even when these are supplemented by tests. But research by Schmidt and Hunter (1998) has shown that, on their own, the ability of assessment centres to predict how well someone will perform (predictive validity) is lower than that of intelligence tests combined with structured interviews. Assessment centres are expensive and time-consuming and their use tends to be restricted to large organizations for managerial positions or for graduates.

Graphology

Graphology is a method of drawing conclusions from a candidate's handwriting about his or her personality as a basis for making predictions about future performance in a role. The use of graphology as a selection aid is extensive in France and some other European countries but uncommon in the UK. A number of validity studies have shown that it is a very poor predictor of job performance. Schmidt and Hunter (1998) analysed a number of research projects on the effectiveness of graphology and concluded that whatever limited information about personality or job performance there is in handwriting samples comes from the content and not the characteristics of the handwriting. Variations in handwriting are caused by genetic differences between individuals in fine motor coordination of the finger muscles, not their personality.

Choice of selection methods

There is a choice to be made between the selection methods. The most important criterion is the predictive validity of the method or combination of methods as measured by its predictive validity coefficient – perfect validity is 1.0; no validity is 0.0.

The meta-analysis of the validity of different selection methods conducted by Schmidt and Hunter (1998), which covered 85 years of research findings, produced the following predictive validity coefficients:

Intelligence tests and structured interviews	.63
Intelligence tests and unstructured interviews	.55
Assessment centres and structured interviews	.53
Intelligence tests only	.51
Structured interviews only	.51
Unstructured interviews only	.38
Assessment centres only	.37
Graphology only	.02

Robertson and Smith (2001) added personality assessments to this list, with a validity coefficient of .37

Schmidt and Hunter (1998) established that the reason why intelligence (general mental ability or GMA) is such a good predictor of job performance is because 'more intelligent people acquire job knowledge more rapidly and acquire more of it and it is this knowledge of how to perform the job that causes their job performance to be higher'. Their research clearly indicates that the combination of structured interviews (as described in Chapter 32) and intelligence tests is the most effective in terms of predictive validity.

Dealing with recruitment problems

Every experienced HR professional who is responsible for recruitment and selection will occasionally come across a vacancy that is particularly difficult to fill. In this situation any compromise that involves appointing someone who does not meet the specification must be avoided. To deal with the problem constructively it is necessary to take the following actions.

Dealing with recruitment problems

- Ensure that all the possible sources of candidates have been used.
- Consider any ways in which the advertisement or website entry could be made more attractive.
- Check that the person specification is realistic – that the requirements have not been overstated.
- Consider whether it might be necessary to improve the package offered to candidates – check market rates to ensure that the level of pay and benefits are competitive.
- In discussion with the line manager, examine the possibility of reshaping the role to increase its attractiveness.
- If the worst comes to the worst, and again in discussion with the manager, consider alternative ways of carrying out the work involved with existing staff.

References and offers

After the interviewing and testing procedure has been completed, a provisional decision to make an offer by telephone or in writing can be made. This is normally 'subject to satisfactory references' and the candidate should, of course, be told that these will be taken up. If there is more than one eligible candidate for a job it may be advisable to hold one or two people in reserve. Applicants often withdraw, especially those whose only purpose in applying for the job was to carry out a 'test marketing' operation, or to obtain a lever with which to persuade their present employers to value them more highly.

Checking applications

It is a sad fact that applicants all too often misinform their prospective employers about their education, qualifications and employment record. This was confirmed by a survey carried out by the CIPD (2008a), which found that 25 per cent of employers had to withdraw their offers because applicants had lied or misrepresented their application. It is always advisable to check with universities, professional institutes and previous employers that the facts given by applicants are correct. Other checks can be made such as:

- interview questions about actual (not hypothetical) experiences, with deep probing to ascertain the extent of the individual's personal involvement, decision making and contribution;

- detailed application forms with open-ended questions about specific learning related to the skills, knowledge and competencies required for the vacancies under consideration;
- occupational health screening;
- identity check;
- electoral register check;
- credit reference agency check (especially appropriate for positions in the financial services sector);
- confirmation of previous employment with HM Revenue & Customs or through the Department of Work & Pensions;
- Criminal Records Bureau check;
- Companies House check (for directors); and
- fraud prevention check, including Cifas staff fraud database check (to prevent an employer unwittingly employing people previously dismissed for fraud somewhere else). Cifas is a not-for-profit fraud prevention service.

References

The main purpose of a reference is to obtain in confidence factual information about a prospective employee. This information is straightforward and essential. It is simply necessary to confirm the nature of the previous job, the period of time in employment, the reason for leaving (if relevant), the salary or rate of pay and, possibly, the attendance record.

Opinions about character, competence, performance and suitability are unreliable. Referees are reluctant to commit themselves and they are not in any position to assess suitability – only the prospective employer can do that. Personal referees are, of course, entirely useless. All they prove is that the applicant has at least one or two friends.

A written request for a reference could simply ask the precious employer to confirm the candidate's employment record. More precise answers may be obtained if a standard form is provided for the employer to complete. The questions asked on this form should be limited to the following:

- What was the period of employment?
- What was the job title?
- What work was carried out?
- What was the rate of pay or salary?

- How many days absence over the last 12 months?
- Would you re-employ (if not, why not)?

The last question is important, if it is answered honestly or at all.

Telephone references may save time and may be more reliable. They can be used as an alternative or in addition to written references. Ask factual questions only and keep a record of the conversation.

References – legal aspects

The key legal points that should be considered when asking for or giving references are:

- Once the decision has been made to make an offer, the letter should state that 'this is a provisional offer subject to the receipt of satisfactory references'.
- It has been generally held that there is no common law duty on an employer to provide references for a serving or past employee unless there is a term to that effect in the employment contract. But it has been ruled *(Spring v. Guardian Assurance 1994)* that there might be a moral duty to provide a reference where it is 'natural practice' to require a reference from a previous employer before offering employment, and where the employee could not expect to enter that type of employment without a reference.
- If a reference contains a false or unsubstantiated statement that damages the reputation of the individual, action for damages may result.
- It is possible to succeed in a claim for damages if it can be shown that the reference provided was negligent because reasonable care had not been taken in preparing it, which includes ensuring that it is factually correct.

Confirming the offer

The final stage in the selection procedure is to confirm the offer of employment after satisfactory references have been obtained, and the applicant has passed the medical examination required for pension and life assurance purposes or because a certain standard of physical fitness is required for the work. The contract of employment should also be prepared at this stage.

Contracts of employment

The basic information that should be included in a written contract of employment varies according to the level of the job.

Follow-up

It is essential to follow up newly engaged employees to ensure that they have settled in and to check on how well they are doing. If there are any problems it is much better to identify them at an early stage rather than allowing them to fester.

Following up is also important as a means of checking on the selection procedure. If by any chance a mistake has been made, it is useful to find out how it happened so that the procedure can be improved. Misfits can be attributed to a number of causes, for example inadequate person specification, poor sourcing of candidates, weak advertising, poor interviewing techniques, inappropriate or invalidated tests, or prejudice on the part of the selector.

Recruitment and selection – key learning points

Defining requirements

Requirements are set out in the form of job descriptions or role profiles and person specifications. These provide the information required to draft advertisements, post vacancies on the internet, brief agencies or recruitment consultants and assess candidates by means of interviews and selection tests.

Recruitment planning

A recruitment plan will cover:

- the number and types of employees required to cater for expansion or new developments and make up for any deficits;
- the likely sources of candidates;
- plans for tapping alternative sources;
- how the recruitment programme will be conducted.

Analysing recruitment strengths and weaknesses

The analysis should cover such matters as the national or local reputation of the organization, pay, employee benefits and working conditions, the intrinsic interest of the job, security of employment, opportunities for education and training, career prospects, and the location of the office or plant.

Analysing the requirement

- Establish how many jobs have to be filled and by when.
- Set out information on responsibilities and competency requirements.
- Consider where suitable candidates are likely to come from.
- Define the terms and conditions of the job (pay and benefits).
- Consider what is likely to attract good candidates.

Identifying sources of candidates

Initially, consideration should be given to internal candidates. An attempt can be made to persuade former employees to return to the organization or obtain suggestions from existing employees

Recruitment and selection – key learning points (continued)

(referrals). If these approaches do not work, the main sources of candidates are advertising, online recruiting, agencies and job centres, consultants, recruitment process outsourcing providers and direct approaches to educational establishments.

Advertising

Advertising has traditionally been the most obvious method of attracting candidates and it is still important, although many organizations are outsourcing recruitment to agencies or consultants or using online recruitment. The information in a recruitment advertisement should include:

- the organization;
- the job;
- the person required – qualifications, experience, etc;
- the pay and benefits offered;
- the location;
- the action to be taken.

Online recruitment

Online or e-recruitment uses the internet to advertise or 'post' vacancies, provide information about jobs and the organization and enable e-mail communication to take place between employers and candidates. The latter can apply for jobs online and can e-mail application forms and their CVs to employers or agencies. Tests can be completed online.

Using agencies and job centres

Agencies should be briefed carefully on what is wanted. They produce unsuitable candidates from time to time but the risk is reduced if they are clear about your requirements. The job centres operated by the government are mainly useful for manual and clerical workers and sales or call centre assistants.

Using recruitment consultants

Recruitment consultants generally advertise, interview and produce a short-list. They provide expertise and reduce workload.

Selection methods

The aim is to assess the suitability of candidates by predicting the extent to which they will be able to carry out a role successfully. It involves deciding on the degree to which the characteristics of applicants match the person specification and using this assessment to make a choice between candidates.

References and offers

After the interviewing and testing procedure has been completed, a provisional decision to make an offer by telephone or in writing can be made. This is normally 'subject to satisfactory references'. It is essential to check the information provided by candidates on qualifications and their work experience.

Questions

1. What is the difference between recruitment and selection?
2. What are the three 'classic' methods of recruitment and selection and what other approaches are available?
3. From the customer services director: 'We are proposing to open a new call centre on Wearside. We need 50 call centre operators and five supervisors by the end of the year and we want to expand to 200 operators and 18 supervisors by the following year. How do you propose that we should do this?'
4. From the HR director: 'Can you let me have any research evidence that indicates what the most successful approach to recruiting graduates, or combination of approaches, is likely to be?'
5. From the HR director: 'What are the advantages and disadvantages of internet recruiting?'
6. From the HR director: 'I have read that the amount of CV fraud is considerable and rising. What can we do to combat this?'

References

CIPD (2008a) *Survey of Recruitment, Retention and Turnover*, CIPD, London

Munro-Fraser, J (1954) *A Handbook of Employment Interviewing*, Macdonald and Evans, London

Pioro, I and Baum, N (2005) How to design better job application forms, *People Management*, 16 June, pp 42–3

Purcell, J, Kinnie, K, Hutchinson, S, Rayton, B and Swart, J (2003) *People and Performance: How people management impacts on organisational performance*, CIPD, London

Robertson, I T and Smith, M (2001) Personnel selection, *Journal of Occupational and Organizational Psychology*, **74** (4), pp 441–72

Rodger, A (1952) *The Seven-point Plan*, National Institute of Industrial Psychology, London

Schmidt, F L and Hunter, J E (1998) The validity and utility of selection methods in personnel psychology: practical and theoretical implications of 85 years of research findings, *Psychological Bulletin*, **124** (2), pp 262–74

Wood, R and Payne, T (1998) *Competency-based Recruitment and Selection*, Wiley, Chichester

32 Selection Interviewing

Key concepts and terms

- Behavioural-based interview
- Halo effect
- Situational-based interview
- Biographical interview
- Horns effect
- Structured interview

Learning outcomes

On completing this chapter you should be able to define these key concepts. You should also know about:

- The purpose of an interview
- The nature of an interview
- Interviewing arrangements
- Interviewing techniques – starting and finishing
- Selection interviewing skills
- The basis of an interview
- Advantages and disadvantages of interviews
- Planning the interview – structuring and timing
- Interviewing techniques – asking questions
- Coming to a conclusion

Introduction

The interview forms a major part of what is sometimes called the 'classic trio' of selection techniques, the other two being the application form and references (although the latter mainly serve to confirm factual information – they cannot be used reliably to influence choice). Further evidence may be obtained from psychological tests, as described in Chapter 33.

Interviews are an inevitable part of most if not all selection procedures but they are not always reliable as a means of predicting success in a job. They are difficult to do well – a considerable amount of knowledge of the techniques of interviewing and the skills required to apply them is needed. Interviewers need to know what they are looking for and how to set about finding it. They need to plan their interviews in advance, structure them accordingly and record their analyses of candidates against a set of assessment criteria that will have been spelt out in a person specification.

Purpose

The purpose of selection interviews is to obtain and assess information about candidates that will enable a valid prediction to be made of their future performance in the job for which they are being considered in comparison with the predictions made for other candidates. They aim to answer the following fundamental questions.

Selection interviews – three fundamental questions

1. Can candidates do the job – are they competent?
2. Will candidates do the job – are they well-motivated?
3. How will individuals fit into the organization?

The basis of an interview – the person specification

Interviewing involves processing and evaluating evidence about the capabilities of a candidate in relation to a person specification. This might be set out under the following headings, as described in Chapter 31:

- Knowledge – what the individual needs to know to carry out the role.
- Skills and abilities – what the individual has to be able to do to carry out the role.

- Behavioural competencies – the types of behaviour required for successful performance of the role.
- Qualifications and training – the professional, technical or academic qualifications required or the training that the candidate should have undertaken.
- Experience – the types of achievements and activities that would be likely to predict success.
- Specific demands – anything that the role holder will be expected to achieve in specified areas, eg develop new markets or products, improve sales, productivity or levels of customer service, introduce new systems or processes.
- Special requirements – travelling, unsocial hours, mobility, etc.

Alternatively, the headings used in the seven-point plan or fivefold grading scheme could be used; these were also given in Chapter 31, in Table 31.1.

The nature of an interview – obtaining the information

Interviews aim to obtain the information required to decide on the extent to which candidates fit a person specification for the job. Some of the evidence will be in the CV and application form, but interviews supplement these data with the more detailed or specific information about experience and personal characteristics that is obtained in a face-to-face meeting. Such a meeting enables judgements to be made by the interviewer on whether the candidate will 'fit' the organization, and by both parties as to how they would get on together. Although these judgements are entirely subjective and are often biased or prejudiced, they will be made.

An interview can be described as a conversation with a purpose. It is a conversation because candidates should be induced to talk freely with their interviewers about themselves, their experience and their careers. But the conversation has to be planned, directed and controlled to achieve the main purpose of the interview, which is to make an accurate assessment of the candidate's suitability for a job.

Interviews can be either structured to a greater or lesser degree, or unstructured. A structured interview is one built around a set of predetermined questions that may be related to the typical situations faced by holders of the role for which the candidate is being considered, or the competencies required as contained in the person specification. An unstructured interview is one that has not been planned by reference to predetermined questions although it may have a sort of structure in the shape of the sequence of areas covered, for example a biographical interview that simply goes progressively through a candidate's education, training and experience.

Interviews focus on experience and personal characteristics to assess the extent to which candidates fit the person specification. They also provide a means of conveying information about the job and the organization.

Experience

Interviews provide an opportunity to establish the extent to which the experience of candidates is useful and relevant. It is necessary to pin people down to obtain explicit statements about what they have been doing and what knowledge and skills they have acquired. Candidates naturally want to present themselves well and this can lead to exaggerated claims about their achievements. Answers to probing questions about what they have done, with examples, must be obtained. Vague statements must not be tolerated.

The extent to which the careers of candidates have progressed smoothly, the reasons for moves between jobs and employers, and any gaps in work experience need to be explored. Redundancy should not be a problem – it can happen to anyone, although if it keeps on happening the interviewer may be tempted to speculate that this is more than just bad luck. Similarly with dismissal, if this comes out. One or perhaps even two dismissals may be understandable if they are attributable to poor performance. But a sequence of them is unacceptable and alarm bells begin to ring if a dismissal was for gross misconduct (although this is unlikely to be revealed, which is where references can be helpful). If candidates have a career history of 'job hopping' (short periods in a number of jobs) it is necessary to find out why. There may be a good explanation when, for example, the candidate has been working on limited-term contracts, but it may indicate instability or consistent failure.

Personal characteristics

Selection interviews provide an opportunity to assess personal characteristics. But impressions, especially first impressions, can make a huge and sometimes misleading impact, although they can be important in jobs where impressing other people is important, eg sales representatives. Intelligence and personality tests can be used to provide more objective information, if they are valid and reliable. Situational and behavioural-based questions in structured interviews, as described later, are also helpful.

Interests and activities outside work

Questions about interests and activities can be useful when interviewing candidates from schools or further and higher education establishments who have had little work experience. They have much less relevance for more experienced candidates although they may give some indication of how well people are motivated if they pursue them actively.

Advantages and disadvantages of interviews

Table 32.1 Advantages and disadvantages of interviews

Advantages of interviews as a method of selection	Disadvantages of interviews as a method of selection
• Provide opportunities for interviewers to ask probing questions about the candidate's experience and to explore the extent to which the candidate's competencies match those specified for the job • Enable interviewers to describe the job (a 'realistic job preview') and the organization in more detail, providing some indication of the terms of the psychological contract • Provide opportunities for candidates to ask questions about the job and to clarify issues concerning training, career prospects, the organization and terms and conditions of employment • Enable a face-to-face encounter to take place so that the interviewer can make an assessment of how the candidate would fit into the organization and what they would be like to work with • Give the candidate the same opportunity to assess the organization, the interviewer and the job	• Can lack validity as a means of making sound predictions of performance, and lack reliability in the sense of measuring the same things for different candidates • Rely on the skill of the interviewer – many people are poor at interviewing, although most think that they are good at it • Do not necessarily assess competence in meeting the demands of the particular job • Can lead to biased and subjective judgements by interviewers

Disadvantages can be alleviated if not entirely removed by, first, using a structured approach that focuses on the competencies required for successful performance and, secondly, by training interviewers. The use of another opinion or opinions can also help to reduce bias, especially if the same structured approach is adopted by all the interviewers. Finally, selection tests, especially those measuring intelligence or general ability, can provide valuable information that supplements the interview (see Chapter 33).

Interviewing arrangements

The interviewing arrangements will depend partly on the procedure being used, which may consist of individual interviews, an interviewing panel, a selection board or some form of assessment centre. In most cases, however, the arrangements for the interviews should conform broadly to the following pattern:

- The candidate who has applied in writing, by e-mail or telephone should be told where and when to come and who to ask for. The interview time should be arranged to fit in with the time it will take to get to the company. It may be necessary to adjust times for those who cannot get away during working hours. If the company is difficult to find, a map should be sent with details of public transport. The receptionist or security officer should be told who is coming. Candidates are impressed to find that they are expected.
- Applicants should have somewhere quiet and comfortable in which to wait for the interview, with reading material available and access to cloakroom facilities.
- The interviewers or interviewing panel should have been well briefed on the programme. Interviewing rooms should have been booked and arrangements made, as necessary, for welcoming candidates, for escorting them to interviews, for meals and for a conducted tour round the company.
- Comfortable private rooms should be provided for interviews with little, if any, distractions around them. Interviewers should preferably not sit behind their desks, as this creates a psychological barrier.
- During the interview or interviews, some time, but not too much, should be allowed to tell candidates about the company and the job and to discuss with them conditions of employment. Negotiations about pay and other benefits may take place after a provisional offer has been made, but it is as well to prepare the ground during the interviewing stage.
- Candidates should be told what the next step will be at the end of the interview. They may be asked at this stage if they have any objections to references being taken up.
- Follow-up studies should be carried out of the performance of successful candidates in their jobs compared with the prediction made at the selection stage. These studies should be used to validate the selection procedure and to check on the capabilities of interviewers.

Briefing interviewers

When making arrangements for an interview it is essential that the people who are going to conduct the interview are properly briefed on the job and the procedures they should use.

Training in interviewing techniques should be an automatic part of the training programmes for managers and team leaders.

It is particularly important that everyone is fully aware of the provisions of the sex, race and disability discrimination Acts and the Age Discrimination Regulations. It is essential that any form of prejudiced behaviour or any prejudiced judgements are eliminated completely from the interview or the subsequent evaluation of the candidate. Even the faintest hint of a sexist, racist or ageist remark must be totally avoided. When recording a decision following an interview it is also essential to spell out the reasons why someone was rejected, making it clear that this was on the grounds of their ability to do the job and not because of their sex, race, disability or age.

Ethical considerations

Another important consideration in planning and executing a recruitment programme is to behave ethically towards candidates. They have the right to be treated with consideration and this includes acknowledging replies, informing them of the outcome of their application without undue delay and responding promptly to requests for information on why they have been turned down.

Planning the interview programme

It is best to leave some time, say 15 minutes, between interviews to allow for comments to be made. There is a limit to how many interviews can be conducted in a day without running out of steam. Holding more than six demanding interviews of, say, one hour each in a day is unwise. Even with less demanding half-hour interviews it is preferable to limit the number to eight or so in a day.

The main dos and don'ts of selection interviews are shown in Table 32.2.

Preparation

Careful preparation is essential and this means a thorough study of the person specification and the candidate's application form and/or CV. It is necessary at this stage to identify those features of the applicant that do not fully match the specification so that these can be probed more deeply during the interview. It can be assumed that the candidate is only being considered because there is a reasonable match, but it is most unlikely that this match will be perfect. It is also necessary to establish if there are any gaps in the job history or items that require further explanation, and to answer the following questions.

Preparing for an interview – four questions

1. What are the criteria to be used in selecting the candidate? These may be classified as essential or desirable and will refer to the knowledge, skill and competency requirements and the experience, qualifications and training that will satisfy those requirements as set out in the person specification.
2. What more do I need to find out at the interview to ensure that the candidate meets the essential selection criteria?
3. What further information do I need to obtain at the interview to ensure that I have an accurate picture of how well the candidate meets the criteria?
4. How am I going to structure the interview in terms of the questions I need to ask and the sequence in which these questions are covered? These may be quite detailed if a highly structured approach is being adopted, as described below. It is essential to probe during an interview to establish what the candidate really can do and has achieved.

Planning an interview

An interview can be divided into the five parts set out below.

The five parts of an interview

1. The welcome and introductory remarks.
2. The major part concerned with obtaining information about the candidate to assess against the person specification.
3. The provision of information to candidates about the organization and the job.
4. Answering questions from the candidate.
5. Closing the interview with an indication of the next step.

Better results will be obtained if the interview is planned using one of the approaches described below or a combination of them. It is also necessary to plan how much time should be taken.

Types of interviews

The basic types of interviews are:

1. Biographical interviews, which either start at the beginning (education) and go on sequentially to the end (the current or last job or the most recent educational experience) or do this in reverse order, ie starting with the current or most recent job and working backwards.
2. Structured interviews built around a set of predetermined questions that may be related to the competencies required as contained in the person specification (structured behavioural-based interviews), or typical situations faced by holders of the role for which the candidate is being considered (structured situational-based interviews) or the headings in the person specification framework.
3. Person specification-based interviews, which are planned to obtain information under each of the headings in the person specification.

1. The biographical interview

The traditional way of structuring an interview is the biographical approach. Many interviewers prefer to proceed in reverse chronological order with experienced candidates, spending most time on the present or recent jobs, giving progressively less attention to the more distant experience, and only touching on education lightly.

There is no one best sequence to follow. What is important is to decide in advance which approach to adopt. It is also important to get the balance right. You should concentrate most on recent experience and not dwell too much on the past. You should allow time not only for candidates to talk about their careers but also to ask probing questions about their experience. You should certainly not spend too much time at the beginning of the interview talking about the company and the job. It is desirable to issue that information in advance to save interview time and to encourage the candidate to ask questions at the end of the interview (the quality of the questions can indicate something about the quality of the candidate).

A biographical approach is logical and provides some element of structure to the interview but it will not produce the desired information unless interviewers are absolutely clear about what they are looking for and are prepared with questions that will elicit the data they need to make a prediction and a selection decision. This means conducting a structured interview as described below in the full sense in which that term is used, ie an interview that is based on situational-based or behavioural-based questions, focusing on one or other or both.

2. Structured behavioural-based interviews

In a behavioural-based interview (sometimes referred to as a 'criterion-referenced interview') the interviewer poses questions or asks for descriptions of how the candidate behaved in particular situations – how he or she dealt with them and how well that behaviour worked. The behaviour is aligned to a behavioural competency that has been defined as a requirement in the person specification. The aim is to collect evidence about how people behave in typical situations on the grounds that such evidence is the best predictor of future behaviour as long as the criteria fit the specified demands of the job.

A list of points to be covered can be drawn up in advance to cover the key competencies set out in the person specification. The following are examples of behavioural questions that might be posed to a candidate for a recruitment adviser post.

Behavioural questions that might be posed to a candidate for a recruitment adviser post

- Can you tell me about any occasion when you have persuaded your fellow team members to do something that at first they didn't really want to do?
- Do people come to you to help solve problems? If so, tell me about a problem you have solved recently.
- Tell me about a time when you used previous experience to solve a problem new to you.
- Tell me about any occasion when you successfully persuaded a line manager to agree to a course of action (eg the use of a particular medium) or to accept a recommendation (eg on a candidate to be short listed).
- Have you ever had to deal with a candidate who has complained bitterly about the selection procedure? If not, how would you deal with such a situation if it did arise?
- Have you ever been in the position when you have been told to do something differently and you were uncomfortable about it? If so, how did you deal with it? If not, what approach would you adopt?
- Tell me about any time when you had to deal with a large influx of requests for recruitment services from line managers. How did you cope? Or if this has not been your experience, how do you think you would try to cope?
- Have you ever felt under tremendous pressure to achieve a result? If so, how did you deal with it?
- Have you ever made a presentation to a group of colleagues or people outside your organization? If so, what approach did you adopt and how well did it work?
- What sorts of achievements give you the greatest satisfaction at work?

Behavioural-based interviews can provide a clear and relevant framework. But preparing for them takes time and interviewers need to be trained in the technique. A fully behavioural or criterion-referenced structure is probably most appropriate for jobs that have to be filled frequently, but even with one-off jobs, the technique of having a set of competency-referenced questions to ask that will be applied consistently to all candidates will improve the reliability of the prediction.

3. Structured situational-based interviews

In a situational-based interview (sometimes described as a 'critical-incident interview') the focus is on a number of situations or incidents in which behaviour can be regarded as being indicative of subsequent performance. Situational-based questions ask candidates how they would handle a hypothetical situation that resembles one they may encounter in the job. For example, sales assistants might be asked how they would respond to rudeness from a customer. Situational questions can provide some insight into how applicants might deal with particular job demands and have the advantage of being work-related. They can also provide candidates with some insight into the sort of problems they might meet in the job. But, because they are hypothetical and can necessarily only cover a limited number of areas, they cannot be relied on by themselves. They could indicate that candidates understand how they might handle one type of situation in theory but not that they would be able to handle similar or other situations in practice. Follow-up questions are needed to explore the response in more detail, thus gaining a better understanding of how candidates might tackle similar problems. The following is an example of a situational-based set of questions to be posed to a candidate for a recruitment adviser post.

Situational-based questions to be posed to a candidate for a recruitment adviser post

- What would you do if you felt that none of the applicants quite met the specification, although one came fairly close?
- How would you deal with a line manager who you believed was significantly overstating the qualifications and experience required for a job?
- What would you say to a candidate if there was an unexplained gap in his or her employment record?
- A line manager has chosen a candidate who you think is clearly unsuitable. What do you do?
- What do you do in a situation where it has not been possible to find a suitable candidate?

- A senior line manager has suggested that you should rely entirely on online recruiting for managers and professional staff and abandon conventional advertising. How do you respond?
- A manager tells you that he thinks a candidate is too old for the job. How do you respond?
- A colleague has suggested that it would be a good idea to check out short-listed candidates on Facebook or MySpace. How would you react to this idea?
- A candidate responds to your questions with monosyllabic answers. How would you draw him or her out?
- You are interviewing someone for a sales assistant post. She does not make a very good impression, being rather hesitant and lacking in confidence, but her track record in sales is good. What do you do?

Structuring within the person specification framework

Person specifications should be set out under a number of standard headings, examples of which were given earlier in this chapter (page 541–42). An interview can be structured to obtain the information needed under each of those headings. Questions are drawn up in advance to elicit this information. These may be specific questions about experience, qualifications, education and training, or behavioural or situational-based questions as described above. The aim is to ensure that when an assessment of the candidate under these headings is made after the interview, all that needs to be known to make a reliable assessment is available.

Choice of approach

The more the interview can be structured by the use of situational- or behavioural-based questions or within a person specification framework the better. Both situational- and behavioural-based questions can be deployed usefully and, as the above examples show, the distinction between them is sometimes small.

In practice, a mix of approaches can be used as long as this is deliberate and planned. A biographical sequence can be used as a framework and questions on different aspects of the person specification can be injected at appropriate moments. These could be specific questions about experience, qualifications and training. Additionally, situational- or behavioural-based questions could be added to obtain a fuller picture of the candidate. Three or four of each of them could be decided in advance and these could be introduced gradually as the occasion arises when discussing the candidate's experience in relation to the requirements of the job.

The alternative is to go through job experience chronologically to establish what the candidate can do and then produce the questions. The latter approach has the merit of ensuring that there are no diversions from the analysis of experience.

Timing the interview

The length of time allowed for an interview will be related to the seniority and complexity of the job. For relatively routine jobs, 20 to 30 minutes may suffice. For more demanding jobs, up to an hour but no more may be necessary.

The bulk of the time – at least 80 per cent – should be allocated to obtaining information from the candidate. The introduction and conclusion should be brief. Preparation involves deciding on the type of interview to be used.

Interview techniques – starting and finishing

You should start interviews by putting candidates at their ease. You want them to provide you with information and they are not going to talk freely and openly if they are given a cool reception.

In the closing stages of the interview candidates should be asked if they have anything they wish to add in support of their application. They should also be given the opportunity to ask questions. At the end of the interview the candidate should be thanked and given information about the next stage. If some time is likely to elapse before a decision is made the candidate should be informed accordingly so as not to be left on tenterhooks. It is normally better not to announce the final decision during the interview. It may be advisable to obtain references and, in any case, time is required to reflect on the information received.

Interviewing techniques – asking questions

As mentioned earlier, an interview is a conversation with a purpose. The interviewee should be encouraged to do most of the talking – one of the besetting sins of poor interviewers is that they talk too much. The interviewer's job is to draw the candidate out at the same time ensuring that the information required is obtained. To this end it is desirable to ask a number of open-ended questions – questions that cannot be answered by yes or no and which promote a full response. But a good interviewer will have an armoury of other types of questions to be asked as appropriate, as described below.

Open questions

Open questions are phrased generally and give no indication of the expected reply; they cannot be answered by yes or no. They encourage candidates to talk, drawing them out and obtaining a full response. Single-word answers are seldom illuminating. It is a good idea to begin the interview with some open questions to obtain a general picture of candidates, thus helping them to settle in. Open questions or phrases inviting a response can be phrased as follows.

Open questions or phrases inviting a response

- I'd like you to tell me about the sort of work you are doing in your present job.
- What do you know about...?
- Could you give me some examples of...?
- In what ways do you think your experience fits you to do the job for which you have applied?
- How have you tackled...?
- What have been the most challenging aspects of your job?
- Please tell me about some of the interesting things you have been doing at work recently.

Open questions can give you a lot of useful information but you may not get exactly what you want, and answers can go into too much detail. For example, the question, 'What has been the main feature of your work in recent months?' may result in a one-word reply – 'marketing', or it may produce a lengthy explanation that takes up too much time. Replies to open questions can get bogged down in too much detail, or miss out some key points. They can come to a sudden halt or lose their way. You need to ensure that you get all the facts, keep the flow going and maintain control. Remember that you are in charge. Hence the value of probing, closed and the other types of questions, which are discussed below.

Probing questions

Probing questions ask for further details and explanations to ensure that you are getting all the facts. You ask them when answers have been too generalized or when you suspect that there may be some more relevant information that candidates have not disclosed. A candidate may claim to have done something and it may be useful to find out more about exactly what contribution was made. Poor interviewers tend to let general and uninformative answers pass by without probing for further details, simply because they are sticking rigidly to a predetermined list of open questions. Skilled interviewers are able to flex their approach to ensure they get the facts while still keeping control to ensure that the interview is completed on time.

A candidate could say to you something like: 'I was involved in a major exercise that produced significant improvements in the flow of work through the factory.' This statement conveys nothing about what the candidate actually did. You have to ask probing questions, such as the examples below.

Probing questions

- You've informed me that you have had experience in... Could you tell me more about what you did?
- What sort of targets or standards have you been expected to achieve?
- How successful have you been in achieving those targets or standards? Please give examples.
- Could you give an example of any project you have undertaken?
- What was your precise role in this project?
- What exactly was the contribution you made to its success?
- What knowledge and skills were you able to apply to the project?
- Were you responsible for monitoring progress?
- Did you prepare the final recommendations in full or in part? If in part, which part?
- Could you describe in more detail the equipment you used?

Closed questions

Closed questions aim to clarify a point of fact. The expected reply will be an explicit single word or brief sentence. In a sense, a closed question acts as a probe but produces a succinct factual statement without going into detail. When you ask a closed question you intend to find out:

- What the candidate has or has not done – 'What did you do then?'
- Why something took place – 'Why did that happen?'
- When something took place – 'When did that happen?'
- How something happened – 'How did that situation arise?'
- Where something happened – 'Where were you at the time?'
- Who took part – 'Who else was involved?'

Hypothetical questions

Hypothetical questions are used in structured situational-based interviews when a situation is described to candidates and they are asked how they would respond. Hypothetical questions can be prepared in advance to test how candidates would approach a typical problem. Such questions may be phrased: 'What do you think you would do if...?' When such questions lie well within the candidate's expertise and experience the answers can be illuminating. But it could be unfair to ask candidates to say how they would deal with a problem without knowing more about the context in which the problem arose. It can also be argued that what candidates say they would do and what they actually do could be quite different. Hypothetical questions can produce hypothetical answers. The best data upon which judgements about candidates can be judged are what they have actually done or achieved. You need to find out if they have successfully dealt with the sort of issues and problems they may be faced with if they join your organization.

Behavioural event questions

Behavioural event questions as used in behavioural-based structured interviews aim to get candidates to tell you how they would behave in situations that have been identified as critical to successful job performance. The assumption upon which such questions are based is that past behaviour in dealing with or reacting to events is the best predictor of future behaviour.

The following are some typical behavioural event questions:

- Could you give an instance when you persuaded others to take an unusual course of action?
- Could you describe an occasion when you completed a project or task in the face of great difficulties?
- Could you describe any contribution you have made as a member of a team in achieving an unusually successful result?
- Could you give an instance when you took the lead in a difficult situation in getting something worthwhile done?

Capability questions

Capability questions aim to establish what candidates know, the skills they possess and use and their competencies – what they are capable of doing. They can be open, probing or closed but they will always be focused as precisely as possible on the contents of the person specification, referring to knowledge, skills and competences. Capability questions are used in behavioural-based structured interviews.

Capability questions should therefore be explicit – focused on what candidates must know and be able to do. Their purpose is to obtain evidence from candidates that show the extent to which they meet the specification in each of its key areas. Because time is always limited it is best to concentrate on the most important aspects of the work and it is always best to prepare the questions in advance. The sort of capability questions you can ask are set out below.

Capability questions

- What do you know about…?
- How did you gain this knowledge?
- What are the key skills you are expected to use in your work?
- How would your present employer rate the level of skill you have reached in…?
- Could you please tell me exactly what sort and how much experience you have had in…?
- Could you tell me more about what you have actually been doing in this aspect of your work?
- Can you give me any examples of the sort of work you have done that would qualify you to do this job?
- What are the most typical problems you have to deal with?
- Would you tell me about any instances when you have had to deal with an unexpected problem or a crisis?

Questions about motivation

The degree to which candidates are motivated is a personal quality to which it is necessary to give special attention if it is to be properly assessed. This is usually achieved by inference rather than direct questions. 'How well are you motivated?' is a leading question that will usually produce the response: 'Highly'. You can make inferences about the level of motivation of candidates by asking questions on the following subjects.

Subjects for motivation questions

- Their career – replies to such questions as: 'Why did you decide to move on from there?' can give an indication of the extent to which they have been well-motivated in progressing their career.
- Achievements – not just 'What did you achieve?' but 'How did you achieve it?' and 'What difficulties did you overcome?'
- Triumphing over disadvantages – candidates who have done well in spite of an unpromising upbringing and relatively poor education may be more highly motivated than those with all the advantages that upbringing and education can bestow, but who have not made good use of these advantages.
- Spare time interests – don't accept at its face value a reply to a question about spare time interests which, for example, reveals that a candidate collects stamps. Find out if the candidate is well-motivated enough to pursue the interest with determination and to achieve something in the process. Expressing interest in jazz is not evidence of motivation. Knowing all about Kansas City jazz, especially the contribution made by Lester Young to the Count Basie Orchestra, and publishing articles in the jazz music press on the subject is at least an example of pursuing an interest vigorously, which is evidence of motivation.

Continuity questions

Continuity questions aim to keep the flow going in an interview and encourage candidates to enlarge on what they have told you, within limits. Here are some examples of continuity questions.

Continuity questions

- 'What happened next?
- 'What did you do then?'
- 'Can we talk about your next job?'
- 'Can we move on now to…?'
- 'Could you tell me more about…?'

It has been said that to keep the conversation going during an interview the best thing an interviewer can do is to make encouraging grunts at appropriate moments. There is more to interviewing than that, but single words or phrases like 'good', 'fine', 'that's interesting', 'carry on' can help things along.

Play-back questions

Play-back questions test your understanding of what candidates have said by putting to them a statement of what it appears they have told you, and asking them if they agree or disagree with your version. For example, you could say: 'As I understand it, you resigned from your last position because you disagreed with your boss on a number of fundamental issues – have I got that right?' The answer might simply be 'Yes' to this closed question, in which case you might probe to find out more about what happened. Or the candidate may reply 'Not exactly' in which case you ask for the full story.

Career questions

As mentioned earlier, questions about the career history of candidates can provide some insight into motivation as well as establishing how they have progressed in acquiring useful and relevant knowledge, skills and experience. You can ask questions such as those given below.

Career questions

- What did you learn from that new job?
- What different skills had you to use when you were promoted?
- Why did you leave that job?
- What happened after you left that job?
- In what ways do you think this job will advance your career?

Focused work questions

These are questions designed to tell you more about particular aspects of the candidate's work history, such as those shown below.

Focused work questions

- How many days absence from work did you have last year?
- How many times were you late last year?
- Have you been absent from work for any medical reason not shown on your application form?
- Do you have a clean driving licence (for those whose work will involve driving)?

Unhelpful questions

Unhelpful questions

- Multiple questions such as, 'What skills do you use most frequently in your job? Are they technical skills, leadership skills, team working skills or communicating skills?' will only confuse candidates. You will probably get a partial or misleading reply. Ask only one question at a time.
- Leading questions that indicate the reply you expect are also unhelpful. If you ask a question such as: 'That's what you think, isn't it?' you will get the reply: 'Yes, I do.' If you ask a question such as: 'I take it that you don't really believe that…?' you will get the reply: 'No, I don't.' Neither of these replies will get you anywhere.

Questions to be avoided

Avoid any questions such as those given below that could be construed as being biased on the grounds of sex, race, disability or age.

Don't ask

- Who is going to look after the children?
- Are you planning to have any more children?
- Are you concerned at all about racial prejudice?

- Would it worry you being the only immigrant around here?
- With your disability, do you think you can cope with the job?
- Do you think that at your time of life you will be able to learn the new skills associated with this job?

Useful questions

Ten useful questions

1. What are the most important aspects of your present job?
2. What do you think have been your most notable achievements in your career to date?
3. What sort of problems have you successfully solved recently in your job?
4. What have you learnt from your present job?
5. What has been your experience in…?
6. What do you know about…?
7. What particularly interests you in this job and why?
8. Now you have heard more about the job, would you please tell me which aspects of your experience are most relevant?
9. What do you think you can bring to this job?
10. Is there anything else about your career that hasn't come out yet in this interview but you think I ought to hear?

Selection interviewing skills

The key interviewing skills are establishing rapport, listening, maintaining continuity, keeping control and note taking.

Establishing rapport

Establishing rapport means establishing a good relationship with candidates – getting on their wavelength, putting them at ease, encouraging them to respond and generally being friendly. This is not just a question of being 'nice' to candidates. If you achieve rapport you are more likely to get them to talk freely about both their strengths and weaknesses.

Good rapport is created by the way in which you greet candidates, how you start the interview and how you put your questions and respond to replies. Questions should not be posed aggressively or imply that you are criticizing some aspect of the candidate's career. Some people like the idea of 'stress' interviews but they are counterproductive. Candidates clam up and gain a negative impression of you and the organization.

When responding to answers you should be appreciative, not critical: 'Thank you, that was very helpful; now can we go on to...?' not 'Well, that didn't show you in a good light, did it?'

Body language can also be important. If you maintain natural eye contact, avoid slumping in your seat, nod and make encouraging comments when appropriate, you will establish better rapport and get more out of the interview.

Listening

If an interview is a conversation with a purpose, as it should be, listening skills are important. You need not only to hear but also to understand what candidates are saying. When interviewing you must concentrate on what candidates are telling you. Summarizing at regular intervals forces you to listen because you have to pay attention to what they have been saying in order to get the gist of their replies. If you play back to candidates your understanding of what they have told you for them to confirm or amend, it will ensure that you have fully comprehended the messages they are delivering.

Maintaining continuity

So far as possible link your questions to a candidate's last reply so that the interview progresses logically and a cumulative set of data is built up. You can put bridging questions to candidates such as: 'Thank you, that was an interesting summary of what you have been doing in this aspect of your work. Now, could you tell me something about your other key responsibilities?'

Keeping control

You want candidates to talk, but not too much. When preparing for the interview you should have drawn up an agenda and you must try to stick to it. Don't cut candidates short too brutally but say something like: 'Thank you, I've got a good picture of that, now what about...?'

Focus on specifics as much as you can. If candidates ramble on a bit, use a pointed question (a 'probe' question) that asks for an example illustrating the particular aspect of their work that you are considering.

Note taking

You won't remember everything that candidates tell you. It is useful to take notes of the key points they make, discreetly, but not surreptitiously. However, don't put candidates off by frowning or tut-tutting when you are making a negative note. It may be helpful to ask candidates if they would mind if you take notes. They can't really object but will appreciate the fact that they have been asked.

Coming to a conclusion

It is essential not to be beguiled by a pleasant, articulate and confident interviewee who is all surface without substance. Beware of the 'halo' effect that occurs when one or two good points are seized upon, leading to the neglect of negative indicators. The opposite 'horns' effect of focusing on the negatives should also be avoided.

Individual candidates should be assessed against the criteria. These could be set under the headings of knowledge and skills, competencies, education, qualifications, training, experience and overall suitability. Ratings can be given against each heading, for example: very acceptable, acceptable, marginally acceptable, and unacceptable. If you have used situational- or behavioural-based questions you can indicate against each question whether the reply was good, just acceptable or poor. These assessments can inform your overall assessment of knowledge, skills and competencies.

Next, compare your assessment of each of the candidates against one another. You can then make a conclusion on those preferred by reference to their assessments under each heading.

In the end, your decision between qualified candidates may well be judgmental. There may be one outstanding candidate but quite often there are two or three. In these circumstances you have to come to a balanced view on which one is more likely to fit the job and the organization and have potential for a long-term career, if this is possible. Don't, however, settle for second best in desperation. It is better to try again.

Remember to make and keep notes of the reasons for your choice and why candidates have been rejected. These together with the applications should be kept for at least six months just in case your decision is challenged as being discriminatory. An example of an interview rating form is given in Figure 32.1.

	very acceptable	acceptable	marginally acceptable	unacceptable	comments
knowledge and skills					
competencies					
education and qualifications					
training					
experience					
overall suitability					

Figure 32.1 Example of an interview rating form

Table 32.2 Dos and don'ts of selection interviewing

Do	Don't
• Plan the interview • Give yourself sufficient time • Use a structured interview approach wherever possible • Create the right atmosphere • Establish an easy and informal relationship – start with open questions • Encourage the candidate to talk • Cover the ground as planned, ensuring that you complete a prepared agenda and maintain continuity • Analyse the candidate's career to reveal strengths, weaknesses and patterns of interest • Ask clear, unambiguous questions • Get examples and instances of the successful application of knowledge and skills and the effective use of capabilities	• Start the interview unprepared • Plunge too quickly into demanding (probe) questions • Ask multiple or leading questions • Pay too much attention to isolated strengths or weaknesses • Allow candidates to gloss over important facts • Talk too much or allow candidates to ramble on • Allow your prejudices to get the better of your capacity to make objective judgements • Fall into the halo or horns effect trap • Ask questions or make remarks that could be construed as in any way discriminatory • Attempt too many interviews in a row

Table 32.2 *continued*

Do	Don't
• Make judgements on the basis of the factual information you have obtained about candidates' experience and attributes in relation to the person specification • Keep control over the content and timing of the interview	

Selection interviewing – key learning points

The purpose of an interview

The purpose of selection interviews is to obtain and assess information about candidates that will enable a valid prediction to be made of their future performance in the job for which they are being considered in comparison with the predictions made for other candidates.

The nature of an interview

Interviewing involves processing and evaluating evidence about the capabilities of a candidate in relation to a person specification. An interview can be described as a conversation with a purpose.

Interviewing arrangements

The interviewing arrangements will depend partly on the procedure being used, which may consist of individual interviews, an interviewing panel, a selection board or some form of assessment centre.

Preparing for the interview

Careful preparation is essential and this means a careful study of the person specification and the candidate's application form and/or CV. It is necessary at this stage to identify those features of the applicant that do not fully match the specification so that these can be probed more deeply during the interview.

Structuring the interview

The five parts are:

1. The welcome and introductory remarks.
2. The major part concerned with obtaining information about the candidate to assess against the person specification.
3. The provision of information to candidates about the organization and the job.
4. Answering questions from the candidate.

Selection interviewing – key learning points (continued)

5. Closing the interview with an indication of the next step.

Types of interviews

Biographical, structured situational-based interviews, structured behavioural-based interviews, person specification framework interviews.

Timing the interview

The length of time allowed for an interview will be related to the seniority and complexity of the job. For relatively routine jobs, 20 to 30 minutes may suffice. For more demanding jobs up to an hour but no more may be necessary.

Interviewing techniques – starting and finishing

Start by putting candidates at their ease. You want them to provide you with information and they are not going to talk freely and openly if they are given a cool reception. In the closing stages of the interview candidates should be asked if they have anything they wish to add in support of their application. They should also be given the opportunity to ask questions. At the end of the interview the candidate should be thanked and given information about the next stage.

Interviewing techniques – asking questions

The interviewer's job is to draw the candidate out, at the same time ensuring that the information required is obtained. To this end it is desirable to ask a number of open-ended questions – questions that cannot be answered by yes or no and that promote a full response. But a good interviewer will have an armoury of other types of questions to be asked as appropriate, ie probing, closed, hypothetical, behavioural event, motivation, playback, continuation, career and focused work questions.

Selection interviewing skills

The key interviewing skills are establishing rapport, listening, maintaining continuity, keeping control and note taking.

Coming to a conclusion

Candidates should be assessed against the criteria. These could be set under the headings of knowledge and skills, competencies, education, qualifications, training, experience and overall suitability.

Questions

1. From a line manager: 'I have heard that the use of structured interviews when selecting people is the most effective method. What are they exactly and how should I use them?'
2. From a fellow member of your CIPD branch: 'It's been decided here that line managers will shortly take more personal responsibility for staff selection. We want to ensure that they do not say things that could lead to claims of discrimination by applicants. Please summarize for me the major dos and don'ts we should warn our managers about.'
3. From a line manager: 'I have heard that it is a good idea to test candidates by asking them hypothetical questions that ask them to say what they would do in a given situation. What are the arguments for and against this?'

33 Selection Tests

Key concepts and terms

- Ability test
- Criterion score
- Intelligence test
- Normal curve
- Personality test
- Psychometric test
- Trait
- Aptitude test
- Intelligence quotient (IQ)
- Norm
- Personality
- Psychological test
- Selection test

Learning outcomes

On completing this chapter you should be able to define these key concepts. You should also know about:

- The types of tests
- Test validity
- Choosing tests
- The characteristics of a good test
- Interpreting test results
- Using tests in a selection procedure

Introduction

Selection tests are used to provide valid and reliable evidence of levels of abilities, intelligence, personality characteristics, aptitudes and attainments. They typically supplement the information obtained from an interview.

Selection tests can be divided into two broad categories: measures of typical performance such as personality inventories that do not have right or wrong answers, and measures of maximum performance that measure how well people can do things, how much they know and the level of their ability, and ask questions for which there are right or wrong or good or bad answers. The latter category can focus on what people are capable of knowing or doing (ability tests) or what they actually know or can do (aptitude or attainment tests).

In this chapter, a distinction is made between psychological or psychometric tests, which measure or assess intelligence or personality, and aptitude tests, which are occupational or job-related tests that assess the extent to which people can do the work. These are dealt with in the first two sections of this chapter. Before using any type of test it is necessary to be aware of the characteristics of a good test and methods of interpreting test results, and these considerations are examined in the following two sections. The chapter concludes with sections dealing with choosing tests, using them in a selection procedure and guidelines on their use.

Psychological tests

Psychological tests use systematic and standardized procedures to measure differences in individual characteristics such as intelligence and personality. They enable selectors to gain a greater understanding of candidates to help in predicting the extent to which they will be successful in a job. Psychological tests are measuring instruments, which is why they are often referred to as psychometric tests. 'Psychometric' literally means mental measurement. For selection purposes, the main types of tests are those used for measuring intelligence and ability and those concerned with assessing personality characteristics.

Intelligence tests

Intelligence tests measure a range of mental abilities which enable a person to succeed at a variety of intellectual tasks using the faculties of abstract thinking and reasoning. They are concerned with general intelligence (termed 'g' by Spearman, 1927, one of the pioneers of intelligence testing) and are sometimes called 'general mental ability' (GMA) tests. Intelligence tests measure abilities while cognitive tests measure an individual's learning in a specific subject area. The meta-analysis conducted by Schmidt and Hunter (1998) showed that intelligence tests had high predictive validity. In fact, when combined with a structured interview, they had the highest predictive value of all the methods of selection they studied.

Intelligence tests contain questions, problems and tasks. The outcome of a test can be expressed as a score that can be compared with the scores of members of the population as a whole or the population of the whole or part of the organization using the test (norms).

The outcome of an intelligence test may sometimes be recorded as an intelligence quotient (IQ), which is the ratio of an individual's mental age to the individual's actual age as measured by an intelligence test. When the mental and actual age correspond, the IQ is100. Scores above 100 indicate that the individual's level of average is above the norm for his or her age, and vice versa. It is usual now for IQs to be directly computed as an IQ test score. It is assumed that intelligence is distributed normally throughout the population; that is, the frequency distribution of intelligence corresponds with the normal curve shown in Figure 33.1.

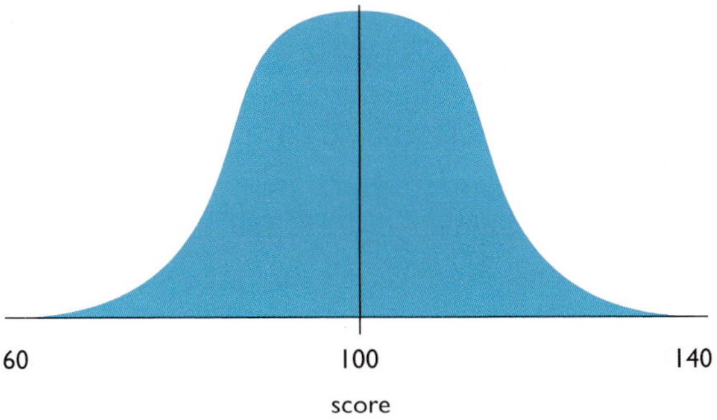

Figure 33.1 A normal curve

The normal curve describes the relationship between a set of observations and measures and the frequency of their occurrence. It indicates that for characteristics such as intelligence that can be measured on a scale, a few people will produce extremely high or low scores and there will be a large proportion of people in the middle. Its most important characteristic is that it is symmetrical – there are an equal number of cases on either side of the mean, the central axis. The normal curve is a way of expressing how scores will typically be distributed; for example, that 60 per cent of the population are likely to get scores between x and y, 20 per cent are likely to get scores below x and 20 per cent are likely to get more than y.

Intelligence tests can be administered to a single individual or to a group. They can also be completed online.

Ability tests

Ability tests establish what people are capable of knowing or doing. Although the term can refer primarily to reasoning ability, the British Psychological Society (2007) refers to ability tests as measuring the capacity for:

- verbal reasoning – the ability to comprehend, interpret and draw conclusions from oral or written language;
- numerical reasoning – the ability to comprehend, interpret and draw conclusions from numerical information;
- spatial reasoning – the ability to understand and interpret spatial relations between objects;
- mechanical reasoning – understanding of everyday physical laws such as force and leverage.

Personality tests

Personality tests attempt to assess the personality of candidates in order to make predictions about their likely behaviour in a role. Personality is an all-embracing and imprecise term that refers to the behaviour of individuals and the way it is organized and coordinated when they interact with the environment. There are many different theories of personality and, consequently, many different types of personality tests. These include self-report personality questionnaires and other questionnaires that measure interests, values or work behaviour.

One of the most generally accepted ways of classifying personality is the five-factor model, which defines the following 'big five' key personality characteristics.

The 'big five' personality characteristics

1. Extraversion/introversion – gregarious, outgoing, assertive, talkative and active (extraversion); or reserved, inward-looking, diffident, quiet, restrained (introversion).
2. Emotional stability – resilient, independent, confident, relaxed; or apprehensive, dependent, under-confident, tense.
3. Agreeableness – courteous, cooperative, likeable, tolerant; or rude, uncooperative, hostile, intolerant.
4. Conscientiousness – hard-working, persevering, careful, reliable; or lazy, dilettante, careless, expedient.
5. Openness to experience – curious, imaginative, willingness to learn, broad-minded; or blinkered, unimaginative, complacent, narrow-minded.

As noted by Schmidt and Hunter (1998), integrity and conscientiousness tests have fairly high predictive validity (0.41 and 0.31 respectively).

Self-report personality questionnaires are commonly used. They usually adopt a 'trait' approach, defining a trait as a fairly independent but enduring characteristic of behaviour that all people display but to differing degrees. Trait theorists identify examples of common behaviour, devise scales to measure these, and then obtain ratings on these behaviours by people who know each other well. These observations are analysed statistically, using the factor analysis technique to identify distinct traits and to indicate how associated groups of traits might be grouped loosely into 'personality types'.

'Interest' questionnaires are sometimes used to supplement personality tests. They assess the preferences of respondents for particular types of occupation and are therefore most applicable to vocational guidance but can be helpful when selecting apprentices and trainees.

'Value' questionnaires attempt to assess beliefs about what is 'desirable or good' or what is 'undesirable or bad'. The questionnaires measure the relative prominence of such values as conformity, independence, achievement, decisiveness, orderliness and goal-orientation.

Personality tests can provide interesting supplementary information about candidates that is free from the biased reactions that frequently occur in face-to-face interviews, but they have to be used with great care. The tests should have been developed by a reputable psychologist or test agency on the basis of extensive research and field testing and they must meet the specific needs of the user. Advice should be sought from a member of the British Psychological Society on what tests are likely to be appropriate.

Aptitude tests

Aptitude tests are job-specific tests designed to predict the potential an individual has to perform tasks within a job. They typically take the form of work sample tests, which replicate an important aspect of the actual work the candidate will have to do, such as using a keyboard or carrying out a skilled task such as repair work. Work sample tests can be used only with applicants who are already familiar with the task through experience or training.

Aptitude tests should be properly validated. This will be the case if a test or a 'test battery' (an associated group of tests) has been obtained from a reputable test agency. Alternatively, a special test can be devised by or for the organization to determine the aptitudes required by means of job and skills analysis. The test is then given to employees already working on the job and the results compared with a criterion, usually managers' or team leaders' ratings. If the correlation between test and criterion is sufficiently high, the test is then given to applicants. To validate the test further, a follow-up study of the job performance of the applicants selected by the test is usually carried out. This is a lengthy procedure, but without it no real confidence can be attached to the results of any aptitude test. Properly validated work sample tests have a high level of predictive validity (0.54 according to Schmidt and Hunter, 1998). The operative words are 'properly validated' – many do-it-yourself tests are worse than useless because this has not happened.

Characteristics of a good test

A good test is one that provides valid data which enable reliable predictions of behaviour or performance to be made and therefore assists in the process of making objective and reasoned decisions when selecting people for jobs. It will be based on research that has produced standardized criteria derived by using the same measure to test a number of representative people to produce a set of 'norms' for comparison purposes. The test should be capable of being objectively scored by reference to the normal or average performance of the group.

The characteristics of a good test

- It is a sensitive measuring instrument that discriminates well between subjects.
- It has been standardized on a representative and sizeable sample of the population for which it is intended so that any individual's score can be interpreted in relation to that of others.
- It is reliable in the sense that it always measures the same thing. A test aimed at measuring a particular characteristic, such as intelligence, should measure the same characteristic when applied to different people at the same or a different time or to the same person at different times.
- It is valid in the sense that it measures the characteristic the test is intended to measure. Thus, an intelligence test should measure intelligence (however defined) and not simply verbal facility. A test meant to predict success in a job or in passing examinations should produce reasonably convincing (statistically significant) predictions.

Types of validity

There are five types of validity:

1. Predictive validity – the extent to which the test correctly predicts future behaviour. To establish predictive validity it is necessary to conduct extensive research over a period of time. It is also necessary to have accurate measures of performance so that the prediction can be compared with actual behaviour.
2. Concurrent validity – the extent to which a test score differentiates individuals in relation to a criterion or standard of performance external to the test. This means comparing the test scores of high and low performances as indicated by the criteria and establishing the degree to which the test indicates who should fit into the high or low performance groups.

3. Content validity – the extent to which the test is clearly related to the characteristics of the job or role for which it is being used as a measuring instrument.
4. Face validity – the extent to which the test 'looks' or 'feels' right in the sense that it is measuring what it is supposed to measure.
5. Construct validity – the extent to which the test measures a particular construct or characteristic. Construct validity is in effect concerned with looking at the test itself. If it is meant to measure numerical reasoning, is that what it measures?

Measuring validity

A criterion-related approach is used to assess validity. This means selecting criteria against which the validity of the test can be measured. These criteria must reflect 'true' performance at work as accurately as possible. A single criterion is inadequate. Multiple criteria should be used. The extent to which criteria can be contaminated by other factors should also be considered and it should be remembered that criteria are dynamic – they will change over time.

Test validity can be expressed as a predictive validity co-efficient in which 1.0 would equal perfect correlation between test results and subsequent behaviour, while 0.0 would equal no relationship between the test and performance. The following rule of thumb guide was produced by Smith (1984) on whether a validity coefficient is big enough:

over 0.50, excellent
0.40–0.49, good
0.30–0.39, acceptable
less than 0.30, poor.

On the basis of the research conducted by Schmidt and Hunter (1998), only work sample tests and intelligence tests with coefficients of 0.54 and 0.51 respectively are excellent.

Interpreting test results

Test results can be interpreted by the use of norms or through criterion scores.

Norms

An individual's score in a test is not meaningful on its own. It needs to be compared with the scores achieved by the population on whom the test was standardized – the norm or reference group. A normative score is read from a norms table and might, for example, indicate that someone has performed the test at a level equivalent to the top 30 per cent of the relevant population.

Criterion scores

Norms simply tell us how someone has performed a test relative to other people. A more powerful approach is to use the relationship between test scores and an indication of what the test is designed to measure, such as job success. This is described as a criterion measure. For example, when the test is validated it might be established that for scores of less than 10 on a test, 50 per cent of people would fail in the job, while the failure rate may be 35 per cent for those who score between 10 and 15 and 20 per cent for those scoring more than 15. The score achieved by the individual would therefore enable a prediction to be made of the likelihood of success.

Choosing tests

It is essential to choose tests that meet the four criteria of sensitivity, standardization, reliability and validity. It is very difficult to achieve the standards required if an organization tries to develop its own test batteries, unless it employs a qualified psychologist or obtains professional advice from a member of the British Psychological Society. This organization, with the support of the reputable test suppliers, exercises rigorous control over who can use what tests and the standard of training required and given. Particular care should be taken when selecting personality tests – there are a lot of charlatans about.

Do-it-yourself tests are always suspect unless they have been properly validated and realistic norms have been established. They should not be used.

The use of tests in a selection procedure

While validated intelligence and personality tests can produce useful data, they should not be relied on entirely. It is best to combine them in a selection procedure with structured interviews.

Tests are often used as part of a selection procedure for occupations where a large number of recruits are required, and where it is not possible to rely entirely on examination results or information about previous experience as the basis for predicting future performance. In these circumstances it is economical to develop and administer the tests, and a sufficient number of cases can be built up for the essential validation exercise. Tests usually form part of an assessment centre procedure.

Intelligence tests are particularly helpful in situations where intelligence is a key factor, but there is no other reliable method of measuring it. It may, incidentally, be as important to use an intelligence test to keep out applicants who are too intelligent for the job as to use one to guarantee a minimal level of intelligence.

Aptitude tests are most useful for jobs where specific and measurable skills are required, such as word-processing and skilled repair work. Personality tests can complement structured interviews and intelligence and aptitude tests. Some organizations use them for jobs such as selling where they believe that 'personality' is important, and where it is not too difficult to obtain quantifiable criteria for validation purposes. They may be used to assess integrity and conscientiousness where these characteristics are deemed to be important.

Tests should be administered only by people who have been trained in what the tests are measuring, how they should be used, and how they should be interpreted.

It is essential to evaluate all tests by comparing the results at the interview stage with later achievements. To be statistically significant, these evaluations should be carried out over a reasonable period of time and cover as large a number of candidates as possible.

In some situations a battery of tests may be used, including various types of intelligence, personality and aptitude tests. These may be a standard battery supplied by a test agency, or a custom-built battery may be developed. The biggest pitfall to avoid is adding extra tests just for the sake of it, without ensuring that they make a proper contribution to the success of the predictions for which the battery is being used.

The CIPD (2007c) has noted that online testing is growing in popularity (25 per cent of respondents to their survey made some use of them). Online tests are most used for recruiting graduates and when high volumes of applicants have to be dealt with.

Good practice in psychological testing

The British Psychological Society and The International Test Commission have respectively produced guidelines on the general use of psychological tests and on the use of online testing.

General use of tests

People who use psychological tests are expected by the British Psychological Society (2007) to:

1. Take steps to ensure that they are able to meet all the standards of competence defined by the British Psychological Society for the relevant Certificate(s) of Competence, and to endeavour, where possible, to develop and enhance their competence as test users.
2. Monitor the limits of their competence in psychometric testing and not to offer services that lie outside their competence nor encourage or cause others to do so.
3. Use tests only in conjunction with other assessment methods and only when their use can be supported by the available technical information.

4. Administer, score and interpret tests in accordance with the instructions provided by the test distributor and to the standards defined by the British Psychological Society.
5. Store test materials securely and to ensure that no unqualified person has access to them.
6. Ensure test results are stored securely, are not accessible to unauthorized or unqualified persons and are not used for any purposes other than those agreed with the test taker.
7. Obtain the informed consent of potential test takers, making sure that they understand why the tests will be used, what will be done with their results and who will be provided with access to them.
8. Ensure that all test takers are well informed and well prepared for the test session, and that all have had access to practice or familiarization materials where appropriate.
9. Give due consideration to factors such as gender, ethnicity, age, disability and special needs, educational background and level of ability in using and interpreting the results of tests.
10. Provide the test taker and other authorized persons with feedback about the results in a form that makes clear the implications of the results, is clear and in a style appropriate to their level of understanding.

Guidelines on the use of online tests

The key points made in the guidelines on the use of online tests produced by The International Test Commission (2005) are:

1. Only use websites supplied by test publishers who offer validated psychometric tests.
2. Tests alone may not provide a complete assessment of an individual as other confirmatory or ancillary information is not included.
3. Provide test-takers with clear instructions on how to take the test.
4. Provide relevant feedback to test-takers.
5. When individuals take an unsupervised test, procedures should be used in the form of a confirmatory test to check whether the test-taker's original responses are consistent with the responses to the confirmatory test.

Selection tests – key learning points

The types of tests

Intelligence, ability, personality and aptitude.

The characteristics of a good test

- It is a sensitive measuring instrument.

Selection tests – key learning points (continued)

- It has been standardized on a representative and sizeable sample of the population for which it is intended.
- It is reliable in the sense that it always measures the same thing.
- It is valid in the sense that it measures the characteristic the test is intended to measure.

Test validity

The five types of validity are: predictive, concurrent, content, face and construct.

Interpreting test results

Test results can be interpreted by the use of norms or through criterion scores.

Choosing tests

It is essential to choose tests that meet the four criteria of sensitivity, standardization, reliability and validity.

Using tests in a selection procedure

While validated intelligence and personality tests can produce useful data they should not be relied on entirely. It is best to combine them in a selection procedure with structured interviews.

Questions

1. What does the term 'validity' mean when applied to selection tests? How can it be measured?
2. What are the advantages and disadvantages of personality tests as a method of selection?
3. From a colleague: 'I have just come back from a spell in our French associated company where they swear by graphology as a method of selection. Is there anything in it for us?'

References

British Psychological Society (2007) *Psychological Testing: A user's guide*, Psychological Testing Centre, Leicester

CIPD (2007c) *Psychological Testing*, CIPD Fact Sheet, www.cipd.co.uk

International Test Commission (2005) *International Guidelines on Computer-based and Internet Delivered Testing*, British Psychological Society, Leicester

Schmidt, F L and Hunter, J E (1998) The validity and utility of selection methods in personnel psychology: practical and theoretical implications of 85 years of research findings, *Psychological Bulletin*, **124** (2), pp 262–74

Smith, M (1984) *Survey Item Blank*, MCB Publications, Bradford

Spearman, C (1927) *The Abilities of Man*, Macmillan, New York

34 Talent Management

Key concepts and terms

- Talent management
- Talent relationship management
- Talent pool
- War for talent

Learning outcomes

On completing this chapter you should be able to define these key concepts. You should also know about:

- The meaning of talent management
- Developing a talent management strategy
- The process of talent management
- Management succession planning

Introduction

The concept of talent management as a process of ensuring that the organization has the talented people it needs only emerged in the late 1990s. It has now been recognized as a major resourcing activity, although its elements are all familiar. Talent management has been called a fad or a fashion, but David Guest argues that: 'talent management is an idea that has been around for a long time. It's been re-labelled, and that enables wise organizations to review what they are doing. It integrates some old ideas and gives them a freshness, and that is good' (Guest cited in Warren 2006, p 29).

This chapter covers the meaning and process of talent management and talent management strategy. An important aspect of talent management – management succession planning – is dealt with at the end of the chapter.

The meaning of talent management

Talented people possess special gifts, abilities and aptitudes which enable them to perform effectively. As defined by the CIPD (2007f), 'Talent consists of those individuals who can make a difference to organizational performance, either through their immediate contribution or in the longer term by demonstrating the highest levels of potential.' Talent management is the process of identifying, developing, recruiting, retaining and deploying those talented people.

The term 'talent management' may refer simply to management succession planning and management development activities, although this notion does not really add anything to these familiar processes except a new, although admittedly quite evocative, name. It is better to regard talent management as a more comprehensive and integrated bundle of activities, the aim of which is to secure the flow of talent in an organization, bearing in mind that talent is a major corporate resource.

However, there are different views about what talent management means. Some follow the lead given by McKinsey & Company, which coined the phrase 'the war for talent' in 1997. A book on this subject by Michaels *et al* (2001) identified five imperatives that companies need to act on if they are going to win the war for managerial talent; these are as follows.

SOURCE REVIEW

Five imperatives for talent management, Michaels *et al* (2001)

1. Creating a winning employee value proposition that will make your company uniquely attractive to talent.
2. Moving beyond recruiting hype to build a long-term recruiting strategy.
3. Using job experience, coaching and mentoring to cultivate the potential in managers.
4. Strengthening your talent pool by investing in A players, developing B players and acting decisively on C players.
5. Central to this approach is a pervasive mindset – a deep conviction shared by leaders throughout the company that competitive advantage comes from having better talent at all levels.

The McKinsey prescription has often been misinterpreted to mean that talent management is only about obtaining, identifying and nurturing high flyers, ignoring the point they made that competitive advantage comes from having better talent at all levels.

Pfeffer (2001) has doubts about the war for talent concept, which he thinks is the wrong metaphor for organizational success. He has expressed the following belief.

SOURCE REVIEW

Doubts about the war for talent concept, Pfeffer (2001)

Fighting the war for talent itself can cause problems. Companies that adopt a talent war mindset often wind up venerating outsiders and downplaying the talent already in the company. They frequently set up competitive zero-sum dynamics that make internal learning and knowledge transfer difficult, activate the self-fulfilling prophesy in the wrong direction (those labelled as less able become less able), and create an attitude of arrogance instead of an attitude of wisdom. For all these reasons, fighting the war for talent may be hazardous to an organization's health and detrimental to doing the things that will make it successful.

HR people also have different views, which state on the one hand that everyone has talent and it is not just about the favoured few, and on the other that you need to focus on the best. As reported by Warren (2006), Laura Ashley, director of talent at newspaper group Metro, believes you must maximize the performance of your workforce as a whole if you are going to maximize the performance of the organization. Alternatively, as also reported by Warren, Wendy Hirsh, principal associate at the Institute for Employment Studies, says it is not helpful to confuse talent management with overall employee development. Both are important, but talent management is best kept clear and focused. Another view was expressed by Thorne and Pellant (2007) who wrote: 'No organization should focus all its attention on development of only part of its human capital. What is important, however, is recognizing the needs of different individuals within its community.'

The general consensus seems to be that while talent management does concentrate on obtaining, identifying and developing people with high potential, this should not be at the expense of the development needs of people generally.

The process of talent management

Talent management takes the form of a 'bundle' of interrelated processes, as shown in Figure 34.1.

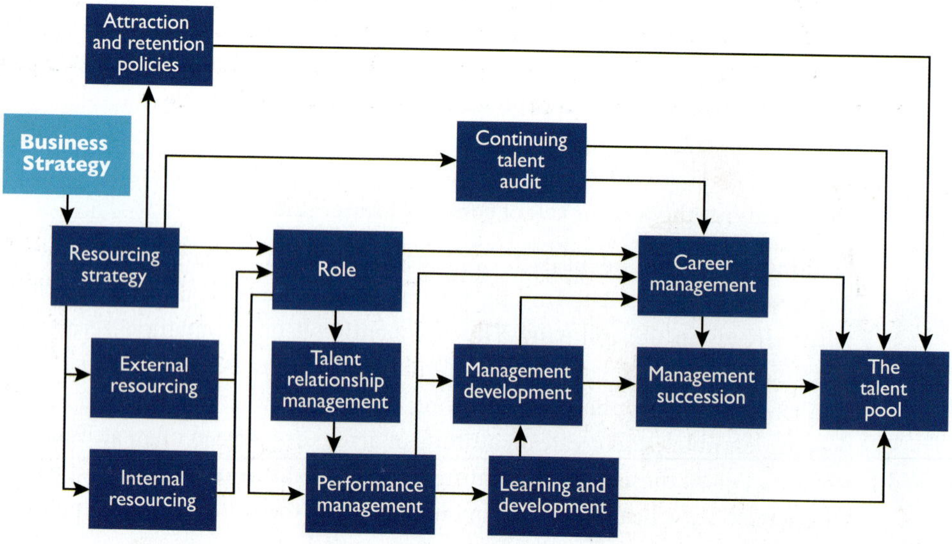

Figure 34.1 The elements of talent management

Talent management starts with the business strategy and what it signifies in terms of the talented people required by the organization. Ultimately, the aim is to develop and maintain a pool of talented people. This is sometimes described as the 'talent management pipe line'. Its elements are described below.

The resourcing strategy

The business plan provides the basis for human resource planning, which defines human capital requirements and leads to attraction and retention policies and programmes for internal resourcing (identifying talented people within the organization and developing and promoting them).

Attraction and retention policies and programmes

These policies and programmes describe the approach to ensuring that the organization both gets and keeps the talent it needs. Attraction policies lead to programmes for external resourcing (recruitment and selection of people from outside the organization). Retention policies are designed to ensure that people remain as committed members of the organization. The outcome of these policies is a talent flow that creates and maintains the talent pool.

Talent audit

A talent audit identifies those with potential and provides the basis for career planning and development – ensuring that talented people have the sequence of experience supplemented by coaching and learning programmes that will fit them to carry out more demanding roles in the future. Talent audits can also be used to indicate the possible danger of talented people leaving (risk analysis) and what action may need to be taken to retain them.

Role design

Talent management is concerned with the roles people carry out. This involves role design – ensuring that roles provide the responsibility, challenge and autonomy required to create role engagement and motivation. It also means taking steps to ensure that people have the opportunity and are given the encouragement to learn and develop in their roles. Talent management policies focus on role flexibility – giving people the chance to develop their roles by making better and extended use of their talents.

Talent relationship management

Talent relationship management is the process of building effective relationships with people in their roles. It is concerned generally with creating a great place to work, but in particular it is about treating individual employees fairly, recognizing their value, giving them a voice and providing opportunities for growth. The aim is to achieve 'talent engagement', ensuring that people are committed to their work and the organization. As Sears (2003) points out, it is 'better to build an existing relationship rather than try to create a new one when someone leaves'.

Performance management

Performance management processes provide a means of building relationships with people, identifying talent and potential, planning learning and development activities, and making the most of the talent possessed by the organization. Line managers can be asked to carry out separate 'risk analyses' for any key staff to assess the likelihood of their leaving. Properly carried out, performance management is a means of increasing the engagement and motivation of people by providing positive feedback and recognition. This is part of a total reward system.

Learning and development

Learning and development policies and programmes are essential components in the process of talent management – ensuring that people acquire and enhance the skills and competencies they need. Policies should be formulated by reference to 'employee success profiles', which are described in terms of competencies and define the qualities that need to be developed. Employee success profiles can be incorporated in role profiles.

Management succession planning

Management succession planning takes place to ensure that, as far as possible, the organization has the managers it requires to meet future business needs.

Career management

Career management, as discussed in Chapter 35, is concerned with the provision of opportunities for people to develop their abilities and their careers in order to ensure that the organization has the flow of talent it needs and to satisfy their own aspirations.

Developing a talent management strategy

A talent management strategy consists of a view on how the processes described above should mesh together with an overall objective – to acquire and nurture talent wherever it is and wherever it is needed by using a number of interdependent policies and practices. Talent management is the notion of 'bundling' in action. The strategy covers the following aims.

The aims of talent management

- Define who the talent management programme should cover.

- Define what is meant by talent in terms of competencies and potential.
- Define the future talent requirements of the organization.
- Develop the organization as an 'employer of choice' – a 'great place to work'.
- Use selection and recruitment procedures that ensure that good quality people are recruited who are likely to thrive in the organization and stay with it for a reasonable length of time (but not necessarily for life).
- Design jobs and develop roles that give people opportunities to apply and grow their skills and provide them with autonomy, interest and challenge.
- Provide talented staff with opportunities for career development and growth.
- Create a working environment in which work processes and facilities enable rewarding (in the broadest sense) jobs and roles to be designed and developed.
- Provide scope for achieving a reasonable balance between working in the organization and life outside work.
- Develop a positive psychological contract.
- Develop the leadership qualities of line managers.
- Recognize those with talent by rewarding excellence, enterprise and achievement.
- Conduct talent audits that identify those with potential and those who might leave the organization.
- Introduce management succession planning procedures that identify the talent available to meet future requirements and indicate what management development activities are required.

The following talent management checklist was developed by the CIPD (2006):

- How are we defining talent and talent management?
- Where do professional and specialist staff fit into our talent management process?
- What are the key features of the external environment and the labour market issues impacting on our talent management task?
- What are the main challenges we're facing in developing a talent pipeline?
- What are we doing to overcome them?
- How do we define and measure aspects of talent, such as potential?

- Are we benchmarking with other organizations?
- Have we clarified for everyone involved the relationship between talent management and other HR initiatives, such as succession planning?
- What tools can be used to identify the right talent and assess potential, employee engagement, etc?
- Are we prepared to train and encourage those responsible for talent management to ask serious questions about performance and potential, and to do something about those not up to the task?
- How is the success of our talent management process measured?
- Do we undertake any systematic evaluation, including calculation of the financial and other benefits of talent management to our organization?

The qualities required

The development and implementation of a talent management strategy requires high quality management and leadership from the top and from senior managers and the HR function. As suggested by Younger *et al* (2007), the approaches required involve emphasizing 'growth from within', regarding talent development as a key element of the business strategy, being clear about the competencies and qualities that matter, maintaining well-defined career paths, taking management development, coaching and mentoring very seriously, and demanding high performance.

Management succession planning

Management succession planning is the process of assessing and auditing the talent in the organization in order to answer three fundamental questions. First, are there enough potential successors available – a supply of people coming through who can take key roles in the longer term? Second, are they good enough? Third, have they the right skills and competencies for the future? At different stages in their careers, potential successors may be ranked in order, such as, a) being ready to do the next job now, b) being ready for a certain higher-grade position in, say, two years' time, c) being ready for job rotation at the same level, and d) being ready for lateral assignments on temporary relief or project work.

Succession planning is based on the information about managers gleaned from supply and demand forecasts, talent audits and performance and potential reviews. In some large organizations in which demand and supply forecasts can be made accurately, highly formalized succession planning processes exist based on the sort of management succession schedule illustrated in Figure 34.2.

MANAGEMENT SUCCESSION SCHEDULE					Department:	Director/manager:		
Existing managers						Potential successors		
Name	Position	Due for replacement	Rating		If promotable to what position and when?	Names: 1st and 2nd choice	Positions	When
			Performance	Potential				

Figure 34.2 Management succession schedule

However, the scope for formal succession planning may be limited in today's more flexible and rapidly changing organizations where elaborate succession plans could be out of date as soon as they are made. In these circumstances, the most that can be done is to use talent management and management development processes to ensure that there are plenty of talented people around in 'talent pools' to fill vacancies as they arise, bearing in mind that the most talented or ambitious individuals may not want to wait very long.

Talent management – key learning points

The meaning of talent management

Talented people possess special gifts, abilities and aptitudes that enable them to perform effectively. Talent management is the process of identifying, developing, recruiting, retaining and deploying those talented people.

The process of talent management

Talent management starts with the business strategy and what it signifies in terms of the

Talent management – key learning points (continued)

talented people required by the organization. Ultimately, its aim is to develop and maintain a pool of talented people. Its elements are resourcing strategies, attraction and retention programmes, role design, talent relationship management, performance management, learning and development, management succession planning and career management.

Developing a talent management strategy

A talent management strategy consists of a view on how the processes described above should mesh together with an overall objective – to acquire and nurture talent wherever it is and wherever it is needed by using a number of interdependent policies and practices. Talent management is the notion of 'bundling' in action.

Management succession planning

Management succession planning is the process of assessing and auditing the talent in the organization in order to answer three fundamental questions: 1) are there enough potential successors available – a supply of people coming through who can take key roles in the longer term; 2) are they good enough; and 3) do they have the right skills and competencies for the future?

Questions

1. From your chief executive: 'What's this I hear about talent management? Is it simply new wine in old bottles as so many "innovative" HR practices seem to be? Is it for us and if so, why and how?' How do you reply?
2. Jeffrey Pfeffer made the following typically trenchant remarks about the notion of 'the war for talent'. What do you think? 'This war-for-talent imagery overlooks the fact that effective teams often outperform even more talented collections of individuals, that individual talent and motivation is partly under the control of what companies do, and that what matters to organizational success is the set of management practices that create the culture. But it is not only that the war for talent is the wrong metaphor for organizational success. Fighting the war for talent itself can cause problems. Companies that adopt a talent war mindset often wind up venerating outsiders and downplaying the talent already inside the company. They frequently set up competitive, zero-sum dynamics that make internal learning and knowledge transfer difficult, activate the self-fulfilling prophecy in the wrong direction, and create an attitude of arrogance instead of

Questions (continued)

an attitude of wisdom. For all of these reasons, fighting the war for talent may be hazardous to an organization's health and detrimental to doing the things that will make it successful.' What do you think?

3. As HR director you have proposed that a formal succession planning process should be introduced. This generated a sceptical response from the finance director who said that it was pointless to plan ahead because, a) we do not know what we want for more than a few months in advance, and b) in his experience it is difficult if not impossible to forecast anyone's potential for promotion. How do you respond?

References

CIPD (2006) *Talent Management: Understanding the dimensions*, CIPD, London

CIPD (2007f) *Talent Management Fact Sheet*, CIPD, London

Michaels, E G, Handfield-Jones, H and Axelrod, B (2001) *The War for Talent*, Harvard Business School Press, Boston, MA

Pfeffer, J (2001) Fighting the war for talent is hazardous to your organization's health, *Organizational Dynamics*, **29** (4), pp 248–59

Sears, D (2003) *Successful Talent Strategies*, American Management Association, New York

Thorne, K and Pellant, A (2007) *The Essential Guide to Managing Talent*, Kogan Page, London

Warren, C (2006) Curtain call, *People Management*, 23 March, pp 24–29

Younger, J, Smallwood, N and Ulrich, D (2007) Developing your organization's brand as a talent developer, *Human Resource Planning*, **30** (2), pp 21–9

35 Career Management

Key concepts and terms

- Career anchors
- Career ladders
- Career paths
- Portfolio career
- Career dynamics
- Career management
- Career planning
- Protean career

Learning outcomes

On completing this chapter you should be able to define these key concepts. You should also know about:

- The aims of career management
- Career development strategy
- Career management policies
- Career stages
- Career management activities
- Self-managed careers

Introduction

Career management is an aspect of talent management but deserves to be considered separately as an important activity in its own right. This chapter starts with a definition of career management and its aims. It then describes the framework of career planning – the stages that careers can follow within an organization and the dynamics that govern career progression. The next section of the chapter covers career management activities, and the chapter ends with a discussion of how people can manage their own careers with help, as required, from the organization.

Career management defined

Career management is concerned with the provision of opportunities for people to develop their abilities and their careers in order to ensure that the organization has the flow of talent it needs and to satisfy their own aspirations. It is about integrating the needs of the organization with the needs of the individual.

An important part of career management is career planning, which shapes the progression of individuals within an organization in accordance with assessments of organizational needs, defined employee success profiles and the performance, potential and preferences of individual members of the enterprise. But career management is also concerned with career counselling to help people develop their careers to their advantage as well as that of the organization.

Aims

For the organization the aim of career management is to meet the objectives of its talent management policies, which are to ensure that there is a talent flow that creates and maintains the required talent pool. For employees the aims of career management policies are: 1) to give them the guidance, support and encouragement they need to fulfil their potential and achieve a successful career with the organization in tune with their talents and ambitions, and 2) to provide those with promise a sequence of experience and learning activities that will equip them for whatever level of responsibility they have the ability to reach.

Career management calls for an approach that explicitly takes into account both organizational needs and employee interests. It calls for creativity in identifying ways to provide development opportunities. Career management policies and practices are best based on an understanding of the stages through which careers progress in organizations.

Career stages

The stages of a career within an organization can be described as a career lifecycle. Hall (1984) set this out as follows.

Career stages

1. Entry to the organization when the individual can begin the process of self-directed career planning.
2. Progress within particular areas of work where skills and potential are developed through experience, training, coaching, mentoring and performance management.
3. Mid-career when some people will still have good career prospects while others may have got as far as they are going to get, or at least feel that they have. It is necessary to ensure that these 'plateaued' people do not lose interest at this stage by taking such steps as providing them with cross-functional moves, job rotation, special assignments, recognition and rewards for effective performance, etc.
4. Later career when individuals may have settled down at whatever level they have reached but are beginning to be concerned about the future. They need to be treated with respect as people who are still making a contribution and given opportunities to take on new challenges wherever this is possible. They may also need reassurance about their future with the organization and what is to happen to them when they leave.
5. End of career with the organization – the possibility of phasing disengagement by being given the chance to work part time for a period before they finally have to go should be considered at this stage.

Career dynamics

Career management should be based on an understanding of career dynamics. This is concerned with how careers progress – the ways in which people move through their careers either upwards when they are promoted, or by enlarging or enriching their roles to take on greater responsibilities or make more use of their skills and abilities. The three stages of career progression – expanding, establishing and maturing – are illustrated in Figure 35.1. This also shows how individuals progress or fail to progress at different rates through these stages.

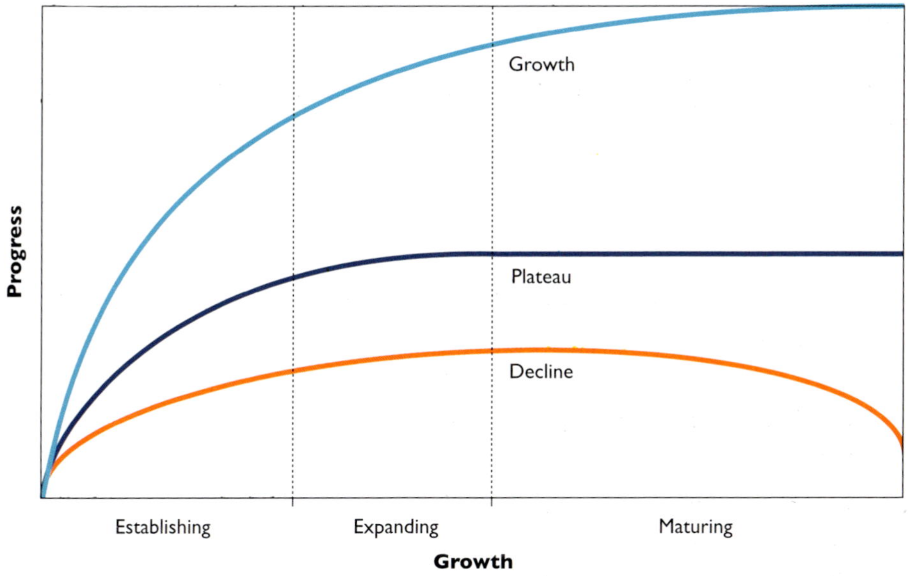

Figure 35.1 Career progression curves

Career development strategy

A career development strategy might include the following activities:

- a policy of promoting from within wherever possible;
- career routes enabling talented people to move from bottom to top of the organization, or laterally in the firm, as their development and job opportunities take them;
- personal development planning as a major part of the performance management process, in order to develop each individual's knowledge and skills;
- systems and processes to achieve sharing and development of knowledge (especially tacit) across the firm;
- multi-disciplinary project teams with a shifting membership in order to offer developmental opportunities for as wide a range of employees as possible.

Career management activities

As described by Hirsh and Carter (2002), career management encompasses recruitment, personal development plans, lateral moves, special assignments at home or abroad, development positions, career bridges, lateral moves and support for employees who want to develop.

Baruch and Peiperl (2000) identified 17 career management practices, and their survey of 194 UK companies established a rank order for their use. The practices are listed below in order, from most frequent to least frequent use.

Career management practices

1. Postings regarding internal job openings.
2. Formal education as part of career development.
3. Performance appraisal as a basis for career planning.
4. Career counselling by manager.
5. Lateral moves to create cross-functional experience.
6. Career counselling by HR department.
7. Retirement preparation programmes.
8. Succession planning.
9. Formal mentoring.
10. Common career paths.
11. Dual ladder career paths (parallel hierarchy for professional staff).
12. Books and/or pamphlets on career issues.
13. Written personal career planning (as done by the organization or personally).
14. Assessment centres.
15. Peer appraisal.
16. Career workshops.
17. Upward (subordinate) appraisal.

The process of career management

The process of career management is illustrated in Figure 35.2.

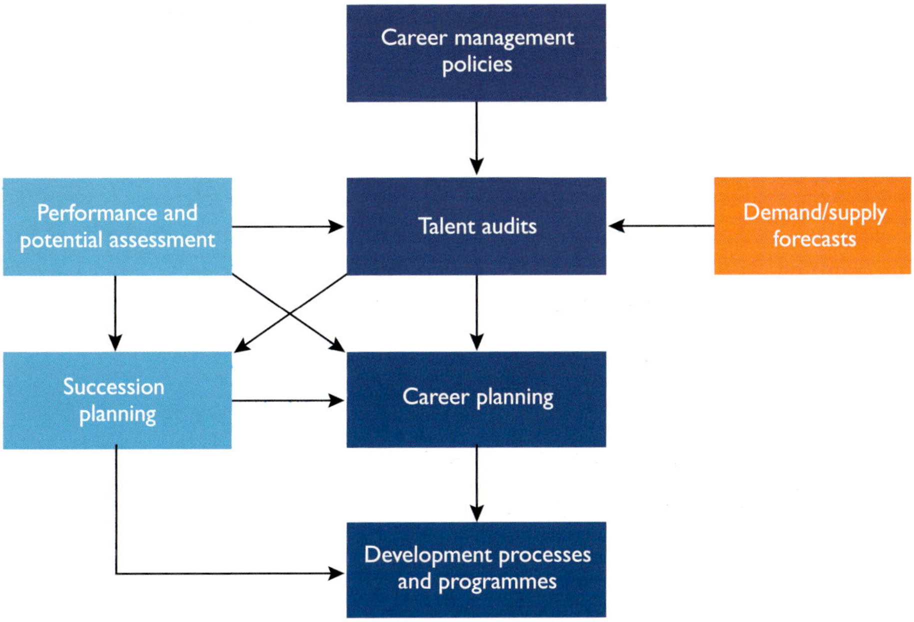

Figure 35.2 The process of career management

Career management policies

The organization needs to decide on the extent to which it 'makes or buys' talented people. Should it grow its own talent (a promotion from within policy) or should it rely on external recruitment (bringing 'fresh blood' into the organization)? The policy may be to recruit potentially high performers who will be good at their present job and are rewarded accordingly. If they are really good, they will be promoted and the enterprise will get what it wants. Deliberately to train managers for a future that may never happen is a waste of time. In contrast and less frequently, employers who believe in long-term career planning develop structured approaches to career management. These include elaborate reviews of performance and potential, assessment centres to identify talent or confirm that it is there, 'high flyer' schemes and planned job moves in line with a predetermined programme.

There may also be policies for dealing with the 'plateaued' manager who has got so far but will get no further. Some managers in this position may be reconciled to reaching that level but continue to work effectively. Others will become bored, frustrated and unproductive, especially rising stars on the wane. The steps that can be taken to deal with this problem include:

- lateral moves into different functional areas or specialized subsidiaries, in order to provide new challenges and career breadth;
- temporary assignments and secondments outside the organization;

- appointments as leaders of project teams set up to deal with performance barriers inside the organization such as the slowness of responses to customer complaints.

Talent audits

These review the stocks of talent available and the flows required by reference to demand and supply forecasts and performance and potential assessments. They provide the basis for succession planning, as described in Chapter 34, and career planning, as covered later in this section.

Performance and potential assessments

The aim of performance and potential assessments is to identify learning and development needs, provide guidance on possible directions in which an individual's career might go, and indicate who has potential for promotion. This information can be obtained from performance management processes, as described in Part VII.

Assessment of potential can be carried out formally by managers following a performance review. They may be asked to identify people who have very high potential, some potential or no potential at all. They may also be asked to indicate when individuals will be ready for promotion and how far they are likely to get. The problem with this sort of assessment is that managers find it difficult to forecast the future for the people they are reviewing – good performance in the current job does not guarantee that individuals will be able to cope with wider responsibilities, especially if this involves moving into management, and managers may not necessarily be aware of the qualities required for longer-term promotion. But the organization does need information on those with potential and assessors should be encouraged at least to indicate that this is someone who is not only performing well in the present job but may well perform well in higher-level jobs. This information can identify those who may be nominated to attend development centres (see Chapter 45), which can be used to establish potential and discuss career plans.

Career planning

Career planning involves the definition of career paths – the routes people can take to advance their careers within an organization. It uses all the information provided by the organization's assessments of requirements, the assessments of performance and potential and management succession plans, and translates it into the form of individual career development programmes and general arrangements for management development, career counselling and mentoring.

It is possible to define career progression in terms of what people are required to know and be able to do to carry out work to progress up the 'career ladder' (the sequence of jobs at increasing levels of responsibility, which constitute a career). These levels can be described as competency bands. For each band, the competencies needed to achieve a move to that level would be defined to produce a career map incorporating 'aiming points' for individuals, as illustrated in Figure 35.3. People would be made aware of the competency levels they must reach in order to achieve progress in their careers. This would help them to plan their own development, although support and guidance should be provided by their managers, HR specialists and, if they exist, management development advisers or mentors. The provision of additional experience and training could be arranged as appropriate, but it would be important to clarify what individual employees need to do for themselves if they want to progress within the organization.

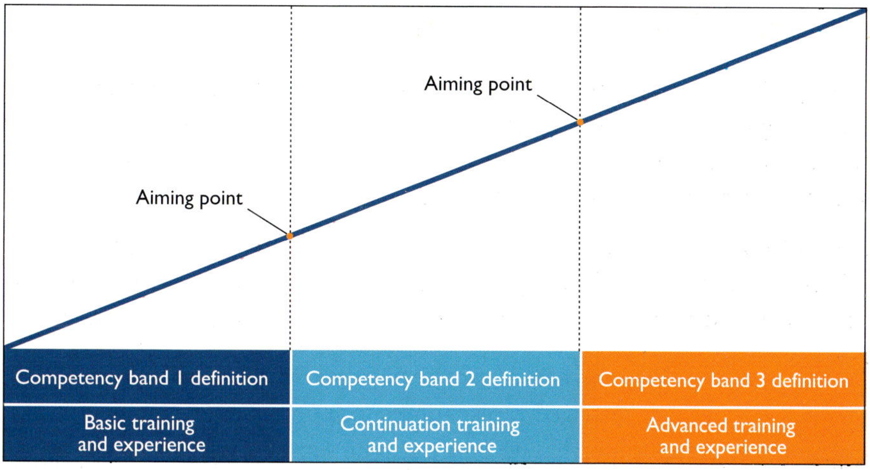

Figure 35.3 Competency band career progression system

As reported by Ready and Conger (2007), at Proctor & Gamble, 'destination jobs' are identified for rising stars, which are attainable only if the employee continues to perform, impress and demonstrate growth potential.

Career family grade structures, as described in Chapter 49, can define levels of competency in each career family and show career paths upwards within families or between families, as illustrated in Figure 35.4.

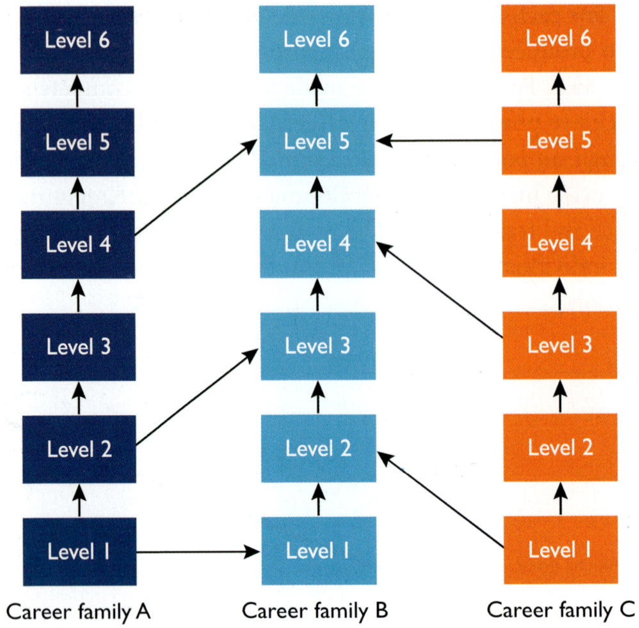

Figure 35.4 Career paths in a career family structure

Formal career planning along these lines may be the ideal but, as noted by Hirsh *et al* (2000), there has been a shift from managed career moves to more open internal job markets. The process of internal job application has become the main way in which employees manage their careers.

Self-managed careers

The organization may need to manage careers as part of its talent management and management succession programmes and can provide support and guidance to people with potential. Ultimately, however, it is up to individuals to manage their own careers within and beyond their present organization. Handy (1984) used the term 'portfolio career' to describe his forecast that people will increasingly change the direction of their careers during the course of their working life. Hall (1996) coined the phrase the 'protean career' in which individuals take responsibility for transforming their career path (the name comes from the Greek god Proteus who could change his shape at will).

Schein (1978) originated the notion of career anchors. He defined them as the self-concept of people consisting of self-perceived talents and abilities, basic values and a sense of motives and needs relating to their careers. As people gain work experience, career anchors evolve and function as stabilizing forces, hence the metaphor of 'anchor'. His original research in the 1970s showed that most people's self-concept revolved round the following categories reflecting their needs.

SOURCE REVIEW

Self-concept categories, Schein (1978)

1. Autonomy/independence.
2. Security/stability.
3. Technical-functional competence.
4. General managerial competence.
5. Entrepreneurial creativity.
6. Service or dedication to a cause.
7. Pure challenge.
8. Lifestyle.

The original concept of career anchors was developed at a time when jobs were relatively static and career paths within and between organizations were fairly easy to map. But as Schein pointed out in an update of his concept in 1996, jobs are increasingly becoming more dynamic and there is a shift from the provision of 'employment security' to 'employability security'. Calling on his experience in administering his career anchor self-analysis exercise, Schein claimed that while each of the anchor categories are still valid, they are more difficult to apply as the world of work and organizational structure become more turbulent.

Although the career anchor is designed as a self-analysis tool it can be used by career counsellors within and outside organizations as the basis for discussing career plans and how they can be realized, but it is necessary to consider the changing perceptions of people about their careers. Research on career anchors in a changing business environment based on interviews with 540 managers, carried out by Kniveton (2004), indicated that younger managers were more oriented towards their own skills and what they could contribute, whereas older managers were more inclined to be aware of the limitations of their role in the organization. It was stressed that this difference needed to be taken into account by those involved in career planning within organizations.

Career management – key learning points

The aims of career management

For the organization, the aim of career management is to meet the objectives of its talent management policies, which are to ensure that there is a talent flow that creates and maintains the required talent pool. For employees, the aims of career management policies are to give them the guidance, support and encouragement they need to fulfil their potential and achieve a successful career with the organization in tune with their talents and ambitions.

Career stages

- Entry to the organization.
- Progress within particular areas of work.
- Mid-career.
- Later career.
- End of career.

Career management activities

The five most common activities are:

1. Postings regarding internal job openings.
2. Formal education as part of career development.
3. Performance appraisal as a basis for career planning.
4. Career counselling by manager.
5. Lateral moves to create cross-functional experience.

Career management policies

The organization needs to decide on the extent to which it 'makes or buys' talented people (ie grows from within or recruits from outside). It also needs policies on talent audits and performance and potential assessments.

Self-managed careers

The organization may need to manage careers as part of its talent management and management succession programmes and can provide support and guidance to people with potential. Ultimately, however, it is up to individuals to manage their own careers within and beyond their present organization.

Questions

1. Drawing upon research findings, how might you use past assessments of an individual's strengths and weaknesses to help clarify their future development?
2. Critically evaluate Schein's concept of career anchors.

Questions (continued)

3. Identify and justify the guidance that you would give to line managers in your organization to ensure that they provide effective career management support to all members of their staff.
4. Review the career paths available for key occupations in your organization. What can be done to improve the process of career development?

References

Baruch, Y and Peiperl, M (2000) Career management practices: an empirical survey and explanations, *Human Resource Management*, **39** (4), pp 347–66

Hall, D T (1984) Human resource development and organizational effectiveness, in (eds) D Fombrun, M A Tichy and M A Devanna, *Strategic Human Resource Management*, Wiley, New York

Hall, D T (1996) *The Career is Dead: Long live the career*, Jossey-Bass, San Francisco, CA

Handy, C (1984) *The Future of Work*, Blackwell, Oxford

Hirsh, W and Carter, A (2002) *New Directions in Management Development*, Paper 387, Institute of Employment Studies

Hirsh, W, Pollard, E and Tamkin, P (2000) Management development, *IRS Employee Development Bulletin*, November, pp 8–12

Kniveton, B H (2004) Managerial career anchors in a changing business environment, *Journal of European Industrial Training*, **28** (7), pp 564–73

Ready, D A and Conger, J A (2007) Make your company a talent factory, *Harvard Business Review*, June, pp 68–77

Schein, E H (1978) *Career Dynamics: Matching individual and organizational needs*, Addison-Wesley, Reading, MA

Schein, E H (1996) *Career Anchors Revisited: Implications for career development in the 21st century*, Society for Organizational Learning, Cambridge, MA

36 Introduction to the Organization

Learning outcomes

On completing this chapter you should know about:

- The aims of induction
- Reception of employees
- Initial briefing
- Formal induction courses
- The importance of induction
- Documentation requirements
- Introduction to the workplace
- On-the-job induction training

Introduction

It is important to ensure that care is taken over introducing people to the organization through effective induction arrangements, as described in this chapter.

Induction: what it is and why it is important

Induction is the process of receiving and welcoming employees when they first join a company and giving them the basic information they need to settle down quickly and happily and start work.

Aims of induction

1. Smooth the preliminary stages when everything is likely to be strange and unfamiliar to the starter.
2. Establish quickly a favourable attitude to the organization in the mind of new employees so that they are more likely to stay.
3. Obtain effective output from the new employee in the shortest possible time.
4. Reduce the likelihood of the employee leaving quickly.

Induction is important because it reduces the cost and inconvenience of early leavers. Employees are far more likely to resign during the initial months after joining the organization. First impressions are important as is the impact of the first four weeks of employment. Such early resignations cause disruption and create recurrent costs such as the costs of obtaining replacements, induction costs – training and the costs of lower productivity from new starters – and the costs arising from the gaps that occur before a leaver is replaced.

These costs can be considerable. The cost for a professional employee could be 75 per cent of annual salary. For a support worker the cost could easily reach 50 per cent of pay. If 15 out of 100 staff paid an average of £20,000 a year leave during a year, the total cost could amount to £150,000 – 7.5 per cent of the pay roll for those staff. It is worth making an effort to reduce that cost; giving more attention to induction pays off. This means considering the reception of newcomers, the information they are given when they join, the initial briefing, how people are introduced to their workplace, a formal induction course and induction training.

Reception

Most people suffer from some feelings of trepidation when they start a new job. However outwardly confident, they may well be asking themselves, what will the company be like? How will my boss behave to me? Will I get on with the other workers? Will I be able to do the job?

These questions may not be answered immediately but at least general fears may be alleviated by ensuring that the first contacts are friendly and helpful.

SOURCE REVIEW

Checklist for reception, Fowler (1996)

- Ensure that the person whom the starter first meets (ie the receptionist, HR assistant or supervisor) knows of their pending arrival and what to do next.
- Set a reporting time, which will avoid the risk of the starter turning up before the reception or office staff arrive.
- Train reception staff in the need for friendly and efficient helpfulness towards new starters.
- If the new starter has to go to another location immediately after reporting, provide a guide, unless the route to the other location is very straightforward.
- Avoid keeping the new starter waiting; steady, unhurried, guided activity is an excellent antidote to first day nerves.

Documentation

A variety of documents may then be issued to employees, including safety rules and safety literature, a company rule book or an employee handbook. The latter should include the following.

Employee handbook contents

- A brief description of the organization.
- Details of basic terms and conditions of employment (hours of work, holidays, pension scheme, insurance, payment arrangements).

- Sickness and absence – notification of absence, leave of absence, certificates, pay.
- Company rules.
- Company procedures – disciplinary, capability and grievance.
- Union and joint consultation arrangements.
- Education and training facilities.
- Health and safety arrangements.
- Medical and first aid facilities.
- Restaurant facilities.

If the organization is not large enough to justify a printed handbook, the least that can be done is to prepare a word-processed summary of this information.

Company induction – initial briefing

Company induction procedures should not rely on the printed word. The member of the HR department or other individual who is looking after new employees should run through the main points with each individual or, when larger numbers are being taken on, with groups of people. In this way, a more personal touch is provided and queries can be answered.

When the initial briefing has been completed, new employees should be taken to their place of work and introduced to their manager or team leader for the departmental induction programme. Alternatively, they may go straight to a training school and join the department later.

Introduction to the workplace

New starters will be concerned about who they are going to work for (their immediate manager or team leader), who they are going to work with, what work they are going to do on their first day and the geographical layout of their place of work (location of entrances, exits, lavatories, restrooms and the canteen).

Some of this information may be provided by a member of the HR department, or an assistant in the new employee's place of work. But the most important source of information is the immediate manager, supervisor or team leader.

The departmental induction programme should, wherever possible, start with the departmental manager, not the immediate team leader. The manager may give only a general welcome and a brief description of the work of the department before handing new employees over to their team leaders for the more detailed induction. But it is important for the manager to be involved at this stage so that he or she is not seen as a remote figure by the new employee. At least this means that the starter will not be simply a name or a number to the manager.

The detailed induction is probably best carried out by the immediate team leader, who should have the following five main aims.

Induction to the workplace – aims

1. Put the new employee at ease.
2. Interest the employee in the job and the organization.
3. Provide basic information about working arrangements.
4. Indicate the standards of performance and behaviour expected from the employee.
5. Tell the employee about training arrangements and how he or she can progress in the company.

The team leader should introduce new starters to their fellow team members. It is best to get one member of the team to act as a guide or 'starter's friend'. There is much to be said for these initial guides being people who have not been long with the organization. As relative newcomers they are likely to remember all the small points that were a source of worry to them when they started work, and so help new employees to settle in quickly.

Formal induction courses

Formal induction courses can provide for new starters to be assembled in groups so that a number of people can be given consistent and comprehensive information at the same time that may not be forthcoming if reliance is placed solely on team leaders. A formal course is an opportunity to deliver messages about the organization, its products and services, its mission and values, using a range of media such as DVDs and other visual aids that would not be available within departments. But formal induction courses cannot replace informal induction arrangements at the workplace where the most important need – settling people well – can best be satisfied.

On-the-job induction training

Most new starters other than those on formal training schemes will learn on-the-job, although this may be supplemented with special off-the-job courses to develop particular skills or knowledge. On-the-job training can be haphazard, inefficient and wasteful. A planned, systematic approach is desirable. This can incorporate an assessment of what the new starter needs to learn, the use of designated and trained colleagues to act as guides and mentors, and coaching by team leaders or specially appointed and trained departmental trainers.

These on-the-job arrangements can be supplemented by self-managed learning arrangements by offering access to flexible learning packages and by providing advice on learning opportunities.

Introduction to the organization – key learning points

The aims of induction

- Smooth the preliminary stages when everything is likely to be strange and unfamiliar to the starter.
- Establish quickly a favourable attitude to the organization in the mind of new employees so that they are more likely to stay.
- Obtain effective output from the new employee in the shortest possible time.
- Reduce the likelihood of the employee leaving quickly.

The importance of induction

Induction is important because it reduces the cost and inconvenience of early leavers. Employees are far more likely to resign during the initial months after joining the organization. First impressions are important as are the impact of the first four weeks of employment. Such early resignations cause disruption and create recurrent costs.

Reception of employees

Ensure that the first contacts are friendly and helpful.

Documentation

A variety of documents can be issued to employees, including safety rules and safety literature, a company rule book or an employee handbook.

Initial briefing

Company induction procedures should not rely on the printed word. The member of the HR department or other individual who is looking after new employees should run through the main points with each individual or, when larger numbers are being taken on, with groups of people.

Introduction to the organization – key learning points (continued)

Introduction to the workplace

New starters will be concerned about who they are going to work for (their immediate manager or team leader), who they are going to work with, what work they are going to do on their first day and the geographical layout of their place of work (location of entrances, exits, lavatories, restrooms and the canteen).

Formal induction courses

Formal induction courses can provide for new starters to be assembled in groups so that a number of people can be given consistent and comprehensive information at the same time that may not be forthcoming if reliance is placed solely on team leaders. A formal course is an opportunity to deliver messages about the organization, its products and services, its mission and values.

On-the-job induction training

Most new starters other than those on formal training schemes will learn on-the-job, although this may be supplemented with special off-the-job courses to develop particular skills or knowledge.

Questions

1. Why is it important to get induction right?
2. What are the essential elements of induction?
3. How should people be introduced to their workplace?

Reference

Fowler, A (1996) *Induction*, IPD, London

37

Release from the Organization

Learning outcomes

On completing this chapter you will know about:

- Redundancy
- Retirement
- Dismissal

Introduction

One of the most demanding areas of human resource management in organizations is in handling arrangements for releasing people through redundancy, dismissal or retirement. This chapter deals with these issues in turn.

Redundancy

Redundancy takes place when the organization as a whole is going through a downsizing exercise, when structural changes are being made, following mergers and acquisitions, and when individual jobs are no longer needed. If, unfortunately, redundancy has to take place, it is necessary to plan ahead – seeking and implementing methods of avoiding redundancy as far as possible, making arrangements for voluntary redundancy and helping people to find jobs (outplacement). HR usually has the onerous responsibility of handling the redundancy itself if all else fails.

Planning ahead

Planning ahead means that future reductions in people needs are anticipated and steps are taken to minimize compulsory redundancies. This can be done by allowing the normal flow of leavers (natural wastage) to reduce or even eliminate the need for redundancy, calling in outsourced work, reducing or eliminating overtime, reducing the number of part-timers and temporary staff, work-sharing (two people splitting one job between them), or, more reluctantly, temporary layoffs.

Voluntary redundancy

Asking for volunteers – with a suitable payoff – is another way of reducing compulsory redundancies. The disadvantage is that the wrong people might go, ie the good workers who find it easy to get other work. It is sometimes necessary to go into reverse and offer such people a special loyalty bonus if they stay on.

Outplacement

Outplacement is about helping redundant employees to find other work. It means helping them to cope with the trauma of redundancy through job shops and by counselling, often through specialized outplacement consultants.

Job shops

Help may be provided on an individual basis through counselling or outplacement consultants, but in larger scale redundancies 'job shops' can be set up. The staff of the job shop, who may be from HR or are sometimes members of a specialized outplacement consultancy, scour the travel-to-work area seeking job opportunities, match people to jobs and arrange interviews.

Counselling

Counselling involves help and advice in identifying possible moves, preparing CVs and how to make the best impression in interviews. Counselling may be provided by HR staff but there is much to be said for using specialized outplacement consultants.

Outplacement consultants

Outplacement consultants provide counselling on how people can make the best use of what they can offer to other employers. They can be helped to identify their strengths and achievements, the type of job they are qualified to do and the sort of employer who is most likely to want people with their experience and qualifications. Assistance can be provided in preparing what is sometimes called an 'achievement CV', which spells out what the individual has been successful in and prompts the thought in the employer's mind that 'what the individual has done for them he or she can do for us'.

Dismissal

Dismissal takes place when an employer terminates the employment of someone with or without notice. A contract can be terminated as a result of demotion or transfer as well as dismissal. People can be 'constructively dismissed' if they resign because of their employer's unreasonable behaviour.

The principles of natural justice

- Individuals should know the standards of performance they are expected to meet and the rules to which they are expected to conform.
- They should be given a clear indication of where they are failing or what rules they have broken.
- Except in cases of gross misconduct, they should be given an opportunity to improve before disciplinary action is taken.

Dismissals should be handled in accordance with the principles of natural justice. These principles should form the basis of a disciplinary procedure, which is staged as follows.

Stages in a disciplinary procedure

1. An informal discussion on the problem.
2. A first written warning.
3. A final written warning.
4. Dismissal or action short of dismissal such as loss of pay or demotion.

If an employee faces serious disciplinary action such as dismissal the minimum statutory procedure should be followed, which involves:

Step 1: a written note to the employee setting out the allegation and the basis for it.
Step 2: a meeting to consider and discuss the situation.
Step 3: a right of appeal including an appeal meeting.

Employees should be reminded of their right to be accompanied by a colleague or employee representative in disciplinary hearings.

Managers and team leaders should be made aware of the procedure and told what authority they have to take action. It is advisable to have all written warnings and any final action approved by a higher authority. In cases of gross misconduct, managers and team leaders should be given the right to suspend if higher authority is not available, but not to dismiss. The importance of obtaining and recording the facts should be emphasized. Managers should always have a colleague with them when issuing a final warning and should make a note to file of what was said on the spot.

Retirement

Retirement is a major change and should be prepared for. Retirement policies need to specify:

- when people are due to retire;
- the circumstances, if any, in which they can work beyond their normal retirement date;

- the provision of pre-retirement training on such matters as finance, insurance, state pension rights and other benefits, health, working either for money or for a voluntary organization, and sources of advice and help;
- the provision of advice to people about to retire.

Release from the organization – key learning points

Redundancy

If, unfortunately, redundancy has to take place, it is necessary to plan ahead – seeking and implementing methods of avoiding redundancy as far as possible, making arrangements for voluntary redundancy and helping people to find jobs (outplacement). HR usually has the onerous responsibility of handling the redundancy itself if all else fails.

Dismissal

Dismissal takes place when an employer terminates the employment of someone with or without notice. A contract can be terminated as a result of demotion or transfer as well as dismissal. People can be 'constructively dismissed' if they resign because of their employer's unreasonable behaviour.

Retirement

Retirement policies need to specify:

- when people are due to retire;
- the circumstances, if any, in which they can work beyond their normal retirement date;
- the provision of pre-retirement training on such matters as finance, insurance, state pension rights and other benefits, health, working either for money or for a voluntary organization, and sources of advice and help;
- the provision of advice to people about to retire.

Questions

1. How should planning ahead for redundancy take place?
2. What are the stages in a disciplinary procedure?
3. What should retirement policies specify?

Part VII

Performance Management

Performance management processes have come to the fore in recent years as means of providing a more integrated and continuous approach to the management of performance than was provided by previous isolated and often inadequate merit rating or performance appraisal schemes. Performance management is based on the principle of management by agreement or contract rather than management by command. It emphasizes development and the initiation of self-managed learning plans as well as the integration of individual and corporate objectives. It can, in fact, play a major role in providing for an integrated and coherent range of human resource management processes that are mutually supportive and contribute as a whole to improving organizational effectiveness.

Part VII contents

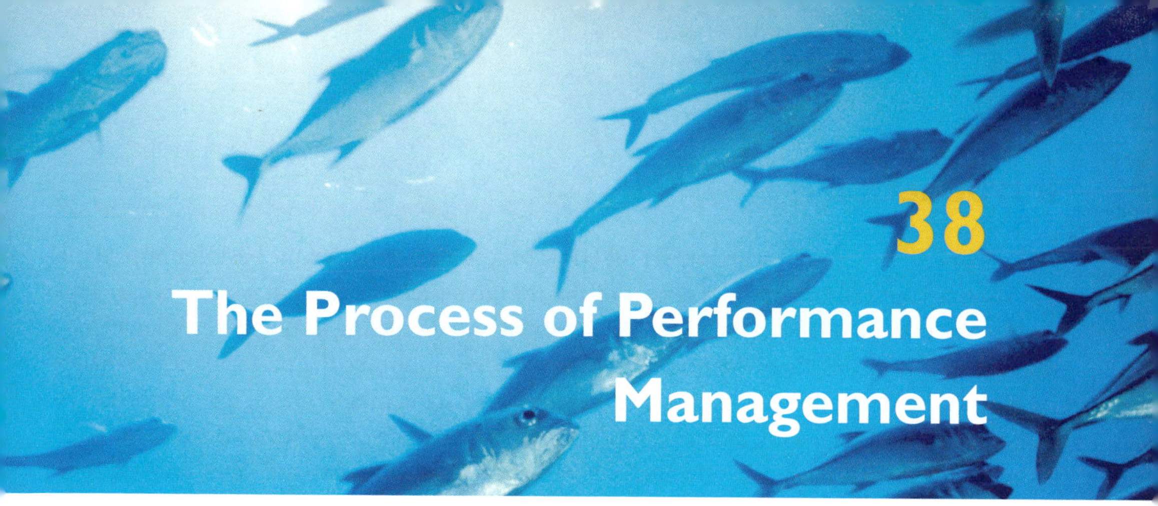

38 The Process of Performance Management

Key concepts and terms

- Control theory
- Objectives
- Performance management
- Social cognitive theory
- Goal theory
- Performance appraisal
- Personal development planning
- SMART objectives

Learning outcomes

On completing this chapter you will know about:

- Objectives of performance management
- The performance management cycle
- Types of objectives
- Managing performance throughout the year
- Rating performance
- Introducing performance management
- Characteristics of performance management
- Performance and development agreements
- Performance planning
- Reviewing performance
- Dealing with under-performers
- Line managers and performance management

Introduction

Performance management is an important HRM process that provides the basis for improving and developing performance and is part of the reward system in its most general sense. This chapter starts by defining performance management and discussing its objectives, characteristics and underpinning theories. It continues with a description of the performance management cycle and its three constituents: performance agreement, managing performance continuously, and reviewing and assessing performance. Finally, the chapter deals with managing under-performers, introducing performance management and the role of line managers.

Performance management defined

Performance management is a systematic process for improving organizational performance by developing the performance of individuals and teams. It is a means of getting better results by understanding and managing performance within an agreed framework of planned goals, standards and competency requirements. As Weiss and Hartle (1997) commented, performance management is: 'A process for establishing a shared understanding about what is to be achieved and how it is to be achieved, and an approach to managing people that increases the probability of achieving success.'

The main concerns of performance management

Performance management is concerned with:

- aligning individual objectives to organizational objectives and encouraging individuals to uphold corporate core values;
- enabling expectations to be defined and agreed in terms of role responsibilities and accountabilities (expected to do), skills (expected to have) and behaviours (expected to be);
- providing opportunities for individuals to identify their own goals and develop their skills and competencies.

It is sometimes assumed that performance appraisal is the same thing as performance management. But there are significant differences. Performance appraisal can be defined as the formal assessment and rating of individuals by their managers at or after a review meeting. It has been discredited because too often it has been operated as a top-down and largely bureaucratic system owned by the HR department rather than by line managers. As Armstrong and Murlis (1998) asserted, performance appraisal too often degenerated into 'a dishonest annual ritual'.

In contrast performance management is a continuous and much wider, more comprehensive and more natural process of management that clarifies mutual expectations, emphasizes the support role of managers who are expected to act as coaches rather than judges and focuses on the future.

Objectives of performance management

The overall objective of performance management is to develop the capacity of people to meet and exceed expectations and to achieve their full potential to the benefit of themselves and the organization. Performance management provides the basis for self-development but importantly, it is also about ensuring that the support and guidance people need to develop and improve is readily available.

SOURCE REVIEW

Performance management objectives – respondents to the 2005 e-reward survey

- Align individual and organizational objectives – 64 per cent.
- Improve organizational performance – 63 per cent.
- Improve individual performance – 46 per cent.
- Provide the basis for personal development – 37 per cent.
- Develop a performance culture – 32 per cent.
- Inform contribution/performance pay decisions – 21 per cent.

The following is a typical statement of objectives from one respondent to the e-reward survey: 'To support culture change by creating a performance culture and reinforcing the values of the organization with an emphasis on the importance of these in getting a balance between "what" is delivered and "how" it is delivered.'

Characteristics of performance management

Performance management is a planned process of which the five primary elements are agreement, measurement, feedback, positive reinforcement and dialogue. It is concerned with measuring outcomes in the shape of delivered performance compared with expectations expressed as objectives (management by objectives). In this respect it focuses on targets, standards and performance measures or indicators. It is based on the agreement of role requirements, objectives and performance improvement and personal development plans. It provides the setting for ongoing dialogues about performance, which involves the joint and continuing review of achievements against objectives, requirements and plans.

It is also concerned with inputs and values. The inputs are the knowledge, skills and behaviours required to produce the expected results. Developmental needs are identified by defining these requirements and assessing the extent to which the expected levels of performance have been achieved through the effective use of knowledge and skills and through appropriate behaviour that upholds core values.

Performance management is not just a top-down process in which managers tell their subordinates what they think about them, set objectives and institute performance improvement plans. It is not something that is done *to* people. As Buchner (2007) emphasizes, performance management should be something that is done *for* people and in partnership with them.

Performance management is a continuous and flexible process that involves managers and those whom they manage acting as partners within a framework that sets out how they can best work together to achieve the required results. It is based on the principle of management by contract and agreement rather than management by command. It relies on consensus and cooperation rather than control or coercion.

Performance management focuses on future performance planning and improvement and personal development rather than on retrospective performance appraisal (Armstrong, 2006). It functions as a continuous and evolutionary process in which performance improves over time. It provides the basis for regular and frequent dialogues between managers and individuals about performance and development needs based on feedback and self-assessment. It is mainly concerned with individual performance but it can also be applied to teams. The emphasis is on development, although performance management is an important part of the reward system through the provision of feedback and recognition and the identification of opportunities for growth. It may be associated with performance- or contribution-related pay but its developmental aspects are much more important.

Underpinning theories

The following three theories underpinning performance management have been identified by Buchner (2007).

Goal theory

Goal theory, as developed by Latham and Locke (1979), highlights four mechanisms that connect goals to performance outcomes: 1) they direct attention to priorities; 2) they stimulate effort; 3) they challenge people to bring their knowledge and skills to bear to increase their chances of success; and 4) the more challenging the goal, the more people will draw on their full repertoire of skills. This theory underpins the emphasis in performance management on setting and agreeing objectives against which performance can be measured and managed.

Control theory

Control theory focuses attention on feedback as a means of shaping behaviour. As people receive feedback on their behaviour they appreciate the discrepancy between what they are doing and what they are expected to do and take corrective action to overcome the discrepancy. Feedback is recognized as a crucial part of performance management processes.

Social cognitive theory

Social cognitive theory was developed by Bandura (1986). It is based on his central concept of self-efficacy. This suggests that what people believe they can or cannot do powerfully impacts on their performance. Developing and strengthening positive self-belief in employees is therefore an important performance management objective.

The performance management cycle

Performance management takes the form of a continuous self-renewing cycle, as illustrated in Figure 38.1 and described below.

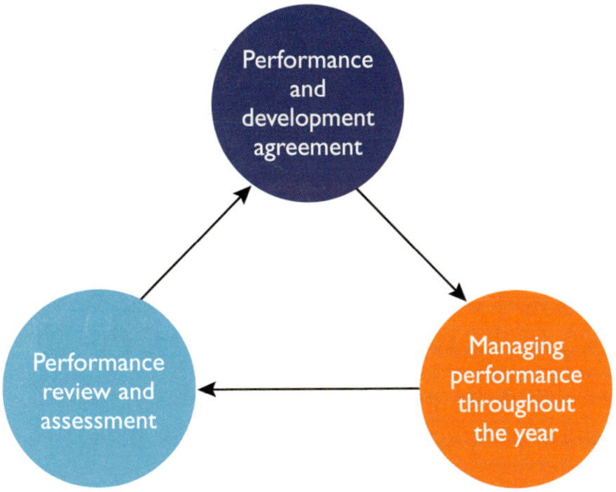

Figure 38.1 The performance management cycle

Performance and development agreements

Performance and development agreements form the basis for development, assessment and feedback in the performance management process. They define expectations in the form of a role profile, which sets out role requirements in terms of key result areas and the competencies required for effective performance. The role profile provides the basis for agreeing objectives and methods of measuring performance and assessing the level of competency reached. The performance agreement incorporates any performance improvement plans that may be necessary and a personal development plan. It describes what individuals are expected to do but also indicates what support they will receive from their manager.

Performance agreements emerge from the analysis of role requirements and the performance review. An assessment of past performance leads to an analysis of future requirements. The two processes can take place at the same meeting.

Defining role requirements

The foundation for performance management is a role profile, which defines the role in terms of the key results expected, what role holders need to know and be able to do (technical competencies), and how they are expected to behave in terms of behavioural competencies and upholding the organization's core values. Role profiles need to be updated every time a formal performance agreement is developed. Guidelines on preparing role profiles and an example are given in Chapter 26.

Objectives

Objectives or goals describe something that has to be accomplished. Objectives setting that results in an agreement on what the role holder has to achieve is an important part of the performance management processes of defining and managing expectations and forms the point of reference for performance reviews.

Types of objectives

- Ongoing role or work objectives – all roles have built-in objectives that may be expressed as key result areas in a role profile.
- Targets – these define the quantifiable results to be attained as measured in such terms as output, throughput, income, sales, levels of service delivery and cost reduction.
- Tasks/projects – objectives can be set for the completion of tasks or projects by a specified date or to achieve an interim result.

- Behavioural – behavioural expectations are often set out generally in competency frameworks but they may also be defined individually under the framework headings. Competency frameworks may deal with areas of behaviour associated with core values, for example teamwork, but they often convert the aspirations contained in value statements into more specific examples of desirable and undesirable behaviour, which can help in planning and reviewing performance.

Criteria for objectives

Many organizations use the following SMART mnemonic to summarize the criteria for objectives:

S = Specific/stretching – clear, unambiguous, straightforward, understandable and challenging.
M = Measurable – quantity, quality, time, money.
A = Achievable – challenging but within the reach of a competent and committed person.
R = Relevant – relevant to the objectives of the organization so that the goal of the individual is aligned to corporate goals.
T = Time framed – to be completed within an agreed timescale.

Measuring performance in achieving objectives

Measurement is an important concept in performance management. It is the basis for providing and generating feedback, it identifies where things are going well to provide the foundations for building further success, and it indicates where things are not going so well, so that corrective action can be taken.

Measuring performance is relatively easy for those who are responsible for achieving quantified targets, for example sales. It is more difficult in the case of knowledge workers, for example scientists. But this difficulty is alleviated if a distinction is made between the two forms of results – outputs and outcomes. An output is a result that can be measured quantifiably, while an outcome is a visible effect that is the result of effort but cannot necessarily be measured in quantified terms.

There are components in all jobs that are difficult to measure quantifiably as outputs, but all jobs produce outcomes even if they are not quantified. It is therefore often necessary to measure performance by reference to what outcomes have been attained in comparison with what outcomes were expected, and the outcomes may be expressed in qualitative terms as a standard or level of competency to be attained. That is why it is important when agreeing objectives to answer the question, 'How will we know that this objective has been achieved?' The answer needs to be expressed in the form, 'Because such and such will have happened.' The 'such and such' will be defined either as outputs in such forms as meeting or exceeding a quantified target, completing a project or task satisfactorily (what is 'satisfactory' having been defined), or as outcomes in such forms as reaching an agreed standard of performance, or delivering an agreed level of service.

However, when assessing performance it is also necessary to consider inputs in the shape of the degree of knowledge and skill attained and behaviour that is demonstrably in line with the standards set out in competency frameworks and statements of core values. Behaviour cannot be measured quantitatively but it can be assessed against definitions of what constitutes good and not so good behaviour, and the evidence that can be used to make that assessment can be identified.

Performance planning

The performance planning part of the performance management sequence involves agreement between the manager and the individual on what the latter needs to do to achieve objectives, raise standards, improve performance and develop the required competencies. It also establishes priorities – the key aspects of the job to which attention has to be given. The aim is to ensure that the meaning of the objectives, performance standards and competencies as they apply to everyday work is understood. They are the basis for converting aims into action.

Agreement is also reached at this stage on how performance will be measured and the evidence that will be used to establish levels of competence. It is important that these measures and evidence requirements should be identified and fully agreed now because they will be used by individuals as well as managers to monitor and demonstrate achievements.

Personal development planning

A personal development plan provides a learning action plan for which individuals are responsible with the support of their managers and the organization. It may include formal training but, more importantly, it will incorporate a wider set of learning and development activities such as self-managed learning, coaching, mentoring, project work, job enlargement and job enrichment. If multi-source assessment (360-degree feedback) is practised in the organization this will be used to discuss development needs.

The development plan records the actions agreed to improve performance and to develop knowledge, skills and capabilities. It is likely to focus on development in the current job – to improve the ability to perform it well and also, importantly, to enable individuals to take on wider responsibilities, extending their capacity to undertake a broader role. This plan therefore contributes to the achievement of a policy of continuous development that is predicated on the belief that everyone is capable of learning more and doing better in their jobs. The plan will also contribute to enhancing the potential of individuals to carry out higher-level jobs.

Managing performance throughout the year

Perhaps one of the most important concepts of performance management is that it is a continuous process that reflects normal good management practices of setting direction, monitoring and measuring performance and taking action accordingly. Performance management should not be imposed on managers as something 'special' they have to do. It should instead be treated as a natural function that all good managers carry out.

This approach contrasts with that used in conventional performance appraisal systems, which were usually built around an annual event, the formal review, which tended to dwell on the past. This was carried out at the behest of the personnel department, often perfunctorily, and then forgotten. Managers proceeded to manage without any further reference to the outcome of the review and the appraisal form was buried in the personnel record system.

To ensure that a performance management culture is built and maintained, performance management has to have the active support and encouragement of top management who must make it clear that it is regarded as a vital means of achieving sustained organizational success. They must emphasize that performance management is what managers are expected to do and that their performance as managers will be measured by reference to the extent to which they do it conscientiously and well. Importantly, the rhetoric supporting performance management must be converted into reality by the deeds as well as the words of the people who have the ultimate responsibility for running the business.

The sequence of performance management activities as described in this chapter does no more than provide a framework within which managers, individuals and teams work together in whatever ways best suit them to gain better understanding of what is to be done, how it is to be done and what has been achieved. This framework and the philosophy that supports it can form the basis for training newly appointed or would-be managers in this key area of their responsibilities. It can also help in improving the performance of managers who are not up to standard in this respect.

A formal, often annual, review is still an important part of a performance management framework but it is not the most important part. Equal, if not more, prominence is given to the performance agreement and the continuous process of performance management.

Reviewing performance

Although performance management is a continuous process it is still necessary to have a formal review once or twice a year. This provides a focal point for the consideration of key performance and development issues. The performance review meeting is the means through which the five primary performance management elements of agreement, measurement, feedback, positive reinforcement and dialogue can be put to good use. It leads to the completion of the performance management cycle by informing performance and development agreements. It involves some form of assessment, as considered in the next section of this chapter.

The review should be rooted in the reality of the individual's performance. It is concrete, not abstract and it allows managers and individuals to take a positive look together at how performance can become better in the future and how any problems in meeting performance standards and achieving objectives can be resolved. Individuals should be encouraged to assess their own performance and become active agents for change in improving their results. Managers should be encouraged to adopt their proper enabling role; coaching and providing support and guidance.

There should be no surprises in a formal review if performance issues have been dealt with as they should have been – as they arise during the year. Traditional appraisals are often no more than an analysis of where those involved are now, and where they have come from. This static and historical approach is not what performance management is about. The true role of performance management is to look forward to what needs to be done by people to achieve the purpose of the job, to meet new challenges, to make even better use of their knowledge, skills and abilities, to develop their capabilities by establishing a self-managed learning agenda and to reach agreement on any areas where performance needs to be improved and how that improvement should take place. This process also helps managers to improve their ability to lead, guide and develop the individuals and teams for whom they are responsible.

The most common practice has traditionally been to have one annual review, which was the practice of 44 per cent of the respondents to the 2008 IRS survey (Wolff, 2008). But twice-yearly reviews are becoming more common (39 per cent of the IRS respondents). These reviews lead directly into the conclusion of a performance agreement (at the same meeting or later). It can be argued that formal reviews are unnecessary and that it is better to conduct informal reviews as part of normal good management practice to be carried out as and when required. Such informal reviews are valuable as part of the continuing process of performance management (managing performance throughout the year, as discussed in the previous chapter). But there is everything to be said for an annual or half-yearly review that sums up the conclusions reached at earlier reviews and provides a firm foundation for a new performance agreement and a framework for reviewing performance informally, whenever appropriate.

Criteria for reviewing performance

The criteria for reviewing performance should be balanced between:

- achievements in relation to objectives;
- the level of knowledge and skills possessed and applied (competences or technical competencies);

- behaviour in the job as it affects performance (competencies);
- the degree to which behaviour upholds the core values of the organization;
- day-to-day effectiveness.

The criteria should not be limited to a few quantified objectives as has often been the case in traditional appraisal schemes. In many cases the most important consideration will be the job holders' day-to-day effectiveness in meeting the continuing performance standards associated with their key tasks. It may not be possible to agree meaningful new quantified targets for some jobs every year. Equal attention needs to be given to the behaviour that has produced the results as to the results themselves.

Conducting a performance review meeting

There are 12 golden rules for conducting performance review meetings.

1. *Be prepared.* Managers should prepare by referring to a list of agreed objectives and their notes on performance throughout the year. They should form views about the reasons for success or failure and decide where to give praise, which performance problems should be mentioned and what steps might be undertaken to overcome them. Thought should also be given to any changes that have taken place or are contemplated in the individual's role and to work and personal objectives for the next period.

   Individuals should also prepare in order to identify achievements and problems, and to be ready to assess their own performance at the meeting. They should also note any points they wish to raise about their work and prospects.

2. *Work to a clear structure.* The meeting should be planned to cover all the points identified during preparation. Sufficient time should be allowed for a full discussion – hurried meetings will be ineffective. An hour or two is usually necessary to get maximum value from the review.

3. *Create the right atmosphere.* A successful meeting depends on creating an informal environment in which a full, frank but friendly exchange of views can take place. It is best to start with a fairly general discussion before getting into any detail.

4. *Provide good feedback.* Individuals need to know how they are getting on. Feedback should be based on factual evidence. It refers to results, events, critical incidents and significant behaviours that have affected performance in specific ways. The feedback should be presented in a manner that enables individuals to recognize and accept its factual nature – it should be a description of what has happened, not a judgement. Positive feedback should be given on the things that the individual did well in addition to areas for improvement. People are more likely to work at improving their performance and developing their skills if they feel empowered by the process.

5. *Use time productively.* The reviewer should test understanding, obtain information, and seek proposals and support. Time should be allowed for the individual to express his or her views fully and to respond to any comments made by the manager. The meeting should take the form of a dialogue between two interested and involved parties both of whom are seeking a positive conclusion.
6. *Use praise.* If possible, managers should begin with praise for some specific achievement, but this should be sincere and deserved. Praise helps people to relax – everyone needs encouragement and appreciation.
7. *Let individuals do most of the talking.* This enables them to get things off their chest and helps them to feel that they are getting a fair hearing. Use open-ended questions (ie questions that invite the individual to think about what to reply rather than indicating the expected answer). This is to encourage people to expand.
8. *Invite self-assessment.* This is to see how things look from the individual's point of view and to provide a basis for discussion – many people underestimate themselves. Ask questions such as those given below.

Self-assessment questions

- How well do you feel you have done?
- What do you feel are your strengths?
- What do you like most/least about your job?
- Why do you think that project went well?
- Why do you think you didn't meet that target?

9. *Discuss performance not personality.* Discussions on performance should be based on factual evidence, not opinion. Always refer to actual events or behaviour and to results compared with agreed performance measures. Individuals should be given plenty of scope to explain why something did or did not happen.
10. *Encourage analysis of performance.* Don't just hand out praise or blame. Analyse jointly and objectively why things went well or badly and what can be done to maintain a high standard or to avoid problems in the future.
11. *Don't deliver unexpected criticisms.* There should be no surprises. The discussion should only be concerned with events or behaviours that have been noted at the time they took place. Feedback on performance should be immediate; it should not wait until the end of the year. The purpose of the formal review is to reflect briefly on experiences during the review period and on this basis to look ahead.

12. *Agree measurable objectives and a plan of action.* The aim should be to end the review meeting on a positive note.

These golden rules may sound straightforward and obvious enough but they will only function properly in a culture that supports this type of approach. This emphasizes the importance of getting and keeping top management support and the need to take special care in developing and introducing the system and in training managers and their staff.

Assessing performance

Most performance management schemes include some form of rating, which is usually carried out during or after a performance review meeting. The rating indicates the quality of performance or competence achieved or displayed by an employee by selecting the level on a scale that most closely corresponds with the view of the assessor on how well the individual has been doing. A rating scale is supposed to assist in making judgements and it enables those judgements to be categorized to inform performance or contribution pay decisions, or simply to produce an instant summary for the record of how well or not so well someone is doing.

The rationale for rating

There are four arguments for rating:

1. It recognizes the fact that we all form an overall view of the performance of the people who work for us and that it makes sense to express that view explicitly against a framework of reference rather than hiding it. Managers can thus be held to account for the ratings they make and be required to justify them.
2. It is useful to sum up judgements about people – indicating who are the exceptional performers or under-performers and who are the reliable core performers so that action can be taken (developmental or some form of reward).
3. It is impossible to have performance or contribution pay without ratings – there has to be a method that relates the size of an award to the level of individual achievement. However, many organizations with contribution or performance pay do not include ratings as part of the performance management process – 23 per cent of the respondents to the e-reward 2005 survey.
4. It conveys a clear message to people on how they are doing and can motivate them to improve performance if they seek an answer to the question, 'What do I have to do to get a higher rating next time?'

Types of rating scales

Rating scales can be defined alphabetically (a, b, c, etc), or numerically (1, 2, 3, etc). Initials (ex for excellent, etc) are sometimes used in an attempt to disguise the hierarchical nature of the scale. The alphabetical or numerical points scale points may be described adjectivally, for example, a = excellent, b = good, c =satisfactory and d= unsatisfactory.

Alternatively, scale levels may be described verbally as in the following example:

- Exceptional performance: Exceeds expectations and consistently makes an outstanding contribution that significantly extends the impact and influence of the role.
- Well-balanced performance: Meets objectives and requirements of the role; consistently performs in a thoroughly proficient manner.
- Barely effective performance: Does not meet all objectives or role requirements of the role; significant performance improvements are needed.
- Unacceptable performance: Fails to meet most objectives or requirements of the role; shows a lack of commitment to performance improvement, or a lack of ability, which has been discussed prior to the performance review.

The e-reward 2005 survey of performance management found that overall ratings were used by 70 per cent of respondents, and the most popular number of levels was five (43 per cent of respondents). However, some organizations are settling for three levels. There is no evidence that any single approach is clearly much superior to another, although the greater the number of levels the more is being asked of managers in the shape of discriminatory judgement. It does, however, seem to be preferable for level definitions to be positive rather than negative and for them to provide as much guidance as possible on the choice of ratings. It is equally important to ensure that level definitions are compatible with the culture of the organization and that close attention is given to ensuring that managers use them as consistently as possible.

Problems with rating

Ratings are largely subjective and it is difficult to achieve consistency between the ratings given by different managers (ways of achieving consistent judgements are discussed below). Because the notion of 'performance' is often unclear, subjectivity can increase. Even if objectivity is achieved, to sum up the total performance of a person with a single rating is a gross over-simplification of what may be a complex set of factors influencing that performance – to do this after a detailed discussion of strengths and weaknesses suggests that the rating will be a superficial and arbitrary judgement. To label people as 'average' or 'below average', or whatever equivalent terms are used, is both demeaning and demotivating.

The whole performance review meeting may be dominated by the fact that it will end with a rating, thus severely limiting the forward-looking and developmental focus of the meeting, which is all-important. This is particularly the case if the rating governs performance or contribution pay increases.

Achieving consistency in ratings

The problem with rating scales is that it is very difficult, if not impossible without very careful management, to ensure that a consistent approach is adopted by managers responsible for rating, and this means that performance or contribution pay decisions will be suspect. It is almost inevitable that some people will be more generous, while others will be harder on their staff. Some managers may be inconsistent in the distribution of ratings to their staff because they are indulging in favouritism or prejudice.

Ratings can, of course, be monitored and challenged if their distribution is significantly out of line, and computer-based systems have been introduced for this purpose in some organizations. But many managers want to do the best for their staff, either because they genuinely believe that they are better or because they are trying to curry favour. It can be difficult in these circumstances to challenge them. The basic methods for increasing consistency described below are training, calibration and monitoring. More draconian methods of achieving consistency, also described below, are forced distribution and forced ranking.

Training

Training can take place in the form of 'consistency' workshops for managers who discuss how ratings can be objectively justified and test rating decisions on simulated performance review data. This can build a level of common understanding about rating levels.

Calibration (peer reviews)

Groups of managers meet to review the pattern of each other's ratings and challenge unusual decisions or distributions. This process of calibration or peer reviews is time-consuming but is possibly the best way to achieve a reasonable degree of consistency, especially when the group members share some knowledge of the performances of each other's staff as internal customers.

Monitoring

The distribution of ratings is monitored by a central department, usually HR, which challenges any unusual patterns and identifies and questions what appear to be unwarrantable differences between departments' ratings.

Forced distribution

Forced distribution means that managers have to conform to a laid down distribution of ratings between different levels. The pattern of distribution may correspond to the normal curve of distribution that has been observed to apply to IQ scores, although there is no evidence that performance in an organization is distributed normally – there are so many other factors at work such as recruitment and development practices. A typical normal distribution of ratings is: A=5 per cent, B = 15 per cent C = 60 per cent, D = 15 per cent and E = 5 per cent. This is similar to the academic practice of 'rating on the curve', which distributes grades in accordance with the distribution represented by the normal or bell-shaped curve.

Forced distribution achieves consistency of a sort, but managers and staff rightly resent being forced into this sort of straightjacket. Only 8 per cent of the respondents to the CIPD 2004 performance management survey (Armstrong and Baron, 2004) used forced distribution.

Forced ranking

Forced ranking is a development of forced distribution. It is sometimes called the 'vitality curve'. It is more common in the United States than in the UK. Managers are required to place their staff in order from best to worst. Rankings can be generated directly from the assignment of employees to categories (eg A, B and C) or indirectly through the transformation of performance ratings into groups of employees. The problem with forced ranking, as with forced distribution and other overall rating systems, is that the notion of performance is vague. In the case of ranking it is therefore unclear what the resulting order of employees truly represents. If used at all, ranks must be accompanied by meaningful performance data.

Some organizations, mainly in the United States, have gone as far as adopting the practice of terminating annually the employment of 5 to 10 per cent of the consistently lowest performers. It is claimed that this practice 'raises the bar', ie it is said that it improves the overall level of performance in the business. There is no evidence that this is the case.

Visual methods of assessment

An alternative approach to rating is to use a visual method of assessment. This takes the form of an agreement between the manager and the individual on where the latter should be placed on a matrix or grid, as illustrated in Figure 38.2. A 'snapshot' is thus provided of the individual's overall contribution that is presented visually and as such provides a better basis for analysis and discussion than a mechanistic rating. The assessment of contribution refers to outputs and to behaviours, attitudes and overall approach.

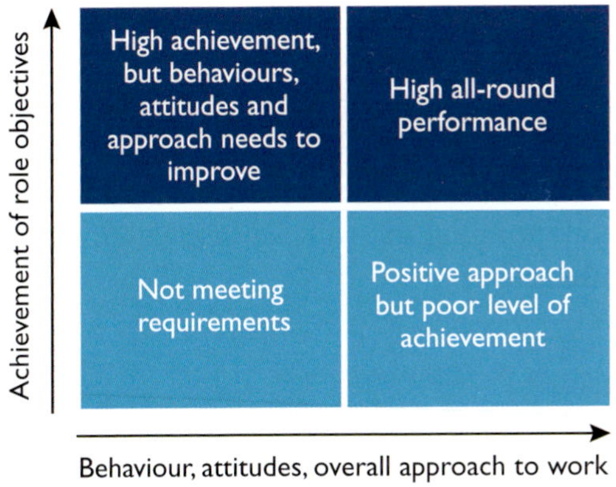

Figure 38.2 Performance matrix

The review guidelines accompanying the matrix are as follows.

You and your manager need to agree an overall assessment. This will be recorded in the summary page at the beginning of the review document. The aim is to get a balanced assessment of your contribution through the year. The assessment will take account of how you have performed against the responsibilities of your role as described in the Role Profile; objectives achieved and competency development over the course of the year. The assessment will become relevant for pay increases in the future.

The grid on the annual performance review summary is meant to provide a visual snapshot of your overall contribution. This replaces a more conventional rating scale approach. It reflects the fact that your contribution is determined not just by results, but also by your overall approach towards your work and how you behave towards colleagues and customers.

The evidence recorded in the performance review will be used to support where your manager places a mark on the grid.

Their assessment against the vertical axis will be based on an assessment of your performance against your objectives, performance standards described in your role profile, and any other work achievements recorded in the review. Together these represent 'outputs'.

The assessment against the horizontal axis will be based on an overall assessment of your performance against the competency level definitions for the role.

Note that someone who is new in the role may be placed in one of the lower quadrants but this should not be treated as an indication of development needs and not as a reflection on the individual's performance.

Conclusions on ratings

Many organizations retain ratings because they perceive that the advantages outweigh the disadvantages. But organizations that want to emphasize the developmental aspect of performance management and play down, even eliminate, the performance pay element, will be convinced by the objections to rating and will dispense with them altogether, relying instead on overall analysis and assessment.

Dealing with under-performers

The improvement of performance is a fundamental part of the continuous process of performance management. The aim should be the positive one of maximizing high performance, although this involves taking steps to deal with under-performance. When managing under-performers remember the advice given by Handy (1989), which was that this should be about 'applauding success and forgiving failure'. He suggests that mistakes should be used as an opportunity for learning – 'something only possible if the mistake is truly forgiven because otherwise the lesson is heard as a reprimand and not as an offer of help'.

When dealing with poor performers, note should be made of the following comments by Risher (2003): 'Poor performance is best seen as a problem in which the employer and management are both accountable. In fact, one can argue that it is unlikely to emerge if people are effectively managed.' This is another way of expressing the old Army saying: 'There are no bad soldiers, only bad officers.'

Managing under-performers is therefore a positive process that is based on feedback throughout the year and looks forward to what can be done by individuals to overcome performance problems and, importantly, how managers can provide support and help. The five basic steps required to manage under-performers are as follows:

1. *Identify and agree the problem.* Analyse the feedback and, as far as possible, obtain agreement from the individual on what the shortfall has been. Feedback may be provided by managers but it can in a sense be built into the job. This takes place when individuals are aware of their targets and standards, know what performance measures will be used and either receive feedback/control information automatically or have easy access to it. They will then be in a position to measure and assess their own performance and, if they are well-motivated and well-trained, take their own corrective actions. In other words, a self-regulating feedback mechanism exists. This is a situation managers should endeavour to create on the grounds that prevention is better than cure.
2. *Establish the reason(s) for the shortfall.* When seeking the reasons for any shortfalls the manager should not be trying crudely to attach blame. The aim should be for the manager and the individual jointly to identify the facts that have contributed to the problem. It is

on the basis of this factual analysis that decisions can be made on what to do about it by the individual, the manager or the two of them working together.

It is necessary first to identify any causes external to the job and outside the control of either the manager or the individual. Any factors that are within the control of the individual and/or the manager can then be considered. What needs to be determined is the extent to which the reason for the problem is because the individual:

- did not receive adequate support or guidance from his or her manager;
- did not fully understand what he or she was expected to do;
- could not do it – ability;
- did not know how to do it – skill;
- would not do it – attitude.

3. *Decide and agree on the action required.* Action may be taken by the individual, the manager or both parties. This could include:

   - the individual taking steps to improve skills or change behaviour;
   - the individual changing attitudes – the challenge is that people will not change their attitudes simply because they are told to do so; they can only be helped to understand that certain changes to their behaviour could be beneficial not only to the organization but also to themselves;
   - the manager providing more support or guidance;
   - the manager and the individual working jointly to clarify expectations;
   - the manager and the individual working jointly to develop abilities and skills – this is a partnership in the sense that individuals will be expected to take steps to develop themselves but managers can give help as required in the form of coaching, training and providing additional experience.

   Whatever action is agreed, both parties must understand how they will know that it has succeeded. Feedback arrangements can be made but individuals should be encouraged to monitor their own performance and take further action as required.

4. *Resource the action.* Provide the coaching, training, guidance, experience or facilities required to enable agreed actions to happen.
5. *Monitor and provide feedback.* Both managers and individuals monitor performance, ensure that feedback is provided or obtained and analysed, and agree on any further actions that may be necessary.

Introducing performance management

The programme for introducing performance management should take into account the fact that one of the main reasons why it fails is that either line managers are not interested, or they don't have the skills, or both. It is important to get buy-in from top management so that their leadership can encourage line managers to play their part. To ensure buy-in, the process has to be simple (not too much paper) and managers have to be convinced that the time they spend will pay off in terms of improved performance. The demanding skills of concluding performance agreements, setting objectives, assessing performance, giving feedback and coaching need to be developed by formal training supplemented by coaching and the use of mentors.

Excellent practical advice on introducing performance management or making substantial changes to an existing scheme was given by the respondents to the e-reward 2005 survey. Comments in the form of dos and don'ts are set out below in the order of frequency with which they were mentioned.

Introducing performance management – dos and don'ts

Do:

- consult/involve;
- communicate (process and benefits);
- align and ensure relevance to organizational/business/ stakeholder needs;
- get ownership from line managers;
- monitor and evaluate;
- plan and prepare carefully;
- run a pilot scheme;
- treat as a business process;
- define performance expectations;
- get buy-in from senior management;
- keep it simple;
- ensure clear purpose and processes;
- align to culture;
- align with other HR processes;
- clarify link to reward;
- be realistic about the scale and pace of change;
- make the process mandatory.

Don't:

- just make it a form-filling, paper-intensive exercise;
- make it too complicated;

- rush in a new system;
- keep changing the system;
- link to pay;
- neglect communication, consultation and training;
- provide training;
- underestimate the time it takes to introduce;
- assume managers have the skills required;
- blindly follow others;
- assume that everyone wants it.

Examples of comments

- You can never do enough training/coaching of both staff and line managers. You can never do too much communication on the new changes.
- Ensure the process is seen as a business one not an HR process.
- Keep it simple and concentrate on the quality going into the process rather than the design of the process itself (although the design must be appropriate to the organization).
- Engage all managers in why it is important and ensure that they have the necessary understanding and skills to carry out the process. Get buy-in and tailor it to the specific needs of the organization. Get the support of key stakeholders, such as the union, from the start, and get them to work with you to sell the scheme. Agree the overall objectives and guiding principles with all concerned. Keep employees informed and ensure the message is consistent throughout.
- Understand clearly why you are doing it and the desired objectives. Engage others in design of the scheme. Communicate purpose, etc clearly.
- Don't expect that staff will leap for joy at the prospect of another way they would see of criticizing them in their job. Start your change management process where you think the staff are, not where you've assumed they are.
- Don't assume that what seems obvious and logical to you, as an HR manager, will also seem logical to other managers and staff. Don't get caught up in HR-speak and become precious about the differences between 'performance management' and 'appraisals' or between a 'personal development/learning plan' and a 'training plan'. As HR professionals we may be able to eloquently argue the subtle differences and merits of each – for most people the distinction is absolutely meaningless!
- Don't just make it a form-filling exercise – you need to gain the belief from managers that the system is beneficial otherwise it won't work.

- Don't put in a lengthy complicated process – it will become a chore to do rather than a meaningful exercise.
- Don't make HR own the initiative – it is a business improvement model and one which the business needs to manage.
- Don't assume that managers have the requisite skills to manage performance fairly and equitably, embark upon such an initiative without clear goals and without the support of respected key players in the organization, set the wheels in motion until extensive briefings/training have been completed.
- Don't underestimate the amount of work involved!
- Don't expect it to work quickly. It takes a few years to embed performance management in the organization's ethos.

Line managers and performance management

Line managers are crucial to the success of performance management, but there are problems. The e-reward 2005 survey of performance management established that the top four issues concerning respondents about their performance management processes were:

1. Line managers do not have the skills required – 88 per cent.
2. Line managers do not discriminate sufficiently when assessing performance – 84 per cent.
3. Line managers are not committed to performance management – 75 per cent.
4. Line managers are reluctant to conduct performance management reviews – 74 per cent.

When asked how they coped with these problems, respondents emphasized the importance of doing the following.

Gaining the commitment of line managers and enhancing their skills

- Involve line managers in the development and introduction of performance management.
- Train and coach line managers – existing managers and, importantly, potential and newly appointed managers.
- Getting top management to stress the importance they attach to performance management – by example as well as exhortation.

- Keep it simple – do not impose a bureaucratic system.
- Emphasize whenever possible that performance management is a normal process of management and that one of the criteria for assessing the performance of managers is how well they do it.
- Do whatever can be done to persuade line managers that formal performance reviews need not be stressful occasions if they are conducted properly but can in fact provide 'quality time' for the two parties to engage in a dialogue about performance and development opportunities (eliminating formal ratings helps).

The process of performance management – key learning points

Objectives of performance management

The overall objective of performance management is to develop the capacity of people to meet and exceed expectations and to achieve their full potential to the benefit of themselves and the organization. Performance management provides the basis for self-development but, importantly, it is also about ensuring that the support and guidance people need to develop and improve is readily available.

Characteristics of performance management

Performance management is a planned process of which the five primary elements are agreement, measurement, feedback, positive reinforcement and dialogue.

The performance management cycle

Performance management takes the form of a continuous self-renewing cycle: performance and development agreement; managing performance throughout the year; and performance review and assessment.

Performance and development agreements

Performance and development agreements form the basis for development, assessment and feedback in the performance management process. They define expectations in the form of a role profile, which sets out role requirements in terms of key result areas and the competencies required for effective performance. The role profile provides the basis for agreeing objectives and methods of measuring performance and assessing the level of competency reached. The performance agreement incorporates any performance improvement plans that may be necessary and a personal development plan.

Types of objectives

- Ongoing role or work.

The process of performance management – key learning points (continued)

- Tasks/projects.
- Behavioural.

Performance planning

The performance planning part of the performance management sequence involves agreement between the manager and the individual on what the latter needs to do to achieve objectives, raise standards, improve performance and develop the required competencies.

Managing performance throughout the year

Performance management is a continuous process that reflects normal good management practices of setting direction, monitoring and measuring performance and taking action accordingly.

Reviewing performance

Although performance management is a continuous process it is still necessary to have a formal review once or twice a year. This provides a focal point for the consideration of key performance and development issues.

Rating performance

Rating scales can be defined alphabetically (a, b, c, etc), or numerically (1, 2, 3, etc). Initials (ex for excellent, etc) are sometimes used in an attempt to disguise the hierarchical nature of the scale. The alphabetical or numerical points scale points may be described adjectivally, for example, a = excellent, b = good, c =satisfactory and d= unsatisfactory.

Dealing with under-performers

Managing under-performers is a positive process based on feedback throughout the year and looks forward to what can be done by individuals to overcome performance problems and, importantly, how managers can provide support and help.

Introducing performance management

The programme for introducing performance management should take into account the fact that one of the main reasons it fails is that either line managers are not interested, or they don't have the skills, or both. It is important to get buy-in from top management so that their leadership can encourage line managers to play their part.

Line managers and performance management

Line managers are crucial to the success of performance management. But there can be problems with their commitment and skills and it is necessary to involve them in developing the process, provide training and guidance, gain top management support, keep the process simple, emphasize that performance reviews provide for quality time with their staff and need not be stressful if conducted properly.

Questions

1. David Guest wrote in 1987 that, 'Performance management has a poor record of success, and the temptation is to engage in a spiral of control in an attempt to extract more effort and ever higher performance from employees through policies and practices that may succeed only in further de-motivating and which are, thereby, ultimately self-defeating.' To what extent is this true today? Justify your answer by reference to experience in your organization and recent research.
2. From your chief executive: 'About your proposal that we should introduce a performance management system. I thought we already had a performance appraisal system, so what's the difference and why is performance management better?' Reply.
3. Comment on the following conclusions about performance management reached by Latham *et al* (2007): 'The answers required to move the field of performance management forward are much less straightforward than the questions. We know a great deal more about ways to manage the performance of an individual than about ways to manage a team. We know what to observe and how to observe an individual objectively. We are at a loss as to how to overcome political considerations that lead people not to do so. Advances in knowledge have been made with regard to technology that managers embrace to assist in the appraisal process, and that in the eyes of employees, their managers misuse. We know that making decisions is inherent in performance management, yet solutions to decision-making errors remain a mystery. Great strides in this domain include recognition that ongoing performance management is more effective than an annual appraisal in bringing about a positive change in an employee's behaviour, and that context must be taken into account in doing so.'
4. From the managing director to the HR director: 'We went to all that time and trouble (and cost) last year to introduce your all-singing and all-dancing performance management system but what I am hearing is that with a few notable exceptions our line managers are either not capable of doing it properly or are not inclined to do it or both. What are you going to do about it?' Draft your reply.

References

Armstrong, M (2006) *Performance Management*, 3rd edn, Kogan Page, London

Armstrong, M and Baron, A (2004) *Managing Performance: Performance management in action*, CIPD, London

Armstrong, M and Murlis, H (1998) *Reward Management*, 4th edn, Kogan Page, London

Bandura, A (1986) *Social Boundaries of Thought and Action*, Prentice Hall, Englewood Cliffs, NJ

Buchner, T W (2007) Performance management theory: a look from the performer's perspective with implications for HRD, *Human Resource Development International*, **10** (1), pp 59–73

e-reward (2005) *Survey of Performance Management*, e-reward.co.uk, Stockport

Guest, D E (1987) Human resource management and industrial relations, *Journal of Management Studies*, **14** (5), pp 503–21

Handy, C (1989) *The Age of Unreason*, Business Books, London

Latham, G and Locke, R (1979) Goal setting – a motivational technique that works, *Organizational Dynamics*, Autumn, pp 68–80

Latham, G, Sulsky, L M and Macdonald, H (2007) Performance management, in (eds) P Boxall, J Purcell and P Wright, *Oxford Handbook of Human Resource Management*, Oxford University Press, Oxford

Risher, H (2003) Re-focusing performance management for high performance, *Compensation & Benefits Review*, October, pp 20–30

Weiss, T B and Hartle, F (1997) *Re-engineering Performance Management, Breakthroughs in achieving strategy through people*, St Lucie Press, Boca Raton, FL

Wolff, C (2008) Managing employee performance, *IRS Employment Review*, issue 890, pp 1–12

39

360-Degree Feedback

Learning outcomes

On completing this chapter you should know about:

- The process of 360-degree feedback
- 360-degree methodology
- Use of 360-degree feedback
- Advantages and disadvantages of 360-degree feedback

Introduction

360-degree feedback, also known as multi-source assessment, is a process in which someone's performance is assessed and feedback is given by a number of people who may include their manager, subordinates, colleagues and customers. Assessments take the form of ratings against various performance dimensions. The term '360-degree feedback' is sometimes used loosely to describe upward feedback where this is given by subordinates to their managers. This is the most common approach and is more properly described as 180-degree feedback. Feedback may be presented direct to individuals, or to their managers, or both. Expert counselling and coaching for individuals as a result of the feedback may be provided by a member of the HR department or an outside consultant. 360-degree feedback or a variant of it was used by 30 per cent of the respondents to the 2005 e-reward survey.

Use of 360-degree feedback

360-degree feedback recognizes the complexity of management and the value of input from various sources – it is axiomatic that managers should not be assessing behaviours they cannot observe, and the leadership behaviours of subordinates may not be known to their managers.

It is used for a number of purposes. Research conducted by the Ashridge Management Research Group (Handy *et al*, 1996) found that typically, 360-degree feedback forms part of a self-development or management development programme. The 45 users covered by the survey fell into the following groups:

- 71 per cent used it solely to support learning and development;
- 23 per cent used it to support a number of HR processes such as appraisal, resourcing and succession planning;
- 6 per cent used it to support pay decisions.

360-degree feedback – methodology

360-degree feedback processes usually obtain data from questionnaires that measure from different perspectives the behaviours of individuals against a list of competencies. In effect, they ask for an evaluation: 'How well does... do...?' The competency model may be one developed within the organization or the competency headings may be provided by the supplier of a questionnaire. A typical questionnaire may cover aspects of performance such as leadership, teamwork, communication, organizational skills, decisiveness, drive and adaptability.

Ratings

Ratings are given by the generators of the feedback on a scale against each heading. This may refer both to importance and performance, rating the importance of each item on a scale of 1 (not important) to 6 (essential), and performance on a scale of 1 (weak in this area) to 6 (outstanding).

Data processing

Questionnaires are normally processed with the help of software developed within the organization or, most commonly, provided by external suppliers. This enables the data collection and analysis to be completed swiftly, with the minimum of effort and in a way that facilitates graphical as well as numerical presentation.

Graphical presentation is preferable as a means of easing the process of assimilating the data. The simplest method is to produce a profile, as illustrated in Figure 39.1

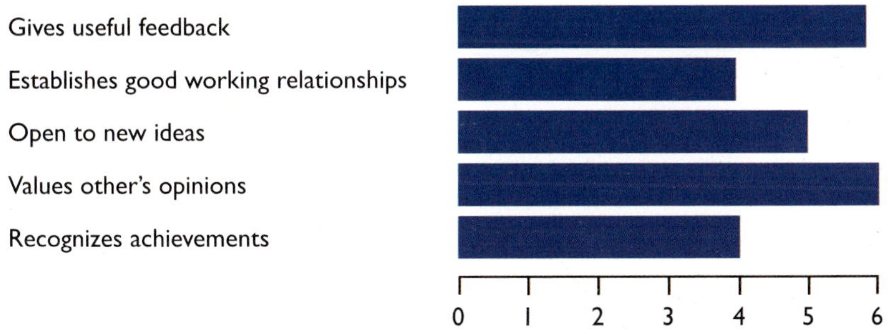

Figure 39.1 360-degree feedback profile

Some of the proprietary software presents feedback data in a much more elaborate form.

Feedback

The feedback is often anonymous and may be presented to the individual (most commonly), to the individual's manager (less common) or to both the individual and the manager. Some organizations do not arrange for feedback to be anonymous. Whether or not feedback is anonymous depends on the organization's culture – the more open the culture, the more likely is the source of feedback to be revealed.

Action

The action generated by the feedback will depend on the purposes of the process, ie development, appraisal or pay. If the purpose is primarily developmental, the action may be left to individuals as part of their personal development plans, but the planning process may be shared between individuals and their managers if they both have access to the information. Even if the data only go to the individual they can be discussed in a performance review meeting so that joint plans can be made, and there is much to be said for adopting this approach.

360-degree feedback – advantages and disadvantages

Advantages and disadvantages

Advantages:

- Individuals get a broader perspective of how they are perceived by others than previously possible.
- It gives people a more rounded view of their performance.
- Increased awareness of and relevance of competencies.
- Increased awareness by senior management that they too have development needs.
- Feedback is perceived as more valid and objective, leading to acceptance of results and actions required.

Disadvantages:

- People do not always give frank or honest feedback.
- People may be put under stress in receiving or giving feedback.
- Lack of action following feedback.
- Over-reliance on technology.
- Too much bureaucracy.

The disadvantages can all be minimized if not avoided completely by careful design, communication, training and follow-up.

Development and implementation

To develop and implement 360-degree feedback the following steps need to be taken:

1. Define objectives – it is important to define exactly what 360-degree feedback is expected to achieve. It will be necessary to spell out the extent to which it is concerned with personal development, appraisal or pay.

2. Decide on recipients – who will be at the receiving end of feedback. This may be an indication of who will eventually be covered after a pilot scheme.

3. Decide on who will give the feedback – the individual's manager, direct reports, team members, other colleagues or internal and external customers. A decision will also have to be made on whether HR staff or outside consultants should take part in helping managers to make use of the feedback. A further decision will need to be made on whether or not the feedback should be anonymous (it usually is).

4. Decide on the areas of work and behaviour on which feedback will be given – this may be in line with an existing competency model or it may take the form of a list of headings for development. Clearly, the model should fit the culture, values and type of work carried out in the organization, but it might be decided that a list of headings or questions in a software package would be acceptable, at least to start with.

5. Decide on the method of collecting the data – the questionnaire could be designed in-house or a consultant's or software provider's questionnaire could be adopted, with the possible option of amending it later to produce a better fit.

6. Decide on data analysis and presentation – again, the decision is on developing the software in-house or using a package. Most organizations installing 360-degree feedback do, in fact, purchase a package from a consultancy or software house. The aim should be to keep it as simple as possible.

7. Plan initial implementation programme – it is desirable to pilot the process, preferably at top level or with all the managers in a function or department. The pilot scheme will need to be launched with communication to those involved about the purpose of 360-degree feedback, how it will work and the part they will play. The aim is to spell out the benefits and, as far as possible, allay any fears. Training in giving and receiving feedback will also be necessary.

8. Analyse outcome of pilot scheme – the reactions of those taking part in a pilot scheme should be analysed and necessary changes made to the process, the communication package and the training.

9. Plan and implement full programme – this should include briefing, communicating, training and support from HR and, possibly, the external consultants.

10. Monitor and evaluate – maintain a particularly close watch on the initial implementation of feedback, but monitoring should continue. This is a process that can cause anxiety and stress, or produce little practical gain in terms of development and improved performance for a lot of effort.

360-degree feedback – criteria for success

- It has the active support of top management who themselves take part in giving and receiving feedback and encourage everyone else to do the same.
- There is commitment everywhere else to the process based on briefing, training and an understanding of the benefits to individuals as well as the organization.
- There is real determination by all concerned to use feedback data as the basis for development.
- Questionnaire items fit or reflect typical and significant aspects of behaviour.
- Items covered in the questionnaire can be related to actual events experienced by the individual.
- Comprehensive and well-delivered communication and training programmes are followed.
- No one feels threatened by the process – this is usually often achieved by making feedback anonymous and/or getting a third-party facilitator to deliver the feedback.
- Feedback questionnaires are relatively easy to complete (not unduly complex or lengthy, with clear instructions).
- Bureaucracy is minimized.

360-degree feedback – key learning points

The process of 360-degree feedback

360-degree feedback, also known as multi-source feedback, is a process in which someone's performance is assessed and feedback is given by a number of people who may include their manager, subordinates, colleagues and customers.

Use of 360-degree feedback

360-degree feedback recognizes the complexity of management and the value of

360-degree feedback – key learning points (continued)

input from various sources. Mainly used for learning and development.

360-degree methodology

360-degree feedback processes usually obtain data from questionnaires that measure from different perspectives the behaviours of individuals against a list of competencies.

Advantages and disadvantages of 360-degree feedback

Main advantages – individuals get a broader perspective of how they are perceived by others than previously possible and therefore obtain a more rounded view of their performance. Main disadvantages – people do not always give frank or honest feedback and people may be put under stress in receiving or giving feedback.

Questions

1. From the chief executive to the HR director: 'Based on your knowledge of other organizations and research, I should like a report from you on the advantages and disadvantages of 360-degree feedback.' Respond.
2. From a friend who is Human Resources Manager for a law firm: 'I need your help. Our partners are contemplating the introduction of 360-degree appraisal, and have asked my advice about the benefits and the dangers. This subject is new to me, so what can you tell me, based on your own knowledge of the relevant research and the experience of other organizations?' Respond.
3. From the head of reward to the HR director: 'Why don't we use the outcome of our 360-degree feedback system to contribute to the annual appraisal rating and through that to performance-related pay decisions?' Draft your response.

References

e-reward (2005) *Survey of Performance Management*, e-reward.co.uk, Stockport

Handy, L, Devine, M and Heath, L (1996) *360-Degree Feedback: Unguided missile or powerful weapon?*, Ashridge Management Group, Berkhamstead

Part VIII

Learning and Development

Learning and development strategies and practices as described in this part aim to ensure that people in the organization acquire and develop the knowledge, skills and competencies they need to carry out their work effectively and advance their careers to their own benefit and that of the organization.

The term 'learning and development' has largely replaced that of 'human resource development' (HRD). The terms are sometimes used interchangeably, although the introduction of 'learning' has emphasized the belief that what matters for individuals is that they are given the opportunity to learn, often for themselves but with guidance and support, rather than just being on the receiving end of training administered by the organization. This change has been reinforced by the importance attached to understanding how people learn and to the concepts of organizational learning and the learning organization.

Part VIII contents

Learning and development activities and methods are described in Appendix D.

learning and development strategy

40 Learning and Development Strategy

Key concepts and terms

- Learning culture
- Learning organization
- Learning and development strategy
- Strategic human resource development

Learning outcomes

On completing this chapter you should be able to define these key concepts. You should also know about:

- The features of a learning and development strategy
- The contents of a learning and development strategy
- The concept of the learning organization and its relevance
- Learning and development philosophy
- The nature of a learning culture
- How learning and development activities contribute to firm performance

Introduction

Learning and development strategy represents the approach an organization adopts to ensure that now and in the future, learning and development activities support the achievement of its goals by developing the skills and capacities of individuals and teams. It can be described similarly as strategic human resource development, defined as follows.

SOURCE REVIEW

Strategic human resource development defined, Walton (1999)

Strategic human resource development involves introducing, eliminating, modifying, directing and guiding processes in such a way that all individuals and teams are equipped with the skills, knowledge and competences they require to undertake current and future tasks required by the organization.

In this chapter the term 'learning and development strategy' is used as it represents more accurately current thinking on this subject. The chapter covers the features and basis of such a strategy and the concepts of a learning culture and the learning organization that are associated with the strategy. It is completed with a discussion of the impact learning and development activities make on organizational performance.

Features of a learning and development strategy

A learning and development strategy should be business-led in the sense that it is designed to support the achievement of business goals by promoting human capital advantage. But it should also be people-led, which means taking into account the needs and aspiration of people to grow and develop. Achieving the latter aim, of course, supports the achievement of the former.

Learning and development strategy is underpinned by a philosophy and its purpose is to operationalize that philosophy. It is fundamentally concerned with creating a learning culture that will encourage learning and will provide the basis for planning and implementing learning activities and programmes. This concept of a learning culture is associated with that of the learning organization.

Learning and development philosophy

A learning and development philosophy expresses the beliefs of an organization on the role of learning and development, its importance and how it should take place. It can be expressed in the following terms:

- Learning and development activities make a major contribution to the successful attainment of the organization's objectives, and investment in them benefits all the stakeholders of the organization.
- Learning and development plans and programmes should be integrated with and support the achievement of business and human resource strategies.
- Learning and development should be performance-related – designed to achieve specified improvements in corporate, functional, team and individual performance, and make a major contribution to bottom-line results.
- Everyone in the organization should be encouraged and given the opportunity to learn – to develop their skills and knowledge to the maximum of their capacity.
- Personal development processes provide the framework for individual and self-directed learning.
- While the need to invest in learning and development is recognized, the prime responsibility for development rests with individual employees, who will be given the guidance and support of their manager and, as necessary, members of the HR department.

Contents of the learning and development strategy

The learning and development strategy should incorporate the elements set out below.

Elements of the learning and development strategy

- The learning and development philosophy of the organization.
- The aims of the learning and development strategy.
- The priorities for learning and development.
- How, broadly, it is intended these aims will be achieved through the creation of a learning culture, formal learning and development programmes, coaching, personal development planning, and self-directed learning.
- The responsibilities for learning and development as shared between top management, line management, individual employees, and members of the HR or learning and development function.

- The resources required for learning and development – financial budgets, training facilities, external help.
- The success criteria for learning and development.
- How the effectiveness of learning and development in meeting these criteria will be measured and evaluated.

Learning culture

A learning culture is one that promotes learning because it is recognized by top management, line managers and employees generally as an essential organizational process to which they are committed and in which they engage continuously.

Reynolds (2004) describes a learning culture as a 'growth medium', which will 'encourage employees to commit to a range of positive discretionary behaviours, including learning' and which has the following characteristics: empowerment not supervision, self-managed learning not instruction, long-term capacity building not short-term fixes. He suggests that to create a learning culture it is necessary to develop organizational practices that raise commitment amongst employees and 'give employees a sense of purpose in the workplace, grant employees opportunities to act upon their commitment, and offer practical support to learning'.

SOURCE REVIEW

Developing a learning culture, Reynolds (2004)

1. Develop and share the vision – belief in a desired and emerging future.
2. Empower employees – provide 'supported autonomy'; freedom for employees to manage their work within certain boundaries (policies and expected behaviours) but with support available as required.
3. Adopt a facilitative style of management in which responsibility for decision making is ceded as far as possible to employees.
4. Provide employees with a supportive learning environment where learning capabilities can be discovered and applied, eg peer networks, supportive policies and systems, protected time for learning.
5. Use coaching techniques to draw out the talents of others by encouraging employees to identify options and seek their own solutions to problems.
6. Guide employees through their work challenges and provide them with time, resources and, crucially, feedback.

7. Recognize the importance of managers acting as role models: 'The new way of thinking and behaving may be so different that you must see what it looks like before you can imagine yourself doing it. You must see the new behaviour and attitudes in others with whom you can identify' (Schein, 1990).
8. Encourage networks – communities of practice.
9. Align systems to vision – get rid of bureaucratic systems that produce problems rather than facilitate work.

The learning organization

The concept of the learning organization has caught the imagination of many people since it was first popularized by Senge (1990) who described it as follows.

SOURCE REVIEW

The learning organization, as defined by Senge (1990)

The learning organization is one 'where people continually expand their capacity to create the results they truly desire, where new and expansive patterns of thinking are nurtured, where collective aspiration is set free, and where people are continually learning how to learn together'.

Pedler *et al* (1991) state that a learning organization is one 'which facilitates the learning of all its members and continually transforms itself'. Wick and Leon (1995) refer to a learning organization as one that 'continually improves by rapidly creating and refining the capabilities required for future success'.

As Harrison (2000) comments, the notion of the learning organization remains persuasive because of its 'rationality, human attractiveness and presumed potential to aid organizational effectiveness and advancement'. However, Scarborough *et al* (1999) argue that 'the dominant perspective [of the learning organization concept] is that of organization systems and design'.

Little attention seems to be paid to what individuals want to learn or how they learn. The idea that individuals should be enabled to invest in their own development seems to have escaped learning organization theorists who are more inclined to focus on the imposition of learning by the organization, rather than creating a climate conducive to learning. This is a learning culture, a concept that has much more to offer than that of the learning organization.

Viewing organizations as learning systems is a limited notion. Argyris and Schon (1996) contend that organizations are products of visions, ideas, norms and beliefs so that their shape is much more fragile than the organization's material structure. People act as learning agents for the organization in ways that cannot easily be systematized. They are not only individual learners but also have the capacity to learn collaboratively. Organization learning theory, as described in Chapter 44, analyses how this happens and leads to the belief that it is the culture and environment that are important, not the systems approach implied by the concept of the learning organization.

The notion of a learning organization is somewhat nebulous. It incorporates miscellaneous ideas about human resource development, systematic training, action learning, organizational development and knowledge management, with an infusion of the precepts of total quality management. But they do not add up to a convincing whole. Easterby-Smith (1997) argues that attempts to create a single best practice framework for understanding the learning organization are fundamentally flawed. There are other problems with the concept: it is idealistic, knowledge management models are beginning to supersede it, few organizations can meet the criteria and there is little evidence of successful learning organizations. Prescriptions from training specialists and management consultants abound but, as Sloman (1999) asserts, they often fail to recognize that learning is a continuous process, not a set of discrete training activities.

Burgoyne (1999), one of the earlier exponents of the learning organization notion, has admitted that there has been some confusion about it and that there have been substantial naiveties in most of the early thinking. He believes that the concept should be integrated with knowledge management initiatives so that different forms of knowledge can be linked, fed by organizational learning and used in adding value.

The contribution of learning and development to organizational performance

Studies on the relationship between learning and development activities and organizational performance have included those by Benabou (1996) and Clarke (2004). The research by Benabou examined the impact of various training programmes on the business and financial results at 50 Canadian organizations. The conclusion reached was that in most cases a well-designed training programme can be linked to improvements in business results and that return on investment in training programmes is very high. But Benabou referred to the following limitations.

SOURCE REVIEW

Limitations of research into the link between learning and development and performance, Benabou (1996)

Regardless of the approach taken, the effects of an HRD program cannot be pinpointed with complete accuracy. The findings provide evidence that positive results stemmed from training programs, but not the clear proof that only a control group would have provided. Considering the methodology used (multiple raters and instruments, experts, warnings to subtract effects of other factors that influence overall results), the researchers are confident, however, that assessors provided reliable estimates. The objective of measuring business results and the costs and benefits of training is to get people in the HRD field to think rigorously about the costs and effects of what they are doing. This level of training evaluation provides a fair and objective approach to making decisions about people and programs, even with conservative data and known limitations. But trainers must be humble when presenting documented benefits. Organizational results are rarely achieved solely through training. The findings here support the view that for training to have positive effects, supporting structures must be in place throughout the organization. The study also found that business results are easier to evaluate when organizations conduct a thorough needs assessment before developing and delivering training.

A national survey of training evaluation in specialized healthcare organizations (hospices) conducted by Clarke (2004) showed that while there appeared to be some links between training and performance it was not possible to reach firm conclusions about causality. However, the study reached the important finding that where organizations undertake assessment of their training and development (both formal and informal learning) then there is a greater belief in the positive impact training and development has in the organization.

While it is possible and highly desirable to evaluate learning, as described in Chapter 42, establishing a link between learning and organizational performance is problematic. It may be difficult to distinguish between cause and effect. Hendry and Pettigrew (1986) warn that it is risky to adopt simplistic views that training leads to improved business performance because it is more likely that successful companies will under certain conditions increase their training budget. A further complication was identified by Tsang (1997), who made the following comment.

SOURCE REVIEW

Conditions required for learning and development to improve performance, Tsang (1997)

Setting aside the complexities of putting the lessons learnt into practice (ie the problem of implementation), learning will automatically lead to better performance only when the knowledge obtained is accurate. If the problem of implementation is taken into consideration as well, even accurate learning is neither a necessary nor a sufficient condition for improving performance.

Harrison (2005) posed the question on what the learning and development implications of such research are and answered it as follows.

SOURCE REVIEW

The implications of learning and development research, Harrison (2005)

It has not yet yielded enough clear evidence of a direct link between individual learning and improvements in organizational performance (however that is defined). However L&D activity does consistently emerge as a crucial intervening factor. In the Bath studies two HR practices were identified as being particularly powerful in influencing employee attitudes and creating positive discretionary behaviour: careers (in the sense of a 'developing future') and training. In other words, the L&D processes that help to activate the people-performance link are those that 'hold the promise of learning to do things better, or doing new things. It is the sense of progression and purpose that is important, especially in linking to organizational commitment' (Purcell *et al* 2003, p 73).

Learning and development strategy – key learning points

The features of a learning and development strategy

A learning and development strategy should be business-led in the sense that it is designed to support the achievement of business goals by promoting human capital advantage. But it should also be people-led, which means taking into account the needs

Learning and development strategy – key learning points (continued)

and aspirations of people to grow and develop.

Learning and development philosophy

A learning and development philosophy expresses the beliefs of an organization on the role of learning and development, its importance and how it should take place.

The contents of a learning and development strategy

The aims and priorities of the strategy, how it is to be achieved, responsibilities and resources and success criteria.

The nature of a learning culture

A learning culture is one that promotes learning because it is recognized by top management, line managers and employees generally as an essential organizational process to which they are committed and in which they engage continuously.

The concept of the learning organization and its relevance

A learning organization is one 'which facilitates the learning of all its members and continually transforms itself' (Pedler *et al*, 1991). However, the notion of a learning organization is somewhat nebulous.

How learning and development activities contribute to firm performance

While it is possible and highly desirable to evaluate learning, establishing a link between learning and organizational performance is problematic, although research has shown that learning and development can be a crucial intervening factor.

Questions

1. You have been asked to deliver a session at a students' evening in your CIPD branch on the gap between learning and development strategy and practice and what can be done about it. It has been suggested that it would be helpful to those attending if you referred to the lessons learnt from research. Prepare the session outline.
2. From your chief executive to the head of learning and development: 'We need to be certain that our learning and development strategy supports the achievement of the business strategy. In what ways can it do this?'
3. From a friend studying human resource management: 'I note that everyone is now talking about "learning and development". I gather that they used to talk about "human

Questions (continued)

resource development" (many still do) and training (also still common). Has there been some sort of progression from training via human resource development to learning and development? If so, what are the differences?' Reply.

References

Argyris, C and Schon, D A (1996) *Organizational learning: A theory of action perspective*, Addison Wesley, Reading, MA

Benabou, C (1996) Assessing the impact of training programs on the bottom line, *National Productivity Review*, **15** (3), pp 91–9

Burgoyne, J (1999) Design of the times, *People Management*, 3 June, pp 39–44

Clarke, N (2004) HRD and the challenges of assessing learning in the workplace, *International Journal of Training and Development*, **8** (2), pp 140–56

Easterby-Smith, M (1997) Disciplines of organizational learning: contributions and critiques, *Human Relations*, **50** (9), pp 1085–113

Harrison, R (2000) *Employee Development*, 2nd edn, IPM, London

Harrison, R (2005) *Learning and Development*, 4th edn, CIPD, London

Hendry, C and Pettigrew, A (1986) The practice of strategic human resource management, *Personnel Review*, **15**, pp 2–8

Pedler, M, Burgoyne, J and Boydell, T (1991) *The Learning Company: A strategy for sustainable development*, McGraw-Hill, Maidenhead

Purcell, J, Kinnie, K, Hutchinson, S, Rayton, B and Swart, J (2003) *People and Performance: How people management impacts on organisational performance*, CIPD, London

Reynolds, J (2004) *Helping People Learn*, CIPD, London

Scarborough, H, Swan, J and Preston, J (1999) *Knowledge Management: A literature review*, Institute of Personnel and Development, London

Schein, E H (1990) Organizational culture, *American Psychologist*, **45**, pp 109–19

Senge, P (1990) *The Fifth Discipline: The art and practice of the learning organization*, Doubleday, London

Sloman, M (1999) Seize the day, *People Management*, 20 May, p 31

Tsang, E W (1997) Organizational learning and the learning organization: a dichotomy between descriptive and prescriptive research, *Human Relations*, **50** (1), pp 73–89

Walton, J (1999) *Strategic Human Resource Development*, Financial Times/Prentice Hall, Harlow

Wick, C W and Leon, L S (1995) Creating a learning organisation: from ideas to action, *Human Resource Management*, Summer, pp 299–311

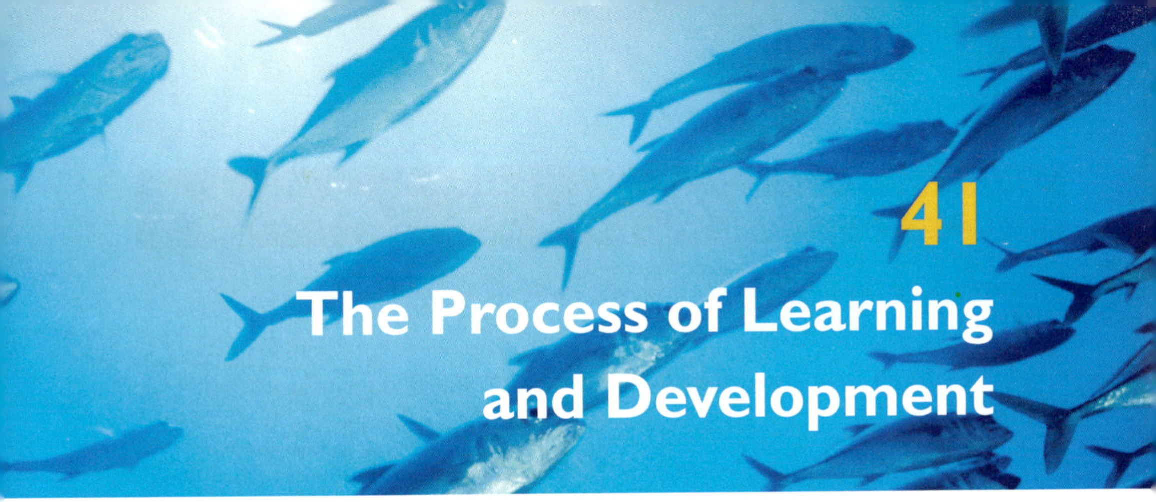

41 The Process of Learning and Development

Key concepts and terms

- Bite-sized training
- Blended learning
- Coaching
- Connectivity
- Criterion behaviour
- Development
- Experiential learning
- Formal learning
- Informal learning
- Instruction
- Just-in-time training
- Learning
- Learning contract
- Learning culture
- Learning and development
- Learning management system
- Learning portal
- Mentoring
- Personal development plan
- Planned experience
- Self-directed (self-managed) learning
- Self-paced learning
- Self-reflective learning
- Systematic training
- Terminal behaviour
- Training

Learning outcomes

On completing this chapter you should be able to define these key concepts. You should also know about:

- The distinction between learning and training
- E-learning
- Self-directed learning
- Planned experience
- Transferring training
- Informal and formal learning
- Blended learning
- Personal development planning
- Training
- Effective training practices

Introduction

The purpose of this chapter is to define and explain the processes and approaches involved in learning and development including informal and formal learning, e-learning, blended learning, development and training. Putting these into practice through identifying learning needs, planning and implementing learning and development programmes and evaluating learning is dealt with in Chapter 42.

Learning and development defined

Learning and development is the process of acquiring and developing knowledge, skills, capabilities, behaviours and attitudes through learning or developmental experiences. It is concerned with ensuring that the organization has the knowledgeable, skilled, engaged and committed workforce it needs.

Learning

Learning is the means by which a person acquires and develops new knowledge, skills, capabilities, behaviours and attitudes. As explained by Honey and Mumford (1996): 'Learning has happened when people can demonstrate that they know something that they did not know before (insights, realizations as well as facts) and when they can do something they could not do before (skills).'

Learning is a continuous process that not only enhances existing capabilities but also leads to the development of the skills, knowledge and attitudes that prepare people for enlarged or higher-level responsibilities in the future.

Development

Development is concerned with ensuring that a person's ability and potential are grown and realized through the provision of learning experiences or through self-directed (self-managed) learning. It is an unfolding process that enables people to progress from a present state of understanding and capability to a future state in which higher-level skills, knowledge and competencies are required.

Training

Training involves the application of formal processes to impart knowledge and help people to acquire the skills necessary for them to perform their jobs satisfactorily.

Comparison of learning and training

Learning should be distinguished from training. 'Learning is the process by which a person constructs new knowledge, skills and capabilities, whereas training is one of several responses an organization can undertake to promote learning' (Reynolds *et al*, 2002).

The encouragement of learning makes use of a process model, which is concerned with facilitating the learning activities of individuals and providing learning resources for them to use. Conversely, the provision of training involves the use of a content model, which means deciding in advance the knowledge and skills that need to be enhanced by training, planning the programme, deciding on training methods and presenting the content in a logical sequence through various forms of instruction.

A distinction is made by Sloman (2003) between learning, which 'lies within the domain of the individual' and training ,which 'lies within the domain of the organization'. Today the approach is to focus on individual learning and ensure that it takes place when required – 'just-for-you' and 'just-in-time' learning.

Elements of learning and development

The elements of learning and development as explained in this chapter and Chapter 45 (Management Development) are shown in Figure 41.1.

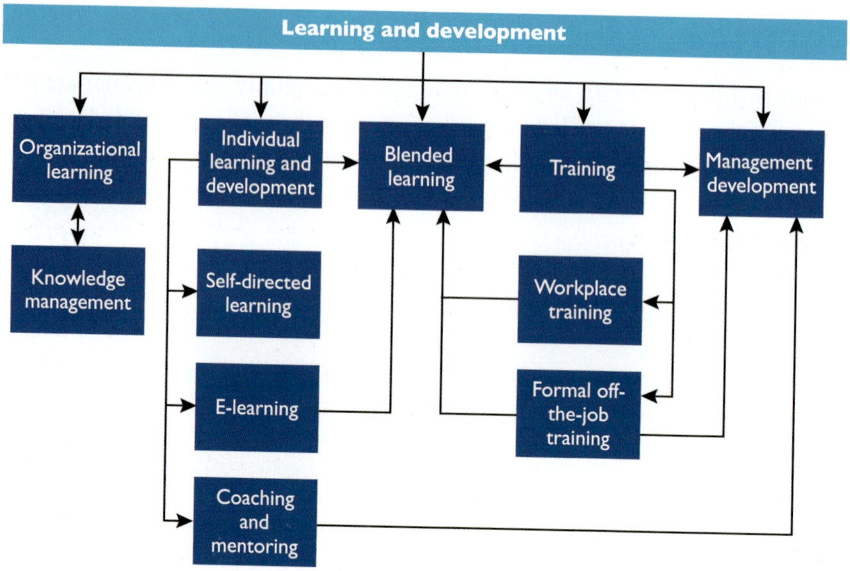

Figure 41.1 Elements of learning and development

Approaches to learning and development

Learning and development can be formal or informal and can use computer, networked and web-based technology (e-learning). Its effectiveness is increased by joining up different methods of learning and development (blended learning) and by encouraging self-directed learning. Approaches to learning and development are underpinned by theories of how individuals learn and the concept of organizational learning, which are covered in Chapters 43 and 44.

Informal and formal learning

As discussed below, a distinction can usefully be made between informal, workplace and formal learning but there is in fact a spectrum from highly informal to highly formal approaches.

Informal learning

Informal learning is experiential learning. It takes place while people are learning on-the-job as they go along. Most learning does not take place in formal training programmes. People can learn 70 per cent of what they know about their job informally.

A study by Eraut *et al* (1998) established that in organizations adopting a learner-centred perspective, formal education and training provided only a small part of what was learnt at work.

Most of the learning described to the researchers was non-formal, neither clearly specified nor planned. It arose naturally from the challenges of work. Effective learning was, however, dependent on the employees' confidence, motivation and capability. Some formal training to develop skills (especially induction training) was usually provided, but learning from experience and other people at work predominated. Reynolds (2004) notes that:

> *The simple act of observing more experienced colleagues can accelerate learning; conversing, swapping stories, cooperating on tasks and offering mutual support deepen and solidify the process... This kind of learning – often very informal in nature – is thought to be vastly more effective in building proficiency than more formalized training methods.*

Advantages and disadvantages of informal learning

Advantages:

- Learning efforts are relevant and focused in the immediate environment.
- Understanding can be achieved in incremental steps rather than in indigestible chunks.
- Learners define how they will gain the knowledge they need – formal learning is more packaged.
- Learners can readily put their learning into practice.

Disadvantages:

- It may be left to chance – some people will benefit, some won't.
- It can be unplanned and unsystematic, which means that it will not necessarily satisfy individual or organizational learning needs.
- Learners may simply pick up bad habits.

Workplace learning

Informal learning occurs in the workplace but there are a number of specific ways in which learning can be enhanced. The most important of these are coaching and mentoring, but other methods are job rotation, job shadowing, bite-sized learning through e-learning, cross-functional or cross-site project work.

The characteristics of workplace learning were explained by Stern and Sommerlad (1999) as follows.

SOURCE REVIEW

Characteristics of workplace learning, Stern and Sommerlad (1999)

1. The workshop as a site for learning. In this case, learning and working are spatially separated with some form of structured learning activity occurring off or near the job. This may be in a company training centre or a 'training island' on the shop floor where the production process is reproduced for trainees.
2. The workplace as a learning environment. In this approach, the workplace itself becomes an environment for learning. Various on-the-job training activities take place which are structured to different degrees. Learning is intentional and planned, aimed at training employees by supporting, structuring and monitoring their learning.
3. Learning and working are inextricably mixed. In this case, learning is informal. It becomes an everyday part of the job and is built into routine tasks. Workers develop skills, knowledge and understanding through dealing with the challenges posed by the work. This can be described as continuous learning. As Zuboff (1988) put it: 'Learning is not something that requires time out from being engaged in productive activity; learning is the heart of productive activity.'

Formal learning

Formal learning is planned and systematic. It makes use of structured training programmes consisting of instruction and practice that may be conducted on- or off-the-job. Experience may be planned to provide opportunities for continuous learning and development. Formal learning and developmental activities may be used such as action learning, coaching, mentoring and outdoor learning, as described in Appendix D. The organization may have its own training centre. Some large companies have corporate universities (see Appendix D)

Spectrum of learning – from informal to formal

The distinction between formal and informal learning may not always be precise. Watkins and Marsick (1993) described a spectrum of learning from informal to formal as follows:

- unanticipated experiences and encounters that result in learning as an incidental by-product, which may or may not be consciously recognized;
- new job assignments and participation in teams, or other job-related challenges that provide for learning and self-development;

- self-initiated and self-planned experiences, including the use of media and seeking out a coach or mentor;
- total quality or improvement groups/active learning designed to promote continuous learning for continuous improvement;
- providing a framework for learning associated with personal development planning or career planning;
- the combination of less-structured with structured opportunity to learn from these experiences;
- designed programmes of mentoring, coaching or workplace learning;
- formal training programmes or courses involving instruction.

Informal and formal learning compared

A comparison between informal and formal learning is shown in Table 41.1.

Table 41.1 Characteristics of formal and informal learning

Informal learning	Formal learning
Highly relevant to individual needs	Relevant to some, not so relevant to others
Learners learn according to need	All learners learn the same thing
May be small gap between current and target knowledge	May be variable gaps between current and target knowledge
Learner decides how learning will occur	Trainer decides how learning will occur
Immediate applicability ('just-in-time' learning)	Variable times, often distant
Learning readily transferable	Problems may occur in transferring learning to the workplace
Occurs in work setting	Often occurs in non-work setting

This comparison is weighted in favour of informal learning, but as mentioned above there are disadvantages. Informal learning used to be anathematized as 'sitting by Nellie' (this was when Nellie was a fairly common name) meaning that trainees were left to their own devices to pick up bad habits from their neighbours. It can be argued that formal training has its limits but at least it is planned and systematic. In fact, the systematic training movement of the 1960s (discussed later in this chapter) was a revulsion from traditional laissez faire approaches. Informal training has a lot of advantages but as explained below, it should not be allowed to take place in a haphazard way.

Making informal learning work

- Analyse the knowledge, skills and abilities (KSAs) required.
- Define how these KSAs will be acquired: eg initial instruction and coaching from a supervisor; demonstration, coaching and mentoring from a colleague; the preparation of personal development or self-directed learning plans; planned programmes for acquiring knowledge and skills; blending informal on-the-job learning with other learning processes such as e-learning and formal training courses.
- Ensure that line managers and supervisors are aware of their responsibilities for the provision of learning opportunities and have the skills required, eg coaching and instructing skills.
- Where a department or unit has regular large influxes of trainees, appoint a full- or part-time training supervisor to oversee all training activities.
- Follow up to ensure that learning is taking place.

The approaches describe above use a number of formal methods described later in this chapter and in Appendix D, but the essential nature of informal learning – that it is about learning through experience on-the-job – is unaffected. The more formal approaches are there simply to enhance experiential learning.

E-learning

E-learning was defined by Pollard and Hillage (2001) as 'the delivery and administration of learning opportunities and support via computer, networked and web-based technology to help individual performance and development'. E-learning enhances learning by extending and supplementing face-to-face learning rather than replacing it. It enables learning to take place when it is most needed (just in time as distinct from just in case) and when it is most convenient. Learning can be provided in short segments or bites that focus on specific learning objectives. It is 'learner-centric' in that it can be customized to suit an individual's learning needs – learners can choose different learning objects within an overall package. The main potential drawbacks are the degree of access to computers, the need for a reasonable degree of literacy, the need for learners to be self-motivated, and the time and effort required to develop and update e-learning programmes.

E-learning programmes may cover common business applications and processes, induction programmes and, frequently, IT skills development. They are not so effective for developing soft skills such as team building, communication or presentation, which rely on interpersonal contact. But programmes can still present basic principles that can prepare people for practical face-to face sessions, provide reinforcement through post-event reading, help with self-assessment and lead to chatroom support.

Commonly, candidates raised issues about computer access and IT literacy, cost, time and self-motivation levels. Too few candidates considered the types of learning suited to/not suited to the e-learning approach.

The basic principle of e-learning is 'connectivity' – the process by which computers are networked, share information and connect people to people. This is provided for by what is often called 'the e-learning landscape or architecture', which refers to the hardware, software and connectivity components required to facilitate learning. In designing the system, consideration has to be given to 'functionality' – what each part is expected to do.

The main components of the e-learning 'landscape' are:

- The learning management system (LMS) – this provides users with access to various learning processes and enables self-paced e-learning to take place. It can also help with administration, including curriculum management, and course publishing.
- The learning content management system (LCMS) – this provides an authoring system for course or programme preparation, a collection of learning objects or modules (sometimes called a 'repository') and a means of sending a completed course to a delivery system (sometimes called a delivery interface).
- Learning portals – these are access points to learning information and services that enable learners to locate content.

The e-learning process

The e-learning process comprises defining the system, encouraging access, advising and assisting individual learners, and encouraging and facilitating the creation of learning communities. E-learning focuses on the learner. It provides a means of satisfying individual learning needs. But individual learning may be supplemented by participation in learning groups or communities of interest in which members both gain and share knowledge.

The emphasis is on self-paced learning – learners control the rate at which they learn although they may be given targets for completion and guidance from tutors on how they should learn. However, while self-paced learning is encouraged and provided for, the impact of e-learning is strongly influenced by how well support is provided to learners. It is the effectiveness of this support rather than the sophistication of the technology that counts. The quality of the content is important but it will be enhanced by support from tutors or 'e-moderators'. The latter, as described by Salmon (2001), preside over the activities of a learning group in 'knowledge exchange forums', arranging contributions and information sharing and providing guidance and comments as appropriate.

E-learning programme content

E-learning programmes can be used for 'bite-sized' training, ie training to develop a particular skill or area of knowledge. Programmes may consist of generic content purchased from suppliers, but most organizations prefer customized web-based modules developed either in-house or outsourced to software firms that produce material to a specified design. The content should be constructed in accordance with the pedagogic principles set out below.

Principles for e-learning programmes

- Learners must be stimulated by the learning process.
- The programme and content should be seen to be intrinsically relevant, the method of presentation should be interesting, use should be made of graphics, animations, audio, interactive simulations, scenarios, case studies, projects, question and answer sessions and problem-solving activities where appropriate – the programme should not simply involve 'page turning'.
- Learners must be encouraged to respond to stimuli and should be engaged in the learning process.
- Learners should understand their learning goals, preferably working them out for themselves but with help where necessary.
- The programme should be constructed in incremental steps and presented in 'bite-sized chunks' or modules, each with clear objectives and outcomes.
- Learners should be able to plan their learning (self-paced learning).
- Learners must be able to measure their own progress but should be given feedback as well.
- Learners should be encouraged to reflect on what they are learning by reference to their own experience.

The content can be prepared with the help of authoring tools such as Macromedia (Authorware and Flash).

Delivery of e-learning

E-learning is delivered through websites and the intranet; CD-ROMs are also used extensively. Provision can be made for online coaching and discussion forums. The content can be delivered through PowerPoint, video and audio clips, drag and drop questions, PDF files, links to websites, and web-enabled forums and learning communities.

Blended learning

Blended learning is the use of a combination of learning methods to increase the overall effectiveness of the learning process by providing for different parts of the learning mix to complement and support one another. A blended learning programme might be planned for an individual using a mix of self-directed learning activities defined in a personal development plan, e-learning facilities, group action learning activities, coaching or mentoring, and instruction provided in an in-company course or externally. Generic training for groups of people might include e-learning, planned instruction programmes, planned experience and selected external courses. Within a training course a complementary mix of different training activities might take place, for example a skills development course for managers or team leaders might include some instruction on basic principles but much more time would be spent on case studies, simulations, role playing and other exercises.

Self-directed learning

Self-directed or self-managed learning involves encouraging individuals to take responsibility for their own learning needs, either to improve performance in their present job or to develop their potential and satisfy their career aspirations. It can also be described as self-reflective learning (Mezirow, 1985), which is the kind of learning that involves encouraging individuals to develop new patterns of understanding, thinking and behaving

Self-directed learning can be based on a process of recording achievement and action planning that involves individuals reviewing what they have learnt, what they have achieved, what their goals are, how they are going to achieve those goals and what new learning they need to acquire. The learning programme can be 'self-paced' in the sense that learners can decide for themselves, up to a point, the rate at which they work and are encouraged to measure their own progress and adjust the programme accordingly.

Self-directed learning is based on the principle that people learn and retain more if they find things out for themselves. But they still need to be given guidance on what to look for and help in finding it. Learners have to be encouraged to define, with whatever help they may require, what they need to know to perform their job effectively. They need to be provided with guidance on where they can get the material or information that will help them to learn and how to make good use of it. Personal development plans, as described later in this chapter, can provide a framework for this process. They also need support from their manager and the organization with the provision of coaching, mentoring and learning facilities, including e-learning.

Development

Development takes the form of learning activities that prepare people to exercise wider or increased responsibilities. In development programmes there is an emphasis on self-directed learning as described above, personal development planning (together with learning contracts) and planned learning from experience.

Personal development planning

Personal development planning is carried out by individuals with guidance, encouragement and help from their managers as required. A personal development plan sets out the actions people propose to take to learn and to develop themselves. They take responsibility for formulating and implementing the plan but they receive support from the organization and their managers in doing so. The purpose is to provide what Tamkin *et al* (1995) call a 'self-organized learning framework'.

Stages of personal development planning

1. Analyse current situation and development needs. This can be done as part of a performance management process.
2. Set goals. These could include improving performance in the current job, improving or acquiring skills, extending relevant knowledge, developing specified areas of competence, moving across or upwards in the organization, or preparing for changes in the current role.
3. Prepare action plan. The action plan sets out what needs to be done and how it will be done under headings such as outcomes expected (learning objectives), the development activities, the responsibility for development (what individuals are expected to do and the support they will get from their manager, the HR department or other people), and timing. A variety of activities tuned to individual needs should be included in the plan, for example observing what others do, project work, planned use of e-learning programmes and internal learning resource

centres, working with a mentor, coaching by the line manager or team leader, experience in new tasks, guided reading, special assignments and action learning. Formal training to develop knowledge and skills may be part of the plan but it is not the most important part.

4. Implement. Take action as planned.

The plan can be expressed in the form of a learning contract, as described below.

Learning contracts

A learning contract is a formal agreement between the manager and the individual on what learning needs to take place, the objectives of such learning and what part the individual, the manager, the learning and development function or a mentor will play in ensuring that learning happens. The partners to the contract agree on how the objectives will be achieved and their respective roles. It will spell out learning programmes and indicate what coaching, mentoring and formal training activities should be carried out. It is, in effect, a blueprint for learning.

Planned experience

Planned experience is the process of deciding on a sequence of experience that will enable people to obtain the knowledge and skills required in their jobs and prepare them to take on increased responsibilities. This enables experiential learning to take place to meet a learning specification. A programme is drawn up that sets down what people are expected to learn in each department or job in which they are given experience. This should spell out what they are expected to discover for themselves. A suitable person (a mentor) should be available to see that people in a development programme are given the right experience and opportunity to learn, and arrangements should be made to check progress. A good way of stimulating people to find out for themselves is to provide them with a list of questions to answer. It is essential, however, to follow up each segment of experience to check what has been learnt and, if necessary, modify the programme.

Training

Training is the use of systematic and planned instruction activities to promote learning. The approach can be summarized in the phrase 'learner-based training'. It is one of several responses an organization can undertake to promote learning.

As Reynolds (2004) points out, training has a complementary role to play in accelerating learning: 'It should be reserved for situations that justify a more directed, expert-led approach rather than viewing it as a comprehensive and all-pervasive people development solution.' He also commented that the conventional training model has a tendency to 'emphasize subject-specific knowledge, rather than trying to build core learning abilities'.

The justification for training

Formal training is indeed only one of the ways of ensuring that learning takes place, but it can be justified in the following circumstances.

Justifying training

- The work requires skills that are best developed by formal instruction.
- Different skills are required by a number of people, which have to be developed quickly to meet new demands and cannot be acquired by relying on experience.
- The tasks to be carried out are so specialized or complex that people are unlikely to master them on their own initiative at a reasonable speed.
- Critical information must be imparted to employees to ensure they meet their responsibilities.
- A learning need common to a number of people has to be met that can readily be dealt with in a training programme, for example induction, essential IT skills, communication skills.

Transferring training

It has been argued (Reynolds, 2004) that: 'The transfer of expertise by outside experts is risky since their design is often removed from the context in which work is created.' This is a fundamental problem and applies equally to internally run training courses where what has been taught can be difficult for people to apply in the entirely different circumstances in their workplace. Training can seem to be remote from reality and the skills and knowledge acquired can appear to be irrelevant. This particularly applies to management or supervisory training but even the manual skills learnt in a training centre may be difficult to transfer.

This problem can be tackled by making the training as relevant and realistic as possible, anticipating and dealing with any potential transfer difficulties. Individuals are more likely to apply learning when they do not find it too difficult, believe what they learnt is relevant, useful and transferable, are supported by line managers, have job autonomy, believe in themselves, and are committed and engaged. Transfer is also more likely if systematic training and 'just-in-time training' approaches are used, as described below.

Systematic training

Training should be systematic in that it is specifically designed, planned and implemented to meet defined needs. It is provided by people who know how to train and the impact of training is carefully evaluated. The concept was originally developed for the industrial training boards in the 1960s and consists of a simple four-stage model, as illustrated in Figure 41.2:

1. Identify training needs.
2. Decide what sort of training is required to satisfy these needs.
3. Use experienced and trained trainers to implement training.
4. Follow up and evaluate training to ensure that it is effective.

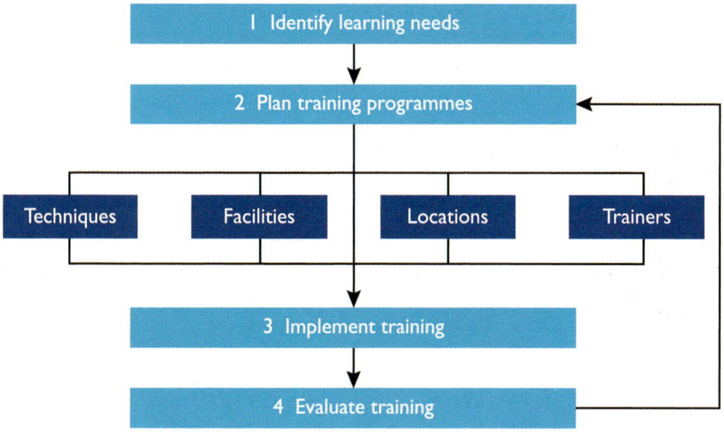

Figure 41.2 Systematic training model

Just-in-time training

Just-in-time training is training that is closely linked to the pressing and relevant needs of people by its association with immediate or imminent work activities. It is delivered as close as possible to the time when the activity is taking place. The training will be based on an identification of the latest requirements, priorities and plans of the participants, who will be briefed on the live situations in which their learning has to be applied. The training programme will take account of any transfer issues and aim to ensure that what is taught is seen to be applicable in the current work situation.

Bite-sized training

Bite-sized training involves the provision of opportunities to acquire a specific skill or a particular piece of knowledge in a short training session that is focused on one activity such as using a particular piece of software, giving feedback, or handling an enquiry about a product or service of the company. It is often carried out through e-learning. It can be a useful means of developing a skill or understanding through a concentrated session or learning activity without diversions and is readily put to use in the workplace. But it can be weak in expanding individuals' intellectual capacity and holistic (or 'whole view') understanding of the business – essential qualities to enable employees to respond creatively to the challenges of today's knowledge economy. It can also be facile and too restricted and relies on the support of line managers, which is not always forthcoming. It is best for training employees in straightforward techniques that they can use immediately in their work or to complement, not replace, longer courses or developmental processes.

Types of training

Training programmes or events can be concerned with any of the following:

- manual skills, including modern apprenticeships (see Appendix D);
- IT skills;
- team leader or supervisory training;
- management training;
- interpersonal skills, eg leadership, team-building, group dynamics, neuro-linguistic programming;
- personal skills, eg assertiveness, coaching, communicating, time management;
- training in organizational procedures or practices, eg induction, health and safety, performance management, equal opportunity or managing diversity policy and practice.

Effective training practices

Effective training uses the systematic approach defined above with an emphasis on skills analysis. The purpose of the training should be clearly defined in terms of the behaviour required as a result of training. This can be expressed as a statement along the lines of: 'On completing this training the participant will be able to…'. Defining expected behaviours will provide the basis for evaluation, which is an essential element in the achievement of successful training.

The process of learning and development – key learning points

The distinction between learning and training

Learning should be distinguished from training. 'Learning is the process by which a person constructs new knowledge, skills and capabilities, whereas training is one of several responses an organization can undertake to promote learning' (Reynolds *et al*, 2002).

Informal and formal learning

Formal learning is planned and systematic. It makes use of structured training programmes consisting of instruction and practice that may be conducted on- or off-the-job. Informal learning is experiential learning. It takes place while people are learning on-the-job as they go along.

E-learning

E-learning provides for learning via computer, networked and web-based technology. The process comprises defining the system, encouraging access, advising and assisting individual learners and encouraging and facilitating the creation of learning communities. E-learning focuses on the learner. It provides a means of satisfying individual learning needs.

Blended learning

Blended learning is the use of a combination of learning methods to increase the overall effectiveness of the learning process by providing for different parts of the learning mix to complement and support one another. A blended learning programme might be planned for an individual using a mix of self-directed learning activities defined in a personal development plan, e-learning facilities, group action learning activities, coaching or mentoring, and instruction provided in an in-company course or externally.

Self-directed learning

Self-directed or self-managed learning involves encouraging individuals to take responsibility for their own learning needs, either to improve performance in their present job or to develop their potential and satisfy their career aspirations. It can also be described as self-reflective learning, which is the kind of learning that involves encouraging individuals to develop new patterns of understanding, thinking and behaving.

Personal development planning

Personal development planning is carried out by individuals with guidance, encouragement and help from their managers as required. A personal development plan sets out the actions people propose to take to learn and to develop themselves. They take responsibility for formulating and implementing the plan but they receive support from the organization and their managers in doing so.

The process of learning and development – key learning points (continued)

Planned experience

Planned experience is the process of deciding on a sequence of experience that will enable people to obtain the knowledge and skills required in their jobs and prepare them to take on increased responsibilities. This enables experiential learning to take place in order to meet a learning specification.

Justifying training

Training can be justified when:

- The work requires skills that are best developed by formal instruction.
- Different skills are required by a number of people, which have to be developed quickly to meet new demands and cannot be acquired by relying on experience.
- The tasks to be carried out are specialized or complex.
- Critical information must be imparted to employees to ensure they meet their responsibilities.
- A learning need common to a number of people has to be met.

Transferring training

Training can seem to be remote from reality and the skills and knowledge acquired can appear to be irrelevant. This particularly applies to management or supervisory training but even the manual skills learnt in a training centre may be difficult to transfer. This problem can be tackled by making the training as relevant and realistic as possible, anticipating and dealing with any potential transfer difficulties.

Effective training practices

- The purpose of the training should be clearly defined.
- Every opportunity should be taken to embed learning at work.
- The training techniques used should be appropriate to the purpose of the course and to the characteristics of participants.

Questions

1. From a colleague who has just transferred into the learning and development department from the people resourcing department: 'I am getting confused. Please would you explain to me the difference between learning, development and training and why it is important to distinguish between them.'
2. You have been asked to contribute to a learning and development seminar on the theme, 'Informal learning is all very well but aren't we in danger of leaving it all to chance?' Draft your outline contribution.
3. Your postgraduate HRM course supervisor has set you the following task: 'Explain why the concept of e-learning was greeted with such enthusiasm a few years ago as the ultimate answer to learning, yet many people believe that it has not lived up to its promise. Refer to any evidence from research or known practice or your own experience to establish the extent to which this belief is well-founded. If it is, what can be done about it? If not, what lessons can be learnt from those who have successfully used e-learning?'
4. From the HR director to the head of learning and development: 'We must develop coaching as a key learning and development process for middle management. Use an evidence-based management approach to identify ways in which we can ensure that coaching is carried out to high and consistent standards.'
5. Look into the concept of blended learning. What does it mean? What are its advantages and disadvantages?
6. Critically evaluate the concept of a learning organization.

References

Eraut, M J, Alderton, G, Cole, G and Senker, P (1998) *Development of Knowledge and Skills in Employment*, Economic and Social Research Council, London

Honey, P and Mumford, A (1996) *The Manual of Learning Styles*, 3rd edn, Honey Publications, Maidenhead

Mezirow, J A (1985) A critical theory of self-directed learning, in (ed) S Brookfield, *Self-directed Learning: From theory to practice*, Jossey-Bass, San Francisco, CA

Pollard, E and Hillage, J (2001) *Explaining e-Learning*, Report No 376, Institute for Employment Studies, Brighton

Reynolds, J (2004) *Helping People Learn*, CIPD, London

Reynolds, J, Caley, L and Mason, R (2002) *How Do People Learn?* CIPD, London

Salmon, G (2001) Far from remote, *People Management*, 27 September, pp 34–36

Sloman, M (2003) E-learning: stepping up the learning curve, *Impact*, CIPD, January, pp 16–17

Stern, E and Sommerlad, E (1999) *Workplace Learning, Culture and Performance*, IPD, London
Tamkin, P, Barber, L and Hirsh, W (1995) *Personal Development Plans: Case studies of practice*, The Institute for Employment Studies, Brighton
Watkins, K and Marsick, V (1993) *Sculpting the Learning Organization*, Falmer Press, London
Zuboff, S (1988) *In the Age of the Smart Machine*, Basic Books, New York

42

Learning and Development Programmes and Events

Key concepts and terms

- Cost/benefit analysis
- Learning evaluation
- Learning specification
- Return on investment
- Discretionary learning
- Learning needs analysis
- Return on expectations
- Self-directed learning

Learning outcomes

On completing this chapter you should be able to define these key concepts. You should also know about:

- The business case for learning and development
- Responsibility for learning
- Evaluating learning
- Planning and delivering learning programmes and events
- Analysing learning needs

Introduction

This chapter starts with an overview of the process of planning a learning and development programme or a learning event. A learning and development programme is a sequence or group of learning activities that take place over a period of time. A learning event is a specific learning activity that might take the form of a course designed to meet established learning needs.

In the first part of this chapter consideration is given to the preparation of a business case for learning, the sequence of activities required to plan the programme or event including who is responsible for ensuring that learning takes place. The next part deals with the delivery of learning programmes and events and the criteria for their effectiveness. The final two parts of the chapter are concerned with two fundamental activities that govern the planning and implementation of learning programmes and events, namely identifying learning needs and evaluating the effectiveness of learning activities.

The business case for learning and development

The business case for learning and development should demonstrate how learning, training and development programmes will meet business needs. Kearns and Miller (1997) go as far as to claim that: 'If a business objective cannot be cited as a basis for designing training and development, then no training and development should be offered.'

A cost/benefit analysis is required, which compares the benefits expressed in quantified terms as far as possible that will result from the learning activity. The business case has to convince management that there will be an acceptable return on the investment (RoI) in learning and training programmes and events. It can be difficult to produce realistic figures, although the attempt is worth making with the help of finance specialists. The case for investing in learning and development can refer to any of the following potential benefits.

Potential benefits provided by learning and development activities

- Improve individual, team and corporate performance in terms of output, quality, speed and overall productivity.
- Attract high quality employees by offering them learning and development opportunities, increasing their levels of competence and enhancing their skills, thus enabling them to obtain more job satisfaction, to gain higher rewards and to progress within the organization.

- Provide additional non-financial rewards (growth and career opportunities) as part of a total reward policy (see Chapter 46).
- Improve operational flexibility by extending the range of skills possessed by employees (multi-skilling).
- Increase the commitment of employees by encouraging them to identify with the mission and objectives of the organization.
- Help to manage change by increasing understanding of the reasons for change and providing people with the knowledge and skills they need to adjust to new situations.
- Provide line managers with the skills required to manage and develop their people.
- Help to develop a positive culture in the organization, one, for example, that is oriented towards performance improvement.
- Provide higher levels of service to customers.
- Minimize learning costs (reduce the length of learning curves).

Planning and delivering learning programmes and events

The actions required are as follows.

1. Establish learning needs

Methods of doing this are described in the penultimate part of this chapter.

2. Define learning objectives

It is essential to be clear about what the programme or event is required to achieve – its learning objectives and outcomes. These are defined to satisfy established learning needs and to provide the basis for planning content and evaluating results.

Objectives can be defined as criterion behaviour (the performance standards or changes in behaviour on the job to be achieved if a learning process is to be regarded as successful) and terminal behaviour (what actually happened following the learning event). Any gap between criterion and terminal behaviour will indicate deficiencies in the programme. A behavioural objective could be set out as follows.

Example of a behavioural learning objective

At the end of the programme managers will be able to take greater responsibility for the development of their staff. Indicative activities will include:

- the conduct of satisfactory performance and development reviews;
- the agreement of personal development plans;
- enabling team members to carry out self-directed learning activities;
- the ability to use coaching skills to improve performance.

3. Decide on content

The content of the programme or event will clearly be governed by whatever those attending need to know or be able to do as set out in the learning objectives. It is important not to try to achieve too much in any one event. There is a limit to how much people can absorb at any one time and an even greater limit to how much they can put into effect. The content of the training should be related to the work contexts of the participants. Ideally, their work should be made a central feature of the subject matter. Every opportunity should be taken to embed learning at work.

4. Decide on methods of delivery

The methods used to deliver learning should be appropriate to the purpose of the course and to the characteristics of participants – their jobs, learning needs, previous experience, level of knowledge and skills, and how receptive they will be to being taught (motivated to learn). A blended learning approach should be adopted, as described in Chapter 41. Account must be taken of how people learn and the conditions for effective learning, as set out in Chapter 43.

Every opportunity should be taken to embed learning at work. It is particularly important in management, supervisory and interpersonal skills training to provide ample time for participation and active learning through discussion, case studies and simulations. Lectures should form a minor part of the course. Good instructional techniques, as described in Appendix D, should be used in skills training.

The design of the programme or event should take account of the principles of learning. The following guidelines, based on the ideas of Gagne (1977), have been produced by Harrison (2005).

SOURCE REVIEW

Guidance on the design and delivery of learning events, Gagne (1977) and Harrison (2005)

- Design an appropriate structure and culture – how the event will be shaped and the desirable climate of relationships.
- Stimulate the learners – ensure that learners believe that their needs are being catered for. Get them involved. Focus on key learning points.
- Help understanding – check understanding regularly and vary the learning pace to ensure that it is absorbed.
- Incorporate appropriate learning activities – these should include situations or the use of knowledge and skills that learners perceive to be relevant to their jobs.
- Build on existing learning – find out what people know and do and build on that so that they can incorporate new learning, or recognize that they are irrelevant and allow them gradually to fall away.
- Guide the learners – give them regular feedback and guidance on the learning process.
- Ensure that learning is retained – enable learners to practise and consolidate their skills, bearing in mind the phenomenon of the learning curve (see Chapter 43). Provide feedback and praise as appropriate.
- Ensure transfer of learning – successful transfer of learning from the event to the workplace depends on the extent to which the event has been relevant to the learners' needs, the learners have been able to acquire the knowledge and skills covered in the programme, they have been stimulated throughout the programme and are encouraged and enabled to put their learning into practice.

5. Decide on the location and facilities required, the budget and who delivers the programme

The programme could take place on- or off-the-job, in-house or at an external centre. The facilities will be determined by the planned learning methods, and their availability will influence the location. At this stage it is also necessary to cost the programme and prepare a financial budget. The programme could be delivered by the organization's own learning and development staff or outsourced in whole or in part to outside training providers. Line managers may usefully take part as long as they are reasonably proficient as instructors, trainers or coaches.

6. Prepare information on the programme or event

This will set out its objectives, content and methods as a guide to nominating managers and potential participants.

7. Deliver the learning

This should not present too many problems if the planning and preparation for the programme or event have been carried out systematically. However, a flexible approach is desirable because all learning events vary according to the characteristics of the learners whose learning needs and reactions will vary. Fine tuning will be necessary throughout the programme.

8. Evaluate the learning

The criteria for an effective learning programme or event are set out below. Systematic methods of evaluation are described in the last part of this chapter.

What makes a learning and development programme or event effective?

- The event or programme is based on a thorough evaluation of learning needs.
- Clear objectives have been set for the outcomes of the event or programme.
- Standards are set for the delivery of the event or programme.
- Success criteria and methods of measuring success have been established.
- A blend of learning and development methods are used – informal and formal – that are appropriate for the established needs of those taking part.
- The responsibilities for planning and delivering the programme or event have been clarified.
- Those responsible for the learning activity are well-qualified in whatever role they are expected to play.
- Adequate resources have been allocated to the programme or event.
- The programme or event has the support of top management.
- The programme is implemented effectively as planned, within its budget and in accordance with the defined standards.

- The application of the programme or event is regularly monitored to ensure that it meets the defined objectives and standards.
- The achievements of the programme or event are evaluated against the success criteria and swift corrective action is taken to deal with any problems.

Responsibility for the implementation of learning

Individuals should be expected to take a considerable degree of responsibility for managing their own learning (self-directed or discretionary learning) but they need the help and support of their line managers and the organization, including the learning and development function. Line managers have a key role in planning and facilitating learning by conducting performance and development reviews, agreeing learning contracts and personal development plans with their staff, and helping staff to implement those plans through the provision of learning opportunities and coaching. But they have to be encouraged to do this. They should understand that the promotion of learning is regarded as an important aspect of their responsibilities and that their performance in carrying it out will be assessed. They also need guidance on how they should carry out their developmental role.

Responsibility for learning and development is being increasingly placed on managers and employees rather than learning and development professionals. The latter are becoming learning facilitators rather than training providers or instructors. The direct role of training is becoming less important. As Stewart and Tansley (2002) point out, training specialists are focusing on learning processes, rather than the content of training courses. Carter *et al* (2002) argue that 'The shifting organizational forms of training, coupled with multiple delivery methods, are not leading to a single new role for the trainer, but rather an array of different role demands.' These roles include facilitator and change agent.

As facilitators, learning and development specialists analyse learning needs and make proposals on how these can best be satisfied. They provide facilities such as learning resource centres and e-learning programmes and plan and implement training interventions, often outsourcing training to external providers. Importantly, they provide guidance to line managers and help them to develop their skills in assessing development needs, personal development planning and coaching. Additionally, they are there to give advice and help to individuals on their learning plans.

Identifying learning needs

All learning activities need to be based on an understanding of what needs to be done and why it needs to be done. The purpose of the activities must be defined and this is only possible if the learning needs of the organization and the groups and individuals within it have been identified and analysed.

The basis of learning needs analysis

Learning needs analysis is often described as the process of identifying the learning gap – the gap between what is and what should be, as illustrated in Figure 42.1.

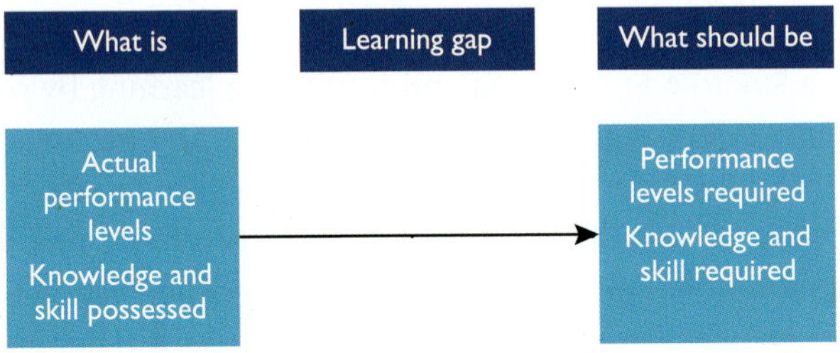

Figure 42.1 The learning gap

But this 'deficiency model' of training – only putting things right that have gone wrong – is limited. Learning is much more positive than that. It should be concerned with identifying and satisfying development needs – fitting people to take on extra responsibilities, increasing all-round competence, equipping people to deal with new work demands, multi-skilling, and preparing people to take on higher levels of responsibility in the future.

Areas for learning needs analysis

Learning needs should be analysed, first, for the organization as a whole – corporate needs; second, for departments, teams, functions or occupations within the organization – group needs; and third, for individual employees – individual needs. These three areas are interconnected, as shown in Figure 42.2. The analysis of corporate needs will lead to the identification of learning needs in different departments or occupations, while these in turn will indicate what individual employees need to learn. The process also operates in reverse. As the needs of individual employees are analysed separately, common needs emerge that can be dealt with on a group basis. The sum of group and individual needs will help to define corporate needs, although there may be some superordinate learning requirements that can be related only to the company as a whole to meet its business development needs – the whole learning plan may be greater than the sum of its parts.

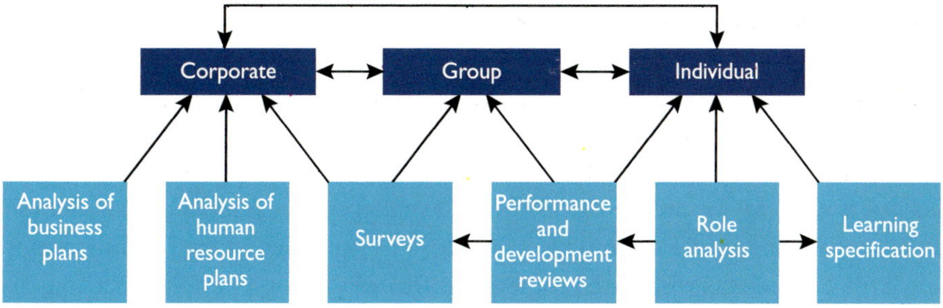

Figure 42.2 Learning needs analysis – areas and methods

These areas of analysis are discussed below.

Analysis of business and human resource plans

Business and HR plans should indicate in general terms the types of skills and competencies that may be required in the future and the numbers of people with those skills and competencies who will be needed. These broad indicators have to be translated into more specific plans that cover, for example, the outputs from training programmes of people with particular skills or a combination of skills (multi-skilling).

Surveys

Special surveys may be carried out that analyse the information from a number of sources, eg performance reviews, to identify corporate and group learning and training needs. This information can be usefully supplemented by interviewing people to establish their views about what they need to learn. But they often find it difficult to articulate learning needs and it is best to lead with a discussion of the work they do and identify any areas where they believe that their performance and potential could be improved by a learning or training programme.

An analysis should also be made of any areas where future changes in work processes, methods or job responsibilities are planned, and of any common gaps in skills or knowledge or weaknesses in performance that indicate a learning need. Further information should be derived from the evaluation of training, as described at the end of this chapter.

Performance and development reviews

The performance management processes should be a prime source of information about individual learning and development needs. The performance management approach to learning concentrates on the preparation of performance improvement programmes, personal development plans and learning contracts, which lead to jointly determined action plans. The emphasis is on identifying learning needs for continuous development or to produce specific improvements in performance.

Role analysis

Role analysis is the basis for preparing role profiles that provide a framework for analysing and identifying learning needs. Role profiles set out the key result areas of the role but, importantly, also define the competencies required to perform the role. A good performance management process will ensure that role profiles are updated regularly and the performance review will be built round an analysis of the results achieved by reference to the key result areas and agreed objectives. The competency framework for the role is used to assess the level of competency displayed in achieving, or as the case may be, not achieving those results. An assessment can then be made of any learning required to develop levels of competency. Ideally, this should be a self-assessment by individuals, who should be given every encouragement to identify learning needs for themselves. These can be discussed with the individuals' manager and agreement reached on how the learning needs should be met, by the individuals through self-managed learning and/or with the help and support of their managers. The output of role analysis could be a learning specification, as illustrated in Figure 42.3.

Learning Specification	
Role: Product Manager	**Department:** Marketing
What the role holder must understand	
Learning outcomes	**Learning methods**
• The product market	• Coaching: Marketing Manager and Advertising Manager
• The product specification	• Coaching: Operations Manager
• Market research availability	• Coaching: Market Research Manager
• Interpretation of marketing data	• Coaching: Market Research Manager
• Customer service requirements	• Customer Service Manager
• Techniques of product management	• Institute of Marketing courses
What the role holder must be able to do	
Learning outcomes	**Learning methods**
• Prepare product budget	• Coaching: Budget Accountant
• Prepare marketing plans	• Coaching: Mentor
• Conduct market reviews	• Coaching: Market Research Department
• Prepare marketing campaigns	• Read: Product Manager's Manual
• Specify requirements for advertisements and promotional material	• Read: Product Manager's Manual
• Liaise with advertising agents and creative suppliers	• Attachment to agency
• Analyse results of advertising campaigns	• Coaching: Mentor, read analyses
• Prepare marketing reports	• Read: previous reports; observe: marketing review meetings

Figure 42.3 A learning specification

Evaluation of learning

It is important to evaluate learning in order to assess its effectiveness in producing the outcomes specified when the activity was planned and to indicate where improvements or changes are required to make the training even more effective.

SOURCE REVIEW

Learning evaluation, Tamkin *et al* (2002)

Learning can be modelled as a chain of impact from the planning of learning to meet organizational or individual learning needs to the learning that takes place in a learning event, from learning to changed behaviour, and from changed behaviour to impact on others and the organization as a whole.

It is at the planning stage that the basis upon which each category of learning programme or event is to be evaluated should be determined. This means defining expectations in the form of the impact that the event will make in terms of criterion and terminal behaviour. The aim is to establish the extent to which the event has achieved its purpose. At the same time, it is necessary to consider how the information required for evaluation should be obtained and analysed.

The significance of learning evaluation

Evaluation is an integral feature of learning activities. In essence, it is the comparison of objectives with outcomes to answer the question of how far the event has achieved its purpose. The setting of objectives and the establishment of methods of measuring results are, or should be, an essential part of the planning stage of any learning and development programme. Evaluation provides guidance on what needs to be done to ensure that learning activities are effective.

Approach to evaluation

The areas that need to be evaluated are:

- Planning – the extent to which needs were properly evaluated and objectives set.

- Conduct – how well the programme or event was organized and managed, the degree to which the inputs and methods were appropriate and effective, and its cost compared with the budget.
- Reactions – what participants felt about the event.
- Outcomes – the impact the event made on individual, departmental and organizational performance. The levels at which this can take place were defined by Hamblin in 1974 and in a better known version, Kirkpatrick in 1994.

Levels of evaluation, Hamblin (1974)

The five evaluation levels identified by Hamblin are:

1. Reactions – what participants think of the learning experience, the quality of the speakers and the relevance of the content. This may be recorded on an evaluation form, sometimes called a 'happy sheet'.
2. Learning – an assessment of what participants have learnt on the programme.
3. Job behaviour – the extent to which participants have applied their learning on-the-job.
4. Organization – the impact of changes in the job behaviour of participants on the effectiveness of the department or function in which they work.
5. Ultimate value – the extent to which the organization has benefited from the learning event in terms of profitability, growth or survival.

As Hamblin points out, the five levels are links in a chain: training leads to reactions, which lead to learning, which leads to changes in the organization, which lead to changes in the achievement of ultimate goals. But the chain can be snapped at any link. Trainees can react favourably to an event – they can 'enjoy it' – but learn little or nothing. They can learn something but cannot, will not, or are not allowed to apply it. It is applied but does little good in the participants' area. It does some good in the area but does not further the objectives of the organization.

Evaluation can take place at any level. Ideally it should focus on levels four and five, but this can be difficult. In practice evaluation often goes no further than level one, but at least it should try to move on to levels two and three and make some attempt to evaluate at higher levels, especially when the learning programme is extensive and addresses issues of importance to the organization as a whole.

Levels of evaluation, Kirkpatrick (1994)

The four levels of evaluation suggested by Kirkpatrick are as follows.

Level 1: Reaction – at this level, evaluation measures how those who participated in the training have reacted to it. In a sense, it is a measure of immediate customer satisfaction. Kirkpatrick suggests the following guidelines for evaluating reactions:

- determine what you want to find out;
- design a form that will quantify reactions;
- encourage written comments and suggestions;
- get 100 per cent immediate response;
- get honest responses;
- develop acceptable standards;
- measure reactions against standards, and take appropriate action;
- communicate reactions as appropriate.

Research by Warr *et al* (1970) has shown that there is relatively little correlation between learner reactions and measures of training, or subsequent measures of changed behaviour. But as Tamkin *et al* (2002) claim, despite this, organizations are still keen to get reactions to training, and used with caution this can produce useful information on the extent to which learning objectives were perceived to be met and why.

Level 2: Evaluate learning – this level obtains information on the extent to which learning objectives have been attained. It will aim to find how much knowledge was acquired, what skills were developed or improved, and the extent to which attitudes have changed in the desired direction. So far as possible, the evaluation of learning should involve the use of tests before and after the programme – paper and pencil, oral or performance tests.

Level 3: Evaluate behaviour – this level evaluates the extent to which behaviour has changed as required when people attending the programme have returned to their jobs. The question to be answered is the extent to which knowledge, skills and attitudes have been transferred from the classroom to the workplace. Ideally, the evaluation should take place both before and after the training. Time should be allowed for the change in behaviour to take place. The evaluation needs to assess the extent to which specific learning objectives relating to changes in behaviour and the application of knowledge and skills have been achieved.

Level 4: Evaluate results – this is the ultimate level of evaluation and provides the basis for assessing the benefits of the training against its costs. The objective is to determine the added value of learning and development programmes – how they contribute to raising organizational performance significantly above its previous level. The evaluation has to be based on 'before' and 'after' measures and has to determine the extent to which the fundamental objectives of the training have been achieved in areas such as increasing sales, raising productivity, reducing accidents or increasing customer satisfaction. Evaluating results is obviously easier when they can be quantified. However, it is not always easy to prove the contribution to improved results made by training as distinct from other factors and, as Kirkpatrick says, 'Be satisfied with evidence, because proof is usually impossible to get.' Perhaps the most powerful method of demonstrating that learning programmes pay is to measure the return on investment, as discussed below.

Kirkpatrick's system is slightly simpler than Hamblin's, which may explain why it is so popular. But the difficulty of moving beyond level one still applies. That is why there have been moves to use an overall measure such as return on investment or return on expectations.

Return on investment as a method of evaluation

Return on investment (RoI) is advocated by some commentators as a means of assessing the overall impact of training on organizational performance. It is calculated as:

$$\frac{\text{Benefits from training (£)} - \text{costs of training (£)}}{\text{costs of training (£)}} \times 100$$

Kearns and Miller (1997) believe that only this sort of measure is useful in evaluating the overall impact of training. They argue that particular measures should be used to evaluate specific training; for example, if development aims to bring about greater awareness of customers then it should still be measured by the eventual effect on customer spend, customer satisfaction and number of customers.

The pressure to produce financial justifications for any organizational activity, especially in areas such as learning and development, has increased the interest in RoI. The problem is that while it is easy to record the costs it is much harder to produce convincing financial assessments of the benefits. Kearns (2005) provides a response to this concern:

> *All business is about the art of speculation and the risk of the unknown. The trick here is not to try and work to a higher standard of credibility than anyone else in the organization. If accountants are prepared to guess about amortization costs or marketing directors to guess about market share why should a trainer not be prepared to have a guess at the potential benefits of training?*

He recommends the use of 'a rule of thumb' when using RoI to the effect that any training should improve the performance of trainees by at least 1 per cent. Thus if the return on sales training is being measured, the benefits could be calculated as 1 per cent of profit on sales.

Return on expectations

The evaluation of learning has traditionally concentrated on the Hamblin or Kirkpatrick 'levels' approach. But there is a trend to concentrate more on the validation of the total learning process and on the outcomes of learning, which means focusing on return on expectation measures that assess the extent to which the anticipated benefits of any learning investment have been realized. This starts with a definition of expectations – a statement of what the learning event is aiming to achieve at the individual, departmental and, importantly, organizational level. This would also involve deciding how achievement will be measured – the success criteria. These criteria would be used as the basis for evaluation. At the organizational level, for example, they could be improvements in the level of customer service, a return on investment target, or increased productivity. As Sloman (2007) emphasizes: 'We must enter into a dialogue with our key stakeholders to find out where they believe that learning can make a strategic impact. This must then determine how we measure and report on learning.'

Application of evaluation

As Reid *et al* (2004) comment: 'The more care that has been taken in the assessment of needs and the more precise the objectives, the greater will be the possibility of effective evaluation.' This is the basis for conducting evaluation at various levels.

It could be argued that the only feedback from evaluation that matters is the results in terms of improved unit or organizational performance that learning brings. But if this is hard to measure, a learning event could still be justified in terms of any actual changes in behaviour that the programme was designed to produce. This is based on the assumption that the analysis of learning needs indicated that this behaviour is more than likely to deliver the desired results. Similarly, at the learning level, if a proper analysis of knowledge, skills and attitude requirements and their impact on behaviour has been conducted, it is reasonable to assume that if the knowledge, etc has been acquired, behaviour is likely to change appropriately. Finally, if all else fails, reactions are important in that they provide immediate feedback on the quality of training given (including the performance of the trainer), which can point the way to corrective action.

Learning and development programmes and events – key learning points

Preparing the business case for learning and development

The business case for learning and development should demonstrate how learning, training and development programmes will meet business needs.

Planning and delivering learning programmes and events

The stages are:

- identify learning needs;
- define learning objectives;
- decide on content;
- decide on methods of delivery;
- decide on location, facilities, the budget and who delivers the programme;
- prepare information about the programme or event;
- deliver the programme or event;
- evaluate learning.

Main criteria for effectiveness

- The programme is based on a thorough evaluation of learning needs.

Learning and development programmes and events – key learning points (continued)

- Clear objectives have been set for the outcomes of the programme.
- Standards are set for the delivery of the programme.
- Success criteria and methods of measuring success have been established.
- A blend of learning and development methods are used – informal and formal – that are appropriate for the established needs of those taking part.
- The outcome of the programme is evaluated.

Responsibility for learning

While individuals should be expected to take a considerable degree of responsibility for managing their own learning, they need the help and support of their line managers and the organization, including the L&D function. Line managers have a key role in planning and facilitating learning by conducting performance and development reviews, agreeing learning contracts and personal development plans with their staff, and helping staff to implement those plans through the provision of learning opportunities and coaching. Learning and development professionals are becoming learning facilitators rather than training providers or instructors.

The basis of learning needs analysis

All learning activities need to be based on an understanding of what needs to be done and why it needs to be done. The purpose of the activities must be defined and this is only possible if the learning needs of the organization and the groups and individuals within it have been identified and analysed.

Areas for learning needs analysis

Learning needs should be analysed, first, for the organization as a whole – corporate needs; second, for departments, teams, functions or occupations within the organization – group needs; and third, for individual employees – individual needs.

The significance of learning evaluation

Evaluation is an integral feature of learning activities. In essence, it is the comparison of objectives with outcomes to answer the question of how far the event has achieved its purpose.

Levels of evaluation

The four levels of evaluation defined by Kirkpatrick are: reactions, evaluating learning, evaluating behaviour and evaluating results.

The application of evaluation

As Reid *et al* (2004) comment: 'The more care that has been taken in the assessment of needs and the more precise the objectives, the greater will be the possibility of effective evaluation.' This is the basis for conducting evaluation at various levels.

Questions

1. You are attending an assessment centre for a senior learning and development post and have been asked to make a 10 to 15 minute presentation on 'How to plan an effective learning event'. Outline what you will say and why.
2. Prepare an outline of a 10 to 15 minute talk at a half-day conference for HRM students on methods of identifying learning and development needs. Illustrate the talk with practical examples.
3. The following remarks on learning evaluation were made by Martin Sloman in *People Management* on 29 November 2007: 'For today's training and learning professional, making a "value contribution" calls for a wide-ranging approach that involves aligning learning processes and investment, and investment with the organization's strategic priorities, and establishing, through dialogue with senior decision makers, what are the most relevant evaluation methods for the organization... The key challenge is to understand and respond to the legitimate expectations that key stakeholders, especially senior managers, have in relation to the strategic value of learning.' Comment on the significance of these remarks as the basis for an approach to learning evaluation which, according to some commentators, will replace the Kirkpatrick model and the reliance on return on investment as a measure of effectiveness.

References

Carter, A, Hirsh, W and Aston, J (2002) *Resourcing the Training and Development Function*, Report No 390, Institute of Employment Studies, Brighton

Gagne, R M (1977) *The Conditions of Learning*, 3rd edn, Rinehart and Winston, New York

Hamblin, A C (1974) *Evaluation and Control of Training*, McGraw-Hill, Maidenhead

Harrison, R (2005) *Learning and Development*, 4th edn, CIPD, London

Kearns, P (2005) *Evaluating the ROI from Learning*, CIPD, London

Kearns, P and Miller, T (1997) Measuring the impact of training and development on the bottom line, *FT Management Briefings*, Pitman, London

Kirkpatrick, D L (1994) *Evaluating Training Programmes*, Berret-Koehler, San Francisco, CA

Reid, M A, Barrington, H and Brown, B (2004) *Human Resource Development: Beyond training interventions*, CIPD, London

Sloman, M (2007) Thanks, it's just what I wanted, *People Management*, 29 November, pp 32–34

Stewart, J and Tansley, C (2002) *Training in the Knowledge Economy*, CIPD, London

Tamkin, P, Yarnall, J and Kerrin, M (2002) *Kirkpatrick and Beyond: A review of training evaluation*, Report 392, Institute of Employment Studies, Brighton

Warr, P B, Bird, M W and Rackham, N (1970) *Evaluation of Management Training*, Gower, Aldershot

43 How People Learn

Key concepts and terms

- Affective learning
- Discretionary learning
- Experiential learning
- Learning
- Operant conditioning
- Self-reflective learning
- Cognitive learning
- Experienced worker's standard (EWS)
- Instrumental learning
- The learning curve
- Reinforcement
- Social learning

Learning outcomes

On completing this chapter you should be able to define these key concepts. You should also know about:

- The types of learning
- Learning theories
- Learning to learn
- The implications of learning theory and concepts
- The learning process
- Learning styles
- The motivation to learn

Introduction

An understanding of how people learn is necessary if learning is to take place effectively. The aims of this chapter are to summarize the different ways in which people in general learn – learning theory; describe how individuals learn – their learning styles and 'learning to learn'; and set out the practical implications of these theories, concepts and approaches.

Learning defined

Learning has been defined by Kim (1993) as the process of 'increasing one's capacity to take action'. It can be described as the modification of behaviour through experience. A distinction was made between learning and development by Pedler *et al* (1989), who see learning as being concerned with an increase in knowledge or a higher degree of an existing skill, whereas development is more towards a different state of being or functioning.

Argyris (1993) makes the point that: 'Learning is not simply having a new insight or a new idea. Learning occurs when we take effective action, when we detect and correct error. How do you know when you know something? When you can produce what it is you claim to know.'

Types of learning

1. Instrumental learning – learning how to do the job better once the basic standard of performance has been attained. It is helped by learning on-the-job.
2. Cognitive learning – outcomes based on the enhancement of knowledge and understanding.
3. Affective learning – outcomes based on the development of attitudes or feelings rather than knowledge.
4. Self-reflective learning – developing new patterns of understanding, thinking and behaving and therefore creating new knowledge (Harrison, 2005).

The learning process

Honey (1998) declared that: 'Learning is complex and various, covering all sorts of things such as knowledge, skills, insights, beliefs, values, attitudes and habits.'

Individuals learn for themselves and learn from other people. They learn as members of teams and by interaction with their managers, co-workers and people outside the organization.

People learn by doing and by instruction. The ways in which individuals learn will differ and the extent to which they learn will depend largely on how well they are motivated or self-motivated. Discretionary learning can take place when individuals of their own volition actively seek to acquire the knowledge and skills they need to carry out their work effectively. It should be encouraged and supported.

The effectiveness of learning will be strongly influenced by the context in which it takes place. This includes the values of the organization. Is it truly believed that learning is important as a means of developing a high performance culture and achieving competitive advantage? Is this belief confirmed by actions that encourage and support learning? Is the approach to learning delivery in line with the following beliefs?

SOURCE REVIEW

Conditions for effective learning, Birchall and Lyons (1995)

For effective learning to take place at the individual level it is essential to foster an environment where individuals are encouraged to take risks and experiment, where mistakes are tolerated, but where means exist for those involved to learn from their experiences.

Learning theory

There are a number of learning theories, each of which focuses on different aspects of the learning process as applied to people in general. The main theories are concerned with:

- reinforcement;
- cognitive learning;
- experiential learning;
- social learning.

Reinforcement theory

Reinforcement theory is based on the work of Skinner (1974). It expresses the belief that changes in behaviour take place as a result of an individual's response to events or stimuli and the ensuing consequences (rewards or punishments). Individuals can be 'conditioned' to repeat the behaviour by positive reinforcement in the form of feedback and knowledge of results. This process is known as 'operant conditioning'.

Gagne (1977) later developed his stimulus-response theory, which relates the learning process to a number of factors, including reinforcement, namely:

- drive – there must be a basic need or drive to learn;
- stimulus – people must be stimulated by the learning process;
- response – people must be helped by the learning process to develop appropriate responses, ie the knowledge, skills and attitudes that will lead to effective performance;
- reinforcement – these responses need to be reinforced by feedback and experience until they are learnt.

Cognitive learning theory

Cognitive learning involves gaining knowledge and understanding by absorbing information in the form of principles, concepts and facts and then internalizing it. Learners can be regarded as powerful information processing machines.

Experiential learning theory

People are active agents of their own learning (Reynolds *et al*, 2002). Experiential learning takes place when people learn from their experience by reflecting on it so that it can be understood and applied. Learning is therefore a personal 'construction' of meaning through experience. 'Constructivists' such as Rogers (1983) believe that experiential learning will be enhanced through facilitation – creating an environment in which people can be stimulated to think and act in ways that help them to make good use of their experience.

Social learning theory

Social learning theory states that effective learning requires social interaction. Wenger (1998) suggested that we all participate in 'communities of practice' (groups of people with shared expertise who work together) and that these are our primary sources of learning. Bandura (1977) views learning as a series of information-processing steps set in train by social interactions.

Learning styles

Learning theories describe in general terms how people learn, but individual learners will have different styles – a preference for a particular approach to learning. The two most familiar classifications of learning styles are those produced by Kolb and by Honey and Mumford.

Kolb's learning style inventory

Kolb *et al* (1974) identified a learning cycle consisting of four stages, as shown in Figure 43.1.

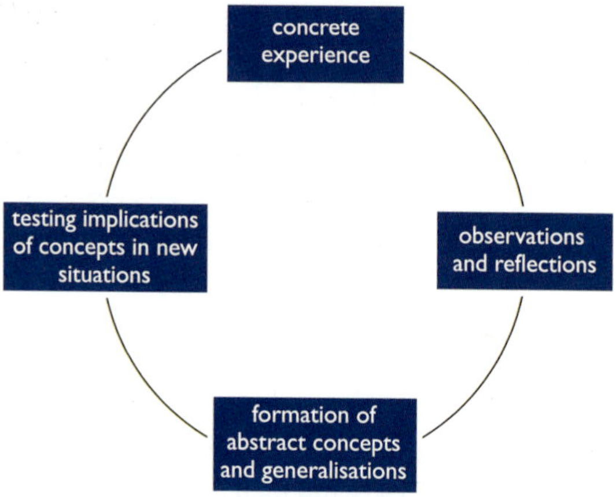

Figure 43.1 The Kolb learning cycle

He defined these stages as follows:

- Concrete experience – this can be planned or accidental.
- Reflective observation – this involves actively thinking about the experience and its significance.
- Abstract conceptualization (theorizing) – generalizing from experience to develop various concepts and ideas that can be applied when similar situations are encountered.
- Active experimentation – testing the concepts or ideas in new situations. This gives rise to a new concrete experience and the cycle begins again.

The key to Kolb's model is that it is a simple description of how experience is translated into concepts that are then used to guide the choice of new experiences. To learn effectively, individuals must shift from being observers to participants, from direct involvement to a more objective analytical detachment. Every person has his or her own learning style and one of the most important arts that trainers have to develop is to adjust their approaches to the learning styles of trainees. Trainers must acknowledge these learning styles rather than their own preferred approach.

Kolb also defined the following learning styles of trainees:

- *Accommodators* who learn by trial and error, combining the concrete experience and experimentation stages of the cycle.
- *Divergers* who prefer concrete to abstract learning situations and reflection to active involvement. Such individuals have great imaginative ability, and can view a complete situation from different viewpoints.
- *Convergers* who prefer to experiment with ideas, considering them for their practical usefulness. Their main concern is whether the theory works in action, thus combining the abstract and experimental dimensions.
- *Assimilators* who like to create their own theoretical models and assimilate a number of disparate observations into an overall integrated explanation. Thus they veer towards the reflective and abstract dimensions.

The Honey and Mumford learning styles

Another analysis of learning styles was made by Honey and Mumford (1996). They identified the following four styles.

SOURCE REVIEW

The Honey and Mumford learning styles

1. *Activists* who involve themselves fully without bias in new experiences and revel in new challenges.
2. *Reflectors* who stand back and observe new experiences from different angles. They collect data, reflect on them and then come to a conclusion.
3. *Theorists* who adapt and apply their observations in the form of logical theories. They tend to be perfectionists.
4. *Pragmatists* who are keen to try out new ideas, approaches and concepts to see if they work.

However, none of these four learning styles is exclusive. It is quite possible that one person could be both a reflector and a theorist and someone else could be an activist/pragmatist, a reflector/pragmatist or even a theorist/pragmatist.

Use of learning style theory

Learning style theory can be used in the design and conduct of learning events or personal development programmes. Learning situations can be designed to fit the learning style of participants. The problem is that people do not necessarily have a single learning style and there will certainly be a large range of styles in any learning group. It may therefore be difficult to fit the approach to the style. Coffield (2005) stressed instead the importance of individuals' 'thinking styles' – that is, their automatic way of organizing and processing information during learning – and of their 'learning strategy', meaning the approach they adopt to try to overcome the limitations of their natural thinking style.

Learning to learn

People learn all the time and through doing so acquire knowledge, skills and insight. But they will learn more effectively if they 'learn how to learn'. As defined by Honey (1998), the process of learning to learn is the acquisition of knowledge, skills and insights about the learning process itself. The aims, as described by Honey, are to:

- provide a basis for organizing and planning learning;
- pinpoint precisely what has been learnt and what to do better or differently as a consequence;
- share what has been learnt with other people so that they benefit;
- check on the quality of what has been learnt;
- transfer what has been learnt and apply it in different circumstances;
- improve the learning process itself so that how people learn, not just what people learn, is given constant attention.

The learning curve

The concept of the learning curve refers to the time it takes an inexperienced person to reach the required level of performance in a job or a task. This is sometimes called the 'experienced worker's standard' (EWS). The standard learning curve is shown in Figure 43.2.

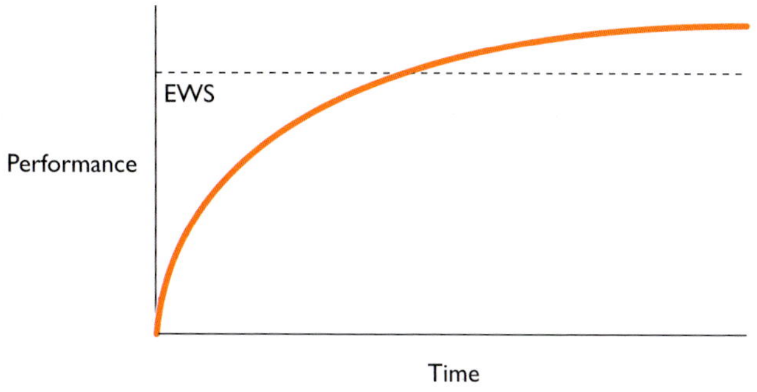

Figure 43.2 A standard learning curve

However, rates of learning vary, depending on the effectiveness of the training, the experience and natural aptitude of the learner and the latter's interest in learning. Both the time taken to reach the experienced worker's standard and the variable speed with which learning takes place at different times, affect the shape of the curve, as shown in Figure 43.3.

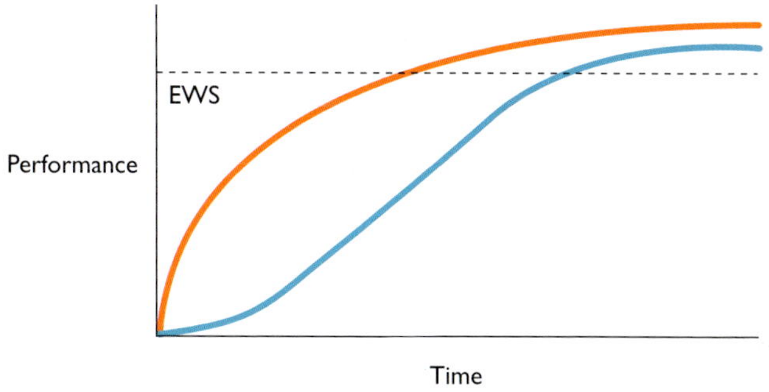

Figure 43.3 Different rates of learning

Learning is often stepped, with one or more plateaus, while further progress is halted. This may be because learners cannot continually increase their skills or speeds of work and need a pause to consolidate what they have already learnt. The existence of steps such as those shown in Figure 43.4 can be used when planning skills training to provide deliberate reinforcement periods when newly acquired skills are practised in order to achieve the expected standards.

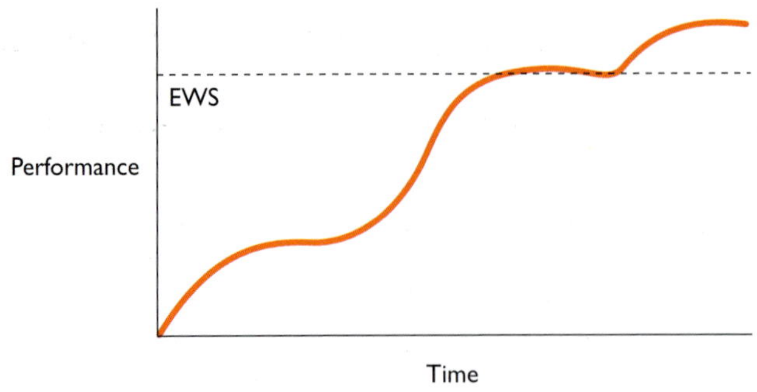

Figure 43.4 A stepped learning curve

When a training module is being prepared that describes what has to be learnt and the training needed to achieve the required levels of skill and speed, it is often desirable to proceed step-by-step, taking one task or part of a task at a time, reinforcing it and then progressively adding other parts, consolidating at each stage. This is called the 'progressive parts method of training'.

The motivation to learn

People will learn more effectively if they are motivated to learn. The motivation to learn can be defined as 'those factors that energize and direct behavioural patterns organized around a learning goal' (Rogers, 1996). As Reynolds *et al* (2002) comment, 'The disposition and commitment of the learner – their motivation to learn – is one of the most critical factors affecting training effectiveness. Under the right conditions, a strong disposition to learn, enhanced by solid experience and a positive attitude, can lead to exceptional performance.'

Two motivation theories, as described in Chapter 18, are particularly relevant to learning. *Expectancy theory* states that goal-directed behaviour is driven by the expectation of achieving something the individual regards as desirable. If individuals feel that the outcome of learning is likely to benefit them they will be more inclined to pursue it. When they find that their expectations have been fulfilled, their belief that learning is worthwhile will be reinforced. *Goal theory* states that motivation is higher when individuals aim to achieve specific goals, when these goals are accepted and, although difficult, are achievable, and when there is feedback on performance. Learning goals may be set for individuals (but to be effective as motivators they must be agreed) or individuals may set their own goals (self-directed learning).

The implications of learning theory and concepts

The practical implications of the learning theories described above are summarized in Table 43.1.

Table 43.1 The implications of learning theory and concepts

Theory/concept	Content	Practical implications
The process of learning	Learning is complex and is achieved in many different ways The context is important	Different learning needs require different learning methods, often in combination Learning effectiveness depends on the extent to which the organization believes in learning and supports it
Reinforcement theory	Behaviours can be strengthened by reinforcing them with positive feedback (conditioning)	Reinforcement theory underpins training programmes concerned with developing skills through instruction. In these, the learner is conditioned to make a response and receives immediate feedback, and progress is made in incremental steps, each directed to a positive outcome
Cognitive learning theory	Learners acquire understanding that they internalize by being exposed to learning materials and by solving problems	The knowledge and understanding of learners can be enriched and internalized by presenting them with learning materials (eg e-learning). Case studies, projects and problem-solving activities can also be used for this purpose Self-directed learning, personal development planning activities and discovery learning processes with help from facilitators, coaches or mentors are underpinned by cognitive learning theory
Experiential learning theory	People learn by constructing meaning and developing their skills through experience	Learning through experience can be enhanced by encouraging learners to reflect on and make better use of what they learn through their own work and from other people. Self-directed learning and personal development planning activities with help from facilitators, coaches or mentors are also underpinned by experiential learning theory, as is action learning

Table 43.1 *continued*

Theory/concept	Content	Practical implications
Social learning theory	Learning is most effective in a social setting. Individual understanding is shaped by active participation in real situations	Learning can be encouraged in communities of practice and in project teams and networks
Learning styles	Every person has their own learning style	Learning programmes need to be adjusted to cope with different learning styles. Trainers have also to flex their methods. People will learn more effectively if they are helped to 'learn how to learn' by making the best use of their own style but also by experimenting with other styles
The learning curve	The time required to reach an acceptable standard of skill or competence, which varies between people. Learning may proceed in steps with plateaus rather than being a continuous process	Recognize that progress may vary and may not be continuous. Enable learners to consolidate their learning and introduce reinforcement periods in training programmes to recognize the existence of learning steps and plateaus
The motivation to learn	People need to be motivated to learn effectively	Learners should be helped to develop learning goals and to understand the benefits to them of achieving them. Performance management processes leading to personal development plans can provide a means of doing this

How people learn – key learning points

The types of learning

Instrumental learning, cognitive learning, affective learning and self-reflective learning.

The learning process

Individuals learn for themselves and learn from other people. They learn as members of teams and by interaction with their

How people learn – key learning points (continued)

managers, co-workers and people outside the organization. People learn by doing and by instruction. The ways in which individuals learn will differ and the extent to which they learn will depend largely on how well they are motivated or self-motivated.

Learning theories

Reinforcement, cognitive learning, experiential learning and social learning.

Learning styles

Learning theories describe in general terms how people learn, but individual learners will have different styles – a preference for a particular approach to learning. The two most familiar classifications of learning styles are those produced by Kolb and by Honey and Mumford.

Learning to learn

People learn all the time and through doing so acquire knowledge, skills and insight. But they will learn more effectively if they 'learn how to learn'. As defined by Honey (1998), the process of learning to learn is the acquisition of knowledge, skills and insights about the learning process itself.

The motivation to learn

People will learn more effectively if they are motivated to learn. The motivation to learn can be defined as 'those factors that energize and direct behavioural patterns organized around a learning goal' (Rogers, 1996).

The implications of learning theory and concepts

See Table 43.1.

Questions

1. What are the main types of learning and how can they be put to use on a learning event?
2. Your local newspaper is publishing a supplement on learning and development and has asked you to write a brief piece on what, in your experience and that of relevant research, are the key factors that determine how well people learn. Draft an outline of your article.
3. Critically evaluate a learning style model such as Honey and Mumford's as a basis for designing learning events and processes.

References

Argyris, C (1993) *Knowledge for Action: A guide to overcoming barriers to organizational change*, Jossey Bass, San Francisco, CA

Bandura, A (1977) *Social Learning Theory*, Prentice-Hall, Englewood Cliffs, NJ

Birchall, D and Lyons, L (1995) *Creating Tomorrow's Organisation*, Pitman, London

Coffield, J (2005) Thinking styles, *People Management*, 15 June, p 24

Gagne, R M (1977) *The Conditions of Learning*, 3rd edn, Rinehart and Winston, New York

Harrison, R (2005) *Learning and Development*, 4th edn, CIPD, London

Honey, P (1998) The debate starts here, *People Management*, 1 October, pp 28–29

Honey, P and Mumford, A (1996) *The Manual of Learning Styles*, 3rd edn, Honey Publications, Maidenhead

Kim, D H (1993) The link between individual and organizational learning, *Sloane Management Review*, **35** (1), pp 37–50

Kolb, D A, Rubin, I M and McIntyre, J M (1974) *Organizational Psychology: An experimental approach*, Prentice Hall, Englewood Cliffs, NJ

Pedler, M, Boydell, T and Burgoyne, J (1989) Towards the learning company, *Management Education and Development*, **20** (1), pp 1–8

Reynolds, J, Caley, L and Mason, R (2002) *How Do People Learn?*, CIPD, London

Rogers, A (1996) *Teaching Adults*, Open University Press, London

Rogers, C R (1983) *Freedom to Learn*, Merrill, Columbus, OH

Skinner, B F (1974) *About Behaviourism*, Cape, London

Wenger, E (1998) *Communities of Practice: Learning, meaning and identity*, Cambridge University Press, Cambridge

44 Organizational Learning

Key concepts and terms

- Adaptive learning
- Evaluative enquiry
- Organizational capability
- Resource capability
- Strategic choice
- Double-loop learning
- Generative learning
- Organizational learning
- Single-loop learning

Learning outcomes

On completing this chapter you should be able to define these key concepts. You should also know about:

- The process of organizational learning
- Organizational learning and the learning organization
- Outcomes of organizational learning

Introduction

Organizational learning theory is concerned with how learning takes place in organizations. It focuses on collective learning but takes into account the proposition made by Argyris (1992) that organizations do not perform the actions that produce the learning; it is individual members of the organization who behave in ways that lead to it, although organizations can create conditions that facilitate such learning. The concept of organizational learning recognizes that the way in which this takes place is affected by the context of the organization and its culture. In this chapter organizational learning is defined, consideration is given to the outcomes and process of organizational learning, the principles of organizational learning are summarized and the process of evaluative enquiry as a basis for organizational learning is described. At the end of the chapter the concepts of organizational learning and the learning organization are compared. These are often confused.

Organizational learning defined

Organizational learning is concerned with the development of new knowledge or insights that have the potential to influence behaviour. It has been defined by Marsick (1994) as a process of: 'Coordinated systems change, with mechanisms built in for individuals and groups to access, build and use organizational memory, structure and culture to develop long-term organizational capacity.' Organizational learning takes place within the wide institutional context of inter-organizational relationships and 'refers broadly to an organization's acquisition of understanding, know-how, techniques and practices of any kind and by any means' (Argyris and Schon, 1996). Organizational learning theory examines how in this context individual and team learning can be translated into an organizational resource and is therefore linked closely to knowledge management processes (see Chapter 12).

It is emphasized by Harrison (1997) that organizational learning is not simply the sum of the learning of individuals and groups across the organization. She comments that: 'Many studies (see for example Argyris and Schon, 1996) have confirmed that without effective processes and systems linking individual and organizational learning, the one has no necessary counterpart with the other.'

SOURCE REVIEW

Principles of organizational learning, Harrison (1997)

1. The need for a powerful and cohering vision of the organization to be communicated and maintained across the workforce in order to promote awareness of the need for strategic thinking at all levels.
2. The need to develop strategy in the context of a vision that is not only powerful but also open-ended and unambiguous. This will encourage a search for a wide rather than a narrow range of strategic options, will promote lateral thinking and will orient the knowledge-creating activities of employees.
3. Within the framework of vision and goals, frequent dialogue, communication and conversations are major facilitators of organizational learning.
4. It is essential continuously to challenge people to re-examine what they take for granted.
5. It is essential to develop a conducive learning and innovation climate.

The process of organizational learning

Organizational learning can be characterized as an intricate three-stage process consisting of knowledge acquisition, dissemination and shared implementation (Dale, 1994). Knowledge may be acquired from direct experience, the experience of others or organizational memory.

Argyris (1992) suggests that organizational learning occurs under two conditions: first when an organization achieves what is intended, and second when a mismatch between intentions and outcomes is identified and corrected. He distinguishes between single-loop and double-loop learning. These two types of learning have been described as adaptive or generative learning.

Single-loop or adaptive learning is incremental learning that does no more than correct deviations from the norm by making small changes and improvements without challenging assumptions, beliefs or decisions. As suggested by Argyris (1992), organizations where single-loop learning is the norm, define the 'governing variables' ie what they expect to achieve in terms of targets and standards, and then monitor and review achievements and take corrective action as necessary, thus completing the loop.

Double-loop or generative learning involves challenging assumptions, beliefs, norms and decisions rather than accepting them. On this basis, learning through the examination of the root causes of problems so that a new learning loop is established goes far deeper than the traditional learning loop provided by single-loop or instrumental learning. It occurs when the monitoring process initiates action to redefine the 'governing variables' to meet the new situation, which may be imposed by the external environment. The organization has learnt something new about what has to be achieved in the light of changed circumstances and can then decide how this should be done. This learning is converted into action. The process is illustrated in Figure 44.1.

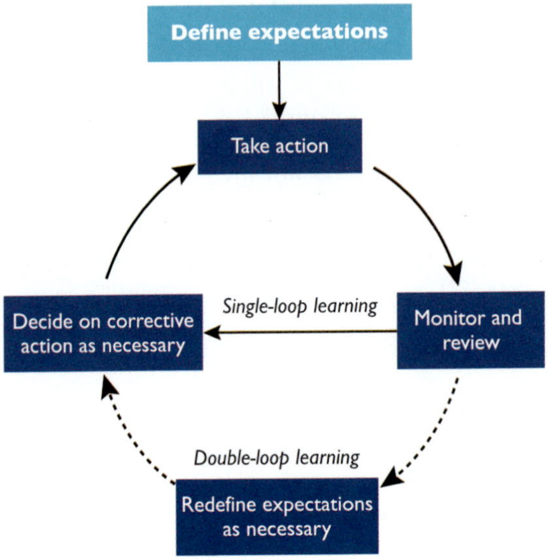

Figure 44.1 Single- and double-loop learning

As Easterby-Smith and Araujo (1999) commented, single-loop learning could be linked to incremental change 'where an organization tries out new methods and tactics and attempts to get rapid feedback on their consequences in order to be able to make continuous adjustments and adaptations'. In contrast, double-loop learning is associated 'with radical change, which might involve a major change in strategic direction, possibly linked to replacement of senior personnel, and wholesale revision of systems'. It is generally assumed that double-loop learning is superior, but there are situations when single-loop learning may be more appropriate.

Strategic choice

The concept of strategic choice in organizational learning was developed by Child (1997). He suggested that in making choices about their priorities, policies, actions and structures, organizations evaluate information from their internal and external environment in order to identify opportunities and problems. This encourages a learning process that proceeds towards action and outcomes through debate, negotiation and the exercise of choice.

Outcomes of organizational learning

Organizational learning outcomes contribute to the development of a firm's resource capability. This is in accordance with one of the basic principles of human resource management, namely that it is necessary to invest in people in order to develop the intellectual capital required by the organization and thus increase its stock of knowledge and skills. As stated by Ehrenberg and Smith (1994), human capital theory indicates that: 'The knowledge and skills a worker has – which comes from education and training, including the training that experience brings – generate productive capital.'

Pettigrew and Whipp (1991) believe that the focus of organizational learning should be on developing 'organizational capability'. This means paying attention to the intricate and often unnoticed or hidden learning that takes place and influences what occurs within the organization. 'Hidden learning' is acquired and developed in the normal course of work by people acting as individuals and, importantly, in groups or 'communities of practice' (Wenger and Snyder, 2000).

Evaluative enquiry

Evaluative enquiry is a method of enhancing organizational learning. It requires organization members to critically consider what they think, say and do in the context of the work environment.

The process of evaluative enquiry

Evaluative enquiry involves:

- asking questions;
- identifying and challenging values, beliefs and assumptions;
- reflection;
- dialogue;
- collecting, analysing and interpreting data;
- action planning;
- implementation.

Organizational learning and the learning organization

The notion of the learning organization as described in Chapter 40 is sometimes confused with the concept of organizational learning. However, as Harrison (2000) points out: 'Too often... it is assumed that the terms "the learning organization" and "organizational learning" are synonymous. They are not.'

Easterby-Smith and Araujo (1999) explain that the literature on organizational learning focuses on the 'observation and analysis of the processes of individual and collective learning in organizations', whereas the learning organization literature is concerned with 'using specific diagnostic and evaluative tools which can help to identify, promote and evaluate the quality of the learning processes inside organizations'. In other words, organizational learning is about how people learn in organizations and the learning organization concept is about what organizations should do to facilitate the learning of their members.

Organizational learning – key learning points

The process of organizational learning

Organizational learning can be characterized as an intricate three-stage process consisting of knowledge acquisition, dissemination and shared implementation. Argyris (1992) suggests that organizational learning occurs under two conditions: first when an organization achieves what is intended, and second when a mismatch between intentions and outcomes is identified and corrected. He distinguishes between single-loop and double-loop learning.

Outcomes of organizational learning

Organizational learning outcomes contribute to the development of a firm's resource-based capability. This is in accordance with one of the basic principles of human resource management, namely that it is necessary to invest in people in order to develop the intellectual capital required by the organization and thus increase its stock of knowledge and skills.

Organizational learning and the learning organization

Organizational learning is about how people learn in organizations; the learning organization concept is about what organizations should do to facilitate the learning of their members.

Questions

1. What, if anything, is the difference between the concepts of organizational learning and the learning organization?
2. What are single- and double-loop learning and what is the significance of these concepts in relation to the design of learning programmes and events?
3. How does the process of knowledge management contribute to organizational learning?

References

Argyris, C (1992) *On Organizational Learning*, Blackwell, Cambridge, MA

Argyris, C and Schon, D A (1996) *Organizational Learning: A theory of action perspective*, Addison Wesley, Reading, MA

Child, D (1997) Strategic choice in the analysis of action, structure, organizations and environment: retrospective and prospective, *Organizational Studies*, **18** (1), pp 43–76

Dale, M (1994) Learning organizations, in (eds) C Mabey and P Iles, *Managing Learning*, Routledge, London

Easterby-Smith, M and Araujo, J (1999) Organizational learning: current debates and opportunities, in (eds) M Easterby-Smith, J Burgoyne and L Araujo, *Organizational Learning and the Learning Organization*, Sage, London

Ehrenberg, R G and Smith, R S (1994) *Modern Labor Economics*, Harper Collins, New York

Harrison, R (1997) *Employee Development*, IPM, London

Harrison, R (2000) *Employee Development*, 2nd edn, IPM, London

Marsick, V J (1994) Trends in managerial invention: creating a learning map, *Management Learning*, **21** (1) pp 11–33

Pettigrew, A and Whipp, R (1991) *Managing Change for Competitive Success*, Blackwell, Oxford

Wenger, E and Snyder, W M (2000) Communities of practice: the organizational frontier, *Harvard Business Review*, January–February, pp 33–41

45 Management Development

Key concepts and terms

- Action learning
- Management development
- Development centre
- Management succession planning

Learning outcomes

On completing this chapter you should be able to define these key concepts. You should also know about:

- Management development policy
- How managers learn and develop
- Informal approaches to management development
- An integrated approach to management development
- Criteria for management development
- Management development strategy
- Formal approaches to management development
- Development centres
- Responsibility for management development

Introduction

Management development is concerned with improving the performance of managers in their present roles and preparing them to take on greater responsibilities in the future. It has been described by Mumford and Gold (2004) as 'an attempt to improve managerial effectiveness through a learning process'. Management development activities are associated with talent management, as described in Chapter 34.

A systematic approach to management development is necessary because the increasingly onerous demands made on line managers mean that they require a wider range of developed skills than ever before.

SOURCE REVIEW

The abilities managers need, Tamkin *et al* (2003)

- To empower and develop people – understand and practise the process of delivering through the capability of others.
- To manage people and performance – managers increasingly need to maintain morale whilst also maximizing performance.
- To work across boundaries, engaging with others, working as a member of a team, thinking differently about problems and their solutions.
- To develop relationships and a focus on the customer, building partnerships with both internal and external customers.
- To balance technical and generic skills – the technical aspects of management and the management of human relationships.

This chapter covers management development policy and strategy, approaches to management development and the responsibility for management development.

Management development policy

A management development policy provides guidelines on the approach an organization adopts to the development of its managers. It is operationalized by a management development strategy. Mabey and Thompson (2000) state that management development policy consists of three variables: 1) the existence of written management development policy statements, 2) the degree of organizational priority given to management development, and 3) who takes responsibility for driving management development in the organization (the individual or the organization).

This is how a large engineering company expressed its management development policy.

Management development policy

- The main long-term object of management development is to find ways in which the company can produce, mainly from within, a supply of managers better equipped for their jobs at all levels.
- The principal method by which managers can be equipped is by ensuring that they gain the right variety of experience, in good time, in the course of their career. This experience can be supplemented – but never replaced – by courses carefully timed and designed to meet particular needs.
- The foundation of management development must be a policy of management succession, ie a system which ensures that men and women of promise, from the shop floor upwards, are given the sequence of experience which will equip them for whatever level of responsibility they have the ability to reach.

Management development strategy

A management development strategy will be concerned with the programmes the organization proposes to implement to develop its managers. It will be business-led even though it may focus on the development of individual performance and potential. The business has to decide what sort of managers it needs to achieve its strategic goals and the business must decide how it can best obtain and develop these managers. Even when the emphasis is on self-development, as it should be, the business must still indicate the directions in which self-development should go, possibly in the broadest of terms, but explicitly nonetheless.

The strategy will be based on an analysis of the future needs for managers that is conducted by means of human resource planning and talent management (see Chapters 29 and 34). Forecasts can be made of the numbers and types of managers required to meet business needs and to cater for management succession. It is also necessary to assess the skills and competencies managers will need to meet future demands and challenges arising from competitive pressures, new product-market strategies and the introduction of new technology. This can be done through performance management processes that identify development needs and potential, and lead to the agreement of personal development plans.

Priorities for management development

Hirsh *et al* (2000) suggest a number of priorities for management development. These are:

- combining a strong corporate architecture for management development with a capability for 'just in time' training and local delivery to meet specific business needs;
- providing better information and advice for individual managers on how to think about their future direction in career terms and their learning needs;
- mainstreaming the skills required to manage self-development and to support the development of others; these skills include those of 'manager as coach' but also go wider and include informal career mentoring;
- finding ways of delivering more stretching and stimulating management development to the whole population of managers, not just those in very senior posts or identified as 'high potential'.

Approaches to management development

The approach adopted by the organization is to provide support through a range of related activities such as performance management, development centres, personal development planning, coaching and mentoring. A rigid, organization-wide programme is not essential, although management development interventions such as those described in this chapter need to be made.

The extent to which management development activities are programmed depends on the organization: its technology, its environment and the type of managers it employs. A traditional bureaucratic/mechanistic type of organization may be inclined to adopt a more programmed approach, complete with a wide range of courses, inventories, replacement charts, career plans and results-oriented review systems. An innovative and organic type of organization may dispense with some or all of these mechanisms. Its approach would be to provide its managers with the opportunities, challenge and guidance they require, seizing the chance to give people extra responsibilities, and ensuring that they receive the coaching and encouragement they need. There may be no replacement charts, inventories or formal appraisal schemes, but people know how they stand, where they can go and how to get there.

The approach to management development should be based on an understanding of how managers learn and develop, and of the use of formal and informal methods of development and development centres.

How managers learn and develop

It has often been said that managers learn to manage by managing – in other words, 'experience is the best teacher'. This is largely true, but some people learn much better than others. After all, a manager with 10 years' experience may have had no more than one year's experience repeated 10 times.

Differences in the ability to learn arise because some managers are naturally more capable or more highly motivated than others, while some will have had the benefit of the guidance and help of an effective boss who is fully aware of his or her responsibilities for developing managers. The saying quoted above could be expanded to read: 'Managers learn to manage by managing under the guidance of a good manager.' The operative word in this statement is *good*. Some managers are better at developing people than others, and one of the aims of management development is to get all managers to recognize that developing their staff is an important part of their job. For senior managers to say that people do not learn because they are not that way inclined, and to leave it at that, is to neglect one of their key responsibilities – to improve the performance of the organization by doing whatever is practical to improve the effectiveness and potential of its managers.

However, to argue that managers learn best 'on the job' should not lead to the conclusion that managers should be left entirely to their own devices or that management development should be a haphazard process. The organization should try to evolve a philosophy of management development that ensures that deliberate interventions are made to improve managerial learning. Revans (1989) wanted to take management development back into the reality of management and out of the classroom, but even he believed that deliberate attempts to foster the learning process through 'action learning' (see Appendix D) are necessary.

Formal approaches to management development

Management development should be based on the identification of development needs through performance management or a development centre making use of the following formal approaches.

Formal approaches to management development

- Coaching and mentoring.
- The use of performance management processes to provide feedback and satisfy development needs.
- Planned experience, which includes job rotation, job enlargement, taking part in project teams or task groups, 'action learning', and secondment outside the organization.

- Formal training by means of internal or external courses.
- Structured self-development following a self-directed learning programme set out in a personal development plan and agreed as a learning contract with the manager or a management development adviser.
- Competency frameworks can be used as a means of identifying and expressing development needs and pointing the way to self-managed learning programmes or the provision of learning opportunities by the organization.

Informal approaches to management development

Informal approaches to management development make use of the learning experiences that managers come across during the course of their everyday work. Managers are learning every time they are confronted with an unusual problem, an unfamiliar task or a move to a different job. They then have to evolve new ways of dealing with the situation. They will learn if they analyse what they did to determine how and why it contributed to its success or failure. This retrospective or reflective learning will be effective if managers can apply the lessons successfully in the future.

Experiential and reflective learning is potentially the most powerful form of learning. It comes naturally to some managers. They seem to absorb, unconsciously and by some process of osmosis, the lessons from their experience, although in fact they have probably developed a capacity for almost instantaneous analysis that they store in their mental databank and which they can retrieve whenever necessary.

Ordinary mortals, however, either find it difficult to do this sort of analysis or do not recognize the need. This is where informal or at least semi-formal approaches can be used to encourage and help managers to learn more effectively.

Informal approaches to management development

- Getting managers to understand their own learning styles so that they can make the best use of their experience and increase the effectiveness of their learning activities – the manager's self-development guide by Pedler *et al* (1994) provides an excellent basis for this important activity.
- Emphasizing self-assessment and the identification of development needs by getting managers to assess their own performance against agreed objectives and

analyse the factors that contributed to effective or less effective performance – this can be provided through performance management.

- Getting managers to produce their own personal development plans – self-directed learning programmes.
- Encouraging managers to discuss their own problems and opportunities with their manager, colleagues or mentors to establish for themselves what they need to learn or be able to do.

Development centres

Development centres consist of a concentrated (usually one or two days) programme of exercises, tests and interviews designed to identify managers' development needs and to provide counselling on their careers. They offer participants the opportunity to examine and understand the competencies they require now and in the future. Because 'behaviour predicts behaviour', centres offer opportunities for competencies to be observed in practice. Simulations of various kinds are therefore important features – these are a combination of case studies and role playing designed to obtain the maximum amount of realism. Participants are put into the position of practising behaviour in conditions very similar to those they will meet in the course of their everyday work. An important part of the centre's activities will be feedback reviews, counselling and coaching sessions conducted by the directing staff.

Development centres use similar techniques to assessment centres, but in the latter the organization 'owns' the results for selection or promotion purposes, while in the former the results are owned by the individual as the basis for self-managed learning.

The integrated approach to management development

An integrated approach to management development will make judicious use of both informal and formal methods and, possibly, in larger organizations, development centres. The five governing principles are set out below:

The reality of management

The approach to management development should avoid making simplistic assumptions about what managers need to know or do, based on the classical analysis of management as the processes of planning, organizing, directing and controlling. In reality managerial work is relatively disorganized and fragmented, and this is why many practising managers reject the facile solutions suggested by some formal management training programmes. As Kanter (1989) has said: 'Managerial work is undergoing such enormous and rapid change that many managers are reinventing their profession as they go.'

Relevance

It is too easy to assume that all managers have to know all about such techniques as balance sheet analysis, discounted cash flow, economic value-added, etc. These can be useful but they may not be what managers really want. Management development processes must be related to the needs of particular managers in specific jobs. Those needs should include not only what managers should know now but also what they should know and be able to do in the future, if they have the potential. Thus, management development may include 'broadening programmes' aimed at giving managers an understanding of the wider, strategic issues that will be relevant at higher levels in the organization.

Self-development

Managers should be encouraged to develop themselves (self-directed development) and helped to do so. Performance management and mentoring can provide this guidance. Programmes can be set out in personal development plans.

Experiential learning

If learning can be described as the modification of behaviour through experience then the principal method by which managers can be equipped is by providing them with the right variety of experience, in good time, in the course of their careers, and by helping them to learn from that experience. Action learning, as described in Appendix D, is a good method of doing this.

Formal training

Courses can supplement but never replace experience and they must be carefully timed and selected or designed to meet particular needs.

Responsibility for management development

The traditional view is that the organization need not concern itself with management development. The natural process of selection and the pressure of competition will ensure the survival of the fittest. Managers, in fact, are born not made. Cream rises to the top (but then so does scum). Management development is not a separate activity to be handed over to a specialist and forgotten or ignored. The success of a management development programme depends on the degree to which all levels of management are committed to it. The development of subordinates must be recognized as a natural and essential part of any manager's job, but the lead must come from the top.

Management development was seen in its infancy as a mechanical process using management inventories, multicoloured replacement charts, 'Cooks tours' for newly recruited graduates, detailed job rotation programmes, elaborate points schemes to appraise personal characteristics, and lots of formal courses operating on the 'sheep-dip' principle (ie everyone undergoes them).

The role of the organization and individuals

The true role of the organization in management development lies somewhere between these two extremes. On the one hand, it is not enough, in conditions of rapid growth (when they exist) and change, to leave everything to chance – to trial and error. On the other hand, elaborate management development programmes cannot successfully be imposed on the organization. As Peter Drucker wisely said many years ago (1955): 'Development is always self-development. Nothing could be more absurd than for the enterprise to assume responsibility for the development of a man (sic). The responsibility rests with the individual, his abilities, his efforts.' But he went on to say:

> *Every manager in a business has the opportunity to encourage individual self-development or to stifle it, to direct it or to misdirect it. He should be specifically assigned the responsibility for helping all men working with him to focus, direct and apply their self-development efforts productively. And every company can provide systematic development challenges to its managers.*

The ability to manage is essentially something that individuals mainly develop for themselves while carrying out their normal duties. But they will do this much better if they are given encouragement, guidance and opportunities by their company and managers. In McGregor's (1960) phrase: managers are grown – they are neither born nor made. The role of the company is to provide conditions favourable to faster growth, and these conditions are very much part of the environment and organization climate of the company and the management style of the chief executive. The latter has the ultimate responsibility for management development. McGregor (1960) made this point as follows.

SOURCE REVIEW

McGregor (1960) on the individual's responsibility for management development

The job environment of the individual is the most important variable affecting his (sic) development. Unless that environment is conducive to his growth, none of the other things we do to him or for him will be effective. This is why the 'agricultural' approach to management development is preferable to the 'manufacturing' approach. The latter leads, among other things, to the unrealistic expectation that we can create and develop managers in the classroom.

It is remarkable that today some people are still reciting these well-established principles as if they had just discovered them.

The role of management

Management development is not a separate activity to be handed over to a specialist and forgotten or ignored. Its success depends upon the degree to which it is recognized as an important aspect of the business strategy – a key process aimed at delivering results. Top management must therefore be committed to it. Senior managers should recognize that an important aspect of their jobs is to play an active part in developing their managers, although those managers should take the main responsibility for their own development with help and support as required.

The role of HR and learning and development specialists

However, HR and learning and development specialists still have an important role to play. They:

- interpret the needs of the business and advise on how management development strategies can play their part in meeting these needs;
- act as advocates of the significance of management development as a business-led activity and make proposals on formal and informal approaches to management development;
- develop in conjunction with line management competency frameworks that can provide a basis for management development;

- encourage managers to carry out their developmental activities and provide guidance as required;
- provide help and encouragement to managers in preparing and pursuing their self-directed learning activities;
- act as coaches or mentors to individual managers or groups of managers;
- plan and conduct formal learning events.

Criteria for management development

The effectiveness and value of any approach to management development include the extent to which it:

- links to organizational goals and context – and so has relevance for the organization as well as for individuals;
- builds on and develops the qualities, skills and attitudes of participants;
- is supported by appropriate HR policies to do with recruitment and selection, reward, talent management and succession planning;
- has the full commitment of those responsible for the operation of the process;
- is motivating to those encouraged to participate in it.

Management development – key learning points

Management development policy

A management development policy provides guidelines on the approach an organization adopts to the development of its managers. It is operationalized by a management development strategy.

Management development strategy

A management development strategy will be concerned with the programmes the organization proposes to implement to develop its managers.

How managers learn and develop

Managers learn to manage by managing under the guidance of a good manager.

Formal approaches to management development

- Coaching and mentoring.
- Performance management.
- Planned experience.
- Formal training.
- Structured self-development.

Management development – key learning points (continued)

Informal approaches to management development

Informal approaches to management development make use of the learning experiences that managers come across during the course of their everyday work.

Development centres

Development centres consist of a concentrated (usually one or two days) programme of exercises, tests and interviews designed to identify managers' development needs and to provide counselling on their careers.

An integrated approach to management development

An integrated approach to management development will make judicious use of both informal and formal methods and, possibly, in larger organizations, development centres.

Responsibility for management development

Individual managers are largely responsible for their own development but need guidance, support and encouragement from their own managers and the HR function.

Questions

1. Someone once said in arguing against a laissez faire approach to management development that 'cream rises to the top but then so does scum'. What arguments would you use in favour of planned management development?
2. Peter Drucker wrote (1955): 'Development is always self-development. Nothing could be more absurd than for the enterprise to assume responsibility for the development of a man (sic). The responsibility rests with the individual, his abilities, his efforts.' Douglas McGregor also wrote (1960) that, 'The job environment of the individual is the most important variable factor affecting his (sic) development. Unless that environment is conducive to his growth, none of the other things we do to him or for him will be effective. This is why the "agricultural" approach to management development is preferable to the "manufacturing" approach. The latter leads, among other things, to the unrealistic expectation that we can create and develop managers in the classroom.' Apart from the use of the masculine pronoun, how relevant are these comments today? If they are relevant, what do they tell us about management development policies?

Questions (continued)

3. From your managing director: 'We recruit a lot of able graduates every year but as your figures tell me, few of them stay long enough to become managers and in my experience not many of them make good managers. I am not in favour of lots of formal and often irrelevant training courses. What else can we do?'

References

Drucker, P (1955) *The Practice of Management*, Heinemann, London

Hirsh, W, Pollard, E and Tamkin, P (2000) Management development, *IRS Employee Development Bulletin*, November, pp 8–12

Kanter, R M (1989) *When Giants Learn to Dance*, Simon & Schuster, London

Mabey, C and Thompson, A (2000) The determinants of management development: the views of MBA graduates, *British Journal of Management*, **11** (3), pp S3–S16

McGregor, D (1960) *The Human Side of Enterprise*, McGraw-Hill, New York

Mumford, A and Gold, J (2004) *Management Development: Strategies for action*, CIPD, 2004

Pedler, M, Burgoyne J and Boydell, T (1994) *A Manager's Guide to Self Development*, McGraw Hill, Maidenhead

Revans, R W (1989) *Action Learning*, Blond and Briggs, London

Tamkin, P, Hirsh, W and Tyers, C (2003) *Chore to Champion: The making of better people managers*, Report 389, Institute of Employment Studies, Brighton

Part IX

Rewarding People

Rewarding people involves reward management processes concerned with the design, implementation and maintenance of reward systems that are geared to the improvement of organizational, team and individual performance. It includes both financial and non-financial rewards. The US term 'compensation' is sometimes used as an alternative to reward but it seems to imply that work is an unpleasant necessity for which people have to be compensated rather than spending their time more profitably elsewhere.

Reward management is treated in this handbook as very much part of an HRM approach to managing people. The essential features of this approach are that it:

- supports the achievement of the business strategy;
- is integrated with other HRM strategies, especially those concerning human resource development;
- is based on a well-articulated philosophy – a set of beliefs and assumptions that are consistent with the HRM philosophies of the business and underpin the ways in which it proposes to reward its employees;
- adopts a 'total reward' perspective that recognizes that there are many other and possibly more powerful ways of rewarding people besides financial rewards;
- appreciates that if HRM is about investing in human capital, from which a reasonable return is required, then it is proper to reward people differentially according to their contribution (ie the return on investment they generate);
- focuses on the development of the skills and competencies of employees in order to increase the resource-based capability of the firm (pay for competency or skill);
- is itself an integrated process that can operate flexibly;
- supports other key HRM initiatives in the fields of resourcing, employee development and employee relations.

Part IX contents

46 Reward Management

Key concepts and terms

- Base pay
- Contingent pay
- Employee benefits
- Grade and pay structure
- Job evaluation
- Market rate analysis
- Non-financial rewards
- Relational rewards
- Reward management
- Reward strategy
- Reward system
- Total remuneration
- Total reward
- Transactional rewards

Learning outcomes

On completing this chapter you should be able to define these key concepts. You should also know about:

- The aims of reward management
- The economic theories explaining pay levels
- The content of reward strategy
- Developing reward strategies
- Implementing reward strategy
- The philosophy of reward management
- Total reward
- Guiding principles for reward
- Components of an effective reward strategy
- Developing line management capability

Introduction

This chapter provides an overview of reward management. The concept of reward management, its aims and its philosophy, are discussed initially. Reference is also made to the economic factors that affect levels of pay. This is followed by a description of the elements of a reward management system and the concept of total reward. The chapter continues with an examination of the process of strategic reward and concludes with a discussion of the role of line managers in reward management.

Reward management defined

Reward management is concerned with the formulation and implementation of strategies and policies in order to reward people fairly, equitably and consistently in accordance with their value to the organization. It deals with the development of reward strategies and the design, implementation and maintenance of reward systems (reward processes, practices and procedures) which aim to meet the needs of both the organization and its stakeholders. Reward can be regarded as the fundamental expression of the employment relationship.

The aims of reward management

- Reward people according to what the organization values and wants to pay for.
- Reward people for the value they create.
- Reward the right things to convey the right message about what is important in terms of behaviours and outcomes.
- Develop a performance culture.
- Motivate people and obtain their commitment and engagement.
- Help to attract and retain the high quality people the organization needs.
- Develop a positive employment relationship and psychological contract.
- Align reward practices with both business goals and employee values; as Duncan Brown (2001) emphasizes, the 'alignment of your reward practices with employee values and needs is every bit as important as alignment with business goals, and critical to the realization of the latter'.
- Operate fairly – people feel that they are treated justly in accordance with what is due to them because of their value to the organization (the 'felt-fair' principle of Eliot Jaques (1961).

- Apply equitably – people are rewarded appropriately in relation to others within the organization, relativities between jobs are measured as objectively as possible and equal pay is provided for work of equal value.
- Function consistently – decisions on pay do not vary arbitrarily and without due cause between different people or at different times.
- Operate transparently – people understand how reward processes operate and how they are affected by them.

The philosophy of reward management

Reward management is based on a well-articulated philosophy – a set of beliefs and guiding principles that are consistent with the values of the organization and help to enact them. These include beliefs in the need to achieve fairness, equity, consistency and transparency in operating the reward system. The philosophy recognizes that if HRM is about investing in human capital from which a reasonable return is required, then it is proper to reward people differentially according to their contribution (ie the return on investment they generate).

The philosophy of reward management recognizes that it must be strategic in the sense that it addresses longer-term issues relating to how people should be valued for what they do and what they achieve. Reward strategies and the processes that are required to implement them have to flow from the business strategy.

Reward management adopts a 'total reward' approach which emphasizes the importance of considering all aspects of reward as a coherent whole which is integrated with other HR initiatives designed to achieve the motivation, commitment, engagement and development of employees. This requires the integration of reward strategies with other human resource management (HRM) strategies, especially those concerning human resource development. Reward management is an integral part of an HRM approach to managing people.

The philosophy will be affected by the business and HR strategies of the organization, the significance attached to reward matters by top management and the internal and external environment of the organization. The external environment includes the levels of pay in the labour market (market rates) and it is helpful to be aware of the economic theories that explain how these levels are determined as summarized in Table 46.1.

Table 46.1 Economic theories explaining pay levels

Name of theory	Summary of theory	Practical significance
The law of supply and demand	Other things being equal, if there is a surplus of labour and supply exceeds the demand, pay levels go down; if there is a scarcity of labour and demand exceeds the supply, pay goes up	Emphasizes the importance of labour market factors in affecting market rates
Efficiency wage theory	Firms will pay more than the market rate because they believe that high levels of pay will contribute to increases in productivity by motivating superior performance, attracting better candidates, reducing labour turnover and persuading workers that they are being treated fairly. This theory is also known as 'the economy of high wages'	Organizations use efficiency wage theory (although they will not call it that) when they formulate pay policies that place them as market leaders or at least above the average
Human capital theory	Workers have a set of skills developed by education and training that generates a stock of productive capital	Employees and employers each derive benefits from investment in creating human capital. The level of pay should supply both parties with a reasonable return on that investment
Agency theory	The owners of a firm (the principals) are separate from the employees (the agents). This difference can create 'agency costs' because the agents may not be as productive as the principals. The latter therefore have to devise ways of motivating and controlling the efforts of the former	A system of incentives is needed to motivate and reward acceptable behaviour. This process of 'incentive alignment' consists of paying for measurable results that are deemed to be in the best interests of the owners
The effort bargain	Workers aim to strike a bargain about the relationship between what they regard as a reasonable contribution and what their employer is prepared to offer to elicit that contribution	Management has to assess what level and type of inducements it has to offer in return for the contribution it requires from its workforce

The reward system

A reward system consists of a number of interrelated processes and activities which combine to ensure that reward management is carried out effectively to the benefit of the organization and the people who work there. These are described below.

Reward strategy

Reward strategy sets out what the organization intends to do in the longer term to develop and implement reward policies, practices and processes which will further the achievement of its business goals.

Reward policies

Reward policies address the following broad issues:

- the level of rewards taking into account 'market stance' – how internal rates of pay should compare with market rates, eg aligned to the median or the upper quartile rate;
- achieving equal pay;
- the relative importance attached to external competitiveness and internal equity;
- the approach to total reward;
- the scope for the use of contingent rewards related to performance, competence, contribution or skill;
- the role of line managers;
- transparency – the publication of information on reward structures and processes to employees.

Total reward

Total reward is the combination of financial and non-financial rewards available to employees.

Total remuneration

Total remuneration is the value of all cash payments (total earnings) and benefits received by employees.

Base or basic pay

The base rate is the amount of pay (the fixed salary or wage) that constitutes the rate for the job. It may be varied according to the grade of the job or, for manual workers, the level of skill required.

Base pay will be influenced by internal and external relativities. The internal relativities may be measured by some form of job evaluation. External relativities are assessed by tracking market rates. Alternatively, levels of pay may be agreed through collective bargaining with trade unions or by reaching individual agreements.

Base pay may be expressed as an annual, weekly or hourly rate. For manual workers this may be an hourly rate which is called a time rate. Allowances for overtime, shift working, unsocial hours or increased cost of living in London or elsewhere may be added to base pay. The base rate may be adjusted to reflect increases in the cost of living or market rates by the organization unilaterally or by agreement with a trade union.

Job evaluation

Job evaluation is a systematic process for defining the relative worth or size of jobs within an organization in order to establish internal relativities and provide the basis for designing an equitable grade structure, grading jobs in the structure and managing relativities. It does not determine the level of pay directly. Job evaluation can be analytical or non-analytical. It is based on the analysis of jobs or roles which leads to the production of job descriptions or role profiles. Job evaluation is described in Chapter 47.

Market rate analysis

Market rate analysis is the process of identifying the rates of pay in the labour market for comparable jobs to inform decisions on levels of pay within the organization. A policy decision may be made on how internal rates of pay should compare with external rates – an organization's market stance. Market rate analysis is described in Chapter 48.

Grade and pay structures

Jobs may be placed in a graded structure according to their relative size. Pay levels in the structure are influenced by market rates. The pay structure may consist of pay ranges attached to grades which provide scope for pay progression based on performance, competence, contribution or service. Alternatively, 'spot rates' or 'individual job grades' structure may be used for all or some jobs in which no provision is made for pay progression in a job. The various types of grade and pay structures are described in Chapter 49.

Contingent pay

Additional financial rewards may be provided that are related to performance, competence, contribution, skill or service in the grade. These are referred to as 'contingent pay'. Contingent payments may be added to base pay, ie 'consolidated'. If such payments are not consolidated (ie paid as cash bonuses) they are described as 'variable pay'. Contingent pay schemes are described in Chapter 50.

Employee benefits

Employee benefits include pensions, sick pay, insurance cover, company cars and a number of other 'perks' as described in Chapter 52. They comprise elements of remuneration additional to the various forms of cash pay and also include provisions for employees that are not strictly remuneration, such as annual holidays.

Performance management

Performance management processes (see Part VII)) define individual performance and contribution expectations, assess performance against those expectations, provide for regular constructive feedback and result in agreed plans for performance improvement, learning and personal development. They are a means of providing non-financial motivation and may also inform contingent pay decisions.

Non-financial rewards

Rewards which do not involve any direct payments and often arise from the work itself, for example, achievement, autonomy, recognition, scope to use and develop skills, training, career development opportunities and high quality leadership.

The interrelationships of these elements of the reward system are shown in Figure 46.1.

Total reward

The concept of total reward is exerting considerable influence on reward management. This section of the chapter begins by defining what it means. The importance of the concept is then explained and the section continues with an analysis of the components of total reward. It concludes with a description of how a total reward approach to reward management can be developed.

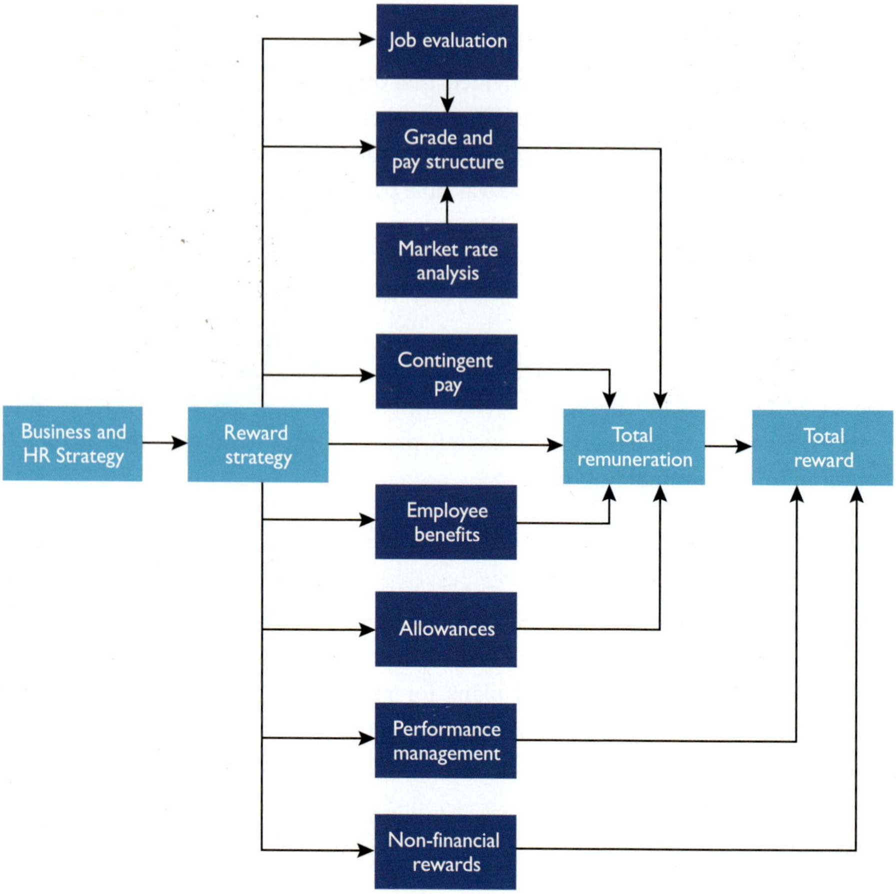

Figure 46.1 The reward management system: elements and interrelationships
(Source: Armstrong, 2007)

Total reward defined

As defined by Manus and Graham (2003), total reward 'includes all types of rewards – indirect as well as direct, and intrinsic as well as extrinsic'. Each aspect of reward, namely base pay, contingent pay, employee benefits and non-financial rewards, which include intrinsic rewards from the work itself, are linked together and treated as an integrated and coherent whole. Total reward combines the impact of the two major categories of reward: 1) transactional rewards – tangible rewards arising from transactions between the employer and employees concerning pay and benefits, and 2) relational rewards – intangible rewards concerned with learning and development and the work experience; see Figure 46.2.

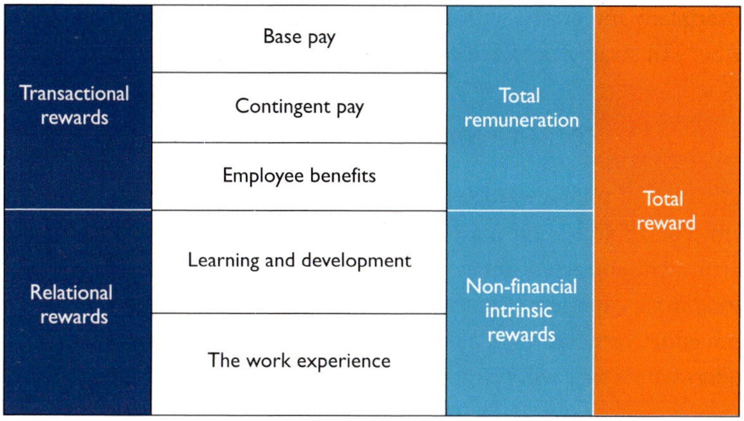

Figure 46.2 The components of total reward

A total reward approach is holistic; reliance is not placed on one or two reward mechanisms operating in isolation, account is taken of every way in which people can be rewarded and obtain satisfaction through their work. The aim is to maximize the combined impact of a wide range of reward initiatives on motivation, commitment and job engagement. As Sandra O'Neal (1998) has explained: 'Total reward embraces everything that employees value in the employment relationship'.

An equally wide definition of total reward is offered by WorldatWork (2000) who state that total rewards are 'all of the employer's available tools that may be used to attract, retain, motivate and satisfy employees.

SOURCE REVIEW

Total reward, defined by Thompson (2002)

Definitions of total reward typically encompass not only traditional, quantifiable elements like salary, variable pay and benefits, but also more intangible non-cash elements such as scope to achieve and exercise responsibility, career opportunities, learning and development, the intrinsic motivation provided by the work itself and the quality of working life provided by the organization'.

The conceptual basis of total rewards is that of configuration or 'bundling', so that different reward processes are interrelated, complementary and mutually reinforcing. Total reward strategies are vertically integrated with business strategies, but they are also horizontally integrated with other HR strategies to achieve internal consistency.

The significance of total reward

Essentially, the notion of total reward says that there is more to rewarding people than throwing money at them. For O'Neal (1998), a total reward strategy is critical to addressing the issues created by recruitment and retention as well as providing a means of influencing behaviour: 'It can help create a work experience that meets the needs of employees and encourages them to contribute extra effort, by developing a deal that addresses a broad range of issues and by spending reward dollars where they will be most effective in addressing workers' shifting values.'

SOURCE REVIEW

A powerful argument for total rewards, Pfeffer (1998b)

Creating a fun, challenging, and empowered work environment in which individuals are able to use their abilities to do meaningful jobs for which they are shown appreciation is likely to be a more certain way to enhance motivation and performance – even though creating such an environment may be more difficult and take more time than simply turning the reward lever.

The benefits of a total reward approach are:

- Greater impact – the combined effect of the different types of rewards will make a deeper and longer-lasting impact on the motivation and commitment of people.
- Enhancing the employment relationship – the employment relationship created by a total rewards approach makes the maximum use of relational as well as transactional rewards and will therefore appeal more to individuals.
- Flexibility to meet individual needs – as pointed out by Milkovich and Bloom (1998): 'Relational rewards may bind individuals more strongly to the organization because they can answer those special individual needs'.
- Talent management – relational rewards help to deliver a positive psychological contract and this can serve as a differentiator in the recruitment market which is much more difficult to replicate than individual pay practices. The organization can become an 'employer of choice' and 'a great place to work' thus attracting and retaining the talented people it needs.

The Towers Perrin model of total reward

A Towers Perrin model of total reward is shown in Figure 46.3.

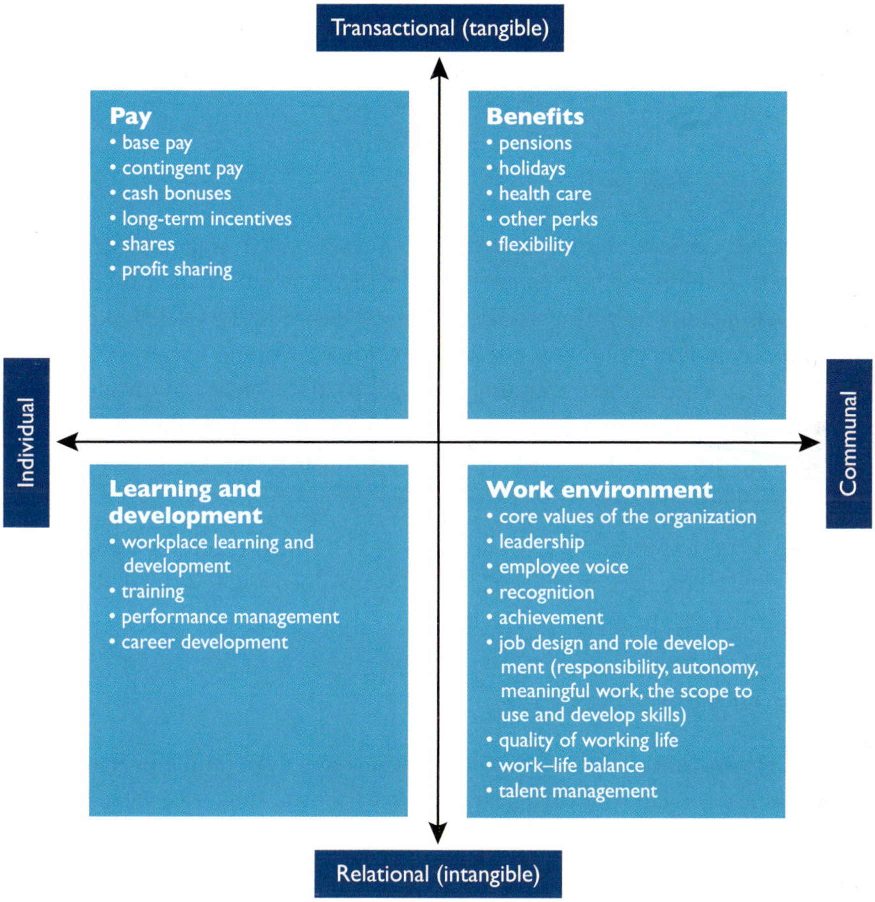

Figure 46.3 Model of total reward

The upper two quadrants – pay and benefits – represent transactional rewards. These are financial in nature and are essential to recruit and retain staff but can be easily copied by competitors. By contrast, the relational (non-financial) rewards produced by the lower two quadrants are essential to enhancing the value of the upper two quadrants. The real power, as Thompson (2002) states, comes when organizations combine relational and transactional rewards.

Reward strategy

Reward strategies provide answers to two basic questions: 1) where do we want our reward practices to be in a few years' time? and 2) how do we intend to get there? They therefore deal with both ends and means. As an end they describe a vision of what reward processes will look like in a few years' time. As a means, they show how it is expected that the vision will be realized.

Reward strategy defined

Reward strategy is a declaration of intent which defines what the organization wants to do in the longer term to develop and implement reward policies, practices and processes which will further the achievement of its business goals and meet the needs of its stakeholders. It provides a sense of purpose and direction and a framework for developing reward policies, practices and process. It is based on an understanding of the needs of the organization and its employees and how they can best be satisfied. It is also concerned with developing the values of the organization on how people should be rewarded and formulating guiding principles which will ensure that these values are enacted.

Reward strategy is underpinned by a reward philosophy which expresses what the organization believes should be the basis upon which people are valued and rewarded. Reward philosophies are often articulated as guiding principles.

Why have a reward strategy?

In the words of Brown (2001): 'Reward strategy is ultimately a way of thinking that you can apply to any reward issue arising in your organization, to see how you can create value from it.'

Arguments for developing reward strategies

- You must have some idea where you are going, or how do you know how to get there, and how do you know that you have arrived (if you ever do)?
- Pay costs in most organizations are by far the largest item of expense – they can be 60 per cent and often much more in labour intensive organizations – so doesn't it make sense to think about how they should be managed and invested in the longer term?
- There can be a positive relationship between rewards, in the broadest sense, and performance, so shouldn't we think about how we can strengthen that link?

- As Cox and Purcell (1998) write: 'The real benefit in reward strategies lies in complex linkages with other human resource management policies and practices'. Isn't this a good reason for developing a reward strategic framework which indicates how reward processes will be associated with HR processes so that they are coherent and mutually supportive?

The content of reward strategy

Reward strategy may be a broad-brush affair simply indicating the general direction in which it is thought reward management should go. Additionally or alternatively, reward strategy may set out a list of specific intentions dealing with particular aspects of reward management.

Broad-brush reward strategy

A broad-brush reward strategy may commit the organization to the pursuit of a total rewards policy. The basic aim might be to achieve an appropriate balance between financial and non-financial rewards. A further aim could be to use other approaches to the development of the employment relationship and the work environment which will enhance commitment and engagement and provide more opportunities for the contribution of people to be valued and recognized.

Examples of other broad strategic aims include: 1) introducing a more integrated approach to reward management – encouraging continuous personal development and spelling out career opportunities; 2) developing a more flexible approach to reward which includes the reduction of artificial barriers as a result of over-emphasis on grading and promotion; 3) generally rewarding people according to their contribution; 4) supporting the development of a performance culture and building levels of competence; and 5) clarifying what behaviours will be rewarded and why.

Specific reward initiatives

The selection of reward initiatives and the priorities attached to them will be based on an analysis of the present circumstances of the organization and an assessment of the needs of the business and its employees. The following are examples of possible specific reward initiatives, one or more of which might feature in a reward strategy:

- the replacement of present methods of contingent pay with a pay for contribution scheme;
- the introduction of a new grade and pay structure, eg a broad-graded or career family structure;

- the replacement of an existing decayed job evaluation scheme with a computerized scheme which more clearly reflects organizational values;
- the improvement of performance management processes so that they provide better support for the development of a performance culture and more clearly identify development needs;
- the introduction of a formal recognition scheme;
- the development of a flexible benefits system;
- the conduct of equal pay reviews with the objective of ensuring that work of equal value is paid equally;
- communication programmes designed to inform everyone of the reward policies and practices of the organization;
- training, coaching and guidance programmes designed to increase line management capability (see also the last section of this chapter).

Guiding principles for reward

Guiding principles define the approach an organization takes to dealing with reward. They are the basis for reward policies and provide guidelines for the actions contained in the reward strategy. They express the reward philosophy of the organization – its values and beliefs about how people should be rewarded.

Members of the organization should be involved in the definition of guiding principles which can then be communicated to everyone to increase understanding of what underpins reward policies and practices. However, employees will suspend their judgement of the principles until they experience how they are applied. What matters to them are not the philosophies themselves but the pay practices emanating from them and the messages about the employment 'deal' that they get as a consequence. It is the reality that is important, not the rhetoric.

Reward guiding principles

- Develop reward policies and practices which support the achievement of business goals.
- Provide rewards which attract, retain and motivate staff and help to develop a high performance culture.
- Maintain competitive rates of pay.
- Reward people according to their contribution.

- Recognize the value of everyone who is making an effective contribution, not just the exceptional performers.
- Allow a reasonable degree of flexibility in the operation of reward processes and in the choice of benefits by employees.
- Devolve more responsibility for reward decisions to line managers.

Developing reward strategy

The formulation of reward strategy can be described as a process for developing and defining a sense of direction. The main phases are:

1. The diagnosis phase, when reward goals are agreed, current policies and practices assessed against them, options for improvement considered and any changes agreed.
2. The detailed design phase when improvements and changes are detailed and any changes tested (pilot testing is important).
3. The final testing and preparation phase.
4. The implementation phase, followed by ongoing review and modification.

A logical step-by-step model for doing this is illustrated in Figure 46.4. This incorporates ample provision for consultation, involvement and communication with stakeholders who include senior managers as the ultimate decision makers as well as employees and line managers.

In practice, however, the formulation of reward strategy is seldom as logical and linear a process as this. As explained in Chapter 3, strategies evolve. Reward strategists have to respond to changes in organizational requirements which are happening all the time. They need to track emerging trends in reward management and may modify their views accordingly, as long as they do not leap too hastily on the latest bandwagon.

It may be helpful to set out reward strategies on paper for the record and as a basis for planning and communication. But this should be regarded as no more than a piece of paper that can be torn up when needs change – as they will – not a tablet of stone.

Components of an effective reward strategy

Brown (2001) has suggested that effective reward strategies have three components:

1. They have to have clearly defined goals and a well-defined link to business objectives.

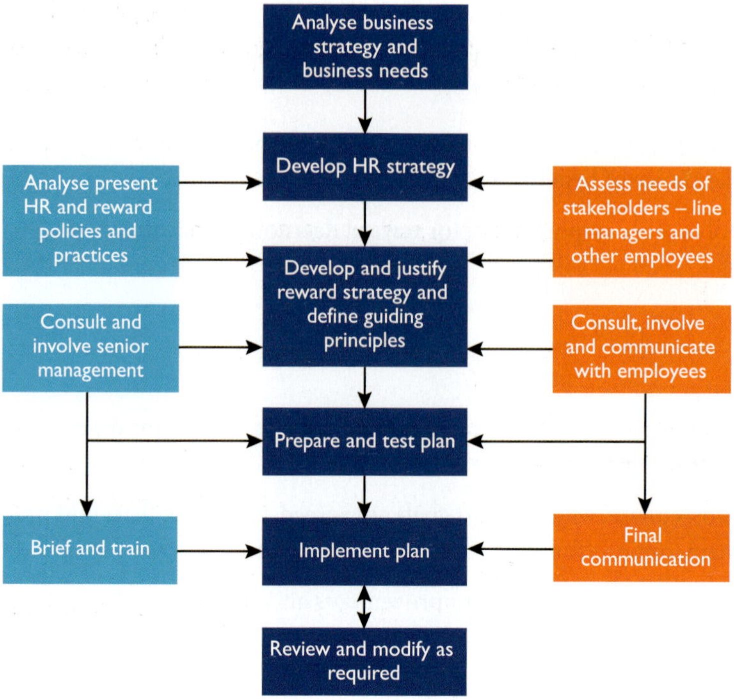

Figure 46.4 A model of the reward strategy development process

2. There have to be well-designed pay and reward programmes, tailored to the needs of the organization and its people, and consistent and integrated with one another.
3. Perhaps most important and most neglected, there needs to be effective and supportive HR and reward processes in place.

Implementing reward strategy

The aim of implementation is to make the reward strategy an operating reality by building the capacity of the organization to put into practice the proposals worked out in the development stage. As Armstrong and Brown (2007) stress: 'It is always essential to design with implementation in mind'.

Purcell (1999) believes that the focus of strategy should be on implementation. As explained by Thompson and Strickland (1990): 'Implementation entails converting the strategic plan into action and then into results'. An effective reward strategy is a living process and, in the words of Rosabeth Moss Kanter (1984), an 'action vehicle'. Formulation is easy; implementation is hard. A pragmatic approach is required – what's good is what works.

Implementing reward strategy is much more about process than design – how it will be done rather than what will be done. The principles of procedural and distributive justice apply.

People must feel that the procedures used to determine their grades, pay level and pay progression are fair, equitable, applied consistently and transparent. They must also feel that the awards distributed to them are just in terms of their contribution and value to the organization.

Reward management and line management capability

The trend is to devolve more responsibility for managing reward to line managers. Some will have the ability to respond to the challenge and opportunity; others will be incapable of carrying out this responsibility without close guidance from HR; some may never be able to cope. Managers may not always do what HR expects them to do and if compelled to, they may be half-hearted about it. This puts a tremendous onus on HR and reward specialists to develop line management capability, to initiate processes which can readily be implemented by line managers, to promote understanding by communicating what is happening, why it is happening and how it will affect everyone, to provide guidance and help where required and to provide formal training as necessary.

Reward management – key learning points

The aims of reward management

The three most important aims of reward management are to:

1. Reward people according to what the organization values and wants to pay for.
2. Reward people for the value they create.
3. Reward the right things to convey the right message about what is important in terms of behaviours and outcomes.

The philosophy of reward management

A belief in the need to achieve fairness, equity, consistency and transparency in operating the reward system.

The economic theories explaining pay levels

See Table 46.1.

Total reward

Each aspect of reward, namely base pay, contingent pay, employee benefits and non-financial rewards, which include intrinsic rewards from the work itself, are linked together and treated as an integrated and coherent whole.

Broad-brush reward strategies

To achieve an appropriate balance between financial and non-financial rewards, develop commitment and engagement and provide more opportunities for the contribution of people to be valued and recognized.

Reward management – key learning points (continued)

Specific reward strategy areas

Could include the introduction of a new contingent pay scheme, a new pay structure or job evaluation.

Guiding principles for reward

Three key guiding principles are:

1. Develop reward policies and practices which support the achievement of business goals.
2. Provide rewards which attract, retain and motivate staff and help to develop a high performance culture.
3. Maintain competitive rates of pay.

Developing reward strategies

The formulation of reward strategy can be described as a process for developing and defining a sense of direction. The main phases are: diagnosis, detailed design, final testing and preparation, and implementation.

Components of an effective reward strategy

According to Brown (2001) an effective strategy is one in which there are clearly defined goals and a well-defined link to business objectives; well-designed pay and reward programmes, tailored to the needs of the organization and its people, and consistent and integrated with one another; and effective and supportive HR and reward processes in place.

Implementing reward strategy

The aim of implementation is to make the reward strategy an operating reality by building the capacity of the organization to put into practice the proposals worked out in the development stage.

Developing line management capability

HR and reward specialists need to develop line management capability by initiating processes which can readily be implemented by line managers, promoting understanding by communicating what is happening, why it is happening and how it will affect everyone, providing guidance and help where required and providing formal training as necessary.

Questions

1. You have been invited to give a brief talk to your local CIP branch entitled 'Total reward systems: how employees benefit'. Outline and justify the main points you would include in the talk.

Questions

2. What are the key areas in which reward policies need to be formulated? Illustrate your answer with examples from your own organization.
3. Drawing on research evidence and good practice, review reward strategies in your organization in terms of their impact on organizational performance. Outline any changes that you think are necessary.
4. In his highly influential book, *Strategic Pay*, 1990, Ed Lawler wrote that: 'The challenge is to develop pay programmes that support and reinforce the business objectives of the organization and the kind of culture, climate and behaviour that are needed for the organization to be effective'. How can reward policies and practices support the achievement of business goals?
5. In another influential book, *The New Pay*, 1992, Jay Schuster and Patricia Zingheim wrote that: 'Employees have the right to determine whether the values, culture and reward systems of the organization match their own'. What does that tell us about an organization's reward practices?

References

Armstrong, M (2007) *A Handbook of Employee Reward*, 2nd ed, Kogan Page, London

Bloom, M and Milkovich, G T (1998) Rethinking international compensation, *Compensation & Benefits Review*, **30** (1), pp 15–23

Brown, D (2001) *Reward Strategies; From intent to impact*, CIPD, London

Cox, A and Purcell, J (1998) Searching for leverage: pay systems, trust, motivation and commitment in SMEs', in S J Perkins and St John Sandringham (eds) *Trust, Motivation and Commitment*, Strategic Remuneration Centre, Faringdon

Jaques, E (1961) *Equitable Payment*, Heinemann, London

Kanter, R M (1984) *The Change Masters*, Allen & Unwin, London

Lawler, E (1990) *Strategic Pay: Aligning organizational strategies and pay systems*, Jossey-Bass, San Francisco, CA

Manus, T M and Graham, M D (2003) *Creating a Total Rewards Strategy*, American Management Association, New York

O'Neal, S (1998) The phenomenon of total rewards, *ACA Journal*, **7** (3), pp 8–14

Pfeffer, J (1998b) Six dangerous myths about pay, *Harvard Business Review*, May/June, pp 109–19

Purcell, J (1999) Best practice or best fit: chimera or cul-de-sac, *Human Resource Management Journal*, **9** (3), pp 26–41

Schuster, J R and Zingheim, P K (1992) *The New Pay*, Lexington Books, New York

Thompson, A A and Strickland, A J (1990) *Strategic Management: Concepts and cases*, Irwin, Georgetown, Ontario

Thompson, M (2002) *High Performance Work Organization in UK Aerospace*, The Society of British Aerospace Companies, London

Thompson, P (2002) *Total Reward*, CIPD, London

WorldatWork (2000) *Total Rewards: From Strategy to Implementation*, WorldatWork, Scottsdale, AZ

47 Job Evaluation

Key concepts and terms

- Analytical job evaluation
- Analytical job matching
- Benchmark job
- Computer-aided job evaluation
- Explicit weighting
- Extreme market pricing
- Factor (job evaluation)
- Factor comparison
- Factor level
- Factor plan
- Going rates
- Implicit weighting
- Internal benchmarking
- Internal relativities
- Job classification
- Job evaluation
- Job ranking
- Job size
- Job slotting
- Job worth
- Market driven
- Market pricing
- Market rates
- Non-analytical job evaluation
- Paired comparison ranking
- Point-factor job evaluation
- Proprietary brand
- Tailor-made job evaluation scheme
- Weighting

Learning outcomes

On completing this chapter you should be able to define these key concepts. You should also know about:

- The aims of job evaluation
- Analytical job evaluation schemes
- Market pricing
- Comparison of schemes
- Designing analytical schemes
- Equal pay considerations
- Approaches to job evaluation
- Non-analytical job evaluation schemes
- Computer-aided job evaluation
- Choice of approach
- Design programme

Introduction

Decisions about what jobs are worth take place all the time. The decisions may be made informally, based on assumptions about the value of a job in the marketplace or in comparison with other jobs in the organization. Or it may be a formal approach, either some type of job evaluation, as described in this chapter, or a systematic comparison with market rates. It has been asserted by Gupta and Jenkins (1991) that the basic premise of job evaluation is that certain jobs 'contribute more to organizational effectiveness and success than others, are worth more than others and should be paid more than others'.

Evaluating 'worth' leads directly or indirectly to where a job is placed in a level or grade within a hierarchy and can therefore determine how much someone is paid. The performance of individuals also affects their pay, but this is not a matter for job evaluation, which is concerned with valuing the jobs people carry out, not how well they perform their jobs.

This chapter covers a definition of job evaluation, formal and informal approaches, analytical and non-analytical formal schemes, market pricing, computer-aided job evaluation, making the choice between approaches, introducing a new or substantially revised scheme and equal pay considerations.

Job evaluation defined

Job evaluation is a systematic process for defining the relative worth or size of jobs within an organization in order to establish internal relativities.

Aims of job evaluation

- Establish the relative value or size of jobs (internal relativities) based on fair, sound and consistent judgements.
- Produce the information required to design and maintain equitable and defensible grade and pay structures.
- Provide as objective as possible a basis for grading jobs within a grade structure, thus enabling consistent decisions to be made about job grading.
- Enable sound market comparisons with jobs or roles of equivalent complexity and size.
- Be transparent – the basis upon which grades are defined and jobs graded should be clear.
- Ensure that the organization meets equal pay for work of equal value obligations.

The last aim is important. In its *Good Practice Guide on Job Evaluation Schemes Free of Sex Bias* the Equal Opportunities Commission (2003) stated that: 'Non-discriminatory job evaluation should lead to a payment system which is transparent and within which work of equal value receives equal pay regardless of sex.'

Approaches

Approaches to establishing the worth of jobs fall broadly into two categories: formal and informal.

Formal job valuation

Formal approaches use standardized methods to evaluate jobs that can be analytical or non-analytical. Such schemes deal with internal relativities and the associated process of establishing and defining job grades or levels in an organization.

An alternative approach is 'extreme market pricing' in which formal pay structures and individual rates of pay are entirely based on systematically collected and analysed information on market rates and no use is made of job evaluation to establish internal relativities. Extreme market pricing should be distinguished from the process of collecting and analysing market rate data used to establish external relativities, having already determined internal relativities through formal job evaluation.

In the 1980s and 1990s formal job evaluation fell into disrepute because it was alleged to be bureaucratic, time-consuming and irrelevant in a market economy where market rates dictate internal rates of pay and relativities. However, job evaluation is still practised widely (60 per cent of the respondents to the 2007 e-reward job evaluation survey had a formal scheme) and, indeed, its use is extending, not least because of the pressures to achieve equal pay. Although formal job evaluation may work systematically it should not be treated as a rigid, monolithic and bureaucratic system. It should instead be regarded as an approach that may be applied flexibly. Process – how job evaluation is used – can be more important than the system itself when it comes to producing reliable and valid results.

Informal job evaluation

Informal approaches price jobs either on the basis of assumptions about internal and external relativities or simply by reference to going or market rates when recruiting people, unsupported by any systematic analysis. There are, however, degrees of informality. A semi-formal approach might require some firm evidence to support a market pricing decision and the use of role profiles to provide greater accuracy to the matching process.

Analytical job evaluation schemes

Analytical job evaluation is based on a process of breaking whole jobs down into a number of defined elements or factors such as responsibility, decisions and the knowledge and skill required. These are assumed to be present in all the jobs to be evaluated. In point-factor and fully analytical matching schemes, jobs are then compared factor by factor either with a graduated scale of points attached to a set of factors or with grade or role profiles analysed under the same factor headings.

The advantages of an analytical approach are that first, evaluators have to consider each of the characteristics of the job separately before forming a conclusion about its relative value, and second, they are provided with defined yardsticks or guidelines that help to increase the objectivity and consistency of judgements. It can also provide a defence in the UK against an equal pay claim. The main analytical schemes as described below are point-factor rating, analytical matching and factor comparison.

Point-factor rating

Point-factor schemes are the most common forms of analytical job evaluation. They were used by 70 per cent of the respondents to the e-reward 2007 job evaluation survey who had job evaluation schemes. The basic methodology is to break down jobs into factors. These are the elements in a job such as the level of responsibility, knowledge and skill or decision making that represent the demands made by the job on job holders. For job evaluation purposes it is assumed that each of the factors will contribute to the value of the job and is an aspect of all the jobs to be evaluated but to different degrees.

Each factor is divided into a hierarchy of levels. Definitions of these levels are produced to provide guidance on deciding the degree to which the factor applies in the job to be evaluated. Evaluators consult the role profile or job description, which should ideally analyse the role in terms of the scheme's factors. They then refer to the level definitions for each factor and decide which one best fits the job.

A maximum points score is allocated to each factor. The scores available may vary between different factors in accordance with beliefs about their relative significance. This is termed 'explicit weighting'. If the number of levels varies between factors this means that they are implicitly weighted because the range of scores available will be greater in the factors with more levels.

The total score for a factor is divided between the levels to produce the numerical factor scale. Progression may be arithmetic, eg 50, 100, 150, 200 and so on, or geometric, eg 50, 100, 175, 275. In the latter case, more scope is given to recognize senior jobs with higher scores.

The complete scheme consists of the factor and level definitions and the scoring system (the total score available for each factor and distributed to the factor levels). This comprises the 'factor plan'.

Jobs are 'scored' (ie allocated points) under each factor heading on the basis of the level of the factor in the job. This is done by comparing the features of the job with regard to that factor with the factor level definitions to find out which definition provides the best fit. The separate factor scores are then added together to give a total score that indicates the relative value of each job and can be used to place the jobs in rank order. An unweighted factor plan is illustrated in Table 47.1. In this example, the evaluations are asterisked and the total score would be 400 points.

Table 47.1 A factor plan

Factors	Levels and scores					
	1	2	3	4	5	6
Expertise	20	40	60*	80	100	120
Decisions	20	40	60	80*	100	120
Autonomy	20	40	60	80*	100	120
Responsibility	20	40	60	80*	100	120
Interpersonal skills	20	40	60	80	100*	120

A point-factor scheme can be operated manually – a 'paper' scheme – or computers can be used to aid the evaluation process, as described later in this chapter.

Analytical job matching

Like point-factor job evaluation, analytical job matching is based on the analysis of a number of defined factors. There are two forms of analytical matching. One is role profile to grade/level profile matching; the other is role profile to benchmark role profile.

In *role to grade analytical matching*, profiles of roles to be evaluated are matched to grade, band or level profiles. Reference is made to a grade structure incorporating the jobs covered by the evaluation scheme. This consists of a sequence or hierarchy of grades, bands or levels that have been defined analytically in terms of a set of factors that may correspond to the job evaluation factors in a point-factor scheme or a selection of them. They may also or alternatively refer to levels of competency and responsibility, especially in job and career family structures. Information on roles is obtained by questionnaires or interviews and role profiles are produced for the jobs to be evaluated under the same headings as the grade or level profiles. The role profiles are then 'matched' with the range of grade or level profiles to establish the best fit and thus grade the job.

In *role to role analytical matching*, role profiles for jobs to be evaluated are matched analytically with benchmark role profiles. A benchmark job is one that has already been graded as a result of an initial job evaluation exercise. It is used as a point of reference with which other roles or jobs can be compared and valued. Thus, if role A has been evaluated and placed in grade 3 and there is a good fit between the factor profile of role B and that of role A, then role B will also be placed in grade 3. Roles are analysed against a common set of factors or elements. Generic role profiles, ie those covering a number of like roles, will be used for any class or cluster of roles with essentially the same range of responsibilities such as team leaders or personal assistants. Role to role matching may be combined with role to grade matching.

Analytical matching can be used to grade jobs or place them in levels following the initial evaluation of a sufficiently large sample of benchmark jobs, ie representative jobs that can provide a valid basis for comparisons. This can happen in big organizations when it is believed that it is not necessary to go through the whole process of point-factor evaluation for every job, especially where 'generic' roles are concerned. When this follows a large job evaluation exercise such as the NHS, the factors used in analytical matching may be the same as those in the point-factor job evaluation scheme that underpins the analytical matching process and can be invoked to deal with difficult cases or appeals. In some matching schemes the number of factors may be simplified, for example the HERA scheme for higher education institutions clusters related factors together, reducing the number of factors from seven to four. However, analytical matching may not necessarily be underpinned by a point-factor evaluation scheme and this can save a lot of time in the design stage as well as when rolling out the scheme.

Factor comparison

The original factor comparison method compared jobs factor by factor using a scale of money values to provide a direct indication of the rate for the job. It was developed in the United States but is not used in the UK. The Hay Guide Chart Profile method (a 'proprietary brand' of job evaluation) is described by the Hay Group as a factor comparison scheme but, apart from this, the only form of factor comparison now in use is graduated factor comparison, which compares jobs factor by factor with a graduated scale. The scale may have only three value levels – for example lower, equal, higher – and no factor scores are used. This is a method often used by the independent experts engaged by employment tribunals to advise on an equal pay claim. Their job is simply to compare one job with one or two others, not to review internal relativities over the whole spectrum of jobs in order to produce a rank order.

Tailor-made, ready-made and hybrid schemes

Any of the schemes referred to above can be 'tailor-made' or 'home grown' in the sense that they are developed specifically by or for an organization, a group of organizations or a sector, eg further education establishments. The 2007 e-reward survey showed that only 20 per cent of the schemes were tailor-made. A number of management consultants offer their own 'ready-made' schemes or 'proprietary brands'. Consultants' schemes tend to be analytical (point-factor, factor comparison or matching) and may be linked to a market rate database. As many as 60 per cent of the respondents to the e-reward survey used these schemes.

Hybrid schemes are consultants' schemes that have been modified to fit the particular needs of an organization – 20 per cent of the e-reward respondents had such schemes. Typically, the modification consists of amendments to the factor plan or, in the case of Hay, to the Hay Guide Chart.

Non-analytical schemes

Non-analytical job evaluation schemes enable whole jobs to be compared in order to place them in a grade or a rank order – they are not analysed by reference to their elements or factors. They can stand alone or be used to help in the development of an analytical scheme. For example, the paired comparison technique described later can produce a rank order of jobs that can be used to test the outcomes of an evaluation using an analytical scheme. It is therefore helpful to know how non-analytical schemes function even if they are not used as the main scheme.

Non-analytical schemes operate on a *job to job* basis in which a job is compared with another job to decide whether it should be valued more, less, or the same (ranking and 'internal benchmarking' processes). Alternatively, they may function on a *job to grade* basis in which judgements are made by comparing a whole job with a defined hierarchy of job grades (job classification) – this involves matching a job description to a grade description. The e-reward 2007 survey showed that only 14 per cent of respondents' schemes were non-analytical.

Non-analytical schemes are relatively simple but rely more on subjective judgements than analytical schemes. Such judgements will not be guided by a factor plan and do not take account of the complexity of jobs. There is a danger therefore of leaping to conclusions about job values based on *a priori* assumptions that could be prejudiced. For this reason, non-analytical schemes do not provide a defence in a UK equal pay case.

There are four main types of non-analytical schemes: job classification, job ranking, paired comparison (a statistical version of ranking), and internal benchmarking.

1. Job classification

This approach is based on a definition of the number and characteristics of the levels or grades in a grade and pay structure into which jobs will be placed. The grade definitions may refer to such job characteristics as skill, decision making and responsibility but these are not analysed separately. Evaluation takes place by a process of non-analytical matching or 'job slotting'. This involves comparing a 'whole' job description, ie one not analysed into factors, with the grade definitions to establish the grade with which the job most closely corresponds. The difference between job classification and role to grade analytical matching as described above is that in the latter case, the grade profiles are defined analytically, ie in terms of job evaluation factors, and analytically defined role profiles are matched with them factor by factor. However, the distinction between analytical and non-analytical matching can be blurred when the comparison is made between formal job descriptions or role profiles that have been prepared in a standard format, which includes common headings for such aspects of jobs as levels of responsibility or knowledge and skill requirements. These 'factors' may not be compared specifically but will be taken into account when forming a judgement. But this may not satisfy the UK legal requirement that a scheme must be analytical to provide a defence in an equal pay claim.

2. Job ranking

Whole-job ranking is the most primitive form of job evaluation. The process involves comparing whole jobs with one another and arranging them in order of their perceived value to the organization. In a sense, all evaluation schemes are ranking exercises because they place jobs in a hierarchy. The difference between simple ranking and analytical methods such as point-factor rating is that job ranking does not attempt to quantify judgements. Instead, whole jobs are compared – they are not broken down into factors or elements although, explicitly or implicitly, the comparison may be based on some generalized concept such as the level of responsibility. Job ranking or paired comparison ranking as described below is sometimes used as a check on the rank order obtained by point-factor rating.

3. Paired comparison ranking

Paired comparison ranking is a statistical technique used to provide a more sophisticated method of whole-job ranking. It is based on the assumption that it is always easier to compare one job with another than to consider a number of jobs and attempt to build up a rank order by multiple comparisons.

The technique requires the comparison of each job as a whole, separately, with every other job. If a job is considered to be of a higher value than the one with which it is being compared it receives two points; if it is thought to be equally important, it receives one point; if it is regarded as less important, no points are awarded. The scores are added for each job and a rank order is obtained.

Paired comparisons can be done factor by factor and in this case can be classified as analytical. A simplified example of a paired comparison ranking is shown in Table 47.2.

Table 47.2 A paired comparison

Job reference	a	b	c	d	e	f	Total score	Ranking
A	–	0	1	0	1	0	2	5=
B	2	–	2	2	2	0	8	2
C	1	0	–	1	1	0	3	4
D	2	0	1	–	2	0	5	3
E	1	0	1	0	–	0	2	5=
F	2	2	2	2	2	–	10	1

The advantage of paired comparison ranking over normal ranking is that it is easier to compare one job with another rather than having to make multiple comparisons. But it cannot overcome the fundamental objections to any form of whole-job ranking – that no defined standards for judging relative worth are provided and it is not an acceptable method of assessing equal value or comparable worth. There is also a limit to the number of jobs that can be compared using this method – to evaluate 50 jobs requires 1,225 comparisons. Paired comparisons are occasionally used analytically to compare jobs on a factor by factor basis.

4. Internal benchmarking

Internal benchmarking means comparing the job under review with any internal job that is believed to be properly graded and paid (an internal benchmark) and placing the job under consideration into the same grade as that job. It is what people often do intuitively when they are deciding on the value of jobs, although it is not usually dignified in job evaluation circles as a formal method of job evaluation. The comparison is made on a whole-job basis without analysing the jobs factor by factor. It can be classified as a formal method if there are specific procedures for preparing and setting out role profiles and for comparing profiles for the role to be evaluated with standard benchmark role profiles.

Market pricing

Market pricing is the process of obtaining information on market rates (market rate analysis) to inform decisions on pay structures and individual rates of pay. It is called 'extreme market pricing' when market rates are the sole means of deciding on internal rates of pay and relativities, and conventional job evaluation is not used. An organization that adopts this method is said to be 'market driven'. This approach has been widely adopted in the United States. It is associated with a belief that 'the market rules, ok', disillusionment with what was regarded as bureaucratic job evaluation, and the enthusiasm for broad-banded pay structures. It is a method that often has appeal at board level because of the focus on the need to compete in the marketplace for talent.

Market rate analysis as distinct from extreme market pricing may be associated with formal job evaluation. The latter establishes internal relativities and the grade structure, and market pricing is used to develop the pay structure – the pay ranges attached to grades. Information on market rates may lead to the introduction of market supplements for individual jobs or the creation of separate pay structures (market groups) to cater for particular market rate pressures.

The acceptability of either form of market pricing is dependent on the availability of robust market data and, when looking at external rates, the quality of the job to job matching process, ie comparing like with like. It can therefore vary from analysis of data by job titles to detailed matched analysis collected through bespoke surveys focused on real market equivalence. Extreme market pricing can provide guidance on internal relativities even if these are market driven. But it can lead to pay discrimination against women where the market has traditionally been discriminatory and it does not satisfy UK equal pay legislation. To avoid a successful equal pay claim in the UK, any difference in pay between men and women carrying out work of equal value based on market rate considerations has to be 'objectively justified', ie the employment tribunal will need to be convinced that this was not simply a matter of opinion and that adequate evidence from a number of sources was available. In such cases, the tribunal will also require proof that there is a business case for the market premium to the effect that the recruitment and retention of essential people for the organization was difficult because pay levels were uncompetitive.

Computer-aided job evaluation

Computer-aided job evaluation uses computer software to convert information about jobs into a job evaluation score or grade. It is generally underpinned by a conventional point-factor scheme. The 'proprietary brands' offered by consultants are often computer-aided. Computers may be used simply to maintain a database recording evaluations and their rationale. In the design stage they can provide guidance on weighting factors through multiple regression analysis, although this technique has been largely discredited and is little used now.

Methodology

The software used in a fully computer-aided scheme essentially replicates in digital form the thought processes followed by evaluators when conducting a 'manual' evaluation. It is based on defined evaluation decision rules built into the system shell. The software typically provides a facility for consistency checks by, for example, highlighting scoring differences between the job being evaluated and other benchmark jobs.

The two types of computer-aided evaluation are: 1) Schemes in which the job analysis data is either entered direct into the computer or transferred to it from a paper questionnaire. The computer software applies predetermined rules to convert the data into scores for each factor and produce a total score. This is the most common approach. 2) Interactive computer-aided schemes in which the job holder and his or her manager sit in front of a PC and are presented with a series of logically interrelated questions, the answers to which lead to a score for each of the built-in factors in turn and a total score.

The case for computer-aided job evaluation

A computer-aided scheme can achieve greater consistency than when a panel of evaluators uses a paper scheme – with the help of the computer the same input information gives the same output result. It can also increase the speed of evaluations, reduce the resources required and provide facilities for sorting, analysing, reporting on the input information and system outputs and record keeping (database).

The case against computer-aided job evaluation

For some organizations the full approach is too expensive and elaborate for them to be bothered with it. Others do not want to abandon the involvement of employees and their representatives in the traditional panel approach. There is also the problem of transparency in some applications. This is sometimes called 'the black box effect' – those concerned have difficulty in understanding the logic that converts the input information to a factor level score. Interactive systems such as those offered by Pilat Consultants (Gauge) and Watson Wyatt aim to overcome this difficulty. It is perhaps for these reasons that less than half the respondents to the 2007 e-reward survey had computer-aided schemes and over half of those used computers simply to maintain job evaluation records.

Choice of approach

The fundamental choice is between using formal or informal methods of valuing roles. This may not be a conscious decision. A company may use informal methods simply because that's what it has always done and because it never occurs to its management that there is an alternative. But it may decide deliberately that an informal or semi-formal approach fits its circumstances best. The advantages and disadvantages of each approach are summarized in Table 47.3. These need to be examined in the light of criteria for choice such as those set out below and compared with the objectives of the scheme and the context in which it will be used.

Criteria for choice

- *Thorough in analysis and capable of impartial application* – the scheme should have been carefully constructed to ensure that its methodology is sound and appropriate in terms of all the jobs it has to cater for. It should also have been tested and trialled to check that it can be applied impartially to those jobs.
- *Appropriate* – it should cater for the particular demands made on all the jobs to be covered by the scheme.
- *Comprehensive* – the scheme should be applicable to all the jobs in the organization covering all categories of staff and, if factors are used, they should be common to all those jobs. There should therefore be a single scheme that can be used to assess relativities across different occupations or job families and to enable benchmarking to take place as required.
- *Transparent* – the processes used in the scheme from the initial role analysis through to the grading decision should be clear to all concerned. If computers are used, information should not be perceived as being processed in a 'black box'.
- *Non-discriminatory* – the scheme should meet equal pay for work of equal value requirements.
- *Ease of administration* – the scheme should not be too complex or time-consuming to design or implement.

Table 47.3 Comparison of different job evaluation methods

Scheme	Characteristics	Advantages	Disadvantages
Point-factor rating	An analytical approach in which separate factors are scored and added together to produce a total score for the job that can be used for comparison and grading purposes	As long as it is based on proper job analysis, point-factor schemes provide evaluators with defined yardsticks that help to increase the objectivity and consistency of judgements and reduce the over-simplified judgement made in non-analytical job evaluation. They provide a defence against equal value claims as long as they are not in themselves discriminatory	Can be complex and give a spurious impression of scientific accuracy – judgement is still needed in scoring jobs. Not easy to amend the scheme as circumstances, priorities or values change
Analytical matching	Grade profiles are produced that define the characteristics of jobs in each grade in a grade structure in terms of a selection of defined factors. Role profiles are produced for the jobs to be evaluated set out on the basis of analysis under the same factor headings as the grade profiles. Role profiles are 'matched' with the range of grade profiles to establish the best fit and thus grade the job	If the matching process is truly analytical and carried out with great care, this approach saves time by enabling the evaluation of a large number of jobs, especially generic ones, to be conducted quickly and in a way that should satisfy equal value requirements	The matching process could be more superficial and therefore suspect than evaluation through a point-factor scheme. In the latter approach there are factor level definitions to guide judgements and the resulting scores provide a basis for ranking and grade design, which is not the case with analytical matching. Although matching on this basis may be claimed to be analytical, it might be difficult to prove this in an equal value case

Table 47.3 *continued*

Scheme	Characteristics	Advantages	Disadvantages
Job classification	Non-analytical – grades are defined in a structure in terms of the level of responsibilities involved in a hierarchy. Jobs are allocated to grades by matching the job description with the grade description (job slotting)	Simple to operate; standards of judgement when making comparisons are provided in the shape of the grade definitions	Can be difficult to fit complex jobs into a grade without using over-elaborate grade definitions; the definitions tend to be so generalized that they are not much help in evaluating borderline cases or making comparisons between individual jobs; does not provide a defence in an equal value case
Combined approach	Point-factor rating is used to evaluate benchmark posts and design the grade structure, and the remaining posts are graded either by analytical matching or job classification	Combines the advantages of both methods	Can be more complex to explain and administer. If job classification is used rather than analytical matching the disadvantages set out above apply, so there may be more of a need to revert to the full point-factor scheme in the event of disagreement
Ranking	Non-analytical – whole job comparisons are made to place them in rank order	Easy to apply and understand	No defined standards of judgement; differences between jobs not measured; does not provide a defence in an equal value case
Internal bench-marking	Jobs or roles are compared with benchmark jobs that have been allocated into grades on the basis of ranking or job classification and placed in whatever grade provides the closest match of jobs. The job descriptions may be analytical in the sense that they cover a number of standard and defined elements	Simple to operate; facilitates direct comparisons, especially when the jobs have been analysed in terms of a set of common criteria	Relies on a considerable amount of judgement and may simply perpetuate existing relativities; dependent on accurate job/role analysis; may not provide a defence in an equal value case

The decision may be to use one approach, for example point-factor rating or analytical matching. But an increasing number of organizations are combining the two: using point-factor rating to evaluate a representative sample of benchmark jobs (ie jobs that can be used as points of comparison for other jobs) and, to save time and trouble, evaluating the remaining jobs by means of analytical matching.

Making the choice

The overwhelming preference for analytical schemes shown by the e-reward 2007 survey suggests that the choice is fairly obvious. The advantages of using a recognized analytical approach that satisfies equal value requirements appear to be overwhelming. Point-factor schemes were used by 70 per cent of those respondents and others used analytical matching, often in conjunction with the points scheme.

There is something to be said for adopting point-factor methodology as the main scheme but using analytical matching in a supporting role to deal with large numbers of generic roles not covered in the original benchmarking exercise. Analytical matching can be used to allocate generic roles to grades as part of the normal job evaluation operating procedure to avoid having to resort to job evaluation in every case. The tendency in many organizations is to assign to job evaluation a supporting role of this nature rather than allowing it to dominate all grading decisions and thus involve the expenditure of much time and energy.

Designing an analytical point-factor job evaluation scheme

The process of designing a point-factor job evaluation scheme is demanding and time-consuming, as stressed by Armstrong and Cummins (2008). The design and process criteria and the design and implementation programme are considered below.

Design and process criteria

It is necessary to distinguish between the design of a scheme and the process of operating it in accordance with the principles set out below. Equal pay considerations have to be taken into account in both design and process.

Design principles

- The scheme should be based on a thorough analysis of the jobs to be covered and the types of demands made on those jobs to determine what factors are appropriate.

- The scheme should facilitate impartial judgements of relative job size.
- The factors used in the scheme should cover the whole range of jobs to be evaluated at all levels without favouring any particular type of job or occupation and without discriminating on the grounds of sex, race, disability or for any other reason – the scheme should fairly measure features of female-dominated jobs as well as male-dominated jobs.
- Through the use of common factors and methods of analysis and evaluation, the scheme should enable benchmarking to take place of the relativities between jobs in different functions or job families.
- The factors should be clearly defined and differentiated – there should be no double counting.
- The levels should be defined and graduated carefully.
- Sex bias must be avoided in the choice of factors, the wording of factor and level definitions and the factor weightings – checks should be carried out to identify any bias.

Process principles

- The scheme should be transparent; everyone concerned should know how it works – the basis upon which the evaluations are produced.
- Appropriate proportions of women, those from ethnic minorities and people with disabilities should be involved in the process of developing and applying job evaluation.
- The quality of role analysis should be monitored to ensure that analyses produce accurate and relevant information that will inform the job evaluation process and will not be biased.
- Consistency checks should be built into operating procedures.
- The outcomes of evaluations should be examined to ensure that sex or any other form of bias has not occurred.
- Particular care is necessary to ensure that the outcomes of job evaluation do not simply replicate the existing hierarchy – it is to be expected that a job evaluation exercise will challenge present relativities.
- All those involved in role analysis and job evaluation should be thoroughly trained in the operation of the scheme and in how to avoid bias.

- Special care should be taken in developing a grade structure following a job evaluation exercise to ensure that grade boundaries are placed appropriately and that the allocation of jobs to grades is not in itself discriminatory.
- There should be scope for the review of evaluations and for appeals against gradings.
- The scheme should be monitored to ensure that it is being operated properly and that it is still fit for its purpose.

The design and implementation programme

The design and implementation of a point-factor job evaluation scheme can be a time-consuming affair. In a large organization it can take two years or more to complete a project. Even in a small organization it can take several months. Many organizations seek outside help from management consultants or ACAS in conducting the programme. An example of a programme is given in Figure 47.1.

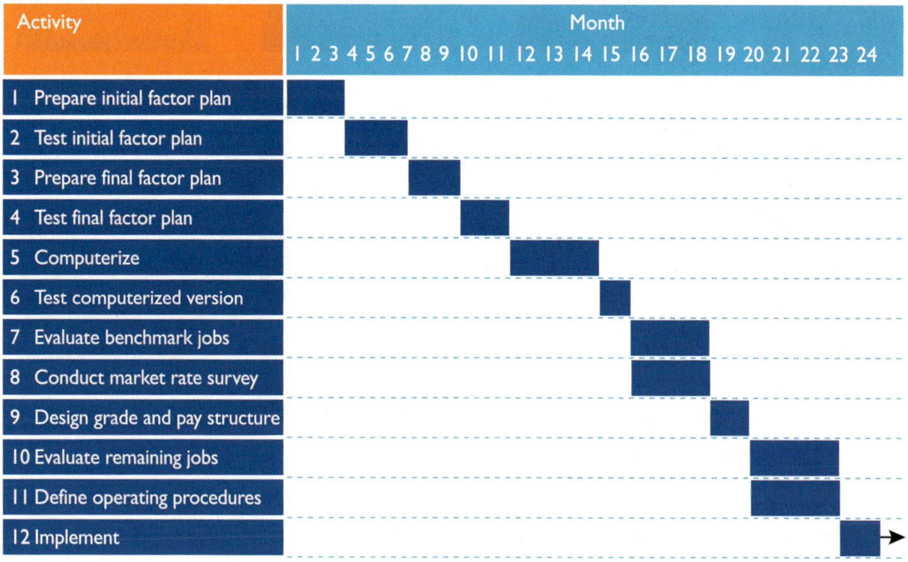

Figure 47.1 A typical job evaluation programme

Activities 1 to 6 form the initial design phase and activities 7 to 12 form the application of the design and implementation phases. Full descriptions of these phases follow.

The scheme design programme

Figure 47.2 shows the steps required to design a point-factor job evaluation scheme.

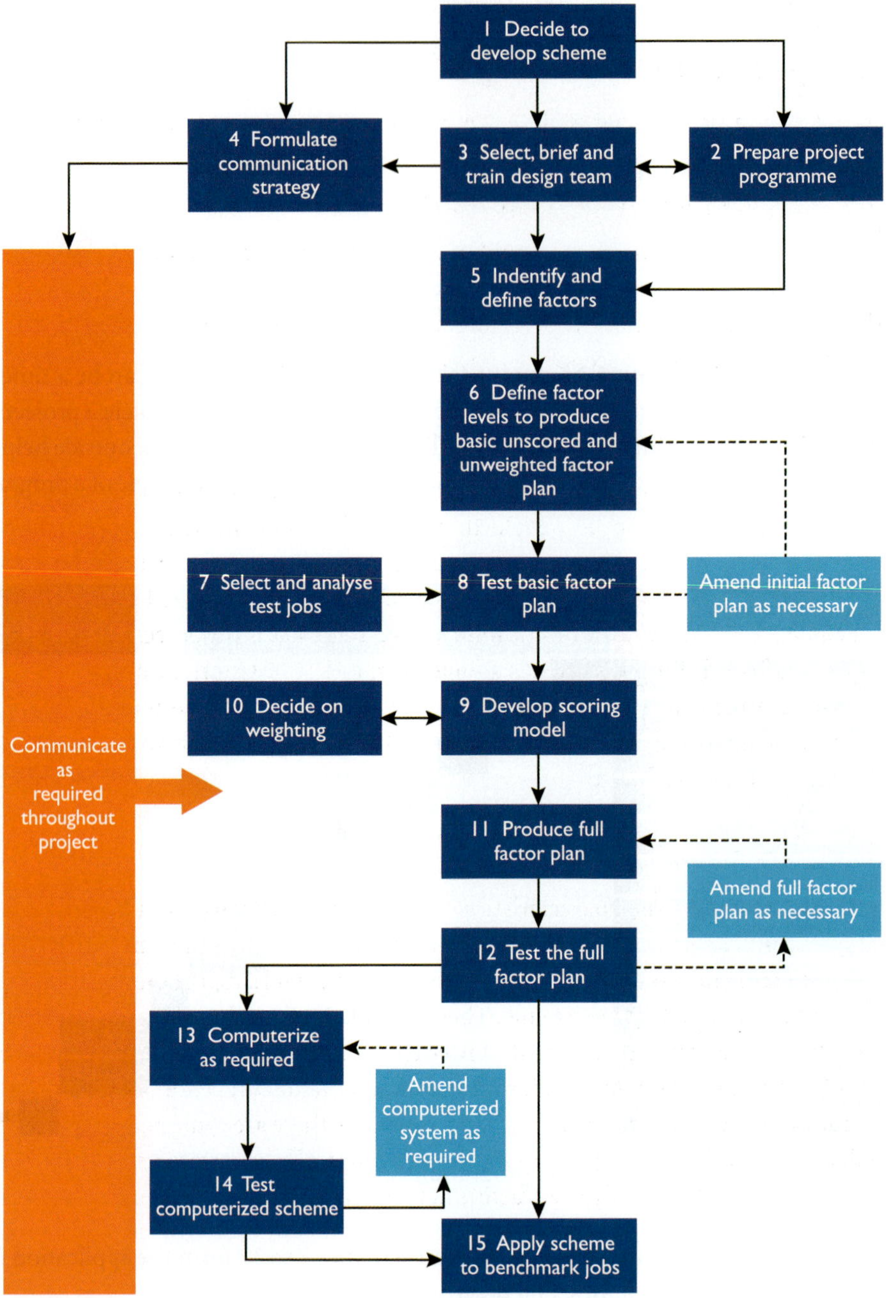

Figure 47.2 Point-factor job evaluation scheme design sequence

Step 1. Decide to develop scheme

The decision to develop a new point-factor job evaluation scheme follows an analysis of the existing arrangements, if any, for job evaluation, and a diagnosis of any problems.

Step 2. Prepare detailed project programme

The detailed project programme could be set out in a chart as illustrated in Table 47.1.

Step 3. Select, brief and train design team

The composition of the design team should have been determined broadly at Step 1. Members are usually nominated by management and the staff or union(s) (if they exist). It is very desirable to have a representative number of women and men and the major ethnic groups employed in the organization. It is also necessary to appoint a facilitator.

Step 4. Formulate communication strategy

It is essential to have a communication strategy. The introduction of a new job evaluation will always create expectations. Some people think that they will inevitably benefit from pay increases; others believe that they are sure to lose money. It has to be explained carefully, and repeatedly, that no one should expect to get more and that no one will lose. The strategy should include a preliminary communication setting out what is proposed and why and how people will be affected. Progress reports should be made at milestones throughout the programme, for example when the factor plan has been devised. A final communication should describe the new grade and pay structure and spell out exactly what is to happen to people when the structure is introduced.

Step 5. Identify and define factors

Job evaluation factors are the characteristics or key elements of jobs that are used to analyse and evaluate jobs in an analytical job evaluation scheme. The factors must be capable of identifying relevant and important differences between jobs that will support the creation of a rank order of jobs to be covered by the scheme. They should apply equally well to different types of work including specialists and generalists, lower level and higher level jobs, and not be biased in favour of one sex or group. Although many of the job evaluation factors used across organizations capture similar job elements (this is an area where there are some enduring truths), the task of identifying and agreeing factors can be challenging. The e-reward survey (2007) established that the 10 most frequently used factors in tailor-made analytical schemes, in rank order, were as follows.

SOURCE REVIEW

The 10 most frequently used factors in tailor-made analytical schemes in rank order, e-reward survey (2007)

1. Knowledge and skills.
2. Responsibility.
3. Problem solving.
4. Decision making.
5. People management.
6. Relationships/contacts.
7. Working conditions.
8. Mental effort.
9. Impact.
10. Creativity.

Step 6. Define factor levels to produce the basic factor plan

The factor plan is the key job evaluation document. It guides evaluators on making decisions about the levels. The basic factor plan defines the levels within each of the selected factors. A decision has to be made on the number of levels (often five, six or seven), which has to reflect the range of responsibilities and demands in the jobs covered by the scheme.

Step 7. Select and analyse test jobs

A small representative sample of jobs should be identified to test the scheme. A typical proportion would be about 10 per cent of the jobs to be covered. These are then analysed in terms of the factors.

Step 8. Test basic factor plan

The factors forming the basic factor plan are tested by the design team on a representative sample of jobs. The aim of this initial test is to check on the extent to which the factors are appropriate, cover all aspects of the jobs to be evaluated, are non-discriminatory, avoid double counting and are not compressed unduly. A check is also made on level definitions to ensure that they are worded clearly, graduated properly and cover the whole range of demands applicable to the jobs to be evaluated so that they enable consistent evaluations to be made.

Step 9. Develop scoring model

The aim is to design a point-factor scheme that will operate fairly and consistently to produce a rank order of jobs, based on the total points score for each job. Each level in the factor plan has to be allocated a points value so that there is a scoring progression from the lowest to the highest level.

Step 10. Decide on the factor weighting

Weighting is the process of attaching more importance to some factors. Explicit weighting takes place in a point-factor scheme when the maximum points available for what are regarded as more important factors are increased. Implicit weighting takes place when some factors have more levels than others but the same scoring progression per level exists as in the other factors.

Step 11. Prepare full factor plan

The outcome of Steps 9 and 10 is the full scored and weighted factor plan, which is tested in Step 12.

Step 12. Test the full factor plan

The full factor plan incorporating a scoring scheme and either explicit or implicit weighting is tested on the same jobs used in the initial test of the draft factors. Further jobs may be added to extend the range of the test.

Step 13. Computerize

The steps set out above will produce a paper-based scheme and this is still the most popular approach. The e-reward survey (2003) found that only 28 per cent of respondents with job evaluation schemes used computers to aid evaluation. But full computerization can offer many advantages including greater consistency, speed and the elimination of much of the paper work. There is also the possibility of using computers to help manage and support the process without using computers as a substitute for grading design teams.

Computer-aided schemes use the software provided by suppliers but the system itself is derived from the paper-based scheme devised by the methods set out above. No job evaluation design team is required to conduct evaluations but it is necessary to set up a review panel that can validate and agree the outcomes of the computerized process. No one likes to feel that a decision about their grade has been made by a computer on its own and hard lessons have been learnt by organizations that have ended up with fully automated but discriminatory systems.

Step 14. Test the computerized scheme

The computerized scheme is tested to ensure that it delivers an acceptable rank order.

Step 15. Apply and implement

When the final design of the paper or computerized scheme has been tested and shown as satisfactory, the application and implementation programme can begin. This involves the evaluation of a representative sample of benchmark jobs followed by the evaluation of the remaining jobs.

Designing an analytical matching job evaluation scheme

The sequence of actions required to design an analytical matching scheme is shown in Figure 47.3. These may follow the development of a point-factor scheme, the factors in which would be used in the matching process.

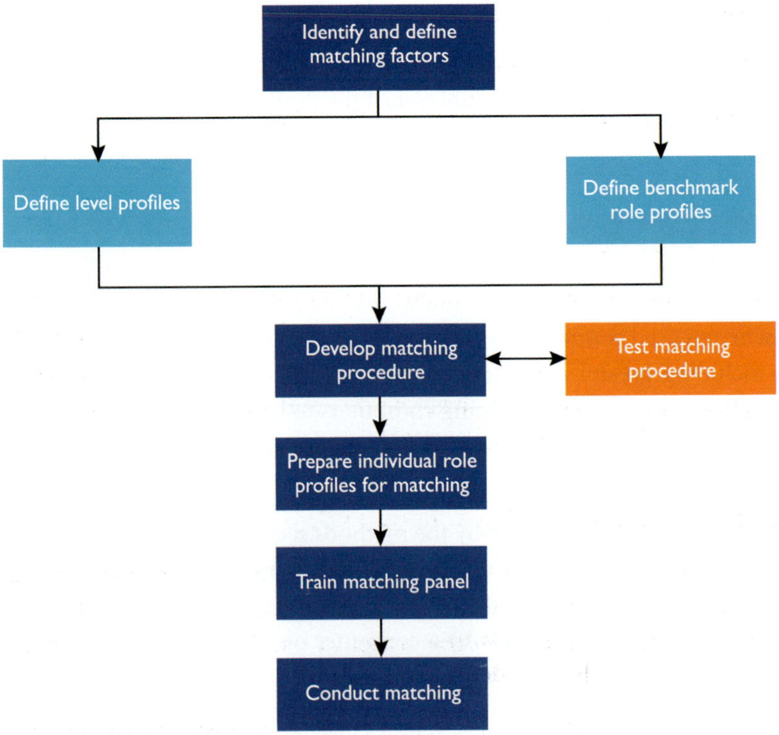

Figure 47.3 Analytical matching job evaluation scheme design sequence

Equal pay considerations

Job evaluation has particular significance when it refers to the achievement of equal pay for work of equal value between women and men. Its role in achieving equal pay is carried out in many countries within the framework of equal pay legislation. Article 2 of the 1951 ILO's Equal Remuneration Convention states that:

> *Each member shall, by means appropriate to the methods in operation for determining rates of remuneration, promote and, in so far as is consistent with such methods, ensure the application to all workers of the principle of equal remuneration for men and women workers for work of equal value.*

One hundred and sixty-three countries have ratified this convention including Albania, Kazakhstan and the United Kingdom but not the United States.

Equal pay legislation in the UK

In the UK equal pay legislation as summarized below is based on Article 142 of the Treaty of Maastricht, which was extended by the EU Equal Pay Directive of 1975. The basic provision of the legislation is that anyone is entitled to equal pay with a comparator when they are carrying out:

- like work, meaning the same or very similar work;
- work rated as equivalent under a job evaluation study;
- work of equal value.

The 1970 Equal Pay Act

This Act effectively outlawed separate women's rates of pay by introducing an implied equality clause into all contracts of employment. It also provided two grounds on which an applicant could take a claim to an Industrial (now Employment) Tribunal for equal pay with a comparator of the opposite sex: 1) 'like work', meaning the same or very similar work, and 2) 'work rated as equivalent' under a job evaluation 'study'.

The Equal Pay (Amendment) Regulations 1983

These regulations were introduced to conform to the European Directive. They provide that women are entitled to the same pay as men (and vice versa) where the work is of equal value 'in terms of the demands made on a worker under various headings, for instance, effort, skill, decision'.

This removed the barrier built into the Act that had prevented women claiming equal pay where they were employed in women's jobs and no men were employed in the same work. Now any woman could claim equal pay with any man and vice versa, subject to the rules about being in the same employment. Equal value claims can be brought even if there are no job evaluation arrangements, although the existence of a non-discriminatory analytical job evaluation scheme that has been applied properly to indicate that the jobs in question are not of equal value can be a defence in an equal value case.

The amendment also provided for the assignment of 'independent experts' by employment tribunals to assess equality of value between claimant and comparator under such headings as effort, skill and decision without regard to the cost or the industrial relations consequences of a successful claim.

Employment Act 2002

One of the biggest barriers to bringing equal pay claims has been a lack of access to information regarding other people's pay. The Equal Pay (Questions and Replies) Order 2003 of the Employment Act 2002 provided for an equal pay questionnaire that can be used by an employee to request information from their employer about whether their remuneration is equal to that of named colleagues. Unions may also lodge these forms on behalf of their members.

Managing the risk of equal pay claims

Equal pay claims can be time-consuming and, if successful, can be hugely expensive, especially in UK public sector organizations with powerful and active trade unions. Some organizations in low risk situations may be convinced that they are doing enough about ensuring equal pay without introducing job evaluation. Others have decided that because their business imperatives are pressing they are prepared to accept a measure of risk in their policy on equal pay. Some, regrettably, may not care. But if there is medium or high risk then action needs to be taken to minimize it. Equal pay risk management means following the design and process criteria for job evaluation mentioned earlier in this chapter and conducting equal pay reviews to establish the extent to which there is pay discrimination.

Equal pay risk assessment involves considering two factors: 1) the risk of having to defend an equal pay claim, and 2) the risk of a claim being successful. Assessing the risk of a claim means first analysing the extent to which there is unequal pay and if it does exist, diagnosing the cause(s). For example, these could be any of the following:

- different base rates of pay for work of equal value;
- disproportionate distribution of men or women at the upper or lower part of a pay range or an incremental scale, bearing in mind that this is a major cause of unequal pay;
- men or women placed at higher points in the scale on appointment or promotion;
- men or women receive higher merit or performance pay awards or benefit more from accelerated increments;

- market supplements applied differentially to men or women;
- 'red or green circling' applied in a way that results in pay discrimination between men and women doing work of equal value or like work;
- a discriminating job evaluation scheme in terms of factors or weightings, or the job evaluation scheme being applied in a discriminatory way.

Secondly, assessing the risk of a claim means considering the possibility of an individual initiating action on his or her own, or trade unions taking action on behalf of their members. Individual actions may come out of the blue, but the individual may have raised an equal pay grievance formally or informally and line managers should understand that they must report this immediately to HR or senior management. The likelihood of trade union action will clearly be higher when there is a strong union with high penetration in the organization, which is often the case in the public sector. But any union member can seek help from her or his union. Even if the union is not recognized for negotiating purposes it can still provide support.

Conclusions

It could be claimed that every time a decision is made on what a job should be paid a form of job evaluation is needed. Job evaluation is therefore unavoidable, but it should not be an intuitive, subjective and potentially biased process. The aim is to develop an appropriate scheme that functions analytically, fairly, systematically, consistently, transparently and, so far as possible, objectively, without being bureaucratic, inflexible or resource-intensive. There are six ways of achieving this aim.

Six ways of developing an appropriate job evaluation scheme

1. Use a tested and relevant analytical job evaluation scheme to inform and support the processes of designing grade structures, grading jobs, managing relativities and ensuring that work of equal value is paid equally.
2. Use analytical matching underpinned by a point-factor scheme.
3. Ensure that job evaluation is introduced and managed properly.
4. Consider using computers to speed up processing and decision making while at the same time generating more consistent evaluations and reducing bureaucracy.
5. Recognize that thorough training and continuing guidance for evaluators is essential, as is communication about the scheme, its operation and objectives to all concerned.

6. Review the operation of the scheme regularly to ensure that it is not decaying, continues to be appropriate and trusted and is not discriminatory.

Job evaluation – key learning points

The aims of job evaluation

- Establish the relative value or size of jobs.
- Produce the information required to design grade and pay structures.
- Provide as objective as possible a basis for grading jobs.
- Enable sound market comparisons with jobs or roles of equivalent complexity and size.
- Be transparent – the basis upon which grades are defined and jobs graded should be clear.
- Ensure that the organization meets equal pay for work of equal value obligations.

Approaches to job evaluation

Informal approaches price jobs either on the basis of assumptions about internal and external relativities or simply by reference to the 'going' or market rates. Formal approaches use standardized methods to evaluate jobs, which can be analytical or non-analytical. Such schemes deal with internal relativities and the associated process of establishing and defining job grades or levels in an organization.

Analytical job evaluation schemes

Analytical job evaluation is based on a process of breaking down whole jobs into a number of defined elements or factors such as responsibility, decisions and the knowledge and skill required. These are assumed to be present in all the jobs to be evaluated. In point-factor and fully analytical matching schemes, jobs are then compared factor by factor either with a graduated scale of points attached to a set of factors or with grade or role profiles analysed under the same factor headings.

Non-analytical job evaluation schemes

Non-analytical job evaluation schemes enable whole jobs to be compared in order to place them in a grade or a rank order – they are not analysed by reference to their elements or factors.

Market pricing

Market pricing is the process of obtaining information on market rates (market rate analysis) to inform decisions on pay structures and individual rates of pay. This is called 'extreme market pricing' when market rates are the sole means of deciding on internal rates of pay and relativities, and conventional job evaluation is not used.

Job evaluation – key learning points (continued)

Computer-aided job evaluation

Computer-aided job evaluation uses computer software to convert information about jobs into a job evaluation score or grade. It is generally underpinned by a conventional point-factor scheme.

Comparison of schemes

The features, advantages and disadvantages of each of the main schemes are summarized in Table 47.3.

Choice of approach

The overwhelming preference for analytical schemes shown by the e-reward 2007 survey suggests that the choice is fairly obvious. The advantages of using a recognized analytical approach that satisfies equal value requirements appear to be overwhelming. Point-factor schemes were used by 70 per cent of those respondents and others used analytical matching, often in conjunction with the points scheme.

Designing analytical schemes

The design sequence is shown in Figures 47.2 and 47.3.

Equal pay considerations

Job evaluation has particular significance when it refers to the achievement of equal pay for work of equal value between women and men. Women should be paid the same rate as men when they are carrying out 'like work', 'work rated as equivalent', or 'work of equal value'.

Questions

1. What is the distinction between analytical and non-analytical job evaluation and what are the advantages and disadvantages of both approaches?
2. What is 'extreme market pricing'? Why is it used by many organizations as a basis for valuing jobs and what are the problems this approach might create?
3. How do you ensure that a job evaluation scheme is not discriminatory?

References

Armstrong, M and Cummins, A (2008) *Valuing Roles*, Kogan Page, London

Equal Opportunities Commission (2003) *Good Practice Guide on Job Evaluation Schemes Free of Sex Bias*, EOC, London e-reward (2003) *Research Report No 10*, e-reward.co.uk, Stockport

e-reward (2007) *Survey of Job Evaluation*, e-reward.co.uk, Stockport

Gupta, N and Jenkins, G D (1991) Practical problems in using job evaluation to determine compensation, *Human Resource Management Review*, **1** (2), pp 133–44

48 Market Rate Analysis

Key concepts and terms

- Arithmetic mean or average
- Capsule job description
- Inter-quartile range
- Lower quartile
- Market rate survey
- Median
- Benchmark jobs
- Derived market rate
- Job matching
- Market rate
- Market stance
- Upper quartile

Learning outcomes

On completing this chapter you should be able to define these key concepts. You should also know about:

- The aims of market rate analysis
- Factors affecting the validity and reliability of market rate data
- Uses of benchmark jobs
- Interpreting and presenting market rate data
- The concept of a market rate
- Job matching
- Sources of data
- Using survey data

Introduction

Market rate analysis is conducted through surveys that produce data on the levels of pay and benefits for similar jobs in comparable organizations. It is the basis either for extreme market pricing, as defined in Chapter 47, or for maintaining competitive rates of pay and benefits and deciding on pay ranges in a grade and pay structure.

Aims of market analysis

- Obtain relevant, accurate and representative data on market rates.
- Compare like with like, in terms of data, regional and organizational variations and, importantly, type and size of job or role.
- Obtain information that is as up to date as possible.
- Interpret data in a way that clearly indicates the action required.

Decisions on levels of pay following market rate analysis will be guided by the pay policy of the organization or its 'market stance' – ie how it wants its pay levels to relate to market levels.

Effective market rate analysis depends on understanding the concept of a market rate and the factors affecting the validity and reliability of market rate data, as considered in the first two parts of this chapter. The rest of the chapter deals with selecting the benchmark jobs used for comparison, the sources of market rate data and how they should be interpreted, presented and used.

The concept of a market rate

People often refer to the 'market rate' but it is a much more elusive concept than it seems. There is no such thing as a definitive market rate for any job, even when comparing identically sized organizations in the same industry and location. There are local markets and there are national markets, and none of them is perfect in the economist's sense. Different market information sources for the same types of jobs produce different results because of variations in the sample, the difficulty of obtaining precise matches between jobs in the organization and jobs elsewhere (job matching), and timing (the dates on which the data are collected may differ).

This means that market rate analysis is most unlikely to produce information on the rate for the job. The possibly incomplete data from a number of sources, some more reliable than others, has to be interpreted to indicate what the organization should do about it. Data may be available for some jobs but not for others, which are unique to the organization.

Factors determining the validity and reliability of market rate data

1. Job matching – the extent to which the external jobs with which the internal jobs are being compared are similar, ie like is being compared with like.
2. Sample frame – the degree to which the sample of organizations from which the data have been collected is fully representative of the organizations with which comparisons need to be made in such terms as sector, technology or type of business, size and location.
3. Timing – the extent to which the information is up to date or can be updated reliably. By their very nature, published surveys, upon which many people rely, can soon become out of date. This can happen the moment they are produced – pay levels may have changed and people may have moved in or out since the date of the survey. While it is not possible to overcome this completely, as data must be gathered and analysed, surveys that aim to have as short a time as possible between data collection and the publication of results are likely to be of more use than those with longer lead times. Estimates can be made of likely movements since the survey took place, but they are mainly guesswork.

Job matching

Inadequate job matching is a major cause of inaccuracies in the data collected by market analysis. So far as possible the aim is to match the jobs within the organization and those outside (the comparators) so that like is being compared with like. It is essential to avoid crude and misleading comparisons based on job titles alone or vague descriptions of job content. It is first necessary to ensure that a broad match is achieved between the organization and the types of organizations used as comparators in terms of sector, industry classification, size and location.

The next step is to match jobs within the organizations concerned. The various methods, in ascending order of accuracy, are:

1. Job title: this can be misleading. Job titles by themselves give no indication of the range of duties or the level of responsibility and are sometimes used to convey additional status to employees or their customers unrelated to the real level of work done.
2. Brief description of duties and level or zone of responsibility: national surveys frequently restrict their job-matching definitions to a two- or three-line description of duties and an indication of levels of responsibility in rank order. The latter is often limited to a one-line

definition for each level or zone in a hierarchy. This approach provides some guidance on job matching, which reduces major discrepancies, but it still leaves considerable scope for discretion and can therefore provide only generalized comparisons.

3. Capsule job descriptions: club (see below) or specialist 'bespoke' surveys frequently use capsule job descriptions that define main responsibilities and duties in about 100 to 200 words. To increase the refinement of comparisons, modifying statements may be made indicating where responsibilities are higher or lower than the norm. Capsule job descriptions considerably increase the accuracy of comparisons as long as they are based on a careful analysis of actual jobs and include modifying statements. But they are not always capable of dealing with specialist jobs and the accuracy of comparisons in relation to levels of responsibility may be limited, even when modifiers are used.
4. Full role profiles, including a factor analysis of the levels of responsibility involved, may be used in special surveys when direct comparisons are made between jobs in different organizations. They can be more accurate on a one-for-one basis but their use is limited because of the time and labour involved in preparing them. A further limitation is that comparator organizations may not have available, or be prepared to make available, their own full role profiles for comparison.
5. Job evaluation: can be used in support of a capsule job description or a role profile to provide a more accurate measure of relative job size. A common method of evaluation is necessary. An increasing number of international and UK consultancies now claim to be able to make this link, either through a point-factor scheme or a matching approach, even though they do not necessarily restrict survey participation only to those organizations that are prepared to conduct a full evaluation process. This approach will further increase the accuracy of comparisons but the degree of accuracy will depend on the quality of the job evaluation process.

Use of benchmark jobs

A market rate survey should aim to collect data on a representative sample of benchmark jobs that will be used to provide guidance on the design of a pay structure (see Chapter 49) or as a basis for market pricing. The jobs selected should be ones for which it is likely that market data will be available. There are usually some jobs that are unique to the organization and for which comparisons cannot be made. When conducting a market pricing exercise it is necessary to make a judgement on the positioning of these jobs in the structure on the basis of comparisons with the benchmark jobs. A point-factor evaluation scheme, if available, helps to make these comparisons more accurate.

Sources of market data

There is a wide variety of sources of varying quality. They include published surveys, special surveys conducted by the organization, 'pay clubs' (groups of organizations that exchange information on pay and benefits) and advertisements.

Because it is unlikely that precise job matching, a perfect sample and coincidence of timing will be achieved, it is best to obtain data from more than one source. Ultimately, a judgement has to be made about market levels of pay and this will be helped if a range of information is available that enables a view to be taken on what should be regarded as 'the market rate' for internal use. This is more convincing if it has been derived from a number of sources. For example, published market data can be supplemented by specialist surveys covering particular jobs. Should the quality of job matching be important, an individual survey can be conducted or a salary club can be joined, if there is room. If a number of sources is used, the objective justification for any market supplement or premium (an addition to the normal rate for the job to reflect the market value of a job) that might create unequal pay must be made.

In choosing data sources it is important to take account of how easily replicable the analysis will be in future years. Trends can only be identified if a consistent set of sources is used, and if those sources are reasonably stable.

Published surveys

Published surveys are readily accessible and are usually based on a large sample. If the information can be obtained online, so much the better. But they have to be relevant to the needs of the organization and particular attention should always be paid to the range of data and the quality of job matching. Published surveys are of widely varying content, presentation and quality and are sometimes expensive. They can be national, local, sector, industrial or occupational.

When selecting a published survey the following guidelines should be used:

- Does it cover relevant jobs in similar organizations?
- Does it provide the information on the pay and benefits required?
- Are there enough participants to provide acceptable comparisons?
- So far as can be judged, is the survey conducted properly in terms of its sampling techniques and the quality of job matching?
- Is the survey reasonably up to date?
- Are the results well presented?
- Does it provide value for money?

As a starting point to identifying a relevant survey, look at the regular reviews included in publications from Incomes Data Services (IDS) and Industrial Relations Services (IRS). Pay analyst IDS also publishes a directory that brings together information on virtually every available survey of salaries and benefits produced in the UK, providing an unmatched guide to data sources. It currently lists some 290 surveys of salaries and benefits from 76 UK survey producers, covering national, local, benefit and international surveys, and gives details of employee groups and jobs covered by each survey, sample size, date of the survey data and the length and price of the report. Subscribers to the directory can also access it online and search for data by job title, type of benefit, sector, UK region or overseas region. Contact www.salarysurveys.info.

Consultants' databases

Many consultancies concerned with reward management have databases of market rates produced by their own surveys and contacts, and are often linked to their proprietary job evaluation scheme.

Special surveys

Special surveys can be 'do it yourself' affairs or they can be conducted for you by management consultants. The latter method costs more but it saves a lot of time and trouble, and some organizations may be more willing to respond to an enquiry from a reputable consultant.

Conducting a special survey

1. Decide what information is wanted.
2. Identify the 'benchmark' jobs for which comparative pay data are required. This could have been done as part of a job evaluation exercise, as described in Chapter 47.
3. Produce capsule job descriptions for those jobs.
4. Identify the organizations that are likely to have similar jobs.
5. Contact those organizations and invite them to participate. It is usual to say that the survey findings will be distributed to participants (this is the quid pro quo) and that individual organizations will not be identified.
6. Provide participants with a form to complete together with guidance notes and capsule job descriptions. This includes provision for participants to indicate by a + or – whether the size or scope of the job is larger or smaller than the capsule job

description indicates. Give them a reasonable amount of time to complete and return the form, say two to three weeks.

7. Analyse the returned forms and distribute a summary of the results to participants.

Special surveys can justify the time and trouble, or expense, by producing usefully comparable data. It may, however, be difficult to get a suitable number of participants to take part, either because organizations cannot be bothered or because they are already members of a survey club or take part in a published survey.

Club surveys

Club surveys (pay clubs) are conducted by a number of organizations who agree to exchange information on pay in accordance with a standard format and on a regular basis. They have all the advantages of special surveys plus the additional benefits of saving a considerable amount of time and providing regular information. It is well worth joining one if you can. If a suitable club does not exist you could always try to start one, but this takes considerable effort.

Advertisements

Many organizations rely on the salary levels published in recruitment advertisements. But these can be very misleading as you will not necessarily achieve a good match and the quoted salary may not be the same as what is finally paid. However, although it is highly suspect, data from advertisements can be used to supplement other more reliable sources.

Other market intelligence

Other market intelligence can be obtained from the publications of Incomes Data Services and Industrial Relations Services. This may include useful information on trends in the 'going rate' for general, across-the-board pay increases that can be used when deciding on what sort of uplift, if any, is required to pay scales.

The features of the main sources and their advantages and disadvantages are listed in Table 48.1.

Table 48.1 Analysis of market rate data sources

Source	Brief description	Advantages	Disadvantages
Online data	Access data from general surveys	Quick, easy, can be tailored	May not provide all the information required
General national published surveys	Available for purchase – provide an overall picture of pay levels for different occupations in national and regional labour markets	Wide coverage, readily available, continuity allows trend analyses over time, expert providers	Risk of imprecise job matching, insufficiently specific, quickly out of date
Local published surveys	Available for purchase – provide an overall picture of pay levels for different occupations in the local labour market	Focus on local labour market especially for administrative staff and manual workers	Risk of imprecise job matching, insufficiently specific, quickly out of date, providers may not have expertise in pay surveys
Sector surveys	Available for purchase – provide data on a sector such as charities	Focus on a sector where pay levels may differ from national rates, deal with particular categories in depth	Risk of imprecise job matching, insufficiently specific, quickly out of date
Industrial/ occupational surveys	Surveys, often conducted by employer and trade associations, on jobs in an industry or specific jobs	Focus on an industry, deal with particular categories in depth, quality of job matching may be better than general or sector surveys	Job matching may still not be entirely precise; quickly out of date
Management consultants' databases	Pay data obtained from the databases maintained by management consultants	Based on well researched and matched data. Often highly tailored to specific market segments	Only obtainable from specific consultants and often confidential to participants. Can be expensive
Special surveys	Surveys specially conducted by an organization	Focused, reasonably good job matching, control of participants, control of analysis methodology	Takes time and trouble, may be difficult to get participation, sample size may therefore be inadequate. May not be repeated, therefore difficult to use for ongoing pay management

Table 48.1 *continued*

Source	Brief description	Advantages	Disadvantages
Pay clubs	Groups of employers who regularly exchange data on pay levels	Focused, precise job matching, control of participants, control of analysis methodology, regular data, trends data, more information may be available on benefits and pay policies	Sample size may be too small, involve a considerable amount of administration, may be difficult to maintain enthusiasm of participants
Published data in journals	Data on settlements and pay levels available from IDS or IRS, and on national trends in earnings from the New Earnings Survey	Readily accessible	Mainly about settlements and trends, little specific well matched information on pay levels for individual jobs
Analysis of recruitment data	Pay data derived from analysis of pay levels required to recruit staff	Immediate data	Data random and can be misleading because of small sample. Can be distorted if applicants inflate their salary history or if data geared to recruitment salaries
Job advertisements	Pay data obtained from job advertisements	Readily accessible, highly visible (to employees as well as employers), up to date. Data can be quite specific for public and voluntary sector roles	Job matching very imprecise, pay information may be misleading
Other market intelligence	Pay data obtained from informal contacts or networks	Provide good background	Imprecise, not regularly available

Interpreting and presenting market rate data

Market rate data need to be interpreted by reference to the details provided from each source and by assessments of their reliability, accuracy and relevance. If data have been obtained from a number of sources these will also have to be interpreted to produce a derived market rate that will be used as the basis of comparison.

Data can be presented as measures of central tendency or measures of dispersion. Measures of central tendency consist of the arithmetic mean (average) and the median – the middle item in a distribution of individual items. The latter is the most commonly used measure because it avoids the distortions to which arithmetic averages are prone.

Measures of dispersion consist of:

- the upper quartile – the value above which 25 per cent of the individual values fall (this term is often used more loosely to indicate any value within the top 25 per cent);
- the lower quartile – the value below which 25 per cent of the individual values fall;
- the interquartile range – the difference between the upper and lower quartiles.

Using survey data

The use of market survey data as a guide to pay levels is a process based on judgement and compromise. Different sources may produce different indications of market rate levels. As a result you may have to produce what might be described as a 'derived' market rate based on an assessment of the relative reliability of the data. This would strike a reasonable balance between the competing merits of the different sources used. This is an intuitive process.

Once all the data available have been collected and presented in the most accessible manner possible (ie job by job for all the areas the structure is to cover), reference points can be determined for each pay range in a graded pay structure, as described in Chapter 49. This process will take account of the place in the market the business wishes to occupy, ie its market 'stance' or 'posture'.

Market rate analysis – key learning points

The aims of market rate analysis

- Obtain relevant, accurate and representative data on market rates.
- Compare like with like, in terms of data, regional and organizational variations and, importantly, type and size of job or role.

Market rate analysis – key learning points (continued)

- Obtain information that is as up to date as possible.
- Interpret data in a way that clearly indicates the action required.

The concept of a market rate

People often refer to the 'market rate' but it is a much more elusive concept than it seems. There is no such thing as a definitive market rate for any job, even when comparing identically sized organizations in the same industry and location. This means that market rate analysis is most unlikely to produce information on the rate for the job.

Factors affecting the validity and reliability of market rate data

The accuracy of job matching, the degree to which the sample frame (the elements in the sample) are representative and the extent to which the survey is up to date.

Job matching

Inadequate job matching is a major cause of inaccuracies in the data collected by market analysis. So far as possible the aim is to match the jobs within the organization and those outside (the comparators) so that like is being compared with like.

Use of benchmark jobs

A market rate survey should aim to collect data on a representative sample of benchmark jobs that will be used to provide guidance on the design of a pay structure or as a basis for market pricing.

Sources of data

Described in Table 48.1.

Interpreting and presenting market rate data

Market rate data need to be interpreted by reference to the details provided from each source and by assessments of their reliability, accuracy and relevance. If data have been obtained from a number of sources these will also have to be interpreted to produce a derived market rate that will be used as the basis of comparison.

Using survey data

The use of market survey data as a guide to pay levels is based on judgement and compromise. Different sources may produce different indications of market rate levels. As a result a 'derived' market rate based on an assessment of the relative reliability of the data often has to be estimated. This would strike a reasonable balance between the competing merits of the different sources used. It is an intuitive process.

Questions

1. From a senior line manager: 'You keep on telling me that there is no such thing as the market rate. I find that difficult to understand especially when I know that you spend quite a lot of time and presumably money in analysing what other organizations pay. Could you explain to me what you mean?'
2. From a line manager: 'I attach a collage of job advertisements that prove my contention that we are seriously underpaying my key staff.' How do you reply?
3. At a careers evening a bright young teenager points to a claim in your company literature that your pay package is in the upper quartile range. She asks what that means and why it matters. How would you explain the term and the organization's policy to her?

49 Grade and Pay Structures

Key concepts and terms

- Broad-banded structure
- Broad-graded structure
- Career family structures
- Compa-ratio
- Differential
- Grade boundary
- Grade drift
- Grade structure
- Grade and pay structure
- Increment
- Individual job grades
- Job family
- Job family structure
- Market anchor
- Market group
- Mid-point
- Mid-point management
- Multi-graded structure
- Pay spine
- Pay structure
- Reference point
- Span
- Zone (in a broad band)

Learning outcomes

On completing this chapter you should be able to define these key concepts. You should also know about:

- Guiding principles for grade and pay structures
- Designing grade and pay structures
- Types of grade and pay structures

Introduction

Grade and pay structures provide a logically designed framework within which an organization's pay policies can be implemented. They enable the organization to determine where jobs should be placed in a hierarchy, define pay levels and the scope for pay progression, and provide the basis upon which relativities can be managed, equal pay achieved and the processes of monitoring and controlling the implementation of pay practices can take place. Grade and pay structures also enable organizations to communicate the career and pay opportunities available to employees.

Although this chapter is mainly concerned with grade and pay structures, reference will be made to the other pay arrangements of spot rates and individual job grades which, although not strictly structures, do represent methods frequently used by organizations to indicate how much a job or a person should be paid.

The chapter starts with definitions of grade and pay structures and the other pay arrangements. This is followed by a list of guiding principles for grade and pay structures and descriptions of each type of structure or arrangement, namely multi-graded, broad-graded and broad-banded structures, job and career families, pay spines, spot rates and individual job grades. The chapter is completed with a section on the design of structures.

Definitions

Grade structure

A grade structure consists of a sequence or hierarchy of grades, bands or levels into which groups of jobs that are broadly comparable in size are placed. There may be a single structure that contains grades or bands and which is defined by their number and width (width is the scope the grade or band provides for pay progression). Alternatively the structure may be divided into a number of job or career families consisting of groups of jobs where the essential nature and purpose of the work are similar but the work is carried out at different levels.

Pay structure

A pay structure defines the different levels of pay for jobs or groups of jobs by reference to their relative internal value as determined by job evaluation, to external relativities as established by market rate surveys and, sometimes, to negotiated rates for jobs. It provides scope for pay progression in accordance with performance, competence, contribution or service.

There may be a single pay structure covering the whole organization or there may be one structure for staff and another for manual workers, but this is becoming less common. There has in recent years been a trend towards 'harmonizing' terms and conditions between different groups of staff as part of a move towards 'single status'. This has been particularly evident in many public sector organizations in the UK, supported by national agreements on single status. Executive directors are sometimes treated separately where reward policy for them is decided by a remuneration committee of non-executive directors.

A grade structure becomes a pay structure when pay ranges, brackets or scales are attached to each grade, band or level. In some broad-banded structures, as described below, reference points and pay zones may be placed within the bands and these define the range of pay for jobs allocated to each band. Examples of grade and pay structures are given in Armstrong and Brown (2001).

Spot rates

A spot rate is the rate for a job or an individual that is not fitted into a grade or band in a conventional grade structure and does not allow any scope for pay progression.

Individual job grades

Individual job grades are essentially spot rates to which a defined pay range on either side of the rate has been attached to provide scope for pay progression.

Guiding principles for grade and pay structures

Grade and pay structures should:

- be appropriate to the culture, characteristics and needs of the organization and its employees;
- facilitate the management of relativities and the achievement of equity, fairness, consistency and transparency in managing gradings and pay;
- be capable of adapting to pressures arising from market rate changes and skill shortages;
- facilitate operational flexibility and continuous development;
- provide scope as required for rewarding performance, contribution and increases in skill and competence;
- clarify reward, lateral development and career opportunities;
- be constructed logically and clearly so that the basis upon which they operate can readily be communicated to employees;
- enable the organization to exercise control over the implementation of pay policies and budgets.

Types of grade and pay structure

The types of pay structures as described below are multi-graded, broad-graded, broad-banded, job family, career family and pay spine.

Multi-graded structure

A multi-graded structure, as illustrated in Figure 49.1 (sometimes called a narrow-graded structure) consists of a sequence of job grades into which jobs of broadly equivalent value are placed. There may be 10 or more grades and long-established structures, especially in the public sector, may have as many as 18 or even more grades. Grades may be defined by a bracket of job evaluation points so that any job for which the job evaluation score falls within the points bracket for a grade would be allocated to that grade. Alternatively, grades may be defined by grade definitions or profiles that provide the information required to match jobs set out under job demand factor headings (analytical matching). This information can be supplemented by reference to benchmark jobs that have been already graded as part of the structure design exercise.

'Mid-point management' techniques are often used to analyse and control pay policies by comparing actual pay with the reference point that is regarded as the policy pay level. 'Compa-ratios' can be used. These measure the relationship between actual and policy rates of pay as a percentage. If the two coincide, the compa-ratio is 100 per cent. Compa-ratio analysis can establish how pay practice (actual pay) compares with pay policy (the rate for a person who is fully qualified and competent in his or her job).

The problem with multi-graded structures is that they encourage 'grade drift', ie unjustified upgradings. This takes place because it is difficult to differentiate between successive grades even with the help of job evaluation.

Broad-graded structures

Broad-graded structures, as illustrated in Figure 49.2, have six to nine grades rather than the 10 or more grades contained in multi-graded structures. They may include 'reference points' or 'market anchors' that indicate the rate of pay for a fully competent performer in the grade and are aligned to market rates in accordance with 'market stance' policy. The grades and pay ranges are defined and managed in the same way as multi-graded structures (ie mid-point management) except that the increased width of the grades means that organizations sometimes introduce mechanisms to control progression in the grade so that staff do not inevitably reach its upper pay limit. The mechanisms available consist of:

- Reference point control – scope is provided for progression according to competence by increments to the reference point. Thereafter, individuals may earn cash bonuses for high achievement that may be consolidated up to the maximum pay for the grade if high achievement levels are sustained.

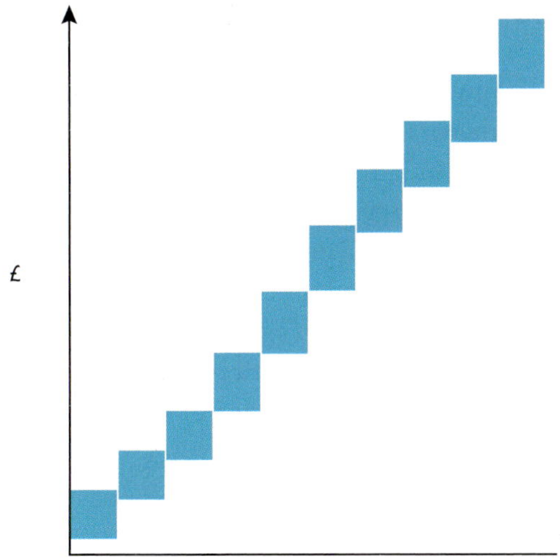

Figure 49.1 A multi-graded structure

- Threshold control – a point is defined in the pay range beyond which pay cannot increase unless individuals achieve a defined level of competence and achievement.
- Segment or zone control – an extension of threshold control that involves dividing the grade into a number, often three, segments or zones.

Broad-graded structures are used to overcome or at least alleviate the grade drift problem endemic in multi-graded structures. If the grades are defined, it is easier to differentiate them, and matching (comparing role profiles with grade definitions or profiles to find the best fit) becomes more accurate. But it may be difficult to control progression and this would increase the costs of operating them, although these costs could be offset by better control of grade drift.

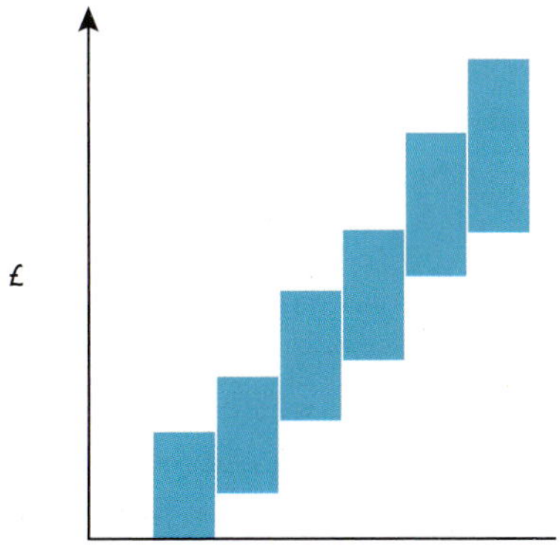

Figure 49.2 A board-graded structure

Broad-banded structures

Broad-banded structures compress multi-graded structures into four or five 'bands', as illustrated in Figure 49.3. The process of developing broad-banded structures is called 'broad-banding'. In its original version, a broad-banded structure contained no more than five bands, each with, typically, a span of 70 to 100 per cent. Bands were unstructured and pay was managed much more flexibly than in a conventional graded structure (no limits may be defined for progression that depended on competence and the assumption of wider role responsibilities) and much more attention was paid to market rates, which governed what were in effect the spot rates for jobs within bands. Analytical job evaluation was often felt to be unnecessary because of the ease with which jobs could be allocated to one of a small number of bands.

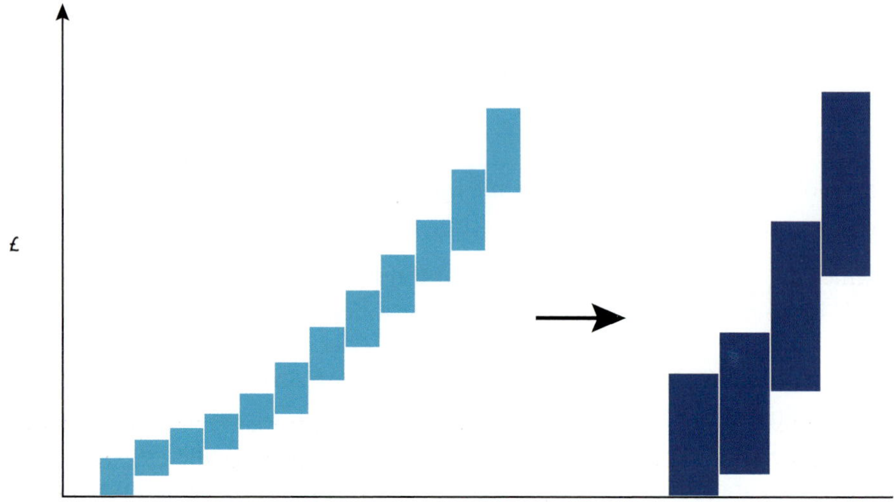

Figure 49.3 Narrow- and broad-banded structures

The difference between this original concept of broad bands and broad grades is that the latter still generally adopt a fairly conventional approach to pay management by the use of analytical job evaluation, mid-point management and compa-ratio analysis techniques. Structures with six or seven grades are sometimes described as broad-banded even when their characteristics are typical of broad grades.

However, structure often crept in to broad bands. It started with reference points aligned to market rates around which similar roles could be clustered. These were then extended into zones for individual jobs or groups of jobs, which placed limits on pay progression, as illustrated in Figure 49.4. Job evaluation was increasingly used to define the boundaries of the band and to size jobs as a basis for deciding where reference points should be placed in conjunction with market pricing. The original concept of broad-banding was therefore eroded as more structure was introduced and job evaluation became more prominent to define the structure and meet equal pay requirements. Zones within broad bands began to look rather like conventional grades.

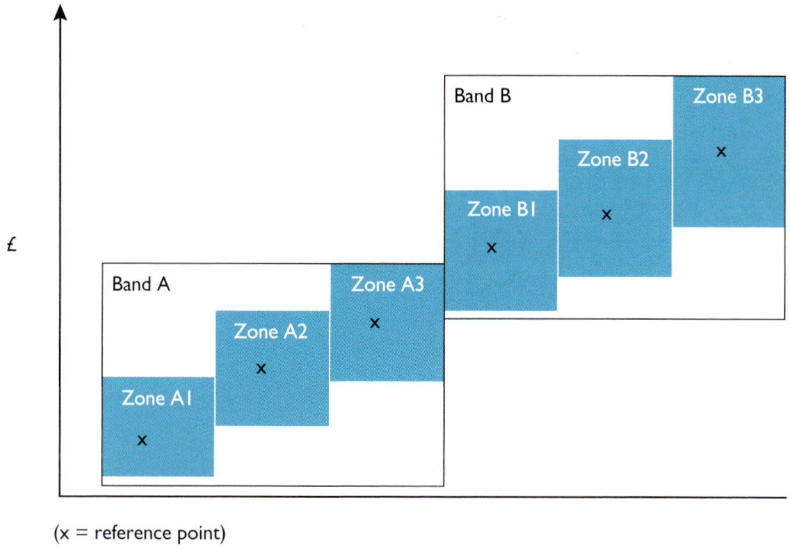

Figure 49.4 A broad-banded structure with zones

Job family structures

Job families consist of jobs in a function or occupation such as marketing, operations, finance, IT, HR, administration or support services that are related through the activities carried out and the basic knowledge and skills required, but in which the levels of responsibility, knowledge, skill or competence levels required differ. In a job family structure, as shown in Figure 49.5, different job families are identified and the successive levels in each family are defined by reference to the key activities carried out and the knowledge, skills or competences required to perform them effectively. They therefore define career paths – what people have to know and be able to do to advance their career within a family and to develop career opportunities in other families. Typically, job families have between six and eight levels as in broad-graded structures. Some families may have more levels than others.

In contrast to career family structures (see below) each family in a job family structure may in effect have its own pay structure that takes account of different levels of market rates between families (this is sometimes called a 'market group'). The level or grade structures may also differ between families to reflect any special family role characteristics. Because the size of jobs and rates of pay can vary between the same levels in different job families, there may be no read-across between them unless use is made of analytical job evaluation.

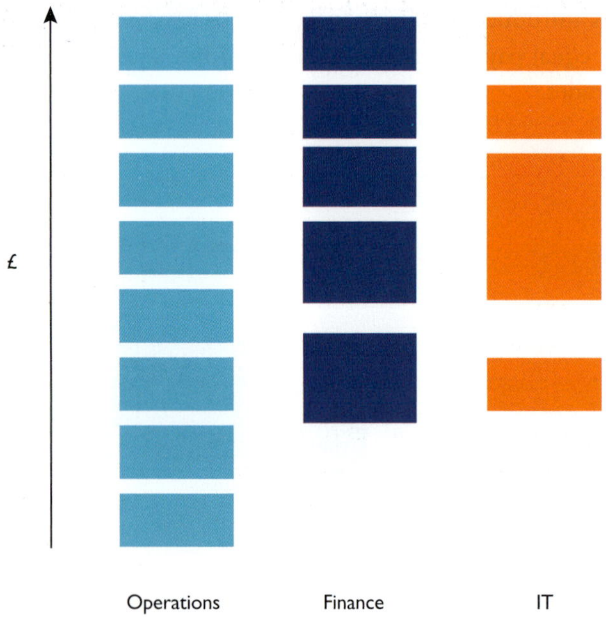

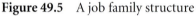

Figure 49.5 A job family structure

Career family structures

Career family structures, as shown in Figure 49.6, resemble job family structures in that there are a number of different 'families'. The difference is that in a career family, jobs in the corresponding levels across each of the career families are within the same size range and, if an analytical job evaluation scheme is used, this is defined by the same range of scores. Similarly, the pay ranges in corresponding levels across the career families are the same, although to deal with market pressures, market supplements or premiums may be added for individual jobs to the normal pay range for their level. In effect, a career structure is a single-graded structure in which each grade has been divided into families.

Career family structures focus on career mapping and career development as part of an integrated approach to human resource management. This is as important a feature of career families as the pay structure element, possibly even more so.

Pay spines

Pay spines are found in the public sector or in agencies and charities that have adopted a public sector approach to reward management. As illustrated in Figure 49.7, they consist of a series of incremental 'pay points' extending from the lowest to the highest paid jobs covered by the structure. Typically, pay spine increments are between 2.5 and 3 per cent. They may be standardized from the top to the bottom of the spine, or the increments may vary at different levels,

£

Operations	Finance	IT
Level 1	Level 1	Level 1
Level 2	Level 2	Level 2
Level 3	Level 3	Level 3
Level 4	Level 4	Level 4
Level 5	Level 5	Level 5
Level 6	Level 6	Level 6

job evaluation points

Figure 49.6 A career family structure

sometimes widening towards the top. Job grades are aligned to the pay spine and the pay ranges for the grades are defined by the relevant scale of pay points. The width of grades can vary and job families may have different pay spines. Progression through a grade is based on service, although an increasing number of organizations provide scope for accelerating increments or providing additional increments above the top of the scale for the grade to reward merit.

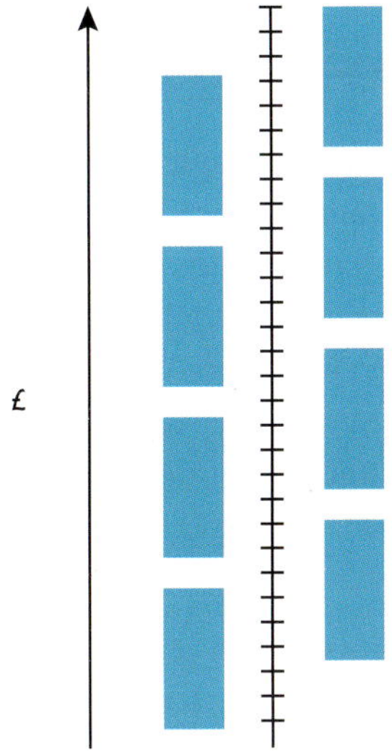

Figure 49.7 A pay spine

Spot rates

Some organizations do not have a graded structure at all for any jobs or for certain jobs such as directors. Instead they use 'spot rates'. They may also be called the 'rate for the job', more typically for manual jobs where there is a defined skilled or semi-skilled market rate that may be negotiated with a trade union. Spot rates are quite often used in retail firms for customer service staff.

Spot rates are sometimes attached to a person rather than a job. Unless they are negotiated, rates of pay and therefore relativities are governed by market rates and managerial judgement. Spot rates are not located within grades and there is no defined scope for progression while on the spot rate. There may, however, be scope for moving on to higher spot rates as skill, competence or contribution increases. Job holders may be eligible for incentive bonuses on top of the spot rate.

Spot rates may be used where there is a very simple hierarchy of jobs, as in some manufacturing and retailing companies. They may be adopted by organizations that want the maximum amount of scope to pay what they like. They often exist in small or start-up organizations that do not want to be constrained by a formal grade structure and prefer to retain the maximum amount of flexibility. But they can result in serious inequities that may be difficult to justify.

Individual job grades

Individual job grades are, in effect, spot rates to which a defined pay range of, say, 20 per cent on either side of the rate has been attached to provide scope for pay progression based on performance, competence or contribution. Again, the midpoint of the range is fixed by reference to job evaluation and market rate comparisons.

Individual grades are attached to jobs not people, but there may be more flexibility for movement between grades than in a conventional grade structure. This can arise when people have expanded their role and it is considered that this growth in the level of responsibility needs to be recognized without having to upgrade the job. Individual job grades may be restricted to certain jobs, for example more senior managers, where flexibility in fixing and increasing rates of pay is felt to be desirable. They provide for greater flexibility than more conventional structures but can be difficult to manage and justify and can result in pay inequities. The 'zones' that are often established in broad-banded structures have some of the characteristics of individual job grades.

A summary of the features of the different pay structures, their advantages and disadvantages and when they may be appropriate is given in Table 49.1.

Incidence of different types of structure

The incidence of different types of structure and pay arrangements as established by the 2008 e-reward survey is shown in Figure 49.8. Broad-graded structures are now the most popular. They are replacing narrow-graded structures rather than broad-banding, which is relatively little used. There are a fair number of job family structures but few career family structures.

Table 49.1 Summary analysis of different grade and pay structures

Type	Features	Advantages	Disadvantages	When appropriate
Multi-graded	• A sequence of job grades – 10 or more • Narrow pay ranges, eg 20–40% • Progression usually linked to performance	• Clearly indicate pay relativities • Facilitate control • Easy to understand	• Create hierarchical rigidity • Prone to grade drift • Inappropriate in a de-layered organization	• In a large bureaucratic organization with well defined hierarchies • When close and rigid control is required • When some but not too much scope for pay progression related to performance or contribution is wanted
Broad-graded	• A sequence of between 6 and 9 grades • Fairly broad pay ranges, eg 40–50% • Progression linked to contribution and may be controlled by thresholds or zones	• As for narrow-graded structures but in addition: – the broader grades can be defined more clearly – better control can be exercised over grade drift	• Too much scope for pay progression • Control mechanisms can be provided but they can be difficult to manage • May be costly	• Desirable to define and differentiate grades more accurately as an aid to better precision when grading jobs • Grade drift problems exist • More scope wanted to reward contribution
Broad-banded	• A series of, often, 5 or 6 'broad' bands • Wide pay bands – typically between 50% and 80% • Progression linked to contribution and competence	• More flexible • Reward lateral development and growth in competence • Fit new style organizations	• Create unrealistic expectations of scope for pay rises • Seem to restrict scope for promotion • Difficult to understand • Equal pay problems	• In de-layered, process-based, flexible organizations • Where more flexibility in pay determination is wanted • Where the focus is on continuous improvement and lateral development

Table 49.1 *continued*

Type	Features	Advantages	Disadvantages	When appropriate
Job family	• Separate grade and pay structures for job families containing similar jobs • Progression linked to competence and/or contribution	• Can appear to be divisive • May inhibit lateral career development • May be difficult to maintain internal equity between job families	• Facilitate pay differentiation between market groups • Define career paths against clear criteria	• When there are distinct market groups which need to be rewarded differentially • Where there are distinct groups of jobs in families
Pay spine	• A series of incremental pay points covering all jobs • Grades may be superimposed • Progression linked to service	• Easy to manage • Pay progression not based on managerial judgement	• No scope for differentiating rewards according to performance • May be costly as staff drift up the spine	• In a public sector or voluntary organization where this is the traditional approach and it therefore fits the culture • Where it is believed to be impossible to measure differential levels of performance fairly and consistently

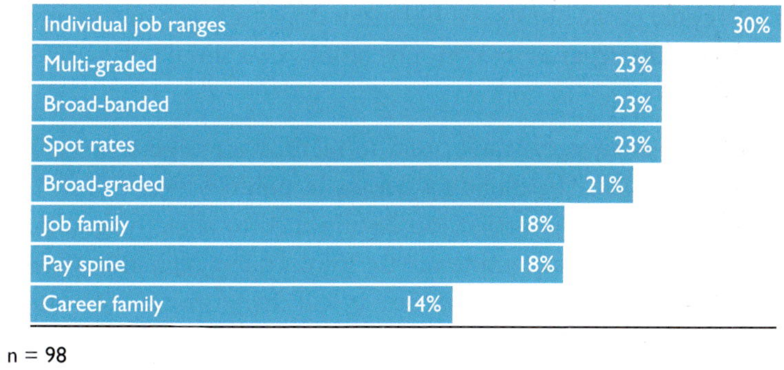

Figure 49.8 Incidence of grade and pay structures

Designing grade and pay structures

There is a choice of structure, as shown in Table 49.1, and whichever structure is selected, there will be a number of design options. The first decision to make is where to place grade boundaries which, as described below, is usually informed by a job evaluation exercise. Decisions on grade boundaries will be influenced by considerations affecting the number and width of grades. Further options exist on the pay structure concerning the differentials between grades, the degree to which there should be overlap between grades, if any, and the method of pay progression within grades. In broad-banded structures there is also choice on the infrastructure (the use of reference points or zones), and in career or job family structures there are options concerning the number of families, the composition of families and the basis upon which levels should be defined.

Deciding on grade boundaries

A grade boundary is the point between one grade and the next higher or lower grade, which is defined as a rate of pay and a points score if a points evaluation scheme is used to determine grades. The boundaries therefore define the span of a grade in those terms. An analytical job evaluation exercise will produce a rank order of jobs according to their job evaluation scores. A decision then has to be made on where the boundaries that will define grades should be placed in the rank order. So far as possible, boundaries should divide groups or clusters of jobs that are significantly different in size so that all the jobs placed in a grade are clearly smaller than the jobs in the next higher grade and larger than the jobs placed in the next lower grade.

Fixing grade boundaries is one of the most critical aspects of grade structure design following an analytical job evaluation exercise. It requires judgement – the process is not scientific and it is rare to find a situation where there is one right and obvious answer. In theory, grade boundaries could be determined by deciding on the number of grades in advance and then dividing the rank order into equal parts. But this would mean drawing grade boundary lines arbitrarily and the result could be the separation of groups of jobs that should properly be placed in the same grade.

The best approach is to analyse the rank order to identify any significant gaps in the points scores between adjacent jobs. These natural breaks in points scores will then constitute the boundaries between clusters of jobs that can be allocated to adjacent grades. A distinct gap between the highest rated job in one grade and the lowest rated job in the grade above will help to justify the allocation of jobs between grades. It will therefore reduce boundary problems leading to dissatisfaction with gradings when the distinction is less well defined. Provisionally, it may be decided in advance when designing a conventional graded structure that a certain number of grades is required, but the gap analysis will confirm the number of grades that is appropriate, taking into account the natural divisions between jobs in the rank order. However, the existence of a number of natural breaks cannot be guaranteed, which means that judgement has to be exercised as to where boundaries should be drawn when the scores between adjacent jobs are close. In cases where there are no obvious natural breaks, the guidelines that should be considered when deciding on boundaries are as follows.

Guidelines for deciding on grade boundaries

- Jobs with common features as indicated by the job evaluation factors are grouped together so that a distinction can be made between the characteristics of the jobs in different grades – it should be possible to demonstrate that the jobs grouped into one grade resemble each other more than they resemble jobs placed in adjacent grades.
- The grade hierarchy should take account of the organizational hierarchy, ie jobs in which the job holder reports to a higher level job holder should be placed in a lower grade, although this principle should not be followed slavishly when an organization is over-hierarchical with, perhaps, a series of one-over-one reporting relationships.
- The boundaries should not be placed between jobs mainly carried out by men and jobs mainly carried out by women.
- The boundaries should ideally not be placed immediately above jobs in which large numbers of people are employed.
- The grade width in terms of job evaluation points should represent a significant step in demand as indicated by the job evaluation scheme.

Number of grades, levels or bands

The considerations to be taken into account when deciding on the number of grades, levels or bands are given below.

The considerations to be taken into account when deciding on the number of grades

- The range and types of roles to be covered by the structure.
- The range of pay and job evaluation points scores to be accommodated.
- The number of levels in the organizational hierarchy (this will be an important factor in a broad-banded structure).
- Decisions on where grade boundaries should be placed following a job evaluation exercise that has produced a ranked order of jobs – this might identify the existence of clearly defined clusters of jobs at the various levels in the hierarchy between which there are significant differences in job size.
- The fact that within a given range of pay and responsibility, the greater the number of grades the smaller their width, and vice versa – this is associated with views on what is regarded as the desirable width of a range, taking into account the scope for progression, the size of increments in a pay spine and equal pay issues.
- The problem of 'grade drift' (unjustified upgradings in response to pressure, lack of promotion opportunities or because job evaluation has been applied laxly), which can be increased if there are too many narrow grades.

Width of grades or pay ranges

The factors affecting decisions on the width of grades or pay ranges are as follows.

The factors affecting decisions on the width of grades or bands

- Views on the scope that should be allowed for performance, contribution or career progression within grades.
- Equal pay considerations – wide grades, especially extended incremental scales, are a major cause of pay gaps between men and women simply because women,

who are more likely to have career breaks than men, may not have the same opportunity as men to progress to the upper regions of the range; male jobs may therefore cluster towards the top of the range while women's may cluster towards the bottom.

- Decisions on the number of grades – the greater the number the smaller the width.
- Decisions on the value of increments in a pay spine – if it is believed that the number of increments should be restricted, for equal pay or other reasons, but that the number of grades should also be limited, then it is necessary to increase the value of the increments.
- In a broad-banded structure, the range of market rates and job evaluation scores covering the jobs allocated to the band.

Differentials between pay ranges

Differentials between pay ranges should provide scope to recognize increases in job size between successive grades. If differentials are too close – less than 10 per cent – many jobs become borderline cases, which can result in a proliferation of appeals and arguments about grading. Large differentials below senior management level of more than 25 per cent can create problems for marginal or borderline cases because of the amount at stake. Experience has shown that in most organizations with conventional grade structures a differential of between 16 and 20 per cent is appropriate except, perhaps, at the highest levels.

Pay range overlap

There is a choice on whether or not pay ranges should overlap and, if so, by how much. The amount of overlap, if any, is a function of range width and differentials. Large overlaps of more than 10 per cent can create equal pay problems where, as is quite common, men are clustered at the top of their grades and women are more likely to be found at the lower end.

Pay progression

There is a choice of methods of pay progression between the fixed service-related increments common in the public sector, and the other forms of contingent pay, namely performance, competency or contribution-related, as described in Chapter 50.

The grade and pay structure design process

An analytical job evaluation scheme is usually the basis for designing a graded structure and it can be used in the initial stages of designing a broad-banded or career/job family structure. In the case of graded structures, decisions on the number and width of grades are generally based on an analysis of the rank order of scores produced by job evaluation.

This approach is used less often in the design of broad-banded or career/job family structures where the most common method is to make a provisional advance decision on the number of bands or career family levels, and then position roles in bands (often by reference to market rates), or allocate roles into levels by an 'analytical job matching' process, as described in Chapter 47. Job evaluation may only be used at a later stage to validate the positioning of roles in bands or the allocation of jobs to family levels, check on relativities and, sometimes, define the bands or levels in job evaluation score terms. The initial decision on the number of bands or levels and their definition may, however, be changed in the light of the outcome of the allocation, matching and evaluation processes.

More rarely, the grade and pay structure design is conducted by means of a non-analytical job evaluation schemes (see Chapter 47), which defines a number of single grades. Jobs are then slotted into the grades by reference to the grade definitions. The basic sequence of steps for designing a grade and pay structure is illustrated in Figure 49.9. Note the emphasis on communication and involvement at all stages.

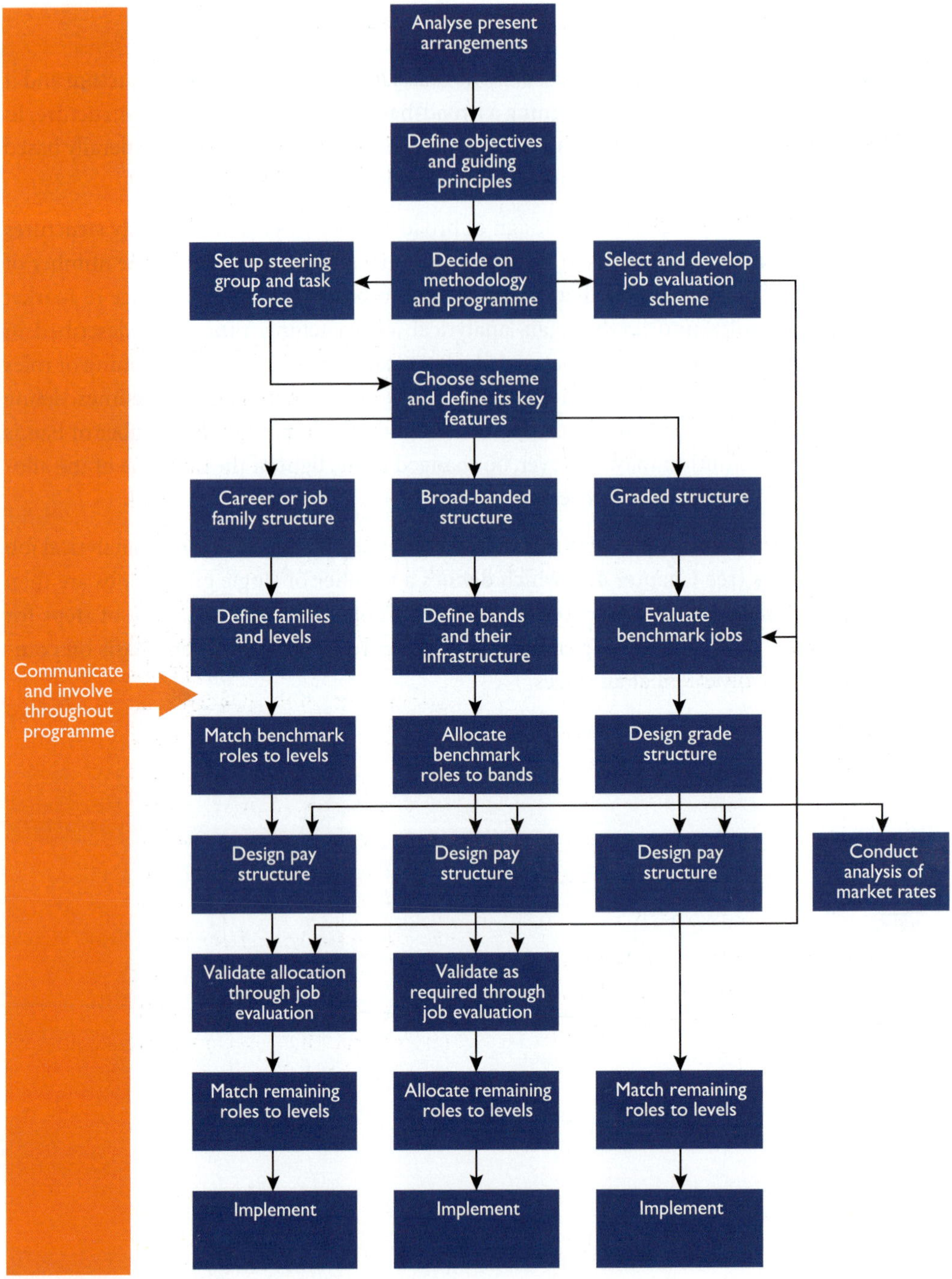

Figure 49.9 Flow chart: design of a new grade and pay structure

Grade and pay structures – key learning points

Guiding principles for grade and pay structures

Grade and pay structures should:

- be appropriate to the culture, characteristics and needs of the organization and its employees;
- facilitate the management of relativities and the achievement of equity, fairness, consistency and transparency in managing gradings and pay;
- be capable of adapting to pressures arising from market rate changes and skill shortages;
- facilitate operational flexibility and continuous development;
- provide scope as required for rewarding performance, contribution and increases in skill and competence;
- clarify reward, lateral development and career opportunities;
- be constructed logically and clearly so that the basis upon which they operate can readily be communicated to employees;
- enable the organization to exercise control over the implementation of pay policies and budgets.

Types of grade and pay structures

Summarized in Table 49.1.

Designing grade and pay structures

There is a choice of structure, as shown in Table 49.1, and whichever structure is selected, there will be a number of design options. The first decision to make is where to place grade boundaries, which is usually informed by a job evaluation exercise. Decisions on grade boundaries will be influenced by considerations affecting the number and width of grades. Further options exist on the pay structure concerning the differentials between grades, the degree to which there should be overlap between grades, if any, and the method of pay progression within grades. In broad-banded structures there is also choice on the infrastructure (the use of reference points or zones), and in career or job family structures there are options concerning the number of families, the composition of families and the basis upon which levels should be defined.

Questions

1. From the senior representative of your staff union: 'We are very concerned about this proposal that the company should introduce a broad-banded pay structure. We

Questions (continued)

understand that such structures are governed mainly by market rate comparisons that lead to internal inequities and discrimination against women. We would like to hear what you have to say about this.' How do you reply?

2. From the HR director to the head of reward: 'It appears from your statistics that a lot of appeals against grading using our somewhat outdated job evaluation scheme are being successful. This must be leading to grade drift. What can we do about it?'
3. From the head of learning and development to the head of reward: 'I have read recently that there are such things as career family structures that can provide the basis for career planning and development. What are the benefits we may gain from moving to that type of structure from our existing graded structure? Are there any drawbacks?'

Reference

Armstrong, M and Brown, D (2001) *Pay: The New Dimensions*, CIPD, London

e-reward (2008) *Survey of Grade and Pay Structures*, e-reward.co.uk, Stockport

50 Contingent Pay

Key concepts and terms

- Bonus
- Contingent pay
- Incentives
- Rewards
- Variable pay
- Competency-related pay
- Contribution-related pay
- Performance-related pay
- Skills-based pay

Learning outcomes

On completing this chapter you should be able to define these key concepts. You should also know about:

- The basis of contingent pay
- Arguments for contingent pay
- Alternatives to contingent pay
- Types of individual contingent pay
- Developing and implementing individual contingent pay
- Bonus schemes
- Organization-wide bonus schemes
- Contingent pay as a motivator
- Argument against contingent pay
- Criteria for success
- Readiness for individual contingent pay
- Service-related pay
- Team pay
- Choice of approach

Introduction

The term 'contingent pay' is used in this chapter to describe any formal pay scheme that provides for payments on top of the base rate, which are linked to the performance, competency, contribution or skill of people. Contingent pay can apply to individuals (individual contingent pay) or teams, or it can operate on an organization-wide basis. It is either consolidated in the base rate so that pay progresses within a pay range or it is paid as a non-consolidated cash bonus (the latter arrangement is called 'variable pay').

Pay can be related to service. This is dealt with in this chapter, but it is not regarded as contingent pay in the sense defined above as it does not relate to performance, contribution, competency or skill. The comments made about contingent pay as a motivator and the advantages and disadvantages of contingent pay do not therefore apply to pay related to service.

Contingent pay is concerned with answering the two fundamental reward management questions: what do we value? What are we prepared to pay for? Contingent pay schemes are based on measurements or assessments. These may be expressed as ratings that are converted by means of a formula to a payment. Alternatively, there may be no formal ratings and pay decisions are based on broad assessments rather than a formula.

This chapter examines contingent pay as a motivator, its advantages and disadvantages, and criteria for success. It then describes the different forms of contingent pay and how to choose and develop them. Incentives for sales staff and manual workers are covered in Chapter 51.

Contingent pay as a motivator

Many people see pay related to performance, competency, contribution or skill as the best way to motivate people. But it is simplistic to assume that it is only the extrinsic motivators in the form of pay that create long-term motivation. The total reward concept, as explained in Chapter 46, emphasizes the importance of non-financial rewards as an integral part of a complete package. The intrinsic motivators that can arise from the work itself and the working environment may have a deeper and longer-lasting effect.

Incentives and rewards

When considering contingent pay as a motivator, a distinction should be made between financial incentives and rewards.

Financial incentives are designed to provide direct motivation. They tell people how much money they will get in the future if they perform well – 'Do this and you will get that.' A shop floor payment-by-results scheme or a sales representative's commission system are examples of financial incentives.

Financial rewards act as indirect motivators because they provide a tangible means of recognizing achievements, as long as people expect that what they do in the future will produce something worthwhile, as expectancy theory suggests. Rewards can be retrospective – 'You have achieved this, therefore we will pay you that.' But rewards can also be prospective: 'We will pay you more now because we believe you have reached a level of competency that will produce high levels of performance in the future.'

Arguments for and against contingent pay

Arguments for

The most powerful argument for contingent pay is that those who contribute more should be paid more. It is right and proper to recognize achievement with a financial and therefore tangible reward. This is preferable to paying people just for 'being there', as happens in a service-related system. Other typical arguments in favour of using contingent pay are set out below.

SOURCE REVIEW

Reasons in order of importance for using contingent pay given by respondents to the e-reward 2004 survey

1. To recognize and reward better performance.
2. To attract and retain high quality people.
3. To improve organizational performance.
4. To focus attention on key results and values.
5. To deliver a message about the importance of performance.
6. To motivate people.
7. To influence behaviour.
8. To support cultural change.

Arguments against

The main arguments against individual contingent pay are that:

- the extent to which contingent pay schemes motivate is questionable – the amounts available for distribution are usually so small that they cannot act as an incentive;
- the requirements for success as set out below are exacting and difficult to achieve;

- money by itself will not result in sustained motivation – as Kohn (1993) points out, money rarely acts in a crude, behaviourist, Pavlov's dog manner;
- people react in widely different ways to any form of motivation – it cannot be assumed that money will motivate all people equally, yet that is the premise on which contribution pay schemes are based;
- financial rewards may possibly motivate those who receive them but they can demotivate those that don't, and the numbers who are demotivated could be much higher than those who are motivated;
- contingent pay schemes can create more dissatisfaction than satisfaction if they are perceived to be unfair, inadequate or badly managed and, as explained below, they can be difficult to manage well;
- contingent pay schemes depend on the existence of accurate and reliable methods of measuring performance, competency, contribution or skill, which might not exist;
- contingent pay decisions depend on the judgement of managers which, in the absence of reliable criteria, could be partial, prejudiced, inconsistent or ill-informed;
- the concept of contingent pay is based on the assumption that performance is completely under the control of individuals when in fact it is affected by the system in which they work;
- contingent pay, especially performance-related pay schemes, can militate against quality and teamwork.

A number of commentators have argued forcibly against contingent pay, especially in the form of performance-related pay. Two of the most prominent have been Alfie Kohn and Jeffrey Pfeffer.

Kohn (1993) contended that financial rewards 'do not create lasting satisfaction; they merely and temporarily change what we do... rewards, like punishment, may actually undermine the intrinsic motivation that results in optimal performance'. Pfeffer (1998b) listed in the *Harvard Business Review* his fifth and sixth myths of pay as follows:

> Myth # 5: Individual incentive pay improves performance. Reality: Individual incentive pay, in reality, undermines performance of both the individual and the organization. Many studies strongly suggest that this form of reward undermines teamwork, encourages a short-term focus, and leads people to believe that pay is not related to performance at all but to having the 'right' relationships and an ingratiating personality.
>
> Myth # 6: People work for money. Reality: People do work for money – but they work even more for meaning in their lives. In fact, they work to have fun. Companies that ignore this fact are essentially bribing their employees and will pay the price in a lack of loyalty and commitment.

Another powerful argument against contingent pay is that it has proved difficult to manage. Organizations, including the Civil Service, rushed into performance-related pay (PRP) in the 1980s without really understanding how to make it work. Inevitably problems of implementation arose. Studies such as those conducted by Bowey (1982), Kessler and Purcell (1992), Marsden and Richardson (1994) and Thompson (1992a, 1992b) have all revealed these difficulties. Failures are usually rooted in implementation and operating processes, especially those concerned with performance management, the need for effective communication and involvement, and line management capability.

The last factor is crucial. The success of contingent pay rests largely in the hands of line managers. They have to believe in it as something that will help them as well as the organization. They must also be good at practising the crucial skills of agreeing targets, measuring performance fairly and consistently, and providing feedback to their staff on the outcome of performance management and its impact on pay. Line managers can make or break contingent pay schemes.

Wright (1991) has summed it all up: 'Even the most ardent supporters of performance-related pay recognize that it is difficult to manage well,' and Oliver (1996) made the point that 'performance pay is beautiful in theory but difficult in practice'.

Conclusions on the effectiveness of contingent pay

A study by Brown and Armstrong (1999) into the effectiveness of contingent pay as revealed by a number of research projects produced two overall conclusions: 1) contingent pay cannot be endorsed or rejected universally as a principle, and 2) no type of contingent pay is universally successful or unsuccessful. They concluded their analysis of the research findings by stating that 'the research does show that the effectiveness of pay-for-performance schemes is highly context and situation-specific; and it has highlighted the practical problems which many companies have experienced with these schemes'.

Alternatives to contingent pay

The arguments against contribution pay set out above convince many people that it is unsatisfactory; but what is the alternative? One answer is to rely more on non-financial motivators, but it is still necessary to consider what should be done about pay. The reaction in the 1990s to the adverse criticisms of PRP was to develop the concept of competency-related pay, which fitted in well with the emphasis on competencies. This approach, as described later, in theory overcame some of the cruder features of PRP but still created a number of practical difficulties and has never really taken off. In the late 1990s the idea of contribution-related pay emerged, as advocated by Brown and Armstrong (1999). This combines the output-driven focus of PRP with the input (competency) oriented focus of competency-related pay and has proved to be much more appealing than either performance- or competence-related pay.

However, many people still have reservations about this approach from the viewpoint of achieving the fair and consistent measurement of contribution. So what are the alternatives? Team pay is often advocated because it removes the individualistic aspect of PRP and accords with the belief in the importance of teamwork, but although team pay is attractive, it is often difficult to apply and it still relies on performance measurement.

The traditional alternative is service-related pay, as described later in this chapter. This certainly treats everyone equally (and therefore appeals to trade unions) but pays people simply for being there, and this could be regarded as inequitable in that rewards take no account of relative levels of contribution. The other common alternative is a spot rate system, as described in Chapter 49. Most people, though, want and expect a range of base pay progression, however that is determined, and spot rates are not much used in larger organizations except for senior managers, shop floor and sales staff.

Criteria for success

In spite of the powerful arguments against contingent pay, many organizations and the people who work in them feel that it is right and proper that people who contribute more should be paid more. But to be 'right and proper' the process for deciding on who gets contingent pay when it is paid to individuals and teams and how much they get should be fair, consistent and in accordance with the principles of distributive justice, ie that people feel that they have been treated justly, that rewards have been distributed in accordance with their contribution, that they receive what was promised to them and they get what they need.

These are exacting criteria. If the objective is to make contingent pay an incentive, the criteria are even more exacting. These are as follows:

1. Individuals should have a clear line of sight between what they do and what they will get for doing it (see Figure 50.1). This expresses the essence of expectancy theory: that motivation only takes place when people expect that their effort and contribution will be rewarded. The reward should be clearly and closely linked to accomplishment or effort – people know what they will get if they achieve defined and agreed targets or standards and can track their performance against them.
2. Rewards are worth having.
3. Fair and consistent means are available for measuring or assessing performance, competence, contribution or skill.
4. People must be able to influence their performance by changing their behaviour and developing their competences and skills.
5. The reward should follow as closely as possible the accomplishment that generated it.

Figure 50.1 Line of sight model

These are ideal requirements and few schemes meet them in full. That is why individual or team contingent pay arrangements as described below can often promise more than they deliver.

Performance-related pay

Methods of operating performance-related pay (PRP) vary considerably, but its typical features are summarized in Figure 50.2 and described below.

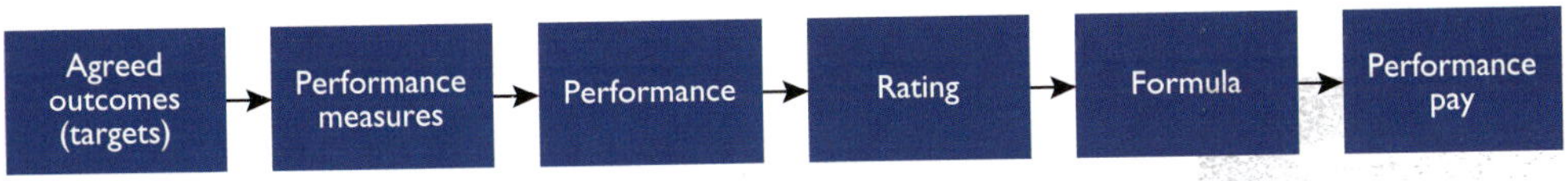

Figure 50.2 Performance-related pay

Basis of scheme

Pay increases are related to the achievement of agreed results defined as targets or outcomes. Scope is provided for consolidated pay progression within pay brackets attached to grades or levels in a graded or career family structure, or zones in a broad-banded structure. Such increases are permanent – they are seldom if ever withdrawn. Alternatively or additionally, high levels of performance or special achievements may be rewarded by cash bonuses that are not consolidated and have to be re-earned. Individuals may be eligible for such bonuses when they have reached the top of the pay bracket for their grade, or when they are assessed as being fully competent, having completely progressed along their learning curve. The rate of pay for someone who reaches the required level of competence can be aligned to market rates according to the organization's pay policy.

Pay progression

The rate and limits of progression through pay ranges or brackets are typically but not inevitably determined by performance ratings that are often made at the time of the performance management review but may be made separately in a special pay review. The e-reward 2004 survey found that the average increase was 3.9 per cent.

A formula in the shape of a pay matrix is often used to decide on the size of increases. This indicates the percentage increase payable for different performance ratings according to the position of the individual's pay in the pay range (see also Chapter 53).

Pay progression in a graded structure is typically planned to decelerate through the grade for two reasons. First, it is argued in line with learning curve theory, that pay increases should be higher during the earlier period in a job when learning is at its highest rate. Second, it may be assumed that the central or reference point in a grade represents the market value of fully competent people. According to the pay policy of the organization, this may be at or higher than the median. Especially in the latter case, it may be believed that employees should progress quite quickly to that level but, beyond it, they are already being paid well and their pay need not increase so rapidly. This notion may be reasonable, but it can be difficult to explain to someone why they get smaller percentage increases when they are performing well at the upper end of their scale.

Some organizations do not base PRP increases on formal ratings and instead rely on a general assessment of how much the pay of individuals should increase by reference to performance, potential, the pay levels of their peers and their 'market worth' (the rate of pay it is believed they could earn elsewhere).

Conclusions on PRP

PRP has all the advantages and disadvantages listed for contingent pay. Many people feel the latter outweigh the former. It has attracted a lot of adverse comment, primarily because of the difficulties organizations have met in managing it. Contribution-related pay schemes are becoming more popular.

Competency-related pay

The main features of competency-related pay schemes are illustrated in Figure 50.3 and described below.

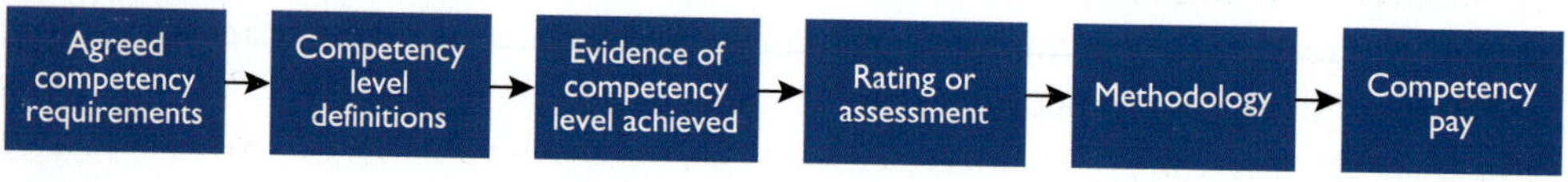

Figure 50.3 Competency-related pay

Basis of scheme

People receive financial rewards in the shape of increases to their base pay by reference to the level of competence they demonstrate in carrying out their roles. It is a method of paying people for the ability to perform now and in the future. As in the case of PRP, scope is provided for consolidated pay progression within pay brackets attached to grades or levels in a narrow graded or career family structure, or zones in a broad-banded structure (competency pay is often regarded as a feature of such structures).

Pay progression

The rate and limits of progression through the pay brackets can be based on ratings of competency using a pay matrix, but they may be governed by more general assessments of competency development.

Conclusions on competency-related pay

Competency-related pay is attractive in theory because it can be part of an integrated competency-based approach to HRM. However, the idea of competency-related pay raises two questions. The fundamental question is, 'What are we paying for?' Are we paying for competencies, ie how people behave, or competences, ie what people have to know and be able to do to perform well? If we are rewarding good behaviour then a number of difficulties arise. It has been suggested by Sparrow (1996) that these include the performance criteria on which competencies are based, the complex nature of what is being measured, the relevance of the results to the organization, and the problem of measurement. He concluded that 'we should avoid over-egging our ability to test, measure and reward competencies'.

Other fundamental objections to the behavioural approach have been raised by Lawler (1993). He expresses concern about schemes that pay for an individual's personality traits and emphasizes that such plans work best 'when they are tied to the ability of an individual to perform a particular task and when there are valid measures available of how well an individual can perform a task'. He also points out that 'generic competencies are not only hard to measure, they are not necessarily related to successful task performance in a particular work assignment or work role'.

This raises the second question: 'Are we paying for the possession of competence or the use of competencies?' Clearly it must be the latter. But we can only assess the effective use of competence by reference to performance. The focus is therefore on results and if that is the case, competency-related pay begins to look suspiciously like performance-related pay. It can be said that the difference between the two in these circumstances is all 'smoke and mirrors'. Competency-related pay could be regarded as a more acceptable name for PRP. Competency-related pay sounds like a good idea but it has never been taken up to a great extent because of the problems mentioned above.

Contribution-related pay

Contribution-related pay, as modelled in Figures 50.4 and 50.5, is a process for making pay decisions based on assessments of both the outcomes of the work carried out by individuals and the inputs in terms of levels of competency that have influenced these outcomes. In other words, it pays not only for what they do but how they do it. Contribution-related pay focuses on what people in organizations are there to do, that is, to contribute by their skill and efforts to the achievement of the purpose of their organization or team.

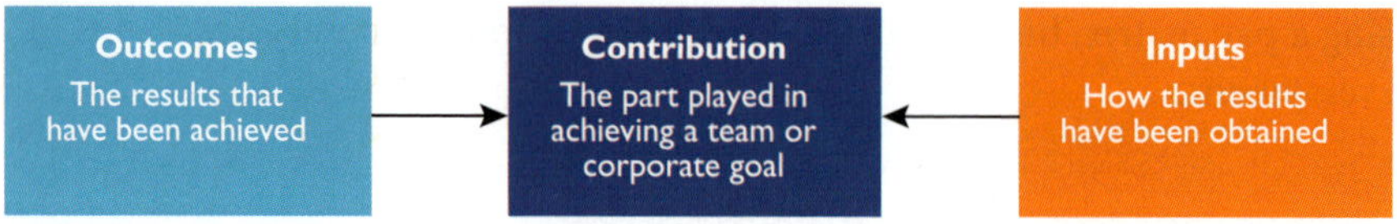

Figure 50.4 Contribution pay model (1)

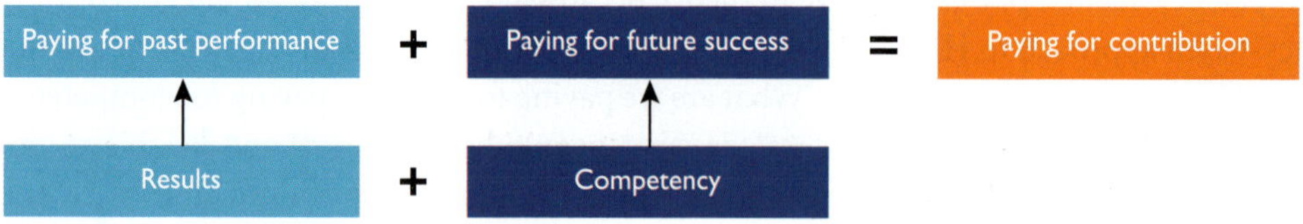

Figure 50.5 Contribution pay model (2)

The case for contribution-related pay was made by Brown and Armstrong (1999) as follows.

SOURCE REVIEW

The case for contribution-related pay, Brown and Armstrong (1999)

Contribution captures the full scope of what people do, the level of skill and competence they apply and the results they achieve, which all contribute to the organization achieving its long-term goals. Contribution pay works by applying the mixed model of performance management: assessing inputs and outputs and coming to a conclusion on the level of pay for people in their roles and their work; both to the organization and in the market; considering both past performance and their future potential.

Main features

Contribution-related pay rewards people for both their performance (outcomes) and their competency (inputs). Pay awards can be made as consolidated pay increases, but in some schemes there is also scope for cash bonuses. The features of contribution-related pay are illustrated in Figure 50.6.

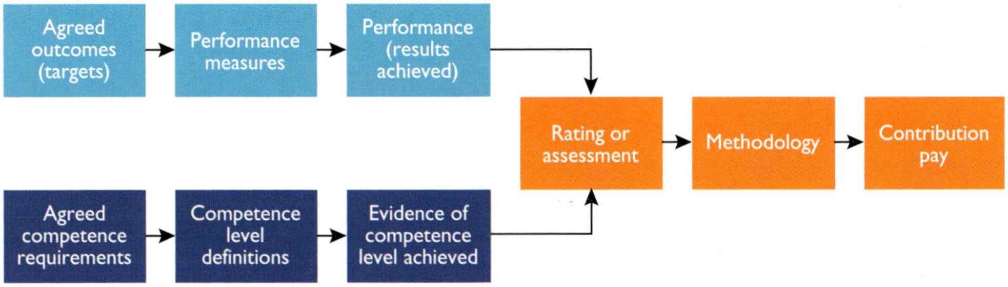

Figure 50.6 Contribution-related pay

A 'pay for contribution' scheme incorporating consolidated increases and cash bonuses developed for the Shaw Trust is modelled in Figure 50.7.

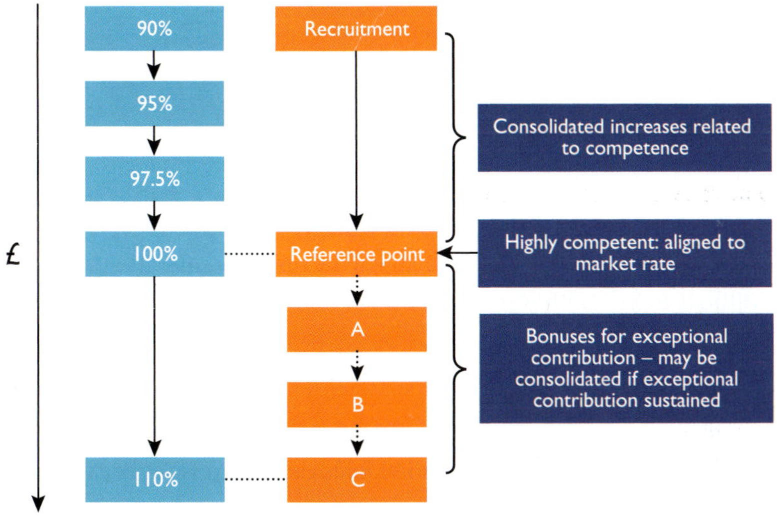

Figure 50.7 Contribution-related pay model

Skill-based pay

Definition

Skill-based pay provides employees with a direct link between their pay progression and the skills they have acquired and can use effectively. It focuses on what skills the business wants to pay for and what employees must do to demonstrate them. It is therefore a people-based rather than a job-based approach to pay. Rewards are related to the employee's ability to apply a wider range or a higher level of skills to different jobs or tasks. It is not linked simply with the scope of a defined job or a prescribed set of tasks.

A skill may be defined broadly as a learnt ability that improves with practice in time. For skill-based pay purposes, the skills must be relevant to the work. Skill-based pay is also known as 'knowledge-based pay', but the terms are used interchangeably, knowledge being regarded loosely as the understanding of how to do a job or certain tasks.

Application

Skill-based pay was originally applied mainly to operatives in manufacturing firms, but it has been extended to technicians and workers in retailing, distribution, catering and other service industries. The broad equivalent of skill-based pay for managerial, professional and administrative staff and knowledge workers is competence-related pay, which refers to expected behaviour as well as, often, to knowledge and skill requirements. There is clearly a strong family resemblance between skill- and competence-related pay – each is concerned with rewarding the person as well as the job. But they can be distinguished both by the way in which they are applied, as described below, and by the criteria used.

Main features

Skill-based pay works as follows:

- Skill blocks or modules are defined. These incorporate individual skills or clusters of skills that workers need to use and which will be rewarded by extra pay when they have been acquired and the employee has demonstrated the ability to use them effectively.
- The skill blocks are arranged in a hierarchy with natural break points between clearly definable different levels of skills.
- The successful completion of a skill module or skill block will result in an increment in pay. This will define how the pay of individuals can progress as they gain extra skills.
- Methods of verifying that employees have acquired and can use the skills at defined levels are established.
- Arrangements for 'cross-training' are made. These will include learning modules and training programmes for each skill block.

Conclusions

Skill-based pay systems are expensive to introduce and maintain. They require a considerable investment in skill analysis, training and testing. Although in theory a skill-based scheme will pay only for necessary skills, in practice individuals will not be using them all at the same time and some may be used infrequently, if at all. Inevitably, therefore, payroll costs will rise. If this increase is added to the cost of training and certification, the total of additional costs may be considerable. The advocates of skill-based pay claim that their schemes are self-financing because of the resulting increases in productivity and operational efficiency. But there is little evidence that such is the case. For this reason, skill-based schemes have never been very popular in the UK and some companies have discontinued them.

Readiness for individual contingent pay

The 10 questions to be answered when assessing readiness for pay related to performance, competency, contribution or skill are:

1. Is it believed that contingent pay will benefit the organization in the sense of enhancing its ability to achieve its strategic goals?
2. Are there valid and reliable means of measuring performance?
3. Is there a competency framework and are there methods of assessing levels of competency objectively (or could such a framework be readily developed)?
4. Are there effective performance management processes that line managers believe in and carry out conscientiously?
5. Are line managers willing to assess performance or contribution and capable of doing so?
6. Are line managers capable of making and communicating contingent pay decisions?
7. Is the HR function capable of providing advice and guidance to line managers on managing contingent pay?
8. Can procedures be developed to ensure fairness and consistency in assessments and pay decisions?
9. Are employees and trade unions willing to accept the scheme?
10. Do employees trust management to deliver the deal?

Developing and implementing individual contingent pay

If it is decided to use individual contingent pay, the 10 steps required are as follows.

Developing and implementing individual contingent pay

1. Assess readiness.
2. Analyse culture, strategy and existing processes, including the grade and pay structure, performance management and methods of progressing pay or awarding cash bonuses.
3. Decide which form of contingent pay is most appropriate.
4. Set out aims that demonstrate how contribution pay will help to achieve the organization's strategic goals.
5. Communicate aims to line managers and staff and involve them in the development of the scheme.
6. Determine how the scheme will operate.
7. Develop or improve performance management processes covering the selection of performance measures, decisions on competence requirements, methods of agreeing objectives, and the procedure for conducting joint reviews.
8. Pilot-test the scheme and amend as necessary.
9. Provide training to all concerned.
10. Launch the scheme and evaluate its effectiveness after the first review.

Service-related pay

Service-related pay provides fixed increments that are usually paid annually to people on the basis of continued service either in a job or a grade in a pay spine structure. Increments may be withheld for unacceptable performance (although this is rare) and some structures have a 'merit bar' that limits increments unless a defined level of 'merit' has been achieved. This is the traditional form of contingent pay and is still common in the public and voluntary sectors and in education and the health service, although it has largely been abandoned in the private sector.

Arguments for

Service-related pay is supported by many unions because they perceive it as being fair – everyone is treated equally. It is felt that linking pay to time in the job rather than performance or competence avoids the partial and ill-informed judgements about people that managers are prone to make. Some people believe that the principle of rewarding people for loyalty through continued service is a good one. It is also easy to manage; in fact, it does not need to be managed at all.

Arguments against

The arguments against service-related pay are that:

- it is inequitable in the sense that an equal allocation of pay increases according to service does not recognize the fact that some people will be contributing more than others and should be rewarded accordingly;
- it does not encourage good performance, indeed, it rewards poor performance equally;
- it is based on the assumption that performance improves with experience, but this is not automatically the case;
- it can be expensive – everyone may drift to the top of the scale, especially in times of low staff turnover, but the cost of their pay is not justified by the added value they provide.

The arguments against service-related pay have convinced most organizations, although some are concerned about managing any other form of contingent-pay schemes. They may also have to face strong resistance from their unions and can be unsure of what exit strategy they should adopt if they want to change. They may therefore stick with the status quo.

Summary of individual contingent pay schemes

The features, advantages, disadvantages and the appropriateness of individual contingent pay schemes and service-related pay are set out in Table 50.1.

Bonus schemes

Bonus schemes provide cash payments to employees that are related to the performance of themselves, their organization or their team, or a combination of two or more of these. Bonuses are often referred to as 'variable pay' or 'pay-at-risk'.

A defining characteristic of a bonus is that it is not consolidated into base pay. It has to be re-earned, unlike increases arising from individual contingent pay schemes such as performance or contribution-related pay or pay related to service, which are consolidated. Such payments have been described as 'gifts that go on giving' on the grounds that a reward for, say, one year's performance is continued in subsequent years even if the level of performance has not been sustained.

Table 50.1 Summary of contingent pay and service-related pay schemes

Type of scheme	Main features	Advantages	Disadvantages	When appropriate
Performance-related pay	Increases to basic pay or bonuses are related to assessment of performance	• May motivate (but this is uncertain) • Links rewards to objectives • Meets the need to be rewarded for achievement • Delivers message that good performance is important and will be rewarded	• May not motivate • Relies on judgements of performance, which may be subjective • Prejudicial to teamwork • Focuses on outputs, not quality • Relies on good performance management processes • Difficult to manage well	• For people who are likely to be motivated by money • In organizations with a performance-oriented culture • When performance can be measured objectively
Competency-related pay	Pay increases are related to the level of competence	• Focuses attention on need to achieve higher levels of competence • Encourages competence development • Can be integrated with other applications of competency-based HR management	• Assessment of competence levels may be difficult • Ignores outputs – danger of paying for competences that will not be used • Relies on well-trained and committed line managers	• As part of an integrated approach to HRM where competencies are used across a number of activities • Where competence is a key factor, where it may be inappropriate or hard to measure outputs • Where well-established competency frameworks exist

Table 50.1 *continued*

Type of scheme	Main features	Advantages	Disadvantages	When appropriate
Contribution-related pay	Increases in pay or bonuses are related both to inputs (competence) and outputs (performance)	Rewards people not only for what they do but how they do it	As for both PRP and competence-related pay – it may be hard to measure contribution and it is difficult to manage well	When it is believed that a well-rounded approach covering both inputs and outputs is appropriate
Skill-based pay	Increments related to the acquisition of skills	Encourages and rewards the acquisition of skills	Can be expensive when people are paid for skills they don't use	On the shop floor or in retail organizations
Service-related pay	Increments related to service in grade	No scope for bias, easy to manage	Fails to reward those who contribute more	Where this is a traditional approach and trade unions oppose alternatives

Cash bonuses may be the sole method of providing people with rewards in addition to their base pay, or they may be paid on top of individual contingent pay. 'Combination' bonus schemes combine schemes for rewarding individual performance with those for rewarding either team or organizational performance.

Team-based pay

Team-based pay provides rewards to teams or groups of employees carrying out similar and related work that is linked to the performance of the team. Performance may be measured in terms of outputs and/or the achievement of service delivery standards. The quality of the output and the opinion of customers about service levels are also often taken into account.

Team pay is usually paid in the form of a bonus that is shared amongst team members in proportion to their base rate of pay (much less frequently, it is shared equally). Individual team members may be eligible for competence-related or skill-based pay, but not for performance-related pay.

Advantages and disadvantages of team pay

Advantages of team pay:

- Encourages effective team working and cooperative behaviour.
- Clarifies team goals and priorities.
- Enhances flexible working within teams.
- Encourages multi-skilling.
- Provides an incentive for the team collectively to improve performance.
- Encourages less effective team members to improve to meet team standards.

Disadvantages of team pay:

- It only works in cohesive and mature teams.
- Individuals may resent the fact that their own efforts are not rewarded specifically.
- Peer pressure that compels individuals to conform to group norms could be undesirable.

Conditions suitable for team pay

Team pay is more likely to be appropriate when:

- teams can be readily identified and defined;
- teams are well-established;
- the work carried out by team members is interrelated – team performance depends on the collective efforts of team members;
- targets and standards of performance can be determined and agreed readily with team members;
- acceptable measurements of team performance compared with targets and standards are available;
- generally, the formula for team pay meets the criteria for performance pay.

Organization-wide bonus schemes

Organization-wide bonus schemes pay sums of money to employees that are related to company or plant-wide performance. They are designed to share the company's prosperity with its employees and thus to increase their commitment to its objectives and values. Because they do not relate reward directly to individual effort they are not effective as direct motivators, although gainsharing schemes can focus directly on what needs to be done to improve performance and so get employees involved in productivity improvement or cost-reduction plans. The two main types of schemes are gainsharing and profit sharing.

Gainsharing

Gainsharing is a formula-based company- or factory-wide bonus plan that provides for employees to share in the financial gains resulting from increases in added value or another measure of productivity. The link between their efforts and the payout can usefully be made explicit by involving them in analysing results and identifying areas for improvement.

Profit sharing

Profit sharing is the payment to eligible employees of sums in the form of cash or shares related to the profits of the business. The amount shared may be determined by a published or unpublished formula, or entirely at the discretion of management. Profit sharing differs from gainsharing in that the former is based on more than improved productivity. A number of factors outside the individual employee's control contribute to profit, while gainsharing aims to relate its payouts much more specifically to productivity and performance improvements within the control of employees. It is not possible to use profit sharing schemes as direct incentives as for most employees the link between individual effort and the reward is so remote. But they can increase identification with the company and many organizations operate profit sharing schemes because the management believes that it should share the company's success with its employees.

Share ownership schemes

There are two main forms of share ownership plans: share incentive plans (SIPS) and save-as-you-earn (SAYE) schemes. These can be HMRC-approved and, if so, produce tax advantages as well as linking financial rewards in the longer term to the prosperity of the company.

Share incentive plans

Share incentive plans must be HMRC-approved. They provide employees with a tax-efficient way of purchasing shares in their organization to which the employer can add 'free', 'partnership' or 'matching' shares.

Save-as-you-earn schemes

Save-as-you-earn schemes must be HMRC-approved. They provide employees with the option to buy shares in the company in three, five or seven years' time at today's price or a discount of up to 20 per cent of that price. Purchases are made from a savings account from which the employee pays an agreed sum each month. Income tax is not chargeable when the option is granted.

Choice of approach to contingent pay

The first choice is whether or not to have contingent pay related to performance, competence, contribution or skill. Public or voluntary sector organizations with fixed incremental systems (pay spines), where progression is solely based on service, may want to retain them because they do not depend on possibly biased judgements by managers and they are perceived as being fair – everyone gets the same – and easily managed. However, the fairness of such systems can be questioned. Is it fair for a poor performer to be paid more than a good performer simply for being there?

The alternative to fixed increments is either spot rates or some form of contingent pay. Spot rate systems in their purest form are generally only used for senior managers, shop floor or retail workers, and in smaller organizations and new businesses where the need for formal practices has not yet been recognized.

If it is decided that a more formal type of contingent pay for individuals should be adopted, the choice is between the various types of performance, competency-related or contribution-related pay and skill-based pay, as summarized in Table 50.1. The alternative to individual contingent pay is team pay. Pay related to organizational performance is another alternative, although some organizations have such schemes in addition to individual contingent pay. Bonuses may be paid in addition to or as an alternative to consolidated pay, and individual bonuses can be combined with team or organizational bonus schemes.

Contingent pay – key learning points

The basis of contingent pay

Contingent pay is concerned with answering the two fundamental reward management questions: 1) What do we value? 2) What are we prepared to pay for? Schemes are based on measurements or assessments.

Contingent pay as a motivator

Many people see contingent pay as the best way to motivate people. But it is simplistic to assume that it is only the extrinsic motivators in the form of pay that create long-term motivation. The total reward concept emphasizes the importance of non-financial rewards as an integral part of a complete package.

Argument for contingent pay

The most powerful argument for contingent pay is that those who contribute more should be paid more.

Arguments against contingent pay

The main arguments against contingent pay are: 1) the extent to which contingent pay schemes motivate is questionable – the amounts available for distribution are usually so small that they cannot act as an incentive, 2) the requirements for success are exacting and difficult to achieve, and 3) money by itself will not result in sustained motivation.

Alternatives to contingent pay

Service-related pay or spot rates.

Criteria for success

Individuals should have a clear line of sight between what they do and what they will get for doing it; the rewards are worth having; fair and consistent means are available for measuring or assessing performance, competence, contribution or skill; people must be able to influence their performance; and the reward should follow as closely as possible the accomplishment that generated it.

Types of individual contingent pay

A summary of contingent pay schemes is given in Table 50.1.

Assess readiness

Consider the extent to which contingent pay will benefit the organization, can be based on reliable methods of measuring performance and/or competency, can be managed effectively (by line managers and HR), will be accepted by trade unions and employees.

Contingent pay – key learning points (continued)

Developing and implementing individual contingent pay

Assess readiness, analyse requirements, decide on most appropriate approach, define aims, communicate aims, design scheme, development assessment processes, pilot-test, provide training, and launch and evaluate the scheme.

Service-related pay

Service-related pay provides fixed increments that are usually paid annually to people on the basis of continued service either in a job or a grade in a pay spine structure.

Bonus schemes

Bonus schemes provide cash payments to employees that are related to the performance of themselves, their organization or their team, or a combination of two or more of these. Bonuses are often referred to as 'variable pay' or 'pay-at-risk'.

Team pay

Team-based pay provides rewards to teams or groups of employees carrying out similar and related work that is linked to the performance of the team.

Organization-wide bonus schemes

These include profit sharing, gainsharing and employee share schemes.

Choice of approach

If it is decided that a more formal type of contingent pay for individuals should be adopted, the choice is between the various types of performance, competency-related or contribution-related pay and skill-based pay. The alternative to individual contingent pay is team pay. Pay related to organizational performance is another alternative, although some organizations have such schemes in addition to individual contingent pay. Bonuses may be paid in addition to or as an alternative to consolidated pay, and individual bonuses can be combined with team or organizational bonus schemes.

Questions

1. Thompson (1998) commented that: 'Research on the efficacy of performance pay in delivering higher trust, commitment and motivation tends to suggest that at best individual performance-related pay is neutral in its effects and at worst highly destructive.' Give your reactions to this statement based on your own experience or understanding of the impact of performance pay.
2. You have been asked to talk for 30 minutes or so to a group of first-year business management students at your local university about the arguments for and against performance-related pay. Prepare an outline of your talk, which should incorporate evidence from research or experience to support your case.
3. From a senior colleague: 'I don't believe that our performance-related pay scheme is working. I have just been involved in updating our competency framework and I have heard that such frameworks are being used by other organizations as the basis for pay related to competency. What do you think of this idea? I would be interested in any evidence you can produce to support your views.'
4. From your chief executive: 'Everyone extols the virtues of teams and there seem to be many good arguments against individual performance pay. We have many well-established teams and we believe in good teamwork. What is the business case for team pay? Are there any reasons why we should not follow that route?'

References

Bowey, A (1982) *The Effects of Incentive Pay Systems*, Department of Employment, Research Paper No 36, DOE, London

Brown, D and Armstrong, M (1999) *Paying for Contribution*, Kogan Page, London

e-reward (2004) *Survey of Contingent Pay*, e-reward.co.uk, Stockport

Kessler, J and Purcell, J (1992) Performance-related pay: objectives and application, *Human Resource Management Journal*, **2** (3), pp 16–33

Kohn, A (1993) Why incentive plans cannot work, *Harvard Business Review*, September–October, pp 54–63

Lawler, E E (1993) Who uses skill-based pay, and why, *Compensation & Benefits Review*, March–April, pp 22–26

Marsden, D and Richardson, R (1994) Performing for pay?, *British Journal of Industrial Relations*, **32**,(2), pp 243–61

Oliver, J (1996) Cash on delivery, *Management Today*, August, pp 6–9

Pfeffer, J (1998b) Six dangerous myths about pay, *Harvard Business Review*, May/June, pp 109–19

Sparrow, P R (1996) Too true to be good, *People Management*, December, pp 22–27

Thompson, M (1992a) *Pay and Performance: The employee experience*, Institute of Manpower Studies, Brighton

Thompson, M (1992b) *Pay and Performance: The employer experience*, Institute of Manpower Studies, Brighton

Thompson, M (1998) Trust and reward, in (eds) S Perkins and St John Sandringham, *Trust, Motivation and Commitment: A reader*, Strategic Remuneration Research Centre, Faringdon

Wright, V (1991) Performance-related pay, in (ed) F Neale, *The Handbook of Performance Management*, IPM, London

51 Rewarding Special Groups

Learning outcomes

On completing this chapter you should know about:

- Elements of directors' and senior executives' pay
- Types of payment for manual workers
- Payment and incentive schemes for sales staff
- Payment by results schemes

Reward management for directors and executives

Principles of corporate governance relating to remuneration of directors

The key principles of corporate governance as it affects the remuneration of directors, which emerged from various reviews, namely the Cadbury, Greenbury and Hampel Reports, are as follows:

- Remuneration committees should consist exclusively of non-executive directors. Their purpose is to provide an independent basis for setting the salary levels and the rules covering incentives, share options, benefit entitlements and contract provisions for executive directors. Such committees are accountable to shareholders for the decisions they take and the non-executive directors who sit on them should have no personal financial interests at stake. They should be constituted as sub-committees of company boards and boards should elect both the chairman and the members.
- Remuneration committees must provide a remuneration package sufficient to attract, retain and motivate directors, but should avoid paying more than is necessary. They should be sensitive to wider issues, eg pay and employment conditions elsewhere in the company.
- Remuneration committees should take a robust line on the payment of compensation where performance has been unsatisfactory.
- Performance-related elements should be designed to align the interests of directors and shareholders.
- Any new longer-term incentive arrangement should, preferably, replace existing executive share option plans, or at least form part of an integrated approach that should be approved by shareholders.
- The pension consequences and associated costs to the company of increases in base salary should be considered.
- Notice or service contract periods should be set at, or reduced to, a year or less. However, in some cases periods of up to two years may be acceptable.

Elements of directors' and senior executives' pay

The main elements of directors' and senior executives' pay are basic pay, bonus or incentive schemes, share option and share ownership schemes.

Basic pay

Decisions on the base salary of directors and senior executives are usually founded on largely subjective views about the market worth of the individuals concerned. Remuneration on joining the company is commonly settled by negotiation, often subject to the approval of a remuneration committee. Reviews of base salaries are then undertaken by reference to market movements and success as measured by company performance. Decisions on base salary are important not only in themselves but also because the level may influence decisions on the pay of both senior and middle managers. Bonuses are expressed as a percentage of base salary, share options may be allocated as a declared multiple of basic pay and, commonly, the pension will be a proportion of final salary.

Bonus schemes

Virtually all major employers in the UK (90 per cent according to recent surveys by organizations such as Monks and Hay) provide annual incentive (bonus) schemes for senior executives. Bonus schemes provide directors and executives with cash sums based on the measures of company and, frequently, individual performance.

Typically, bonus payments are linked to achievement of profit and/or other financial targets and they are sometimes 'capped', ie a restriction is placed on the maximum amount payable. There may also be elements related to achieving specific goals and to individual performance.

Share option schemes

Many companies have share option schemes, which give directors and executives the right to buy a block of shares on some future date at the share price ruling when the option was granted. They are a form of long-term incentive on the assumption that executives will be motivated to perform more effectively if they can anticipate a substantial capital gain when they sell their shares at a price above that prevailing when they took up the option.

Executive restricted share schemes

Under such schemes free shares are provisionally awarded to participants. These shares do not belong to the executive until they are released or vested; hence they are 'restricted'. The number of shares actually released to the executive at the end of a defined period (usually three or, less commonly, five years) will depend on performance over that period against specific targets. Thereafter there may be a further retention period when the shares must be held, although no further performance conditions apply.

Reward management for sales representatives

There are no hard-and-fast rules governing how sales representatives should be paid. It depends on the type of company, the products or services it offers its customers, and the nature of the sales process – how sales are organized and made. The different methods are described in Table 51.1.

Table 51.1 Summary of payment and incentive arrangements for sales staff

Method	Features	Advantages	Disadvantages	When appropriate
Salary only	Straight salary, no commission or bonus	Encourage customer service rather than high pressure selling; deal with the problem of staff who are working in a new or unproductive sales territory; protect income when sales fluctuate for reasons beyond the individual's control	No direct motivation through money; may attract under-achieving people who are subsidized by high achievers; increases fixed costs of sales because pay costs are not flexed with sales results	When representing the company is more important than direct selling; staff have little influence on sales volume (they may simply be 'order takers'); customer service is all-important
Salary plus commission	Basic salary plus cash commission calculated as a percentage of sales volume or value	Direct financial motivation is provided related to what sales staff are there to do, ie generate sales; but they are not entirely dependent on commission – they are cushioned by their base salary	Relating pay to the volume or value of sales is too crude an approach and may result in staff going for volume by concentrating on the easier to sell products, not those generating high margins; may encourage high-pressure selling as in some financial services firms in the 1980s and 1990s	When it is believed that the way to get more sales is to link extra money to results, but a base salary is still needed to attract the many people who want to be assured of a reasonable basic salary that will not fluctuate but who still aspire to increase that salary by their own efforts

Table 51.1 *continued*

Method	Features	Advantages	Disadvantages	When appropriate
Salary plus bonus	Basic salary plus cash bonus based on achieving and exceeding sales targets or quotas and meeting other selling objectives	Provide financial motivation but targets or objectives can be flexed to ensure that particular sales goals are achieved, eg high-margin sales, customer service	Do not have a clear line of sight between effort and reward; may be complex to administer; sales representative may find them hard to understand and resent the use of subjective judgements on performance other than sales	When flexibility in providing rewards is important; it is felt that sales staff need to be motivated to focus on aspects of their work other than simply maximizing sales volume
Commission only	Only commission based on a percentage of sales volume or value is paid, there is no basic salary	Provide a direct financial incentive; attract high performing sales staff; ensure that selling costs vary directly with sales; little direct supervision required	Lead to high-pressure selling; may attract the wrong sort of people who are interested only in money and not customer service; focus attention on high volume rather than profitability	When sales performance depends mainly on selling ability and can be measured by immediate sales results; staff are not involved in non-selling activities; continuing relationships with customers are relatively unimportant
Additional non-cash rewards	Incentives, prizes, cars, recognition, opportunities to grow	Utilize powerful non-financial motivators	May be difficult to administer; do not provide a direct incentive	When it is believed that other methods of payment need to be enhanced by providing additional motivators

Paying manual workers

The pay of manual workers takes the form of time rates, also known as day rates, day work, flat rates or hourly rates. Incentive payments by means of payment-by-results schemes may be made on top of a base rate.

Time rates

These provide workers with a predetermined rate for the actual hours they work. Time rates on their own are most commonly used when it is thought that it is impossible or undesirable to use a payment-by-results system, for example in maintenance work. From the viewpoint of employees, the advantage of time rates is that their earnings are predictable and steady and they do not have to engage in endless arguments with rate fixers and supervisors about piece rates or time allowances. The argument against them is that they do not provide a direct incentive relating the reward to the effort or the results. Two ways of modifying the basic time rate approach are to adopt high day rates, as described below, or measured day work.

Time rates may take the form of what are often called 'high day rates'. These are higher than the minimum time rate and may contain a consolidated bonus rate element. The underlying assumption is that higher base rates will encourage greater effort without the problems created when operating an incentive scheme. High day rates are usually above the local market rates, to attract and retain workers.

Payment-by-result schemes

Payment-by-result (PBR) schemes provide incentives to workers by relating their pay or, more usually, part of their pay to the number of items they produce or the time taken to do a certain amount of work. The main types of PBR or incentive schemes for individuals are piece work, work measured schemes, measured day work and performance-related pay. Team bonus schemes are an alternative to individual PBR and plant-wide schemes can produce bonuses that are paid instead of individual or team bonuses, or in addition to them. Each of these methods is described in Table 51.2, together with an assessment of their advantages and disadvantages for employers and employees, and when they are appropriate.

Table 51.2 Comparison of shop floor payment-by-results schemes

Scheme	Main features	For employers		For employees		When appropriate
		Advantages	Disadvantages	Advantages	Disadvantages	
Piece work	Bonus directly related to output	Direct motivation; simple, easy to operate	Lose control over output; quality problems	Predict and control earnings in the short term; regulate pace of work themselves	More difficult to predict and control earnings in the longer term; work may be stressful and produce RSI	Fairly limited application to work involving unit production controlled by the person eg agriculture, garment manufacture
Work-measured schemes	Work measurement used to determine standard output levels over a period or standard times for job/tasks; bonus based by reference to performance ratings compared with actual performance or time saved	Provides what appears to be a 'scientific' method of relating reward to performance; can produce significant increases in productivity, at least in the short term	Schemes are expensive, time-consuming and difficult to run and can too easily degenerate and cause wage drift because of loose rates	Appear to provide a more objective method of relating pay to performance; employees can be involved in the rating process to ensure fairness	Ratings are still prone to subjective judgement and earnings can fluctuate because of changes in work requirements outside the control of employees	For short-cycle repetitive work where changes in the work mix or design changes are infrequent, down time is restricted, and management and supervision are capable of managing and maintaining the scheme

Table 51.2 *continued*

Scheme	Main features	For employers		For employees		When appropriate
		Advantages	Disadvantages	Advantages	Disadvantages	
Measured day work	Pay fixed at a high rate on the understanding that a high level of performance against work-measured standards will be maintained	Employees are under an obligation to work at the specified level of performance	Performance targets can become easily attained norms and may be difficult to change	High predictable earnings are provided	No opportunities for individuals to be rewarded in line with their own efforts	Everyone must be totally committed to making it work; high standards of work measurement are essential; good control systems to identify shortfalls on targets
Performance-related pay	Payments on top of base rate are made related to individual assessments of performance	Reward individual contribution without resource to work measurement; relevant in high technology manufacturing	Measuring performance can be difficult; no direct incentive provided	Opportunity to be rewarded for own efforts without having to submit to a pressured PBR system	Assessment informing performance pay decisions may be biased, inconsistent or unsupported by evidence	As part of a reward harmonization (shop floor and staff) programme; as an alternative to work measured schemes or an enhancement of a high day rate system

Table 51.2 *continued*

Scheme	Main features	For employers		For employees		When appropriate
		Advantages	Disadvantages	Advantages	Disadvantages	
Group or team basis	Groups or teams are paid bonuses on the basis of their performance as indicated by work measurement ratings or the achievement of targets	Encourage team co-operation and effort; not too individualized	Direct incentive may be limited; depends on good work measurement or the availability of clear group output or productivity targets	Bonuses can be related clearly to the joint efforts of the group; fluctuations in earnings minimized	Depend on effective work measurement, which is not always available; individual effort and contribution not recognized	When team working is important and team efforts can be accurately measured and assessed; as an alternative to individual PBR if this is not effective
Factory wide bonuses	Bonuses related to plant performance – added value or productivity	Increase commitment by sharing success	No direct motivation	Earnings increased without individual pressure	Bonuses often small and unpredictable	As an addition to other forms of incentive when increasing commitment is important

Rewarding special groups – key learning points

Elements of directors' and senior executives' pay

Basic pay, bonus schemes, share options, executive restricted share schemes.

Payment and incentive schemes for sales staff

Summarized in Table 51.1.

Types of payment for manual workers

The pay of manual workers takes the form of time rates, also known as day rates, day work, flat rates or hourly rates. Incentive payments by means of payment-by-results schemes may be made on top of a base rate.

Payment-by-results schemes

Payment-by-result (PBR) schemes provide incentives to workers by relating their pay or, more usually, part of their pay to the number of items they produce or the time taken to do a certain amount of work. The main types of PBR or incentive schemes for individuals are piece work, work measured schemes, measured day work and performance-related pay.

Questions

1. What is the function of a remuneration committee?
2. What are the advantages and disadvantages for employers and employees of work-measured payment by result schemes?
3. What are the main methods of rewarding sales staff?

52 Employee Benefits, Pensions and Allowances

Key concepts and terms

- Defined benefit pension scheme (final salary)
- Employee benefits
- Pension scheme
- Stakeholder pension
- Defined contribution pension scheme (money purchase)
- Flexible benefits
- Segmentation
- Total reward statement

Learning outcomes

On completing this chapter you should be able to define these key concepts. You should also know about:

- Objectives of employee benefits
- Flexible benefits
- Types of pension scheme
- Total reward statement
- Main types of employee benefits
- What pension schemes provide
- Communicating pensions policies
- Types of allowances

Employee benefits

Employee benefits are elements of remuneration given in addition to the various forms of cash pay. They also include items that are not strictly remuneration such as annual holidays.

Objectives

The objectives of the employee benefits policies and practices of an organization are to:

- provide a competitive total remuneration package that both attracts and retains high-quality employees;
- provide for the personal needs of employees;
- increase the commitment of employees to the organization;
- provide for some people a tax-efficient method of remuneration.

Note that these objectives do not include 'motivate employees'. This is because the normal benefits provided by a business seldom make a direct and immediate impact on performance. They can, however, create more favourable attitudes towards the business, which can improve commitment and organizational performance in the longer term.

Main types of employee benefits

Benefits can be divided into the following categories:

- Pension schemes: these are generally regarded as the most important employee benefit and are described in the next part of this chapter.
- Personal security: these are benefits that enhance the individual's personal and family security with regard to illness, health, accident or life insurance.
- Financial assistance: loans, house purchase schemes, relocation assistance and discounts on company goods or services.
- Personal needs: entitlements that recognize the interface between work and domestic needs or responsibilities, eg holidays and other forms of leave, child care, career breaks, retirement counselling, financial counselling and personal counselling in times of crisis; fitness and recreational facilities.
- Company cars and petrol: still a much appreciated benefit in spite of the fact that cars are now more heavily taxed.
- Other benefits that improve the standard of living of employees such as subsidized meals, clothing allowances, refund of telephone costs, mobile phones (as a 'perk' rather than a necessity) and credit card facilities.

- Intangible benefits: characteristics of the organization that contribute to the quality of working life and make it an attractive and worthwhile place in which to be employed.

Benefits provision

The CIPD 2008b reward survey established that some of the most popular benefits for all sectors were:

Pensions – 97 per cent.
25 days or more paid leave – 84 per cent.
Childcare vouchers – 62 per cent.
Life assurance – 59 per cent.
Car allowance – 57 per cent.
Health and well-being benefits – 57 per cent.
Mobile phones – 54 per cent.
Enhanced maternity/paternity leave – 54 per cent.

Company cars were popular in manufacturing and production (75 per cent of respondents) but did not appear in the top 10 benefits in other sectors.

Flexible benefits

Flexible benefit schemes (sometimes called 'cafeteria systems') allow employees to decide, within certain limits, on the make-up of their benefits package. Schemes can provide for a choice within benefits or a choice between benefits. Employees are allocated an individual allowance to spend on benefits. This allowance can be used to switch between benefits, to choose new ones or to alter the rate of cover within existing benefits. Some core benefits such as sick pay may lie outside the scheme and cannot be 'flexed'. Employees can shift the balance of their total reward package between pay and benefits, either adding to their benefits allowance by sacrificing salary or taking any unspent benefit allowance as cash.

Segmentation

Segmentation involves the identification of the special individuals or groups of employees who create the most value and providing them with an individualized (and better) reward package. It allows employers to tailor their reward programmes to the needs and wants of their employees of choice. However, segmentation can damage morale. It creates an elite group and may be perceived as a form of favouritism.

Taxation

It should be remembered that most benefits are taxable as 'benefits in kind', the notable exceptions being approved pension schemes, meals where these are generally available to employees, car parking spaces, professional subscriptions and accommodation where this is used solely for performing the duties of the job.

Pensions

Pensions provide an income to employees when they retire and to their surviving dependant on the death of the employee, and deferred benefits to employees who leave. Schemes offered by organizations (occupational pensions), as distinct from state pensions, are funded by contributions from the organization and usually, but not always, the employee. Pensions are the most significant benefit and are a valuable part of the total reward package, but they are perhaps the most complex part.

Why occupational pensions are provided

Pensions are provided because they demonstrate that the organization is a good employer concerned about the long-term interests of its employees who want the security provided be a reasonable pension when they retire. Good pension schemes help to attract and retain high-quality people by maintaining competitive levels of total remuneration. But they can be expensive and funding problems can arise, especially in defined benefit (final salary schemes).

What pension schemes provide

The range and level of benefits from pension schemes depend on the type of scheme and the level of contributions. In general, schemes provide the following benefits.

Pension scheme benefits

- Benefits on retirement – these are related to the final salary of individuals when they retire or the amount that has been paid into a defined contribution scheme while the individuals were members.
- Benefits on death – the pensions of widows or widowers and children are normally related to the member's anticipated pension; the most common fraction is half.
- Benefits on leaving an employer – individuals leaving an employer can elect to take one of the following options: a deferred pension from the occupational scheme they are leaving, the transfer of the pension entitlement from the present employer to the new employer (but this is not always possible), or refund of their contributions, but only if they have completed less than two years' membership of the pension scheme.

The main types of schemes are described below.

Defined benefit (final salary) schemes

The main features of a defined benefit scheme are as follows.

Pension entitlement on retirement

- On retiring, the employee is entitled to a pension that is calculated as a fraction of final salary (on retirement or an average of the last two or three years) multiplied by the length of pensionable service.
- The maximum proportion of salary allowed by HMRC is two-thirds of final salary after 40 years service.
- The amount of the pension depends on the final salary, the value of the annuity that provides the pension and the accrual rate. The accrual rate refers to the fraction of final salary that can be earned per year of service. When a pension is described as 1/60th it means that 40 years service would produce a two-thirds of final salary pension, and 30 years would produce a pension of half the final salary. This is a fairly typical fraction in private sector firms.

Employer and employee contributions

Employer contributions can be a fixed percentage of salary. Alternatively, the percentage increases with service or is a multiple of the employee's contribution (eg the employer contributes 15 per cent if the employee contributes 5 per cent). Employee contribution rates vary considerably, ranging from 3 to 15 per cent with a median of around 8 per cent.

Pension fund

Employee and employer contributions are paid into a combined fund, and there is no direct link between fund size and the pensions paid. The money remaining in the fund after any lump sums have been taken out is invested in an annuity to provide a regular income, the amount of which may be revised upwards periodically to compensate for inflation.

Dependants

Dependants are entitled to a percentage of the employee's pension entitlement if he or she dies during retirement or in service with the company.

Lump sum

Part of the pension may be exchanged for a tax-free lump sum up to a maximum under HMRC rules of 1/80th per year for up to 40 years service.

Defined contribution (money purchase) schemes

The main features of defined contribution schemes are as follows.

Pension entitlement

The employee receives a pension on retirement that is related to the size of the fund accumulated by the combined contributions of the employee and employer. The amount of the pension depends on the size of contributions, the rate of return on the investment of the accumulated fund, and the rate of return on an annuity purchased by the employer. It is not related to the employee's final salary.

Contributions

The employer contributes a defined percentage of earnings, which may be fixed, age-related or linked to what the employee pays. The 2003 survey by the National Association of Pension Funds found that the level of employer contribution averages 6 per cent. The employee also contributes a fixed percentage of salary.

Pension fund

The contributions are invested and the money is used at retirement to purchase a regular income, usually via an annuity contract from an insurance company. The retirement pension is therefore whatever annual payment can be purchased with the money accumulated in the fund for a member.

Members have individual shares of the fund, which represent their personal entitlements and which will directly determine the pensions they receive.

Dependants

Dependants receive death in service and death in retirement pensions.

Lump sum

One-quarter of the pension can be taken as a tax-free lump sum on retirement.

Comparison of defined benefits and defined contribution schemes

Defined benefit

- A guaranteed pension is provided to employees.
- Benefits are defined as a fraction of final salary.

- Employer costs are not fixed or predictable.
- Employer takes financial risk.
- Benefits are designed for long-serving employees.
- Early leavers lose.

Defined contribution

- The pension provided for the employee is uncertain.
- Benefits are purchased using an accumulation of contributions invested.
- Employer costs are fixed and predictable.
- Employee takes financial risk.
- Benefits are not designed for long-serving employees.
- Early leavers do not lose.

Many companies are dubious about the financial wisdom of final salary provision. Defined benefit schemes provide much more value to older and longer-serving employees but the costs involved and greater labour mobility have led some employers to question this emphasis, particularly in newer industries with young, high-turnover workforces.

However, defined benefit schemes are still the most popular, especially in the public sector. The CIPD (2008b) Reward Survey found that 53 per cent of employers had such schemes while 22 per cent had defined contribution schemes.

Stakeholder pension

A stakeholder pension is a government sponsored scheme, primarily designed for lower paid employees. Employers who do not provide a suitable pension scheme for their employees are required by law to offer access to a stakeholder scheme. A stakeholder pension is a defined contribution arrangement that satisfies certain conditions, designed to ensure that it provides good value for money and that members' interests are protected. The most important provision is that contributions from members should be flexible – they must be free to pay whatever contributions they wish, when they wish.

Communicating pensions policies

The pension benefits provided by employers should be developed as an important part of a coherent total reward package. Good schemes demonstrate that employers care about the future security and well-being of their employees, and pensions are a valuable means of gaining and keeping employee commitment to the organization. Younger and more mobile employees are often indifferent to pensions but the older they get the more they are concerned, and these mature employees contribute largely to organizational success.

Careful consideration needs to be given to telling employees about the scheme. They need to know how it works and how it benefits them – it is too easy for employees to take pensions for granted. It is particularly important to communicate the reasons for any changes, and staff should be involved in discussing the reasons for the proposed arrangements and given the opportunity to comment on them.

Total reward statements

Employees tend not to appreciate the value of the benefits provided for them by their employers. To overcome this problem many companies are now issuing total reward statements that spell how much more the company provides for its employees than their pay.

Allowances

Allowances are paid in addition to basic pay for special circumstances (such as living in London) or features of employment (overtime, shifts or working unsocial hours). They may be determined unilaterally by the organization but they are often the subject of negotiation. The main types of allowances are:

- Location allowances – London and large town allowances to compensate for higher costs of living.
- Overtime payments – most manual workers are eligible for paid overtime as well as many staff employees up to management level. Higher-paid staff may receive time off in lieu if they work longer hours. Typically, organizations that make overtime payments give time and a half as an overtime premium from Monday to Saturday, with double time paid on Sundays and statutory holidays. Some firms also pay double time from around noon on Saturday. Work on major statutory holidays such as Christmas Day and Good Friday often attracts higher overtime premiums.
- Shift payments are made at rates that usually vary according to the shift arrangement. A premium of, say, one-third of basic pay may be given to people working nights, while those on an early or late day shift may receive less – say, one-fifth of basic pay.
- Working conditions allowances may be paid where the work is unpleasant.
- Subsistence allowances may be paid for accommodation and meals when working away from home.

- Stand-by and call-out allowances may be made to those who have to be available to come in to work when required.

Employee benefits, pensions and allowances – key learning points

Objectives of employee benefits

- Provide a competitive total remuneration package.
- Provide for the personal needs of employees.
- Increase the commitment of employees to the organization.
- Provide for some people a tax-efficient method of remuneration.

Main types of employee benefits

Pensions, financial assistance, personal needs, company cars.

Flexible benefits

Flexible benefit schemes (sometimes called 'cafeteria systems') allow employees to decide, within certain limits, on the make-up of their benefits package. Schemes can allow for a choice within benefits or a choice between benefits. Employees are allocated an individual allowance to spend on benefits. This allowance can be used to switch between benefits, to choose new ones, or to alter the rate of cover within existing benefits.

What pension schemes provide

Pensions provide an income to employees when they retire and to their surviving dependant/s on the death of the employee, and deferred benefits to employees who leave.

Types of pension scheme

The main types of pensions are defined benefit pension schemes (final salary), defined contribution pension schemes (money purchase) and stakeholder pensions.

Communicating pensions policies

Careful consideration needs to be given to telling employees about the scheme. They need to know how it works and how it benefits them – it is too easy for employees to take pensions for granted.

Total reward statement

Employees tend not to appreciate the value of the benefits provided for them by their employers. To overcome this problem many companies are now issuing total reward statements that spell how much more the company provides for its employees than their pay.

Types of allowances

Location, overtime, shift, working conditions, subsistence, stand-by.

Questions

1. From your chief executive: 'How does a flexible benefits scheme work and how would we benefit from introducing one?'
2. From the local paper: 'We are running a section on employee benefits and pensions. Could you write a short piece on the differences between defined benefit and defined contribution pension schemes and why many of the former are being abandoned?'
3. From the finance director: 'I am sure most of our employees do not appreciate the value of the benefits they receive. What can we do to remedy this situation?'

Reference

CIPD (2008b) *Reward Survey*, CIPD, London

53 Managing Reward Systems

Key concepts and terms

- Added value
- Compa-ratio
- Pay matrix
- Attrition
- Mid-point management
- Total payroll budget

Learning outcomes

On completing this chapter you should be able to define these key concepts. You should also know about:

- Reward forecasting
- Compa-ratio analysis
- Assessing added value
- Conducting individual pay reviews
- Managing the development of reward systems
- Communicating to employees
- Reward budgets
- Attrition analysis
- Conducting general pay reviews
- Reward procedures
- Devolution of pay decisions to line managers

Introduction

Reward management involves the management of complex systems. This is a demanding requirement involving control, evaluation, pay reviews, procedures, the allocation of responsibility and communicating to employees, as explained in this chapter.

Controlling reward

The implementation of reward policies and procedures should be monitored and controlled to ensure that value for money is obtained. Control is easier if the grade and pay structure is well defined and clear guidelines exist on how it and the benefits arrangements should be managed. Control should be based on forecasts, budgets and costings, as described below, and by monitoring and evaluating the implementation of reward policies, as discussed in the next part of this chapter.

Reward forecasts

It is necessary to forecast future payroll costs taking into account the number of people employed and the impact of pay reviews and contingent pay awards. The cost implications of developments such as a revised job evaluation scheme, a new grade and pay structure or a flexible benefits scheme also have to be forecast.

Reward budgets

Pay review budgets set out the increase in payroll costs that will result for either general or individual pay reviews and are used for cost forecasts generally and as the basis for the guidelines issued to line managers on conducting individual reviews.

Total payroll budgets are based on the number of people employed in different jobs and their present and forecast rates of pay. In a budgetary control system they are aggregated from the budgets prepared by departmental managers, but HR provides guidance on the allowances that should be made for pay increases. The aim is to maintain control over payroll costs and restrain managers from the temptation to overpay their staff.

Costing reward processes

Proposed changes to the reward system need to be costed for approval by senior management. The costs would include development costs such as consultants' fees, software, literature, additional staff and, possibly, the opportunity costs arising when staff are seconded to a development project.

Implementation costs also have to be projected. A new grade and pay structure, for example, can easily result in an increase to the payroll of 3 or 4 per cent. New contingent pay schemes may also cost more, although the aim should be to make them self-financing.

Monitoring and evaluating reward policies and practices

The effectiveness of reward policies and practices should be monitored and evaluated against the requirements of the organization. Evaluation should compare outcomes with the objectives set for the new practice (this is why setting objectives for reward initiatives is so important). Monitoring is carried out through compa-ratio analysis, attrition analysis, assessing added value and the use of attitude surveys.

Compa-ratio analysis

A compa-ratio (short for 'comparative ratio') measures the relationship in a graded pay structure between actual and policy rates of pay as a percentage. The policy value used is the mid-point or reference point in a pay range, which represents the 'target rate' for a fully competent individual in any job in the grade. This point is aligned with market rates in accordance with the organization's market stance.

Compa-ratios can be used to define the extent to which pay policy is achieved (the relationship between the policy and actual rates of pay). The analysis of compa-ratios indicates what action may have to be taken to slow down or accelerate increases if compa-ratios are too high or too low compared with the policy level. This is sometimes called 'midpoint management'. Compa-ratios can also be used to measure where an individual is placed in a pay range and therefore provide information on the size of pay increases when a pay matrix is used, as described later in this chapter.

Compa-ratios are calculated as follows:

$$\frac{\text{actual rate of pay}}{\text{mid or reference point of range}} \times 100$$

A compa-ratio of 100 per cent means that actual pay and policy pay are the same. Compa-ratios that are higher or lower than 100 per cent mean that, respectively, pay is above or below the policy target rate. For example, if the target (policy) rate in a range were £20,000 and the average pay of all the individuals in the grade were £18,000, the compa-ratio would be 90 per cent. Compa-ratios establish differences between policy and practice. The reasons for such differences need to be established.

Analysing attrition

Attrition or slippage takes place when employees enter jobs at lower rates of pay than the previous incumbents. If this happens payroll costs will go down, given an even flow of starters and leavers and a consistent approach to the determination of rates of pay. In theory attrition can help to finance pay increases within a range. It has been claimed that fixed incremental systems can be entirely self-financing because of attrition, but the conditions under which this can happen are so exceptional that it probably never happens.

Attrition can be calculated by the formula: total percentage increase to payroll arising from general or individual pay increases minus total percentage increase in average rates of pay. If it can be proved that attrition is going to take place, the amount involved can be taken into account as a means of at least partly financing individual pay increases. Attrition in a pay system with regular progression through ranges, and a fairly even flow of starters and leavers, is typically between 2 and 3 per cent but this should not be regarded as a norm.

Assessing added value

Assessing the added value (ie the value for money) provided by existing practices or by new practices when they are implemented is a major consideration when monitoring and evaluating reward management processes. Evaluating the cost of innovations may lead to the reconsideration of proposals to ensure that they will provide added value. Evaluating the value for money obtained from existing reward practices leads to the identification of areas for improvement.

Affordability is, or should be, a major issue when reviewing reward management developments and existing practices. Added value is achieved when the benefits of a reward practice either exceed its cost or at least justify the cost. At the development stage it is therefore necessary to carry out cost/benefit assessments. The two fundamental questions to be answered are, 'What business needs will this proposal meet?' and 'How will the proposal meet the needs?' The costs and benefits of existing practices should also be assessed on the same basis.

Attitude surveys

An attitude survey is a valuable means of evaluating and monitoring reward practices by assessing the views of those at the receiving end of pay policies as a basis for taking action.

Conducting pay reviews

Pay reviews are general or 'across-the-board' reviews in response to movements in the cost of living or market rates, following pay negotiations with trade unions, individual reviews that determine the pay progression of individuals in relation to their performance or contribution, or individual reviews. They are one of the most visible aspects of reward management (the other is job grading) and are an important means of implementing the organization's reward policies and demonstrating to employees how these policies operate.

Employees expect that general reviews will maintain the purchasing power of their pay by compensating for increases in the cost of living. They will want their levels of pay to be competitive with what they could earn outside. They will also want to be rewarded fairly and equitably for the contribution they make.

General reviews

General reviews take place when employees are given an increase in response to general market rate movements, increases in the cost of living, or union negotiations. General reviews are often combined with individual reviews, but employees are usually informed of both the general and individual components of any increase they receive. Alternatively the general review may be conducted separately to enable better control to be achieved over costs and to focus employees' attention on the performance-related aspect of their remuneration.

Some organizations have completely abandoned the use of across-the-board reviews. They argue that the decision on what people should be paid should be an individual matter, taking into account the personal contribution people are making and their 'market worth' – how they as individuals are valued in the marketplace. This enables the organization to adopt a more flexible approach to allocating pay increases in accordance with the perceived value of individuals to the organization.

The steps required to conduct a general review

1. Decide on the budget.
2. Analyse data on pay settlements made by comparable organizations and rates of inflation.
3. Conduct negotiations with trade unions as required.
4. Calculate costs.
5. Adjust the pay structure – by either increasing the pay brackets of each grade by the percentage general increase or by increasing pay reference points by the overall percentage and applying different increases to the upper or lower limits of the bracket, thus altering the shape of the structure.
6. Inform employees.

Individual reviews

Individual pay reviews determine contingent pay increases or bonuses. The e-reward 2004 survey of contribution pay found that the average size of contingent pay awards made by respondents was 3.3 per cent. Individual awards may be based on ratings, an overall assessment that does not depend on ratings, or ranking, as discussed below.

Individual pay reviews based on ratings

Managers propose increases on the basis of their performance management ratings within a given pay review budget and in accordance with pay review guidelines. Forty-two per cent of the respondents to the CIPD 2003 performance management survey (Armstrong and Baron, 2004) used ratings to inform contingent pay decisions. Approaches to rating were discussed in Chapter 38.

There is a choice of methods. The simplest way is to have a direct link between the rating and the pay increase, for example:

Rating	Percentage increase
A	6
B	4
C	3
D	2
E	0

A more sophisticated approach is to use a pay matrix, as illustrated in Table 53.1. This indicates the percentage increase payable for different performance ratings according to the position of the individual's pay in the pay range. This is sometimes referred to as an individual 'compa-ratio' and expresses pay as a percentage of the midpoint in a range. A compa-ratio of 100 per cent means that the salary would be at the midpoint.

Many people argue that linking performance management too explicitly to pay prejudices the essential developmental nature of performance management. However, realistically it is accepted that decisions on performance-related or contribution-related increases have to be based on some form of assessment. One solution is to 'decouple' performance management and the pay review by holding them several months apart, and 45 per cent of the respondents to the CIPD 2003 survey (Armstrong and Baron, 2004) separated performance management reviews from pay reviews (43 per cent of the respondents to the e-reward 2004 survey separated the review). There is still a read-across but it is not so immediate. Some try to do without formulaic approaches (ratings and pay matrices) altogether, although it is impossible to dissociate contingent pay completely from some form of assessment.

Table 53.1 A pay matrix

	Percentage pay increase according to performance rating and position in pay range (compa-ratio)			
Rating	Position in pay range			
	80%-90%	91%-100%	101%-110%	111%-120%
Excellent	12%	10%	8%	6%
Very effective	10%	8%	6%	4%
Effective	6%	4%	3%	0
Developing	4%	3%	0	0
Ineligible	0	0	0	0

Doing without ratings

Twenty-seven per cent of the respondents to the 2004 e-reward survey of contingent pay did without ratings. The percentage of respondents to the 2003 CIPD performance management survey who did not use ratings was 52 per cent (this figure is too high to be fully reliable and may have been inflated by those who treat service-related increments, which do not depend on ratings, as contingent pay). One respondent to the e-reward survey explained that in the absence of ratings, the approach they used was 'informed subjectivity', which meant considering ongoing performance in the form of overall contribution.

Some companies adopt what might be called an 'holistic' approach. Managers propose where people should be placed in the pay range for their grade, taking into account their contribution and pay relative to others in similar jobs, their potential, and the relationship of their current pay to market rates. The decision may be expressed in the form of a statement that an individual is now worth £30,000 rather than £28,000. The increase is 7 per cent, but what counts is the overall view about the value of a person to the organization, not the percentage increase to that person's pay.

Ranking

Ranking is carried out by managers who place staff in a rank order according to an overall assessment of relative contribution or merit and then distribute performance ratings through the rank order. The top 10 per cent could get an A rating, the next 15 per cent a B rating, and so on. The ratings determine the size of the reward. A forced ranking or 'vitality curve' system may be used to compel managers to conform to predetermined proportions of staff in each grade. But ranking depends on fair, consistent and equitable assessments, which cannot be guaranteed, and assumes that there is some sort of standard distribution of ability across the organization, which may not be the case.

Guidelines for managers on conducting individual pay reviews

Whichever approach is adopted, guidelines have to be issued to managers on how they should conduct reviews. These guidelines will stipulate that they must keep within their budgets and may indicate the maximum and minimum increases that can be awarded with an indication of how awards could be distributed, eg when the budget is 4 per cent overall, it might be suggested that a 3 per cent increase should be given to the majority of their staff and the others given higher or lower increases as long as the total percentage increase does not exceed the budget. Managers in some companies are instructed that they must follow a forced pattern of distribution (a forced choice system) but only 8 per cent of the respondents to the 2003 CIPD survey (Armstrong and Baron, 2004) used this method. To help them to explore alternatives, managers may be provided with a spreadsheet that contains details of the existing rates of staff and which can be used to model alternative distributions on a 'what if' basis. Managers may also be encouraged to 'fine tune' their pay recommendations to ensure that individuals are on the right track within their grade according to their level of performance, competence and time in the job compared with their peers. To do this, they need guidelines on typical rates of progression in relation to performance, skill or competence, and specific guidance on what they can and should do. They also need information on the positions of their staff in the pay structure in relation to the policy guidelines.

Conducting individual pay reviews

Steps required to conduct individual pay review

1. Agree budget.
2. Prepare and issue guidelines on the size, range and distribution of awards and on methods of conducting the review.
3. Provide advice and support.
4. Review proposals against budget and guidelines and agree modifications to them if necessary.
5. Summarize and cost proposals and obtain approval.
6. Update payroll.
7. Inform employees.

It is essential to provide advice, guidance and training to line managers as required. Some managers will be confident and capable from the start. Others will have a lot to learn.

Reward procedures

Reward procedures deal with grading jobs, fixing rates of pay and handling appeals.

Grading jobs

The procedures for grading jobs set out how job evaluation should be used to grade a new job or re-grade an existing one. A point-factor evaluation scheme that has defined grades may be used for all new jobs and to deal with requests for re-grading. However, an analytical matching process (see Chapter 47) may be used to compare the role profiles of the jobs to be graded with grade or level profiles, or profiles of benchmark jobs. This is likely to be the case in large organizations and for broad-banded structures.

Fixing rates of pay on appointment

The procedure should indicate how much freedom line managers and HR have to pay above the minimum rate for the job. The freedom may be limited to, say, 10 per cent above the minimum or two or three pay points on an incremental scale. More scope is sometimes allowed to respond to market rate pressures or to attract particularly well-qualified staff by paying up to the reference point or target salary in a pay range, subject to HR approval and bearing in mind the need to provide scope for contingent pay increases. If recruitment supplements or premiums are used, the rules for offering them to candidates must be clearly defined.

Promotion increases

The procedure will indicate what is regarded as a meaningful increase on promotion, often 10 per cent or more. To avoid creating anomalies, the level of pay has to take account of what other people are paid who are carrying out work at a similar level and it is usual to lay down a maximum level that does not take the pay of the promoted employee above the reference point for the new range.

Appeals

It is customary to include the right to appeal against gradings as part of a job evaluation procedure. Appeals against pay decisions are usually made through the organization's grievance procedure.

Managing the development of reward systems

As Brown (2001) has noted: 'Underneath the glossy jargon in the policy documentation, the reality is that changing pay and benefits practices is a sensitive, difficult and time-consuming exercise.' As a senior reward practitioner explained to e-reward (2003):

> *A key challenge is getting the people in all of the different departments involved in the project – recruitment, employment policy, internal communications, human resources and reward – to work together. If change strategies do not carry everyone in the organization willingly forward, the process can be painful and even damaging. So it's vital that the reward manager builds relationships with the right people. You need to get key individuals to work together without them feeling that they are losing control of their initiatives. Never underestimate the value of in-depth employee consultation. It is necessary to spend money on professional research – market research, HR consultants to design and facilitate focus groups – as though you are conducting a market research exercise. Employees are consumers. You need to sell the initiative to them and help them understand why it is taking place.*

Developing reward systems is indeed a complex process, as illustrated in Figure 53.1. Throughout the sequence of events shown there, it is essential to communicate with and involve the stakeholders – top management, line managers, employees and employee representatives.

Devolution to line managers of responsibility for reward

The trend is to devolve more authority to line managers for pay decisions dealing with pay increases awarded in periodical individual pay reviews and, less commonly, fixing rates of pay on appointment or promotion. Authority is generally constrained by the requirement to keep within strictly defined budget limits. Line managers will be required to make decisions that are in accordance with policy guidelines. The amount of authority devolved can vary widely.

Reasons for devolution

The reasons for devolving more authority for pay decisions to line managers are as follows:

- the trend generally to devolve more decision-making authority and accountability to line managers;

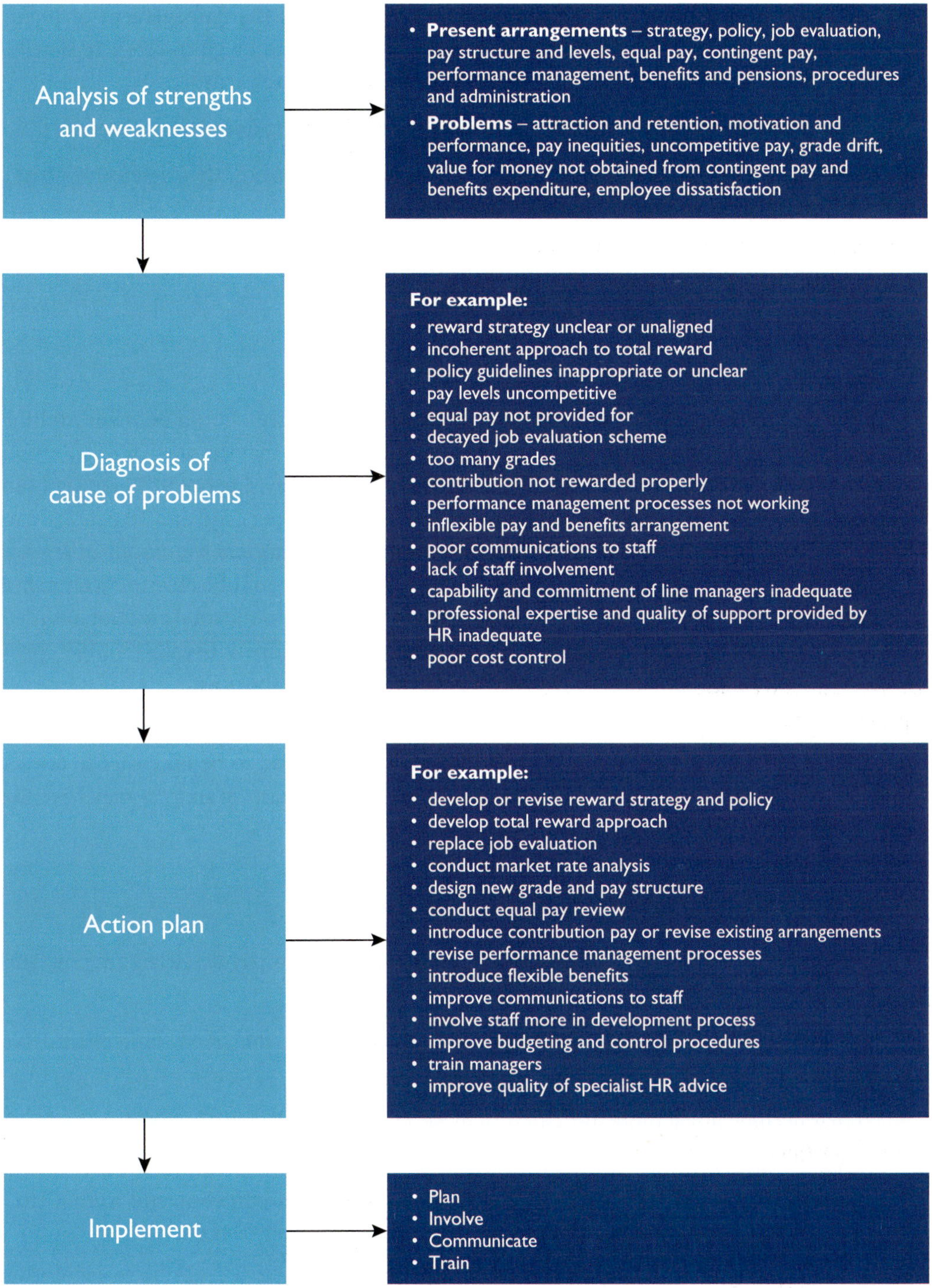

Figure 53.1 Development of reward system

- the belief that if managers are to be held accountable for the management of their resources and the performance of their teams they ought to be given scope to determine, within the guidelines, how team members should be rewarded;
- delayering in organizations has forced more decision making onto line managers;
- a generally more flexible approach to reward management means that rigid centralized control of pay is no longer appropriate;
- line managers are close to individual employees and are in the best position to know how they should be valued.

Guidelines

Pay review guidelines can spell out the basis upon which decisions should be made and the way awards should be distributed. For example, it might be stated that the normal distribution of awards is as follows: 70 per cent receive the average reward of, say, 3 per cent; 20 per cent can be given an above average award of, say, between 4 per cent and 6 per cent; and 10 per cent can be given a below average reward. If the policy is to provide a reasonable amount of leeway, these guidelines might be treated as indicative only; managers would be able to recommend deviations from them as long as these were objectively justified and the total amount awarded to their staff did not exceed the budget. In addition, the HR department usually monitors proposed increases and asks managers to justify any deviations from the norm.

Guidelines on fixing salaries may limit the discretion to pay more than a defined amount, eg up to 10 per cent above the pay range minimum, if this is believed to be necessary to attract someone or provide a person with an adequate promotion increase. Managers may have the right to make out a case for paying more.

Problems with devolution

The arguments for devolving more authority to line managers for pay decisions are powerful but there are a number of problems, namely:

- the danger of managers making biased, unfair or ill-informed judgements is increased;
- it may become much more difficult to achieve a reasonable degree of consistency across departments;
- it is difficult to achieve the right balance between centralized direction and control (to achieve consistency) and freedom for managers to make their own decisions.

Dealing with the problems

It would be most unusual for any organization to give unlimited freedom to line managers. The least that can be done is to control payroll costs by requiring managers to keep within their budgets. Beyond that, in any organization where top management does not operate hands-on control of all decisions (which means almost every organization), there have to be some guidelines, such as those mentioned above and explained in more detail earlier in this chapter (fixing rates of pay) and individual pay reviews. The culture of the organization and its management style will determine how exacting those guidelines will be but, if it is believed that devolution is desirable, then some freedom to act should be provided within the guidelines. However, it is still necessary for the HR department to monitor proposed increases. Such monitoring might have to be fairly tight when devolution first takes place or for newly appointed managers, although it should be relaxed when it is believed that managers will act responsibly.

Communicating to employees

Transparency is important. Employees need to know how reward policies will affect them and how pay and grading decisions have been made. They need to be convinced that the system is fair.

Communicating to employees collectively

Employees and their representatives should be informed about the guiding principles and policies that underpin the reward system and the reward strategies that drive it. They should understand the grade and pay structure, how grading decisions are made, including the job evaluation system, how their pay can progress within the structure, the basis upon which contingent pay increases are determined, and policies on the provision of benefits including details of a flexible benefits scheme if one is available.

Communicating to individual employees

Individual employees should understand how their grade, present rate of pay and pay increases have been determined and the pay opportunities available to them – the scope for pay progression and how their contribution will be assessed through performance management. They should be informed of the value of the benefits they receive so that they are aware of their total remuneration and, if appropriate, how they can exercise choice over the range or scale of their benefits through a flexible benefits scheme.

Managing reward systems – key learning points

Reward forecasting

It is necessary to forecast future payroll costs, taking into account the number of people employed and the impact of pay reviews and contingent pay awards.

Reward budgets

Pay review budgets set out the increase in payroll costs that will result for either general or individual pay. Total payroll budgets are based on the number of people employed in different jobs and their present and forecast rates of pay.

Compa-ratio analysis

Compa-ratios can be used to define the extent to which pay policy is achieved (the relationship between the policy and actual rates of pay) The analysis of compa-ratios indicates what action may have to be taken to slow down or accelerate increases if compa-ratios are too high or too low compared with the policy level.

Attrition analysis

Attrition can be calculated by the formula: total percentage increase to payroll arising from general or individual pay increases minus total percentage increase in average rates of pay. If it can be proved that attrition is going to take place, the amount involved can be taken into account as a means of at least partly financing individual pay increases.

Assessing added value

Assessing the added value (ie the value for money) provided by existing practices or by new practices when they are implemented is a major consideration when monitoring and evaluating reward management processes.

Conducting general pay reviews

General reviews take place when employees are given an increase in response to general market rate movements, increases in the cost of living, or union negotiations. The steps are:

1. Decide on the budget.
2. Analyse data on pay settlements.
3. Conduct negotiations with trade unions.
4. Calculate costs.
5. Adjust the pay structure.
6. Inform employees.

Conducting individual pay reviews

1. Agree budget.
2. Prepare and issue guidelines on the size, range and distribution of awards and on methods of conducting the review.
3. Provide advice and support.
4. Review proposals against budget and guidelines and agree modifications to them if necessary.
5. Summarize and cost proposals and obtain approval.
6. Update payroll.
7. Inform employees.

Managing reward systems – key learning points (continued)

Reward procedures

Reward procedures deal with grading jobs, fixing rates of pay and handling appeals.

Managing the development of reward systems

See Figure 53.1.

Devolution of pay decisions to line managers

The trend is to devolve more authority to line managers for pay decisions dealing with pay increases awarded in periodical individual pay reviews and, less commonly, fixing rates of pay on appointment or promotion. But it is necessary to ensure that decisions are fair and consistent.

Communicating to employees

Transparency is important. Employees need to know how reward policies will affect them and how pay and grading decisions have been made. They need to be convinced that the system is fair.

Questions

1. From a member of your CIPD branch: 'I have just been asked to take on responsibility for reward management. One of the things my predecessor mentioned was the importance of keeping the midpoint management system going. Can you please tell me what midpoint and midpoint management are and why they are important?'
2. From the director of finance: 'Please tell me what steps can be taken to control the ever-increasing costs arising from our pay arrangements. As a local authority we seem to be landed with a fixed incremental system which, as labour turnover is low, means that the majority of people are at or near the top of their scale without, as I see it, necessarily having earned it in terms of value-adding performance'.
3. From the chief executive: 'What are the arguments for and against instituting a fixed distribution system for performance ratings to improve our ability to control payroll costs?'
4. From the director of personnel: 'Please let me know how you propose to ensure that the introduction of our new broad-graded pay structure runs smoothly.'

References

Armstrong, M and Baron, A (2004) *Managing Performance: Performance management in action*, CIPD, London

Brown, D (2001) *Reward Strategies: From intent to impact*, CIPD, London

e-reward (2003) *Research Report No 10*, e-reward.co.uk, Stockport

e-reward (2004) *Survey of Contingent Pay*, e-reward.co.uk, Stockport

Part X

Employee Relations

Employee or employment relations are concerned with generally managing the employment relationship with particular reference to terms and conditions of employment, issues arising from employment, providing employees with a voice and communicating with employees. Employees are dealt with either directly or through collective agreements where trade unions are recognized.

Employee relations cover a wider spectrum of the employment relationship than industrial relations, which are essentially about what goes on between management and trade union representatives and officials. This wider definition recognizes the move away from collectivism towards individualism in the ways in which employees relate to their employers.

Part X contents

54 The Employee Relations Framework

Key concepts and terms

- Collective bargaining
- Conjunctive bargaining
- Cooperative bargaining
- Custom and practice
- Distributive bargaining
- Employee relations
- Industrial relations
- Integrative bargaining
- Internal regulation
- Job regulation
- Mutuality
- Pluralist view
- Procedural rules
- Social partnership
- Stakeholder theory
- Substantive rules
- Unitary view
- Voluntarism

Learning outcomes

On completing this chapter you should be able to define these key concepts. You should also know about:

- The elements of employee relations
- Regulations and rules in industrial relations
- Unitary and pluralist views of employee relations
- Individualism and collectivism
- The HRM approach to employee relations
- Developments in industrial relations
- Industrial relations as a system of rules
- Collective bargaining
- Social partnership
- Voluntarism
- The context of industrial relations
- The parties to employee relations

Introduction

Employee or employment relations are concerned with managing and maintaining the employment relationship, which involves handling the pay–work bargain, dealing with employment practices, terms and conditions of employment, issues arising from employment, providing employees with a voice and communicating with employees. They consist of the approaches and methods adopted by employers to deal with employees either collectively through their trade unions or individually.

The term 'employee relations' encompasses that of industrial relations, which are about relationships between managements and trade unions involving collective agreements, collective bargaining, disputes resolution and dealing with issues concerning the employment relationship and the working environment. The processes involved in industrial relations are dealt with in Chapter 55.

The purpose of this chapter is to provide a general introduction to the complex subject of employee relations, the elements of which are discussed below.

The basis of employee relations

Employee relations are basically about the pay–work bargain – the agreement made between employers and employees whereby the former undertakes to pay for the work done by the latter. Fundamentally, many employers simply want employees who will do what they are told without costing too much. They want engagement and commitment. In contrast, employees want a say in how much they are rewarded, their terms and conditions of employment and the way in which their work is organized. They want good working conditions, security of employment, a healthy and safe working environment and the scope to raise and resolve grievances. Conflicts of interest can arise between employers and employees on these issues, and these conflicts are resolved by the various employee relations processes described in this chapter and Chapter 55.

Parties to the employment relationship

As Farnham (2000) puts it, employee relations deal with the interactions amongst the parties to the employment relationship. These consist of three groups: employers and employees, the parties who act on their behalf (trade unions and employer associations) and the third-party role played by the state agencies and the EU institutions. He points out that within organizations employee relations practices are the product of a number of factors, namely:

- the interests of the buyers and sellers of labour services (or human resources skills);
- the agreements and rules made by them and their agents;

- the conflict-resolving processes that are used;
- the external influences affecting the parties making employment decisions.

Purpose of employee relations

The purpose of employee relations is to provide for effective and consistent procedures for rule-making, consistency in dealing with employee relations issues, fairness, processes that can affect and improve employee behaviour or mechanisms to resolve differences/disputes. The value-added outcomes that can result from good employee relations include improved morale and commitment, fewer grievances, productivity increases and better control of labour costs.

Elements of employee relations

The elements of employee relations are summarized below.

Elements of employee relations

- The formal and informal employment policies and practices of the organization.
- The development, negotiation and application of formal systems, rules and procedures for collective bargaining, handling disputes and regulating employment. These serve to determine the reward for effort and other conditions of employment, to protect the interests of both employees and their employers, and to regulate the ways in which employers treat their employees and how the latter are expected to behave at work.
- The bargaining structures, recognition and collective agreements and practices that have evolved to enable the formal system to operate.
- Policies and practices for employee voice and communications.
- The informal as well as the formal processes that take place in the shape of continuous interactions between managers and team leaders or supervisors on the one hand and employee representatives and individuals on the other. These may happen within the framework of formal agreements but are often governed by custom and practice and the climate of relationships that has been built up over the years.
- The philosophies and policies of the major players in the industrial relations scene: the government of the day, management and the trade unions.

- A number of parties, each with different roles. These consist of the state, management, employer's organizations, the trade unions, individual managers and supervisors, HR managers, employee representatives or shop stewards and employees.
- The legal framework.
- A number of institutions such as in the UK, the Advisory, Conciliation and Arbitration Service (ACAS) and the employment tribunals.
- The Directives produced by the EC.

The chapter concentrates on the industrial relations aspects of employee relations. Other aspects of employee relations are dealt with in Chapters 55 to 57. Industrial relations theory is strongly influenced by the concept that it is based on a system of rules, as described below.

Industrial relations as a system of rules

The systems theory of industrial relations, as propounded by Dunlop (1958), states that industrial relations can be regarded as a system or web of rules regulating employment and the ways in which people behave at work. According to this theory, the role of the system is to produce the regulations and procedural rules that govern how much is distributed in the bargaining process and how the parties involved, or the 'actors' in the industrial relations scene, relate to one another. Dunlop explained that the output of the system takes the following form.

SOURCE REVIEW

Output of the industrial relations system, Dunlop (1958)

The regulations and policies of the management hierarchy; the laws of any worker hierarchy; the regulations, degrees, decisions, awards or orders of governmental agencies; the rules and decisions of specialized agencies created by the management and worker hierarchies; collective bargaining arrangements and the customs and traditions of the workplace and work community.

The system is expressed in many formal or informal guises: in legislation and statutory orders, in trade union regulations, in collective agreements and arbitration awards, in social conventions, in managerial decisions, and in accepted 'custom and practice'. The 'rules' may be defined and coherent, or ill-defined and incoherent. Within a plant the rules may mainly be concerned with doing no more than defining the status quo that both parties recognize as the norm from which deviations may be made only by agreement. In this sense, therefore, an industrial relations system is a normative system where a norm can be seen as a rule, a standard, or a pattern for action that is generally accepted or agreed as the basis upon which the parties concerned should operate. Trade unions will always be anxious to preserve any aspects of custom and practice beneficial to their members and resist attempts by management to make changes.

Criticisms of the system of rules theory

However, the systems theory of industrial relations has been criticized. Kochan *et al* (1986) see a more active as opposed to merely adaptive role for management because they are in a strong position to exercise strategic choice. They also believe that there are more interrelated levels of industrial relations. In addition to the functional level of collective bargaining there is the strategic (corporate) level and the workplace level (supervisory style, participation, job design and work organization). Because these work levels interact and, because different ideologies dominate each level, instability and conflict are inevitable. It is only at the functional level, ie the level of collective bargaining, that there is a need for a collective ideology to bind the system together.

Schilstra (1998) criticized the Dunlop systems theory because behavioural factors are virtually absent, it concentrates on rules and procedures as outputs and does not explain how the rules are determined, and the focus on rules and job regulation as the outputs of the system concentrates on accommodation and equilibrium, not on conflict and change.

The theory is right to emphasize the importance of rules in the context of traditional industrial relations and, as described below, they still play a significant role. But it does not sufficiently take into account the distribution of power between management and trade unions nor the impact of the state. Neither does it adequately explain the role of the individual in industrial relations.

Regulations and rules in industrial relations

Job regulation aims to provide a framework of minimum rights and rules. These may provide for internal or external regulation, contain substantive or procedural rules or be expressed in the form of collective agreements or custom and practice, as described below.

Internal and external regulation

Internal regulation is concerned with procedures for dealing with grievances, redundancies, or disciplinary problems, and rules concerning the operation of the employment relationship and the rights of shop stewards. External regulation is carried out by means of employment legislation, the rules of trade unions and employers' associations, and the regulative content of procedural or substantive rules and agreements.

Substantive and procedural rules

Substantive rules settle the rights and obligations attached to jobs. It is interesting to note that in the UK, the parties to collective agreements have tended to concentrate more on procedural than on substantive rules. In the United States, where there is greater emphasis on fixed-term agreements, the tendency has been to rely more on substantive rules.

Procedural rules are intended to regulate relationships, especially those involving conflict, between the parties to collective bargaining, and when their importance is emphasized, a premium is being placed on industrial peace.

Collective agreements

A collective agreement is a formal agreement between management and trade unions dealing with terms and conditions of employment or other aspects of the relationships between the two parties. The forms of collective agreement are described in Chapter 55.

Custom and practice

The term 'custom and practice' refers to the unwritten rules on how industrial relations and employment issues should be dealt with that have been built up and accepted by management and the trade unions over time. Custom and practice is an implied contractual term when it meets the following criteria: 1) the practice is definite and can be defined, 2) it is reasonable to all the parties concerned, and 3) it is applied so that the parties to employee relations know the practice exists. Once established, trade unions generally want to hang onto custom and practice. If management wants to change it, they expect something in return.

Collective bargaining

The industrial relations system is regulated by collective bargaining, defined by Flanders (1970) as a social process that 'continually turns disagreements into agreements in an orderly fashion'.

Collective bargaining is the establishment by negotiation and discussion of agreement on matters of mutual concern to employers and unions covering the employment relationship and terms and conditions of employment. It therefore provides a framework within which the views of management and unions about disputed matters that could lead to industrial disorder can be considered, with the aim of eliminating the causes of the disorder. Collective bargaining is a joint regulating process, dealing with the regulation of management in its relationships with work people as well as the regulation of conditions of employment. It has a political as well as an economic basis – both sides are interested in the distribution of power between them as well as the distribution of income.

Collective bargaining can be regarded as an exchange relationship in which wage–work bargains take place between employers and employees through the agency of a trade union. Traditionally, the role of trade unions as bargaining agents has been perceived as being to offset the inequalities of individual bargaining power between employers and employees in the labour market.

Collective bargaining can also be seen as a political relationship in which trade unions, as Chamberlain and Kuhn (1965) noted, share industrial sovereignty or power over those who are governed, the employees. The sovereignty is held jointly by management and union in the collective bargaining process.

Above all, collective bargaining is a power relationship that takes the form of a measure of power-sharing between management and trade unions (although recently the balance of power has shifted markedly in the direction of management).

Bargaining power

The extent to which industrial sovereignty is shared by management with its trade unions (if at all) depends upon the relative bargaining powers of the two parties. Bargaining power can be defined as the ability to induce the other side to make a decision or take a course of action that it would otherwise be unwilling to make. Each side is involved in guessing the bargaining preferences and bargaining power of the other side.

As Fox and Flanders (1969) commented: 'Power is the crucial variable which determines the outcome of collective bargaining'. It has been suggested by Hawkins (1979) that a crucial test of bargaining power is 'whether the cost to one side in accepting a proposal from the other is higher than the cost of not accepting it'. Singh (1989) has pointed out that bargaining power is not static but varies over time. He also noted that:

> *Bargaining power is inherent in any situation where differences have to be reconciled. It is, however, not an end in itself and negotiations must not rely solely on bargaining power. One side may have enormous bargaining power, but to use it to the point where the other side feels that it is impossible to deal with such a party is to defeat the purpose of negotiations.*

Atkinson (1989) asserts that:

- What creates bargaining power can be appraised in terms of subjective assessments by individuals involved in the bargaining process.
- Each side can guess the bargaining preferences and bargaining power of the other side.
- There are normally a number of elements creating bargaining power.

Forms of collective bargaining

Collective bargaining takes two basic forms, as identified by Chamberlain and Kuhn (1965).

1. Conjunctive bargaining, which 'arises from the absolute requirement that some agreement – any agreement – may be reached so that the operations on which both are dependent may continue', results in a 'working relationship in which each party agrees, explicitly or implicitly, to provide certain requisite services, to recognize certain seats of authority, and to accept certain responsibilities in respect of each other'. In other words, both parties are seeking to reach agreement.
2. Cooperative bargaining, in which it is recognized that each party is dependent on the other and can achieve its objectives more effectively if it wins the support of the other.

Walton and McKersie (1965) made the distinction between distributive bargaining, defined as the 'complex system of activities instrumental to the attainment of one party's goals when they are in basic conflict with those of the other party', and integrative bargaining, defined as the 'system of activities which are not in fundamental conflict with those of the other party and which therefore can be integrated to some degree'. These activities aim to define 'an area of common concern, a purpose'.

The unitary and pluralist views

There are two basic views expressed about the basis of the relationship between management and trade unions in particular or employees in general: the unitary and the pluralist perspectives (a concept originally developed by Fox, 1966).

The unitary view

The unitary view is one typically held by management who see their function as that of directing and controlling the workforce to achieve economic and growth objectives. To this end, management believes that it is the rule-making authority. Management tends to view the enterprise as a unitary system with one source of authority – itself – and one focus of loyalty – the organization. It extols the virtue of teamwork, where everyone strives jointly to a common objective, everyone pulls their weight to the best of their ability, and everyone accepts their place and function gladly, following the leadership of the appointed manager or supervisor. These are admirable sentiments, but they sometimes lead to what McClelland (1963) referred to as an orgy of 'avuncular pontification' on the part of the leaders of industry.

The unitary view, which is essentially autocratic and authoritarian, has sometimes been expressed in agreements as 'management's right to manage'. The philosophy of HRM with its emphasis on commitment and mutuality owes much to the unitary perspective.

It was claimed by Edwards (1990) in line with labour process theory, that relationships between capital and labour are ones of 'structured antagonism'. Although as the revisionist labour process theorists Thompson and Harley (2007) comment: 'In the employment relationship there will always be (actual and potential) conflict, but simultaneously there will be shared interests.'

The pluralist view

The pluralist view, as described by Fox (1966), is that an industrial organization is a plural society, containing many related but separate interests and objectives that must be maintained in some kind of equilibrium. In place of a corporate unity reflected in a single focus of authority and loyalty, management has to accept the existence of rival sources of leadership and attachment. It has to face the fact that in Drucker's (1951) view, a business enterprise has a triple personality: it is at once an economic, a political and a social institution. In the first, it produces and distributes incomes. In the second, it embodies a system of government in which managers collectively exercise authority over the managed, but are also themselves involved in an intricate pattern of political relationships. Its third personality is revealed in the organization's community, which evolves from below out of face-to-face relations based on shared interests, sentiments, beliefs and values among various groups of employees.

Pluralism conventionally regards the workforce as being represented by 'an opposition that does not seek to govern' (Clegg, 1976). Pluralism, as described by Cave (1994), involved:

> *a balance of power between two organized interests and a sufficient degree of trust within the relationship (usually) for each side to respect the other's legitimate and, on occasions, separate interests, and for both sides to refrain from pushing their interest separately to the point where it became impossible to keep the show on the road.*

It has been noted by Guest (1995) that: 'The tradition of bargaining at plant or even organization level has reinforced a pluralistic concept.' The concept of pluralism underpins that of social partnership, as discussed below.

The concept of social partnership

Social partnership is the concept that, as stakeholders, the parties involved in employee relations should aim to work together to the greater good of all. It has been defined by Ackers and Payne (1998) as 'a stable, collaborative relationship between capital and labour, as represented by an independent trade union, providing for low social conflict and significant worker influence on business decision making through strong collective bargaining'. The then General Secretary of the TUC, John Monks, wrote in 1996, 'The trade union movement is uniquely placed to create a new social and political settlement based on solidarity and justice. To achieve this great prize we have to work through dialogue, cooperation and compromise – a social partnership.'

The concept of social partnership is rooted in stakeholder theory as originally formulated by Freeman (1984). Donaldson and Preston (1995) define the theory as representing the corporation as a 'constellation of cooperative and competitive interests'. They explain that:

> *stakeholders are identified by their interest in the corporation, whether or not the corporation has any interests in them. Each group of stakeholder merits consideration because of its own sake and not merely because of its ability to further the interests of some other group, such as the shareholders.*

As Hampden-Turner (1996) commented: 'Stakeholders include at least five parties: employees, shareholders, customers, community and government. Wealth is created when all work together.' The Industrial Partnership Association (1996) stated that the concept of social partnership could be applied to create a favourable industrial relations terrain in which there was:

- a new approach to relationships at work;
- security of employment and job flexibility;
- sharing in the success of the organization;
- information, consultation and employee involvement;
- representation of the workforce.

The concept of social partnership can be put into practice through partnership agreements, as described in Chapter 55.

Individualism and collectivism

Purcell (1987) argues that the distinction between pluralist and unitary frames of management has 'provided a powerful impetus to the debate about management style, but the mutually exclusive nature of these categories has limited further development'. Moreover, wide variations can be found within both the unitary and the pluralist approach. He therefore suggests an alternative distinction between 'individualism' – policies focusing on individual employees and 'collectivism' – the extent to which groups of workers have an independent voice and participate in decision making with managers. He believes that companies can and do operate on both these dimensions of management style.

Voluntarism and its decline

The essence of the systems theory of industrial relations is that the rules are jointly agreed by the representatives of the parties to employment relations; an arrangement which, it is believed, makes for readier acceptance than if they were imposed by a third party such as the state. This concept of voluntarism was defined by Kahn-Freund (1972) as 'the policy of the law to allow the two sides by agreement and practice to develop their own norms and their own sanctions and to abstain from legal compulsion in their collective relationship'. It was, in essence, voluntarism that came under attack by government legislation from 1974 onwards, including the principle of 'immunities' for industrial action and the closed shop.

The HRM approach to employee relations

The philosophy of human resource management has been translated into the following prescriptions that constitute the HRM model for employee relations.

The HRM model of employee relations

- A drive for commitment – winning the 'hearts and minds' of employees to get them to identify with the organization, to exert themselves more on its behalf and to remain with the organization, thus ensuring a return on their training and development.
- An emphasis on mutuality – getting the message across that 'we are all in this together' and that the interests of management and employees coincide (ie a unitarist approach).
- The organization of complementary forms of communication such as team briefings, alongside traditional collective bargaining – ie approaching employees directly as individuals or in groups rather than through their representatives.

- A shift from collective bargaining to individual contracts.
- The use of employee involvement techniques such as improvement groups.
- Continuous pressure on quality – total quality management.
- Increased flexibility in working arrangements, including multi-skilling, to provide for the more effective use of human resources, sometimes accompanied by an agreement to provide secure employment for the 'core' workers.
- Emphasis on teamwork.
- Harmonization of terms and conditions for all employees.

The key contrasting dimensions of traditional industrial relations and HRM have been presented by Guest (1995), as set out below.

SOURCE REVIEW

Dimensions of industrial relations and HRM, Guest (1995)

Dimension	Industrial Relations	HRM
Psychological contract	Compliance	Commitment
Behaviour references	Norms, custom and practice	Values/mission
Relations	Low trust, pluralist, collective	High trust, unitarist, individual
Organization design	Formal roles, hierarchy, division	Flexible roles, flat structure of labour, managerial control, teamwork/ autonomy, self control

Guest notes that this model aims to support the achievement of the three main sources of competitive advantage identified by Porter (1985) namely: innovation, quality and cost leadership. Innovation and quality strategies require employee commitment, while cost leadership strategies are believed by many organizations to be only achievable without a union. 'The logic of a market-driven HRM strategy is that where high organizational commitment is sought, unions are irrelevant. Where cost advantage is the goal, unions and industrial relations systems appear to carry higher costs.'

An HRM approach is still possible if trade unions are recognized by the organization. In this case, the employee relations strategy might be to marginalize or at least side-step them by dealing directly with employees through involvement and communications processes.

The context of industrial relations

Industrial relations are conducted within the external context of the national political and economic environment, the international context and the internal context of the organization.

The political context

The political context is formed by the government of the day. The Conservative administrations from 1979 onwards set out to curb the power of the trade unions through legislation, and succeeded to a degree. The Labour Government since 1997 has not made any other major changes to the existing trade union legislation.

The economic context

Perhaps the most significant feature of the changing economic environment from the industrial relations viewpoint has been the drastic cutbacks in manufacturing industry, where unions have traditionally been strongly organized.

The European context

Employee relations in the UK are affected by European Union regulations and initiatives. A number of Articles in the original treaty of Rome referred to the promotion of improvements in working conditions and the need to develop dialogue between the two sides of industry. The conduct of employee relations in Britain is increasingly being affected by EC Directives such as those concerning works councils and working hours.

The organizational context

The need to 'take cost out of the business' has meant that employers have focused on the cost of labour – usually the highest and most easily reduced cost, hence 'the lean organization' movement and large-scale redundancies, especially in manufacturing. There has been pressure for greater flexibility and increased management control of operations, which has had a direct impact on employee relations policies and union agreements.

The widespread introduction of new technology and IT has aimed to increase productivity by achieving higher levels of efficiency and reducing labour costs. Organizations are relying more on a core of key full-time employees, leaving the peripheral work to be undertaken by subcontractors and the increasing numbers of part-timers – women and men. This has reduced the number of employees who wish to join unions or remain trade union members.

Developments in industrial relations

Developments in the practice of industrial relations since the 1960s can be divided into the following phases:

1. The traditional system existing prior to the 1970s.
2. The Donovan analysis of 1968.
3. The interventionist and employment protection measures of the 1970s.
4. The 1980s programme for curbing what were perceived by the Conservative government to be the excesses of rampant trade unionism.
5. Developments since the 1980s.
6. The findings of the Workplace Employee Relations Survey (WERS) 2004.

1. The traditional system – to 1971

Relations prior to 1971 and indeed for most of the 1970s could be described as a system of collective representation designed to contain conflict. Voluntary collective bargaining between employers and employees' associations was the central feature of the system, and this process of joint regulation (the regulation of terms and conditions of employment by agreement between management and trade unions) was largely concerned with pay and basic conditions of employment, especially hours of work in industry, and legal abstention on the part of the state and the judiciary. During this period and, in fact, for most of the century, the British system of industrial relations was characterized by a tradition of voluntarism.

2. The Donovan analysis

The high incidence of disputes and strikes, the perceived power of the trade unions and some well-publicized examples of shop steward militancy (although the majority were quite amenable) contributed to the pressure for the reform of industrial relations which led to the setting up of the Donovan Commission (the Royal Commission on Industrial Relations, 1968). This concluded that the formal system of industry-wide bargaining was breaking down. Its key findings were that, at plant level, bargaining was highly fragmented and ill-organized, based on informality and custom and practice. The Commission's prescription was for a continuation of voluntarism, reinforced by organized collective bargaining arrangements locally, thus relieving trade unions and employers' associations of the 'policing role', which they so often failed to carry out. This solution involved the creation of new, orderly and systematic frameworks for collective bargaining at plant level by means of formal negotiation and procedural agreements.

Since Donovan, comprehensive policies, structures and procedures to deal with pay and conditions, shop steward facilities, discipline, health and safety, etc have been developed at plant level to a substantial extent. The support provided by Donovan to the voluntary system of industrial relations was, however, underpinned by a powerful minority note of reservation penned by Andrew Shonfield in the report of the Royal Commission. He advocated a more interventionist approach, which began to feature in Government policies in the 1970s.

3. Interventionism in the 1970s

The received wisdom in the 1960s, as reflected in the majority Donovan report, was that industrial relations could not be controlled by legislation. But the Industrial Relations Act introduced by the Conservative Government in 1971 ignored this belief and drew heavily on Shonfield's minority report. It introduced a strongly interventionist legal framework to replace the voluntary regulation of industrial relations systems. Trade unions lost their general immunity from legal action and had to register under the Act if they wanted any rights at all. Collective agreements were to become legally binding contracts and a number of 'unfair industrial practices' were proscribed. Individual workers were given the right to belong or not belong to a trade union, although no attempt was made to outlaw the closed shop. But the Act failed to make any impact; being ignored or side-stepped by both trade unions and employers, although it did introduce the important general right of employees 'not to be unfairly dismissed'.

The Labour Government of 1974 promptly repealed the 1971 Industrial Relations Act and entered into a 'social contract' with the trade unions that incorporated an agreement that the TUC would support the introduction of a number of positive union rights. These included a statutory recognition procedure and in effect meant that the unions expressed their commitment to legal enforcement as a means of restricting management's prerogatives.

Statutory rights were also provided for minimum notice periods, statements of terms and conditions, redundancy payments and unfair dismissal.

4. The 1980s – curbing the trade unions

The strike-ridden 'winter of discontent' in 1978 and the return of a Conservative Government in 1979 paved the way for the ensuing step-by-step legislation that continued throughout the 1980s and into the early 1990s. The ethos of the Conservative Governments in the 1980s was summed up by Phelps Brown (1990) as follows:

People are no longer seen as dependent on society and bound by reciprocal relationship to it; indeed the very notion of society is rejected. Individuals are expected to shift for themselves and those who get into difficulties are thought to have only themselves to blame. Self-reliance, acquisitive individualism, the curtailment of public expenditure, the play of market forces instead of the restraints and directives of public policy, the prerogatives of management instead of the power of the unions, centralization of power instead of pluralism.

The legislation on trade unions followed this ethos, and was guided by an ideological analysis expressed in the 1981 Green Paper on Trade Union Immunities as follows: 'Industrial relations cannot operate fairly and efficiently or to the benefit of the nation as a whole if either employers or employees collectively are given predominant power – that is, the capacity effectively to dictate the behaviour of others.'

The Government described industrial relations as 'the fundamental cause of weakness in the British economy', with strikes and restrictive practices inhibiting the country's ability to compete in international markets. The balance of bargaining power was perceived to have moved decisively in favour of trade unions, which were described as 'irresponsible, undemocratic and intimidatory', while the closed shop was described as being destructive of the rights of the individual worker.

5. Developments since the 1980s

In their analysis of the industrial relations scene, Kessler and Bayliss (1992) commented that 'the needs of employers have increasingly been towards enterprise orientated rather than occupationally orientated trade unions'. They also noted that: 'It is clear that the significance of industrial relations in many firms has diminished. It is part of a management controlled operation – a branch of human resource management. It is no longer a high profile problem-ridden part of personnel management as it so often was in the 1970s.'

Guest (1995) noted that the industrial relations system may continue as a largely symbolic 'empty shell', insufficiently important for management to confront and eliminate, but retaining the outward appearance of health to the casual observer: 'Management sets the agenda, which is market-driven, while industrial relations issues are relatively low on the list of concerns.'

Rousseau (2001) noted that in the United States there had been a shift from general (negotiated at the centre) to idiosyncratic contracts (negotiated at the local level between line managers and employees). However, in the UK, research by Blanden *et al* (2006) established that in the private sector there had been a slight fall in de-recognition but a relatively large increase in recognition.

6. Workplace Employee Relations Survey (WERS) 2004

The findings of this survey showed some significant changes from the 1998 survey. Most striking of all, perhaps, was the continuing decline of collective labour organization. Employees were less likely to be union members than they were in 1998; workplaces were less likely to recognize unions for bargaining over pay and conditions; collective bargaining was less prevalent. Even so, the rate of decline seemed to have slowed down from that seen in earlier periods and the joint regulation of terms and conditions remains a reality for many employees in Britain: one-half of employees were employed in workplaces with a recognized trade union; one-third were union members; and 40 per cent had their pay set through collective bargaining.

The parties to employee relations

The parties to employee relations are:

- the government;
- the trade unions;
- employee representatives or shop stewards;
- the Trade Union Congress (the TUC);
- staff associations;
- management;
- employers' organizations;
- the Confederation of British Industry;
- various institutions, agencies and officers;
- the European Union;
- the HR function.

The role of each of these parties is summarized below.

The government

The government plays multiple roles in shaping employee relations. These include being a major employer in its own right that sets standards of good employee relations practice, and acting as a paymaster in both the public sector and through private contractor services of employment, as an economic manager by influencing prices and wages, as a rule maker and legislator of employment rights and standards, and as a peace maker by providing services such as conciliation and arbitration.

The trade unions

Traditionally the fundamental purpose of trade unions is to promote and protect the interests of their members. They are there to redress the balance of power between employers and employees. As Emmott (2008) comments: 'Trade unionism has always been about power. The aim of trade unions is to redress the imbalance of power between employer and employee and this remains the fundamental basis for their existence.' Unions have been described by Ackers and Payne (1998) as 'essentially collective self-help bodies'. The basis of the employment relationship is the contract of employment. But this is not a contract between equals. Employers are almost always in a stronger position to dictate the terms of the contract than individual employees.

Trade unions, as indicated by Freeman and Medoff (1984), provide workers with a 'collective voice' to make their wishes known to management and thus bring actual and desired conditions closer together. This applies not only to terms of employment such as pay, working hours and holidays, but also to the way in which individuals are treated in such aspects of employment as the redress of grievances, discipline and redundancy. Trade unions also exist to let management know that there will be, from time to time, an alternative view on key issues affecting employees. More broadly, unions may see their role as that of participating with management on decision making on matters affecting their members' interests.

Within this overall role, trade unions have had two specific roles, namely: 1) to secure, through collective bargaining, improved terms and conditions for their members, and 2) to provide protection, support and advice to their members as individual employees. An additional role, that of providing legal, financial and other services to their members, has come to the fore more recently.

The key reasons why people may join a trade union include obtaining external support and protection from employment problems or seeking improvements in pay and terms and conditions. They may also join because union membership is common at a workplace or because of a belief in unionism.

Trade union structure

Trade unions are run by full-time central and, usually, district officials. There may be local committees of members. There is usually a general secretary who exercises control over the union and in the words of one union leader, Clive Jenkins, 'sits on the tip of a pyramid of organized indignation'. National officials may conduct industry-wide or major employer pay negotiations, while local officials may not be involved in plant negotiations unless there is a 'failure to agree' and the second stage of a negotiating procedure is invoked. Major employers who want to introduce significant changes in agreements or working arrangements may deal direct with national officials.

The state of the trade unions in the UK

The density of trade union membership in the UK declined from 32.4 in 1995 to 28.0 per cent in 2007 (union density is defined in *Labour Market Trends* as the proportion of the population in question who are union members – union membership is defined as the actual number of people who are members of a trade union). UK union density in the private sector was 16.1 per cent in 2007, a decline of 5.3 per cent from 1995. Density is much higher in the public sector (59.0 per cent) and actually rose by 0.3 per cent from 2006 although since 1995 it has fallen by 2.3 per cent. In both the public and private sectors, union density was higher for males than for females. In the private sector union density for males was 18.5 per cent compared to 12.8 per cent for females. In the public sector, male density was 61.3 per cent compared to 57.8 per cent for females.

The trade union movement is now dominated by the large general unions and the recently merged craft unions. The reasons for the decline in the private sector are not primarily disenchantment with the trade unions, or the impact of trade union legislation, or large-scale de-recognitions. The more important causes are structural and economic, namely:

- a shift in the economy away from large-scale manufacturing industries (traditionally heavily unionized) to the service industries (traditionally non-unionized);
- the trend to decentralize organizations;
- a decline in the number of workplaces employing large numbers of people;
- growing numbers of office and part-time workers;
- the impact of unemployment.

The differences between the private and public sectors are reflected in the figures for industrial disputes. Strikes are uncommon across most of the private sector, whereas in the public sector, industrial action – or the threat of it – remains relatively high on the agenda.

The actions taken by the unions to counteract this trend have included mergers to increase their perceived power and enable them to operate more cost-effectively, recruitment drives in non-unionized sectors (not very successful), and what used to be known as 'enterprise trade unionism' or 'the new reality'. The latter approach emphasizes the valuable role that unions can play as partners in the workplace, helping to manage change and improving productivity. It has been the basis for single union-deals, single-table bargaining, new-style agreements and partnership agreements, as described in Chapter 55. These approaches have worked in some instances, but many employers have remained unconvinced that the unions can play a positive role.

Employee representatives

Employee representatives or shop stewards are involved in discussing issues of mutual concern with management, and attending works councils and joint consultative committees. They may also be involved in settling disputes, resolving collective grievances, and representing individual employees with grievances or other disciplinary matters. If their union has negotiating rights, they will take part in collective bargaining often with the advice of union officials.

At one time, shop stewards were the ogres of the industrial relations scene. Undoubtedly there have been cases of excessively militant shop stewards and some may still exist. But employee representatives are there to be forthright when they have to be in taking up issues with management that concern their members. Where there are recognized trade unions, management have generally appreciated the value of employee representatives as points of contact and channels of communication. Their role may extend beyond the traditional areas of terms and conditions of employment and employment security to other matters that concern the workforce such as learning and development and health and safety.

Trade union learning representatives

Trade union learning representatives generate demand for learning among members, advise about learning, identify the learning needs of members, negotiate agreements incorporating learning, sit on joint learning or training committees, and work with employers to introduce and monitor learning and development initiatives that benefit members. Some of the difficulties encountered by learning representatives include reaching a wide range of members/ employers, employer resistance where unions are recognized, a limited role where there is no union recognition, and problems in small and medium-sized enterprises.

Health and safety representatives

Health and safety representatives:

- make representations to management on any matter affecting the health and safety of employees;
- cooperate with management in developing and promoting health and safety measures;
- take part in health and safety audits and inspections;
- sit on health and safety committees.

They can make a substantial contribution to creating and maintaining healthy and safe systems of work.

The Trade Union Congress (TUC)

The TUC acts as the collective voice of the unions. Its roles are to:

- represent the British trade union movement in the UK and internationally;
- conduct research and develop policies on trade union, industrial, economic and social matters and to campaign actively for them;
- regulate relationships between unions;
- help unions in dispute;
- provide various services (eg research) to affiliated unions.

International union organizations

The two main international union organizations are the European Trade Union Confederation and the International Trade Union Confederation. At present neither of these makes much impact on the UK, but this could change.

Staff associations

Staff associations are sometimes formed to represent employees in the absence of unions. They may sometimes have representational or even negotiating rights, but they seldom have anything like the real power possessed by a well-organized and supported trade union. They are often suspected by employees as being no more than management's poodle. Management have sometimes encouraged the development of staff associations as an alternative to trade unions, but this strategy has not always worked. In fact, in some organizations the existence of an unsatisfactory staff association has provided an opportunity for a trade union to gain membership and recognition. Staff associations have their uses as channels of communication and representatives can play a role in consultative processes and representing colleagues who want to take up grievances or who are being subject to disciplinary proceedings.

The role of management

The balance of power, especially in the private sector, has shifted to management, who now have more choice over how they conduct relationships with their employees. But the evidence is that there has been no concerted drive by management to de-recognize unions. As Kessler and Bayliss (1992) pointed out:

> *If managers in large establishments and companies wanted to make changes they looked at ways of doing so within the existing arrangements and if they could produce the goods they used them. Because managers found that the unions did not stand in their way they saw no reason for getting rid of them.*

They argued that management's industrial relations objectives are now generally to control the work process, secure cost-effectiveness, reassert managerial authority and move towards a more unitary and individualistic approach.

Storey (1992a) found in most of the cases he studied that there was a tendency for management to adopt HRM approaches to employee relations while still co-existing with the unions. But they gave increasing weight to systems of employee involvement, in particular communication, which by-pass trade unions.

Employers' organizations

Traditionally, employers' organizations have bargained collectively for their members with trade unions and have in general aimed to protect the interests of those members in their dealings with unions. Multi-employer or industry-wide bargaining, it was believed, allowed companies to compete in product markets without undercutting their competitors' employment costs and prevented the trade unions 'picking off' individual employers in a dispute.

The trend towards decentralizing bargaining to plant level has reduced the extent to which employers' organizations fulfil this traditional role, although some industries such as building and electrical contracting, with large numbers of small companies in competitive markets, have retained their central bargaining function, setting a floor of terms and conditions for the industry.

The Confederation of British Industry (CBI)

The CBI is a management organization that is only indirectly concerned with industrial relations. It provides a means for its members to influence economic policy and provides advice and services to them, supported by research.

Institutions, agencies and officers

There are a number of bodies and people with a role in employee relations in the UK, as described below.

The Advisory Conciliation and Arbitration Service (ACAS)

ACAS was created by the government but functions independently. It has three main statutory duties:

- to resolve disputes;
- to provide conciliatory services for individuals in, for example, unfair dismissal cases;
- to give advice, help and information on industrial relations and employment issues.

ACAS helps to resolve disputes in three ways: collective conciliation, arbitration (using arbitrators appointed by ACAS) and mediation.

The Central Arbitration Committee (CAC)

The CAC is an independent arbitration body. It mainly deals with trade union recognition and disclosure of information for collective bargaining purposes. In a trade dispute the parties can ask ACAS to refer the dispute to the CAC.

Employment tribunals

Employment tribunals are independent judicial bodies that deal with disputes on employment matters such as unfair dismissal, equal pay, sex and race discrimination and employment protection provisions. They have a legally qualified chair and two other members, one an employer, the other a trade unionist.

The Employment Appeal Tribunal (EAT)

The EAT hears appeals from the decisions of industrial tribunals on questions of law only.

The Certification Officer

The Certification Officer:

- ensures that the statutory provisions for union political funds and union amalgamations are complied with;
- maintains lists of trade unions and employers' associations and ensures that their accounts are audited;
- reimburses the expenses incurred by independent unions in conducting secret ballots;
- deals with complaints by members that a union has failed to comply with the provisions for certain union elections.

The Commissioner for the Rights of Trade Union Members

The Commissioner has two duties: to assist union members wanting to take legal action against a union arising from an alleged or threatened breach of a member's statutory union membership rights, and to assist members who complain that a union has failed to observe the requirements of its own rule book.

The European Union

The main EU legislative instruments are:

- Directives: instruments to transfer EC employment policy into domestic legislation. Crucially, member states can adapt the core principles of a Directive to suit national customs and laws (examples include age discrimination, employee works councils, employee information and consultation, parental leave, and working time).
- Regulations: these tend to take immediate effect and are often of a technical nature for legal compliance.
- Decisions/Directions: these apply to member states that may be called to account for breach of certain EC Directives or regulations.
- Framework Agreements: the EU partners (for example, UNICE, ETUC) can initiate negotiations and agree a framework agreement. Once adopted, a framework agreement can substitute as legislation.

Role of members of the HR function in employee relations

Members of the HR function provide advice and help but do not do the jobs of line managers for them. However, they may well be the main channel through which the management deals with unions and their representatives. They are usually responsible for maintaining participation and involvement processes and for managing employee communication. They should play a major part in developing employee relations policies.

Employee relations framework – key learning points

The elements of employee relations

The main elements are the formal and informal employment policies and practices of the organization, the development, negotiation and application of formal systems, and the bargaining structures, recognition and procedural agreements and practices that have evolved to enable the formal system to operate.

Industrial relations as a system of rules

Industrial relations can be regarded as a system or web of rules regulating employment and the ways in which people behave at work.

Regulations and rules in industrial relations

Job regulation aims to provide a framework of minimum rights and rules. Internal regulation is concerned with procedures for dealing with grievances, redundancies or disciplinary problems, and rules concerning the operation of the pay system and the rights of shop stewards. External regulation is carried out by means of employment legislation, the rules of trade unions and

Employee relations framework – key learning points (continued)

employers' associations, and the regulative content of procedural or substantive rules and agreements. The regulations and rules may be expressed in collective agreements or exist as custom and practice.

Collective bargaining

Collective bargaining is the establishment by negotiation and discussion of agreement on matters of mutual concern to employers and unions, covering the employment relationship and terms and conditions of employment.

Unitary and pluralist views of employee relations

In the unitary view, management tends to view the enterprise as a unitary system with one source of authority – itself – and one focus of loyalty – the organization. The pluralist view is that an industrial organization is a plural society, containing many related but separate interests and objectives that must be maintained in some kind of equilibrium.

Social partnership

Social partnership is the concept that, as stakeholders, the parties involved in employee relations should aim to work together to the greater good of all. It has been defined by Ackers and Payne (1998) as 'a stable, collaborative relationship between capital and labour, as represented by an independent trade union, providing for low social conflict and significant worker influence on business decision making through strong collective bargaining'.

Individualism and collectivism

A distinction can be made between 'individualism' – policies focusing on individual employees, and 'collectivism' – the extent to which groups of workers have an independent voice and participate in decision making with managers (Purcell, 1987).

Voluntarism

This concept of voluntarism was defined by Kahn-Freund (1972) as 'the policy of the law to allow the two sides by agreement and practice to develop their own norms and their own sanctions and to abstain from legal compulsion in their collective relationship'.

The HRM approach to employee relations

Emphasis on commitment, mutuality, communication, individual contracts, involvement, quality, flexibility, teamwork and harmonization.

The context of industrial relations

Industrial relations are conducted within the external context of the national political and economic environment, the international context and the internal context of the organization.

Developments in industrial relations

Developments in the practice of industrial relations since the 1950s can be divided into the following phases:

Employee relations framework – key learning points (continued)

- The traditional system existing prior to the 1970s.
- The Donovan analysis of 1968.
- The interventionist and employment protection measures of the 1970s.
- The 1980s programme for curbing what were perceived by the Conservative Government to be the excesses of rampant trade unionism.
- Developments since the 1980s. 'Management sets the agenda, which is market-driven, while industrial relations issues are relatively low on the list of concerns' (Guest, 1995).
- The findings of the Workplace Employee Relations Survey (WERS) 2004.

The parties to employee relations

The government, trade unions, shop stewards or employee representatives, the Trade Union Congress (the TUC), staff associations, management, employers' organizations, the Confederation of British Industry (CBI), various agencies and institutions (eg ACAS, Employment Tribunals), and officers, the EU and the HR function.

Questions

1. From a tutor at the local further education college: 'I'd be most grateful if you would talk to my business management study on the subject of "Obtaining added value from good employee relations". Prepare an outline of your talk.
2. From the managing director of a subsidiary company: 'I have just finished a negotiating session with our trade union. I was surprised when they opposed vehemently what I thought was a minor change in working arrangements. They said that the existing arrangements were long established "custom and practice". What does this phrase mean and why does the union think it so important?'
3. From the chair of your local CIPD branch: 'We are proposing to hold a debate on the motion that: "Collective bargaining is no longer relevant today and is a waste of time for all concerned." I am not sure what your views on this are but I would like you to either propose or oppose the motion.' Before deciding whether to propose or oppose, you have decided to set down the arguments both for and against the motion. Do so.

Questions (continued)

4. You have been invited to address a meeting of the local Chamber of Commerce on the theme of the future of trade unions. Making use of recent research, outline what you will say.

References

Ackers, P and Payne, J (1998) British trade unions and social partnership: rhetoric, reality and strategy, *International Journal of Human Resource Management*, **9** (3), pp 529–49

Atkinson, G (1989) *The Effective Negotiator*, Negotiating Systems Publications, Newbury

Blanden, J, Machin, S and Reenen, J V (2006) Have unions turned the corner? New evidence on recent trends in union recognition in UK firms, *British Journal of Industrial Relations*, **44** (2), pp 169–90

Cave, A (1994) *Organizational Change in the Workplace*, Kogan Page, London

Chamberlain, N W and Kuhn, J (1965) *Collective Bargaining*, McGraw-Hill, New York

Clegg, H (1976) *The System of Industrial Relations in Great Britain*, Blackwell, Oxford

Donaldson, T and Preston, L E (1995) The stakeholder theory of the corporation: concepts, evidence and implications, *Academy of Management Review*, **20** (1), pp 65–91

Drucker, P (1951) *The New Society*, Heinemann, London

Dunlop, J T (1958) *Industrial Relations Systems*, Holt, New York

Edwards, P K (1990) Understanding conflict in the labor process: the logic and anatomy of struggle, in *Labor Process Theory*, Macmillan, London

Emmott, M (2008) Is there a return to 'old style industrial relations?, *Impact*, February, pp 6–7

Farnham, D (2000) *Employee Relations in Context*, 2nd edn, CIPD, London

Flanders, A (1970) *Management and Unions: The theory and reform of industrial relations*, Faber and Faber, London

Fox, A (1966) *Industrial Sociology and Industrial Relations*, Royal Commission Research Paper No 3, HMSO, London

Fox, A and Flanders, A (1969) Collective bargaining: from Donovan to Durkheim, in (ed) A Flanders, *Management and Unions*, Faber and Faber, London

Freeman, R E (1984) *Strategic Management: A stakeholder perspective*, Prentice Hall, Englewood Cliffs, NJ

Freeman, R E and Medoff, J (1984) *What do Unions do?*, Basic Books, New York

Guest, D E (1995) Human resource management: trade unions and industrial relations, in (ed) J Storey, *Human Resource Management; A critical text*, Routledge, London

Hampden-Turner, C (1996) The enterprising stakeholder, *The Independent*, 5 February, p 8

Hawkins, K A (1979) *A Handbook of Industrial Relations Practice*, Kogan Page, London

Industrial Partnership Association (1996) *Towards Industrial Partnership*, IPA, London

Kahn-Freund, O (1972) *Labour and the Law*, Stevens, London

Kessler, S and Bayliss, F (1992) *Contemporary British Industrial Relations*, Macmillan, London

Kochan, T A, Katz, H and McKersie, R (1986) *The Transformation of American Industrial Relations*, Basic Books, New York

McClelland, G (1963) Editorial, *British Journal of Industrial Relations*, June, p 278

Monks, J (1996) The TUC's stake in Mr Blair, *The Times*, 17 January, p 12

Phelps Brown, H (1990) The counter revolution of our time, *Industrial Relations*, **29** (1), pp 306–20

Porter, M E (1985) *Competitive Advantage: Creating and sustaining superior performance*, New York, The Free Press

Purcell, J (1987) Mapping management styles in employee relations, *Journal of Management Studies*, September, pp 78–91

Rousseau, D M (2001) The idiosyncratic deal: flexibility versus fairness, *Organizational Dynamics*, **29** (4), pp 260–73

Royal Commission on Industrial Relations (1968) *Report*, HM Stationery Office, London

Schilstra, K (1998) *Industrial Relations and Human Resource Management*, Tinbergen Institute Research Series No 185, Thela Thesis, Amsterdam

Singh, R (1989) Negotiations, in (ed) B Towers, *A Handbook of Industrial Relations Practice*, Kogan Page, London

Storey, J (1992a) *New Developments in the Management of Human Resources*, Blackwell, Oxford

Thompson, P and Harley, B (2007) HRM and the worker: labour process perspectives, in (eds) P Boxall, J Purcell and P Wright, *Oxford Handbook of Human Resource Management*, Oxford University Press, Oxford

Walton, R E and McKersie, R B (1965) *Behavioural Theory of Labour Negotiations*, McGraw-Hill, New York

WERS (2004) *Workplace Employee Relations Survey*, HMSO, Norwich

55 Employee Relations Processes

Key concepts and terms

- Arbitration
- Aspiration grid
- Bargaining
- Check-off system
- Collective agreement
- Collective bargaining
- Conciliation
- Convergent negotiation
- Dispute resolution
- Divergent negotiation
- Employee relations
- Employee relations climate
- Harmonization
- Industrial relations
- Mediation
- Negotiation
- New-style agreements
- Partnership agreements
- Procedural agreements
- Single status
- Single-table bargaining
- Single-union deal
- Substantive agreements

Learning outcomes

On completing this chapter you should be able to define these key concepts. You should also know about:

- Employee relations policies
- Union recognition
- Dispute resolution
- Negotiating and bargaining
- Managing without unions
- Handling employment issues
- Employee relations strategies
- Collective bargaining outcomes
- Informal employee relations procedures
- Managing with unions
- The state of employment relations

Introduction

Employee relations processes consist of the approaches, methods and procedures adopted by employers to deal with employees either collectively through their trade unions or individually. As described in this chapter, many of these processes are concerned with industrial relations and include dealings between management and trade unions involving collective agreements, collective bargaining, disputes resolution and handling issues concerning the employment relationship and the working environment. This chapter starts with a review of employee relations policies and strategies and the employee relations climate. It then covers the various processes of union recognition, collective bargaining, negotiating and the state of employment relations.

Employee relations policies

Approaches to employee relations

1. Adversarial: the organization decides what it wants to do, and employees are expected to fit in. Employees only exercise power by refusing to cooperate.
2. Traditional: a good day-to-day working relationship, but management proposes and the workforce reacts through its elected representatives.

3. Partnership: the organization involves employees in the drawing up and execution of organization policies, but retains the right to manage.
4. Power sharing: employees are involved in both day-to-day and strategic decision making.

Adversarial approaches are less common now than in the 1960s and 1970s. The traditional approach is still the most typical but more interest is being expressed in partnership, as discussed later in this chapter. Power sharing is rare.

Nature and objectives of employee relations policies

Against the background of a preference for one of the four approaches listed above, employee relations policies express the philosophy of the organization on what sort of relationships between management and employees and their unions are wanted, and how the pay–work bargain should be managed. A social partnership policy, as described in Chapter 54, will aim to develop and maintain a positive, productive, cooperative and trusting climate of employee relations.

The objectives of employee relations policies may include maintaining good relations with staff and their unions, developing a cooperative and constructive employee relations climate, the effective management of the work process, the control of labour costs, and the development of an engaged and committed workforce.

When they are articulated, policies provide guidelines for action on employee relations issues and can help to ensure that these issues are dealt with consistently. They provide the basis for defining management's intentions (its employee relations strategy) on key matters such as union recognition and collective bargaining.

Policy areas

The areas covered by employee relations policies are shown below.

Areas covered by employee relations policies

- Trade union recognition – whether trade unions should be recognized or derecognized, which union or unions the organization would prefer to deal with, and whether or not it is desirable to recognize only one union for collective bargaining and/or employee representational purposes.

- Collective bargaining – the extent to which it should be centralized or decentralized and the scope of areas to be covered by collective bargaining.
- Employee relations procedures – the nature and scope of procedures for redundancy, grievance handling and discipline.
- Participation and involvement – the extent to which the organization is prepared to give employees a voice on matters that concern them.
- Partnership – the extent to which a partnership approach is thought to be desirable.
- The employment relationship – the extent to which terms and conditions of employment should be governed by collective agreements or based on individual contracts of employment (ie collectivism versus individualism).
- Harmonization of terms and conditions of employment for staff and manual workers.
- Working arrangements – the degree to which management has the prerogative to determine working arrangements without reference to trade unions or employees (this includes job-based or functional flexibility).

When formulating policies in these areas organizations may be consciously or unconsciously deciding on the extent to which they want to adopt the HRM approach to employee relations. As described in Chapter 54, this emphasizes commitment, mutuality and forms of involvement and participation, which means that management approaches and communicates with employees directly rather than through their representatives.

Policy choices

The following four policy options for organizations on industrial relations and HRM have been described by Guest (1995).

1. The new realism – a high emphasis on HRM and industrial relations

The aim is to integrate HRM and industrial relations. A review of new collaborative arrangements in the shape of single-table bargaining (IRS, 1993) found that they were almost always the result of employer initiatives, but that both employers and unions seem satisfied with them. They have facilitated greater flexibility, more multi-skilling, the removal of demarcations and improvements in quality. They can also extend consultation processes and accelerate moves towards single status.

2. Traditional collectivism – priority to industrial relations without HRM

This involves retaining the traditional pluralist industrial relations arrangements within an eventually unchanged industrial relations system. Management may take the view in these circumstances that it is easier to continue to operate with a union, since it provides a useful, well-established channel for communication and for the handling of grievance, discipline and safety issues.

3. Individualized HRM – high priority to HRM with no industrial relations

According to Guest, this approach is not very common, except in North American-owned firms. It is, he believes, 'essentially piecemeal and opportunistic'.

4. The black hole – no industrial relations

This option is becoming more prevalent in organizations in which HRM is not a policy priority for management but where they do not see that there is a compelling reason to operate within a traditional industrial relations system. When such organizations are facing a decision on whether or not to recognize a union, they are increasingly deciding not to do so.

Employee relations strategies

Employee relations strategies set out how employee relations policy objectives are to be achieved. The intentions expressed by employee relations strategies may direct the organization towards any of the following.

Employee relations strategy areas

- Altering the forms of recognition, including single-union recognition, or derecognition.
- Changes in the form and content of procedural agreements.
- New bargaining structures, including decentralization or single-table bargaining.
- The achievement of increased levels of commitment through involvement or participation.
- Deliberately by-passing trade union representatives to communicate directly with employees.

- Increasing the extent to which management controls operations in such areas as flexibility.
- Developing a 'partnership' with trade unions, recognizing that employees are stakeholders and that it is to the advantage of both parties to work together (this could be described as a unitarist strategy aiming at increasing mutual commitment).
- Generally improving the employee relations climate, as discussed below, to produce more harmonious and cooperative relationships.

Employee relations climate

The employee relations climate of an organization represents the perceptions of management, employees and their representatives about the ways in which employee relations are conducted and how the various parties (managers, employees and trade unions) behave when dealing with one another. An employee relations climate may be created by the management style adopted by management (see below) or by the behaviour of the trade unions or employee representatives (cooperative, hostile, militant, etc) or by the two interacting with one another. It can be good, bad or indifferent according to perceptions about the extent to which:

- management and employees trust one another;
- management treats employees fairly and with consideration;
- management is open about its actions and intentions – employee relations policies and procedures are transparent;
- harmonious relationships are generally maintained on a day-to-day basis, which results in willing cooperation rather than grudging submission;
- conflict, when it does arise, is resolved without resort to industrial action and resolution is achieved by integrative processes that result in a 'win-win' solution;
- employees are generally committed to the interests of the organization and, equally, management treats them as stakeholders whose interests should be protected as far as possible.

Management style

The term 'management style' refers to the overall approach the management of an organization adopts to the conduct of employee relations. It was defined by Purcell (1987) as 'the existence of a distinctive set of guiding principles, written or otherwise, which set parameters to and signposts for management action in the way employees are treated and particular events handled'.

Purcell and Sisson (1983) identified five typical styles:

1. Authoritarian – employee relations are not regarded as important and people issues are not attended to unless something goes wrong.
2. Paternalistic – in some ways this resembles the authoritarian style but a more positive attitude to employees is adopted.
3. Consultative – trade unions are welcomed and employee consultation is a high priority.
4. Constitutional – there is a trade union presence but the management style tends to be adversarial.
5. Opportunistic – management style is determined by local circumstances which determines whether or not unions are recognized and the extent to which employee involvement is encouraged.

Purcell (1987) gave further attention to management style. He described two major dimensions: 1) individualism, which refers to the extent to which personnel policies are focused on the rights and capabilities of individual workers, and 2) collectivism, which is concerned with the extent to which management policy is directed towards inhibiting or encouraging the development of collective representation by employees and allowing employees a collective voice in management decision making. According to Purcell, style is a deliberate choice linked to business policy. Organizations may choose to focus on one or both aspects. Not all firms have a distinctive preferred management style.

Improving the climate

Improvements to the climate can be attained by developing fair employee relations policies and procedures and implementing them consistently. Line managers and team leaders who are largely responsible for the day-to-day conduct of employee relations need to be educated and trained on the approaches they should adopt. Transparency should be achieved by communicating policies to employees, and commitment increased by involvement and participation processes. Problems that need to be resolved can be identified by simply talking to employees, their representatives and their trade union officials. Importantly, as discussed below, the organization can address its obligations to the employees as stakeholders and take steps to build trust.

An ethical approach

Businesses aim to achieve prosperity, growth and survival. Ideally, success should benefit all the stakeholders in the organization – owners, management, employees, customers and suppliers, but the single-minded pursuit of business objectives can act to the detriment of employees' well-being and security. There may be a tension between accomplishing business purposes and the social and ethical obligations of an organization to its employees. The chances of attaining a good climate of employee relations are slight if no attempt is made to recognize and act on an organization's duties to its members.

An ethical approach will be based on high-commitment and high-involvement policies. The commitment will be mutual and the arrangements for involvement will be genuine, ie management will be prepared not only to listen but to act on the views expressed by employees or at least, if it cannot take action, the reasons will be explained. It will also be transparent and, although the concept of a 'job for life' may no longer be valid in many organizations, at least an attempt will be made to maintain 'full employment' policies.

Union recognition

An employer fully recognizes a union for the purposes of collective bargaining when pay and conditions of employment are jointly agreed between management and trade unions. Partial recognition takes place when employers restrict trade unions to representing their members on issues arising from employment. Full recognition therefore confers negotiating (and representational) rights on unions. Partial recognition only gives unions representational rights. The following discussion of union recognition is only concerned with the much more common practice of full recognition. Unions can be de-recognized, although as noted by Blanden *et al* (2006) this is happening less frequently.

Factors influencing recognition or de-recognition

Employers are in a strong position now to choose whether they recognize a union or not, which union they want to recognize and the terms on which they would grant recognition, for example a single union and a no-strike agreement.

When setting up on greenfield sites, employers may refuse to recognize unions. Alternatively, they hold 'beauty contests' to select the union they prefer to work with and which will be prepared to reach an agreement in line with what management wants.

An organization deciding whether or not to recognize a union will take some or all of the following factors into account:

- the perceived value or lack of value of having a process for regulating collective bargaining;
- if there is an existing union, the extent to which management has freedom to manage, for example to change working arrangements and introduce flexible working or multi-skilling;

- the history of relationships with the union;
- the proportion of employees who are union members and the degree to which they believe they need the protection their union provides; a decision on de-recognition has to weigh the extent to which its perceived advantages outweigh the disadvantages of upsetting the status quo;
- any preferences as to a particular union, because of its reputation or the extent to which it is believed a satisfactory relationship can be maintained.

In deliberating recognition arrangements, employers may also consider entering into a 'single-union deal', as described below.

Collective bargaining arrangements

Collective bargaining involves employers and unions reaching agreement on terms and conditions of employment and the ways in which employment issues such as disputes, grievances and disciplinary matters should be resolved. Bargaining arrangements result in collective agreements, which are formal agreements between management and trade unions dealing with terms and conditions of employment or other aspects of the relationships between the two parties. They may be substantive agreements dealing with terms and conditions of employment, or they may be procedural agreements dealing with the procedures for collective bargaining – these are sometimes called framework agreements because they provide a structure for the bargaining process.

Collective bargaining involves the following main features:

- parties – at least two sides;
- an agreed procedure whereby the parties relate to each other – and the negotiation of framework agreements and consultation;
- outcomes – a collective agreement;
- the existence of sanctions designed to change the attitude or position of the other party.

The considerations to be taken into account in developing and managing collective bargaining arrangements are the level at which bargaining should take place, single-table bargaining where a number of unions are recognized in one workplace, and dispute resolution.

Bargaining levels

There has been a pronounced trend away from multi-employer bargaining, especially in the private sector. This has arisen because of decentralization and a reluctance on the part of central management to get involved.

Single-table bargaining

Single-table bargaining brings all the unions in an organization together as a single bargaining unit. The main reason organizations advance for wanting this arrangement is their concern that existing multi-unit bargaining arrangements not only are inefficient in terms of time and management resources but are also a potential source of conflict. They may also want to achieve major changes in working practices, or introduce harmonized or single-status conditions which, it is believed, can only be achieved through single-table bargaining.

Marginson and Sisson (1990), however, identified the following critical issues that need to be resolved if single-table bargaining is to be introduced successfully.

SOURCE REVIEW

Requirements for single-table bargaining to be introduced successfully, Marginson and Sisson (1990)

- The commitment of management to the concept.
- The need to maintain levels of negotiation that are specific to particular groups below the single bargaining table.
- The need to allay the fears of managers that they will not be able to react flexibly to changes in the demand for specific groups of workers.
- The willingness of management to discuss a wider range of issues with union representatives – this is because single-table bargaining adds to existing arrangements a top tier in which matters affecting all employees, such as training, development, working time and fringe benefits can be discussed.
- The need to persuade representatives from the various unions to forget their previous rivalries, sink their differences and work together (not always easy).
- The need to allay the fears of trade unions that they may lose representation rights and members, and of shop stewards that they will lose the ability to represent members effectively.

These are formidable requirements to satisfy, and however desirable single-table bargaining may be, it will never be easy to introduce or to operate.

Collective bargaining outcomes

The formal outcomes of collective bargaining are substantive agreements, procedural agreements, single-union deals, new-style agreements, partnership agreements and employee relations procedures.

Substantive collective agreements

Substantive agreements are the outcome of collective bargaining. They set out agreed terms and conditions of employment covering pay and working hours and other aspects such as holidays, overtime regulations, flexibility arrangements and allowances. They are not legally enforceable. A substantive agreement may detail the operational rules for a payment-by-results scheme, which could include arrangements for timing or re-timing and for payments during waiting time or on new work that has not been timed. Substantive agreements can also deal with the achievement of single status or harmonization.

Single status is the removal of differences in basic conditions of employment to give all employees equal status. This leads to harmonization, ie the adoption of a common approach and criteria to pay and conditions for all employees. Many organizations such as local government authorities negotiated a single-status deal, which means putting all employees into the same pay and grading structure.

Procedural collective agreements

Procedural agreements set out the methods to be used and the procedures or rules to be followed in the processes of collective bargaining and the settlement of industrial disputes. Their purpose is to regulate the behaviour of the parties to the agreement, but they are not legally enforceable and the degree to which they are followed depends on the goodwill of both parties or the balance of power between them. Procedural and substantive agreements are seldom broken and, if so, never lightly – the basic presumption of collective bargaining is that both parties will honour agreements that have been made freely between them. An attempt to make collective agreements legally enforceable in the 1971 Industrial Relations Act failed because employers generally did not seek to enforce its provisions. They readily accepted union requests for a clause in agreements to the effect that: 'This is not a legally enforceable agreement', popularly known as a TINALEA clause.

A typical procedure agreement contained the following sections:

- a preamble defining the objectives of the agreement;
- a statement that the union is recognized as a representative body with negotiating rights;
- a statement of general principles, which may include a commitment to use the procedure (a no-strike clause) and/or a status quo clause that restricts the ability of management to introduce changes outside negotiated or customary practice;

- a statement of the facilities granted to unions, including the rights of shop stewards and the right to hold meetings;
- provision for joint negotiating committees (in some agreements);
- a grievance or disputes procedure (see Chapter 61);
- provision for terminating the agreement.

The scope and content of such agreements can, however, vary widely. Some organizations have limited recognition to the provision of representational rights only, others have taken an entirely different line in concluding single-union deals which, when they first emerged in the 1980s, were sometimes referred to as the 'new realism'.

Single-union deals

Single-union deals have the following typical features:

- a single union representing all employees, with constraints put on the role of full-time union officials;
- flexible working practices – agreement to the flexible use of labour across traditional demarcation lines;
- single status for all employees – the harmonization of terms and conditions between manual and non-manual employees;
- an expressed commitment by the organization to involvement and the disclosure of information in the form of an open communication system and, often, a works council;
- the resolution of disputes by means of devices such as arbitration, a commitment to continuity of production and a 'no-strike' provision.

Single-union deals have generally been concluded on greenfield sites, often in the UK by Japanese firms. A 'beauty contest' may be held by the employer to select a union from a number of contenders. Thus, the initiative is taken by the employer, which can lay down radical terms for the agreement.

New-style agreements

The so-called 'new-style agreements' emerged in the 1990s. As described by Farnham (2000), a major feature of these agreements is that their negotiating and disputes procedures are based on the mutually accepted 'rights' of the parties expressed in the recognition agreement. The intention is to resolve any differences of interests on substantive issues between the parties by regulations, with pendulum arbitration (see later) providing a resolution of those issues where differences exist. New-style agreements will typically include provision for single-union recognition, single status, labour flexibility, company council and a no-strike clause to the effect that issues should be resolved without resource to strikes. The term is not much used nowadays – some or all of these provisions may still be included in agreements but they are not described as 'new-style'.

Partnership agreements

Partnership agreements are based on the concept of social partnership, as discussed in Chapter 54. The TUC has been enthusiastic in its support of them. In industrial relations a partnership arrangement is one in which both parties (management and the trade union) agree to work together to their mutual advantage and to achieve a climate of more cooperative and therefore less adversarial industrial relations. A partnership agreement may include undertakings from both sides; for example, management may offer job security linked to productivity and the union may agree to new forms of work organization that might require more flexibility on the part of employees.

Five key values for partnership have been set down by Rosow and Casner-Lotto (1998):

1. Mutual trust and respect.
2. A joint vision for the future and the means to achieve it.
3. Continuous exchange of information.
4. Recognition of the central role of collective bargaining.
5. Devolved decision making.

Their research in the United States indicated that if these matters were addressed successfully by management and unions, then companies could expect productivity gains, quality improvements, a better motivated and committed workforce and lower absenteeism and turnover rates.

Forms of partnership agreements

There is no standard format for partnership agreements although they tend to have a number of common features which, as listed by Reilly (2001), are:

- Mutuality – both sides recognize that there are areas of commonality, of shared interest.
- Plurality – it is recognized that there are areas of difference as well as areas of common interest.

- Trust and respect – for the intentions of the other side and for legitimate differences in interests.
- Agreement without coercion – there is an intention to solve problems through consensus, recognizing business and employee needs.
- Involvement and voice – opportunities are provided for employees to shape their work environment and have their opinions heard.
- Individualist and collectivist dimension – this is achieved through direct and indirect (ie representative) forms of employee involvement.

Benefits of partnership agreements

The benefits of partnership agreements include management and unions working together, cooperation and mutuality being preferable to an adversarial approach and conflict in the employment relationship. Change is introduced through discussion and agreement rather than by coercion or power. Any additional costs arising from single status can be offset because single status facilitates improved customer service. Partnerships can also promote openness on problems of mutual concern, provide effective communication between employer and union, and involve union and employees in proposals for change at an early stage, as well as help promote employment security.

The effectiveness of partnership agreements

Partnership agreements sound like a good thing but Bacon and Storey (2000) concluded from their research that 'although some companies may espouse partnership, there is evidence that underlying attitudes towards joint governance may be little changed'. Research by Kelly (2004) into 22 UK firms with partnership agreements found that in industries marked by employment decline, partnership firms often have shed jobs at a faster rate than non-partnership firms. However, in expanding sectors, partnership firms have created jobs at a faster rate than non-partnership firms. There is no discernible impact of partnership on either wage settlements or union density. He concluded that: 'Because of the evidence on labour outcomes, and given the economic and institutional constraints on partnership agreements, they [the agreements] seem unlikely to figure as a major component of the revitalization of the union movement.'

An analysis by Guest *et al* (2008) of evidence from the 2004 Workshop Employee Relations Survey suggested that partnership practice remains relatively undeveloped and that it is only weakly related to trust between management and employee representatives and to employees' trust in management. Direct forms of participation generally have a more positive association with trust than representative forms. The case for partnership and more particularly representative partnership as a basis for mutuality and trust is not supported by this evidence.

On the other hand, studies by Haynes and Allen (2001) at Tesco and Legal and General have highlighted potential benefits for unions and employees. However, as Roche and Geary (2004) found from their research, the outcomes are likely to be linked to the nature of the specific agreements, rationale, context, business environment, day-to-day processes and relationships within organizations espousing partnership, rather than the actual text of an agreement.

Employee relations procedures

Employee relations procedures are those agreed by management and trade unions to regulate the ways in which management handles certain industrial relations and employment processes and issues. The main employee relations procedures, as described in Chapter 61, are those concerned with grievances, discipline and redundancy. Disputes procedures are usually contained within an overall procedural agreement. In addition, agreements are sometimes reached on health and safety procedures.

Dispute resolution

The aim of collective bargaining is, of course, to reach agreement, preferably to the satisfaction of both parties. Grievance or negotiating procedures provide for various stages of 'failure to agree' and often include a clause providing for some form of dispute resolution in the event of the procedure being exhausted. The processes of dispute resolution are conciliation, arbitration and mediation.

Conciliation

Conciliation is the process of reconciling disagreeing parties. It is carried out by a third party, often an ACAS conciliation officer, who acts in effect as a go-between, attempting to get the employer and trade union representatives to agree on terms. Conciliators can only help the parties to come to an agreement. They do not make recommendations on what that agreement should be; that is the role of an arbitrator.

The incentives to seek conciliation are the hope that the conciliator can rebuild bridges and the belief that a determined, if last minute, search for agreement is better than confrontation, even if both parties have to compromise.

Arbitration

Arbitration is the process of settling disputes by getting a third party, the arbitrator, to review and discuss the negotiating stances of the disagreeing parties and make a recommendation on the terms of settlement that is binding on both parties who therefore lose control over the settlement of their differences.. The arbitrator is impartial and the role is often undertaken by ACAS officials, although industrial relations academics are sometimes asked to act in this capacity. Arbitration is the means of last resort for reaching a settlement, where disputes cannot be resolved in any other way.

Procedure agreements may provide for either side unilaterally to invoke arbitration, in which case the decision of the arbitrator is not binding on both parties. The process of arbitration in its fullest sense, however, only takes place at the request of both parties who agree in advance to accept the arbitrator's findings. ACAS will only act as an arbitrator if the consent of both parties is obtained, conciliation is considered, any agreed procedures have been used to the full, and a failure to agree has been recorded.

The notion of pendulum or final offer arbitration emerged in the 1980s and 1990s. It increases the rigidity of the arbitration process by allowing an arbitrator no choice but to recommend either the union's or the employer's final offer – there is no middle ground. The aim is to get the parties to avoid adopting extreme positions. The benefit of signing up to pendulum arbitration as the final stage of a disputes procedure is the so-called 'shock effect' of the likelihood of entering a win/loss scenario. This, it is argued, provides a strong incentive for the parties to settle their differences themselves. The threat of pendulum arbitration coming into play should reduce the gap in the position between the parties; the smaller the gap the greater the risk of not settling and being exposed to an 'all or nothing' situation.

However, the evidence from the Workshop Employee Relations Survey (2004) is that the full version of pendulum arbitration as defined above is rare.

Mediation

Mediation is a form of arbitration, although it is stronger than conciliation. It takes place when a third party (often ACAS) helps the employer and the union by making recommendations which, however, they are not bound to accept. Mediation means that the employer retains control of the situation by being free to reject or accept the mediator's recommendations. It is cheap and informal relative to an employment tribunal and offers a quick resolution to problems, privacy and confidentiality.

Informal employee relations processes

The formal processes of union recognition, collective bargaining and dispute resolution described earlier in this chapter provide the framework for industrial relations in so far as this is concerned with agreeing terms and conditions of employment and working arrangements and settling disputes. But within or outside that framework, informal employee relations processes are taking place continuously.

Informal employee relationships happen whenever a line manager or team leader is handling an issue in contact with a shop steward, an employee representative, an individual employee or a group of employees. The issue may concern methods of work, allocation of work and overtime, working conditions, health and safety, achieving output and quality targets and standards, discipline or pay (especially if a payment-by-results scheme is in operation, which can generate continuous arguments about times, standards, re-timings, payments for waiting time or when carrying out new tasks, and fluctuations or reductions in earnings because of alleged managerial inefficiency).

Line managers and supervisors handle day-to-day grievances arising from any of these issues and are expected to resolve them to the satisfaction of all parties without involving a formal grievance procedure. The thrust for devolving responsibility to line managers for HR matters has increased the onus on them to handle employee relations effectively. A good team leader will establish a working relationship with the shop steward representing his or her staff, which will enable issues arising on the shop floor or with individual employees to be settled amicably before they become a problem.

Creating and maintaining a good employee relations climate in an organization may be the ultimate responsibility of top management, advised by HR specialists. But the climate will be strongly influenced by the behaviour of line managers and team leaders. The HR function can help to improve the effectiveness of this behaviour by identifying and defining the competencies required, advising on the selection of supervisors, ensuring that they are properly trained, encouraging the development of performance management processes that provide for the assessment of the level of competence achieved by line managers and team leaders in handling employee relations, or by providing unobtrusive help and guidance as required.

Other features of the industrial relations scene

There are three features of the industrial relations scene that are important, besides the formal and informal processes discussed above. These features are union membership arrangements within the organization, the 'check-off' system, and strikes and other forms of industrial action (which should more realistically be called 'industrial inaction' if it involves a 'go slow' or 'work to rule').

Union membership within organizations

The closed shop, which enforced union membership within organizations, has been made illegal. But many managers prefer that all their employees should be in the union because on the whole it makes their life easier to have one channel of representation to deal with industrial relations issues and also because it prevents conflict between members and non-members of the union.

The 'check-off' system

The 'check-off' is a system that involves management in deducting the subscriptions of trade union members on behalf of the union. It is popular with unions because it helps to maintain membership and provides a reasonably sure source of income. Management has generally been willing to cooperate as a gesture of good faith to their trade union. They may support a check-off system because it enables them to find out how many employees are union members. Employers also know that they can exert pressure in the face of industrial action by threatening to end the check-off. However, the Trade Union and Employment Rights Act 1993 provides that if an employer is lawfully to make check-off deductions from a worker's pay there must be prior written consent from the worker and renewed consent at least every three years. This three-year renewal provision may inhibit the maintenance of the system.

Strikes

Strikes are the most politically charged of all the features of industrial relations. The Conservative Government in the 1980s believed that 'strikes are too often a weapon of first rather than last resort'. However, those involved in negotiation – as well as trade unions – have recognized that a strike is a legitimate last resort if all else fails. It is a factor in the balance of power between the parties in a negotiation and has to be taken into account by both parties.

Unlike other Western European countries, there is no legal right in Britain for workers or their unions to take strike action. What has been built up through common law is a system of legal liability that suspended union liability for civil wrongs, or 'torts', as long as industrial action falls within the legal definition of a trade dispute and takes place 'in contemplation of furtherance of a trade dispute'.

The Conservative Government's 1980s and 1990s legislation has limited this legal immunity to situations where a properly conducted ballot has been carried out by the union authorizing or endorsing the action and where the action is between an employer and their direct employees, with all secondary or sympathy action being unlawful. Immunity is also removed if industrial action is taken to impose or enforce a closed shop or where the action is unofficial and is not repudiated in writing by the union. The impact of this law is to deter the calling of strikes without careful consideration of where the line of legal immunity is now drawn and of the likely result of a secret ballot. But the secret ballot can in effect legitimize strike action.

The number of strikes and the proportion of days lost through strike action have diminished significantly in the UK since the 1970s. This reduction has been caused more by economic pressures than by the legislation. Unions have had to choose between taking strike action, which could lead to closure, or survival on the terms dictated by employers with fewer jobs. In addition, unions in manufacturing found that their members who remained in jobs did well out of local productivity bargaining and threatened strike action.

Negotiating and bargaining

Collective bargaining requires the exercise of negotiating and bargaining skills. This section covers the processes of negotiation and bargaining and the conventions and skills involved.

The process of negotiation

Negotiation takes place when two parties meet to reach an agreement concerning a proposition, such as a pay claim, one party has put to the other. Negotiation can be convergent when both parties are equally keen to reach a win-win agreement (in commercial terms, a willing buyer/willing seller arrangement). It can be divergent when one or both of the parties aim to win as much as they can from the other while giving away as little as possible. This can become a zero-sum game where the winner takes all and the loser gets nothing although, fortunately, this is seldom the case in pay negotiations.

Negotiations in an industrial relations setting differ from commercial negotiations, as shown in Table 55.1.

Table 55.1 Industrial relations negotiations/commercial negotiations

Industrial relations negotiations	Commercial negotiations
• Assume an ongoing relationship – negotiators cannot walk away • The agreement is not legally binding • Conducted on a face-to-face basis • Carried out by representatives responsible to constituents • Make frequent use of adjournments • May be conducted in an atmosphere of distrust, even hostility	• Negotiators can walk away • The contract is legally binding • May be conducted at a distance • Carried out directly with the parties being responsible to a line manager • Usually conducted on a continuing basis • Usually conducted on a 'willing buyer/willing seller' basis

In negotiations on pay or other terms and conditions of service, management represents the employer's interests and employee representatives represent the interests of employees. Both sides are of equal status.

Negotiations take place in an atmosphere of uncertainty. Neither side knows how strong the other side's bargaining position is or what it really wants and will be prepared to accept. Negotiations are conducted in four stages.

1. Initial steps

In a pay negotiation, unions making the claim will define three things: a) the target they would like to achieve, b) the minimum they will accept, and c) the opening claim they believe will most likely lead to achieving the target. Employers define three related things: a) the target settlement they would like to achieve, b) the maximum they would be prepared to concede, and c) the opening offer that will provide them with sufficient room to manoeuvre in reaching their target. The difference between a union's claim and an employer's offer is the negotiating range. If the maximum the employer will offer exceeds the minimum the union will accept, the difference will be the settlement range, in which case a settlement will be easily reached. If, however, the maximum the employer will offer is less than the minimum the union will accept, negotiations will be more difficult and a settlement will only be reached if the expectations of either side are adjusted during the bargaining stage. The extent to which this will happen depends on the relative power of the two parties.

Preparation for negotiation by either party involves:

- deciding on the strategy and tactics to be used;
- listing the arguments to be used in supporting their case;
- listing the arguments or counter-arguments the other party is likely to use;
- obtaining supporting data;
- selecting the negotiating team, briefing them on the strategy and tactics, and rehearsing them in their roles.

2. Opening

Tactics in the opening phase of a negotiation can be as follows:

- open realistically and move moderately;
- challenge the other side's position as it stands; do not destroy their ability to move;
- observe behaviour, ask questions and listen attentively in order to assess the other side's strengths and weaknesses, their tactics and the extent to which they may be bluffing;
- make no concessions at this stage;
- be non-committal about proposals and explanations – do not talk too much.

3. Bargaining

After the opening moves, the main bargaining phase takes place in which the gap is narrowed between the initial positions, and there are attempts to persuade each other that their case is strong enough to force the other side to close at a less advantageous point than they had planned. Bargaining is often as much about concealing as revealing – keeping arguments in reserve to deploy when they will make the greatest impact.

The following tactics can be employed:

- always make conditional proposals: 'If you will do this, then I will consider doing that' – the words to remember are: 'if... then...';
- never make one-sided concessions: always trade off against a concession from the other party: 'If I concede x, then I expect you to concede y';
- negotiate on the whole package: negotiations should not allow the other side to pick off item by item (salami negotiation);
- keep the issues open to extract the maximum benefit from potential trade-offs.

There are certain bargaining conventions that experienced negotiators follow because they appreciate that by so doing they create an atmosphere of trust and understanding, which is essential to the sort of stable bargaining relationship that benefits both sides. Some of the more generally accepted conventions are:

- Whatever happens during the bargaining, both parties are hoping to reach a settlement.
- Negotiators should show that they respect the views of the other side and take them seriously even if they disagree with them.
- While it is preferable to conduct negotiations in a civilized and friendly manner, attacks, hard words, threats and controlled losses of temper may be used by negotiators to underline determination to get their way and to shake their opponent's confidence and self-possession. But these should be treated by both sides as legitimate tactics and should not be allowed to shake the basic belief in each other's integrity or desire to settle without taking drastic action.
- Off-the-record discussions ('corridor negotiations') can be mutually beneficial as a means of probing attitudes and intentions and smoothing the way to a settlement, but they should not be referred to specifically in formal bargaining sessions unless both sides agree in advance.
- Each side should be prepared to move from its original position.
- It is normal, although not inevitable, for the negotiation to proceed by alternate offers and counter-offers from each side, which lead steadily towards a settlement.
- Third parties should not be brought in until both sides agree that no further progress can be made without them.
- Concessions, once made, cannot be withdrawn.

- If negotiators want to avoid committing themselves to 'a final offer' with the risk of devaluing the term if they are forced to make concessions, they should state as positively as they can that this is a far as they can go. But bargaining conventions allow further moves from this position on a quid pro quo basis.
- Firm offers must not be withdrawn.
- The final agreement should mean exactly what it says. There should be no trickery and the agreed terms should be implemented without amendment.
- So far as possible the final settlement should be framed and communicated in such a way as to reduce the extent to which the other part loses face or credibility.

When bargaining, the parties have to identify the basis for a possible agreement; that is, the common ground. One way of doing this, as described by Gennard and Judge (2005), is to use the aspiration grid technique. The grid sets out the parameters for the anticipated outcome of the negotiations. It shows the expected issues one of the parties is prepared to trade as well as the anticipation of the attitude to the bargaining agenda of the other party. The grid gives the parameters within which the forthcoming bargaining sessions might be expected to develop. It helps to identify the information required from the other party and the information required to be conveyed by one party to the other party. If the receipt of this information shows expectations as to the behaviour of the other party to be wrong, then the aspiration grid has to be reassessed and modified.

4. Closing

There are various closing techniques:

- Make a concession from the package, preferably a minor one, which is traded off against an agreement to settle. The concession can be offered more positively than in the bargaining stage: 'If you will agree to settle at x then I will concede y.'
- Do a deal, split the difference or bring in something new, such as extending the settlement timescale, agreeing to back-payments, phasing increases, or making a joint declaration of intent to do something in the future.
- Summarize what has happened so far, emphasize the concessions that have been made and the extent of the movement from the original position, and indicate that the limit has been reached.
- Apply pressure through a threat of the dire consequences that will follow if a 'final' claim is not agreed or a 'final offer' is not accepted.

Employers should not make a final offer unless they mean it. If it is not really their final offer and the union calls their bluff, they may have to make further concessions and their credibility will be undermined. Each party will attempt to force the other side into revealing the extent to which they have reached their final position. But negotiators should not allow themselves to be pressurized; they have to use their judgement on when to say 'this is a far as we can go'. That judgement will be based on their understanding that the stage when a settlement is possible has been reached.

Negotiating and bargaining skills

The skills required to be effective in negotiations and bargaining are:

- Analytical ability – the capacity to assess the factors that affect the negotiating stance and tactics of both parties.
- Empathy – the ability to put oneself in the other party's shoes.
- Interactive skills – the ability to relate well with other people.
- Communicating skills – the ability to convey information and arguments clearly, positively and logically.
- Keeping cards close to the chest – not giving away what you really want or are prepared to concede until you are ready to do so (in the marketplace it is always easier for sellers to drive a hard bargain with buyers who have revealed somehow that they covet the article).
- Flexible realism – the capacity to make realistic moves during the bargaining process to reduce the claim or increase the offer, which will demonstrate that the bargainer is seeking a reasonable settlement and is prepared to respond appropriately to movements from the other side.

Managing with unions

Ideally, management and trade unions learn to live together, often on a give and take basis, the presumption being that neither would benefit from a climate of hostility or by generating constant confrontation. It would be assumed in this ideal situation that mutual advantage would come from acting in accordance with the spirit as well as the letter of agreed joint regulatory procedures. However, both parties would probably adopt a realistic pluralist viewpoint, recognizing the inevitability of differences of opinion, even disputes, but believing that with goodwill on both sides they could be settled without resource to industrial action.

Of course, the reality in the 1960s and 1970s was often different. In certain businesses, for example in the motor and shipbuilding industries, hostility and confrontation were rife, and newspaper proprietors tended to let their unions walk all over them in the interests of peace and profit.

Times have changed. Trade union power has diminished in the private sector if not in the public sector. Management in the private sector has tended to seize the initiative. They may be content to live with trade unions but they give industrial relations lower priority. They may feel that it is easier to continue to operate with a union because it provides a useful, well-established channel for communication and for the handling of grievance, discipline and safety issues. In the absence of a union, management would need to develop its own alternatives, which would be costly and difficult to operate effectively. The trade union and the shop stewards remain a 'useful lubricant'.

Alternatively, as Smith and Morton (1993) suggest, the management perspective may be that it is safer to marginalize the unions than formally to de-recognize them and risk provoking a confrontation: 'Better to let them wither on the vine than receive a reviving fertilizer.' However, an alternative view was advanced by Purcell (1979), who argued that management will have greater success in achieving its objectives by working with trade unions, in particular by encouraging union membership and participation in union affairs.

The pattern varies considerably but there is general agreement based on studies such as the Workplace Industrial Relations Survey that employers have been able to assert their prerogative – 'management must manage' in the workplace. They seem generally to have regained control over how they organize work, especially with regard to the flexible use of labour and multi-skilling. The 'status quo' clause, typical of many agreements in the engineering industry, whereby management could not change working arrangements without union agreement, has virtually disappeared.

Four types of industrial relations management have been identified by Purcell and Sisson (1983):

1. Traditionalists, who have unitary beliefs and are anti-union with forceful management.
2. Sophisticated paternalists, who are essentially unitary but they do not take it for granted that their employees accept the organization's objectives or automatically legitimize management decision making. They spend considerable time and resources in ensuring that their employees adopt the right approach.
3. Sophisticated moderns, who are either constitutionalists, where the limits of collective bargaining are codified in an agreement but management is free to take decisions on matters which are not the subject of such an agreement; or consultors, who accept collective bargaining but do not want to codify everything in a collective agreement, and instead aim to minimize the amount of joint regulation and emphasize joint consultation with 'problems' having to be solved rather than 'disputes' settled.
4. Standard moderns, who are pragmatic or opportunist. Trade unions are recognized, but industrial relations are seen as primarily fire-fighting and are assumed to be non-problematic unless events prove otherwise. This is by far the most typical approach.

On the whole, pluralism prevails and management and unions will inevitably disagree from time to time on employment issues. The aim is to resolve these issues before they become disputes. This means adopting a more positive partnership approach. Where collective agreements are being made, a cooperative or integrative bargaining philosophy can be adopted that is based on perceptions about the mutual interdependence of management and employees and the recognition by both parties that this is a means to achieve more for themselves. As Ackers and Payne (1998) emphasize: 'Partnership offers British unions a strategy that is not only capable of moving with the times and accommodating new political developments, but allowing them a hand in shaping their own destiny.'

Managing without trade unions

Millward *et al* (1992) established from the third Workshop Industrial Relations Survey that the characteristics of union-free employee relations were as follows.

SOURCE REVIEW

Characteristics of union-free employee relations, Millward *et al* (1992)

- Employee relations were generally seen by managers as better in the non-union sector than in the union sector.
- Strikes were almost unheard of.
- Labour turnover was high but absenteeism was no worse.
- Pay levels were generally set unilaterally by management.
- The dispersion of pay was higher, it was more market-related and there was more performance-related pay. There was also a greater incidence of low pay.
- In general, no alternative methods of employee representation existed as a substitute for trade union representation.
- Employee relations were generally conducted with a much higher degree of informality than in the union sector. In a quarter of non-union workplaces there were no grievance procedures and about a fifth had no formal disciplinary procedures.
- Managers generally felt unconstrained in the way in which they organized work.
- There was more flexibility in the use of labour than in the union sector, which included the greater use of freelance and temporary workers.
- Employees in the non-union sector are two and a half times as likely to be dismissed as those in unionized firms and the incidence of compulsory redundancies is higher.

The survey concluded that many of the differences that exist between unionized and non-unionized workplaces could be explained by the generally smaller size of the non-union firms and the fact that many such workplaces were independent, rather than being part of a larger enterprise. Another characteristic, not mentioned by the survey, is the use by non-unionized firms of personal contracts as an alternative to collective bargaining.

The state of employment relations

A survey conducted in 2008 (CIPD, 2008e) revealed what was on the whole a satisfactory state of employment relationships, as summarized below.

SOURCE REVIEW

2008 Survey of Employment Relations, CIPD – main findings

- Nearly two-thirds of unionized employers describe the relationship between management and the unions as either positive or very positive.
- About a quarter of respondents that recognize unions report that the relationship between management and the unions is neither positive nor negative, while 9 per cent of employers describe relationships with the unions as negative or very negative.
- Half of unionized employers describe personal relations between managers and unions as good, and 44 per cent said they are variable.
- Just 2 per cent of employers say personal relations between managers and union officials are bad, and 3 per cent report they are non-existent.
- Just over 40 per cent of unionized organizations say their relationship with the unions has changed in the last year, with manufacturing and production and public services organizations most likely to report change.
- Among employers citing changes in union relations, 42 per cent report that the relationship has become more negative and 41 per cent of respondents say the opposite.
- Nearly 60 per cent of respondents in organizations that recognize unions think that unions exert a significant or very significant influence on their organization. Just over 40 per cent of respondents say that unions exert little or no significant influence.

- Public sector respondents are most likely to see union influence as strong, with almost three-quarters reporting union influence as significant or very significant.
- A positive net balance of respondents say union influence has become weaker over the last two years.
- Nearly half of respondents that recognize unions say unions take a constructive line when change is proposed, always (6 per cent) or usually (41 per cent). Four in ten employers say unions respond constructively sometimes, 12 per cent report that unions take a constructive line rarely, and just 2 per cent say unions never respond constructively.

Handling employment issues

Management should never act without establishing a just cause for action after a thorough investigation. If it establishes there is a fair and just cause to act, then in carrying out that action it must behave in a fair, reasonable and consistent manner. Employment law says that if management does not behave on the basis of just cause and reasonable behaviour in accordance with the principles of natural justice, then the law will make it do so. For example, the law on dismissal says you must have a fair reason to dismiss (eg unsatisfactory behaviour, lack of capability or redundancy) and in carrying out the dismissal, management must behave reasonably (that is, be procedurally correct).

Employee relations processes – key learning points

Employee relations policies

Employee relations policies express the philosophy of the organization on what sort of relationships between management and employees and their unions is wanted, and how they should be handled. They cover trade union recognition, collective bargaining, employee relations procedures, participation and involvement, partnership, the employment relationship, harmonization and working arrangements.

Employee relations strategies

Employee relations strategies set out how employee relations policy objectives are to be achieved. They cover union recognition, procedural agreements, bargaining structures and other matters concerning relationships with unions and employees such

Employee relations processes – key learning points (continued)

as involvement, communication and partnership.

Union recognition

An employer fully recognizes a union for the purposes of collective bargaining when pay and conditions of employment are jointly agreed between management and trade unions. Partial recognition takes place when employers restrict trade unions to representing their members on issues arising from employment.

Collective bargaining outcomes

These include procedural agreements, substantive agreements, single-union deals, new-style agreements, partnership agreements and employee relations procedures.

Dispute resolution

Dispute resolution processes comprise conciliation, arbitration and mediation.

Informal employee relations

Informal employee relationships happen whenever a line manager or team leader is handling an issue in contact with a shop steward, an employee representative, an individual employee or a group of employees.

Negotiating and bargaining

Negotiations take place in four stages: initial steps, opening, bargaining and closing.

Managing with unions

Working with unions has often meant conflict in the past, but while conflict can never be avoided, a positive partnership approach can be adopted.

Managing without unions

Millward *et al* (1992) established that the characteristics of union-free employee relations were that employee relations were generally seen by managers as better in the non-union sector than in the union sector, employee relations were generally conducted with a much higher degree of informality than in the union sector, managers generally felt unconstrained in the way in which they organized work, and there was more flexibility in the use of labour than in the union sector, which included the greater use of freelance and temporary workers.

Questions

1. You are the people resourcing manager in a medium-sized engineering firm that carries out sub-contract work for the aerospace industry in the UK and abroad. Manufacturing

Questions (continued)

operations are fully computerized and sophisticated capacity planning systems are in use. A trade union representing manufacturing staff (terms and conditions have been harmonized) is recognized. It is quite militant and hotly opposes any attempt to vary custom and practice. The firm's order book is reasonably full and the long-term forecast is good, but demand is subject to marked fluctuations. The manufacturing director e-mails you to say that it will be essential to prepare plans for making short-term adjustments to available capacity. From his previous experience he believes that the ways of doing this include: altering the total hours worked by changing the number of shifts or overtime; employing part-time staff to cover peak demand; scheduling work patterns so that the total workforce available at any time varies in line with varying demand; using outside contractors; adjusting the process, perhaps making larger batches to reduce set-up times; and adjusting equipment and processes to work faster or slower. He asks you to advise him on what the IR implications would be of any of these actions. He also wants your views on how to avoid any negative reactions from the union.

2. From the managing director of a subsidiary company: 'I am due to negotiate with the unions on their pay claim next week. This is my first experience of negotiation. Could you advise me on the approach I should adopt?'

3. From your chief executive: 'What is the case for and against our entering into a partnership agreement with the trade union? I would be interested in any evidence you can get from research or experience elsewhere.'

References

Ackers, P and Payne, J (1998) British trade unions and social partnership: rhetoric, reality and strategy, *International Journal of Human Resource Management*, **9** (3), pp 529–49

Bacon, N and Storey, J (2000) New employee relations strategies in Britain: towards individualism or partnership, *British Journal of Industrial Relations*, **38** (3), pp 407–27

Blanden, J, Machin, S and Reenen, J V (2006) Have unions turned the corner? New evidence on recent trends in union recognition in UK firms, *British Journal of Industrial Relations*, **44** (2), pp 169–90

CIPD (2008e) *Survey of Employment Relations*, CIPD, London

DTI (2004) *Workshop Industrial Relations Survey*, DTI, London

Farnham, D (2000) *Employee Relations in Context*, 2nd edn, CIPD, London

Gennard, J and Judge, G (2005) *Employee Relations*, 3rd edn, CIPD, London

Guest, D E (1995) Human resource management: trade unions and industrial relations, in (ed) J Storey, *Human Resource Management; A critical text*, Routledge, London

Guest, D E, Brown, W, Peccei, R and Huxley, K (2008) Does partnership at work increase trust? An analysis based on the 2004 Workplace Employment Relations Survey, *Industrial Relations Journal*, **39** (2), pp 124–52

Haynes, P and Allen, M (2001) Partnership as a union strategy: a preliminary evaluation, *Employee Relations*, **23** (2), pp 167–87

IRS (1993) Multi-employer bargaining, *Employment Trends*, **544,** pp 6–8

Kelly, J (2004) Social partnership agreements in Britain: labour cooperation and compliance, *Industrial Relations*, **43** (1), pp 267–92

Marginson, P and Sisson, K (1990) Single table talk, *Personnel Management*, May, pp 46–9

Millward, N, Stevens, M, Smart, D and Hawes, W R (1992) *Workplace Industrial Relations in Transition*, Dartmouth Publishing, Hampshire

Purcell, J (1979) A strategy for management control in industrial relations, in (eds) J Purcell and R Smith, *The Control of Work*, Macmillan, London

Purcell, J (1987) Mapping management styles in employee relations, *Journal of Management Studies*, September, pp 78–91

Purcell, J and Sisson, K (1983) Strategies and practice in the management of industrial relations, in (ed) G Bain, *Industrial Relations in Britain*, Blackwell, Oxford

Reilly, P (2001) *Partnership Under Pressure: How does it survive?*, Report No 383, Institute for Employment Studies, Brighton

Roche, W K and Geary, J F (2004) Workforce partnership and the search for dual commitment, in (eds) M Martinez Lucio and M Stuart, *Partnership and Modernisation in Employment Relations*, Routledge, London

Rosow, J and Casner-Lotto, J (1998) *People, Partnership and Profits: The new labor-management agenda*, Work in America Institute, New York

Smith, P and Morton, G (1993) Union exclusion and decollectivisation of industrial relations in contemporary Britain, *British Journal of Industrial Relations*, **31** (1) pp 97–114

WERS (2004) *Workplace Employee Relations Survey*, HMSO, Norwich

56 Employee Voice

Key concepts and terms

- Attitude survey
- Improvement group
- Joint consultation
- Quality circle
- Employee voice
- Involvement
- Participation
- Suggestion scheme

Learning outcomes

On completing this chapter you should be able to define these key concepts. You should also know about:

- The meaning of employee voice
- Expression of employee voice
- Attitude surveys
- Effectiveness of employee involvement and participation
- EU Directives affecting employee voice procedures
- The forms of employee voice
- Joint consultation
- Suggestion schemes
- Planning for voice

Introduction

The phrase 'employee voice' refers to the say employees have in matters of concern to them in their organization. It describes a form of two-way dialogue that allows employees to influence events at work and includes the processes of involvement, participation, upward problem solving and upward communication. This chapter covers the meaning and purpose of employee voice and how it is expressed.

The meaning of employee voice

As defined by Boxall and Purcell (2003): 'Employee voice is the term increasingly used to cover a whole variety of processes and structures which enable, and sometimes empower employees, directly and indirectly, to contribute to decision-making in the firm.' Employee voice can be seen as 'the ability of employees to influence the actions of the employer' (Millward *et al*, 1992). The concept covers the provision of opportunities for employees to register discontent, express complaints or grievances and modify the power of management, and sometimes brings collective and individual techniques into one framework. Direct employee voice involves contacts between management and employees without the involvement of trade unions. Union voice is expressed through representatives and can be power-based.

Dundon *et al* (2004) suggested the following meanings of direct and union employee voice.

SOURCE REVIEW

The meaning of employee voice, Dundon *et al* (2004)

- Expression of individual dissatisfaction raised with line manager or through grievance procedure.
- Expression of collective dissatisfaction raised by trade unions through collective bargaining or industrial action.
- Contribution to management decision making through upward problem solving, suggestion schemes and attitude surveys.
- Demonstration of mutuality through partnership agreements, joint consultative committees and works councils.

The forms of employee voice

The elements of employee voice are:

- Participation, which is about employees playing a greater part in the decision-making process by being given the opportunity to influence management decisions and to contribute to the improvement of organizational performance. As Williams and Adam-Smith (2006) explain, the term 'participation' refers to arrangements that give workers some influence over organizational and workplace decisions.
- Involvement, which is the process through which management allows employees to discuss with them issues that affect them. Williams and Adam-Smith (2006) suggest that this term is most usefully applied to management initiatives that are designed to further the flow of communication at work as a means of enhancing the organizational commitment of employees.

As defined by Marchington *et al* (2001), these elements of employee voice can be categorized as representative participation and upward problem solving.

Representative participation

- Joint consultation – a formal mechanism that provides the means for management to consult employee representatives on matters of mutual interest (discussed in more detail below).
- Partnership schemes – these emphasize mutual gains and tackling issues in a spirit of cooperation rather than through traditional, adversarial relationships.
- European Works Councils – these may be set up across European sites as required by EU legislation.
- Collective representation – the role of trade unions or other forms of staff association in collective bargaining and representing the interests of individual employees and groups of employees. This includes the operation of grievance procedures.

Upward problem solving

- Upward communication, which is any means through which employees can make representations to management about their concerns through their representatives, through established channels (consultative committees, grievance procedures, 'speak-up' programmes, etc) or informally.
- Attitude surveys – seeking the opinions of staff through questionnaires (discussed in more detail below).

- Suggestion schemes – the encouragement of employees to make suggestions, often accompanied by rewards for accepted ideas (discussed in more detail below).
- Project teams – getting groups of employees together with line managers to develop new ideas, processes, services or products or to solve problems (quality circles and improvement groups come into this category, although the former have often failed to survive as a specific method of involvement).

The framework for employee voice

The framework for employee voice has been modelled by Marchington *et al* (2001) as shown in Figure 56.1.

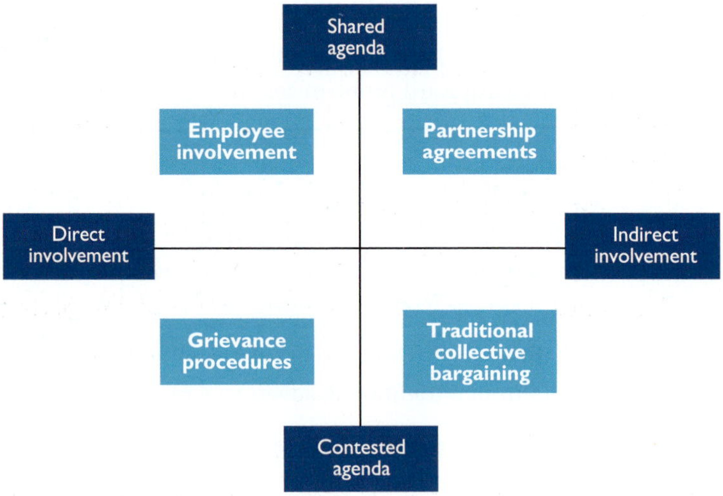

Figure 56.1 A framework for employee voice

This framework identifies two dimensions of voice: 1) individual employees, and 2) collective – union and other representation. The shared agenda of involvement and partnership is a form of upward problem solving. This is on the same axis as the contested agenda of grievances and collective bargaining. But these are not absolutes. Organizations will have tendencies toward shared or contested agendas just as there will be varying degrees of direct and indirect involvement, although they are unlikely to have partnership and traditional collective bargaining at the same time. As Kochan *et al* (1986) point out, one of the strongest factors affecting the choice of approach to employee voice is the values held by management towards employees and their unions.

Expression of employee voice

The degree to which employees have a voice will vary considerably. At one end of the scale there will be unilateral management and employees will have no voice at all. At the other end, employees might have complete self-management and control as in a cooperative, although this is very rare. In between, the steps in the degree to which employees have voice, as defined by Boxall and Purcell (2003), are as follows.

SOURCE REVIEW

The degrees to which employees have voice, Boxall and Purcell (2003)

- Little voice – information provided.
- Downward – right to be told.
- Some – opportunity to make suggestions.
- Two way – consulted during decision making.
- Two way plus – consulted at all stages of decision making and implementation.
- A lot – the right to delay a decision.
- Power to affect outcome – the right to veto a decision.
- Substantial – equality or co-determination in decision making.

Levels of employee voice

Involvement and participation takes various forms at different levels in an enterprise, as described below.

The *job level* involves team leaders and their teams, and the processes include the communication of information about work and the interchange of ideas about how the work should be done. These processes are essentially informal.

The *management level* can involve sharing information and decision making about issues that affect the way in which work is planned and carried out, and working arrangements and conditions. There are limits. Management as a whole, and individual managers, must retain authority to do what their function requires. Involvement does not imply anarchy; but it does require some degree of willingness on the part of management to share its decision-making powers. At this level, involvement and participation may become more formalized, through consultative committees, briefing groups or other joint bodies involving management and employees or their representatives.

At the *policy-making level,* where the direction in which the business is going is determined, total participation would imply sharing the power to make key decisions. This is very seldom practised in the UK, although there may be processes for communicating information on proposed plans (which would almost certainly not reveal proposals for acquisitions or disinvestments or anything else where commercial security is vital) and discussing the implications of those plans.

At the *ownership level,* participation implies a share in the equity, which is not meaningful unless the workers have sufficient control through voting rights to determine the composition of the board. This is not a feature of the British employee relations scene.

At one end of the scale, management makes decisions unilaterally; at the other end, in theory, but never in practice except in a worker's cooperative (almost non-existent in the UK), workers decide unilaterally. Between these extremes there is a range of intermediate points, as shown in Figure 56.2. The point on this scale at which participation should or can take place at any level in an organization depends on the attitudes, willingness and enthusiasm of both management and employees. Management may be reluctant to give up too much of its authority except under pressure from the unions (which is less likely today), or from EC Directives on worker consultation.

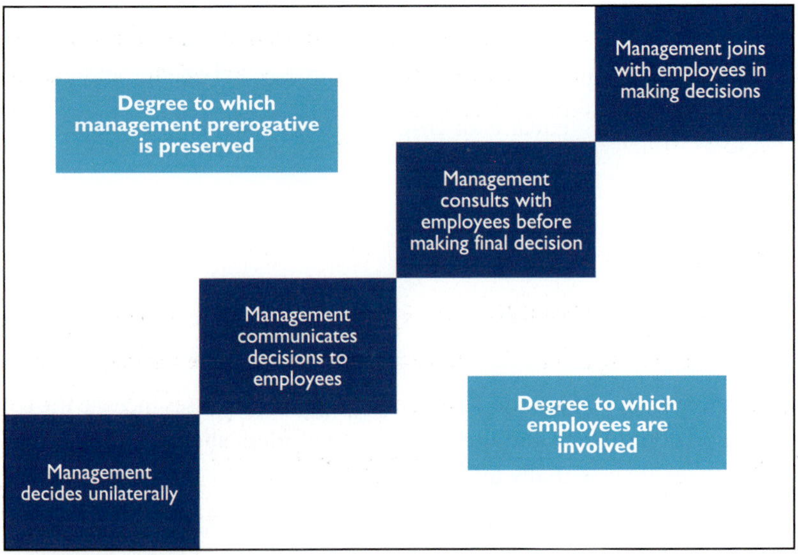

Figure 56.2 Levels of employee voice

Factors affecting choice

Research carried out by Marchington *et al* (1992) identified the following factors that influenced employers to implement employee voice initiatives.

SOURCE REVIEW

Factors influencing employers to implement employee voice initiatives, Marchington *et al* (1992)

- Information and education – a desire to 'educate' employees more fully about aspects of the business and to convince them of the 'logic' of management's actions.
- Secure enhanced employee contributions – seeking employee ideas and using them to improve performance.
- Handling conflict at work and promoting stability – providing a safety-valve for the expression of employees' views.
- A mechanism for channelling employee anxieties and misgivings without their resorting to the disputes procedure and industrial action.

Joint consultation

Joint consultation enables managers and employee representatives to meet on a regular basis in order to exchange views, to make good use of members' knowledge and expertise, and to deal with matters of common interest that are not the subject of collective bargaining. Meaningful consultation involves the actions by management set out below.

Meaningful consultation

- Tell employees what management proposes (not intends) to do.
- Give employees sufficient time to respond to the proposed action.
- Give consideration to the employees' response.
- Explain fully the response of management to the employees' view.

For joint consultation to work well it is first necessary to define, discuss and agree its objectives. These should be related to tangible and significant aspects of the job, the process of management, or the formulation of policies that affect the interests of employees. They should not deal only with peripheral matters such as welfare, social amenities or 'the quality of the sausages in the staff restaurant'. Consultation should take place before decisions are made. Management must believe in and must be seen to believe in involving employees. Actions speak louder than words and management should demonstrate that it will put into effect the joint decisions made during discussions. The unions must also believe in participation as a genuine means of giving them voice and advancing the interests of their members, and not simply as a way of getting more power. They should show by their actions that they are prepared to support unpopular decisions to which they have been a party.

Joint consultation machinery should be in line with any existing systems of negotiation and representation. It should not be supported by management as a possible way of reducing the powers of the union. If this naïve approach is taken, it will fail – it always does. Joint consultation should be regarded as a process of integrative bargaining complementary to the distributive bargaining that takes place in joint negotiating committees. Consultative committees should always relate to a defined working unit, should never meet unless there is something specific to discuss, and should always conclude their meetings with agreed points that are implemented quickly.

Employee and management representatives should be properly briefed and trained and have all the information they require. Managers and team leaders should be kept in the picture and, as appropriate, involved in the consultation process – it is clearly highly undesirable for them to feel that they have been left out.

Attitude surveys

Attitude surveys are a valuable way of involving employees by seeking their views on matters that concern them. Attitude surveys can provide information on the preferences of employees, give warning on potential problem areas, diagnose the cause of particular problems and compare levels of job satisfaction, commitment and morale in different parts of the organization.

Methods of conducting attitude surveys

There are four methods of conducting attitude surveys.

1. By the use of structured questionnaires

These can be issued to all or a sample of employees. The questionnaires may be standardized ones, such as the Brayfield and Rothe Index of Job Satisfaction, or they may be developed specially for the organization. The advantage of using standardized questionnaires is that they have been thoroughly tested and in many cases norms are available against which results can be compared. Additional questions especially relevant to the company can be added to the standard list. A tailor-made questionnaire can be used to highlight particular issues, but it may be advisable to obtain professional help from an experienced psychologist, who can carry out the skilled work of drafting and pilot-testing the questionnaire and interpreting the results. Questionnaires have the advantage of being relatively cheap to administer and analyse, especially when there are large numbers involved. Many organizations use electronic means (the intranet) to seek the views of employees generally or on particular issues. Examples of attitude surveys are given in Appendices A and B.

2. By the use of interviews

These may be 'open-ended' or in-depth interviews in which the discussion is allowed to range quite freely. Or they may be semi-structured in that there is a checklist of points to be covered, although the aim of the interviewer should be to allow discussion to flow around the points so that the frank and open views of the individual are obtained. Alternatively, and more rarely, interviews can be highly structured so that they become no more than the spoken application of a questionnaire. Individual interviews are to be preferred because they are more likely to be revealing, but they are expensive and time-consuming and not so easy to analyse. Discussions through 'focus groups' (ie groups of employees convened to focus their attention on particular issues) are a quicker way of reaching a large number of people, but the results are not so easy to quantify and some people may have difficulty in expressing their views in public.

3. By a combination of questionnaire and interview

This is the ideal approach because it combines the quantitative data from the questionnaire with the qualitative data from the interviews. It is always advisable to accompany questionnaires with some in-depth interviews, even if time permits only a limited sample. An alternative approach is to administer the questionnaire to a group of people and then discuss the reactions to each question with the group. This ensures that a quantified analysis is possible but enables the group, or at least some members of it, to express their feelings more fully.

4. By the use of focus groups

A focus group is a representative sample of employees whose attitudes and opinions are sought on issues concerning the organization and their work. The essential features of a focus group are that it is structured, informed, constructive and confidential.

Assessing results

It is an interesting fact that when people are asked directly if they are satisfied with their job, most of them (70 to 90 per cent) will say they are. This is regardless of the work being done and often in spite of strongly held grievances. The probable reason for this phenomenon is that while most people are willing to admit to having grievances – in fact, if invited to complain, they will complain – they may be reluctant to admit, even to themselves, to being dissatisfied with a job that they have no immediate intention of leaving. Many employees have become reconciled to their work, even if they do not like some aspects of it, and have no real desire to do anything else. So they are, in a sense, satisfied enough to continue, even if they have complaints. Finally, many people are satisfied with their job overall, although they grumble about many aspects of it.

Overall measures of satisfaction do not, therefore, always reveal anything interesting. It is more important to look at particular aspects of satisfaction or dissatisfaction to decide whether or not anything needs to be done. In these circumstances, the questionnaire will indicate only a line to be followed up; it will not provide the answers. Hence the advantage of individual meetings or focus group discussions to explore in depth any issue raised.

Suggestion schemes

Suggestion schemes are established procedures for employees to submit ideas to management with tangible recognition for those suggestions that have merit. They can provide a valuable means for employees to participate in improving the efficiency of the company. Properly organized, they can help to reduce the feelings of frustration endemic in all concerns where people think they have good ideas but cannot get them considered because there are no recognized channels of communication. Normally, only those ideas outside the usual scope of employees' duties are considered, and this should be made clear, as well as the categories of those eligible for the scheme – senior managers are often excluded.

The most common arrangement is to use suggestion boxes with, possibly, a special form for entering a suggestion. Alternatively, or additionally, employees can be given the name of an individual or a committee to whom suggestions should be submitted. Managers and team leaders must be stimulated to encourage their staff to submit suggestions, and publicity in the shape of posters, leaflets and articles in the company magazine should be used to promote the scheme. The publicity should give prominence to the successful suggestions and how they are being implemented.

One person should be made responsible for administering the scheme. He or she should have the authority to reject facetious suggestions, but should be given clear guidance on the routing of suggestions by subject matter to departments or individuals for their comments. The administrator deals with all communication and, if necessary, may go back to the individual who submitted the suggestion to get more details of, for example, the savings in cost or improvements in output that should result from the idea.

It is desirable to have a suggestion committee consisting of management and employee representatives to review suggestions in the light of the comments of any specialist functions or executives who have evaluated them. This committee should be given the final power to accept or reject suggestions but could, if necessary, call for additional information or opinion before making its decision. The committee could also decide on the size of any award within established guidelines, such as a proportion of savings during the first year. There should be a standard procedure for recording the decisions of the committee and informing those who made suggestions of the outcome – with reasons for rejection if appropriate. It is important to take care when explaining to employees that their ideas cannot be accepted so that they are not discouraged.

Effectiveness of employee involvement and participation

Research conducted by Cox *et al* (2006) indicated that to be effective, employee involvement and participation mechanisms have to be embedded in the organization – well established and part of everyday working life. Combinations of involvement and participation practices worked best. The main barriers to effective employee voice appear to be a partial lack of employee enthusiasm, absence of necessary skills to implement and manage employee voice programmes, and issues concerning line managers – such as middle managers acting as blockers through choice or ignorance. Making employee voice effective requires top management support, good leadership skills and finding the right mechanisms for involvement and participation.

Planning for voice

The forms of voice appropriate for an organization depend upon the values and attitudes of management and, if they exist, trade unions, and the current climate of employee relations. Attention has also to be paid to the EU Directives on works councils and information and consultation of employees; see below.

Planning should be based on a review of the existing forms of voice, which would include discussions with stakeholders (line managers, employees and trade union representatives) on the effectiveness of existing arrangements and any improvements required. In the light of these discussions, new or revised approaches can be developed; it will be necessary to brief and train those involved in the part they should play.

EU Directives affecting employee voice procedures

European Works Councils (EWC) Directive

This Directive, put into effect in the UK in 2000, requires works councils to be set up in European undertakings or groups of undertakings as a means of informing or consulting with employees. The Directive covers undertakings, irrespective of ownership, with at least 1,000 employees located in the EU area, of which at least 150 are located in each of two EU countries. The subjects for discussion may include the general economic and financial situation of the business, and other matters with a major impact on employees such as relocations, closures, mergers, collective dismissals and the introduction of new technology. The formation of an EWC can be triggered either by a formal request from employees or by the employer.

Information and Consultation of Employees (ICE) Directive

This Directive was put into effect by UK regulations in 2005. These give employees the right to be informed about the business's economic situation and their employment prospects, and informed and consulted about decisions likely to lead to substantial changes in work relations or contractual relations, including redundancies and transfers. The regulations apply to organizations with 50 or more employees and procedures can be triggered either by a formal request from employees or by the employer.

Employee voice – key learning points

The meaning of employee voice

'Employee voice is the term increasingly used to cover a whole variety of processes and structures which enable, and sometimes empower employees, directly and indirectly, to contribute to decision making in the firm' Boxall and Purcell (2003).

The forms of employee voice

The basic elements of employee voice are participation and involvement. These take the forms of joint consultation, participation, collective representation, upward communication (consultative committees, etc), attitude surveys, suggestion schemes and project teams (quality circles or improvement groups).

Expression of employee voice

The degree to which employees have voice will vary considerably.

Joint consultation

Joint consultation enables managers and employee representatives to meet on a regular basis to exchange views, to make good use of members' knowledge and expertise, and to deal with matters of common interest that are not the subject of collective bargaining.

Attitude surveys

Attitude surveys are a valuable way of involving employees by seeking their views on matters that concern them.

Suggestion schemes

Suggestion schemes can provide a valuable means for employees to participate in improving the efficiency of the company.

Effectiveness of employee involvement and participation (Cox *et al*, 2006)

To be effective, employee involvement and participation mechanisms have to be

Employee voice – key learning points (continued)

embedded in the organization – well established and part of everyday working life. Combinations of involvement and participation practices worked best.

Planning for voice

Planning should be based on a review of the existing forms of voice, which would include discussions with stakeholders (line managers, employees and trade union representatives) on the effectiveness of existing arrangements and any improvements required. In the light of these discussions, new or revised approaches can be developed; it will be necessary to brief and train those involved in the part they should play.

EU Directives affecting employee voice procedures

The two relevant EU Directives are: the European Works Councils (EWC) Directive and the Information and Consultation of Employees (ICE) Directive.

Questions

1. From the operations director: 'The term "employee voice" is being bandied about a lot, but what does it mean?'
2. From a friend studying for her CIPD exams: 'Could you please explain to me the difference between employee involvement and employee participation?'
3. From your chief executive: 'I seem to spend more and more of my time meeting employees in our various consultative committees. Do they really add value to the business? If so, I would like to know how.'

References

Boxall, P F and Purcell, J (2003) *Strategy and Human Resource Management*, Palgrave Macmillan, Basingstoke

Cox, A, Zagelmeyer, S and Marchington, M (2006) Embedding employee involvement and participation at work, *Human Resource Management Journal*, **16** (3), pp 250–67

Dundon, T, Wilkinson, A, Marchington, M and Ackers, P (2004) *The International Journal of Human Resource Management*, **15** (6), pp 1149–70

Kochan, T A, Katz, H and McKersie, R (1986) *The Transformation of American Industrial Relations*, Basic Books, New York

Marchington M, Goodman, J, Wilkinson, A and Ackers, P (1992) *New Developments in Employee Involvement*, HMSO, London

Marchington, M, Wilkinson, A, Ackers, P and Dundon, A (2001) *Management Choice and Employee Voice*, CIPD, London

Millward, N, Stevens, M, Smart, D and Hawes, W R (1992) *Workplace Industrial Relations in Transition*, Dartmouth Publishing, Hampshire

Williams, S and Adam-Smith, D (2006) *Contemporary Employment Relations: A critical introduction*, Oxford University Press, Oxford

57 Employee Communications

Key concepts and terms

- Employee communication
- Speak-up programme
- Consultation
- Team briefing

Learning outcomes

On completing this chapter you should be able to define these key concepts. You should also know about:

- The importance of employee communications
- The approach to communication
- Employee communication strategy
- What should be communicated
- Communication methods

Introduction

Employee communication processes and systems provide for 'two-way communication'. In one direction they enable organizations to inform employees about matters that will interest them. In the other, they provide for upward communication by giving employees a voice, as described in Chapter 56.

Communication should be distinguished from consultation. As the ACAS (2005) guide states, communication is concerned with the exchange of information and ideas within an organization while consultation goes beyond this and involves managers actively seeking and then taking account of the views of employees before making a decision.

The importance of employee communications

Good communication is important for three reasons. First, it is a vital part of any change management programme. If any change is proposed in terms and conditions of employment, HR processes such as contingent pay, working methods, technologies, products and services or organization (including mergers and acquisitions) employees need to know what is proposed and how it will affect them. Resistance to change often arises simply because people do not know what the change is or what it implies for them. Second, commitment to the organization will be enhanced if employees know what the organization has achieved or is trying to achieve and how this benefits them. Third, effective communication generates trust as organizations take the trouble to explain what they are doing and why. However, it should be emphasized that these three benefits of good communication will only be realized in full if employees are given a voice – the opportunity to comment and respond to the information they obtain from management.

What should be communicated?

Management and individual managers need to communicate to employees about terms and conditions of employment, what they are expected to do, learning and development opportunities, the objectives, strategies, policies and performance of the organization, and any proposed changes to conditions of employment, working arrangements and requirements, or the structure and policies of the organization.

Employees need the opportunity to communicate upwards their comments and reactions to what is proposed will happen or what is actually happening in matters that affect them; for example, pay and other terms of employment, working conditions, work–life balance, equal opportunity, job security, health and safety, and learning and development programmes.

Approach to communication

To be effective, communication needs to be clear, easily understood and concise. Information should be presented systematically on a regular basis and be as relevant, local and timely as possible. Empathy is required by management in the sense of appreciating the concerns of employees and what they want and need to hear. Possible reactions to proposed changes should be assessed and anticipated in the communication. Attitude surveys can be used to find out what information employees want and where they feel there are any gaps that need to be filled.

A variety of communication methods will be needed; spoken and written, direct and indirect. Face-to-face communication to individuals or groups is both direct and swift and it provides an opportunity to gauge the reactions of people, who can respond on the spot and ask questions. It should be supplemented by written material or intranet communications where the information is particularly important or complex.

Written communication is most effective when the information is important, the topic requires detailed and accurate explanation, the audience is widespread or large, and there is need for a back-up to face-to-face communication or a permanent record. Judicious use should be made of a mix of face-to-face and written communication, using a selection of the methods described below.

Communication methods

Individual face-to-face communication

This is, of course, the most common method of communication but it can be the most problematic. The quality, accuracy and acceptability of the information depend largely on the skill of the managers or team leaders involved and on their commitment to doing it well. Information can be distorted or plain wrong. Briefing notes are helpful but they will not necessarily be used well. Individual communication is inevitable and necessary but should not be relied upon in isolation when the subject matter is important.

Team briefing

A team briefing aims to overcome the limited scope for communication through individuals or even joint consultative committees by involving everyone in an organization, level by level, in face-to-face meetings to present, receive and discuss information. It operates as follows.

How a team briefing operates

- Organization – covers all levels in the business with the fewest possible steps from top to bottom. There should be between four and 18 in each group and the group should be run by its team leader or manager (who must be given training).
- Subjects – policies, plans, progress and people.
- Operation – work to a brief prepared by the board on key issues. The brief is written up and cascaded down the organization. Briefs are discussed at meetings and comments are fed back to the top to provide for two-way communication.
- Timing and duration – meet when there is something to discuss. Meetings last no more than 20–30 minutes.

Team briefing can work well as long as there is enthusiasm for it at the top that is transmitted throughout the organization. It depends on good briefing and managers or team leaders who have the necessary communication and interpersonal skills.

Consultative committees

Joint consultation provides a channel for two-way communication, but committees are not always effective. Their discussions can be confined to relatively trivial issues and there is still the problem of disseminating information around the organization – committee members cannot do this on their own. Minutes can be posted on notice boards but may not be read. It is better to highlight key points either on notice boards or through other channels.

Notice boards

Notice boards are the most obvious and familiar means of communication but they can too easily be cluttered up with redundant information. It is necessary to control what goes on to boards and ensure that out-of-date or unauthorized notices are removed.

Speak-up programmes

Speak-up programmes provide unique channels for individual employees to raise points with senior management concerning the organization and its plans and policies. This can be through the intranet.

Intranet

Organizations are increasingly relying on an internal e-mail system (the intranet) to communicate information, especially in workplaces where all or most of the employees have access to a computer. The advantage of intranet communication is that it can be transmitted swiftly to a wide audience. It can also be used for two-way communication – employees can be invited to respond to questions or surveys.

A communication dashboard can be created for departmental websites that displays performance metrics in a visual form, as on a car dashboard.

Magazines

Glossy magazines or house journals are obvious ways to keep employees informed about the activities and achievements of the organization. There is, however, a danger of such magazines being more about public relations than about matters of real interest to employees.

Newsletters and bulletins

Newsletters can appear more frequently than magazines and can angle their contents more to the concerns of employees. They may be distributed in addition to a house magazine, treating the latter mainly as a public relations exercise.

Bulletins can be used to give immediate information to employees that cannot wait for the next issue of a newsletter.

Employee communication strategy

A strategy for employee communication will deal with what information the organization wants to give to employees and how it wants to provide it. Provision should also be made for upward communication.

Information to be made available

The strategy should be based on an analysis of what management wants to say and what employees want to hear on a regular basis. It should also cover provision for upwards communication. The analysis could refer to the areas of interest set out earlier in this chapter.

It may also be necessary to develop a specific communication strategy for any proposed major changes to terms and conditions, working arrangements such as downsizing, or organization structure, including mergers and acquisitions. For example, the introduction of a new pay structure is a major change exercise and will need to be supported by a planned communication strategy.

Providing the information

The strategy should cover the mix of methods that will be used to convey the information – face-to-face (individual or team), notice boards, intranet and magazines, newsletters or bulletins.

Upward communication

The strategy should also provide for upward communication through consultative committees, team briefing, speak-up programmes and the intranet.

Employee communication – key learning points

The importance of employee communication

A vital part of a change management programme, increase commitment, generate trust.

What should be communicated

Management and individual managers need to communicate to employees about terms and conditions of employment, what they are expected to do, learning and development opportunities, the objectives, strategies, policies and performance of the organization, and any proposed changes to conditions of employment, working arrangements and requirements, or the structure and policies of the organization. Employees need the opportunity to communicate upwards their comments and reactions to what is proposed will happen or what is actually happening in matters that affect them.

The approach to communication

Communication needs to be clear, easily understood and concise. Information should be presented systematically on a regular basis and be as relevant, local and timely as possible.

Communication methods

Individual face-to-face communication, team briefing, consultative committees, notice boards, speak-up programmes, intranet, magazines, newsletters and bulletins.

Employee communication strategy

A strategy for employee communication will deal with what information the organization wants to give to employees and how it wants to provide it. Provision should also be made for upward communication.

Questions

1. You have been asked to give a talk at your local CIPD branch conference on 'Upwards communication: what does it mean and what is its value to employers and employees?' Prepare an outline of your talk with supporting evidence on good practice from your own organization or elsewhere.
2. From your managing director: 'What's this I hear about team briefing? Is it for us and, if so, how do we benefit?'
3. What are the main barriers to communication and how can they be overcome?

Reference

ACAS (2005) *Guide to Communications*, ACAS, London

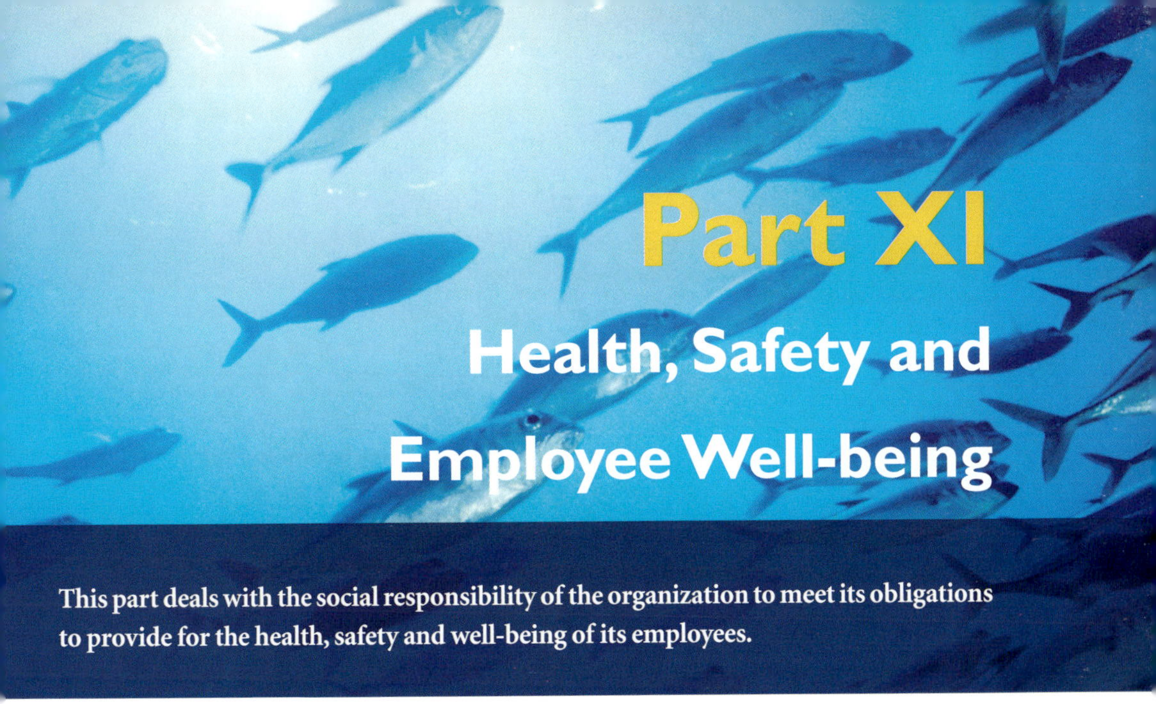

Part XI

Health, Safety and Employee Well-being

This part deals with the social responsibility of the organization to meet its obligations to provide for the health, safety and well-being of its employees.

Part XI contents

58 Health and Safety

Key concepts and terms

- Frequency rate
- Health and safety audit
- Incidence rate
- Occupational hygiene
- Risk
- Severity rate
- Hazard
- Health and safety inspection
- Occupational health programme
- Occupational medicine
- Risk assessment

Learning outcomes

On completing this chapter you should be able to define these key concepts. You should also know about:

- Managing health and safety at work
- Risk assessments
- Health and safety inspections
- Occupational health programmes
- Communicating the need for better health and safety practices
- Organizing health and safety
- Health and safety policies
- Health and safety audits
- Accident prevention
- Measuring health and safety performance
- Health and safety training

Introduction

Health and safety policies and programmes are concerned with protecting employees – and other people affected by what the company produces and does – against the hazards arising from their employment or their links with the company.

Safety programmes deal with the prevention of accidents and with minimizing the resulting loss and damage to people and property. They relate more to systems of work than the working environment, but both health and safety programmes are concerned with protection against hazards, and their aims and methods are clearly interlinked.

Occupational health programmes deal with the prevention of ill-health arising from working conditions. They consist of two elements: 1) occupational medicine, which is a specialized branch of preventive medicine concerned with the diagnosis and prevention of health hazards at work and dealing with any ill-health or stress which has occurred in spite of preventive actions, and 2) occupational hygiene, which is the province of the chemist and the engineer or ergonomist engaged in the measurement and control of environmental hazards.

Managing health and safety at work

It is estimated by the Royal Society for the Prevention of Accidents (2008) that every year in the UK we face the challenge of reducing about 350 fatalities at work, over 36 million days lost due to work-related accidents and ill-health. It has also been estimated by the Health and Safety Executive (2008) that, apart from the pain and misery caused to those directly or indirectly concerned, the total cost to British employers of work-related injury and illness is £6.5 billion a year.

The achievement of a healthy and safe place of work and the elimination to the maximum extent possible of hazards to health and safety is the responsibility of everyone employed in an organization, as well as those working there under contract. But the onus is on management to achieve and indeed go beyond the high standard in health and safety matters required by the legislation – the Health and Safety at Work, etc Act, 1974 and the various regulations laid down in the Codes of Practice.

The importance of healthy and safe policies and practices is, sadly, often underestimated by those concerned with managing businesses and by individual managers within those businesses. But it cannot be emphasized too strongly that the prevention of accidents and elimination of health and safety hazards is a prime responsibility of management and managers in order to minimize suffering and loss.

The achievement of the highest standards of health and safety in the workplace is the moral as well as the legal responsibility of employers – this is the overriding reason. Close and continuous attention to health and safety is important because ill-health and injuries caused by the system of work or working conditions cause suffering and loss to individuals and their dependants. In addition, accidents and absences through ill-health or injuries result in losses and damage for the organization. This 'business' reason is much, much less significant than the 'human' reasons, but it is still a consideration, albeit a tangential one.

Health and safety policies

Written health and safety policies are required to demonstrate that top management is concerned about the protection of the organization's employees from hazards at work and to indicate how this protection will be provided. They are, therefore, first a declaration of intent; second, a definition of the means by which that intent will be realized, and third, a statement of the guidelines that should be followed by everyone concerned – which means all employees – in implementing the policy.

The policy statement should consist of three parts:

1. the general policy statement;
2. the description of the organization for health and safety;
3. details of arrangements for implementing the policy.

The general policy statement

The general policy statement should be a declaration of the intention of the employer to safeguard the health and safety of employees. It should emphasize these fundamental points:

- that the safety of employees and the public is of paramount importance;
- that safety takes precedence over expediency;
- that every effort will be made to involve all managers, team leaders and employees in the development and implementation of health and safety procedures;
- that health and safety legislation will be complied with in the spirit as well as the letter of the law.

Organization

This section of the policy statement should describe the health and safety organization of the business through which high standards are set and achieved by people at all levels in the organization.

This statement should underline the ultimate responsibility of top management for the health and safety performance of the organization. It should then indicate how key management personnel are held accountable for performance in their areas. The role of safety representatives and safety committees should be defined, and the duties of specialists such as the safety adviser and the medical officer should be summarized.

Conducting risk assessments

What is a risk assessment?

Risk assessments are concerned with the identification of hazards and the analysis of the risks attached to them. A hazard is anything that can cause harm (working on roofs, lifting heavy objects, chemicals, electricity, etc). A risk is the chance, large or small, of harm being actually done by the hazard.

The purpose of risk assessments is to initiate preventive action. They enable control measures to be devised on the basis of an understanding of the relative importance of risks. Risk assessments must be recorded if there are five or more employees.

There are two types of risk assessment. The first is quantitative risk assessment, which produces an objective probability estimate based upon risk information that is immediately applicable to the circumstances in which the risk occurs. The second is qualitative risk assessment, which is more subjective and is based on judgement backed by generalized data. Qualitative risk assessment is preferable if the specific data are available. Qualitative risk assessment may be acceptable if there is little or no specific data as long as the assessment is made systematically on the basis of an analysis of working conditions and hazards and informed judgement of the likelihood of harm actually being done.

Risk assessments seek to identify typical hazards – activities where accidents happen, such as those set out below.

Typical hazards – activities where accidents happen

- Receipt of raw materials, eg lifting, carrying.
- Stacking and storage, eg falling materials.
- Movement of people and materials, eg falls, collisions.
- Processing of raw materials, eg exposure to toxic substances.
- Maintenance of buildings, eg roof work, gutter cleaning.
- Maintenance of plant and machinery, eg lifting tackle, installation of equipment.

- Using electricity, eg using hand tools, extension leads.
- Operating machines, eg operating without sufficient clearance, or at an unsafe speed; not using safety devices.
- Failure to wear protective equipment, eg hats, boots, clothing.
- Distribution of products or materials, eg movement of vehicles.
- Dealing with emergencies, eg spillages, fires, explosions.
- Health hazards arising from the use of equipment or methods of working, eg VDUs, repetitive strain injuries from badly designed work stations or working practices.

Most accidents are caused by a few key activities. Assessors should concentrate initially on those that could cause serious harm. Operations such as roof work, maintenance and transport movement cause far more deaths and injuries each year than many mainstream activities.

When carrying out a risk assessment it is also necessary to consider who might be harmed. This does not mean only employees but also visitors, including cleaners and contractors, and the public when calling in to buy products or enlist services.

Hazards should be ranked according to their potential severity as a basis for producing one side of the risk equation. A simple three-point scale can be used such as 'low', 'moderate' and 'high'. A more complex severity rating scale has been proposed by Holt and Andrews (1993), as follows:

- Catastrophic – imminent danger exists, hazard capable of causing death and illness on a wide scale.
- Critical – hazard can result in serious illness, severe injury, property and equipment damage.
- Marginal – hazard can cause illness, injury, or equipment damage, but the results would not be expected to be serious.
- Negligible – hazard will not result in serious injury or illness, remote possibility of damage beyond minor first-aid case.

Assessing the risk

When the hazards have been identified it is necessary to assess how high the risks are. This involves answering three questions:

1. What is the worst result?
2. How likely is it to happen?
3. How many people could be hurt if things go wrong?

A probability rating system can be used such as:

1. Probable – likely to occur immediately or shortly.
2. Reasonably probable – probably will occur in time.
3. Remote – may occur in time.
4. Extremely remote – unlikely to occur.

Taking action

Risk assessment should lead to action. The type of action can be ranked in order of potential effectiveness in the form of the following 'safety precedence sequence'.

Safety precedence sequence

- Hazard elimination – use of alternatives, design improvements, change of process.
- Substitution – for example, replacement of a chemical with one that is less risky.
- Use of barriers – removing the hazard from the worker or removing the worker from the hazard.
- Use of procedures – limitation of exposure, dilution of exposure, safe systems of work (these depend on human response).
- Use of warning systems – signs, instructions, labels (these also depend on human response).
- Use of personal protective clothing – this depends on human response and is used only when all other options have been exhausted.

Monitoring and evaluation

Risk assessment is not completed when action has been initiated. It is essential to monitor the hazard and evaluate the effectiveness of the action in eliminating it or at least reducing it to an acceptable level.

Health and safety audits

Risk assessments identify specific hazards and quantify the risks attached to them. Health and safety audits provide for a much more comprehensive review of all aspects of health and safety policies, procedures and practices programmes. As described by Saunders (1992):

> *A safety audit will examine the whole organization in order to test whether it is meeting its safety aims and objectives. It will examine hierarchies, safety planning processes, decision making, delegation, policy making and implementation as well as all areas of safety programme planning.*

Who carries out a health and safety audit?

Safety audits can be conducted by safety advisers and/or HR specialists, but the more managers, employees and trade union representatives are involved the better. Audits are often carried out under the auspices of a health and safety committee with its members taking an active part in conducting them.

Managers can also be held responsible for conducting audits within their departments and, even better, individual members of these departments can be trained to carry out audits in particular areas. The conduct of an audit will be facilitated if checklists are prepared and a simple form used to record results.

Some organizations also use outside agencies such as the British Safety Institute to conduct independent audits.

What is covered by a health and safety audit?

A health and safety audit should cover the following.

1. Policies

- Do health and safety policies meet legal requirements?
- Are senior managers committed to health and safety?
- How committed are other managers, team leaders and supervisors to health and safety?
- Is there a health and safety committee? If not, why not?
- How effective is the committee in getting things done?

2. *Procedures*

How effectively do the procedures:

- Support the implementation of health and safety policies?
- Communicate the need for good health and safety practices?
- Provide for systematic risk assessments?
- Ensure that accidents are investigated thoroughly?
- Record data on health and safety that is used to evaluate performance and initiate action?
- Ensure that health and safety considerations are given proper weight when designing systems of work or manufacturing and operational processes (including the design of equipment and work stations, the specification for the product or service, and the use of materials)?
- Provide safety training, especially induction training and training when jobs or working methods are changed?

3. *Safety practices*

- To what extent do health and safety practices in all areas of the organization conform to the general requirements of the Health and Safety at Work Act and the specific requirements of the various regulations and Codes of Practice?
- What risk assessments have been carried out? What were these findings? What actions were taken?
- What is the health and safety performance of the organization as shown by the performance indicators? Is the trend positive or negative? If the latter, what is being done about it?
- How thoroughly are accidents investigated? What steps have been taken to prevent their recurrence?
- What is the evidence that managers and supervisors are really concerned about health and safety?

What should be done with the audit?

The audit should cover the questions above but its purpose is to generate action. Those conducting the audit will have to assess priorities and costs and draw up action programmes for approval by the board.

Health and safety inspections

Health and safety inspections are designed to examine a specific area of the organization – an operational department or a manufacturing process – in order to locate and define any faults in the system, equipment, plant or machines, or any operational errors that might be a danger to health or the source of accidents. Health and safety inspections should be carried out on a regular and systematic basis by line managers and supervisors with the advice and help of health and safety advisers. The steps to be taken in carrying out health and safety inspections are as follows:

1. Allocate the responsibility for conducting the inspection.
2. Define the points to be covered in the form of a checklist.
3. Divide the department or plant into areas and list the points to which attention needs to be given in each area.
4. Define the frequency with which inspections should be carried out – daily in critical areas.
5. Use the checklists as the basis for the inspection.
6. Carry out sample or spot checks on a random basis.
7. Carry out special investigations as necessary to deal with special problems such as operating machinery without guards to increase throughput.
8. Set up a reporting system (a form should be used for recording the results of inspections).
9. Set up a system for monitoring that safety inspections are being conducted properly and on schedule and that corrective action has been taken where necessary.

Accident prevention

The prevention of accidents is achieved by the following actions.

Accident prevention actions

- Identify the causes of accidents and the conditions under which they are most likely to occur.
- Take account of safety factors at the design stage – building safety into the system.

- Design safety equipment and protective devices and provide protective clothing.
- Carry out regular risk assessments audits, inspections and checks and take action to eliminate risks.
- Investigate all accidents resulting in damage or harm to establish the cause and to initiate corrective action.
- Maintain good records and statistics in order to identify problem areas and unsatisfactory trends.
- Conduct a continuous programme of education and training on safe working habits and methods of avoiding accidents.
- Encourage approaches to leadership and motivation that do not place excessive demands on people.

Occupational health programmes

Occupational health programmes are designed to minimize the impact of work-related illnesses arising from work. It is estimated by the Royal Society for the Prevention of Accidents (2008) that every year in the UK 30 million working days are lost because of work-related illness. Two million people say they suffer from an illness they believe was caused by their work. Muscular disorders, including repetitive strain injury (RSI) and back pain are by far the most commonly reported illnesses, with 1.2 million affected, and the numbers are rising. The next biggest problem is stress, which 500,000 people say is so bad that it is making them ill. These are large and disturbing figures and they show that high priority must be given to creating and maintaining programmes for the improvement of occupational health.

The control of occupational health and hygiene problems can be achieved by taking the following actions.

The control of occupational health and hygiene problems

- Eliminate the hazard at source through design and process engineering.
- Isolate hazardous processes and substances so that workers do not come into contact with them.
- Change the processes or substances used to promote better protection or eliminate the risk.

- Provide protective equipment, but only if changes to the design, process or specification cannot completely remove the hazard.
- Train workers to avoid risk.
- Maintain plant and equipment to eliminate the possibility of harmful emissions, controlling the use of toxic substances and eliminating radiation hazards.
- Adopt good housekeeping practices to keep premises and machinery clean and free from toxic substances.
- Conduct regular inspections to ensure that potential health risks are identified in good time.
- Carry out pre-employment medical examinations and regular checks on those exposed to risk.
- Ensure that ergonomic considerations (ie, those concerning the design and use of equipment, machines, processes and workstations) are taken into account in design specifications, establishing work routines and training – this is particularly important as a means of minimizing the incidence of RSI.
- Maintain preventive medicine programmes that develop health standards for each job and involve regular audits of potential health hazards and regular examinations for anyone at risk.

Particular attention needs to be exercised on the control of noise, fatigue and stress. The management and control of stress, as considered in Chapter 59, should be regarded as a major part of any occupational health programme.

Measuring health and safety performance

It is essential to measure health and safety performance as a means of identifying in good time where actions are necessary. Account should be taken not only of current and recent figures but also trends. The most common measures are:

- The frequency rate: number of injuries/number of hours worked × 100,000.
- The incidence rate: number of injuries/average number employed during the period × 1,000.
- The severity rate – the days lost through accidents or occupational health problems per 1 million hours worked.

Some organizations adopt a 'total loss control' approach, which covers the cost of accidents to the business under such headings as pay to people off work, damage to plant or equipment and loss of production. A cost severity rate can then be calculated, which is the total cost of accident per million hours worked.

Communicating the need for better health and safety practices

It is necessary to deliver the message that health and safety is important, as long as this supplements rather than replaces other initiatives. The following steps can be taken to increase the effectiveness of safety messages.

Communicating effectively on health and safety

- Avoid negatives – successful safety propaganda should contain positive messages, not warnings of the unpleasant consequences of actions.
- Expose correctly – address the message to the right people at the point of danger.
- Use attention-getting techniques carefully – lurid images may only be remembered for what they are, not for the message they are trying to convey.
- Maximize comprehension – messages should be simple and specific.
- Messages must be believable – they should address real issues and be perceived as being delivered by people (ie managers) who believe in what they say and are doing something about it.
- Messages must point the way to action – the most effective messages call for positive actions that can be achieved by the receivers and will offer them a tangible benefit.

Approaches to briefing staff on the importance of health and safety

Advice to a group of staff on the importance of health and safety in the workplace must be based on a thorough understanding of the organization's health and safety policies and procedures and an appreciation of the particular factors affecting the health and safety of the group of people concerned. The latter can be based on information provided by risk assessments, safety audits and accident reports. But the advice must be positive – why health and safety is important and how accidents can be prevented. The advice should not be over-weighted by awful warnings.

The points to be made include:

- A review of the health and safety policies of the organization with explanations of the reasoning behind them and a positive statement of management's belief that health and safety is a major consideration because: 1) it directly affects the well-being of all concerned, and 2) it can, and does, minimize suffering and loss.
- A review of the procedures used by the organization for the business as a whole and in the particular area to assess risks and audit safety position.
- An explanation of the roles of the members of the group in carrying out their work safely and giving full consideration to the safety of others.
- A reiteration of the statement that one of the core values of the organization is the maintenance of safe systems of work and the promotion of safe working practices.

Health and safety training

Health and safety training is a key part of the preventative programme. It should start as part of the induction course. It should also take place following a transfer to a new job or a change in working methods. Safety training spells out the rules and provides information on potential hazards and how to avoid them. Further refresher training should be provided and special courses laid on to deal with new aspects of health and safety or areas in which safety problems have emerged.

Organizing health and safety

Health and safety concerns everyone in an establishment, although the main responsibility lies with management in general and individual managers in particular. Specific roles as summarized below should be defined:

- *Management* develops and implements health and safety policies and ensures that procedures for carrying out risk assessments, safety audits and inspections are implemented. Importantly, management has the duty of monitoring and evaluating health and safety performance and taking corrective action as necessary.
- *Managers* can exert the greater influence on health and safety. They are in immediate control and it is up to them to keep a constant watch for unsafe conditions or practices and to take immediate action. They are also directly responsible for ensuring that employees are conscious of health and safety hazards and do not take risks.

- *Employees* should be aware of what constitutes safe working practices as they affect them and their fellow workers. While management and managers have the duty to communicate and train, individuals also have the duty to take account of what they have heard and learnt in the ways they carry out their work.
- *Health and safety advisers* advise on policies and procedures and on healthy and safe methods of working. They conduct risk assessments and safety audits and investigations into accidents in conjunction with managers and health and safety representatives, maintain statistics and report on trends and necessary actions.
- *Health and safety representatives* deal with health and safety issues in their areas and are members of health and safety committees.
- *Medical advisers* have two functions: preventive and clinical. The preventive function is most important, especially on occupational health matters. The clinical function is to deal with industrial accidents and diseases and to advise on the steps necessary to recover from injury or illness arising from work. They do not usurp the role of the family doctor in non-work-related illnesses.
- *Safety committees* consisting of health and safety representatives advise on health and safety policies and procedures, help in conducting risk assessments and safety audits, and make suggestions on improving health and safety performance.

Health and safety – key learning points

Managing health and safety at work

The achievement of a healthy and safe place of work and the elimination to the maximum extent possible of hazards to health and safety is the responsibility of everyone employed in an organization, as well as those working there under contract. But the onus is on management to achieve and indeed go beyond the high standard in health and safety matters required by the legislation – the Health and Safety at Work, etc Act, 1974 and the various regulations laid down in the Codes of Practice.

Health and safety policies

Written health and safety policies are required to demonstrate that top management is concerned about the protection of the organization's employees from hazards at work and to indicate how this protection will be provided.

Risk assessments

Risk assessments are concerned with the identification of hazards and the analysis of the risks attached to them. The purpose is to initiate preventive action.

Health and safety audits

Health and safety audits provide for a much more comprehensive review of all aspects of health and safety policies, procedures and practices programmes.

Health and safety – key learning points (continued)

Health and safety inspections

Health and safety inspections should be carried out on a regular and systematic basis by line managers and supervisors with the advice and help of health and safety advisers.

Accident prevention

- Identify the causes of accidents.
- Take account of safety factors at the design stage.
- Design safety equipment and protective devices and provide protective clothing.
- Carry out regular risk assessments audits and inspections and take action to eliminate risks.
- Investigate all accidents.
- Maintain good records and statistics in order to identify problem areas and unsatisfactory trends.
- Conduct a continuous programme of education and training on safe working habits.

Occupational health programmes

- Eliminate the hazard at source through design and process engineering.
- Isolate hazardous processes and substances so that workers do not come into contact with them.
- Change the processes or substances used to promote better protection or eliminate the risk.
- Provide protective equipment, but only if changes to the design, process or specification cannot completely remove the hazard.
- Train workers to avoid risk.

Measuring health and safety performance

This is important as a guide to action, using the standard measures of frequency, incidence and severity rate.

Communicating the need for better health and safety practices

It is necessary to deliver the message that health and safety is important, as long as this supplements rather than replaces other initiatives.

Health and safety training

Health and safety training is a key part of the preventative programme. It should start as part of the induction course. It should also take place following a transfer to a new job or a change in working methods.

Organizing health and safety

Health and safety concerns everyone in an establishment, although the main responsibility lies with management in general and individual managers in particular. The following roles should be defined: managers and employees, health and safety advisers, medical advisers and the health and safety committee.

Questions

1. What are health and safety and occupational health programmes?
2. What is the purpose of health and safety policies?
3. What is the distinction between risk assessments, health and safety audits and health and safety inspections?
4. What steps need to be taken to prevent accidents?
5. How are occupational health problems controlled?

References

Health and Safety Executive (2008) *Annual Report*, HSE, London
Holt, A and Andrews, H (1993) *Principles of Health and Safety at Work*, IOSH Publishing, London
Royal Society for the Prevention of Accidents (2008) *Annual Report*, RoSPA, London
Saunders, R (1992) *The Safety Audit*, Pitman, London

59 Employee Well-being

Key concepts and terms

- Employee assistance programme (EAP)
- Work environment
- Quality of working life
- Work–life balance

Learning outcomes

On completing this chapter you should be able to define these key concepts. You should also know about:

- Reasons for concern with well-being
- The achievement of work–life balance
- Sexual harassment
- Services for individuals
- The significance of the work environment
- Managing stress
- Bullying
- Group employee services

Introduction

Well-being at work exists when people are happy with their lot – what they do, how they are treated, how they get on with others. The well-being of employees depends on the quality of working life provided by their employers – the feelings of satisfaction and happiness arising from the work itself and the work environment. The concept of the quality of working life emerged in the 1970s (Wilson, 1973) but has been less prominent recently, partly because of the preoccupation with work–life balance, which is dealt with later in this chapter. As defined by Taylor (2008) the quality of working life is related to the basic extrinsic job factors of wages, hours and working conditions and the intrinsic factors of the work itself. Warr *et al* (1970) focused their definition on work involvement, intrinsic job motivation, job satisfaction and happiness.

Some time ago Martin (1967) put the case for welfare, as it was then known, as follows: 'People (at work) are entitled to be treated as full human beings with personal needs, hopes and anxieties.' This requirement has not changed since then.

There are three reasons why organizations should be concerned with the well-being of their employees. First, and most importantly, they have a duty of care and this means adopting a socially responsible approach to looking after their people. Second, employers are responsible for creating a good work environment not only because it is their duty to do so but also as part of the total reward system. Third, it is in the interests of employers to do so because this will increase the likelihood of their employees being committed to the organization and help to establish it as a 'best place to work'.

A key aspect of well-being for employees is their health and safety, as covered in Chapter 58. Job design factors, as discussed in Chapter 27, are also important. The other aspects dealt with in this chapter are creating a satisfactory work environment, which includes dealing with how people are treated at work, managing stress, attending to work–life balance issues, providing services for individuals including employee assistance programmes, and group services.

Improving of the work environment

The work environment consists of the system of work, the design of jobs, working conditions and the ways in which people are treated at work by their managers and co-workers. Well-being is achieved when account is taken in designing the work system and the jobs in it of the needs of the people concerned (see Chapter 27). Working conditions need to meet health and safety requirements as listed in Chapter 58. The way people are treated is a matter of managerial behaviour, achieving work–life balance and dealing with issues such as stress, harassment and bullying, as discussed below.

Managerial behaviour

Lawler (2003) suggests that what managers have to do is 'to treat people right'. This means recognizing them as individuals with different needs and wants, rewarding their achievements, helping them to develop, and treating them with consideration as human beings.

Work–life balance

Work–life balance employment practices are concerned with providing scope for employees to balance what they do at work with the responsibilities and interests they have outside work and so reconcile the competing claims of work and home by meeting their own needs as well as those of their employers. The term 'work–life balance' has largely replaced 'family-friendly policy'. As Kodz *et al* (2002) explain, the principle of work–life balance is that: 'There should be a balance between an individual's work and their life outside work, and that this balance should be healthy.'

As defined by the Work Foundation (2003b) the concept of work–life balance is 'about employees achieving a satisfactory equilibrium between work and non-work activities (ie parental responsibilities and wider caring duties, as well as other activities and interests)'. The Work Foundation recommends that practical day-to-day business and related needs should be considered when organizations set about selecting the range of work–life options that should be made available to staff, whether on a collective basis (as, for example, flexitime arrangements) or on an individual level (say, allowing an individual to move to term-time working provisions). Individual requests for a particular working arrangement generally need to be considered on a case-by-case basis, but it is important for a culture to exist that does not discourage employees from making such requests. In addition to fearing the reaction of line managers, the risk of career damage is a common reason for poor take-up of work–life balance arrangements. Line management will need to be convinced that work–life balance measures are important and pay off in terms of increased engagement.

The IRS (2002) considers that 'Flexible working is considered the most practical solution to establishing an effective work–life balance.' The term 'flexible working 'covers flexitime, homeworking, part-time working, compressed working weeks, annualized hours, job sharing and term-time only working. It also refers to special leave schemes that provide employees with the freedom to respond to a domestic crisis or to take a career break without jeopardizing their employment status. However, IRS noted that 'creating an environment in which staff who opt to work flexibly and those who raise work–life issues will require a cultural shift in many organizations, backed by senior level support'.

The Work Foundation (2003b) survey of work–life balance established that the most common work–life balance measures taken by employers were the provision of part-time working (90 per cent), family/emergency leave (85 per cent) and general unpaid leave (78 per cent). Formal policies are most likely to be found in public and voluntary sector organizations (35 per cent) and least likely to be found in manufacturing (14 per cent).

Management resistance is the most common difficulty met in introducing work–life balance policies. However, the work–life balance survey conducted by the DTI in 2003 found that there was a high level of support amongst employers (65 per cent). A large proportion of employers (74 per cent) believed that people who work flexibly are just as likely to be promoted as those who do not. The survey established that the benefits claimed from introducing work–life balance policies were:

- improved productivity and quality of work;
- improved commitment and morale;
- reduced staff turnover;
- reduced casual absence;
- improved utilization of new recruits.

Work–life balance policies can lower absence and help to tackle the low morale and high degrees of stress that can lead to retention problems as employees tire of juggling work and life responsibilities. The research conducted by the Institute of Employment Studies (Kodz *et al*, 2002) identified employees who were staying longer with their firms because of access to flexible working arrangements.

Managing stress

There are four main reasons why organizations should take account of stress and do something about it. First, they have the social responsibility to provide a good quality of working life; second, because excessive stress causes illness; third, because it can result in inability to cope with the demands of the job which, of course, creates more stress, and finally because excessive stress can reduce employee effectiveness and therefore organizational performance.

The ways in which stress can be managed by an organization include the following.

Ways of managing stress

- Job design – clarifying roles, reducing the danger of role ambiguity and conflict and giving people more autonomy within a defined structure to manage their responsibilities.
- Targets and performance standards – setting reasonable and achievable targets that may stretch people but do not place impossible burdens on them.

- Job placement – taking care to place people in jobs that are within their capabilities.
- Career development – planning careers and promoting staff in accordance with their capabilities, taking care not to over- or under-promote.
- Performance management processes, which allow a dialogue to take place between managers and individuals about the latter's work problems and ambitions.
- Counselling – giving individuals the opportunity to talk about their problems with a member of the HR department, or through an employee assistance programme, as described later in this chapter.
- Anti-bullying campaigns – bullying at work is a major cause of stress.
- Management training in what managers can do to alleviate their own stress and reduce it in others.

Sexual harassment

Sadly, sexual harassment has always been a feature of life at work. Perhaps it is not always quite as blatant today as it has been in the past, but it is still there, in more or less subtle forms, and it is just as unpleasant. People subject to sexual harassment can take legal action but it must be the policy of the organization to make it clear that it will not be tolerated, and this policy should be backed up by procedures and practices for dealing with harassment.

Problems of dealing with harassment

There are three problems in dealing with harassment. First, it can be difficult to make a clear-cut case. An accusation of harassment can be hard to prove unless there are witnesses, and those who indulge in this practice usually take care to carry it out on a one-to-one basis. In this situation, it may be a case of one person's word against another's. The harasser, almost inevitably a man, resorts to two defences: one, that it did not take place ('it was all in her mind'); and two, that if anything did take place it was provoked by the behaviour of the female. When this happens, whoever deals with the case has to exercise judgement and attempt, difficult though it may be, to remove any prejudice in favour of the word of the man, the woman, the boss or the subordinate.

The second problem is that victims of sexual harassment are often unwilling to take action and in practice seldom do so. This is because of the actual or perceived difficulty of proving their case. But they may also feel that they will not get a fair hearing and are worried about the effect making such accusations will have on how they are treated by their boss or their colleagues in the future, whether or not they have substantiated their accusation.

The third, and perhaps the most deep-rooted and difficult problem is that sexual harassment may be part of the culture of the organization – 'the way we do things around here'; a norm, practised at all levels.

Solutions

There are no easy solutions to these problems. It may be very hard to eradicate sexual harassment completely, but the effort must be made along the following lines.

Dealing with harassment

1. Issue a clear statement by the chief executive that sexual harassment will not be tolerated.
2. Back up the statement with a policy directive that spells out in more detail that the organization deplores it, why it is not acceptable and what people who believe they are being subjected to harassment can do about it.
3. Reinforce the policy statement by behaviour at senior level that demonstrates that it is not merely words but that these exhortations have meaning.
4. Ensure that the sexual harassment policy is stated clearly in induction courses and is conveyed to everyone on promotion. Reinforce this message by regular reminders.
5. Make arrangements for employees subjected to sexual harassment to seek advice, support and counselling without any obligation to take a complaint forward. They could talk informally with someone in HR. Alternatively, a counsellor (possibly engaged as part of an employee assistance programme) can usefully offer guidance on harassment problems, assist in resolving them informally by seeking, with the agreement of the complainant, a confidential and voluntary interview with the person complained against to achieve a solution without resource to a formal disciplinary procedure, assist in submitting a complaint if the employee wishes to raise it formally, and counselling the parties on their future conduct.
6. Create a special procedure for hearing complaints about sexual harassment. The normal procedure may not be suitable because the harasser could be the employee's line manager. The procedure should provide for employees to bring their complaint to someone of their own sex, should they so choose.

7. Handle complaints about harassment with sensitivity and due respect for the rights of both the complainant and the accused. Ensure that hearings are conducted fairly and both parties are given an equal opportunity to put their case.
8. Where sexual harassment has taken place, crack down on it. It should be stated in the policy that it is regarded as gross misconduct and, if it is proved, makes the individual liable to instant dismissal. Less severe penalties may be reserved for minor cases, but there should always be a warning that repetition will result in dismissal.
9. Ensure that everyone is aware that the organization does take action when required to punish those who indulge in sexual harassment.
10. Provide training to line managers and team leaders to ensure that the policy is properly implemented and to make them aware of their direct responsibility to prevent harassment taking place and to take action if it does.

Bullying

Bullying is a form of harassment and can be very unpleasant. It is perhaps one of the most difficult aspects of employee relationships to control. Like sexual harassment, it can be hard to prove that bullying has taken place and employees may be reluctant to complain about a bullying boss, simply because he or she is a bully. But this does not mean that an organization can ignore the problem. A policy should be published that states that bullying is unacceptable behaviour. People who feel that they are being bullied should have the right to discuss the problem with someone in the HR department or a trained counsellor. Bullies should not be punished automatically. They should initially be helped to acknowledge the impact of their behaviours, and to change. Punishment should be reserved for those who persist in spite of this guidance.

Services for individuals

Services may be provided for individuals to help them deal with their problems. This may involve counselling or personal case work where the aim is as far as possible to get individuals to help themselves. Counselling is a skilled business, and is best carried out by trained people. This is where employee assistance programmes (EAPs) can be useful. EAP services are provided by external agencies that give employees access to counselling through a phone service, although face-to-face counselling may also be offered. Employers can refer employees to the service, which is provided in confidence between the agency and the individual.

The areas where counselling and other forms of help may be provided are as follows.

Areas where counselling and other forms of help may be provided

- Sickness – the provision of help and advice to employees absent from work for long periods due to illness; this might include sick visits.
- Bereavement – advice on how to cope with the death of a partner or close relative.
- Domestic problems – normally they should not be the concern of the employer, but if someone is very distressed help can be offered through a counselling service.
- Retirement – advice can be made available to employees who are about to retire to prepare them for their new circumstances; continued counselling and visiting services can be provided for retired employees.

Group employee services

Group employee services mainly consist of subsidized restaurants, sports and social clubs and child care facilities.

Restaurant facilities are desirable in any large establishment where local facilities are limited. Sports or social clubs should not be laid on because they are 'good for morale'; there is no evidence that they are. They should only be provided if there is a real need for them arising from a lack of local facilities. In the latter case the facilities should be shared with the local community.

Child care facilities are one of the most popular forms of group services if they fill a need that cannot be met easily elsewhere.

Employee well-being – key learning points

Reasons for concern with well-being

- Employers have a duty of care and this means adopting a socially responsible approach to looking after their people.
- Employers are responsible for creating a good work environment, not only because it is their duty to do so but also as part of the total reward system.

Employee well-being – key learning points (continued)

- It is in the interests of employers to do so because this will increase the likelihood of their employees being committed to the organization and help to establish it as a 'best place to work'.

The significance of the work environment

The work environment consists of the system of work, the design of jobs, working conditions and the ways in which people are treated at work by their managers and co-workers. Well-being is achieved when account is taken in designing the work system and the jobs in it of the needs of the people concerned. Working conditions need to meet health and safety requirements. The way people are treated is a matter of managerial behaviour, achieving work-life balance and dealing with issues such as stress, harassment and bullying.

The achievement of work–life balance

Flexible working is the most practical solution to establishing an effective work–life balance. This covers flexitime, homeworking, part-time working, compressed working weeks, annualized hours, job sharing and term-time only working. It also refers to special leave schemes that provide employees with the freedom to respond to a domestic crisis or to take a career break without jeopardizing their employment status.

Managing stress

- Employers have the social responsibility to provide a good quality of working life.
- Excessive stress causes illness.
- Stress can result in inability to cope with the demands of the job, which creates more stress.
- Excessive stress can reduce employee effectiveness and therefore organizational performance.

Sexual harassment

Sexual harassment is difficult to deal with but it is important to make a determined attempt to minimize it through policy statements backed up by special procedures for seeking help and making complaints.

Bullying

A policy should be published that states that bullying is unacceptable behaviour. People who feel that they are being bullied should have the right to discuss the problem with someone in the HR department or a trained counsellor.

Services for individuals

Counselling, possibly through EAP programmes, can be provided for sickness, bereavement, domestic problems and retirement.

Group employee services

These mainly consist of subsidized restaurants, sports and social clubs and child care facilities.

Questions

1. What does employee well-being mean?
2. What is work–life balance and what can be done about it?
3. How can stress be managed?
4. What are employee assistance programmes (EAPs)?

References

DTI (2003) *Work–life Balance Survey 2*, DTI, London

IRS (2002) *Work/life Balance*, IRS, London

Kodz, J, Harper, H and Dench, S (2002) *Work–life Balance: Beyond the rhetoric*, Report 384, Institute of Employment Studies, Brighton

Lawler E E (2003) *Treat People Right! How organisations and individuals can propel each other into a virtuous spiral of success*, Jossey-Bass, San Francisco, CA

Martin, A O (1967) *Welfare at Work*, Batsford, London

Taylor, S (2008) *People Resourcing*, CIPD, London

Warr, P B, Bird, M W and Rackham, N (1970) *Evaluation of Management Training*, Gower, Aldershot

Wilson, N A B (1973) *On the Quality of Working Life*, HMSO, London

Work Foundation (2003b) *Work–life Balance*, Work Foundation, London

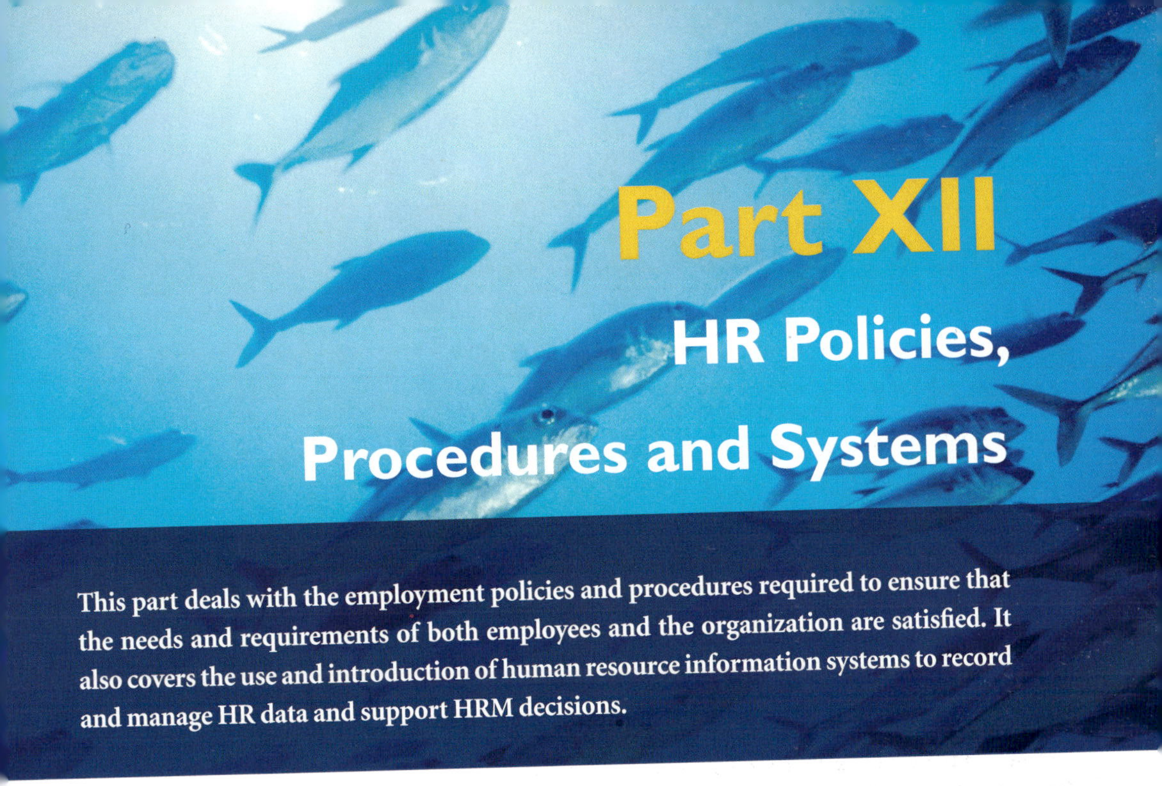

Part XII

HR Policies, Procedures and Systems

This part deals with the employment policies and procedures required to ensure that the needs and requirements of both employees and the organization are satisfied. It also covers the use and introduction of human resource information systems to record and manage HR data and support HRM decisions.

Part XII contents

60 HR Policies

Learning outcomes

On completing this chapter you should know about:

- The reasons for having HR policies
- Specific HR policies
- Implementing HR policies
- Overall HR policy
- Formulating HR policies

Introduction

HR policies are continuing guidelines on how people should be managed in the organization. They define the philosophies and values of the organization on how people should be treated, and from these are derived the principles upon which managers are expected to act when dealing with HR matters. HR policies should be distinguished from procedures, as discussed in Chapter 61. A policy provides generalized guidance on how HR issues should be dealt with; a procedure spells out precisely what steps should be taken to deal with major employment issues such as grievances, discipline, capability and redundancy.

Why have HR policies?

HR policies provide guidelines on how key aspects of people management should be handled. The aim is to ensure that any HR issues are dealt with consistently in accordance with the values of the organization in line with certain defined principles. All organizations have HR policies. Some, however, exist implicitly as a philosophy of management and an attitude to employees that is expressed in the way in which HR issues are handled; for example, the introduction of new technology. The advantage of explicit policies in terms of consistency and understanding may appear to be obvious, but there are disadvantages: written policies can be inflexible, constrictive, platitudinous, or all three. To a degree, policies have often to be expressed in abstract terms and managers do not care for abstractions. But they do want to know where they stand – people like structure – and formalized HR policies can provide the guidelines they need.

Formalized HR policies can be used in induction, team leader and management training to help participants understand the philosophies and values of the organization and how they are expected to behave within that context. They are a means for defining the employment relationship and the psychological contract.

HR policies can be expressed formally as overall statements of the values of the organization or in specific areas, as discussed in this chapter.

Overall HR policy

The overall HR policy defines how the organization fulfils its social responsibilities to its employees and sets out its attitudes towards them. It is an expression of its values or beliefs about how people should be treated. Peters and Waterman (1982) wrote that if they were asked for one all-purpose bit of advice for management, one truth that they could distil from all their research on what makes an organization excellent, it would be: 'Figure out your value system. Decide what the organization stands for.'

Selznick (1957) emphasized the key role of values in organizations when he wrote: 'The formation of an institution is marked by the making of value commitments, that is, choices which fix the assumptions of policy makers as to the nature of the enterprise, its distinctive aims, methods and roles.'

The values expressed in an overall statement of HR policies may explicitly or implicitly refer to the following concepts.

Values expressed in overall HR policy

- Equity – treating employees fairly and justly by adopting an 'even-handed' approach. This includes protecting individuals from any unfair decisions made by their managers, providing equal opportunities for employment and promotion, and operating an equitable payment system.
- Consideration – taking account of individual circumstances when making decisions that affect the prospects, security or self-respect of employees.
- Organizational learning – a belief in the need to promote the learning and development of all the members of the organization by providing the processes and support required.
- Performance through people – the importance attached to developing a performance culture and to continuous improvement; the significance of performance management as a means of defining and agreeing mutual expectations; the provision of fair feedback to people on how well they are performing.
- Quality of working life – consciously and continually aiming to improve the quality of working life. This involves increasing the sense of satisfaction people obtain from their work by, so far as possible, reducing monotony, increasing variety, autonomy and responsibility, avoiding placing people under too much stress and providing for an acceptable balance between work and life outside work.
- Working conditions – providing healthy, safe and, so far as practicable, pleasant working conditions.

These values are espoused by many organizations in one form or another. But to what extent are they practised when making 'business-led' decisions which can, of course, be highly detrimental to employees if, for example, they lead to redundancy? One of the dilemmas facing all those who formulate HR policies is: 'How can we pursue business-led policies focusing on business success and fulfil our obligations to employees in such terms as equity, consideration, quality of working life and working conditions?' To argue, as some do, that HR strategies should be entirely business-led seems to imply that human considerations are unimportant. Organizations have obligations to all their stakeholders, not just their owners.

It may be difficult to express these policies in anything but generalized terms, but employers are increasingly having to recognize that they are subject to external as well as internal pressures that act as constraints on the extent to which they can disregard the higher standards of behaviour towards their employees that are expected of them.

Specific HR policies

The most common areas in which specific HR policies exist are age and employment, AIDS, bullying, discipline, e-mails and the internet, employee development, employee relations, employee voice, employment, equal opportunity, grievances, health and safety, managing diversity, promotion, redundancy, reward, sexual harassment, substance abuse and work–life balance.

Age and employment

The policy on age and employment should take into account the UK legislation on age discrimination and the following facts:

- age is a poor predictor of job performance;
- it is misleading to equate physical and mental ability with age;
- more of the population are living active, healthy lives as they get older.

AIDS

An AIDS policy could include the following points:

- The risk through infection in the workplace is negligible.
- Where the occupation does involve blood contact, as in hospitals, doctors' surgeries and laboratories, the special precautions advised by the Health and Safety Commission will be implemented.
- Employees who know that they are infected with HIV will not be obliged to disclose the fact to the company, but if they do, the fact will remain completely confidential.
- There will be no discrimination against anyone with or at risk of acquiring AIDS.
- Employees infected by HIV or suffering from AIDS will be treated no differently from anyone else suffering a severe illness.

Bullying

An anti-bullying policy will state that bullying will not be tolerated by the organization and that those who persist in bullying their staff will be subject to disciplinary action, which could be severe in particularly bad cases. The policy will make it clear that individuals who are being bullied should have the right to discuss the problem with another person; a representative or a member of the HR function, and to make a complaint. The policy should emphasize that if a complaint is received it will be thoroughly investigated.

Discipline

The disciplinary policy should state that employees have the right to know what is expected of them and what could happen if they infringe the organization's rules. It would also make the point that, in handling disciplinary cases, the organization will treat employees in accordance with the principles of natural justice. It should be supported by a disciplinary procedure (see Chapter 61).

Diversity management

A policy on managing diversity recognizes that there are differences among employees and that these differences, if properly managed, will enable work to be done more efficiently and effectively. It does not focus exclusively on issues of discrimination but instead concentrates on recognizing the differences between people. As Kandola and Fullerton (1994) express it, the concept of managing diversity 'is founded on the premise that harnessing these differences will create a productive environment in which everyone will feel valued, where their talents are fully utilized, and in which organizational goals are met'.

Managing diversity is a concept that recognizes the benefits to be gained from differences. It differs from equal opportunity, which aims to legislate against discrimination, assumes that people should be assimilated into the organization and, often, relies on affirmative action. This point was emphasized by Mulholland *et al* (2005) as follows:

> *The new diversity management thinking suggests that diversity management goes beyond the equal opportunities management considerations as described by the law, and promises to make a positive and strategic contribution to the successful operation of business. So diversity management is being hailed as a proactive, strategically relevant and results-focused approach and a welcome departure from the equal opportunities approach, which has been defined as reactive, operational and sometimes counterproductive.*

A management of diversity policy could:

- acknowledge cultural and individual differences in the workplace;
- state that the organization values the different qualities that people bring to their jobs;
- emphasize the need to eliminate bias in such areas as selection, promotion, performance assessment, pay and learning opportunities;
- focus attention on individual differences rather than group differences.

E-mails and use of the internet

The policy on e-mails could state that the sending or downloading of offensive e-mails is prohibited and that the senders or downloaders of such messages are subject to normal disciplinary procedures. They may also prohibit any internet browsing or downloading of material not related to the business, although this can be difficult to enforce. Some companies have always believed that reasonable use of the telephone is acceptable, and that policy may be extended to the internet.

If it is decided that employees' e-mails should be monitored to check on excessive or unacceptable use, this should be included in an e-mail policy, which would therefore be part of the contractual arrangements. A policy statement could be included to the effect that: 'The company reserves the right to access and monitor all e-mail messages created, sent, received or stored on the company's system.'

Employee development

The employee development policy could express the organization's commitment to the continuous development of the skills and abilities of employees in order to maximize their contribution and to give them the opportunity to enhance their skills, realize their potential, advance their careers and increase their employability both within and outside the organization.

Employee relations

The employee relations policy will set out the organization's approach to the rights of employees to have their interests represented to management through trade unions, staff associations or some other form of representative system. It will also cover the basis upon which the organization works with trade unions, eg emphasizing that this should be regarded as a partnership.

Employee voice

The employee voice policy should spell out the organization's belief in giving employees an opportunity to have a say in matters that affect them. It should define the mechanisms for employee voice such as joint consultation and suggestion schemes.

Employment

Employment policies should be concerned with fundamental aspects of the employment relationship. They should take account of the requirements of relevant UK and European legislation and case law, which is beyond the scope of this handbook to cover in detail. Recent Acts and Regulations that are important include those concerning the minimum wage, working time and part-time workers. The latter is especially significant because it requires that part-time workers should be entitled to the same terms and conditions as full-time workers, including pro rata pay.

Note should also be taken of the UK Human Rights Act (1998), which gave further effect to rights and freedoms guaranteed under the European Convention on Human Rights. However, the rights are essentially civil and political rather than economic or social rights and they only apply to a narrow range of employment. Moreover, they are not directly enforceable against an employer unless it is an 'obvious' public authority. It has, however, been held by the European Court of Human Rights that statutory rights should not be unlawfully dismissed or discriminated against as they can be regarded as 'civil rights'. Provisions inserted into the Employment Rights Act must be interpreted by employment tribunals in a way that is compatible with the European Convention right to freedom of expression. This could apply to whistle-blowing.

Equal opportunity

The equal opportunity policy should spell out the organization's determination to give equal opportunities to all, irrespective of sex, race, creed, disability, age or marital status. The policy should also deal with the extent to which the organization wants to take 'affirmative action' to redress imbalances between the numbers employed according to sex or race or to differences in the levels of qualifications and skills they have achieved.

The policy could be set out as follows:

- We are an equal opportunity employer. This means that we do not permit direct or indirect discrimination against any employee on the grounds of race, nationality, sex, sexual orientation, disability, religion, marital status or age.
- Direct discrimination takes place when a person is treated less favourably than others are, or would be, treated in similar circumstances.
- Indirect discrimination takes place when, whether intentional or not, a condition is applied that adversely affects a considerable proportion of people of one race, nationality, sex, sexual orientation, religion or marital status, or those with disabilities or older employees.
- The firm will ensure that equal opportunity principles are applied in all its HR policies and in particular to the procedures relating to the recruitment, training, development and promotion of its employees.

- Where appropriate and where permissible under the relevant legislation and codes of practice, employees of under-represented groups will be given positive training and encouragement to achieve equal opportunity.

Grievances

The policy on grievances could state that employees have the right to raise their grievances with their manager, to be accompanied by a representative if they so wish, and to appeal to a higher level if they feel that their grievance has not been resolved satisfactorily. The policy should be supported by a grievance procedure (see Chapter 61).

Health and safety

Health and safety policies cover how the organization intends to provide healthy and safe places and systems of work (see Chapter 58).

New technology

A new technology policy statement could state that there will be consultation about the introduction of new technology and the steps that would be taken by the organization to minimize the risk of compulsory redundancy or adverse effects on other terms and conditions or working arrangements.

Promotion

A promotion policy could state the organization's intention to promote from within wherever this is appropriate as a means of satisfying its requirements for high-quality staff. The policy could, however, recognize that there will be occasions when the organization's present and future needs can only be met by recruitment from outside. The point could be made that a vigorous organization needs infusions of fresh blood from time to time if it is not to stagnate. In addition, the policy might state that employees will be encouraged to apply for internally advertised jobs and will not be held back from promotion by their managers, however reluctant the latter may be to lose them. The policy should define the approach the organization adopts to engaging, promoting and training and older employees. It should emphasize that the only criterion for selection or promotion should be ability to do the job, and for training, the belief, irrespective of age, that the employee will benefit.

Redundancy

The redundancy policy should state that the aim of the organization is to provide for employment security. It is the organization's intention to use its best endeavours to avoid involuntary redundancy through its redeployment and retraining programmes. However, if redundancy is unavoidable, those affected will be given fair and equitable treatment, the maximum amount of warning, and every help that can be provided to obtain suitable alternative employment. The policy should be supported by a redundancy procedure (see Chapter 61).

Reward

The reward policy could cover such matters as:

- providing an equitable pay system;
- equal pay for work of equal value;
- paying for performance, competence, skill or contribution;
- sharing in the success of the organization (gainsharing or profit sharing);
- the relationship between levels of pay in the organization and market rates;
- the provision of employee benefits, including flexible benefits, if appropriate;
- the importance attached to the non-financial rewards resulting from recognition of accomplishment, autonomy and the opportunity to develop.

Sexual harassment

The sexual harassment policy should state that:

- Sexual harassment will not be tolerated.
- Employees subjected to sexual harassment will be given advice, support and counselling as required.
- Every attempt will be made to resolve the problem informally with the person complained against.
- Assistance will be given to the employee to complain formally if informal discussions fail.
- A special process will be available for hearing complaints about sexual harassment. This will provide for employees to bring their complaint to someone of their own sex if they so wish.
- Complaints will be handled sensitively and with due respect for the rights of both the complainant and the accused.
- Sexual harassment is regarded as gross misconduct and, if proved, makes the individual liable for instant dismissal. Less severe penalties may be reserved for minor cases, but there will always be a warning that repetition will result in dismissal.

Substance abuse

A substance abuse policy could include assurances that:

- employees identified as having substance abuse problems will be offered advice and help;
- any reasonable absence from work necessary to receive treatment will be granted under the organization's sickness scheme provided that there is full cooperation from the employee;
- an opportunity will be given to discuss the matter once it has become evident or suspected that work performance is being affected by substance-related problems;
- the right to be accompanied by a friend or employee representative in any such discussion;
- agencies will be recommended to which the employee can go for help if necessary;
- employment rights will be safeguarded during any reasonable period of treatment.

Work–life balance

Work–life balance policies define how the organization intends to allow employees greater flexibility in their working patterns so that they can balance what they do at work with the responsibilities and interests they have outside work. The policy will indicate how flexible work practices can be developed and implemented. It will emphasize that the numbers of hours worked must not be treated as a criterion for assessing performance. It will set out guidelines on the specific arrangements that can be made, such as flexible hours, a compressed working week, term-time working contracts, working at home, special leave for parents and carers, career breaks and various kinds of child care.

A flexibility policy will need to take account of the Work and Families Act 2006, an extension of which gives carers the right to request flexible working to care for an elderly or sick relative. This provides for the following actions: 1) the request must be acknowledged in writing; 2) the employee must be notified if not all the required information is provided, so that they can resubmit the application properly completed; 3) if the employee unreasonably refuses to provide the additional information needed, the employer can treat the application as withdrawn; 4) a meeting has to be arranged with the employee within 28 days, to discuss the desired work pattern and consider how it might be accommodated; 5) if the request cannot be accommodated, alternative working arrangements may be discussed and a trial period agreed. In certain circumstances, a solution might be to develop an informal arrangement, outside the legislation, to allow flexible working for a limited period.

Formulating HR policies

HR policies need to address the key HR issues that have been identified in the organization. They must also take account of external influences such as legislation. The maximum amount of consultation should take place with managers, employees and their representatives and the policies should be communicated widely with guidelines on their application. The following steps should be taken when formulating HR policies.

Formulating HR policies

1. Gain understanding of the corporate culture and its shared values.
2. Analyse existing policies – written and unwritten. HR policies will exist in any organization, even if they are implicit rather than expressed formally.
3. Analyse external influences. HR policies are subject to the influence of UK employment legislation, EC employment regulations, and the official Codes of Practice issued by bodies in the UK, such as ACAS (The Advisory, Conciliation and Arbitration Service), the EOC (Equal Opportunities Commission), the CRR (Commission on Racial Relations) and the HSE (Health and Safety Executive). The Codes of Practice issued by relevant professional institutions, such as the CIPD, should also be consulted.
4. Assess any areas where new policies are needed or existing policies are inadequate.
5. Check with managers, preferably starting at the top, on their views about HR policies and where they think they could be improved.
6. Seek the views of employees about the HR policies, especially the extent to which they are inherently fair and equitable and are implemented fairly and consistently. Consider doing this through an attitude survey.
7. Seek the views of union representatives.
8. Analyse the information obtained in the first seven steps and prepare draft policies.
9. Consult, discuss and agree policies with management and union representatives.
10. Communicate the policies with guidance notes on their implementation as required (although they should be as self-explanatory as possible). Supplement this communication with training.

Implementing HR policies

The aim will be to implement policies fairly and consistently. Line managers have an important role in doing this. As pointed out by Purcell *et al* (2003) 'there is a need for HR policies to be designed for and focused on front line managers'. It is they who will be largely responsible for policy implementation. Members of the HR function can give guidance, but it is line managers who are on the spot and have to make decisions about people. The role of HR is to communicate and interpret the policies, convince line managers that they are necessary, and provide training and support that will equip managers to implement them. As Purcell *et al* (2003) emphasize, it is line managers who bring HR policies to life.

HR policies – key learning points

The reasons for having HR policies

HR policies provide guidelines on how key aspects of people management should be handled. The aim is to ensure that any HR issues are dealt with consistently in accordance with the values of the organization in line with certain defined principles.

Overall HR policy

The overall HR policy defines how the organization fulfils its social responsibilities for its employees and sets out its attitudes towards them. It is an expression of its values or beliefs about how people should be treated.

Specific HR policies

Specific HR policies cover age and employment, AIDS, bullying, discipline, e-mails and the internet, employee development, employee relations, employee voice, employment, equal opportunity, grievances, health and safety, managing diversity, promotion, redundancy, reward, sexual harassment, substance abuse and work–life balance.

Formulating HR policies

HR policies need to address the key HR issues that have been identified in the organization. They must also take account of external influences such as legislation. The maximum amount of consultation should take place with managers, employees and their representatives, and the policies should be communicated widely with guidelines on their application.

Implementing HR policies

The aim will be to implement policies fairly and consistently. Line managers have a key role in doing this.

Questions

1. What are HR policies?
2. Why have HR policies?
3. What values may be expressed in overall HR policy?
4. What are the areas in which specific HR policies may be required?
5. How should HR policies be formulated?

References

Kandola, R and Fullerton, J (1994) *Managing the Mosaic: Diversity in action*, Institute of Personnel and Development, London

Mulholland, G, Özbilgin, M and Worman, D (2005) *Managing Diversity: Linking theory and practice to business performance*, CIPD, London

Peters, T and Waterman, R (1982) *In Search of Excellence*, Harper & Row, New York

Purcell, J, Kinnie, K, Hutchinson, S, Rayton, B and Swart, J (2003) *People and Performance: How people management impacts on organisational performance*, CIPD, London

Selznick, P (1957) *Leadership and Administration*, Row, Evanston, Ill

61 HR Procedures

Learning outcomes

On completing this chapter you should:

- Be able to define what HR procedures are
- Know about the main HR procedures: capability, discipline, grievance and redundancy

What are HR procedures?

HR procedures set out the ways in which certain actions concerning people should be carried out by the management or individual managers. In effect they constitute a formalized approach to dealing with specific matters of policy and practice. They should be distinguished from HR policies, as described in Chapter 60. These describe the approach the organization adopts to various aspects of people management and define key aspects of the employment relationship. They serve as guidelines on people management practices but do not necessarily lay down precisely the steps that should be taken in particular situations. Procedures are more exacting: they state what must be done as well as spelling out how to do it.

It is desirable to have the key HR procedures written down to ensure that HR policies are applied consistently and in accordance with both legal requirements and ethical considerations. The existence of a written and well publicized procedure ensures that everyone knows precisely what steps need to be taken when dealing with certain significant and possibly recurring employment issues.

The introduction or development of HR procedures should be carried out in consultation with employees and, where appropriate, their representatives. It is essential to brief everyone on how the procedures operate and they should be published either in an employee handbook or as a separate document. Line managers may need special training on how they should apply the procedures and the HR department should provide guidance wherever necessary. HR will normally have the responsibility of ensuring that procedures are followed consistently.

The main areas where procedures are required are those concerned with handling capability and disciplinary issues, grievances and redundancy.

Capability procedure

Some organizations deal with matters of capability under a disciplinary procedure, but there is a good case to be made for dealing with poor performance issues separately, leaving the disciplinary procedure to be invoked for situations such as poor timekeeping. An example of a capability procedure is given below.

Policy

The company aims are to ensure that performance expectations and standards are defined, performance is monitored and employees are given appropriate feedback, training and support to meet these standards.

Capability Procedure

1. If a manager/team leader believes that an employee's performance is not up to standard an informal discussion will be held with the employee to try to establish the reason and to agree the actions required to improve performance by the employee and/or the manager/team leader. If, however:

   - it is agreed that the established standards are not reasonably attainable, they will be reviewed;
   - it is established that the performance problems are related to the employee's personal life, the necessary counselling/support will be provided;
   - it is decided that the poor performance emanates from a change in the organization's standards, those standards will be explained to the employee and help will be offered to obtain conformity with the standards;
   - it is apparent that the poor performance constitutes misconduct; the disciplinary procedure will be invoked.

2. Should the employee show no (or insufficient) improvement over a defined period (weeks/months), a formal interview will be arranged between the employee (together with a representative if so desired). The aims of this interview will be to:

   - explain clearly the shortfall between the employee's performance and the required standard;
   - identify the cause(s) of the unsatisfactory performance and to determine what, if any, remedial treatment (training, retraining, support, etc) can be given;
   - obtain the employee's commitment to reaching that standard;
   - set a reasonable period for the employee to reach the standard and agree on a monitoring system during that period; and
   - tell the employee what will happen if that standard is not met.

3. The outcome of this interview will be recorded in writing and a copy will be given to the employee.

4. At the end of the review period a further formal interview will be held, at which time:

   - if the required improvement has been made, the employee will be told of this and encouraged to maintain the improvement;
   - if some improvement has been made but the standard has not yet been met, the review period will be extended;

- if there has been no discernible improvement and performance is still well below an acceptable standard this will be indicated to the employee and consideration will be given to whether there are alternative vacancies that the employee would be competent to fill; if there are, the employee will be given the option of accepting such a vacancy or being considered for dismissal;
- if such vacancies are available, the employee will be given full details of them in writing before being required to make a decision;
- in the absence of suitable alternative work, the employee will be informed and invited to give his or her views on this before the final decision is taken.

5. Employees may appeal against their dismissal. The appeal must be made within three working days.

Disciplinary procedure

A disciplinary procedure sets out the stages through which any disciplinary action should proceed. An example is given below.

Disciplinary Procedure (part 1)

Policy

It is the policy of the company that if disciplinary action has to be taken against employees it should:

- be undertaken only in cases where good reason and clear evidence exist;
- be appropriate to the nature of the offence that has been committed;
- be demonstrably fair and consistent with previous action in similar circumstances;
- take place only when employees are aware of the standards that are expected of them or the rules with which they are required to conform;
- allow employees the right to be represented by a representative or colleague during any formal proceedings;
- allow employees the right to know exactly what charges are being made against them and to respond to those charges;
- allow employees the right of appeal against any disciplinary action.

Disciplinary rules

The company is responsible for ensuring that up-to-date disciplinary rules are published and available to all employees. These will set out the circumstances in which an employee could be dismissed for gross industrial misconduct.

Procedure

The procedure is carried out in the following stages:

1. Informal warning. A verbal or informal warning is given to the employee in the first instance or instances of minor offences. The warning is administered by the employee's immediate team leader or manager.

2. Formal warning. A written formal warning is given to the employee in the first instance of more serious offences or after repeated instances of minor offences. The warning is administered by the employee's immediate team leader or manager – it states the exact nature of the offence and indicates any future disciplinary action that will be taken against the employee if the offence is repeated within a specified time limit. A copy of the written warning is placed in the employee's personal record file but is destroyed 12 months after the date on which it was given, if the intervening service has been satisfactory. The employee is required to read and sign the formal warning and has the right to appeal to higher management if he or she thinks the warning is unjustified. The HR Manager should be asked to advise on the text of the written warning.

3. Further disciplinary action. If, despite previous warnings, an employee still fails to reach the required standards in a reasonable period of time, it may become necessary to consider further disciplinary action. The action taken may be up to three days' suspension without pay, or dismissal. In either case the departmental manager should discuss the matter with the HR manager before taking action. Staff below the rank of departmental manager may only recommend disciplinary action to higher management, except when their manager is not present (for example, on night-shift), when they may suspend the employee for up to one day pending an inquiry on the following day. Disciplinary action should not be confirmed until the appeal procedure has been carried out.

Disciplinary Procedure (part 2)

Summary dismissal

An employee may be summarily dismissed (ie given instant dismissal without notice) only in the event of gross misconduct, as defined in company rules. Only departmental managers and above can recommend summary dismissal, and the action should not be finalized until the case has been discussed with the HR Manager and the appeal procedure has been carried out. To enable this review to take place, employees should be suspended pending further investigation, which must take place within 24 hours.

Appeals

In all circumstances, an employee may appeal against suspension, dismissal with notice, or summary dismissal. The appeal is conducted by a member of management who is more senior than the manager who initially administered the disciplinary action. The HR Manager should also be present at the hearing. If he or she wishes, the employee may be represented at the appeal by a fellow employee of his or her own choice. Appeal against summary dismissal or suspension should be heard immediately. Appeals against dismissal with notice should be held within two days. No disciplinary action that is subject to appeal is confirmed until the outcome of the appeal.

If an appeal against dismissal (but not suspension) is rejected at this level, the employee has the right to appeal to the chief executive. The head of HR and, if required, the employee's representative should be present at this appeal.

Grievance procedure

A grievance procedure spells out the policy on handling grievances and the approach to dealing with them. An example of a grievance procedure is given below.

Grievance Procedure

Policy

It is the policy of the company that employees should:

- be given a fair hearing by their immediate supervisor or manager concerning any grievances they may wish to raise;
- have the right to appeal to a more senior manager against a decision made by their immediate supervisor or manager;
- have the right to be accompanied by a fellow employee of their own choice when raising a grievance or appealing against a decision.

The aim of the procedure is to settle the grievance as near as possible to its point of origin.

Procedure

The main stages through which a grievance may be raised are as follows:

1. The employee raises the matter with his or her immediate team leader or manager and may be accompanied by a fellow employee of his or her own choice.
2. If the employee is not satisfied with the decision, the employee requests a meeting with a member of management who is more senior than the team leader or manager who initially heard the grievance. This meeting takes place within five working days of the request and is attended by the manager, the HR Manager or business partner, the employee appealing against the decision, and, if desired, his or her representative. The HR Manager records the results of the meeting in writing and issues copies to all concerned.
3. If the employee is still not satisfied with the decision, he or she may appeal to the appropriate director. The meeting to hear this appeal is held within five working days of the request and is attended by the director, the head of HR, the employee making the appeal, and, if desired, his or her representative. The manager responsible for HR records the result of this meeting in writing and issues copies to all concerned.

Redundancy procedure

A redundancy procedure aims to meet statutory, ethical and practical considerations when dealing with this painful process. An example of a procedure is given below.

Redundancy Procedure (part 1)

Definition

Redundancy is defined as the situation in which management decides that an employee or employees are surplus to requirements in a particular occupation and cannot be offered suitable alternative work.

Employees may be surplus to requirements because changes in the economic circumstances of the company mean that fewer employees are required, or because changes in methods of working mean that a job no longer exists in its previous form. An employee who is given notice because he or she is unsuitable or inefficient is not regarded as redundant and would be dealt with in accordance with the usual disciplinary or capability procedure.

Objectives

The objectives of the procedure are to ensure that:

- employees who may be affected by the discontinuance of their work are given fair and equitable treatment;
- the minimum disruption is caused to employees and the company;
- as far as possible, changes are effected with the understanding and agreement of the unions and employees concerned.

Principles

The principles governing the procedure are as follows:

- The trade unions concerned will be informed as soon as there is a possibility of redundancy.
- Every attempt will be made to:
  - absorb redundancy by the natural wastage of employees;
  - find suitable alternative employment within the company for employees who might be affected, and provide training if this is necessary;
  - give individuals reasonable warning of pending redundancy in addition to the statutory period of notice.
- If alternative employment in the company is not available and more than one individual is affected, the factors to be taken into consideration in deciding who should be made redundant will be:
  - length of service with the company;
  - value to the company;
  - other things being equal, length of service should be the determining factor.
- The company will make every endeavour to help employees find alternative work if that is necessary.

Redundancy Procedure (part 2)

The procedure for dealing with employees who are surplus to requirements is set out below.

Review of employee requirements

Management will continuously keep under review possible future developments that might affect the number of employees required, and will prepare overall plans for dealing with possible redundancies.

Measures to avoid redundancies

If the likelihood of redundancy is foreseen, the company will inform the union(s), explaining the reasons, and in consultation with the union(s) will give consideration to taking appropriate measures to prevent redundancy.

Departmental managers will be warned by the management of future developments that might affect them so that detailed plans can be made for running down the numbers of employees by allowing natural wastage to take place without replacements, retraining, or transfers.

Departmental managers will be expected to keep under review the work situation in their departments so that contingency plans can be prepared and the HR Manager advised of any likely surpluses.

Consultation on redundancies

If all measures to avoid redundancy fail, the company will consult the union(s) at the earliest opportunity in order to reach agreement.

Selection of redundant employees

In the event of impending redundancy, the individuals who might be surplus to requirements should be selected by the departmental manager with the advice of the HR Manager on the principles that should be adopted.

The HR Manager should explore the possibilities of transferring affected employees to alternative work.

The HR Manager should inform management of proposed action (either redundancy or transfer) to obtain approval.

The union(s) will be informed of the numbers affected but not of individual names.

The departmental manager and the HR Manager will jointly interview the employees affected, either to offer a transfer or, if a suitable alternative is not available, to inform them they will be redundant. At this interview, full information should be available to give to the employee on, as appropriate:

- the reasons for being surplus;
- the alternative jobs that are available;
- the date when the employee will become surplus (that is, the period of notice);
- the entitlement to redundancy pay;
- the employee's right to appeal to an appropriate director;
- the help the company will provide.

Redundancy Procedure (part 3)

An appropriate director will hear any appeals with the manager responsible for personnel.

The HR Manager will ensure that all the required administrative arrangements are made.

If the union(s) has/have any points to raise about the selection of employees or the actions taken by the company, these should be discussed in the first place with the HR Manager. If the results of these discussions are unsatisfactory, a meeting will be arranged with an appropriate director.

Alternative work within the company

If an employee is offered and accepts suitable alternative work within the company, it will take effect without a break from the previous employment and will be confirmed in writing. Employees will receive appropriate training and will be entitled to a four-week trial period to see if the work is suitable. This trial period may be extended by mutual agreement to provide additional training. During this period, employees are free to terminate their employment and, if they do, would be treated as if they had been made redundant on the day the old job ended. They would then receive any redundancy pay to which they are entitled.

Alternative employment

Employees for whom no suitable work is available in the company will be given reasonable opportunities to look for alternative employment.

Questions

1. What are HR procedures?
2. What are the characteristics of a good procedure?
3. What would you expect a capability procedure to cover?
4. What would you expect a disciplinary procedure to cover?
5. What would you expect a grievance procedure to cover?
6. What would you expect a redundancy procedure to cover?

62 HR Information Systems

Key concepts and terms

- e-HR
- Functionality
- Intranet
- Enterprise resource planning (ERP) system
- HR information system (HRIS)
- Self-service

Learning outcomes

On completing this chapter you should be able to define these key concepts. You should also know about:

- Reasons for using an HRIS
- Features of an HRIS
- Functions of an HRIS
- Introducing an HRIS

Introduction

An HR information system (HRIS) is a computer-based information system for managing the administration of HR processes and procedures. Tannenbaum (1990) defined an HRIS as any system that helps an organization to 'acquire, store, manipulate, analyse, retrieve and distribute information about an organization's human resources'. Kettley and Reilly (2003) defined an HRIS as 'a fully integrated, organization-wide network of HR-related data, information, services, tools and transactions'.

The term 'e-HR' refers in more general terms to the use of computer technology within the HR function.

Reasons for introducing an HRIS

The CIPD (2007d) survey established that the top 10 reasons for introducing an HRIS were:

1. To improve quality of information available.
2. To reduce administrative burden on the HR department.
3. To improve speed at which information is available.
4. To improve flexibility of information to support business planning.
5. To improve services to employees.
6. To produce HR metrics.
7. To aid human capital reporting.
8. To improve productivity.
9. To reduce operational costs.
10. To manage people's working time more effectively.

The functions of an HRIS

The functions that an HRIS can perform (its 'functionality') are set out below. They cover almost every aspect of HRM.

The functions that an HRIS can perform

- absence recording and management;
- employee surveys;
- e-learning;
- expenses;
- job evaluation;
- intranet;
- manager and employee self-service;
- online recruitment;
- payroll administration;
- pensions and benefits administration;
- total reward statements;
- employee records;
- employee turnover analysis;
- equal opportunity modelling;
- HR planning and forecasting;
- knowledge management;
- manage diversity;
- metrics and human capital reporting;
- online performance management systems and 360-degree feedback;
- pay reviews;
- reward modelling.

The CIPD survey found that the 10 most popular uses to which respondents put their HRIS were:

1. Absence management.
2. Training and development.
3. Rewards.
4. Managing diversity.
5. Recruitment and selection.
6. Other (usually payroll).
7. Appraisal/performance management.
8. HR planning.
9. Knowledge management.
10. Expenses.

Features of an HRIS

The features of particular interest in an HRIS system are the use of software, integration with other IT systems in the organization, use of the intranet and provisions for self-service.

Use of software

It is customary to buy software from an external supplier. There is a choice between buying a 'vanilla system' (ie an 'off-the-shelf' system without any upgrades) or customize the supplier's system to meet specified business requirements. Extensive customization can make future upgrades problematic and expensive, so it is important to limit it to what is absolutely necessary.

If an external supplier is used, the choice should be made as follows:

- research HR software market through trade exhibitions and publications;
- review HR processes and existing systems;
- produce a specification of system requirements;
- send an invitation to tender to several suppliers;
- invite suppliers to demonstrate their products;
- obtain references from existing customers, including site visits;
- analyse and score the product against the specification.

Integration

Enterprise resource planning (ERP) systems integrate all data and processes of an organization into a unified system with the same database. HR systems are not frequently integrated to this extent, although they often link payroll administration with other HR functions. As the CIPD (2005b) pointed out, integration of the HR system with IT systems in the wider organization so that they can 'talk to one another' will aid human capital reporting, comply with supply-chain partner requirements, improve profitability, reduce headcount and deliver against economic criteria. However, many HR functions retain stand-alone systems, because they believe integration would compromise their own system, potential lack of confidentiality and the cost and perceived risks involved.

Intranet

An intranet system is one where computer terminals are linked so that they can share information within an organization or within part of an organization. The scope of the information that can be shared across terminals can be limited to preserve confidentiality and this security can be enhanced by using passwords. HR intranet systems can be used for purposes such as updating personal details, applications for internal jobs online, requests for training, access to e-learning, administration of queries and communication.

Self-service

A human resource self-service system (HRSS) allows managers and employees access to information and the facility to interact with the system to input information or make choices of their own. This can operate through an HR portal (a site that functions as a point of access to information on the intranet) that may be specially designed to produce a brand image of the HR function. This is sometimes referred to as a business to employees (B2E) portal.

For managers, self-service means that they can access information immediately. This might be HR metrics (human capital reporting measures) in such areas as absenteeism, personal details, performance management data, learning and development progress, and pay (as a basis for pay reviews). They can also input data on their staff. This facilitates the devolution of responsibility to line managers and reduces the administrative burden on HR.

Employees can also access information, input data about themselves, request training and apply for jobs online.

Introducing an HRIS

The steps required are illustrated in Figure 62.1.

The following tips on introducing an HRIS were provided by respondents to the CIPD survey.

SOURCE REVIEW

Tips on introducing an HRIS, CIPD (2005b)

- Make sure you really know what you need now, and what you are likely to need in the near future so you can give clear guidelines to the software provider.
- Involve end-users and other stakeholders in the decision-making process.
- It's useful to include a member of staff with IT expertise on the decision-making team, even if they're not HR professionals.
- Go for something clear and straightforward that adds value. Don't go for all the 'bells and whistles'; they may cost more, take more time to administer and you will probably end up not using them anyway.

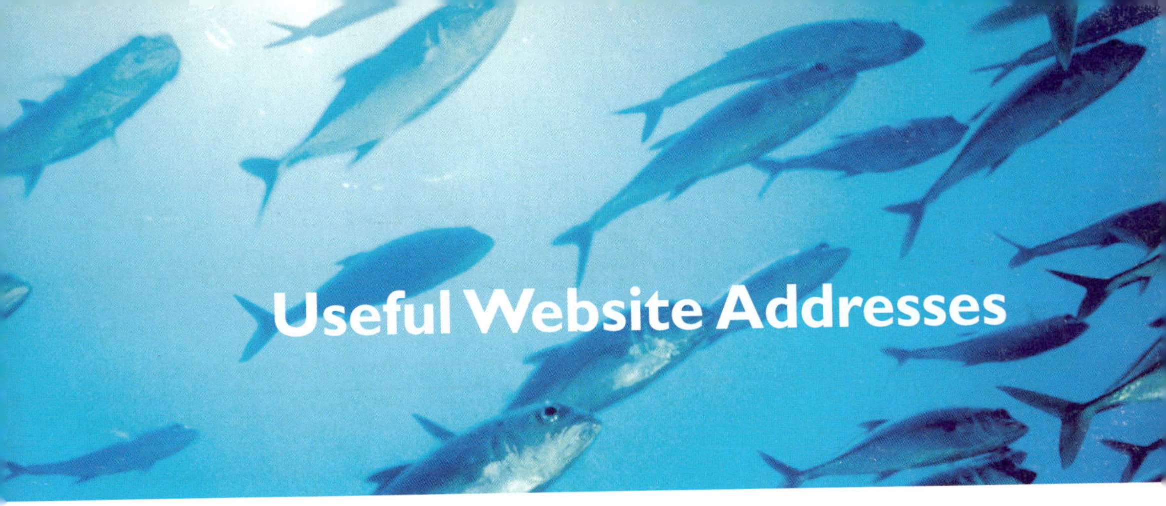

Useful Website Addresses

Michael Armstrong	http://www.michaelarmstrong@lycos.co.uk
Aston Business School	http://www.abs.ast.ac.uk
Birkbeck College	http://www.bbk.ac.uk
Birmingham Business School	http://www.business.bham.ac.uk
Cardiff Business School	http://www.cardiff.ac.uk
Chartered Institute of Personnel and Development	http://www.cipd.co.uk
Chartered Management Institute	http://www.managers.org.uk
Cranfield School of Management	http://www.som.cranfield.ac.uk
Deloitte	http://www.deloitte.com
Durham Business School	http://www.dur.ac.uk
Equality and Human Rights Commission	http://www.equalityhumanrights.com
Edinburgh Business School	http://www.ebsglobal.net
e-reward	http://www.e-reward.co.uk
Ernst & Young	http://www.ey.com
Harvard Business School	http://www.hbs.edu
Hay Group	http://www.haygroup.co.uk
Henley Management College	http://www.henleymc.ac.uk
Humanus Consultants	ann@humanus.biz
Hewitt Associates	http://www.hewitt.com
Incomes Data Services	http://www.incomesdata.co.uk
Institute for Employment Studies	http://www.employment-studies.co.uk

Industrial Relations Services (IRS)	http://www.irs.com
The International Journal of Human Resource Management	http://www.tandf.co.uk/journals/routledge/09585192.html
Kings College London	http://www.kcl.ac.uk
Kingston Business School	http://www.kingston.ac.uk/business
Kogan Page Ltd	www.koganpage.com
Learning and Skills Council	http://www.lsc.gov.uk
Leeds Business School	http://www.leeds.ac.uk
Leeds Metropolitan Business School	http://www.lmu.ac.uk
Leicester Business School	http://www.dmu.ac.uk
London Business School	http://www.lbs.lon.ac.uk
London Metropolitan Business School	London.met.ac.uk
London School of Economics	http://www.lse.ac.uk
Manchester Business School	http://www.mbs.ac.uk
Mercer Consulting	http://www.mercerhr.com
Middlesex Business School	http://www.mubs.mdx.ac.uk
Newcastle Business School	http://www.newcastlebusinessschool.ac.uk
New Earnings Survey	http://www.statistics.gov.uk
Nottingham Business School	http://www.bs.ac.uk
People Management	http://www.peoplemanagement.co.uk
Personnel Today	http://www.personneltoday.com
Portsmouth Business School	http://www.port.ac.uk
PricewaterhouseCoopers	http://www.pwc.com
Queens University Business School	http://www.qub.ac.uk
Roffey Park Institute	http://www.roffeypark.com
Society for Human Resource Management (USA)	www.shrm.org
Strathclyde Business School	http://www.strath.ac.uk
Towers Perrin	http://www.towersperrin.com
Trades Union Congress	http://www.tuc.org.uk

Warwick Business School	http://www.wbs.ac.uk
Watson Wyatt	http://www.watsonwyatt.com
Westminster Business School	http://www.wmin.ac.uk
The Work Foundation	http://www.theworkfoundation.com

Subject Index

Author Index